ALPHABET

to

INTERNET

Mediated Communication in Our Lives

Irving Fang
Professor Emeritus
University of Minnesota

rada press

Library of Congress Cataloging-in-Publication Data

Fang, Irving E.

Alphabet to Internet : mediated communication in our lives / Irving Fang.

p. cm.

Includes bibliographical references and index.

ISBN-13: 978-1-933011-90-5

ISBN-10: 1-933011-90-4

1. Mass media—History. I. Title.

P90.F264 2008

302.2309--dc22

2006030032

rada press, inc.

1277 Fairmount Avenue

St. Paul, Minnesota 55105-2702

eMail: orders@radapress.com

www. radapress.com

Printed in the United States of America

CONTENTS

ACKNOWLEDGEMENTS

A number of people contributed information or critiqued manuscript chapters. I wish to thank Nielsjacob Andersen, Donald Browne, Lisa Burns, Dane Claussen, Eva von Dassow, Mathias Diederich, Arthur Goldberg, William Huntzicker, Michael Keith, Richard Kielbowicz, Marie Mater, Roger Mellen, Nora Paul, Daisy Pellant, Ron-Michael Pellant, Phil Tichenor, Sarah Shaw, and Sam Stewart.

A particular debt of gratitude is owed to Michael Sobocinski for his editor's eagle eye.

The author alone is responsible for any errors.

William Wells designed the cover.

ALSO BY IRVING FANG:
Those Radio Commentators!

Television News (2 editions)

Television News, Radio News (2 editions)

The Computer Story (for younger readers)

Pictures (for younger readers)

A History of Mass Communication: Six Information Revolutions

The Story of Communication (with Ann Norris, an 11-book series)

Stone Thrower (under pseudonym Alexander Start)

INTRODUCTION

MEDIATED COMMUNICATION ENVELOPS US, replacing older ways of living. On a Friday evening in 1975 at the start of my first trip to Asia, I got off the bus in downtown Taipei, the capital of Taiwan, to a strange sight. The streets were bubbling with people enjoying themselves. Lots of people. Shopkeepers stood outside their stores and gossiped. Couples walked arm in arm and window-shopped. High heels clicking on the sidewalk, young women went by. Mothers chatted, barely mindful of playing children. The sight of so many people, young and old, enjoying shopping, chatting, eating, or just strolling amazed me, because it was beyond anything I had seen in the United States, including downtown New York and San Francisco. Most American city streets in the United States were scarcely populated in the evening. With a few exceptions, most downtowns did not bubble. None matched what I was seeing. Americans were home watching television. A walk along any American urban residential street would reveal the bluish glow from television sets in darkened rooms of house after house. At that time Taipei, I learned, had three government-controlled television stations and poor programs.

It didn't take a rocket scientist to conclude that urban-dwelling Americans like me had exchanged the lifestyle these Taiwanese had for the undeniable pleasure of watching TV. We gained something, but it was in exchange for something else. There could be no clearer lesson in how a communication medium alters behavior and separates people from one another. Arguably the most powerful image that television can present is not *on* the screen, but is the viewer sitting in front of the set, staring fixedly *at* the screen.

According to a report, when one family in a research study agreed to give up television for a month, a participant said the result was like a death in his family. But television is not the only medium of communication to form the building blocks of our daily routine. In the evenings. we can hardly wait to get back to that can't-put-down book, or climb on a treadmill with iTunes on the iPod, or head to the mall for that movie someone "texted" us about instead of staying in because our must-see program comes on at 8, because we can tape or TiVo that.

Communication media loom larger in our daily lives than most of us realize. In many ways they have altered the human condition. We spend much of each day with mediated communication. As evidence, add up all the hours you spend daily with one form of media or another, from the

While we don't all have a house that's the equivalent of Willy Wonka's chocolate factory, the American family is living more than ever in a multi-screen world.

We're checking out video clips at YouTube.com while reading a book. Googling via text message while Googling on laptops. Playing video games during commercial breaks of "Ugly Betty."

And as those habits reshape our lives and the industries that give us electronic information and entertainment, they also are creating new debate:

Do so many screens make us smarter, savvier human beings or drooling zombies?[1]

—Neal Justin

morning alarm clock radio to the nightime program, the novel, or the shopping channel that lulls you to sleep. Obviously, it was not always like this.

Mediated communication—this transmission and delivery of information, opinion, and entertainment from a distance—is baked into our lives today, too consequential to be mere convenience or diversion. It is with the devices and content of mediated communication that so many of us spend so many of our hours and acquire so much of what we think, and think about. In short, media truly matter.

The pace of the changes in our lifetime due to mediated communication is accelerating. We—all of humankind—are living during what has been described as an "Information Age"; we are identified as members of an "Information Society." To some degree, almost everyone is touched by these changes.

We hold opinions by the dozen. How did we acquire our political views? Our religious convictions? Our moral standards? Our assumptions about people who belong to another group than ours? How do we know what we know? In the post-industrialized world of the twenty-first century, the answers are influenced by the undeniable fact that *most of what we know and most of what we believe we have learned through mediated communication.*

The mediated communication tools that we use vary from person to person, and the content certainly varies, but a common factor is that the time spent with the means of bringing or storing information grows with education. The better educated we are, the more we rely—and are dependent—on the tools of communication. That is how we became educated in the first place, and how we stay current. Only the smallest fraction of what an educated person knows in today's world comes from direct experience. Even when we can truly say that our knowledge and opinions have come from parents, teachers, friends, and the leaders of our special communities, it is reasonable to ask how they received what they imparted to us.

Why should it matter to us that we have learned from books, newspapers, and the movies rather than through our senses? What difference does it make that our opinions were filtered through the Internet rather than through personal experience? Is it significant that so much of each day is spent with television or a video game rather than sitting at the feet of a village elder?

The answers lie partly in the sheer size and diversity of our knowledge, because we must simply accept most of it. We could not function if we had to question everything. A second answer is that some of the information derived through a medium may have attached strings that deserve attention. Another answer is that anything that occupies so much of our time is worth examining. Finally, it is important to recognize that mediated communication brings changes to our lives. Knowing this is a first step in determining how to improve what we get.

It would be pointless just to look at mediated communication as a whole and conclude that, taken all in all, our lives are different. Comparing, say, a well-to-do, plugged-in youth of an advanced society today with a member of an illiterate village can hold no interest. Of more significance is recognizing how the successive means of communicating information have changed us. Between sitting before a village elder and sitting before a plasma screen, each new means has affected our lives in specific ways.

Where does mass communication end and personal life begin? What is Facebook.com? What are YouTube and all the other personal sites where users provide intimate content? The entire concept of Web 2.0 is its personal nature within the larger mass communication framework.

Hundreds of departments and schools and colleges of mass communication examine communication in a world that has changed so much and so rapidly that even the schools' own names are obsolescent. If the subject ever was really limited to "mass" communication as contrasted with "personal" communication, it no longer is. What the schools teach is *mediated* communication; that is, communication employing an external medium between sender and receiver. Some schools are meeting the challenge of change in the naming of courses, just as high school libraries have been renaming themselves "media centers."

Boundaries and definitions blur in distinguishing media tools, like the Internet, from mediated content, like blogs. Mail and email can be identified both as technologies and the content of technologies. They are also examples of both mass and personal communication. Blogs—the online diary and commentary websites—can be both personal and mass within the same blog. Is email mass or personal communication? That depends on the number of people to whom it is addressed. The World Wide Web is considered a mass medium, but AOL among others offers personalized news reports, and CNN has personalized a video news service. Magazines, a mass medium by anyone's definition, are moving toward advertising tailored to the subscriber. If radio is a mass medium, where do Internet radio stations with miniscule audiences fit in?

It is "mass" when groups with similar interests are pulled together in cyberspace by what are referred to as "taste tribes." But is it "personal" when hundreds of thousands of online video gamers shatter into chatrooms for one-to-one conversations that have occasionally culminated in marriage proposals, an action about as personal as actions get?

You can learn more about how Americans live just by looking at the backgrounds of YouTube videos—those rumpled bedrooms and toy-strewn basement rec rooms—than you could from 1,000 hours of network television.

And we didn't just watch, we also worked.[2]

—Time

The unification of human civilization through modern communications and transportation means that there is no part of mankind that is not aware of the scientific method and its potential, even if that part is currently incapable of generating technology or applying it successfully.

— Francis Fukuyama

Whether it is a Match.com-inspired marriage proposal to one person or a spam offer of a Nigerian fortune to a hundred thousand, an email message uses such media as telephone infrastructure, computer servers, and communication satellites.

Distinctions were blurry even before we embarked on the digital highway. The postal service has for more than two centuries been a shared medium. That is how newspapers, later joined by magazines and catalogues, reached their readers, tucked in the mailbox next to a cousin's hand-written letter about the new baby. The point of all this is not to seek precise nomenclature, but to take note of the shifting under the very feet of those who study media.

A new kind of flip has been taking place, comparable in its scope to the "Negroponte flip" (*see Chapter 5*), but dug more deeply into social behavior. It can be stated like this: *what is mass is rapidly becoming personal; what is personal is rapidly becoming mass.* In the capacity to address smaller and smaller groups, down to the individual, mass communication is personal. In the insertion of mediated communication into even the most personal corners of daily life, the personal morphs into the mass. Examples of the former have been given. Examples of the latter include cell phone texting in place of face-to-face conversation, and identifying personal worth in terms of mediated celebrity, cleverly brought out in such films as *To Die For* and *Little Miss Sunshine*. I also recall a crowd of journalists at the airport for the arrival in New York of Robert Kennedy's body from Los Angeles, all turning to watch the event on a small monitor, as if only television validated the mournful occasion.

The purpose of this book is to look back at how mediated communication developed and to take note of the changes in human life that resulted each time that a new invention or a new method took hold across the land.

Chapter 1, "Writing: Holding Thought in Our Hands," traces writing from tokens at burial sites and scratches on jars in ancient Sumer to the output of Greek writing, and the application of writing in the great Asian empires. Knowledge now crossed distances and generations without the memory loss of oral communication.

Chapter 2, "Printing: Reproducing Information," surveys printing from its first uses in China and Korea to Europe, where printing by movable type replaced a tradition of centuries of patient labor in monasteries needed to copy manuscripts by hand. The chapter touches on how the invention of printing in Europe underlay the great religious and intellectual movements that led the medieval world into the modern era. The chapter also looks at the introduction of paper, the hand-maiden of printing.

CHAPTER 3, "EXTENDING READING" continues the chronicle of printing. The introduction of newspapers, magazines, and books are here. So are public libraries, the penny press, news services, the reporter, and the typewriter. All contributed to the reasons that we, today, are part of a literate society.

CHAPTER 4, "MAIL: HAULING INFORMATION," follows the trail of the post, an often overlooked part of the communication narrative. Postal services began sometime during the long dawn of recorded history, first for government use, then gradually for commercial and personal uses. From ocean crossings to the pony express and the postage stamp, the story of mail fascinates.

CHAPTER 5, "TELEGRAPH AND TELEPHONE WIRES: REMOVING DISTANCE," takes up both wired and cell phone communication. They have made time and distance vanish. With the telephone, personal separation no longer seemed permanent. Today, the cell phone is having its greatest effects in some of the world's poorest places.

CHAPTER 6, "PHOTOGRAPHY: CAPTURING THE EYE," looks at picture taking from ancient chemical observations to point-and-shoot digital cameras. Photographs hold our memories. They open the world to us, aiding understanding in a hundred ways. They show the face of injustice and neglect, and that has led to social change. The copier and holography are briefly examined. So is a different way to "capture the eye," the cartoon.

CHAPTER 7, "MOTION PICTURES: SHARING EMOTIONS," is about the art of motion photography from its start to the desktop video boom. The chapter recalls the days of the movies as entertainment for the working poor who crowded into nickelodeons for the pleasure that silent films gave them. Genre, censorship, the drive-in, and video recording are among topics touched on here.

CHAPTER 8, "RECORDING: CAPTURING THE EAR," looks back at sound recording, from Edison's first "whooooo" to the issues of downloading and piracy. The effects of recording on music itself are considered, and so are the changes in how we choose to entertain ourselves.

CHAPTER 9, "RADIO: HEARING VOICES," tunes in on radio from point-to-point dots and dashes to broadcasting that provided "free" entertainment during the Depression, and on to the "narrowcasting" that we have today, and to satellite transmission. Radio continues to be an unfolding tale.

One might presume that the technology revolution of the late twentieth century has increased our ability to preserve our history and cultural artifacts. In actuality, mankind is doing a terrible job. As more information is created and data standards evolve and progress, more information is being lost. Digital standards come and go within a few years' time. Already, some of NASA's earliest pictures of Earth are no longer accessible. The operating system and format documentation are long gone.[4]

—S.F. SPIRA

CHAPTER 10, "TELEVISION: LEANING BACK," reflects our fascination with "the tube." The chapter's title, taken from a comment by Steven Jobs, refers to all the contented couch potatoes and their mostly passive entertainment. But television has been more than that. The chronology starts with pre-television inventions. It concludes with the expansion of cable, TiVo, and other ways the industry is changing.

CHAPTER 11, "COMPUTERS AND THE INTERNET: CHOOSING DIGITS," is about computers, digits and the remarkable time we live in. Desktop publishing, PDAs, the rise of the Internet, the World Wide Web, email, instant messaging, texting, and blogging are considered, along with the problems caused by predators and con artists. It is also about the choices we now have.

CHAPTER 12, "PLAYING GAMES" taps into video games, their brief but explosive history, their problems, and their benefits. The opening sentence explains its purpose: "If our culture is determined by our storytellers, we must pay attention to video games."

CHAPTER 13, "PERSUADING THE MULTITUDES," identifies only a few of the many uses of mediated communication to persuade. The chapter argues, "If nothing else is consistent in human history, you can count on the desire of almost everyone to try to convince almost everyone else of something." Briefly touched on in this chapter are newspaper essays, editorials, political cartoons, radio commentaries, political propaganda, advertising, and public relations. The First Amendment, "yellow journalism," and the Fairness Doctrine are noted.

CHAPTER 14, "CROSSING BOUNDARIES," thinks about how mediated communication may intensify the conflicts between the Western and non-Western regions of the world. When part of the world is able to communicate whatever it chooses to the rest of the world, despite strong cultural objections from some of the recipients, disquiet seems inevitable. What are the responses? The chapter also considers how the tools of communication have influenced the migrations of populations within countries and across borders.

CHAPTER 15, "ON MEDIATED COMMUNICATION," tries to find points of cohesion across a vast landscape. It considers the astonishing range of communication choices we now have and what we give up in social cohesion to get them. It is less likely that we gather around the water cooler to talk about what we saw last night.

At the back of the book is "A Timeline of Communication and Culture." The two are so intertwined that trying to separate communication from culture seems futile. The timeline contains more than 5,000 entries.

All historical surveys must suffer from their scant attention to matters about which lifetimes of research have been devoted. What surveys leave out fills libraries. The present work is certainly no exception. The reader finding any information of particular interest is urged to continue to pursue it elsewhere. The books cited in the bibliography offer a start.

This survey has of necessity been limited in its geographical scope. Countries beyond the United States have their own rich histories of mediated communication in addition to the history that we all have in common, such as the start of writing and printing. With apologies, readers must look elsewhere for this information.

The story of mediated communication is so vast as almost to define history itself. To bring at least a semblance of order to that world and its effects on all of us, let us begin in ancient Sumer, when we human beings first learned how to grasp a thought in our hands.

*A man has perished and his
body has become earth. All his
relatives have crumbled to dust.
It is writing that makes him
remembered.*

— An Egyptian
Scribe, 2000 B.C.E.

WRITING:
HOLDING THOUGHT IN
OUR HANDS

EXPLORER ROBERT PEARY ASKED an Inuit guide, a man who lived by hunting, "What are you thinking?" "I do not have to think," the guide replied, "I have plenty of meat."

The hunter-gatherer, who lives from day to day, may not be a long term planner. The farmer, who lives by planting, must be. Out of his preparation comes security, the storage of grains, the raising of livestock, and the seeds of what we call civilization.

When nomadic tribes of hunter gatherers decided to settle in fertile foothills or river valleys and deltas to plant crops and tend animals in order to accumulate for themselves a steady supply of food, they created communities that merged into clans, then into states. So it came to pass in the Nile delta of Egypt, along the great watersheds of the Indus in northwest India, the Yellow in China, and the lands drained by the Tigris and Euphrates in Mesopotamia.

Communities grew, conquests united them, and commerce spread. They needed to keep records. For many centuries in a number of places, black marks placed on a wall by a skilled hand had taken the shape of an animal, or a distinctive mark scratched on a pottery jar filled with oil identified its owner. Marks would be used in the making of calendars, astronomic observations, and lists of a ruler's achievements.

In this way, speech was captured. Fixing the spoken word would change the human condition. Voltaire called writing "the painting of the voice." According to one theory, the history of producing and storing knowledge in the form of tokens representing numbers and goods began about 8000 B.C.E. in Sumer, possibly in towns along the Euphrates River.[1] The theory, which is not accepted by all scholars, holds that over many centuries small clay triangles, spheres, cones, and other tokens were molded to represent sheep, measures of grain, jars of oil, and other possessions. These tokens kept track of goods for the purpose of pooling and redistributing the community's resources.[2] Many of the tokens that have been unearthed from this period were found near temples. Sumerian wall reliefs show people delivering their goods to the temple.

FROM CLAY BALL TO TABLET

The shape of the token conveyed its meaning. Starting about 3700 B.C.E., the tokens went into hollow clay balls, a kind of envelope. Sealing the tokens in the ball hid what was inside, which would remain unknown without cracking the ball open. That led to identifying the contents of the ball by fixing an identical token set into the ball's soft clay surface, or by pressing each token against the surface before it hardened, or by scratch marks.

Impressing a *representation* of the token into the wet clay took Sumerians an important step toward actual writing, which has communication as its purpose and seeks to articulate speech. Someone must have realized that if the outside markings carried the meaning, there was no need for the actual tokens inside the hollow ball, nor really any need for the ball itself. The ball was flattened into a tablet that bore the information. Furthermore, the hand that could scratch a representation in wet clay could also incise other signs than tokens. In surviving specimens in museums these shapes do not match the tokens, indicating abstract thought.[3] Here was the hand of a writer.

Most societies chose to scratch marks onto a surface to create pictograms, logograms (word–signs), syllabic signs, or alphabetic signs. What kind of surface? It had to be reasonably permanent, easily transportable, storable, easy to manufacture out of readily available materials, and cheap, unless you were a Chinese emperor and could insist on the best, such as jade, silk, or ivory. Most writing media were ordinary, humble things. What ancient peoples did with them was, eventually, not humble at all. Writing would be the foundation of progress.

At the dawn of recorded history, the strength inherent in mediated communication started to assert itself. In early societies, the reciters of magic oral incantations that placed them richly between ordinary humans and their capricious gods were also keepers of writing and the secret knowledge that writing carried.

Writing gave power to the priests in the Egypt of the early pharaohs as well as to these worthies in many societies as far as Easter Island in the Pacific Ocean. Writing became sacred. Those who could write stood above the illiterate mass of their fellows. The priests were also often the healers. It was to them that the common folk had to appeal. And what will men and women not pay for health and salvation?

It has always been the task of priests to teach. School tablets that survive the centuries show multiplication tables, square and cube roots, and applied geometry. Patriotism and piety were taught, preparing some students for the high profession of scribe.[6] Writing in Sumer dealt with a variety of commercial, governmental, and religious matters. There were stories about gods, kings, heroes, and animals. Proverbs, word lists, and medical remedies were written down.

At about the same time, Egyptian priests were educating boys in temple schools. From the ranks of students came public administrators and new priests. That literacy and education gave them an advantage cannot be

Writing usually arises as societies become more complex.[4]

—Jerrold Cooper

Initially, writing had been "an instrument of power in the hands of small groups of priests, soothsayers and scribes serving deified monarchs." it was the perfect tool for social ascendancy, the expression of a small elite's ideology.[5]

—Steven Fischer

in doubt. A surviving papyrus says, "It is only the learned man who rules himself."[7] Literacy was part of specialized clerical training for work as a government or temple bureaucrat.[8] Instruction in the lower grades was mostly by rote, copying texts on potsherds or limestone flakes. Papyrus was reserved for students in the higher grades.

From 3000 B.C.E., the successive Sumerian, Akkadian, and Babylonian kingdoms of the Near East set down the histories of their city states on clay tablets, a chronicle of coronations, deaths, and glorious military victories. Thousands of clay tablets survive. They are more durable than papyrus or paper, and clay is readily found everywhere, although its limitations as a writing medium are its bulkiness and weight.

In addition to commercial and religious records, the Sumerians produced a body of literature that has been preserved on clay. The ruins at Tello have yielded a collection of more than 30,000 neatly stacked tablets. Many centuries before the Old Testament books, there were tales of creation and a great flood. The Sumerian king Gilgamesh became the hero of a great poem written on clay tablets centuries after his death. The Sumerian king Tammuz became a Babylonian god and entered Greek religion as Adonis.

The non–Semitic Sumerians were conquered by the Akkadians, a Semitic people, who adapted the Sumerian symbols for their own language. Extant clay tablets record these histories in prose and poetry. In the cosmopolitan city of Babylon, the scribes paraded their knowledge by advertising their achievements, much as an M.D. or Ph.D. does today by adding letters to his or her name.

Writing and mathematics began their development at approximately the same time. Numerals were invented about 3100 B.C.E., separating the symbols for sheep and jars of oil from the number of sheep and jars of oil. No doubt counting was done on the fingers before it was recorded on clay. A simple line represented a finger for all numbers up to 9, the sign for 10 was repeated up to 90; a different sign was used for 100, also repeatable. They divided the circle into 360 degrees and the year into 360 days. Division by 12 is the basis for calculating months, hours, minutes, and seconds.

The Roman decimal system also derives from finger counting. The smaller Roman numerals represented fingers. The "V" was a hand. The "X" was two "V's" attached at their points. Getting past 10 to 12 was useful because 12 could be divided by 2, 3, 4, and 6. Past 12 was 13. It could not be divided, so it was useless, a bad number, an unlucky number.

From China to Western Asia and the Near East, writers produced pictographs, simple drawings of objects that the Chinese called *ku–wan*,

CHRONICLES

It is often supposed that writing was devised for the purpose of communicating at a distance—in order to send messages that did not rely upon the memory of the messenger. But this seems to be a case of overlooking the obvious: the sending of messages, and the writing of books for posterity, are happily accidental byproducts. The earliest uses of writing seems to be to communicate things that realy don't have oral equivalents. In Mesopotamia, the earliest documents are business records, quantities of livestock, lists of workers, and their rations and tasks.[9]

—Peter Daniels

The art of writing was still young enough to give its master a high rank in society; it was the open sesame to governmental and sacerdotal office; its possessor never failed to mention the distinction in narrating his deeds, and usually he engraved a notice of it on his cylinder seal.[10]

—Louis Delaporte

or "gesture pictures." Archeological diggings at Uruk showed that the Sumerians advanced to using symbols that might stand for several objects or concepts. In this way writing could communicate ideas. Using the principle of the rebus, picture words could be combined into new words or names. For example, the sign for oil also signified a long "ee." The symbol for arrow was also the syllable "tee."

The Sumerians advanced an additional step with *phonetic* writing, using symbols for spoken language. A symbol now represented a syllable but not a separate sound. (Modern examples of syllabic writing are the two Japanese *kana*.) The Sumerians at first drew strokes on clay tablets with a reed. To avoid pulling up wet clay at every stroke, they designed a writing tool with a wedge tip to produce *cuneiform* writing. With a stylus the scribe kept property records, contracts, and official documents. The stylus became as mighty as the sword.[11]

Cuneiform was the Sumerian gift to the civilizing of mankind.[12] The Babylonian kingdom that was later established in the land of Mesopotamia continued to use clay tablets with cuneiform script.[13]

The most famous document of the Babylonians is Hammurabi's legal code, written during the eighteenth century B.C.E., carved on a cylinder. The "Mighty King of the Four Quarters of the World" set down nearly 300 laws, some of them concerned with 'an eye for an eye." By codifying the laws, Hammurabi would have established that his rule was based justly on law, not arbitrarily on the whim or will of men. That has been the principal benefit of bodies of law ever since.

Babylonians recorded not only abstract religious and philosophical thoughts. They ventured into science by classifying plants, animals, metals, and rocks. They also started a written compilation of works in mathematics, astronomy, and engineering.[14]

FROM SUMER TO EGYPT?

According to a disputed theory, writing began in Sumer and moved southwest to Egypt along the trade routes that had existed since prehistoric times.[15] Writing also arguably moved east to India and China. There, great civilizations grew. However writing arrived, Egypt and China, like Sumer, built writing systems of picture words and syllables.

In Egypt, the hieroglyphs, serving mostly for sacred writing, were inscribed on Egyptian tomb walls and on pottery. Early hieroglyphs listed the names of kings, and tombs carried autobiographies of nonroyal individuals. Later hieroglyphics recorded history, or at times each ruler's versions of history. Hieroglyphics, arguably the most beautiful of all written languages, were used on monuments and tomb walls. Egyptians created hieratic (the later Greek word for "priestly") , a cursive version of hieroglyphics with about 400 signs, a mix of pictograms and consonants. It became the written language of priests, used for ordinary documents and letters. A simplified secular version, demotic (the later Greek word for "popular"), was also used for record keeping and letters. Demotic had some alphabetic characters, yet still not a full alphabet.

Humans have been creative in the practical matter of what to write on. We have used animal skins, bones, reeds, clay, palm leaves, tree bark, wood, wax, metal, stone, seashells, pottery, silk, cotton, jade, and elephant tusks. The "tablets of stone" holding the Ten Commandments were possibly clay. We still call the page of a book a "leaf." The Latin word for the inner bark of a tree is "liber," giving us "library." The Anglo-Saxon word for bark, "boc," gives us "book." The Latin word for "revolve," which is how a scroll is unrolled, gives us "volume," The word "paper" derives from the word "papyrus." The Phœnician city of Byblos, home of traders who carried papyrus from Egypt to the Greek cities, gives us "bible."

Greeks wrote on wood, among other media. Romans coated the wood with wax; by heating the wax, a reply to a letter was written on the same letter while the messenger waited. The first daily news reports, the *Acta Diurna*, on waxed wood tablets were posted in the Roman Forum to let the public know what the Senate was doing.

The first ink was probably Egyptian. Ink was easy to make. Scrape soot from a pot, mix it with water and animal fat or plant sap, and you have ink. Instead of soot, grind some berries and you have colored ink. Chisel a reed to a point, pull a feather from a goose, or tie up a brush of hair snipped from a camel or donkey's tail and you have a pen.

That clay records would survive the wear of centuries did not matter to its users. That it was plentiful and cheap did, although its inconvenience limited its value. No doubt they would have preferred something that was not only plentiful and cheap, but also lightweight and convenient to use.

Egyptians found just that growing ten feet high along the banks of the Nile, the papyrus reed. It then grew nowhere else in the world, From it, peasants constructed boats and huts. Flexible and simple to store, the papyrus sheet took ink easily. It could also be pressed into paper, which Durant whimsically termed "the very stuff (and nonsense) of civilization."[16]

Workers split the stems into thin strips, placed one layer of stems crosswise over another in close-set rows, hammered them gently for a couple of hours, and let them dry in the sun. A seashell or a piece of ivory was used to smooth the resulting sheets. The product of this effort weighed little but lasted for years. Glue fastened the sheets end to end to make a scroll. It could be rolled up for convenient transport and storage. Scribes could fasten the papyrus sheets to form a single piece thirty feet or more

"POPULAR" WRITING

MAKING PAPYRUS

in length, which they rolled around a cylinder of wood, metal or ivory. Scribes tied smaller sheets together by passing a string through holes along one margin, an early form of bookbinding. Egypt was the paper mill to the ancient world.

Ancient Egyptians used a 12-month calendar of thirty days each; around 4,000 B.C.E. they added five days to create a year of 365 days, and actually calculated the need for the equivalent of a leap year. They created writing systems that predated the alphabet and led to it. They may have had the first postal system and the first schools.

CONTROL WEAKENS

Central government control weakened as Egyptian minor officials in the distant provinces of the empire discovered the ease with which they could communicate with each other, and did so by messages written on papyrus. Further weakening the governmental influence was more thought and activity, a change evident in the surviving papyrus documents. Thought gained lightness, according to a theory by Harold Innis, and writing on papyrus was quicker and more relaxed, even hasty, compared to the stiff and formal stone chiseling.[17]

The Theban priests were enraged by the new religion of the pharaoh Amenhotep IV, who renamed himself Akhnaton (or Ikhnaton) and not only worshipped a different god, but began to build a new capital city further down the Nile. When Akhnaton died, the priests got their revenge by erasing every written record of his name that they could lay hands on. In these early days of recorded history, a medium of communication was already playing a political role.

A technological determinist, Innis argued that the concepts of time and space reflect the significance of media to civilization. Clay, and stone are media that emphasize time; that is, time measured over centuries. They are heavy materials are suited for architecture and sculpture. They last. A civilization using clay, like the Sumerian, would be limited in area and would be concerned with religion and morality, which change little over time.

SIGNIFICANCE OF MEDIA

Media that emphasize space, such as papyrus and paper, are lighter and are suited to wide areas in administration and trade. When Julius Caesar conquered Egypt, Rome was assured a limitless supply of papyrus, and this became the basis of a large administrative empire.[18] According to Innis, an empire would be concerned with changing values, such as those of law, administration and politics, which can be applied over vast areas. The introduction of writing, he argued, undermined the magic of the spoken word and the time-based authority and tradition of the elders, leading toward space-based science and secularism.[19]

Beyond the pictogram (a picture represents a word or idea; like hieroglyphics), ideogram (a symbol represents a word or idea, like many

Chinese characters or the symbol for "no" on traffic signs), and the logogram (a symbol representing a spoken word; e.g., "6" represents "six"), there is the phonetic alphabet, written symbols for spoken language. This is a simple, practical system in which one written symbol stands for one spoken sound. A combination of these symbols represents what is spoken aloud.

Although they did not have a full phonetic alphabet, the Egyptians were apparently the first to represent a sound with a sign.[20] The phonetic alphabet may have been invented about 1700 B.C.E. in the copper mining region of the Sinai and Canaan of modern Israel by Semitic language speakers who took a set of hieroglyphic signs and pronounced them as consonants for their own language. According to this theory, the people who did this used the signs to write inscriptions in their own language on religious objects.[21]

There were no vowels in Egyptian script and none in the new consonant alphabet, but what they borrowed efficiently transcribed their spoken language. *One symbol = one sound*. This alphabet, known today as the "Proto-Sinaitic script," would be adopted by one group after another. Each group adjusted what they received to suit the sounds of their own speech.[22]

There are no biblical references to writing until we come to Moses. Canadian scholar Robert Logan theorized that "the phonetic alphabet, monotheism, and codified law were introduced for the first time to the Israelites by Moses at Mount Sinai in the form of the Ten Commandments."[23] If one believes that the sight of God's speech given as marks on tablets convinced idol worshippers to alter their ways, Logan's theory is a powerful affirmation of the potential of communication to effect change.

For believers, it is worth looking at this a little closer. Israelites in Egypt were likely to be illiterate, as were most Egyptians. Writing itself may have been unknown to them. If that were so, to be shown writing and to be told these were the words spoken by God may well have amazed them. *Imagine a god who can speak with his finger! Here is the evidence!*

Why did the phonetic alphabet, one of the most important advances in human history, come out of a remote and relatively unlettered corner of the then civilized world? Why not a center of culture like Thebes? A definitive answer is, of course, not possible. One may guess that the rigidly controlled, centralized education system of the Egyptian empire or the much later Persian empire would not be inclined to change, and would see no need for a simplification that would spread literacy; in fact, just the opposite.

Monotheism. codified law, and the alphabet all at the same moment in history cannot have been coincidental.... It was not the content of the law that was the new element, since the laws of the covenant can largely be traced back to Sumerian and Babylonian codes. What is new and unique is the manner of presentation, namely directly from God, in fact, "written with the finger of God"...[24]

—ROBERT LOGAN

SPEAKING WITH HIS FINGER

The alphabet ended the hegemony of the literate elite. Instead of a complex syllabary of over six hundred cuneiform characters, or six thousand hieroglyphs coupled with rules of grammar that would daunt the most eager student, an alphabet contained a mere twenty-odd letters. Four-year-olds could, did, and do master the alphabet's essentials. People with below-average intelligence could, did, and do learn to read and write alphabets. Thus an empowering skill that had been guarded by a favored few was now accessible to the multitudes…

…Despite the power of the empires that stood behind them, the two pillars of ancient literacy, cuneiform and hieroglyphics, eventually crumbled.[28]

—LEONARD SHLAIN

However, a more practical way to communicate would be as welcome as a more practical way to do anything. Ordinary people, such as copper miners who did not dream of entering the restricted doors of temple schools, could learn this. The alphabet's simplicity enabled them to figure out how to use it.[25]

A version of this system, known as the Canaanite alphabet, was adopted by the seafaring people we know as Phœnicians, who lived along the coastal strips of modern Syria, Lebanon, and Israel.[26] As its use widened, the alphabet inevitably changed. The Hebrew alphabet began with *aleph, bet*. The Greek alphabet began *alpha, beta*. To a Phœnician, *aleph* and *bet* meant, respectively, *ox* and *house*. The original version of *aleph* has the face of an ox. If you invert a capital A, you may see it more clearly. The original *bet*, meaning house, was a square. To this day, many Jewish temples have names that begin *Beth*. The third letter, *C* in the Roman alphabet, is *gamma* in the Greek and *gimmel* in the Hebrew. It meant *camel*.

We speak of the "Phœnician" alphabet, but they did not invent it, just as we speak of "Arabic" numerals that actually originated in India. "The Phœnicians did not create the alphabet," said historian Will Durant, "They marketed it."[27] The Phœnicians, plying trade across the Mediterranean Sea, established colonies in Greece and at Carthage on the North African coast.

Hieroglyphics also traveled south to the kingdom of Kush (in the modern Sudan), where it was converted into both a variation of hieroglyphics and the Meroïtic alphabet of twenty-three letters.

A written language served the purposes of trade and colonization. Writing must have accomplished a variety of tasks, just as it has done ever since because it was a sensible way to communicate and archive information. Communities exposed to a new and better way to do anything will borrow the ideas and adapt them to suit their own lives. Slaves would have carried the king's commands to his governors and generals in the provinces. Government officials would have needed to communicate with other bureaucrats. And would no governor or military commander have written a personal message or a letter of love to someone out of sight but not out of mind?

Research on the island of Crete indicates that Cretans shifted from using hieroglyphics or pictographs to using a linear script of about 200 symbols, still preserved on clay tablets. The so-called "Linear A" script of the Minoan civilization on Crete was followed about 1450 B.C.E. by phonetic syllable writing.[29] The "Linear B" script also included numerals and ideograms (word-signs that stood for concepts, not just things).

It is probable that the Phœnicians gradually brought writing to the Hellenic world in the course of trade and the dispersal of written magic charms.[30] (Priestly charms to ward off illness and danger were also written in China and Japan.) The legendary inventor of the alphabet, King Cadmus, may have been a Phœnician immigrant, not a king at all.[31] A dozen variations of the Phœnician alphabet took root in the warring Greek city-states before one became dominant, the variation that Homer used.

The Greeks added signs for vowels and both expanded and contracted the Phœnician alphabet to create the uniquely Greek phonetic alphabet of 24 letters to reproduce speech better than any previous written language. Unlike the complex Egyptian writing, the Greek phonetic alphabet was a simple tool. *One symbol = one sound.*

GREEKS ADD VOWELS

This in turn led to the Roman alphabet, which was an offshoot of a western Greek alphabet and the Etruscan alphabet, which also had a Phœnician origin. From the Roman alphabet and the Latin language would come other alphabets of Western civilization including the English alphabet. For traders moving among a variety of languages, a phonetic alphabet was a useful tool even if they did not remember everything just as they had learned it. Traders have never been linguistics scholars concerned with the exactness of orthography or the niceties of definitions. Copies of texts contained mistakes. Ears tuned to local dialects misheard pronunciations. As it traveled, the alphabet was altered as well as the languages it supported, but an alphabet can support any language and dialect. Until about 400 B.C.E., at the dawning of the Greek classical era, nearly every Greek city-state had its own alphabet.[32] The letters themselves took on shapes that were unlike the Phœnician letters.

We must not suppose that the alphabet replaced the predominant oral culture of ancient civilizations. Oral societies preserved their histories in what Eric Havelock called "the living memories of successive living people who are young and then old and then die."[33] Tellers of tales relied on rhythm and rhyme in their epic poems, songs, and stories to guide their memories. They felt little need to write anything down, relying on the strength of their memories to preserve their histories and culture.

**ORAL CULTURE
CONTINUES**

Even in organized religion that was founded upon written scriptures, an oral culture breathed. The stories of the Old and New Testaments were told and retold for decades, even centuries before they were committed to parchment, just like the stories of the Trojan War, which was fought several centuries before the Homeric version was set down on papyrus. Indeed, the early writing was meant to be read aloud or sung to the accompaniment of the lyre. Plato mistrusted books and wrote his *Dialogues* as conversations.[34]

The ancient Hebrews, the Greeks, and to some extent the Romans retained their oral traditions even as they gradually introduced written traditions. The wish to write their thoughts broadened in the third century C.E. as scholars tried to find a synthesis between Hebraic religious beliefs at the base of Christianity and the Greek philosophy that undergirded intellectual life in the Roman Empire. Little by little the practice of writing things down on papyrus intruded into the old oral traditions, but did not overwhelm them.

GREEK INFLUENCE

The Greeks would become the teachers, the source of much of the Mediterranean world's culture, knowledge, and education. We speak of "Greco-Roman" culture. Papyrus widened Greek influence. One of Alexander's generals, Ptolemy, began the dynasty that ruled Egypt and controlled the papyrus industry. Greek-controlled Alexandria became the leading source of book publishing and the home of the famed Alexandrian Library, the greatest of the ancient world. Because of papyrus and the phonetic alphabet written on it, Greek knowledge and ideas would travel the world. The Greeks also introduced the reed pen, replacing brushes made of animal hair.

The effects of writing were felt early in Greek history. With the alphabetic script and the availability of papyrus,[35] the *Iliad* and the *Odyssey*, the epic poems of Homer, based on tales that evidently had been repeated orally for the previous four centuries by storytellers, were written down, probably during the eighth century B.C.E. What followed was totally new in the history of the world. It was an outpouring of intellectual, artistic, and political ideas. Scrolls not only circulated in the cities, but also reached isolated scholars thanks to the trading ships plying the Mediterranean, truly the world's first information highway.

Greeks laid offerings before the gods, as have all civilizations in all centuries to this day, but the Greeks went beyond other ancient civilizations to conceive of man's fate as something separate from the sport of capricious gods. They separated mankind and human accomplishments from the world around them, regarding nature as a separate entity worthy of study.

GREEK WRITING

To do all this, they not only communicated orally among themselves, but also committed their thoughts to papyrus. Such writing, which has been of incalculable benefit to later generations, was of value to their own time. A mathematician or astronomer may have sent his observations to a friend from his school days now living in a distant Greek city. Months later a returning ship might bring his old classmate's response, enriching the body of knowledge of both scientists.

Writing using a phonetic alphabet brought change to Mediterranean culture that took it far beyond its use by shepherds, traders, sailors, and copper miners. It did serve the basic needs of the Greeks, but Greek scholars also used writing to produce bodies of work in philosophy, metaphysics, history, science, mathematics, medicine, politics, and plays both comic and tragic. The Greek writers went beyond mundane communication. They wrote to explain the nature of truth and beauty. Their scholars had a genius for abstract thought, rational thought, logical thought, and for plain common sense. Writing helped the Greeks to govern themselves. The Greeks kept their rhetoricians, who taught political argument as an oral art, but the rhetoricians, too, wrote guides to their methods.

For speakers, arguments are not separate from the arguer, because spoken thoughts hover about the speaker; their words never quite leave their source. Writing, on the other hand, standing apart from the writer, allowed the Greeks to conceive of objectivity, separating the knower from what is known. Objective thinking was the portal to the scientific method.[36] Under the pressure of writing, the influence of the schools of rhetoric declined. But that was for the educated class. Among most Greeks, the oral tradition remained. Nevertheless, the Greeks are credited with inventing literacy and the literate basis of modern thinking. Far more than simple pictographs on walls or a tally of accounts, they created a means of surviving their own life span by leaving a legacy of their thoughts, satisfying the unspoken but ever present human need to be remembered.

According to legend, the ibis-headed god of magic, Thoth, told the Egyptian pharaoh Thamos of Thoth's invention of writing. Thamos denounced it because students, "now that they possessed a means of storing up knowledge without trouble, would cease to apply themselves, and would neglect to exercise their memories."[37] In Athens, Socrates opposed the teaching of writing and apparently wrote nothing himself. Socrates predicted that a reliance on writing would weaken memory and he scornfully observed (in Plato's *Protagoras*) that it was not possible to ask a question of a document.

We for whom writing is as natural as breathing are astonished at the memory abilities found in oral cultures. Their human skills lie beyond our technological cultures.[39] On the other hand, writing made it possible to fix information beyond the uncertainties of what the mind retains, to hold information and conclusions in the hand, keep them nearby for reference or send them winging across space and time to be examined in different places and different centuries. Thanks to writing, the human mind is no longer restricted by memory.

Poetic rhythms serve the memory. Then as now, recitation worked best for poetry, which is designed to be heard; writing was suited to prose. Sometimes the oral and the written worked in tandem. Among the

For your invention will produce forgetfulness in the souls of those who have learned it, through lack of practice at using their memory, as through reliance on writing they are reminded from outside by alien marks, not from inside, themselves by themselves: you have discovered an elixir not of memory but of reminding. To your students you give an appearance of wisdom, not the reality of it; having heard much, in the absence of teaching, they will appear to know much when for the most part they know nothing, and they will be difficult to get along with, because they have acquired the appearance of wisdom instead of wisdom itself.[38]

—SOCRATES

Humankind is defined by language, but civilization is defined by writing. Writing made historical records possible...[40]

—PETER DANIELS

Even to ostracize (banish) an undesirable person from Athens for ten years was only possible if 6,000 men each wrote his name, simultaneously, on individual pieces of ostraca (potsherd). Writing, far from being a (semi-) secret art practiced by a specially trained elite, was an essential element of Greek democracy.[46]

—ALBERTINE GAUR

The long history of its praise in the Western tradition is the self-interested product of those who write, but there has always been a party, less audible by the nature of its doctrine, opposed to writing. The Spartan believed that the unrecorded good behavior of citizens, though lost to history, was worth a book full of unrealized ideals.[47]

—ROBERT PATTISON

Greek historians, written history came out of oral sources. Herodotus, Thucydides, and Xenophon preferred spoken eyewitness accounts to documents. Although they themselves wrote, they used only a few written sources. Thucydides transcribed some letters, inscriptions and treaties, but, like Herodotus, preferred oral to written evidence.[41]

Greek writing that promoted critical thought lit Roman thought and, later, all of Western civilization. The famous Socratic dialogues relied on deduction, a method more suited to philosophy than science. Yet, for nearly two thousand years, until Galileo, in preference to observation, experimentation, and inductive reasoning, the schools and scientists of Europe followed Plato and Aristotle in using deduction.

In Athens the copy shops kept busy, and by the fifth century B.C.E. a book market flourished.[42] During the fourth century, Aristotle set about gathering and classifying the body of known knowledge. He could not have done so without a written language and the papyrus to hold it, giving him a permanent record on a storable medium. Because of Aristotle, education in the Greek world would be based on reading, not simply listening to lectures.

Mathematics, medicine, astronomy, geography, and biology advanced because of ideas, conclusions, and reports of experiments written and stored on the transportable medium of papyrus. Cheap and available papyrus has been credited with supporting a burst of lyric poetry.[43] Despite the complaints of Socrates about the dangers of writing, the Greeks, especially the Athenians, had a reading public. In Athens, Syracuse, and other cities a growing number of young citizens came out of schools able to read and write. The numbers of schools increased, and so did the numbers of freeborn boys and girls. They learned by rote memorization, but the literacy base widened.

A further clue that literacy was a central element in government was the Athenian requirement later that magistrates could not apply "an unwritten law."[44]

Until Alexander, the Greeks, of course, never had an empire, as did the Egyptians, the Persians, and the Romans. They existed as quarrelsome city-states held together by trade, a shared culture and a language, both spoken and written, that remained relatively stable for a thousand years.[45] We can better appreciate this when we consider how much English has changed in the six centuries between us and Chaucer, or even the four centuries since Shakespeare. The culture they shared and would pass on to Rome and Western Europe was transmitted in the academies of Athens and other cities to students who carried it back to the far corners of the Hellenic world. It is reasonable to assume that former classmates stayed in touch by letter. Most Greek scientists worked in isolation.[48] They had both papyrus and the shared phonetic alphabet. It seems natural that they corresponded.[49] Greek scholars were prolific writers, and their writing was meant for their contemporaries or to be read aloud in public.[50]

If Athens was enthusiastic about writing as a means of communication, its rival Sparta was not. Athens produced what may still be the greatest concentration of thinkers in the history of the world, but Sparta produced no historian, no philosopher, no scientist or mathematician, no poet or playwright. In fact, writing was forbidden by Lycurgus, reputed founder of the Spartan constitution. He wanted youngsters to learn his city's laws by listening to them and by practice and example, not by reading about them. The laws themselves were never written down. Students were taught to read and write, but sparingly. Few Spartans bought books. Literacy just didn't matter much.

Romans conquered the Greek city-states but Greek would be the language of education, diplomacy, literature, and science in the eastern Mediterranean for another thousand years. All educated Romans learned Greek. Thousands of books were written in Greek long after Athens and the other Greek cities were conquered. Christianity separated from its Jewish roots when it expanded into Greek culture.

The world's first formal educational system was the training of scribes, who were the programmers of the ancient world. Often recruited from among the slaves, scribes enjoyed a higher social status than other slaves because reading and writing were skills often beyond the capacity of masters who could only stare dumbly at the marks on clay or papyrus and depended on their scribes for their financial health. The stylus was as mighty as the sword.

To a household slave, literacy was the path to a better — and longer — life than anything else available, a skill worth acquiring, The scribe kept the accounts, recorded the tribute to tax collectors and priests, noted what was bought, what was sold, and how much was paid. He read and wrote contracts, oversaw commercial dealings, and engaged in exchanges of diplomatic notes. In doing all this, he achieved a measure of influence rare for slaves. When the Greeks and Romans built libraries by copying the texts of books that came their way, slave scribes were the copyists and sometimes the librarians. The clerical, scribal skills also appealed to many of the freeborn. If a scribe considered himself superior to other men, he enjoyed a delusion of the literate that has persisted.

Historian Will Durant imagined the life of a slave scribe:

> *Every visitor to the Louvre has seen the statue of the Egyptian scribe, squatting on his haunches, almost completely nude, dressed*

Most (scribes) after all their technical training, spent their lives writing lists of deliveries of sheep or issues of barley rations and occasionally taking a letter by dictation. The more successful scribes would end up as senior administators in the state bureaucracy...[51]

—C.B.F. WALKER

PATH TO A BETTER LIFE

with a pen behind the ear as reserve for the one he holds in his hand. He keeps record of work done and goods paid, of prices and costs, of profits and loss; he counts the cattle as they move to the slaughter, or corn as it is measured out in sale; he draws up contracts and wills, and makes out his master's income tax; verily there is nothing new under the sun.

He is sedulously attentive and mechanically industrious; he has just enough intelligence not to be dangerous. His life is monotonous, but he consoles himself by writing essays on the hardships of the manual worker's existence, and the princely dignity of those whose food is paper and whose blood is ink.[52]

CLAY TABLETS SURVIVE

Assyrian and Babylonian books were on clay tablets that have survived the centuries. The oldest catalogue of books in existence is Sumerian. It lists sixty-two literary works.[53] The first known, organized library was meant to be used. With a cataloguing system, it was built in Ninevah by kings of the eighth and seventh centuries B.C.E., Sargon, Senacherib, and Assurbanipal. It contained an estimated 20,000 to 25,000 tablets. When the Assyrians conquered Babylon they improved the collection by ransacking the conquered territory for tablets on grammar, poetry, history, science, and religion.[54] This library served to promote the fame of the king, but it also compiled and advanced knowledge. A cadre of educated slaves worked as scribes. The library catalogued its religious, historical, and scientific works.[55] It is not clear who could use the library; high officials probably gained access, but it was unlikely that scholars did.[56]

According to Greek writers, the only sources available, ancient Egyptian temples collected writings on the trappings of religion, such as liturgies and rituals.[57] These were archives, called "houses of life," not true libraries.[58] Of their papyri, nothing remains.

"HOUSES OF LIFE"

We must look to the Greeks for a fuller appreciation of books and knowledge.[59] There were private collections of books by Aristotle and others, and libraries accessible to scholars. A public depository of books was available in Athens by 330 B.C.E. Aristotle is credited with showing the Egyptians how to set up proper libraries instead of mere collections of books. The word "museum" comes from Aristotle's book collection.[60] In trying to gather the world's knowledge, Aristotle apparently had the world's first known private collection of books, the first private library.

For nations stymied by political decisions to block papyrus shipments, parchment was the answer, for sheep were everywhere. The Greek city-state of Pergamum in western Turkey figures in a tale of library intrigue. It seems that the Egyptian pharaoh Ptolemy, Cleopatra's ancestor, grew jealous of the library assembled by King Eumenes II, so he blocked shipments of papyrus to Pergamum. Undaunted by this embargo, the resourceful Eumenes encouraged the mass production of treated animal skins, and that is how parchment came to rival papyrus and, later, paper.[61]

Slowly becoming brittle and disintegrating with age, papyrus would not survive forever. Some old papyri kept under glass in controlled conditions still exist. The sturdier parchment, made from the skin of a sheep, a calf, or a goat, was scraped clean of hair, smoothed with pumice, then finished with chalk and lime. A similar but more expensive surface was vellum, sometimes made from the thin and supple skin of unborn lambs or kids.

Parchment had the advantage over papyrus of allowing writing on both sides and it could be cleaned and reused. It had the disadvantage of a greater physical effort to write on it. The parchment *codex*, the cut and folded pages written on both sides that made up a book, aided the spread of Christianity. By the second century C.E., books of parchment codices of the four Gospels were written in Greek, the language familiar to educated readers across the ancient world.

Intent on ruling in the manner of one of Plato's philosopher-kings, Ptolemy created the greatest of the ancient libraries at the start of the third century B.C.E. The Alexandrian served not only as a library, but also as a university, a research center, and a publishing house. At first the library was just part of the Alexandrian Museum, but as its collection and its fame grew, the library eclipsed the museum in importance. It was open to scholars at a rich time for the communication of knowledge as it was established within half a century of the establishment of Plato's Academy and Aristotle's Lyceum. Dedicated to the Muses, the Alexandrian continued as a center of scholarship, inquiry, and debate for five centuries.

One of its earliest achievements was the translation of the Septuagint, the Old Testament, into Greek. This was not the only scholarship worth remembering. The third librarian of the Alexandria, Eratosthenes, calculated the circumference of the Earth to within 1% by measuring the length of shadows at noon in two cities. Christopher Columbus would not do so well. And nearly two thousand years before Copernicus and Galileo, Aristarchus applied Alexandrian trigonometry to theorize a heliocentric solar system.

The city of Alexandria was one of the large ports of the ancient world, Under the dictate of the Ptolemy dynasty, ships docking at Alexandria were searched for new manuscripts. These would be copied and the original would go to the library. The copy was given to the ship. Ptolemy III wrote a letter addressed to all the kings of the ancient world asking for their books, so they could be copied. Again, reportedly, the originals

**PARCHMENT
AND VELLUM**

**SEARCHING SHIPS
FOR MANUSCRIPTS**

..And what was that mechanism of (Roman) law and administration based upon? Paper, or more exactly, papyrus....

Engraving in stone is for the priests; they have an affinity for spanning eras. But soldiers are no-nonsense managers. They need to deal with the here and now. The alphabet and paper create armies, or rather the bureaucracies which run armies. Paper creates self-contained kingdoms at a distance.[65]

— MARSHALL MCLUHAN AND BRUCE POWERS

were kept and the copies were returned. Pursuing the goal of holding a copy of every book in the world, the library acquired dictionaries, concordances, and encyclopedias.[62]

The great library suffered in 48 B.C.E., when Julius Caesar sailed into Alexandria. Exactly what happened is unclear. According to one account, a fire in the harbor spread to the library, destroying tens of thousands of volumes. Whatever the cause, the destruction led to more library intrigue, this time because of Antony's love for Cleopatra, if the gossips of the time are to be believed. Antony made a personal gift to Cleopatra of the library of Pergamum for the Alexandrian Library. But the Pergamum holdings were Roman state property and not Antony's to give.

How the Alexandrian library was eventually destroyed is still unsettled. Did Christians do it, or Muslims? One version blames the pillage on a mob of Christians in the late fourth century after the Emperor Theodosius ordered the destruction of all pagan temples. Another tale, dated to the twelfth century, places the blame on the Muslim Caliph Omar.[63] Whoever was to blame apparently burned the books for the sake of religious purity. It would not be the last time that books would be burned to please the heavens.

The Roman Empire could boast of growing literacy. By the fourth century C.E., the city of Rome itself had at least twenty-eight libraries with 20,000 or more papyrus rolls each. Throughout the empire there were city and private libraries and book collections. According to Seneca, in wealthy homes, private libraries became as common as baths. A wealthy Roman family or group of families would set up a private school with an educated slave or freedman as teacher. He — always a he — taught the 3R's plus history and obedience. Moral education and patriotism were staples of Roman education. They were taught through both poetry and prose. The first prose novels of romance and adventure appeared. The youngest Romans wrote upon leaves and strips of tree bark. As they advanced, they wrote on wooden tablets covered with wax that could be warmed and smoothed over. Still later, leather, papyrus, and parchment were used. It is said that Mohammed in Arabia dictated portions of the Quran ("Koran" or "Discourse") that were written on parchment, leather, palm leaves, and even bones.

PROSE NOVELS

Caesar's conquest of Egypt assured a steady supply of papyrus for the administration needed to run an empire.[64] The practical, no-nonsense Romans wrote things down and kept records. Because a written script changes much more slowly than speech, written Latin remained fixed while the spoken language was gradually altered in one part of the empire after another, producing the variety of vernacular Romance languages across southern Europe that exists today from Portugal to

Romania. Unlike Greek education, athletic games were generally not part of education in the practical Roman world. Young men broke off their bookish studies to strengthen their bodies by work in the field or the camp, not the gymnasium.

For the small percentage of the populace literate in Greek or Latin and able to afford the hand-written copies, classical verse and prose were available. They could read the epic poems, the tragedies and satires, political speeches, philosophical questions, religious thought, and what passed as scientific knowledge. As it was everywhere, most of the far-flung Roman Empire remained illiterate. Except for the scribe, whose purpose in life required literacy, a literate peasant or slave would have been a stench in the nostrils of an illiterate nobleman. Not many people had ever heard of such a thing as a book.

Europe became divided not only between the Latin Church in Western Europe and the Greek Orthodox Church in the East but also between Muslim and Christian worlds, to say nothing of the Asian worlds of India and China beyond the Arab lands, virtually unknown in Europe. Exports of papyrus from Egypt to Europe dropped sharply after the Muslim conquest of North Africa in the seventh century. With little commerce and much hostility, communication suffered. Where there might have been knowledge, there was ignorance. The Byzantine Empire rose in the east, centered in Constantinople (modern Istanbul), but Rome itself and the Roman Empire that had covered much of Western Europe sank into barbarism. The age of feudalism dawned. The Bible, the Talmud, and the Quran helped to guide what order existed in society. A few scholars who traveled between these mutually hostile worlds translated some of the books of each.[66]

The Talmud ("Teaching") is the body of laws and commentary that sustained the Jews during their centuries of exile and directed them in every aspect of daily life. The Talmud, and the Torah ("Laws") on which it was based, became a portable nation for a people without their own nation. Education was by rote memory. Scholars and rabbis (teachers) were honored for their lifelong study of scripture. During these centuries, Jews fared better under Muslim rule than under Christian rule, and they contributed to Muslim libraries their own studies of medicine and philosophy.

Mohammed was born in 569 when the Roman world was collapsing. As the Quran and literacy spread in the largely illiterate Arab world, literacy was dying in the Christian world. The Muslim world had universities centuries before those in Christian Europe. Muslims learned of the miracle that transformed Mohammed into a literate man. In Sura 96:1 of the Quran, Muslims were urged to read. However, the oral tradition

LIMITED LITERACY

BIBLE, TALMUD, AND QURAN

continued in the hadith, tales of the life of the prophet and those close to him. Several generations passed before they were written down.

MUSLIM EDUCATION

At the age of six, nearly all boys, some girls, and even some slave children began a religious education. As everywhere, the children of the wealthy enjoyed private schooling. In some parts of the Muslim world, the children of Christians and Jews were allowed education in Muslim schools. In other places, they were forbidden to attend. Learning in the lower grades was by rote, the memorization of prayers. Reading was taught, but writing and arithmetic were left for higher grades, including the Arab invention of algebra. At the highest levels, while the Christian world slept or struggled, Muslim scholars moved forward with books on medicine, science, and philosophy. Short stories were popular everywhere. From the story teller's tradition we get the adventures of Sinbad, Aladdin, Ali Baba, and other tales of *The Thousand and One Nights.*

From the eighth to the thirteenth centuries Islamic civilization was superior to what was happening in Europe. Invasions of the Near East and South Asia by Mongols, Tatars, and Turks resulted in huge numbers of deaths and enslavement, and the destruction of the educated Arab and Persian civilizations, including schools and libraries. Scholars and scientists who survived were scattered. Rebuilding proceeded slowly.

The Crusades tried repeatedly to wrest control of Jerusalem and other places holy to Christianity, but ultimately succeeded in drawing a curtain of animosity between the Christian and Muslim worlds. Contemporaneous with the European Middle Ages, the Mogul Empire was formed. During the sixteenth century one of its most famous rulers, Akbar, built a great library of hand-written manuscripts engraved by skillful artists. Printing was brought to him, but he dismissed it as an inferior thing.

PRINTING IS INFERIOR?

To the east, from ancient to medieval times, different histories were played out. The Persians, who for a time sat astride the world's largest empire, chose to use writing for trade but not literature, which they considered effeminate.[67] The Persians also preferred war and conquest to building their own industry. Centuries earlier they had imported much of their scientific knowledge from Babylon. However, they simplified the Babylonian syllabary to 36 signs, which they gradually turned into an alphabet.

Early worship of the sun god Mithra gave way to the worship of Zarathustra, called Zoroaster by the Greeks. The religion had a bible reportedly written originally on thousands of cowhides. Like the Old Testament, it contained prayers, songs, legends, rituals, and moral teachings. It was also similar to the *Vedas*, the sacred writings of the Hindus who dwelled further to the east.

In India, the priestly Hindu caste of Brahmans were taught, in the sacred writing of the *Upanishads*, that true understanding comes from insight, not books or learning. Like the Spartans of ancient Greece, they held writing inferior to speaking. Yet India has a rich literary tradition. According to fable, the elephant-headed Ganesh, god of wisdom, invented writing. For a pencil he broke a tusk. The Brahman priests, who had charge of education, guarded their exclusive right to hear the sacred texts. According to their law, a Shudra, a member of a lower caste, who listened to a reading of the Scriptures, could have his ears filled with molten lead; a Shudra who recited them was to have his tongue split; a Shudra who memorized the Scriptures was to be cut in half. The threats, seldom enforced, assured Brahman control of writing.

A MATTER OF CASTES

Hindus of the lower classes comforted themselves with reciting the many Tantras, with rituals of mysticism, astrology, and magic. As the centuries passed, education under the control of Brahman priests was gradually extended to boys of lower castes, until only the untouchables were denied education. In India, as elsewhere, literacy conferred power, so it was rationed. In the schools the extensive use of poetry eased learning by the usual rote memorization and repetition. Fables and histories, written and read aloud in the West in prose form, were written in poetic form to be read aloud.

If most men in India were illiterate, so were nearly all women, except the few of the very wealthy, and a peculiar class of women, the temple courtesans or temple prostitutes. They were in some ways like Greek hetaerae or Japanese geisha, cultured women who entertained at ceremonies. Their society could be also compared to the Middle Ages in Europe, where women were also kept illiterate except for a few in the nobility.

During many of the centuries of Hinduism, the priests were the learned men, and therefore the scientists and mathematicians as well as the writers. They gave the world grammar, logic, philosophy, fables, and chess. They also gave the world "Arabic" numerals (which came to Europe from the Arabs, but originated in India), the decimal system and the concept of zero. They added to the knowledge of astronomy and medicine. At the time that European scholars were writing in Latin, a language unintelligible to most Europeans, Indian scholars were writing in Sanskrit, a language unintelligible to most Indians. But ordinary people in both cultures would not be denied forever. Just as Latin was transformed into Spanish, Italian, and the other Romance languages, Sanskrit was shaped into Prakrit, Hindi, and other vernaculars. Mixed with the Persian words of the conquering Muslims, it became Urdu, Tamil, Bengali, and a hundred other written and spoken languages of South Asia.

INDIAN LEARNING

The books of Buddhism, a faith that began in India and became a major religion throughout East Asia, were studied extensively. Before there was paper, Buddhists wrote on pages of treated tree bark. The writer used a pen to scratch into the bark, smeared ink over the whole page, then wiped it away, so that the ink remained only in the scratches, a form of lithography.

Writing itself is sacred to several faiths. Jews press their lips to cloth that has touched the cloth cover of hand-written scrolls. At a Buddhist monastery in Gyangze, Tibet, pilgrims crawl beneath stacks of Buddhist scriptures to absorb their wisdom. These practices have continued for centuries.

It has been argued that all human languages can be traced to a common ancestor, but there seem to be at least three distinct, independent origins of ancient writing: the cuneiform writing for the Sumerian language, Chinese, and the Mayan script in Mesoamerica.[68]

The Chinese never adopted a phonetic alphabet, preferring a system derived from pictograms. The picture words denoted their meanings, not their sounds, although a name could be roughly identified in association with the pronunciation of the characters. It is one of the world's most important writing systems, second only to English in its influence. The Chinese written language allows people whose spoken languages are totally dissimilar to communicate by writing out their thoughts. It is not unusual today for a student from Beijing in conversation with a student from Hong Kong to tease out the meaning of a word by tracing the character with a finger.

Although the Chinese written language consists of a bewildering array of 40,000 characters, few scholars attempt to learn all of them. Students are taught a more manageable 214 radicals, which are then combined into compounds. For example, "wife" is represented by the radical for a woman next to radicals for a hand over a broom. "Help" is represented by the radicals for husband and hand. The radicals were designed, no doubt, by men. If the written language seems impossibly confounding to the Western eye, especially when added to the complexity of four to nine tones that the many regional spoken Chinese languages have, the difficulty is softened by Chinese lack of spelling, parts of speech, declensions, conjugations, numbers, cases, tenses, or the other numbing elements of grammar.

The start of Chinese writing is dated to before 1200 B.C.E. It possibly derived, like the Egyptian writing far to the west, from the Sumerian script along trade routes. At least two books, the *Book of Changes* and the *Laws of Chou*, were written in the twelfth century B.C.E. According to a debatable source, a royal library existed in the sixth century B.C.E.,

For generation after generation the writings of the Master were the texts of the official schools, and nearly every lad who came through those schools had learned those texts by heart… With the help of this philosophy China developed a harmonious community life, a zealous admiration for learning and wisdom, and a quiet and stable culture which made Chinese civilization strong enough to survive every invasion, and to remold every invader in its own image…

…It was well fitted to a nation struggling out of chaos and weakness into order and strength, but it would prove a shackle upon a country compelled by international competition to change and grow… It helped to keep women in supine debasement, and its cold perfection froze the nation into a conservatism as hostile to progress as it was favorable to peace.[69]

—WILL DURANT

older than Aristotle's library on the other side of the world; the philosopher known as Lao Tze ("the old master") became fed up with working as the curator of the royal library, and left.[70]

LAO TZE AND CONFUCIUS

There is no doubt about the five books written in the sixth and fifth centuries by Confucius, or about the influence of his writing not only in China, but also in Korea and Japan. Four additional books of his teachings were compiled by his disciples or their disciples, as the fame of the old government official turned teacher spread. Dealing with morality, ethics, social order, and political order, his written legacy of conservative behavior has influenced governments for all the centuries from his day to ours. For much of this period, Confucian thought was the dominant national philosophy. His real influence came after his death. Schools were created to teach his philosophy. Shih Huang-ti, the emperor most credited with building the Great Wall and setting up the recently excavated underground army in Sian, ordered Confucius' books burned. He had Confucian scholars buried alive, but he could not squelch the power of Confucius' writing. When his Ch'in dynasty ended, a new emperor brought the books out of hiding. Confucius' ideas were taught again, and graduates steeped in his learning achieved high office in government. The words, originally written on bamboo strips, were carved into stone so that students could make rubbings forever. Printing has been credited with reviving Confucian thinking and making it the dominant philosophy of East Asia for centuries.

CHINESE LITERATURE

The imperial library of the Han dynasty had more than ten thousand volumes on such subjects as philosophy, mathematics, literature, medicine, and war. Literature depended heavily upon poetry, but not fiction, which was not considered literature until the Mongols brought it in about the time of Marco Polo's sojourn.In the rigidly controlled Chinese society, the medium of writing promised change, but it did not come easily. Except for Confucian schools supported by the state, most schools in China received neither state nor religious aid. Typically, a single poor scholar taught students in a simple room. Even this poverty of education was denied to most boys because of their inability to pay and, as usual, virtually all girls. School days were long, instruction was by rote memorization, and the bamboo cane rested not far from the teacher's hand. The students pushed themselves as well as being pushed because China also offered public examinations open to all males. Those who passed were promoted to a higher, literary class and were eligible for government jobs. Those who failed the exams could try again and again, even into their old age.

Efforts to simplify Chinese writing can be traced back for two thousand years, but they always ran into opposition from conservative scholars. The most recent efforts came under Mao Tse Tung in 1955, with a simplified Chinese script, and 1958, with a Latin script called Pinyin. In the early twentieth century, Western nations and Japan imposed huge financial demands upon a helpless Manchu dynasty government, but remitted much of it with the stipulation that the money be spent educating Chinese students in the universities of the nations returning the funds. Today, the fact that so many Chinese graduate students come to Western universities is a modern extension of an older tradition.

JAPANESE WRITING

Korean and Japanese written languages are derived from the Chinese. Until Buddhist priests from China introduced a written language, Japan had only its own spoken language, possibly a variation of Mongolian or Korean. The Japanese adapted the Chinese character script, which they call "kanji." (Until the eighteenth century. women were forbidden to use it.) In the ninth century the Japanese added hiragana the first of two "kana" syllabaries. Katakana, using straight lines instead of the hiragana cursives, came later in response to foreign incursions.

The sum total is what may be the world's most difficult written language. It is common in modern Japanese writing to use all three writing systems in the same sentence. A Portuguese missionary struggling to translate the Bible into Japanese grumbled that the Devil had invented the Japanese written language to prevent the translation. The Japanese, who take pride in their distinctiveness and their intellectual achievements, seem content with their complex writing system.

Despite—or maybe because of—the complicated written language, Japan has become the most literate nation on Earth. Nearly every child in the nation attends school, and nearly every Japanese man and woman is able to read. Japanese scholars relished the difficulty of their language and rejected all attempts at simplification. In doing so, they were not the first to use language as a way to limit communication.

(Hang'ul) is good for any practical use, and even the sound of the wind, the chirp of birds, the crowing of cocks, and the barking of dogs can be exactly described with it.[71]

— KOREAN KING SEJONG

Because of the complexity of the Chinese written character script, a remarkable Korean king, Sejong II, in the fifteenth century ordered the creation of a simple written alphabet to encourage literacy among commoners in his effort to turn his country from Confucian to Buddhist ideals; hang'ul ("Korean letters"), may be the world's most efficient script for reproducing human speech, an alphabet based on Sanskrit, with eighteen consonants and ten vowels. A simple alphabet or syllabary made written communication possible for the first time for many unlettered people. It allowed a flexible local alternative to the inflexible original imported language. He said he wanted to further education and "to satisfy reason and to reform men's evil nature." However, Chinese characters remained the written language of Korean and Japanese scholars. Kana and hang'ul were for women, children, and commoners.

In the Mesoamerica of the Western Hemisphere, the Incas of Peru had a complex system of color-coded knots on parallel strings called "quipus"; it is believed that the position of the knots, the spacing between them, and their color identified goods and quantities. Some civilizations used the inner bark of trees.

Existing Zapotec and Mayan texts predate 900 C.E. In 2006, digging in Mexico unearthed a stone Olmec table with writing three thousand years old. There are stone historical records identifying royal births, marriages, and deaths, plus records of battles, captives, and the important blood-letting ceremonies. A Spanish missionary in the Yucatan peninsula, displeased with what he came across although it is doubtful that he could read them, wrote in the sixteenth century, "We found a great number of books written with their characters, and because they contained nothing but superstitions and falsehoods about the devil, we burned them all."[72]

WRITING GIVES PERMANENCE TO the system of sounds that is language. Writing is the oldest form of mediated communication, created out of simple technologies and complex language systems, leaving scratches that others may understand. A simple, practical phonetic alphabet, first developed in a remote corner of the civilized world, served practical needs. As its use spread over the centuries, local communities changed the alphabet that they were given so that it fit their own spoken language. At the same time, the oral cultures continued to serve most people.

At first, writing was used to record possessions, list the achievements of rulers, convey messages, and preserve knowledge of ritual, medicine, and the calendar. It would become much more. Armed with the gift of writing, human beings built soaring edifices of thought.

Writing led to new means of education. It led to libraries. The human mind would no longer be restricted by memory's limitations. Writing enabled its users to hold thinking and memory outside the brain, sharing their inferences and deductions with other people in other places. They reflected upon the writings of others, added to them, and packaged knowledge for future generations. Their readers were the first people to learn from those they could not see and may not have known anything about.

In culture after culture, the art of writing communicated and stored information, myths, prejudices, observations, and the gathered knowledge derived from all of these. Occasionally it managed to store wisdom.

WESTERN HEMISPHERE

CONCLUSION

Recognizing the value of those marks on clay or papyrus, men have hoarded them, walled them in, and severely punished anyone who intruded into their mysteries. The priests of many religions, the keepers of the mysteries of the gods, found writing to be a natural fit for them. They guarded the skill jealously, aware of how it conferred power.

Written language undergirds all other mediated communication and, indeed, most of civilization. Yet there have always been societies that lived without writing. A few pockets survive today by the sufferance of the literate, but would anyone who is literate prefer to live as an illiterate? We would not willingly give up the benefits accompanying the ability to read and write. In the presence of so many other communication tools, perhaps we take writing for granted, but to imagine life without the medium of the written word is to carry us into a world difficult to visualize and less desirable to inhabit.

2 PRINTING: REPRODUCING INFORMATION

ACCORDING TO THE ENGLISH scientist Francis Bacon, gunpowder was one of three inventions that changed the world. Knights on horseback, that bulwark of feudalism, could not win against muskets, nor could castle walls withstand what emerged from the cannon's mouth. Bacon said a second invention was the compass. With it, mariners sailed into new worlds with some assurance of returning, and, in doing so, restructured nations. Gunpowder and the compass were invented in China. The third invention, also Chinese, was printing. With it, Europe entered the Modern Age.

It does not take away from the reputation of printing to identify other causes ascribed to the start of the modern world in Christian Europe. Change came on breezes from every direction. Constantinople fell to the Ottoman Turks. Ancient literature was rediscovered. Explorers voyaged to Asia, Africa, and the New World. A merchant class arose to claim its place in society. Nation states swallowed feudal baronies; the papacy was challenged not only by Martin Luther. And there was printing's transformative role.

PRINTING IN ASIA

The actual invention was not the printing press, for presses were commonly used to squeeze grapes for wine and olives for oil. It was movable type. Because the Chinese character set contains as many as 40,000 ideograms rather than the little more than two dozen letters used to make German, English, and other European language words, printing with movable type — typography — was inefficient for Chinese writing. Its eleventh century Chinese inventor, alchemist Pi Shêng, never went past breakable clay type and an inadequate ink. Add to these difficulties a limited run of book copies.[1] The Chinese later made use of wooden movable type and block printing, carving an entire page in a wood block. (The Musée Guimet in Paris holds a collection of 960 wooden movable type pieces of the ancient Uighur alphabet from western China, carved about 250 years before Gutenberg.) Ink, an invention dating at least to 500 B.C.E., may have originated in inked seals used as early as 4000 B.C.E. by Mediterranean civilizations. In Europe, the Romans had experimented with lining up seals, but with papyrus, poor inks, no market, and plenty of slave scribes, the invention of movable type had little chance in ancient Rome. Traders could have introduced seals to the Far East, but block printing. Xylography, as it is formally known, is credited to the inventor Fêng Tao, whose place in Chinese history can be compared to Johannes Gutenberg.[2]

Besides carving blocks of wood into entire pages for books, the Chinese printers carved small blocks to stamp printed charms onto bamboo strips to be worn as amulets to ward off tigers and illness.[3] Stamped with personal information, these pieces of bamboo could serve as passports to ease entry through a city gate.

Schooling and literacy were limited to the sons of the aristocracy in China, as hey were in the rest of the ancient and medieval world. Book printing had little employment beyond government publications. Most printed books were kept as scrolls printed on silk or paper until the tenth century when pages, printed on one side of the paper sheets, were cut into the codex form.

KOREAN MOVABLE METAL TYPE

Korea did more than China with typography two centuries before Gutenberg printed Bibles, and it had some effect. Korea was the first nation to use movable metal type, but these were small, flat squares difficult to bind into a form for the printing process. The printers did not use a press. They laid a sheet of paper on the inked type and rubbed it with a brush.[4] However, printing with carved wooden blocks continued to be the principal printing method until the nineteenth century. Text written on thin paper was placed face down on a wooden block. The paper was rubbed away, and oil was applied to the block to bring out the inked writing. The engraver then cut into the block to leave the written characters in relief. The characters were then inked, moistened paper was laid over them, and a brush pressed the paper onto the block.

That two nations with an extensive written language least suited to printing with movable type should have led the world in inventing it is a curiosity.

Because Korea is a peninsula jutting out of the distant reaches of the Far East, Korean printing was too remote to affect later developments in Europe, but it should not be overlooked. It helped to educate a segment of the local population. Literate parents made sure they raised literate children. The degree of literacy among Koreans has long been a point of national pride. Today, Korean students are among the top scorers in annual international competition.

WHAT DID EUROPE KNOW?

In Europe, the dividing line between the medieval age and the modern age is considered to be Johannes Gutenberg's printing of the 42–line Bible (42 lines per page). Did the German goldsmith and mirror maker know of Asian printing? Maybe not, but even if he had never heard of Cathay, did he know of the printing that had been done there for centuries? Some reasonable suppositions and a few clues indicate that

Gutenberg ought to have known something of block printing, if not of movable type.

Here are some clues. Block printing of images for fabrics, playing cards, and small religious icons was done in Italy, Germany, and Holland during the last half of the fourteenth century.[5] Paper printed on one side and folded over or bound back to back were assembled into "block books."[6] In addition to block books of religious pictures it was alleged that printed obscene pictures were readily available. They were even being sold outside churches, according to an angry complaint.[7] At the same time there were printers in the Muslim world. For religious reasons some Muslims chose not to print books; the sixteenth century Ottoman sultan Selim I ordered anyone caught printing to be put to death. Far to the north, the Mongols, who crossed northern Asia to the gates of Europe, did not have such cultural restrictions. The illiterate Mongols, lacking their own separate written language, borrowed the cultures of their conquered lands, including the printing of Chinese literature in their own Mongol language.[8] Meanwhile, traders on the Silk Road running between China and the Middle East, who did business with Arab middlemen in Baghdad and Damascus, probably carried printed religious images and block–printed playing cards to while away the evening hours.

More clues. Two missionaries, an Italian, Giovanni da Monte Corvino, and a German, Arnold de Cologne, are known to have printed Christian religious images in China. It is possible that they brought those skills back to Europe. Europeans knew that paper money was printed in China and Persia because travelers, including Marco Polo, reported it.[9] Missionaries and other travelers who came home with news of the Chinese invention of paper may have reported that a great number of books were printed in China. A papal envoy to China, John of Plano Carpini, returned with a letter sealed in the Chinese style, ink printed upon paper.

"Europeans could not know nothing about it," Chinese historian Pan Jixing wrote.[10]

Yet clues are not proof. There is no mention in Europe of the Chinese invention of printing until 1546, a century after Gutenberg's 42–line Bible, when the Italian historian Jovius, who examined printed books from China, came to the conclusion that European printing was derived from China.[11] Normally, information about other cultures would be carried by traders. The nature of trade along the Silk Road, the principal route traversed by merchants, was such that little cultural exchange occurred because of the transshipment of goods through the lands of the Middle East. The middlemen blocked direct contacts. Not until the Portuguese expeditions of the 15th century around Africa was this pat-

**BLOCK PRINTING
IN EUROPE**

No positive documentary evidence has yet been found to show that… European block printing came from the Far East at all. But strong circumstantial evidence leads to the conviction that either through Russia, through Europeans in China, through Persia, or through Egypt — perhaps through several or all of these routes — the influence of the block printing of China entered the European world during the time of the Mongol Empire and the years immediately following and had its part in bringing about the rise and gradual development of that activity which in turn paved the way for Gutenberg's invention.[12]

— THOMAS F. CARTER

tern truly broken. The earlier invasions that brought the Mongols to the gates of Europe could have carried much knowledge of Chinese civilization, but terrified Europeans were in no mood for contact and wisdom from the fearsome Mongol horde. The myth about the kingdom of Prester John was believed across Europe. And, as we know, Marco Polo was ridiculed for the tales he brought home.

THE DARK AGES

For those who equate change with progress, the Dark Ages offer an antidote. If communication brought change to the ancient world, its subsequent collapse brought stagnation. With the poison of suspicion marking religious and baronial boundaries, communication over distance dropped. The network of Roman roads, neglected by authorities, infrequently used by travelers, and beset by bandits, crumbled. Schools and literacy were abandoned for their lack of purpose. What happened to the volumes written during the Greek and Roman eras? They disappeared, hidden away or lost forever.

After the fall of Rome, the Roman Catholic Church continued some of the old traditions throughout the vanished empire, including Latin as the written language of the dominant religion. Until the tenth century, the Church numbered years from the date fixed for the creation of the world. Latin was also the language of much of government and schools, and nearly all of law, science, philosophy, and literature. When universities arose in Europe starting in the twelfth century, Latin was the language used. Out in the towns and the countryside, people may have spoken a babble of vernacular languages made all the more separate because the network of Roman roads hd fallen into decay, but all the scholarly books were written in Latin. Even those barbarians who were literate used it. Literacy during the Dark Ages meant knowledge at least of Latin, to which scholars could add Greek and Hebrew, and this knowledge set them apart from, and usually above, the rest of humanity.

(Europe) severed its cultural arteries and relied on internal and local signs and symbols. Europe was stuck in a crippling cultural stasis while the rest of the world, led by Persian and Arab traders, moved on. The Dark Ages in Europe were a time of mass illiteracy and not coincidental concentrations of power among local elites.[13]

–SIVA VAIDHYANATHAN

With the collapse of Roman rule, European civilization entered the Dark Ages. The pursuit of knowledge shrank into the pinpoints of lighted candles in remote monasteries. Monks, chiefly Benedictines, took up the scribe's pen to transfer the writing in the crumbling, old papyrus manuscripts onto parchment that was prepared in or near the monasteries. They huddled over their painstaking illuminations of the Bible, religious commentaries, and, in some orders, copies of works from classical Greece or Rome. A debt of gratitude is owed to monastic scribes and some of the nobles and private booksellers who preserved them. The English scholar Alcuin, who counted Charlemagne himself among his pupils, encouraged monasteries to make copies of classical works. The French scholar Gerbert, who became Pope Sylvester II, collected or copied not only the books of antiquity but also books written by Muslims. The pope in the year 1000, he is considered a humanist who lived nearly a half millennium before humanism.

Not all monasteries were scrupulous about keeping the old writings. The zeal to shield innocent souls from erotic or pagan thoughts led to manuscript bonfires. Because parchment was expensive, some monasteries scraped the ancient ink off parchment scrolls to put religious text on top of it, creating a *palimpsest*. It was not the only destruction of the writings of Greece and Rome. The sacking of libraries by bands of Huns, Normans, Saracens, and Vikings all took their toll, as did fire and decay. We know of some of the lost manuscripts because surviving manuscripts refer to them. As these illiterate marauders gained power, they absorbed the culture along with the treasure of those they conquered. They opened schools for their own children and taught them to read and write.

For nearly a thousand years until the printing press made superfluous their toil, the monasteries kept the sputtering flame of knowledge. In cold and drafty rooms, their fingers stiff and their backs aching, the monks sat hunched over their scriptorium desktops, as they hand–lettered and painted magnificent copies of books for libraries and cathedrals. These scriptoria may have been cold and grim, but they were not silent, for monks customarily mumbled or read aloud as they worked, or they listened to readings accompanying the scratching of their pens on parchment. Their libraries were assembled, book by precious book, for Church scholars and monastery schools that were kept for their novices plus a few boys of noble families who were not destined to become monks. To be a scribe was no longer a mean calling for slaves. It was to do God's work.

The teaching of handwriting can be traced to ancient times, including at least three distinct Roman styles. Charlemagne, the first Holy Roman Emperor, who never learned to write, pulled together a team of monks under the English scholar Alcuin to create a standard style of lettering. Charlemagne thought a single writing style and a common language, Latin, would help unite the various tribes dwelling in the Holy Roman Empire that he had pieced together by force of arms. His "Carolignian" reforms — lower case letters, spacing between words, and punctuation — made reading easier and promoted literacy throughout Europe.

Until Charlemagne, monastic schools provided almost all the education. The schools concentrated on religion and moral training for boys who would enter religious orders. Charlemagne also promoted the opening of schools to permit a more secular general education for both boys and girls. Education was still mostly for the wealthy, but the promising son of a poor family occasionally was accepted. The family eagerly and gratefully sent off their son, the way for him to a better life.

PALIMPSEST

For over five hundred years this achievement (to be able to read and write) was rare in Western Europe. It is a shock to realize that during all this time practically no lay person, from kings and emperors downward, could read or write. Charlemagne learned to read, but he never could write. He had wax tablets beside his bed to practice on, but said he couldn't get the hang of it.[14]

— Kenneth Clark

SEVERE PENALTY FOR OVERDUE BOOK

Barons holding the power of life and death over their subjects saw little need to read and even less to write. Knights were no more literate than their horses. Literacy was for monks or clerks. Laws were based on custom and memory, not written text. Judges were illiterate, testimony was oral, and witnesses swore an oral oath to tell the truth, as they still do. Perhaps what is most remarkable about these centuries is that some learning did exist, remarkable men studied and wrote, and knowledge was communicated through books saved and books newly written. Monasteries treasured their manuscripts so dearly that a borrower who did not return one when promised faced excommunication.

By the thirteenth century, Europe was showing signs of a new, emerging knowledge. The First Crusade had opened a path to the Muslim world. The cultured Christian East that centered on Constantinople was in greater touch with the cultured Christian West centered on Rome. Books in Arabic and Greek, translated into Latin, changed the practice of medicine and even challenged western Christendom. Abélard and Thomas Aquinas brought a rational cast to Church philosophy and drew on Plato and Aristotle. The centuries that we know as the Dark Ages gradually flowed into the Middle Ages. The start of the First Crusade has been considered the turning point. Europe would never be the same.

UNIVERSITIES

The monopoly of the monasteries over book production and distribution had ended with the founding of universities in Western Europe, starting in Bologna in 1158. In the back shops of stationers in university towns, scriveners copied books by hand that were still too expensive for poor students to buy, but students could rent the books and perhaps copy the copies to share among themselves.[15] Not until the printing press did education significantly change. Because there were no public libraries, educated friends loaned books to each other.[16] Book owners regarded books somewhat as we today regard stocks and bonds, as treasures to be sold when cash was needed. Wills mentioned Bibles.

Medieval students began their education in monastery or cathedral schools that imparted such basic knowledge as reading, writing, grammar, singing and knowledge of the calendar. Students then were taught the seven liberal arts, divided into the trivium and the quadrivium. The trivium consisted of grammar, logic, and rhetoric. The quadrivium consisted of arithmetic, geometry, music, and astronomy. Most students were preparing for the priesthood, and the lessons were religious in nature.

The ills and disorders of the fourteenth century could not be without consequence. Times were to grow worse over the next fifty–odd years until at some imperceptible moment, by some mysterious chemistry, energies were refreshed, ideas broke out of the mold of the Middle Ages into new realms, and humanity found itself redirected.[17]

— BARBARA TUCHMAN

Only a small fraction of the population went to school at all, and even fewer attended a university. Universities were a "community of scholars" gathered for the study of theology or the law. They hired their teachers and set up the rules for teaching. Colleges were formed by groups of boys for such practical needs as acquiring food, lodging, and protection. University education began for boys at 13 or 14. Girls did not attend. Professors could not leave without permission under penalty of death.

In the medieval universities and the monasteries before printing, reading did not always mean what we consider reading to mean today. Some books were too expensive for scholars to own. To "read" meant to listen to a teacher or master reading aloud. Books were intended to be read aloud. Printing changed this by making books more affordable. It allowed some readers to absorb books in privacy, instead of being a member of an audience, an early move toward separation from other people that mediated communication encourages.

Printing had caused no problems for the far–reaching Chinese empire. It might not have disturbed Europe either, except that Europe was ripe for change and it was no monolithic empire. In fact, Europe was already changing before printing arrived to accelerate the changes. The ways it was changing made the rapid absorption of printing easier. The Crusades had ended. Knights and peasants alike had returned with fresh plans for their lives. A century earlier the Black Death had stripped Europe's population of one in every three, leading to a labor shortage. Throughout the fourteenth century and into the century of printing, seven popes in Avignon rivaled the popes in Rome. Scandals and corruption of the high–born, banditry by bands of knights, fanaticism, and revolts marked the century. At the edges of Christendom, the fear of the Mongols, of the Ottoman Turks to the east, and of the Arabs from Jerusalem to Spain added to life's unease.

Europe was not a nation or even an idea. It was kingdoms and baronies and cities whose merchants were looking for trade, and more and more knew how to read for themselves in the vernacular language they spoke on the street.

None of this can diminish what Johannes Gutenberg and the printers who followed him accomplished. In the nineteenth century, the French novelist Victor Hugo would give credit to Gutenberg for the invention that ended the Middle Ages: "The Gothic sun set behind the gigantic printing press of Mainz."[19]

The name of Johannes Gutenberg will be forever associated with the invention of printing with movable type, inexactly known as "the inventor of the printing press," yet information about him is slim, based on assumptions and suspected forgeries. The 42–line Bible and the other books he is credited with printing do not mention his name. Little is known for certain beyond a recorded legal action against him that describes his printing shop in his home city of Mainz, Germany.[20] The lawsuit in 1444 identifies two steel alphabets. Around 1450, Gutenberg

It was the invention of the printing press more than any other event that shattered the medieval world and gave rise to modernism; the growth of a reading public led inevitably to the spread of ideas, ideas that contributed to the philosophical and technological innovations that ultimately destroyed the power of the clergy and the nobility and led, also, to new forms of political, economic, social, cultural, and religious systems.[18]

— HERBERT ALTSCHULL

Every aspect of human life was being revolutionized. New technologies were being discovered or ad–opted from distant lands: the water wheel for driving forge hammers, flour mills and mechanical saws; the crane, the wood plane, the weight–regulated clock, the rudder, the compass, gunpowder and paper making. Returning crusaders and merchants brought back unheard of works of astronomy, geography, medicine, mathematics and philosophy which they had acquired from the infidels, and these were eagerly translated and copied in humanist circles. Writing and books were the custodians and mediators of this growing body of knowledge.[21]

— ALBERT KAPR

used movable type to print a Bible of 36 lines per page. Around 1457 or 1458 he printed the 42–line Bible of 1,282 two–column pages. Of these, forty–eight copies are known to exist today.

A PRINTING SYSTEM

Like the Chinese, some Europeans were manufacturing books by block printing, but carving a block of wood for each page ate up hours and strained eyes. The goldsmith Gutenberg, familiar with stamping soft metal with hard metal punches to leave a permanent hallmark, figured out a better way to print by fabricating steel punches of individual letters. This was the type mold. It could stamp impressions again and again in a soft metal like lead. The result is type. Ink on these lead type pieces could print on paper, then be reused for another printing job. Gutenberg had developed a printing *system*. China and Korea had nothing like it. Gutenberg fabricated punches and lead type to exact dimensions like the dies, stamps and punches used by European leather workers, metalsmiths, and pewter makers. Being the same height, the pieces of lead type could be set in rows. The page of type was gripped tightly within a wooden frame. Gutenberg added a linseed oil–varnish ink well suited to print legible impressions from metal type upon paper. He may have gotten the formula from the artists of the fifteenth century who used oil as a paint base. As for the *printing press*, the handpress itself was in common use throughout Europe as a wine press, an oil press, and a linen press to remove wrinkles. The type was inked, then a sheet of damp paper was laid upon it. The press came down, then the sheet was peeled off and hung up to dry, Once dry, it was dampened again for printing on the other side.

Printers were immediately sought out. Printing spread across Western Europe when apprentices learned the craft, acquired sufficient type, then left their masters to start their own shops. Gutenberg's city of Mainz, a printing center, was sacked in 1462 by an invading army, so its printers set up their shops in Italy, where books were in demand because the Medici in Florence and other wealthy nobles patronized the arts.[22] Humanism, with its focus on the here rather than the hereafter, was on the rise, its adherents demanding copies of the ancient classics of Greece and Rome. Printshops opened for business in the university towns of Oxford and Cambridge. Printshops were set up in Paris, 1470; Holland, 1471; Switzerland, 1472; Spain, 1474; England, 1476; Denmark, 1482; Constantinople, 1490. At the same time, more universities were founded. Oxford and Cambridge built five new colleges in two decades. But Eastern Europe and Russia, where few but priests were literate, did almost no printing before the eighteenth century. The first printer in the New World, the Italian Juan Pablos, brought a press, gothic type, paper, and materials for ink–making to Mexico in 1534. In 1550 he sent for Antonio de Espinosa, a type maker and die cutter.

The encounter with books produced a fundamental change in the mind of the reader, who undertakes a one–way journey to a rational, purposive, participatory way of life. From being God's chosen instrument, literacy comes close to replacing the role of religion altogether.[23]

— *David Vincent*

William Caxton brought printing to England, where he chose to use English, rather than Latin, for the nearly one–hundred romances and morality works he published, including the tales of King Arthur. Printers published popular guides to a well–regulated family life, resulting in a collective morality coming from their shops.[24] Yet the Middle Ages were earthy as well as outwardly moral. Along with religious books, bawdy tales sold well, Chaucer's *Canterbury Tales* and Boccaccio's *Decameron* among them.[25]

The merchant booksellers would do well. The authors of books did not fare as well as the booksellers. Recognizing and rewarding authors is part of the shift to a written tradition, where writing is appreciated for itself. The printing press led many would–be authors to want to see their work in print, even if they did not bother identifying themselves in their works. They often went unpaid for what they wrote, unless a wealthy patron sponsored them in return for a printed dedication. The only publications profitable enough to earn fees were popular romances, tales of magic or marvels, and controversial pamphlets that had to be abusive to sell.[26] In the seventeenth century, John Milton was paid just £5 for *Paradise Lost*.

The monks engaged in copying did not disappear, but scribes fell on hard times. It took a printer only two days to equal what a scribe could copy in a year.[27] Hand copying continued, but as everywhere, the high costs of handmade goods reduced the call for their work. A manuscript Bible in 1470 cost five times as much as a printed Bible. Still, early printing fell short of the quality of handwritten copies, and printed books were far from accurate. Printers had limited amounts of lead type, so made–up pages had to be broken down in order that the type could be reused. To reduce mistakes, authors proofread the pages in the midst of the printing process.[28] Books were filled with variants that were printed and inserted in books when errors were uncovered after a page was taken apart.

The scarcity of books at the start of the fifteenth century became a glut at its conclusion. As the variety of available books increased, students could cross–reference between texts.[29] Inevitably, they found errors in the copied and recopied books. Books were being published on such a variety of topics, compared to what had once been available, that knowledge became more specialized and separated. To have a shelf of books on a single subject, such as medicine, would soon be possible.

The most important book printed in the century following Gutenberg was Martin Luther's New Testament written in the German vernacular. The 3,000 copies printed in 1522, sold at a fraction of their publishing cost, were immediately snapped up. The printing press kept turning

THE PLIGHT OF AUTHORS

Books of universal knowledge, mostly dating from the 13th century and written in (or translated from the Latin into) French and other vernaculars for the use of the layman, were literary staples familiar in every country over several centuries. A 14th century man drew also on the Bible, romances, bestiaries, satires, books of astronomy, geography, universal history, church history, rhetoric, law, medicine, alchemy, falconry, hunting, fighting, music, and any number of special subjects.[30]

—BARBARA TUCHMAN

...there are irreversible aspects to the early modern printing revolution. Cumulative processes were set in motion in the mid–fifteenth century, and they have not ceased to gather momentum in the age of the computer printout and the television guide.... Commercial copy centers, for example, have begun to appear within the precincts of modern universities, much as stationers' stalls did near medieval universities.[33]

— Elizabeth Eisenstein

them out. Mostly illiterate in Latin, the German nobles that the Augustinian monk wanted to enlist in his cause could now read the Word of God for themselves. Even illiterates in German could hear others read the Bible aloud in the language they spoke daily. Because Latin was the language of priests, not the street language, the countryside knew only what priests told them about the scriptures. Only the priests possessed the Latin Bibles. Printing gave God's message to everyone.[31]

Luther's use of Gutenberg's invention was not unexpected. The 95 theses that he nailed to the Wittenburg Church door had been circulating widely in print. More than any other single event, the attack it contained on papal abuses and the sale of indulgences by Church officials started the Reformation by releasing pent–up anger against the Church. What quickly followed was a campaign of posters, pamphlets, and caricature drawings, first across Germany and then across the rest of Europe. Printers could hardly keep up. It was ironic that this craft was in the forefront of the attack on indulgences, now being printed instead of hand–written. After all, when there had been a demand for the indulgences that had roused Luther's ire, was it not the printers who produced them?

A second great social movement arose at this time. The Renaissance introduced the classical literature of ancient Greece and Rome to a world largely unaware of the ancient books. An increasingly literate population wanted to read them and to acquire secular learning available in books. The printers obliged. The copyists in the back shops of the booksellers and stationers could not have met such a demand. The spread of books led to a separation from the Church to pursue individual scholarship. The discovery of the ancient texts furthered individual study.

A GROWING LITERACY

A hallmark of the Modern Age, distinguishing it from the Middle Ages, was the growing literacy, thanks to printing and the rise in education that came in its wake. Printing and literacy were two hands washing each other. The more printing, the more literacy; people who could read wanted more to read. The more literacy, the more printing; the market of readers needed to be served. Most people during the Middle Ages had managed to live their lives well enough without reading, let alone writing. They knew where the butcher's shop was without reading a sign saying "Butcher," and even if they did not know or could not tell by a shop's appearance, a sign with a picture of a sheep or pig would inform them. At the start of the sixteenth century, midway between Chaucer and Shakespeare, it was estimated that three out of five English adults were illiterate. Some nobles were proudly so.[32]

One difficulty during the Middle Ages lay in the Latin language that was unfamiliar to almost everyone. Even if literacy were offered, it would have been pointless. Most books were written in Latin, and were unavailable in any case. There were no newspapers or magazines. The Middle Ages existed in an oral world, enriched by preachers, balladeers who brought rhyming news and gossip from village to village, plus the occasional traveling morality plays, although actors were not high in the social order and did not deserve burial in some Christian cemeteries.[34] Women were not encouraged to read, for the skill was considered both unnecessary and potentially harmful to the fairer sex; for centuries it was felt by the generality of literate men that reading romantic fiction was especially risky for women. Reading was regarded as pointless for the working class. Among lower class women, literacy barely existed. If something written needed to be heard, one person could read aloud to many. That was likely to be the priest.

Before Gutenberg nearly all education had been in the hands of the Church. Books were costly, copying was laborious and sometimes careless. Libraries were numerous but small. By the end of the fifteenth century, about 50 years after the publication of the 42–line Bible, an estimated 20 million copies of books of one sort or another had been printed.[35] By the end of the sixteenth century, that number had increased tenfold.[36] Most of these books were printed in one of the vernacular languages of Europe. People who could not read could at least listen in a language they understood, and that led them to unravel for themselves the mystery of the letters on a page, and to be sure that their sons learned. As it was everywhere, the education of daughters fell behind, but even here some progress could be reported.[37]

With the growth of vernacular printing, Latin was ignored except by the Church. Over time, those vernacular languages that did not embrace printing began to disappear. Although the Church warmed to the new technology, the rise of printing shifted a measure of power from prelates and aristocrats to an emerging literate middle class of commoners.

Europe's fragmented baronies, states, and towns spurred the growth of printing, as political entities large and small did whatever was needed to retain power. Increasingly, noble birth mattered less and the ability to read and write mattered more to merchants and to the middle class burghers who sat in city governments where they wielded real power. They could improve their lives, once blocked by the rigid feudalism that allocated an unchangeable fate to man from the day he was born. The nobility who had assumed that their authority came to them by right from God now made sure their sons were educated.[39] At least, most nobles actually read the writing on the wall.

Another change brought about by vernacular printing was a sense of nationalism. The Holy Roman Empire, an attempt to recreate the Roman

As schools multipled and literacy rose, the demand for books increased. The business classes found literacy useful in the operations of industry and trade… By 1300 the time had passed when only the clergy could read.[38]

—Will Durant

As the presses disgorged new printed matter, the yearning for literacy spread like a fever; millions of Europeans led their children to classrooms and remained to learn themselves.[40]

—William Manchester

The introduction of printing in 1476 started the notion of a single system as standard: William Caxton chose for his printing house the system which reflected the speech of the London area. As a result, the spelling of many words became stable for the first time, and the notion of a 'correct' spelling began to grow.[42]

— C.D. SELWYN-JONES

The new presses… probably did not gradually make available to low-born men what had previously been restricted to the high born. Instead, changes in mental habits and attitudes entailed by access to printed materials affected a wide social spectrum from the outset. In fifteenth-century England, for example, mercers and scriveners engaged in a manuscript book trade were already catering to the needs of lowly bakers and merchants as well as to those of lawyers, aldermen and knights.[43]

— ELIZABETH EISENSTEIN

Empire in a Christian world, gave way to nation states. If you read in English, that meant you shared with everyone else who read in English an innate quality that was different from those who read in French or German. Latin was a borderless international language. English identified a population that had a territory and boundaries.[41] Differences in language pointed up differences between peoples who were otherwise much the same. Shakespeare echoed the growing nationalism in Henry V's rousing speech before the battle of Agincourt. France felt the spur of national fervor early in the fifteenth century under the banner of Joan of Arc.

Printing gave a spoken language an aura of legitimacy. If printing codified it, a spoken language was no longer merely a distortion of a nobler language. What followed would be a language structure for a vernacular with rules for orthography and syntax. In England, the relaxed spelling and grammar of Chaucer, who wrote before the invention of printing, had hardened considerably by the time of Shakespeare two centuries later.

Printers struggled to equate what they were hearing with the typeface letters in their job cases, but they were coming to some agreement about how a spoken word ought to appear in print and how words should fit together. A century and a half after Shakespeare, Samuel Johnson would fix definitions in his *Dictionary of the English Language*. But neither he nor Shakespeare's contemporary, Edmund Coote, who preceded him with a spelling book, nor Noah Webster, who followed them in America with a dictionary, took advantage of the opportunity to spell words rationally. Thus, we have "high" and "height," "four" and "forty," "speak" and "speech," and hundreds of other illogical spellings. By then, in France and Italy, lexicons had also been compiled. In France in 1665, the *Journal des savants*, became the first periodical to review books.

(Newer mediated communication would treat Shakespeare's words quite differently. Truncated almost beyond recognition, the words appear today as text messages on cell phones and BlackBerries as a reminder of his most famous lines. Thus, Hamlet muses, "2b? Nt2b???" and Richard III pleads, "Ahors, m'kingdom 4." These abbreviations are part of a British cell phone service for students.)

The imminent conquest of Constantinople by the Ottoman Turks sent scholars and libraries fleeing to the West. They were welcomed in Florence, a center of learning, where they brought ancient Greek texts unknown to the West until then, including copies of the Septuagint, a Greek version of the Hebrew Scriptures. This began the Renaissance, the renewal that flowed from the cities of Italy throughout Western Europe. The Florentine Renaissance brought out not only the ancient classics but also the poetry of Petrarch and the rollicking tales of Boccaccio.

Considering the variety of topics on which books were being printed, there must have been a revival of the ancient sense that reading could be a source of enjoyment as well as of learning. Renaissance scholars cared about literature more than philosophy, and science least of all.[44]

Erasmus, the leading humanist of his day, promoted the translation of the Bible into vernacular languages so that it could be read by the plowboy and the "simplest woman." But the humanists also studied and wrote about the pagan literature of the classical Greeks and Romans, and it was for this that they were denounced by pious reformers.

In Venice, printer Aldus Manutius collected, edited, and printed all the Greek classics he could get his hands on. The results were spread across Western Europe. With the help of Venetian scholars, this first large–scale publishing activity, done for the love of the literature rather than for profit, was a factor in making the Renaissance a pan–European experience, and not just Italian. Printing arrived at the time that Europeans, led by the Portuguese, began their explorations; printed reports added to the fever of interest in the possibilities of new paths to the riches of Asia and new worlds to conquer.

Where the art of printing established itself, an outpouring of books followed. An active book trade led to the founding of new schools to meet a strong demand to be taught reading and writing. Universities opened their doors to the new books and the new learning they contained. Literary academies arose and some private libraries were opened to scholars.

As it always would, printing spread more nonsense than sense. At a time when astronomers peered into the new telescopes to gather observations that would lead Copernicus and Galileo to a heliocentric sky, books of astrology were best sellers. Nostradamus published his prophecies. Widely circulated reports of the activities of devils and witches were read and believed, leading to torture and burnings.

Illiteracy was the norm at the dawn of movable type printing and so was written Latin instead of writing in any vernacular. Literacy has always been a source of power over illiteracy; with Latin as the dominant written language, that power could be restricted. The system was tightly controlled. Although some poor boys might be accorded the favor of monastic or cathedral schooling where they could learn Latin, they were trained for the priesthood.

Movable type printing was a bomb thrown into this world. Its spread was rapid and inexorable. Printing in the vernacular accelerated the danger to the established control of Church and State. The Church's response was to censor what was printed and to use printing for its own purposes, but not to stop it. Church leaders may have concluded they

RENAISSANCE AND HUMANISM

All this ferment led to that rarest of cultural phenomena, an intellectual movement which alters the course of both learning and civilization. Pythagoreans had tried it, four hundred years before the birth of Christ, and failed. So, in the third and fourth centuries, had Manichaeans, Stoics, and Epicureans. But the humanists of the sixteenth century were to succeed spectacularly — so much so that their triumph is unique. They would be followed by other ideologies determined to shape the future — seventeenth–century rationalism, the eighteenth–century Enlightenment, Marxism in the nineteenth century, and, in the twentieth, by pragmatism, determinism, and empiricism. Each would alter the stream of great events, but none would match the achievements of Renaissance humanists.[45]

—WILLIAM MANCHESTER

Curiously, the threat print posed to authority was not that the masses would become voracious readers of incendiary tracts but that the authorities and exegetes from whom they habitually took their opinions would themselves become infected with new ideas.[47]

— ROBERT PATTISON

Printing published — i.e., made available to the public — cheap manuals of instruction in religion, literature, history, and science; it became the greatest and cheapest of all universities, open to all.…

It made the Bible a common possession, and prepared the people for Luther's appeal from the popes to the Gospels to reason.[48]

— WILL DURANT

could not stop printing, nor was it necessary to do so. The printing of indulgences continued.

One should not conclude that members of the Church hierarchy were unanimous in their views about printing, just as clerical disagreements existed in many matters. The Church, which dominated education in Europe during the Middle Ages, gave considerable latitude to scholars to engage in scholarly disputes even though they challenged ecclesiastic doctrine, as long as the scholars wrote in Latin and addressed their views to an educated readership. Before printing, the Church considered books to be the tools of scholars. In short, scholars were relatively free to express themselves as long as the common people were not disturbed. The Church was more concerned with preaching than writing.

A century and a half before Martin Luther, the Church paid full attention when John Wyclif in England, an Oxford don, preached man's direct communication with God and attacked Church corruption. Wyclif led a movement that resulted in two English translations of the Bible, the first vernacular translation of the Bible in more than 1,000 years. His disciples spread his message across England, risking death as heretics. Wyclif's revolt proved to be short–lived, but it was clear that dissension was in the air. However, a successful religious revolt would await the printing press.

From the beginning the presses were tools for promulgating faith and religious points of view. In the nearly seventy years between Gutenberg's printing of the Bible and the printing of Martin Luther's translation of the New Testament, there were about twenty translations of the Bible in German.[46] Instead of depending upon the explanations of priests, common people read for themselves what the Gospels said about the poor and oppressed.

The religious reformers were indifferent to secular learning, one reason that the humanists felt alienated from the Reformation. The two great movements may have been critical of the practices of the Roman Catholic Church, but they were also mistrustful of each other. Reformers saw humanism as a pagan reversion to classical culture. The humanists saw the Reformation as a backsliding to the Dark Ages. Luther exalted faith, was derogatory of scholarship, and had no use for reason as the guide for men's conduct. The humanists had no taste for theology. Heaven and Hell were myths to the humanists, perhaps less real than the myths of Greece and Rome. The reformers left the established Church. The humanists, although they initially praised Luther's attacks on corruption, pulled away from Protestant theology. The two movements occurred during the same historical period, and both used printing extensively to disseminate their literature, but their proponents had little in common beyond a mutual dislike.[49]

Before the invention of printing, when few but Church scholars were literate or had access to books, the ecclesiastical authorities thought little about heresy in books, being more concerned about preachers who spoke to the masses in the common language.[50] Medieval bishops actually supported civil illiteracy.[51]

In the decades after Gutenberg the Church turned to printing. It set up its own printshops, mixing religious with political purposes. With the publication of a Bible in the German vernacular, that relaxed attitude changed because Rome saw it as a challenge to its power as the sole interpreter of God's Word. Church and state were cautious about new religious books in any language but Latin.[52] They had no problem with romances, folk tales, and children's books in the vernacular, but worried about anything that challenged the control of authorities. The archbishop of Mainz, Gutenberg's city, required permission to print any book. One of the principal concerns of the Church about printing had less to do with common people, most of whom were illiterate anyhow, than with priests and monks themselves.

The Inquisition to root out heresy rooted out books as well as human beings. It gathered books to be burned in public bonfires. In 1502, the Church issued a papal bull ordering the burning of all books that questioned ecclesiastic authority, followed in 1516 by a directive banning printing that lacked Church approval. That included William Tyndale's effort. A contemporary of Luther who followed in Wyclif's footsteps, Tyndale had translated much of the Bible into English. The body of Wyclif, who died a natural death, was removed from consecrated ground, but Tyndale was burned at the stake. The burnings of books, pamphlets, and authors limited but did not stop the printing and secret distribution of banned books. One of the few havens for printers and writers was Holland after it won its freedom from Spain in the seventeenth century. The dissidents found their way into Holland, where they not only continued their subversive publishing, but also smuggled their works back into the countries from which they fled. As for Tyndale, a century later his translation found its way, unacknowledged, into the King James Version of the Bible.

Historian Leonard Shlain has gone much further in arguing the negative impact of printing and literacy. He has blamed them as the root of the evils of the Inquisition, the mass burning of witches, and the Thirty Years War with its slaughter of men, women, and children that wiped out entire villages.

Early sixteenth–century Europe was awash with printed versions of traditional Catholic prayers and orders of service. The old church and the new technology (printing) were the closest of allies. The very trigger of the Reformation, the indulgences sold by the Catholic Church to ease the path into heaven and fill the church's coffers, were by the late fifteenth century printed documents.[53]

— ADAM NICOLSON

…in general, before the fourteenth century, the Church was not opposed to Bible reading on the part of the laity. She did not encourage it, for she distrusted popular interpretations of scriptural mysteries.[54]

— WILL DURANT

… suddenly, violent religious persecution erupted all over Europe… Few plausible explanations have emerged as to why this constellation of persecutions should have clustered in the same cultures that gave us the Renaissance, the birth of science, global explorations, and many other pivotal events… I propose that the sixteenth century European nightmare was brought on by Gutenberg's press and the widespread literacy that resulted from it.…

It seemed no country could escape the terrible religious upheaval that inevitably followed the march of the metal letters…

Taken as a whole, the religious wars that wracked Europe in the 150 years after the printing press had transformed European culture can be viewed as a sort of mass madness. They occurred only in those lands impacted by the printing press; the steeper the rise of literacy rates, the more ferocious the religious wars were.[55]

— Leonard Shlain

Yet printing was always easier to control than a sermon, because a printing press can be seized and taxed, and paper can be withheld. Books can be banned. The first *Index of Forbidden Books*, in 1559, identified forty–eight editions of the Bible that Catholics must not read, and banned the publications of sixty–one printers. No Catholic was to read a book that had not received an "imprimatur," meaning "let it be printed." A later pope relaxed the ban, but censorship, which had existed for centuries before the *Index*, remained part of European tradition. The will to censor all media has never fully dissipated, and remains healthy today in several countries. The pages of the centuries are studded with such well–known book burners as Savonarola, an Italian, and Anthony Comstock, an American. Censorship is by no means unique to the Roman Church. Protestant reformers shared and in many cases exceeded the zeal to protect innocent minds from their own version of heresy and sedition as well as all things immoral. The Chinese have been no less adept than Europeans at the task of rooting out sedition. Just a few years ago in Iran, the Ayatollah Khomeini issued a fatwa allowing anyone to kill the author Salman Rushdie. Not only sticks and stones break bones.

If printing was the engine for the European Reformation and Renaissance, it was another Chinese invention that supplied the fuel. The papermaker's art as much as the printer's art led to our modern world. The availability of printed books, made possible by the paper mills of Europe, allowed the growth of literacy, and literacy in turn increased the demand for books, pamphlets, broadsides, and ever more paper. It should come as no surprise that dictatorships control the paper supply in their nations.

While Chinese emperors wrote on jade tablets, and nobles and high government officials wrote on ivory, lower ranking functionaries needed something less expensive, readily available and less difficult to acquire. Their first answer was bamboo, from which they made tablets. A pointed bamboo stylus or another Chinese invention, the camel's hair brush, dipped into a mixture of lampblack and oil or a black varnish provided pen and ink. But like clay tablets for the Babylonians, bamboo tablets had the limitations of weight and bulk.

Paper was a better choice. Its invention in 105 C.E. is credited to Ts'ai Lun, the emperor's minister of public works, a eunuch. Someone else may have actually invented paper, but he gets the credit.[56] Ts'ai Lun reported to the imperial court that he had made a writing surface from a mixture of tree bark, hemp, rags, and fish nets. The inventor shredded his ingredients, beat them into a pulp, spread the pulp in a thin layer, and dried it. The sheets held together and were cut to size. They took ink.

Paper was immediately accepted because it met the obvious need of all governments for surfaces on which to keep records, approve requests, and issue instructions. Scholars wrote and read books made from paper. The followers of Confucius, Lao Tze, and the Buddha copied the sayings of their masters. The conservative ideas of Confucius were published without government objection, but they contained no radical political ideas that might threaten imperial rule. The Chinese published works in medical theory, mathematical theory, philosophy, and technology generally far ahead of anything in the West.[57]

Wood blocks carved with sacred charms were used to stamp pieces of paper that fit into amulets. Just as the Egyptians used papyrus reeds to make their boats and huts as well as their writing surfaces, the Chinese found uses for paper that had nothing to do with communication: shoes, hats, belts, wrapping, wallpaper, napkins, curtains, toilet paper, and even a soldier's armor. Marco Polo expressed his fascination with paper money, a product that led China to several waves of inflation before it was banned upon imperial order.

Its technology a guarded government secret, paper was used in China alone for five centuries until Buddhist priests carried it east to Korea and Japan, and west to the outposts of its empire. The Islamic conquest of the city of Samarkand in 751 turned up some Chinese papermakers, who were taken west as prisoners. Learning the art of fabricating paper, the Arabs set up paper mills in Baghdad and Damascus. The following centuries saw the height of Muslim culture, expressed by a love of learning and great libraries, established from Baghdad to Córdoba, Spain. Paper fit in well, gradually supplanting papyrus as a printing material. A letter of thanks written in Egypt ends, "Pardon the papyrus."[59]

At the time that paper technology was integral to the flowering of Muslim culture, across the great religious divide, festered in its Dark Ages, lay Christian Europe. After the fall of Rome, knowledge moved in opposite directions. Outside monasteries, books and paper were almost unknown. Writing was done on parchment. In the twelfth century, according to a report, a crusader prisoner named Jean Montgolfier escaped from Damascus, where he had been a slave in a paper mill. Finding his way home to France, he set up the first paper mill in Christian Europe. The superiority of paper in taking ink and the lower cost of paper compared to parchment, despite its fragility and rougher surface, soon led to paper mills across Europe. The supply of rags to make paper was far greater than the supply of sheep for parchment and vellum, which continued to be used for luxury editions and for the missals and breviaries that monks were copying. By the thirteenth century the Dark Ages had yielded to the Middle Ages, marked by the growth of cities and the rise of an economy based on cash and trade rather than

The monopoly position of the Bible and the Latin language in the church was destroyed by the press and in its place there developed a widespread market for the Bible in the vernacular and a concern with its literal interpretation.… The effect of the discovery of printing was evident in the savage religious wars of the sixteenth and seventeenth centuries.[58]

— HAROLD INNIS

The greatest pressure of all for literacy, however, was caused by the sudden availability of paper.… As the paper mills spread, so too did the spirit of religious reform.…

As the price of paper continued to fall, the development of eyeglasses intensified the pressure for literacy. Glasses had first appeared in the early fourteenth century, and a hundred years later they were generally available. Their use lengthened the working life of copyist and reader alike. Demand for texts increased.[60]

— JAMES BURKE

Another consequence of cotton production was… an immense increase in worn–out clothes, or rags. Rags were the raw material of the paper–making industry… By 1839, publishing had been revolutionized. Printed matter was now cheap — for the first time in human history literacy could be massively extended through all levels of the population.[62]

— Morse Peckham

Aside from the introduction of the printed book, the demand for paper was felt in many new fields: teaching spread, business transactions became more complex, writing multiplied, and there was a growing need for paper for non–literary uses, by tradesmen, haberdashers, grocers, chandlers. A whole new species of trades was created which depended on paper: carriers, box–makers, playing–card makers, bill–posters and related trades.[63]

— Lucien Febvre and Henri–Jean Martin

land holdings. Well suited to commerce, paper was used for contracts, insurance, bills of lading, and bills of exchange, along with another importation from the East, Arabic numerals. Paper served the needs of merchants, bureaucrats, and scholars. However, it would not find wide use in Christian Europe until the invention of printing.

Not everyone had welcomed paper. It undermined Church control of writing material, for parchment existed primarily under ecclesiastical authority in the monasteries. And it was brought from a pagan culture. The Holy Roman Emperor Frederick II decreed in 1221 that documents written on paper had no legal validity.[61] On the other hand — and there often is the other hand — many churchmen welcomed paper as churchmen two centuries later would welcome printing.

The superiority of paper over parchment was evident in the printing of the Gutenberg Bible. Thirty of the 210 copies were printed on parchment, each requiring the skins of 300 sheep. By the end of the fifteenth century, parchment was seldom used to print books.

As a footnote to the production of paper during the Middle Ages, the first recorded labor strike in history was at a Nuremberg paper mill when workers objected to the owner's demand that they agree never to work for anyone other than the owner and his heirs. The owner imprisoned his workers until they gave in.

Degrees of literacy widened to include merchants and skilled craftsmen, but the cost of paper limited the availability of books. Although cheaper than parchment, paper was made by hand one sheet at a time by a method not much different than the Chinese used in the second century. And it was not cheap. Its cost kept books expensive until the Industrial Revolution of the nineteenth century. For example, a papermaker in England earned between two and three shillings a week by the end of the seventeenth century, when a ream of writing paper — 500 sheets — sold for 20 shillings. In addition, making paper in small batches limited its supply, which was further limited by the quantity of rags a paper mill could locate.

Colonial America got most of its paper from Europe because its own mills were small and inefficient, and the paper was of poor quality. The Philadelphia printer Benjamin Franklin helped to get more paper mills in the colonies, but by the time of the American Revolution, the interruption of supplies from England and the meager colonial output led to a number of colonial newspapers shutting down.

An inventive French paper mill manager, Nickolas Robert, in 1798 figured out how to produce paper in a continuous roll. His invention of a web to pick up the wet pulp instead of workers spreading the pulp on a mesh screen is known as the Fourdrinier machine because he got financing in England from two brothers of that name. It produced as much paper in two days as hand labor produced in three months.

Where to get rags for the paper pulp was a problem for centuries, even though the population explosion that accompanied the Industrial Revolution increased the amount of clothing made, worn, and discarded. Rag buyers from Europe went as far as Asia to acquire worn out clothing. Some European countries passed laws to prohibit the export of their own rags.

The problem of material shortages and soaring prices was finally solved in mid–nineteenth century Germany with methods for converting wood fiber into paper pulp. By the end of the nineteenth century, wood pulp that cost 8½ cents a pound in 1875 could be bought for 1½ cents. Trees, it was felt, were inexhaustible.

Much of Roman civilization was lost to Western Europe during the Dark Ages, including such communication tools as writing, education, and postal service. For nearly a thousand years what little survived was largely confined to monasteries. Feudal rulers had little use for literacy, a skill for monks and clerks.

THE MEDIEVAL WORLD THAT had stood for a thousand years since the fall of Rome crumbled under the pressure of the religious forces of the Reformation and the humanism of the Renaissance, as well as Roman Catholic Church literature, being pumped out by the printing presses. The Church yielded some of its mysteries and its powers. Religious tracts and printed Bibles in the vernacular languages of Europe separated the Reformation from the Middle Ages.

During the same period of history, the medieval alchemists reluctantly gave way to scientific inquiry. Inductive reasoning and newly rediscovered and published literature, moral thinking, and political awareness of classical Greece separated the Renaissance from the Middle Ages.[64] The intellectual ferment would lead in the seventeenth and eighteenth centuries to the Enlightenment, a revolution in human thought with its focus on the here, not the hereafter. Through the extension of literacy and printing, ordinary Europeans would learn to think rationally, to conclude that they were not limited to a fixed station in life, and that change was both possible and desirable. As literacy grew, there was a demand for more books. As more books became available, literacy grew.

Printing, as we know, began in China. One of history's mysteries is whether Europeans connected with it knew of the Chinese invention. The actual invention was the movable type, not the printing press. The European printers used existing wine and linen presses.

People seldom appreciate paper's impact on Western civilization. Parchment and vellum could never have supported mass literacy, worldwide printing, modern offices, newspapers, goverment records, general education, and so on. These are the consequences of paper and the printing press. Indeed, the printing press itself only made practical sense because of paper's availability.[65]

— STEVEN FISCHER

CONCLUSION

Gutenberg's invention — or reinvention — of movable type printing has been identified as the start of the Modern Age. One may ask whether this gives too much credit to printing. Other historical events might be considered the turning point that ended the Medieval Age. The Black Death, Martin Luther's attack on the Roman Church, the fall of Toledo or Constantinople, and the Mongol invasion could be argued as being the straw that broke the back of feudalism. Or was there no single straw? Was the shift so gradual and so spotty that no single event should be credited?

Stretching back to ancient China, printing and its accompanying paper have histories of technological changes that brought social effects in their wake. Besides the technology, printing has required literacy. The full effects of printing have been dampened by censorship, often harsh. These three threads — technology, literacy, censorship — are woven through printing history.

Uniformity of books from copy to copy awaited the invention of printing with movable type. In inventing printing, Gutenberg also invented industrial repetition. Unlike hand copying, with its errors from weary eyes, each printed page was just like the last one. Repeatability in future centuries would be the basis of much of mediated communication, marked in the nineteenth century by William Fox Talbot's invention of photographic prints and Thomas Edison's invention of the phonograph record. Printing brought a sense of change that would give impetus to the advances of mediated communication that to this day continues.

Beyond everything else, wherever it was taken, the printing press opened a pathway to knowledge for broad masses of people. Without printing, information would remain limited and education would remain cramped. With it, the world changed.

3 EXTENDING READING

PRINTING MEANS NOTHING IF you cannot read. Literacy means nothing if you do not choose to read. In time, society would change to disperse the ability to read across a wide population, and reading matter would expand in many directions to interest that population. As these changes took hold, they in turn would change lives.

By the time Gutenberg was printing with movable type in the mid–fifteenth century, Europe was moving toward a more general literacy. Spectacle lenses were ground to make reading easier for those literates who could afford them. Traveling monks, pilgrims, peddlers, couriers, and balladeers brought news and rumor from afar. Organized mail services took root. Several large cities had something called a university. Although the earliest university students studied little outside of theology and law, students eventually wanted books that came not only from monasteries but also from the shops of stationers, and on a wider range of topics.

New kinds of literacy and new forms of expertise frequently accompany new communication media, and did so with printing. Writing brought alphabets and information on subjects that readers knew little about. Priestly scribes gained power; even household slave scribes gained importance.

As the centuries went by, photography brought visual language and, for many years, demanded almost an alchemist's skill at mixing compounds. Computers brought programming languages and, until application programs eased the confusion, computers yielded their results only to the programmers who could talk to them. These experts served as the priests who were positioned between the wondrous devices and those who wished to make use of them. Television and the Internet each have their own special language requirements. So, of course, does every profession.

PRINTING METHODS

Literacy and reading of books increased as printing spread. The humanism of the sixteenth century would be echoed in the Age of Reason of the eighteenth, but for three and a half centuries after Gutenberg, little had changed in printing technology. Printers still inked one page of type at a time and placed a rag–based sheet of paper over it before lowering a platen to make the impression. The result of a day's work at the start of the nineteenth century was a tired arm and a product that was expensive compared to what that new century would bring. Early in the century, as the Industrial Revolution unfolded, the invention of the Fourdrinier machine to produce rolls of paper was followed by steam–powered rotary presses that used the rolls of paper. New presses were made of iron instead of wood. Small printshops used lever–operated presses.

LIMITATIONS OF TYPESETTING

The flat page of lead type was unsuited to the rotary press. Because of the risk that pieces of type might burst their bonds and spill all over the floor, the make–up of a page was limited to single columns tightly bound by column rules, giving the appearance known as a "tombstone" layout because of the heavy, black, single–column headlines sitting above the type. The stereotyping method solved this problem. An impression of a flat page of lead type was made on a cardboard–like mat, which was then put into a semi–circular mold; molten lead was poured into it; the lead hardened and cooled to give the printer an image of the page that could be fit onto the rotary press. Stereotyping also freed the pieces of type in the original page for reuse.

By the nineteenth century's close a typesetting machine had solved the slow process of hand–setting the type. Named for the rows of lead it spit out, the Linotype would be the noisy centerpiece of newspaper production well past the middle of the twentieth century.

PHOTOENGRAVING

The problem of how to put photographs into a newspaper was solved toward the end of the nineteenth century by the photoengraving process. It converted a paper photograph into a photograph on a zinc plate that held ink in the areas that should be dark, and rejected ink in the rest. On March 4, 1880, the *New York Graphic* published a *halftone* engraving of a photo called "Shantytown."

With the addition of other inventions of the Industrial Revolution, such as the telegraph, paper made from trees instead of cloth, typewriters, telephones, and the electric light bulb, the modern newspaper began to take form. Technology in the twentieth century, such as offset lithography, phototypesetting, and the computer, helped to make the newspaper the primary way that the public learned of current events and one of the primary ways that the public was entertained.

FEWER NEWSPAPER READERS NOW

Unfortunately for admirers of the printed page, the second half of the twentieth century, which saw printing technology improved through the computerization of virtually every newspaper function, also saw readership decline. As television newscasts took hold, many struggling metropolitan afternoon newspapers were compelled to merge with their morning competitors. Having replaced the orally delivered news in coffeehouses, the newspaper found itself beset by a new form of orally delivered news.

No user was more sensitive to the price and availability of paper stock than the newspaper industry. The printing, rather than the oral report, of news reached its apex in the century from 1850, after the introduction of the penny press, to 1950, when television news began making inroads into the way that the public wanted to receive its daily report of large and small events.

However, written news goes back much further. It can be traced to the *Acta Diurna* (*Daily Actions*) that Julius Caesar ordered posted at the Forum and around Rome, a gazette of what happened at the Senate plus other matters the government thought the public should know. In China, several centuries later, government officials could read the *tipao* (*palace report*) for government announcements and news from distant provinces of the empire.

Europe during the Middle Ages saw newsletters handwritten at first and printed after Gutenberg's invention spread, along with printed pamphlets and "broadsides" or "broadsheets," a kind of public relations circular that was printed to distribute a particular bit of news or an announcement. Some broadsides were done in rhyme. These printed pamphlets and broadsides were the first means of reaching a dispersed public with information that remained the same from one copy to the next. This did not mean that the news was accurate — only consistent — when there were tales of miracles and monsters.

Newsbooks were the next step on the path to newspapers. These were several pages usually on a single topic, sometimes illustrated with woodcuts. They competed with coffeehouse and tavern gossip. Like the broadside, the newsbook was provided by someone with something to say, often the government reporting a military victory. A further step toward newspapers was the newssheet. These small sheets of paper carried brief but relatively current items on several topics and were sold in Italy for a small coin called a "gazetta." In time, the newssheet itself took a variation of that name.

These newssheets began in Venice, where they carried news from several cities, but not from Venice itself.[1] Printing news or opinions on local matters could easily bring the police. Avoiding risk was a practice that has stood the test of time. Even so, nervous printers changed the name of the publications occasionally, or used no identifying name at all, and tried to stay on the right side of the authorities.

The popularity of newsbooks led in the early seventeenth century to the newspaper, a publication of several pages with a heading and, more or less, a schedule. Germany, Holland, and Switzerland all claim to have been the location of the first newspaper. Soon, newspapers were printed in cities throughout Western Europe. The first newspaper printed in

THE FIRST NEWS PUBLICATIONS

With the diffusion of literacy, the technology of printing, and the development of the modern newspaper, there was, then, the development of the modern notion of "news" itself. Indeed, between, say, about 1780 and 1830, the growth of journals, newsletters, and newspapers was so great in Europe that a fundamentally new social phenomenon came into being — the "news"–reading public.[2]

— ALVIN GOULDNER

Printing did not really develop in America during the eighteenth century until the printers discovered a new source of income — the newspaper... Far from their homeland, in sparsely populated areas, the pioneers felt cut off from contact with the rest of the world; probably that is why the newspaper developed more quickly in America than elsewhere.[4]

— Lucien Febvre and Henri–Jean Martin

the American colonies was a single issue in Boston in 1690 of *Publick Occurrences*, by Benjamin Harris, who had fled from London because the police were after him for his radical writing. Colonial authorities proved no more hospitable to his provocations.

The flimsy early colonial newspapers that followed were adjuncts of printing shops, which needed the income from sales of publications, advertising, and assorted job printing to survive.[3] A shortage of subscribers usually accompanied every newspaper venture, but it was expected that each copy of the newspaper had several readers or listeners.

There were no reporters. The editor, who was often the printer and only direct contributor, filled his publication with gleanings from other newspapers in the colonies and England, including news, opinions, essays, poetry, advertising when he could get any, and, occasionally, a bit of local news, such as the arrival of a ship and its cargo. That was new information. The printer who added one new item to another "new" and still another "new" could offer *news*. The public read the *news* and wanted more.

It was inevitable that newspapers would carry political and religious comments, and particularly the opinions of the printer. As newspapers came to be identified with political factions, they served as a valuable resource for disseminating the views of whatever party sponsored them.

Therefore, it was desirable for a political party to encourage the establishment of sympathetic newspapers. Favored publishers could count on printing contracts from the several levels of government. Another way for a party in power to gain the support of publishers was through the allocation of postmasterships because newspapers depended on mail delivery. *(See the next chapter, "Hauling Information," for more on this.)*

That other source of seventeenth and eighteenth century information for merchants, the coffeehouses, looked with disdain on newspapers, which were altering the habits of their customers. Instead of exchanging news and gossip in a social milieu, people sat quietly to read their newspapers, or read them at home. Although this behavior was more efficient, it was less neighborly. There were complaints about the "sullen silence" of newspaper readers, an example of the intrusive effects of printed materials on some forms of sociability.[5]

The future of information belonged to the newspaper, not the coffeehouse, but that would depend on improving the means of transportation.

The advanced stage coach, improved roads, and the train helped to expand the lines of distribution of the press and release it from the dependence on the coffeehouse which had been the chief means of circulation since Cromwellian days.[6]

— Anthony Smith

In the United States during the nineteenth century, newspapers in the larger cities had evolved into separate businesses, no longer part of printing shops. News was a commodity to be sold, manufactured from the raw material of facts. Sharing the pages of newspapers with the advertising that depended upon news items to attract readers, news could be sold at a profit. News was the product. The newspaper was the package.

In the early decades of the nineteenth century, readers could choose between commercial newspapers, which were about business, and political newspapers, which promoted the views of a political party and disseminated nasty rumors about their opponents. Neither was cheap. Before the penny press, newspapers were available mostly by subscription, not for sale at street corners, although individual copies could be bought for about six cents each. A year's subscription of $6 to $10 was more than a skilled workman earned in a week. Nor did the papers carry news of much interest to working people.

As a result, although a regular readership had developed, a lot of people barely knew what a newspaper was. But cities were growing, public education was advancing, literacy was spreading, and printing methods were improving. Jacksonian democracy infused the new nation with a spirit of equality.

PENNY PRESS

The penny press changed the dynamic by reaching out to the large portion of the population who had little interest in business or national politics, but had a thirst for gossip, sensation, and local news. The penny press satisfied that thirst, competing for the workingman's penny with the apples and small cakes also hawked on city streets.

The Sun, the *New York Morning Herald*, the *New York Tribune*, the *New York Times*, and the penny newspapers that appeared on the streets of other cities were sold by the issue. They were not in competition with the established newspapers that might cost six cents a copy, an expenditure that required some thought. Some established newspapers were available only by subscriptions that might have cost a workman a week's wages.

Wealthy, educated readers who subscribed to the older newspapers occasionally picked up a penny newspaper to read with scorn and to take home for the family's amusement, the way a grocery shopper today might pick up a tabloid at the checkout counter. Yet, intended to attract "the common man," the penny newsapers attracted middle class readers as well.

Politically, the penny papers fit the era of Jacksonian democracy, covering stories with an egalitarian perspective that had largely been missing.

Readers could find out what was happening down the street behind closed doors. They learned what their police and judges were doing.

The English aristocrat who spoke with a sneer about the American press in the nineteenth century could not have lived long enough to see the emergence of the London *Daily Mirror* and other sensational tabloids at home. His contempt would be reflected in aristocratic reactions to other means of communication, from the postage stamp to the public telephone, the silent motion picture, and television.

To the technological determinist, the penny press came about because advances in printing and paper made it possible, ignoring the role of Jacksonian democracy. Sociologist Michael Schudson, on the other hand, argued that the growth of mass democracy, the growth of cities, and the growth of a "market society" led to the success of the penny press, transforming the newspaper from something to be borrowed or read at a club or library to a product one bought for home consumption. He acknowledges that the changes in technology and the spread of literacy were contributing causes.[8]

First published in 1833, the *New York Sun*, hawked on the streets for a penny, tapped a vein of public curiosity involving scandal, crime, and other "human interest" news. The *Sun* and the penny press rivals that followed built up large circulations with a strong emphasis on the unimportant but interesting item. Sharing the pages with sensational stories were advertisements addressed to a mass audience.

The newspapers were read by the working class graduates of a public school system that taught them to read but did not always equip them with a burning thirst for knowledge. The penny press ads were an integral part of the Industrial Revolution through which its readers were living, for mass advertising created the demands leading to the mass consumption needed to support mass production. Newspapers grew fat with advertising.

For the most part, newspapers had been printing old news stories and opinion articles from other newspapers sent through the mails in the system set up in the eighteenth century by Benjamin Franklin for a free exchange of newspapers among editors.

Before the last half of the nineteenth century, news gathering by reporters was little known. Instead, the postman brought the distant newspapers whose articles could be clipped. Then, in the years after Samuel Morse's demonstation in 1844, the telegraph came along, providing the means for fresh reports of distant events. They whetted the public's appetite for more and still more news. The telegraph wires, running alongside the railroad tracks, hummed with daily reports from distant places to towns up and down the line. Improvements in transportation expanded newspaper circulation. Railroads founded new towns, and with them came local newspapers.

News came to have value as a commodity instead of merely supplying the basis for a piece of political partisanship. Like a bushel of oats or a yard of silk, news had become a product, and in a newspaper, ink upon paper, it had the means to be packaged. If news was a product to be packaged in a newspaper and sold to a willing readership, certain stories had more value than others. Local news had more value than distant news of a similar event. Sensational news had more value than dry reports. Reports of battles mattered, the closer the better, and so did exciting news of political events that might impact the readers' lives. Out of an understanding of these relative values, the modern newspaper has evolved, and so have the radio and television newscasts. The significant but dry relating of information never stood a chance.

NEWS AS A COMMODITY

Then as now, reports had more value when the reporter was at the scene of events, sending back dispatches based on personal observation and answers to questions posed to the important players of each drama, even generals at a battlefield or diplomats at a foreign court. The practice of active investigation soon followed and so did a rise in the circulation of newspapers willing to pursue news actively. In response — or self–defense — organizations from police to government to private business learned a myriad of ways to cope with the reporter's questions. A public relations industry developed, and some organizations actually improved what they were doing.

The coming of the telegraph, as we shall see, led to the wire news service, such as the Associated Press (AP). Sent by the clicking telegraph keys, reports of events became standardized, less opinionated, and of more interest to the political spectrum of readers. News stories won a broader array of readers but lost of some of their bite as they rid themselves of their bile. The new mass dailies, the penny press, now sold not just opinions and essays, but facts upon which working–class readers could base decisions and reach their own opinions.

REPORTING

Because a wire news service derives its income from the newspapers it serves, and receives greater income as the number of customers grows, it is not profitable to alienate any of its customers by expressing strong partisan views. A cooperative news agency existing to serve client newspapers profited by attracting still more clients.

Sensibly, the agency tried to please all its customers, or at least as many as possible, which covered a multitude of political leanings on every conceivable issue. This meant reporting facts in a manner that did not display the agency reporter's point of view.

The penny press wanted to appeal to everyone's interest and thus, logically, it stood opposed to anyone's 'special' interest — except of course its own interests, which presumably corresponded to its expressed policy of indifference.[10]

— THEODORE GLASSER

Out of this practical approach, and not from any noble wish for fairness, the concept of objectivity took form. The editorial pages of a newspaper continued to express the publisher's biases, but the wire reports took on a neutral cast, so that the reader could not tell — or should not be able to identify — the reporter's politics on controversy. The stance could be called balanced. Or it could be called indifferent. *Objective reporting*, something rather out of the ordinary, was born.

The brilliant essay, at least in the writer's mind, had to be replaced by a plainer cousin that held facts high and opinion low. The change was needed to take full business advantage of electrical transmission. A neutral, dispassionate view of events had been uncommon in American journalism, but the AP's effort to be impartial continued. Eventually objectivity set the tone for most news reporting.

This standard of objective reporting spread to all the news reports in the newspaper, not just the wire service news, giving news stories the dispassionate appearance they usually have today. The source for this change, the telegraph wire service, was also responsible for what is known as the 5W (who, what, when, where, why) lead and the inverted pyramid structure of a news story (information presented in order of importance), both of them more familiar to American newspaper readers than to readers in Europe, where the opinionated narrative essay proved more stubborn to dislodge.

The 5W lead and the inverted pyramid, developed during the Civil War, may have been due to the unreliability of the telegraph lines. The editor at the receiving end of the telegraph message wanted to be sure that in the very first paragraph he understood the gist of what was happening. (The surprise ending could be left to the popular short stories of O. Henry, the pen name of a former newspaper reporter with a gift for fiction.)

INTO THE TWENTIETH CENTURY

The twentieth century brought enormous changes to the newspaper industry, including the tabloid format and the increase in sensationalism and celebrity reporting to feed the public appetite. The century brought the growth of newspaper chains as part of media empires. Technological changes included a switch from letterpress to offset lithography and, by the end of the century, the introduction of the computer in every nook of newspaper production from the reporter and photographer in the field to the printing of subscribers' addresses. The century also saw the decline of the newspaper as the pre–eminent purveyor of news, first in competition with radio, then television, and, at the end of the century, the rise of the Internet.

Twentieth century publishers paid attention to market research reports that many in their communities wanted the opposite of what editors thought was best for them. The public, especially those who did not pick up a newspaper daily, wanted less foreign and political news, shorter stories, more local news, and more colorful feature news. As has been so often the case in mediated communication, users influenced the direction that media took, and changes followed that serious journalists still bemoan.

Another change has been the increase of what is called "investigative journalism," a departure from objectivity to expose community ills. It is a continuation of the magazine muckraking of about 1900. Even if the news articles do not openly call for fixing the problems that newspapers uncover, the awakened readers and legislators are expected to do so.

INVESTIGATIVE JOURNALISM

News, editorial opinion, and advertising were not the only products a newspaper had to offer as the decades went by. Nor were they the only means to shape attitudes toward political issues. Political columns, political cartoons, photographs, and advice columns have all done their bit to shape attitudes, and so have the comics, ranging across the political specturm from the conservative Orphan Annie to the liberal Doonesbury. The line between information and entertainment was frequently crossed in the never–ending quest for a mass readership. Horoscopes, household hints, and dozens of other features have been added.

Since the start of the twenty–first century, newspaper readership has declined under the onslaught of other communication media for public attention. The much desired readership of middle class people between 18 and 45 was moving to television, magazines, and, most recently, the Internet, where the latest news and a blogosphere of endless numbers of opinions available in print, voice, and video could be reached with a few clicks. The Internet also carried an assault on that newspaper economic mainstay, the classified ad.

READERSHIP DECLINES

What the newspaper has done is to connect readers to their community and, depending upon the newspaper, to the world beyond the horizon. For many generations the newspaper was their primary or, indeed, their only medium of *mass* communication. That is no longer the case, and for the public, particularly the *young* public, a loss of interest in newspapers reflects the changing times.

Unlike newspapers, which provide a connection to a community based on geography, magazines provide a connection based on interest. Of course, that may be a shared interest based on geography, like city magazines, or a shared interest in politics, religion, occupation, social life, hobbies, an endless list. A few general–interest magazines are sold, but millions of readers prefer magazines that address more specific interests, and most of the nineteen thousand magazines published in the United States do that.

MAGAZINES

General interest magazines like *The Saturday Evening Post* were upended not only by the public preference for specialty magazines but also by general interest television in the form of three dominant networks, ABC, CBS, and NBC. In their turn the general interest television networks are being hurt by specialty cable channels. In short, people tend to go where they can get specifically what they want.

INTEREST GROUPS

Breaking the public into interest groups has separated them. The process can be clearly seen in the neighborhood DVD/VCR shop, where shelves full of titles await. The shop–by–mail versions of video rental shops, such as Netflix, do the same thing, which is to fragment the public by appealing to individual tastes.

Who is hurt? Neighborhood movie multiplexes that offer minimal choices. These multiplexes once did the same thing to the downtown or neighborhood single theater that offered no choice at all. The broadcast networks and even the cable channels are being hurt by media that offer more choices. The expanding number of radio stations that advertise their unique "sound," including multi–channel satellite radio, and the expanding number of cable channels are less–than–mute testimony to fragmentation and the desire for choice. Call it the *magazine effect. (This topic will be revisited in later chapters.)*

The magazine was born in England in the eighteenth century as a weekly periodical. The remarkable and busy Daniel Defoe, author of *Robinson Crusoe* and *Moll Flanders*, wrote the first modern newspaper editorial. He founded the *Review* and filled it with essays, some of which he did not write.[11] He is considered a founder of the English novel and, because of his interviews, the founder of modern journalism. And he was a spy.

In England, *The Tatler* and *The Spectator* followed the *Review*. In the American colonies, the Philadelphia printer Benjamin Franklin tried his hand at publishing a magazine. So did other colonial printers, but most failed, even though many newspapers and magazines accepted goods as barter for ad space and subscriptions. At least one Massachusetts publisher offered to accept butter and other groceries as subscription payment.[12] Without advertising or the postal considerations given to newspapers, survival was difficult. The lack of illustrations, except for the occasional woodcut, limited their attraction. So did the poor quality of paper and presses, plus the high circulation costs, Also, magazines were primarily a medium for the well–to–do.

The American magazine was a lady more than it was a gentleman. The growth of the new United States was matched by an increase in the number of weekly, monthly, and quarterly periodicals, including magazines aimed at a readership of women. These continued to reach out to the middle and upper classes. However, their appeal to a genteel reader-

The American newspaper was a workman, sweaty, busy, and shirt–sleeved; the American magazine was a gentleman, serious, sentimental, and sedate.[13]

—CARL BODE

ship had already begun to change with the arrival of the penny press. In England *The Penny Magazine* was written for literate workmen. Religious magazines and those seeking to extend their readership to the working class were early examples of the fragmentation that specialized magazines brought to a community.

Congress extended low–cost mailing privileges to magazines in 1879. By the end of the century, several dozen mass circulation national magazines supported by advertising and displaying lots of photographs were being published. Cyrus Curtis published *The Saturday Evening Post* and *The Ladies Home Journal* on the concept that large circulation magazines could be profitable based on advertising, not subscriptions. His policies allowed him to pay top dollar for the best writing and art, but he saw editorial content as incidental to advertising.

Curtis once asked an audience of advertisers, "Do you know why we publish *The Ladies Home Journal*? The editor thinks it is for the benefit of American women. That is an illusion, but a very proper one for him to have. But I will tell you, the real reason, the publisher's reason, is to give you people who advertise things that American women want and buy a chance to tell them about your products." During World War II, homesick soldiers who received special editions without advertising complained that the ads told them more about home than the editorial content.[14]

"DO YOU KNOW WHY WE PUBLISH?"

No matter how well–heeled first adopters are, media of all kinds in time seek working class users. Simply, there are more of them. A few magazine publishers continued to appeal primarily to a well–educated readership, but success depended on a broader audience. In 1893, publishers Frank Munsey, S.S. McClure, and *Cosmopolitan* editor John Walker engaged in a circulation war that dropped the price of their magazines even below the cost of production. In doing so, they contributed to a societal movement for change in America. They created the first national mass audience. Their magazines built large circulations that commanded high rates for the mass–produced goods their magazines advertised.

Popular taste magazines reached out to all members of the family with articles on the latest trends, sentimental romance fiction, pictures, and exposés, notably in *McClure's Magazine*, by investigative reporters whom Theodore Roosevelt called "muckrakers."

Occupational groups, some exhibiting early traits of professionalism, launched journals. And individuals with faddish interests in such topics as phrenology and medicinal water cures coalesced in loosely knit associations through the pages of their magazines.[15]

— Richard Kielbowicz

The power of muckrakers, expressed through magazines or books, could be formidable. As one example, Upton Sinclair's *The Jungle*, an exposé of the meat packing industry, helped create the climate that led to passage of the Pure Food and Drug Act. It also created a lot of vegetarians.

By the middle of the twentieth century, thousands of trade and specialty magazines were published for targeted readerships. They fared better than *Life, Look, Coronet,* and *The Saturday Evening Post.* Mass circulation popular–taste magazines succumbed to assaults by the new medium of television, which also appealed to popular tastes. A few mass circulation magazines, notably *Reader's Digest,* continued to thrive, but for most magazines, targeted readerships and targeted advertising provided the revenue to be profitable.

News magazines like *Time* and *Newsweek,* bedeviled by the need to compete with daily television newscasts for timely reports, fought back successfully. To speed the process of getting news into readers' hands, they sent pages via communication satellite to regional printing plants, from which magazines with imprinted addresses were flown or trucked to local distribution points to be mailed or thrown on doorsteps. National newspapers like *The Wall Street Journal* chose similar solutions to reach their dispersed readers.

If a common theme can be found in the history of the magazine, it is that targeting to a specific readership succeeds better than trying to reach the most diverse audience possible. Anyone who wants to see the future of television or any other medium of communication might do well to browse magazine racks. Yet what is on display can be only the tiniest fraction of the 3,000 consumer magazines considered of general interest, the more than 8,000 trade magazines, plus hundreds of others on religion, agriculture, and so many other topics.

The fragmentation and recombination of readers into narrow but national and even international interest groups also expressed itself in newsletters. Once mimeographed and stapled, modern newsletters are either slick products that draw on desktop publishing techniques or are sold for online delivery that requires no paper at all. The ranks of newsletter publishers have risen exponentially because of the minimal costs of publication. At the most basic level, "zines," usually published for younger readers on such personal subjects as the publisher's music tastes, are a printed version of Internet blogs.

BOOKS

The subject of books deserves separate consideration. Older than other types of publication by centuries, the book continues as the standard that marks an educated person. Readers who discard a newspaper without a thought and may not keep magazines very long have a more respectful regard for their books. If a book does not sit on a shelf for years, it may be passed along to someone else. It is less likely than other reading media to be thrown away.

Books are no longer the sole repository of the world's knowledge, nor of simple information, the role they filled for centuries. They are still, as they have always been, a source of enormous pleasure as well as a source of learning, yet they now compete with increasing difficulty against other communication media even though their total numbers continue to increase.

Stories written to entertain can be traced back to ancient Greece and beyond. *Gilgamesh* was written in Sumer 5,000 years ago. The earliest Biblical stories were written 3,000 years ago. Satirical writing traces back to ancient times and such authors as Petronius (Satyricon) and Apuleius (The Golden Ass). Many of the great works produced in ancient Greece and Rome did not survive, but those that have are pillars of modern thought. Some of the extant books refer to works that have been lost to the ages.

ANCIENT BOOKS

During the approximately seven centuries from the fall of Rome to the first European universities, book production was literally in the hands of monks patiently doing God's labor in the scriptoria of monasteries. Their "illuminated manuscripts" are works of art, made to be venerated. Creating such a book was a way to worship God. These books were venerated. Monasteries locked them away. The books certainly were not available for the public gaze.

University booksellers with scribal backshops expanded both the quantity of books and the variety of content. So did stationers who sold paper to students who copied books. Returning crusaders brought classical texts from Greek and Roman authors that were copied.

In the Middle Ages, the invention of the chimney increased book reading, as did spectacles. When chimneys in stately mansions heated private rooms, their owners could escape the common room to relax and read in cozy privacy. The book was the original separator between the surrounding environment and the individual, who happily ignored everything but the printed page.

As books became available, the demand grew for more of them. Bibles, prayer books, and collections of religious thought were joined by moral tales and secular works, including books on medicine and mathematics, plus scientific observation. *The Canterbury Tales* was written in the century before Gutenberg. This is not to say that books were easy to find. University students might get their hands on the books they needed, but not others. Most books were still hidden in monasteries, where they were not catalogued. Peasants were probably unaware that such a thing as a book existed, and most people were peasants.

MEDIEVAL BOOK PUBLICATION

Printing presses sharply increased quantity and variety. The printing center at Frankfort held an annual book fair that brought printers, booksellers, collectors and scholars from all over Europe to browse. In this haphazard world of books, something new was printed: a catalogue of the books for sale. Also for sale, for this was an era of global exploration, were printed maps and geography texts. To readers who could not travel, exploring new continents and reading descriptions of the peoples who inhabited them were fascinating topics, and the demand for these books was high.

Before the eighteenth century, no children's books were published, although no doubt the beastiaries, with woodcut drawings about real or mythical animals, would be available for their pleasure and nightmares. As with all medieval writing, these illustrated books made moral points about vice and virtue, of Christ and the Devil.

NOVELS

Novels are a more recent form. Although the *Tale of Genji* is 1,000 years old and *Don Quixote* appeared nearly 400 years ago, its narrative structure pointing to the modern novel, we look to the eighteenth century for complex prose tales of adventure and romance. Rabelais, Cervantes, Chaucer, Boccaccio, and the Lady Murasaki no–Shikibu brilliantly preceded them with book length fictional tales, but the novel was still an unusual literary form when Daniel Defoe wrote of his shipwrecked mariner, and Samuel Richardson told his readers about Pamela, whose virtue was sorely beset.

France, Germany, Russia, and several other nations developed rich traditions of literary fiction. Examining them lies beyond the scope of this book, which will confine itself to a brief look at responses to the English language novel. Written with middle class sensibilities for middle class readers about matters that concerned them, such as social pretensions and the desire to improve one's status in a class–conscious society, the English novels of the eighteenth and nineteenth centuries set new standards for literature. Popular novels were serialized in magazines. To keep the readers buying new issues, writers ended chapters on a note of suspense. It may also explain the large number of chapters.

At home, families read the chapters aloud, an exception to the separation that books often bring. The Bible, when read aloud, and bedtime children's stories are examples of books that bring family members together. In many homes the Bible and an almanac were the only books. Both helped to advance the desire to read.

For generation after generation, (the King James Bible) gave the English, and the English in America, a template against which to measure their own utterances. It was in many households the only book and became itself a spur to literacy. It is surely no coincidence that its creation coincides with the first great surge in literacy levels in England.[16]

— ADAM NICOLSON

The popular novel was not immune to controversy. The popular colonial preacher Jonathan Edwards, known for his fiery sermons, said reading novels was an indulgence leading to a moral decline. Not untypical was this warning, couched in an epistolary novel, from another minister, "The free access which many young people have to romances, novels, and plays has poisoned the mind and corrupted the morals of many a promising youth."[17] In early America, writing tended to be didactic, especially writing for the young. The popular McGuffey Readers promoted hard work, study, good behavior, kindness, and honesty.

For adults in both England and America, novels of sentimentality prevailed. Heavy on emotion, the advance in social status of a central character provided the happy ending. The boy Oliver Twist moves into an upper class life, but there is no help for his friends. Yet, thanks to *Oliver Twist* and other Dickens novels, we have inherited an understanding of the misery, pain, danger, and just plain unfairness of urban life during the Industrial Revolution.

INHERITING UNDERSTANDING

All of this was true, but for many of the people who lived during the Industrial Revolution, the misery of slaving in grim factories and living in unhealthy slums was better than the starvation and cruelty of the village life they gladly abandoned. Recall that Oliver fled *to* London from the countryside.

Dickens' novels continued a tradition of satire that looked at the miserable conditions of the poor and poked fun at social classes and at bureaucratic incompetence and unfairness without the direct frontal attack that might have had police come knocking. His world was the Industrial Revolution, a century when everything, including mediated communication, seemed to change.

Hardly any of the printing technology changed in the 250 years since Gutenberg. During the Industrial Revolution the changes came thick and fast in paper production, printing, the telegraph, photography, and by the end of the century, the telephone, phonograph, typewriter, radio, motion pictures, and major advances in printing. To this list we may add public education, public libraries, mass advertising, cheap book and magazine publishing for the masses, and postal changes that encouraged communication. There were even experiments that would lead to computers, television and tape recording.

For all its ills, the Industrial Revolution saw a rise in literacy among the middle and working classes. Compulsory free education and lending libraries increased an interest in books, though the curse of child labor continued in the United States and Europe for decades to deprive the children of poor families of a chance for meaningful education. Printing and paper grew cheaper. Continuous web papermaking machines and large cylinder presses led to the mass production of cheap books that were put into the roughened hands of people who otherwise could not afford them.

Rapid change continued into the twentieth century. Books have been the beating heart of a culture, but they are also a product to be manufactured and sold at a profit, obeying the laws of economics. During the 1920s and 1930s, the years of boom and bust, mass sellers clashed with publishers and critics who held books to a high standard.

TWENTIETH CENTURY

The Book–of–the–Month Club and The Literary Guild, both started in 1926, became a new way to sell books to middle class readers. By the end of the decade seven more book clubs joined them. Buying books in bulk, printing cheap editions, and selling subscriptions, the clubs sold hundreds of thousands of novels, non–fiction titles, and reference books at prices that bookstores could not match. Department stores advertised popular titles at bargain prices to woo customers into their stores.

THE HIGH COST OF BOOKS

During the Depression of the 1930s, the book business was hurting. Publishers dropped the price of new novels. Because many titles still sold at regular prices, book buyers were confused and angry at the cost of books. An irritated *New York Times* editorial said book prices might be enough to cause "abandonment of the reading habit."[18]

A public appetite for inexpensive, easy–to–read novels filled with action, adventure, and romance led in the nineteenth century to the dime novel, printed on the cheap new wood–pulp paper and glued between lurid color covers. Publishers could sell them so cheaply and still make a profit thanks to such printing advances as big steam–driven presses and stereotyping.

Dime novels first arrived during the Civil War. Union and Confederate soldiers shared an appetite for them. Their popularity with men and boys did not end with the war, but their appearance and tough–male content held little attraction to women readers.

The paperbacks of the twentieth century followed what was by now a tradition of affordable reading. The early decades of the twentieth century saw a new type of fiction directed at a readership described with a sneer as "men who move their lips when they read."

A survey showed that most readers of this cross between books and magazines were working class men with only a grade school education.[19] They were called pulps because of the rough wood–pulp paper they were printed on. Their shiny covers in bright colors usually featured drawings of scantily clad women and men in violent scenes. Priced from a nickel to a quarter, they contained up to 130 pages of short stories that might bear no connection to the garish covers. They carried advertising appealing to working men for physical or mental self–improvement, such as correspondence courses and muscle building.

Leather bindings were no longer common, and cloth covers gave way to paper covers and paperback books. Critics howled, but a great many books were being read by a great many readers. Other twentieth century factors leading to the mass consumption of what had once been entertainment for a small middle class were the condensed novel in publications like *Reader's Digest*, book clubs, and outlets that included school libraries and their book reading campaigns. Neighborhood public libraries set aside reading nooks for adults and children. Bookmobiles traveled rural roads. Discount stores carried inexpensive reprints of popular books. Online resellers such as Amazon.com and the entrepreneurs of eBay peddled books new and used.

In the twenty–first century, despite the competition from other media, books sold well. Two or three of the most popular books could boast sales of more than a million copies each. Meanwhile, books extended their reach through non–print media, particularly audio books that entertained bored drivers on the daily commute.

As it does every year, the Bible continued to far outsell every other book, at about twenty–five million copies a year. Nine of ten American homes had at least one Bible, and the average home had four. Not all were standard Bibles. For men, there was a *Men of Integrity Bible*; for women, a *Woman, thou Art Loosed!* version; for children, *The Super Heroes Bible*. A surfer's Bible is among several dozen others. Like everything else in mediated communication, choice rules.

Technology was altering the book industry. When they came on the market in 2001, ebooks marketed online failed to grab the reader's attention, but their popularity was expected to increase, particularly among students confronted by high textbook costs. An important advantage of books in digital format is increased choice. The traditional economics guiding publishing decisions change when books do not need to be printed on paper.

Downloaded to portable digital readers, ebooks let the reader mark a page, skip ahead, jump back, or read the usual way, one page at a time. A vacationer could carry several books without adding weight. The main disadvantage of these portable devices, besides the initial cost, was that the screen was not always easy to read. In 2006, Sony came out with new display technology that apparently solved this problem.

A printer/binder called the Espresso Book Machine was being tested in 2006; it may be able to print a book that exists in a digital format, print a color cover, and bind it, all for a reasonable price. With printing on demand, it also has the potential to alter the book publishing industry.

Vanity presses have been available to hopeful new authors for decades, turning manuscripts into books in return for hefty fees. Thanks to inexpensive desktop publishing, new ventures can turn out copies for a fraction of that cost. Thousands of new titles are produced each year, many of them sold through online booksellers, totally bypassing the traditional bookstores. Websites such as lulu.com, picaboo.com, and blurb.com help authors to publish their own titles a few copies at a time.

The general principle —that Scripture can be repackaged to meet the demands of an increasingly segmented market—is at the heart of the modern Bible–publishing business…

Wayne Hastings, the publisher of Nelson's Bible division, said, "Look at satellite radio—what is that, a hundred and seventy–eight stations? And it's all niched. We're doing the same thing in Bibles."[20]

—DANIEL RADOSH

While small runs are never cheap, they provide a professional–looking product.

Beyond fiction and education, throughout the centuries a few books changed the way people thought. Isaac Newton's *Principia Mathematica* was one such book. It is arguably the greatest book of science ever written. He established the primacy of scientific investigation and he expanded the boundaries of thought for all who followed.

Adam Smith's *An Inquiry into the Nature and Causes of the Wealth of Nations* became the underpinning of capitalism. Mary Wollstonecraft's *A Vindication of the Rights of Women* began the feminist movement. Charles Darwin's *On the Origin of Species* spread the theory of evolution and with *The Descent of Man* placed humankind as one of many species. He is still challenged by those who feel his theory denies God's words.

Harriet Beecher Stowe's *Uncle Tom's Cabin* contributed to the abolitionist fervor in the years prior to the Civil War. Rachel Carson's *Silent Spring* helped form the environmental movement and led to the banning of DDT and other pesticides that killed birds and entered the human food supply. The feminist movement was enhanced by several books, such as Betty Friedan's *The Feminine Mystique*.

Many other books deserve a place here. To this brief list, at least two pamphlets must be added: Thomas Paine's *Common Sense* and the *Communist Manifesto* by Karl Marx and Friedrich Engels. All these printed works led to changes in the human condition.

THE TYPEWRITER

The typewriter, which produced so many words for more than a century, deserves a few words for itself. The machine gathers dust in the antique shops of the cities of the West, but it can still be found in developing countries doing its job of generating information along the mediated communication trail leading from someone's brain to everyone's eyes. Even in the computer–rich West, a battered typewriter may still be found at the fingertips of a curmudgeon who will have nothing to do with digital media.

The inefficient computer keyboard is the typewriter QWERTY keyboard; it still protects the typist from jamming the keys at the print point by positioning the common letters "a" and "s" under the weak fingers and the uncommon "j" under the strongest finger, an arrangement that also separated the most frequent pairs of letters so that they are struck by alternate hands. The problem persisted after a Cincinnati school for stenographers began teaching a faster, ten–finger method in place of Sholes' two–finger hunt–and–peck style; it was eased by mechanical designs that returned the key bars faster. If the keyboard arrangement does us no favors, each generation learns it because the previous generation is accustomed to it, rather than learning a more efficient keyboard arrangement like the Dvorak system.

The typewriter became more than just a chain in the mediated communication link. When it was introduced in the latter part of the nineteenth century, middle class women in Western societies were not expected to work outside the home. Trapped in Victorian households and dependent upon a husband, father, or brother, some young, moderately educated women were just beginning to break free to seek their own careers as department store clerks, nurses, and telephone operators.

The chance to work in an office as what was originally called a "typewriter" (referring to both the typist and the machine) was a more daring occupational choice because it put a young woman into a workplace where only men were employed, and these men were not related to her. The opportunity for this daring career came to young women because not enough young men were willing to take up the new typing profession. When a branch of the New York YWCA suggested training young women to type, a group of eight quickly formed for a six–month class. Upon graduation, all were hired in one of the few careers open to women that required literacy.

Quite soon women were pouring into offices across the land, not only as typists, but also as secretaries and stenographers, two occupations hitherto limited to men. A few enterprising women set up their own businesses as public typist–stenographers, which further spread the concepts of both the typewriter as a useful machine and the woman as a desirable employee.

The presence of women also changed the atmosphere of the office, a previously Dickensian workplace with a cuspidor for spitting and dark wood that hid the dirt.

The concept of the typewriter, a personal writing machine that would replace a pen that cost a penny, did not catch on immediately. Before the typewriter, offices did not have machinery, but the advantage of machinery to add efficiency became apparent. Typewriters were followed by dictaphones, mimeographs, adding machines, bookkeeping machines, envelope addressers, check writers, and postal meters.

None of this considers the typewriter's role in the chain of activities that carries words from someone's mind to the minds of others. Its widespread adoption was evidence of its advantages, as it overcame the problems of cramped fingers that resulted from writing long documents to the difficulty of reading bad handwriting. Yet,

When the first wave of female typists hit the business office in the 1890s, the cuspidor manufacturers read the sign of doom. They were right. More important, the uniform ranks of fashionable lady typists made possible a revolution in the garment industry. What she wore, every farmer's daughter wanted to wear, for the typist was a popular figure of enterprise and skill. She was a style-maker who was also eager to follow styles. As much as the typewriter, the typist brought into business a new dimension of the uniform, the homogeneous, and the continuous that has made the typewriter indispensable to every aspect of mechanical industry.[21]

—MARSHALL MCLUHAN

"Computers are better," the 9–year–old says, blonde pony tail bobbing behind her. "With typing, you don't have to erase when you make a mistake. You just hit delete, so it's a lot easier."

Such attitudes are worrying to a growing number of parents, educators and historians, who fear that computers are speeding the demise of a uniquely American form of expression. Handwriting experts fear that the wild popularity of email, instant messages and other electronic communication, particularly among kids, could erase cursive within a few decades.[22]

— CBS News Report

as in all changes, the replacement did not come without a cost. The once prized art of penmanship became less important, and there was less talk of writing "in a fine Italian hand." Cursive is still taught to third graders, but with some grumbling in the computer age.

The idea of a writing machine may have originated with an English engineer, Henry Mill, who received a patent but did not construct a machine. During the eighteenth century, actual machines were built in Austria, Switzerland, France, and Italy.

One goal for such a machine was to emboss letters on paper so that the blind could read, an enterprise perhaps motivated by the example of a French youth, Valentin Haüy, who started a school for the blind. A French youth who had gone blind, Louis Braille, attended the school in the nineteenth century, where he improved on Haüy's book embossing code. Another impetus for a writing machine came from the new telegraph industry. Skilled telegraphers could understand messages as fast as the clicks arrived, but could not write them down by hand fast enough.

Patents flew thick and fast in several countries as imaginative citizens thought up machine designs that resembled everything from a small piano (France) to a beauty parlor hair dryer (Russia). The fifty–second typewriter patent issued by the U.S. Patent Office went to Christopher Sholes of Milwaukee, a printer who joined friends in designing a workable machine that sent keys moving up to a print point. Because the key fell back slowly, pulled just by the force of gravity, it was easy for an ascending key to block a descending key; hence the "scientific" design of the keyboard to reduce the number of jams. Incremental improvements by Sholes and his friends were speeded up when the Remington company, maker of guns and sewing machines, took on the new business; the sewing machine foot treadle was adapted as a carriage return. Of the dozens of companies that later manufactured typewriters, IBM made the most changes with its line of electric typewriters, notably the Selectric typing ball.

CONCLUSION

Printing and literacy have always been one hand washing the other. The greater the degree of literacy, the greater the demand for something to read. And the more there was to read, the greater desire to read. The invention of eyeglasses and chimneys (giving heat to private rooms), both invented before Gutenberg's movable type, aided reading for those who could afford them. New forms of printed communication met the demands of expanded communities of the literate: the newspaper, the magazine, the encyclopedia, books of special information. Also, to encourage reading, there was now the public library and the public school.

From a demand that could not be satisfied with the old wooden screw press came such improvements as the iron press and the lever press. A demand for paper came from the increased demand for its principal use, printing. It is altogether likely that the availability of paper in rolls led to the development of rotary printing presses that took advantage of them.

At the start of the nineteenth century nearly all men and most women in the northeastern United States were literate. To learn to read probably took less effort in industrial Europe than in previous centuries because of the greater sense that literacy was a worthwhile skill. Yet, as was noted at the start of this chapter, literacy means nothing if you do not choose to read.

From the start of printing with movable type, to encourage literacy, printers and publishers provided a variety of materials. They produced books and pamphlets in the vernacular. In future centuries, other reading matter would include magazines and novels on topics of interest to readers written in simple and attractive ways.

The greater availability of printed material was a spur to learning. Books like the McGuffey Readers encouraged not only children but their parents to acquire the skill of figuring out the message on the printed page in front of them.

By the middle of the century, nine out of ten white people throughout the expanding nation had at least a basic reading skill. With slavery still in existence in the South, blacks were usually prevented, sometimes violently, from learning to read. Slave owners sensed the danger of literate slaves. Literacy, the ability to both read and write, conferred power on those who possessed it; illiteracy has always been a weakness.

Books had a long history before printing, but readership was limited until printing made them affordable. The Industrial Revolution brought significant advances to both Western Europe and North America. For the first time in history, nations adopted policies of universal education. Everyone, not just the sons of the wealthy, would be given at least a rudimentary education. But education that reached everyone depended on the availability of printed materials. Mechanical advances in printing methods and paper production added the means to the desire to educate the young in every nation that adopted the policy.

However, although students left schools with reading skills, relatively few of them carried away a taste for great literature, high culture, or a wish to expand their knowledge in such realms as science or political philosophy. Publishers were more likely to follow popular tastes than to lead them.

For the majority of people, the penny press served very well. So did most popular magazines and novels that reflect ordinary human concerns and provide escape from humdrum lives. Besides providing mass entertainment, books continue to be the principal vehicle for societal change. In recent years, feminism and the environmental movement have been led by books.

If newspapers, magazines, and books that met a common need for pleasurable reading have lost some readership in recent years, it is because of competition from newer sources of entertainment and information; it is not because readers are less curious.

With the Internet at hand, if students read fewer books and newspapers than their grandparents did, it does not mean they are learning less. They have more choices in their sources. Students today do their research via SparkNotes and the Google search engine, bypassing original texts. Parents who once used CliffNotes to read their Shakespeare assignments and grandparents who got their literature from *Readers Digest* Condensed Books can hardly complain. Choice, not an elevated taste, is transforming mediated communication.

4 MAIL:
HAULING INFORMATION

A COMPARISON OF THE postal service with the radio or television industries may be instructive. Each has had a considerable impact on our world. (Ralph Waldo Emerson called postal service "a first measure of civilization.") Each brings information, entertainment, and advertising to our homes. Each depends upon international agreements, national standards, and some degree of government supervision. Each is built upon broad communication technologies; the most obvious is the postal service's dependence on paper and printing. If the world had never known each of these methods of communication, life would be different and, arguably, inferior.

Of course, distinctions exist among them. The postal service provides more personal, point–to–point communication. Radio and television provide the physical reality of the machine in the living room. Postal service dates to the dawn of history. The broadcast industry does not. The postal service and broadcasting in most countries are government run. The postal service and broadcasting have competitors. Federal Express, United Parcel Service, DHL and the U.S. Postal Service compete heavily.

A closer analogy can be drawn comparing the postal service with the telephone industry, the telegraph, the communication satellite, and the Internet. It was not so long ago that farm families lived isolated lives, their principal links to the outside world coming through the village post office. Today, mail is joined by email, telephones, radio, and television to reach into every corner of the land to connect even the most remote households. If the Internet is an "information highway," so is the postal service, with analogues up and down the line.

Postal service was never a simple matter. It is certainly not simple today. Mail delivery has included carrier pigeons, human runners, fast ponies, slow donkeys, dog sleds, stagecoaches, all manner of boats, trains, trucks and airplanes. The postman now competes in the message delivery business with fax machines, cell phones, instant messaging, email, electronic banking, automated bill payments, and even preprinted inserts in newspapers. The days when almost the only way to send a message was to drop it in a mailbox are long gone. They are unmourned, for the world prefers, as it always does, choice.

The beginnings of postal communication are lost in antiquity. Like language itself, messages would go out in a hundred disorganized ways over the centuries.[1] Surely, their oral delivery came before writing, but it was writing that led to the organized postal service. Throughout history the postman followed two trails, the path of the government and the path of the private citizen and merchant. In some places at various times the two paths were one, but only in the last few centuries, a fraction of postal history, have they merged. Because of necessity and suspicion, governments still keep separate channels.

EARLY POSTS

Postal service is the handmaiden of central government, essential to retaining power. Kings knew that if they wanted to control their land, they had to control communication. The Chinese Empire had an official postal service in the tenth century B.C.E. Confucius spoke of it in the fifth century B.C.E. By the thirteenth century C.E., Kublai Khan had the world's best courier system. A network of 1,400 post houses and relay stations for an estimated 50,000 horses were on duty throughout his empire. Clerks recorded the time of arrival and departure of the riders. Boats waited at river and lake crossings. Camels and carriages hauled ordinary mail as well as passengers. First–class mail, limited to royal and military mail, always went by pony express in relays. A rider who didn't meet his schedule faced a whipping. Marco Polo was sufficiently impressed to include a description in his reflections on the system.

Government postal services in China until recent centuries were meant only for government departments, as they were in other countries, but merchants also used the system, and no doubt love letters sneaked in. To the east, the Japanese postal system was officially limited to government use until a private courier service began in the seventeenth century.

The New World had no horses until European invaders introduced them, so Aztecs, Incas and Mayas employed relay stations of human runners. Certain Native American tribes notched or painted sticks to convey messages. Incas in South America knotted colored quipu cords. In Peru the Chimu tribes wrote in code on lima beans, delivered by runners, though such media had limited use aside from being easily carried. Aztec couriers also delivered freshly caught fish to inland villages, an early parcel post service.

The first record of a written message stamped with a seal and apparently delivered by a courier dates to King Sargon of Babylon, about 2300 B.C.E. (Clay seals bearing his name are housed in the Louvre.) The Egyptians had a relay system that helped maintain central control of their empire. An ancient Egyptian papyrus scroll carries the request, "Write to me by the letter carrier," but it is unclear if the letter carrier is a private messenger or part of a postal service. In the third century B.C.E, Ptolemy II introduced the camel into Egypt and organized a camel post to carry government and commercial messages to the south.

The Old and New Testaments identify letters. King David's letter to the battlefield sealed the fate of Bathsheba's unlucky husband. Dispatches

'First class' business was conveyed on horseback, with relay–stages of 25 miles. But the really important business of Kublai's empire (note: 13th century) was carried by non–stop dispatch–riders carrying the special tablet with the sign of the gerfalcon. At the approach to each post–house the messenger would sound his horn; the ostlers would bring out a ready–saddled fresh horse, the messenger would transfer to it and gallop straight off. Marco affirmed that those courier horsemen could travel 250 or 300 miles in a day.[2]

— THE SILK ROAD
Foundation

are mentioned in the Book of Esther. Job lamented, "My days are swifter than the post," referring to the rapid courier service of biblical days. Paul, of course, sent many letters to groups of the faithful in Judea and Macedonia. Perhaps at the same time, the Assyrians allowed merchants to send letters by government post. These small clay tablets were encased in clay envelopes bearing addresses. Under the rulers Cyrus, Darius, and Xerxes, Persians (in present–day Iran) built roads and established pony express relay stations throughout the empire. According to the Greek historian Xenophon, to interfere with the mail was punishable by death.

Seeing messages carried 200 miles in a day, the Greek historian Herodotus wrote, "Nothing mortal travels so fast as these Persian messengers… And neither snow nor rain nor heat nor gloom of night stays these couriers from the swift completion of their appointed rounds."[3] (The inscription is carved into the stone of the New York Post Office.)

In Homer's day, communication was by messenger or by signal fires from mountain top to mountain top. Ancient Greece, lacking a central government, had no known postal service, but several tales of running messengers have come down to us. The governments of the city states and individual writers relied on ships, runners, or carrier pigeons to move information. Brief announcements might be flashed from hill to hill by fire beacons. The most famous Greek messenger we know, Pheidippides, ran so hard to report the victory at Marathon that he collapsed and died uttering the message "Nike!" — "victory." (The modern marathon races honor his achievement.)

The large Roman postal system, the *cursus publicus*, stretched across the Empire from Egypt to Britain. It was so fast that no postal organization matched its speed for nearly 1,900 years.[4] One reason for those famous Roman roads was the wish to improve the mails. Like Persia, the Roman Empire established relay stations with post–houses that the local population reluctantly maintained. To reach its distant colonies, Rome organized the world's first sea post. It is likely that the English word "post" is derived from the Latin word for relay station, "posita." We use it in "postal," "post office," and, of course, "postage."

In the *Phillipics* of 44 B.C.E., Cicero railed against spying on private letters, but this bureaucratic addiction proved durable. By the fourth century C.E., the emperor Diocletian placed the Roman postal service under an imperial secret service that included officials called "curiosi." Their duties included government spying and catching mail fraud. No doubt they opened letters. More than fifteen hundred years after Cicero, Martin Luther had the same complaint as that Roman senator.

And he wrote in the King Ahasuerus' name, and sealed it with the king's ring, and sent letters by post on horseback and riders on mules, camels, and young dromedaries.

—ESTHER 8:10

And Hezekiah sent to all Israel and Judah, and wrote letters also to Ephraim and Manasseh, that they should come to the house of the Lord at Jerusalem, to keep the Passover unto the Lord God of Israel.

—II CHRONICLES, 30:1

Should a Greek or Roman citizen–farmer wish to take part in public affairs, he had no choice but to leave his farm and move to the city, since he needed a good deal of information to participate effectively in public affairs, while this information was necessarily restricted to those individuals who lived in close proximity to the seat of power.[5]

— RICHARD JOHN

Ordinary citizens of the Roman Empire, forbidden to use the government *cursus publicus*, devised their own means of communication. For distant communication, the writer depended upon traders and ship captains. Contact between Rome and the aristocrats who lived on their estates remained sparse. Country living separated the aristocrat from the politics of Rome as effectively as the Greek aristocrat on his estate separated himself from what was going on in Athens or Syracuse. No equivalent of a newspaper existed. Some of the best and brightest citizens did not participate in government as long as they were out of the city.

Over short distances, servants, usually slaves, carried letters. It was not the softest of jobs, for a slave could be killed if he were caught by his master's enemies but, if he failed to deliver the letters promptly, he could be slain by his irritated master. The phrase "to kill the messenger" recalls the ancient practice of punishing the bearer of bad tidings.

The postal system changed over time, with the unenviable distinction of backsliding during the Dark and Middle Ages. When the Roman Empire collapsed, so did the efficient Roman postal system. Illiterate peasants certainly had no need of a postal service. Hardly anyone else did either. The roads were no longer safe for post riders, nor were they as necessary during the Dark Ages that followed the fall of the Roman Empire. A mailed letter was probably less secure than an Assyrian or Persian letter four thousand years earlier. Walled towns would flourish when literacy and writing were at their lowest point.

A simple alphabet written on easily transportable papyrus and parchment encouraged communication, which was later discouraged by the walled towns and city-states that rose as Rome fell.[6]

–MARSHALL MCLUHAN

During the Dark Ages, postal service could be of little value even for nobles where illiteracy was the norm. Few peasants knew of anything or anyone beyond the place they were born. Unless their lord led them to battle or a crusade, the peasants had no communication with the world outside. They must have enjoyed gossip as much as we do, but they had little chance to receive accurate news from afar, except for what an itinerant priest or traveler might relate. Serfs probably did not know the country in which they lived or the century into which they were born. Life revolved around planting, security around harvesting, and pleasure around festivals. Independent thought had as little meaning as the notion of freedom to choose a government or a religion. You were what God intended.

Four centuries after the fall of Rome came Charlemagne. Conqueror and reformer, he was the first of the Holy Roman Emperors, dreaming of reviving the glory of Rome under the mantle of Christianity. He restored a rudimentary postal system over the old, deteriorating Roman roads. Postal routes and stations were established. Guards charged tolls to keep up the roads and to maintain safety from sunrise to sunset. Charlemagne's postal routes were for government, not public, use, but no doubt private messages found a way of sneaking in. Charlemagne was succeeded by a son, Louis the Pious, who abandoned the postal stations.

HIGHWAY ROBBERY

For centuries, "highway robbery" was more than an expression. An English law dating from the thirteenth century commanded that all persons whose properties adjoined the important Dover Road from London to the south coast must remove all bushes, trees, and dikes within 200 feet of the road. They were favorite places for robbers to lurk. Another term that has come down to us is "mail" itself. In those days of armored knights who went into battle dressed in coats of mail, the carriers put their letters in small metal bags for protection; they carried letters in mail. Postmen also carried knives.

By the twelfth century, monasteries had established regular links with their distant brethren. Written information was borne in the rotula, a round-robin newsletter. The abbot of a monastery would report events on a parchment scroll, such as who had died during the previous year. At the next monastery, the abbot might add a fresh item or two about actual events, plus such entries as "Common report has it that the Antichrist has been born at Babylon."[7]

UNIVERSITY POSTAL SERVICE

Universities, the expansion of towns, and the needs of mercantilism increased the amount of written communication. Peddlers, pilgrims, merchants, and crusaders carried news and private messages across Europe and the Near East. In the thirteenth century at the University of Paris the foundation of a national postal service began under the umbrella of the Roman Catholic Church. It came about because university teachers and students were regarded as ecclesiastics. That gave them royal protection, including safe conduct when they traveled, exclusion from military duty, and exclusion from taxation. To carry mail between the students and their parents, the University of Paris set up a messenger service. The messengers received the same royal guarantees and exemptions that faculty and students enjoyed. In other words, the postmen had some of the privileges of clerics.

As a result of this generous gesture, the inconsequential job of messenger became a coveted position despite the wages; to put it more precisely, the franchise to employ messengers was hugely valuable. As the years passed, the messengers added to their incomes by carrying outside mail, despite restrictions.

NEWS CARRIED BY MINSTRELS

Some news arrived in disorganized ways. Gossip and imaginings of distant events were borne on the lips of traveling minstrels. It was said that jongleurs — minstrels — had such a strong gift of memory that they could hear a rhyming ballad of a thousand lines only once and be able to repeat it without error. The rhymes, of course, aided the memory.

Just as the absence of mail was a mark of the decline of Roman civilization into the Dark Ages, so a growth of mail marked a renewal of civilization into the Middle Ages. The spreading commercial interests of cities and towns led to arrangements to protect their trade with the outside world, particularly against bandits and feudal lords who taxed and sometimes seized goods crossing their lands.

The Hanseatic League, centered in the northern German commercial port towns along the North Sea and Baltic Sea, had a postal service dating to the thirteenth century. The Teutonic knights protected the towns and the couriers who traveled between them. Many secure post houses were located in castles. Hanseatic League arrangements included postal service between the towns and a court reporting system to coordinate judicial decisions. Craft guilds and merchant guilds set up their own mail operations. Service by service, the illiterate feudal age of Europe was giving way to the mercantile age.

The few literate people who could not take advantage of an existing postal system might have sought out a guild or Church courier willing to carry an extra letter for a coin. In time, such a side business was openly incorporated into the organization, and became part of the courier's duty. By 1500, letter routes were open to the public across Europe. Whether any particular region received good courier service or any service at all was often a matter of luck. Some routes were overserviced, but many regions were ignored. Postal fees were based on what the public could bear and could be heavy. If a letter could cause financial damage to the receiver, the person wishing to communicate might have prudent second thoughts about sending it.

When Patience Breton's letter arrived, if it did, her brother would no doubt be happy to have it. But he would be stunned at the fee he would have to pay. It would certainly help him to understand why the various postal systems were anxious to render him service.[8]

— LAURIN ZILLIACUS

Where rival postal systems sprang up, competition could grow nasty, leading to highway ambushes and royal court intrigues. For example, during the English civil war of the seventeenth century, in a battle over who had the franchise for delivering the mail, the Earl of Warwick's men stopped a mail carrier on a rural road and seized his mail. They had not ridden very far when another group of men seized them.

In the fourteenth and fifteenth centuries, the Italian Della Torres family ran a private courier service that over the years spread across Europe. Because they lived near Mount Tasso, they added that name to their own. The courier tied a badger skin over the forehead of his horse because Tasso is also the Italian word for badgers. Rich and powerful, operating under charters of the Holy Roman Empire, the firm, renamed through marriage as Thurn and Taxis, built a swift and dependable postal system across central Europe. It was a pony express, at first serving emperors and military officers. Inevitably, it served merchants as well.

It was a certainty that the invention of printing would expand the use of postal service. Pamphlets and newsletters filled mailbags, along with the hand–written bills, orders, and news sent by the growing middle class of merchants. In an age of paper scarcity, some of the first newsletters were sold with a blank sheet attached, so that the subscriber might write his own letter. In fifteenth century France, Louis XI revived a national postal service strictly for government use, the first national service since the aborted effort by Charlemagne. The king ordered two hundred couriers to be stationed in towns across France to convey royal messages. The king declared that anyone who dared to inject private letters into the service was doomed to be sent to Hell. That was serious, for the Middle Ages acknowledged the divine right of kings. Louis communicated with God.

Fear of Hell did not stop all private communication where a coin or two could change hands. In the year 1600, the Spanish ruler of the Netherlands, the viceroy Cardinal Duke Albrecht VII, legalized what had been an open secret. He gave the Taxis service official permission to charge for private letters. ("Taxi," a word used around the world, derives from the name.) By officially permitting the mingling of government and private mail, a threshold was crossed, Maximilian I of Bavaria set up a similar pattern of posts in the regions of Central Europe under his control. He also turned its operation over to the Taxis family. At first their post did not have permanent routes. Taxis couriers traveled between wherever the king was and wherever messages were supposed to go. By the mid–sixteenth century, Taxis post riders serviced fixed routes from the Netherlands to Italy.

The kings of England employed couriers, dating at least to Henry III in the thirteenth century. By the fifteenth century, horse relay posts had been set up to carry the king's dispatches. Britain officially began a national postal service in 1517 with Henry VIII's appointment of Sir Brian Tukes as its first Master of the King's Posts. Commerce was growing, including trade with other parts of Europe. Universities were established, scholars corresponded with their peers, and students wrote home for money. William Shakespeare mentions the posts in several plays, sometimes in the phrase "post haste." Actual letters, written on parchment and sealed with wax, sometimes bore this request for urgency: "Haste, Post, Haste, for Thye Lyfe, for Thye Lyfe, Haste." Perhaps it helped.

A postal service depended upon the king's permission, which came with a price. A king appointed a postmaster the way a city today grants a franchise to a cable television company. The franchisee paid for an exclusive right to pursue a profitable enterprise. The British royal court called the franchise a "farm" and the franchisee a "farmer." The postal farmer paid rent to the king or the government for the privilege of man-

MINGLING PRIVATE, GOVERNMENT MAIL

There was a stage at Bugshot, where the letters had been carried by Gilbert Berghe, who there handed them over to Thomas Annesley, who carried them to Basynstoke, and thence they were carried by seven further stages to Exeter.[9]

— George Walker

aging the posts in a region. The farmer harvested money from those who used the service. England had many, many postal operators, so money flowed into the royal coffers along many rivulets. For example, one of the less expensive but more efficient private operators, Mathewe deQuester, built a thriving postal business that extended to the continent. The king's master of the posts, Lord Stanhope, complained to King James I that deQuester was cutting into Stanhope's royal charter business. But instead of cracking down on deQuester, the king whose name would one day be placed on a famous version of the Bible, legalized deQuester's company and appointed him to handle all foreign mail. Not all rulers have awarded efficiency so nobly.

Intrigues against royalty were common, so rulers were suspicious of private communication. That famous plotter, Mary Queen of Scots, sent and received letters hidden in beer kegs. England's King Charles II, mindful that his father's head was chopped off during Oliver Cromwell's successful revolt, had spies who opened sealed letters so skillfully that no one could tell that the seal had been tampered with. Nevertheless, despite royal suspicion of private mail service, the need to send letters for trade continued to grow. Starting in 1627, most of the British government and private operations merged into a single State Post, but private services continued as early versions of UPS and Federal Express.

MAIL PRIVACY

The right of privacy for ordinary people is a fairly modern concept, but the notion of an "invasion of privacy" regarding letters may be traced to a Prussian law of 1794. Mail without envelopes is obviously without privacy. Before paper mills, most written correspondence in Europe was on parchment, but an animal skin cannot be folded like a sheet of paper. Even with a seal, a parchment letter invited prying eyes. Nor did paper assure privacy. It could be folded, but most letters were not sent inside envelopes prior to postage stamps. Instead, letters were folded to put the writing inside and show the blank side out for the address, seal, and indication of payment. The widespread preference for envelopes actually began in France about 1845. Five years later envelopes were used everywhere.

SERVICE FOR THE NEW WORLD

The first English colonists in the New World quickly adopted a postal system. In 1639, less than 20 years after the Pilgrims landed on Plymouth Rock, a post office was set up in the tavern and home of Richard Fairbanks of Boston, following the European practice of using taverns and coffeehouses for mail drops. Arriving ship captains were instructed to deliver their packets of mail to Fairbanks and to pick up those bound for Europe. This made him the first postmaster in America. For his troubles, Fairbanks was allotted one penny per letter. Colonial tavern keepers had no responsibility other than to provide a place for colonists to drop off and pick up their mail, often kept in an unlocked leather bag hanging from a nail. Anyone could go through it. From time to time a ship captain just arriving or ready to sail would attend to its contents.

THE COLONIAL POST STARTS

In the colonies as everywhere else, most letters were carried by friends, acquaintances, or trusted strangers. Dependable regular delivery inland would have to wait until postal routes were planned through the wilderness. Even then, many of the trails traveled by the colonial letter carrier on foot or horseback were little more than narrow Indian footpaths.

In 1673, a once–a–month post was set up between New York and Boston. The post rider's trail became known as the Old Boston Post Road, now part of U.S. Highway 1. Four years later Boston merchants convinced the British Crown government to set up a regular postal system with a post office for the colony of Massachusetts. This was the first official postal service in the New World. A Bostonian writing to a Virginian was advised to send the letter by one of the schooners trading up and down the coast, not overland.

A river steamboat in colonial days was part of something new in mail delivery—the private post box. The first post boxes were a row of old boots nailed against a wall at a riverside landing. Each bore the name of a settler. The mail sat in the boot until the settler came to town. A letter to a settler at a remote outpost might sit in a box for six months before the settler picked it up. If it had not been called for in months, the holder of the letter might open it just to learn the most recent news from the city.

THE ATLANTIC CROSSING

In colonial days, the Atlantic crossing was safer, surer, and cheaper than using roads in the colonies. From Boston it cost only two pence to send a letter to England. That same letter from Boston would cost fifteen pence to the closer parts of Pennsylvania and New Jersey. From Boston to New York cost nine pence. Going the other way cost twelve pence. The British Crown created a postal service for all its North American colonies in 1691, but put it in the hands of an Englishman who never bothered crossing the Atlantic to visit the colonies. He was Thomas Neale, who paid 80 cents a year for the franchise, the "farm."

POSTMASTER BEN FRANKLIN

A struggling printer and newspaper publisher in Philadelphia, young Benjamin Franklin was appointed a colonial postmaster as well. In 1737, when he was 31, he was chosen to be postmaster of Philadelphia. It could not have been much of a job, because the colonial postal service was by now a financial mess. Nevertheless, it had its advantages for a newspaper publisher. The former postmaster did not allow his post riders to carry Franklin's newspaper. Franklin had to bribe them until he became the postmaster. When he was promoted, Franklin was fair in dealing with other publishers where rates were concerned. Many colonial newspapers went out postage free at the postmaster's choosing.

Postal officials had the power to order newspapers to pay letter rates or pay on the basis of an agreement between postmaster and publisher. By contrast, when they were one and the same, the postmaster–publisher could reach such an agreement with himself while shaving.

In 1753, having grown wealthy from printing and publishing, Franklin again was promoted by the Crown, this time to be deputy postmaster general for all the colonies in North America, a position he shared with a Virginian. He improved service and began to show a profit, the first surplus in the colonial postal service. Franklin believed that running the postal system only to make money was a ruinous policy. Putting service first, he felt, would ultimately produce a profit through greater use of the mails. He was right, but his arguments fell on deaf ears.

FIRST WOMAN POSTMASTER

During his tenure, Franklin established post roads from Canada to Florida and set up a regular schedule between the colonies and England. He regulated post offices and organized auditing procedures. He ordered land surveys that resulted in shortening several routes. Post riders started hauling mail at night. Under Franklin, the time it took to carry mail on the Philadelphia–New York route was cut in half. He created the position of surveyor, the start of the modern postal inspection service. However, no angel, Franklin engaged in the nepotism common in his day; he appointed his brother John as postmaster in Boston. When John died two years later, Franklin chose John's widow as his successor. Thus, in 1756, Mrs. John Franklin became the first woman postmaster (or postmistress) in America. She was also the first woman to hold public office in America.

From the very beginning the American colonists had resented any attempt to make a profit out of their postal communication. Instinctively they believed in postal service, not postal profits. If the British Government had recognized that instinct and expended money for a real service of inter–communication, it would have changed history. Choosing the other course, the Government hastened and assured it own downfall.[10]

— Clyde Kelley

The Crown mail service, irritating as a burr, added to the colonists' complaints that led to the American Revolution. The British government had never abandoned the idea of squeezing out a profit from its postal service. Queen Anne's Act of 1710 sent rates soaring, doubling the cost of sending a letter from New York to Philadelphia.

As the years went by the colonists grew more convinced that the Crown's colonial post was just another way to tax them. Taxes on newspapers in both England and the colonies were denounced as "taxes on knowledge." The British Parliament should have expected an uproar in its American colonies when it passed the Stamp Act in 1765, taxing newspapers and documents as a means of raising revenue The public outcry, "No taxation without representation" echoed across the colonies. A punitive stamp tax levied in 1714 to bring the press under control forced many newspapers in England to close. The colonial Stamp Act so angered American colonists that the British Parliament withdrew it the following year. Nevertheless, the Stamp Act was one of the causes of discontent that led to the American Revolution and may have provided one of the arguments for freedom of the press in the First Amendment.

(The United States has never instituted a stamp tax on newspapers. In fact, reduced mailing costs continue to benefit printed media. Britain repealed a duty on paper in 1855, its last "tax on knowledge.")

To refuse to use the royal postal service was not only the right thing to do, it also saved money. The colonists ignored the postal laws and sent letters outside the official mails, depriving the Crown of income. By the end of 1775, seven months before war broke out, so few letters were passing through the royal postal service that it was shut down. A patriot postal service, the Constitutional Post, had all the business.

Crown authorities censored the mail and, despite what Franklin accomplished, they dismissed him in 1774 for his revolutionary activities. The stated reason was that he revealed the contents of letters written by loyalists. The real reason was that he was using the colonial postal service to subvert the Crown. Franklin had taken advantage of his position to pressure publishers to support his idea for a union of all the colonies. A year later, with the colonies breaking away from Britain, the newly formed Continental Congress met to create an independent government. Close to the top of the agenda was how to deal with mail.

Recently returned from England, Franklin was appointed to head a committee that recommended creating the position of postmaster general for the 13 colonies. The Second Continental Congress chose Franklin to set up a separate postal system, the best way to get word to colonists who wanted independence. As a basis for the new system, the Continental Congress turned to the popular Constitutional Post that had been swapping revolutionary news from colony to colony. So began the postal service of the United States of America. Under the Continental Congress, Franklin was the new nation's first postmaster general for 16 months.

The colonial mail service had been set up to carry letters. No rates were fixed for mailing newspapers. A postmaster could charge whatever he wanted, but he had to rely on his riders. Without their cooperation publishers were unable to collect from distant subscribers; the publisher would not know when to stop mailing newspapers to a subscriber who had died or moved away. At a time when few letters carried prepaid postage, post riders earned extra money by carrying postage due mail and pocketing what they collected. Stagecoach drivers had a neat trick that allowed them to swear their coaches did not contain mail that they profited from. They hung a pole outside the stagecoach, from which a bag of letters dangled; therefore, the mail was not *in* the coach, so the coach did not *contain* the mail. Franklin managed to eliminate some of these sharp practices that were stifling the flow of information. By assigning postmasters to collect postage and subscription fees, Franklin in effect turned postmasters into publishers' agents. He arranged for

The Committee of Correspondence began operating an intercolonial news exchange in 1771, one of a decidedly partisan flavor... calculated to arouse feelings of hatred for the British.[11]

— RICHARD KIELBOWICZ

MAILING NEWSPAPERS

the free exchange of newspapers among editors. His policies made the American colonial post office the most progressive in the world, well ahead of the postal policies in England.

Franklin has been called the Father of the United States postal service not merely for the work of these months but also for his contributions to the colonial postal service and perhaps for everything else he did in guiding the colonies to nationhood. Not every decision turned out well. When Franklin left for France to represent the emerging nation at the start of the American Revolution, he managed to put his less effective son–in–law, Richard Bache, in his place.

THE POST RIDERS

In early America, as the post riders covered their routes, they collected information that they passed on to editors. Before newspapers hired reporters, these tidbits of fact and gossip became the local news items that endeared local newspapers to their readers. In the years leading up to the Revolution, both the revolutionaries and the British government saw news dissemination as an advantage. The British regarded it as sewing common threads through the far–flung outposts of British North America. The revolutionaries saw a means for spreading propaganda. Couriers for revolutionary Committees of Correspondence occasionally sent bulletins from town to town. The new postal service was a tool they could use to tighten the bonds holding the colonies together and to separate themselves from the motherland.

In combination, newspapers and the postal service were the most important means of informing the public. They remained so for many decades after the United States became a nation. Vestiges of their collaboration lie in the number of newspapers today that have the word "post" in their names. Both the Federalists and their political opponents, the Jeffersonian Republicans, supported postal subsidies for newspapers in a new nation as thinly populated, as spread out, and as different as the various regions of the United States of America. Together, newspapers and the postal service were badly needed national glue.

Competition among newspapers could be nasty. A publisher might get his newspapers delivered if he offered a bribe to the postmaster, but why not become a postmaster? Publishers pulled strings to be appointed postmasters, a position that presented a sure way to get their newspapers delivered and, not incidentally, make life difficult for rival publishers. Some postmaster–publishers were mailing their own newspapers without postage. Others used the office to put rival publishers out of business.[12]

FRANKING THE MAIL

Among the advantages for publishers–postmasters was franking their own mail; that is, sending it free under their signature. Postal law did not specifically address the matter of franking newspapers, but it did permit postmasters to frank their business mail, which they often interpreted liberally as including correspondence relating to their newspapers and indeed the newspapers themselves. They also received news dispatches before their rivals did. As an appointment to a postmastership handed publishers the opportunity to collect fees, it conferred the status of being a representative of the federal government.

Conversely, some postmasters started their own newspapers. Many early newspapers were started as a sideline to a postmasterships, because small towns did not provide enough postal revenue to afford full salary for its postmaster. Presidents appointed postmasters general of their own political party, and these men in turn were apt to appoint publishers of the same party to local postmasterships, so the government knew where the postmaster's sympathies lay. The postal service managed the news both by impeding the delivery of out–of–favor publications and by giving postal advantages to publications that the authorities wished to promote. Often, postmasters who started newspapers refused to hand them over when a new postmaster was appointed, so a new publication was begun.

PUBLISHER– POSTMASTER

Not everyone was pleased with the idea of a public, federally managed postal service. Thomas Jefferson was among those who felt it gave too much power to a central government. While some critics felt that the individual states should operate the postal services, others wanted it left to private business. The individual states and the private business advocates lost out when the Continental Congress in 1782 settled the question of whether the individual states or the federal government would run the postal service for the new nation. It voted to bring together under the federal umbrella the various laws and regulations, the routes and rates, and all else that related to postal service.

In the end the Constitution authorized a national postal service with the sentence, "The Congress shall have power… to establish Post Offices and post Roads." The new Congress set up the General Post Office, but only on an annual basis for five years. The postmaster general reported to the Secretary of the Treasury; he and his postal service would not be subject to state control. In the years to come, the postal service would have an integral role in supporting the provision calling for freedom of the press in the First Amendment of the Bill of Rights.

SUPPORTING THE FIRST AMENDMENT

At the time the Constitution was being adopted, a letter traveling along the main post road from Georgia to Maine might take three weeks to get there, and it wasn't cheap. A one–page letter going up to 30 miles cost six cents, which was a penny more than the cost of a dozen eggs. (The cost of a postage stamp today roughly equals the cost of three eggs; that sum pays for several pages in an envelope, based upon weight.) The same one–page letter going more than 450 miles cost twenty–five cents.

COST OF MAILING A LETTER

A LETTER AS A LUXURY

To avoid paying for a second sheet, letter writers not only wrote small on both sides of the page, but filled up the margins by writing up and down. In 1799 it cost twelve cents to send a two–page letter no more than 60 miles. Or, the same twelve cents would buy a full–course dinner at New York's fashionable Delmonico's Restaurant. Since the government service was by no means the only way to send mail, both dining at Delmonico and mailing a letter through the U.S. Post Office were luxuries. At the same time, laws passed in 1792 and 1794 let newspapers mail a copy up to one hundred miles or anywhere within their state for just one penny. Beyond that, a penny and a half. And, for a number of years, mailing a newspaper within a county was totally free.

One reason for high letter rates was the attitude shared by Alexander Hamilton and others that the postal service should not only pay its way but also should show a profit that would defray other government costs. The old question surfaced: should the Post Office be primarily a service or a money maker? In the end, proposals that came down on the side of profit did not survive in the new Congress. In any case, no great fortunes were at risk. The American postal service at the start of nationhood amounted to little more than the royal "farm" it had once been. Over a period of four decades, it expanded from being a minor part of a colonial bureaucracy to having a central role in an independent nation.[13] In 1789 the new nation's seventy–five post offices in the thirteen states sent letters by post riders along about 2,000 miles of post roads. The nation had a population estimated at 3,500,000. Postal receipts for the entire nation in 1789 were $25,000.

FIRST POSTMASTER GENERAL

The first postmaster general under the U.S. Constitution, Samuel Osgood, set up a charge to newspaper editors of between a penny and a penny and a half per copy, payable in advance. This was the first prepaid postage in the United States; postage stamps would not be introduced for another half century. To ease financial pressures on the Post Office, Congress in 1799 voted that the expenses of postal headquarters should be paid from the Treasury, not from postal revenue.

There were options. Just as in the pre–Revolutionary days of the Crown postal service, private contractors competed vigorously for the coins senders would pay to have their letters carried. Such competition was illegal, but that law was an inconvenience, not a deterrent. Interrupting the U.S. mail was a graver matter. As in many other countries since the Middle Ages, only one penalty existed for interfering with the mails: death. However, the United States had trial by jury, and jurors hesitated to inflict such a dread sentence. At first, Congress voted flogging for a first offense, death for a second. Later, prison sentences were substituted. Until 1872, however, aggravated mail robbery could still bring the death penalty.

"There is an astonishing circulation of letters and newspapers among these savage woods," said the French aristocrat Alexis de Tocqueville as he traveled across the new country. He recorded his observations of the American people with a shrewd, admiring eye. To Tocqueville, that heralded better economic conditions. "I only know of one means of increasing the prosperity of a people… communication," he wrote in *Journey to America*. "In Michigan forests there is not a cabin so isolated, not a valley so wild, that it does not receive letters and newspapers at least once a week; we saw it ourselves."

President Andrew Jackson in 1829 elevated the office of postmaster general to the cabinet. Jackson did not believe that bureaucrats should hold lifetime positions, but he did believe in the "spoils system" of rewarding party supporters, and the Post Office had a lot of jobs to hand out to the party faithful. Under Jackson the Post Office became a greater source of patronage than any other department. It would remain so for decades. Despite presenting himself as a man of the people, the creator of "Jacksonian democracy," our seventh president, opposed lower newspaper postage. That would have brought more opposition Eastern big city newspapers not only to ordinary readers but also to the weekly editors of the frontier communities. Lower postage might spread ideas hostile to Jackson.

POST OFFICE PATRONAGE

One private service, Letter Express, actually offered to buy out the entire U.S. Postal Department. It offered delivery, not then available anywhere in the country, for five cents a letter. Postal officials turned the offer down as fast as possible. One reason was that it would throw 16,000 postmasters out of office. Their positions were too important to political party strength to sell.

Press and post grew side by side, each affecting the other. Thanks to newspapers and mail reaching the cabins scattered across the huge, new land, settlers figured out that they belonged to the national community that was taking shape. They also gradually understood that what the government decided impacted their lives. Federal policies set up then continue to affect Americans today. In 1820, for example, local postmasters were given a directive to encourage subscribers to take local publications instead of distant city newspapers. As an encouragement, some editors increased their local news. It was a commodity in rural towns that city newspapers could not match. Previously, those newspapers had focused on national, international and state capital news to the exclusion of local events. That changed. Local news today is the staple of small town newspapers.

PRESS AND POST GROW TOGETHER

Newspapers in the past relied on the Post Office for many services, including mailed delivery, subscription sales by postmen, favorable postal rates, free exchange of newspapers among editors, and even special exchanges of newspapers from other countries. The free exchange of newspapers among editors was the principal means of moving non–local information to newspapers before the coming of the news services. Congress shut off this benefit in 1873.

SLAVES DELIVER THE MAIL

In colonial Virginia the plantation owners were required by a 1657 law to pass letters and government messages along to the next plantation. It was known as the "tobacco post" because many of the plantations grew the leaf; failure to comply brought a fine of a hogshead (a large cask that holds between 63 and 140 gallons of liquid) of tobacco. Slaves were frequently used in the antebellum South to deliver mail. They carried letters and newspapers between one huge plantation and the next. This practice made some slaveholders uneasy when they reflected that the slaves might acquire enough knowledge to be dangerous. A federal law in 1802 forbade anyone except a free white man to carry the mail, but no doubt the practice of using slaves continued.

"Everything which tends to increase their (the slaves) knowledge of natural rights… or that affords them an opportunity of associating, acquiring, and communicating sentiments, and of establishing a chain or line of intelligence, must increase your hazard, because it increases their means of effecting their object."[14]

— Gideon Granger, Postmaster General

Slaveholders were correct to be worried. From 1835, northern abolitionists flooded the mails going to the South with abolitionist pamphlets. Southerners feared that this literature would set off a slave rebellion. In Charleston, South Carolina, a pro–slavery mob broke into a post office, seized the literature, and burned it. In other parts of the South, postmasters themselves destroyed abolitionist mail.[15] Drums were illegal in much of the American South before the Civil War. Slaveholders were aware of "talking instruments" in the West African tradition and tried in every way possible to stifle communication across distances. Drums could signal insurrection and could conjure collective memories of freedom. They strictly regulated slave culture and outlawed slave literacy. The slaveholders outlawed the instruments, but they could not stop the beat.[16]

For centuries the "post–boy" with his mail pouch was a familiar sight in Europe, sometimes on foot, sometimes poking along on a swayback horse, if artists' sketches of the period can be believed. On his back he slung his post–horn, which he blew to announce his arrival in a village with the mail. He was an easy target for highwaymen.

USING STAGECOACHES

As communication between cities increased, something better was needed. The stagecoach was the answer, but it was not without problems. The coaches changed horses and drivers at fixed stages along the highways that they traveled at more–or–less regular schedules. Stagecoaches carried both passengers and freight, and some carried mail. On good roads in England a coach–and–six (horses) could cover fifty miles in a twelve–hour day, not counting time for meals or changing horses, but roads, even highways, were usually unpaved, rutted, potholed. Streams had to be forded. When rain fell, a coach–and–four or a coach–and–six was needed to drag its heavy load through the mud.

Because roads were in poor condition, twenty miles in a day was hardly unusual. In fact, some roads were so bad that no wheeled traffic ever used them. A guard often sat next to the driver because of highwaymen who were insufficiently troubled by thoughts of the noose. In a foreshadowing of Federal Express, someone in a hurry to get a letter to a distant city would skip the mail coaches and send it by a faster coach despite the sharply higher cost.

At first the American colonial mail was carried between towns by foot and horseback. The years to come would find letters making their way through the system by every conveyance imaginable, including hot air balloons in the countryside and pneumatic tubes in downtown city buildings. Where roads were available, two–wheel sulkies were the next step after horseback, and then four–wheel stagecoaches. Editors and readers pressed for more stagecoaches, a vehicle that came into general use in the United States after 1785, when Congress encouraged the Post Office to extend its service as fast as possible.

PASSENGERS PREFERRED

Passengers shared the coach with mailbags. As the stagecoaches bounced over the rutted roads, the heavy mailbags shifted as if fighting the passengers for the seats. The means of conveyance obviously limited newspaper circulation because newspapers added weight to the postman's load. Even when a subscriber signed up for a newspaper, the postal courier sometimes refused the added weight, so newspapers piled up at loading points. Bags of mail, especially newspapers, were dropped off at a stage office to make room for a passenger plus baggage.

As for magazines, postmasters had the authority to exclude them from delivery if facilities were inadequate. Newspapers and magazines lying on the ground were likely to be pilfered by otherwise honest citizens eager to catch up on events. If they were not stolen, and were eventually delivered, they might be handed over wet and dirty. When a stagecoach arrived with the mail, people would assemble in the marketplace, gathering around the coach as the driver called out the names of people for whom he had newspapers, not unlike mail call in a modern summer camp.

FRONTIER MAIL

As the new nation entered a new century, new roads snaked through every state. Old highways were improved. The establishment of post roads through the wilderness brought the stagecoaches, and it was stagecoaches that brought the newspapers until the railroad tracks were laid. The earliest post roads — any route on which mail in bulk was carried — ran north to south between Eastern cities, then to new cities in the Midwest, and still later between cities in the Midwest and West. Where few post roads existed, there were fewer newspapers.

POST ROADS

In 1803 the Louisiana Purchase opened a huge wilderness to settlers, who poured west by the tens of thousands. They wanted to retain communication with those they left behind, and the United States wanted to keep their loyalty. Obviously, doing so would cost money. Senator John Calhoun in 1817 urged Congress to "...bind the republic together with a perfect system of roads and canals. . . . It is thus that a citizen of the West will read the news of Boston still moist from the press. The mail and the press are the nerves of the body politic."[17]

Pioneers blazing trails through the wilderness, crossing mountains, and clearing forests for farms did not ask much of the government back east. They did ask for mail service, post offices, and post roads. The United States was growing fast and the Post Office struggled to keep up. By 1820, the young United States had more post offices and newspapers per capita than any nation in the world.[18]

BY STEAMBOAT

Steamboats went into passenger service when Robert Fulton steered the Clermont up the Hudson River in 1807. Six years later, steamboats were carrying mail under contract. On inland navigable waters, designated as post roads by Congress in 1823, steamboats were a familiar sight hauling mail along with passengers and freight up and down America's rivers. On canals, mules or draft horses pulled barges carrying mail sacks and goods along the towpaths beside the waterway. It was a slow way to haul mail, but it was free of the mud that stagecoaches had to deal with. For the most part, it was free of highway robbers. They sensibly preferred out–of–the–way paths.

TRAINS CARRY ALL OF IT

The next step in postal service came on two rails. As the decades of the nineteenth century unfolded, iron tracks were laid. The Puffing Billy—a nickname for early trains—replaced the slow coaches jouncing over bad roads. Trains were able to carry all the letters that anyone cared to write, plus all the newspapers and magazines, with no threat to throw them off at the next station in order to make room for passengers. The westward expansion of the railroad solved most of the problems of irregular and unsure newspaper and magazine dissemination. Traveling at unaccustomed speed over long distances, the iron horses carried large quantities of bulky publications. They started mail by rail in 1829 in Pennsylvania. After carrying small amounts of mail for several years, the railroads began in 1836 to get government mail contracts. Two years later all railroads were declared official post roads. Agents were assigned to ride the trains to do whatever business was needed along the way. They opened the mail pouches to separate letters and packages that would be dropped off en route. The rest of the mail was sent to distributing post offices for further sorting. Little by little this work was done on the trains themselves.

Trains and mail went together like ham and eggs. By 1930, more than 10,000 trains carried mail to every hamlet in the nation that rail lines served. Railroad postal service ended as a result of the Transportation Act of 1958, which favored airmail. A dozen years later, almost no first–class mail was carried by train as dependence on airplanes increased. The last railway post office, running between New York and Washington, D.C., quit handling mail in 1977. First class to other mail zones went by air.

POST OFFICES ON TRAINS

Horseless carriages still had not appeared on many American streets when the Post Office Department in 1901 issued its first contract to carry mail by automobile. Buses were equipped as rolling post offices; clerks sorted as the wheels turned. Contracts with haulage companies continued, but postal officials chafed at the high charges and outright fraud. Congress gave its approval in 1914 for the Post Office Department to buy its own vehicles.

News normally took from two to four months to cross the Atlantic Ocean during the Colonial and post–revolutionary years, although a vessel might wait in port for a week or more until its cargo hold filled, and mail was sometimes forgotten on the dock. Mercantilism, the national economic policy that seeks to accumulate wealth by trade, led merchants to set up branch offices in other trading nations during the nineteenth century. Sending mail by ship was chancy, for schedules were erratic. The great sailing ships needed favorable winds, of course, but a ship owner's wish to sail with a full cargo could also delay letters in port and could send the ship from port to port gathering cargo, while the letters sat in the mail packet. The solution was the small, fast packet ship that carried passengers and goods, too, but was first and foremost a ship to carry the mail and to follow a schedule for doing so.

Mail traveling across the seas was sometimes handled in imaginative ways. Ship captains docking to take on casks of fresh water at Cape Town (known as "Table Bay" before it was a town), on the southern tip of Africa, knew that bags of mail waited near a freshwater stream in a hole at the foot of Table Mountain. A stone over the hole had a painted sign, "Hereunder look for letters." This was the place to leave mail and pick up outgoing packages. Eastbound letters were picked up by eastbound ships, which deposited westbound letters under the stone. This post office served not only the colonists in southern Africa but ports as far away as Batavia, in the present Indonesia. The principal users, the English and Dutch, were often at each other's throats in the competition for colonies, but they forwarded each other's mail.

CROSSING OCEANS

An even stranger drop–off point for mail in the nineteenth century was a keg located at the tip of South America for ships hazarding the treacherous Straits of Magellan. The keg was fastened to a spar. For protection it was covered with tar, with a sheet–iron lid held by a leather hinge. For twenty years ships anchored to drop off and pick up mail on their way between the Atlantic and Pacific oceans.

As the nineteenth century unfolded across the new United States, a steady stream of settlers flowed west along wagon trails. Their tales of the Santa Fe, the Oregon, and the Mormon trails form part of the American legend. When they reached their destination and settled down to farm, dig for minerals, hang out medical or law shingles, or start up hardware stores, groceries, and newspapers, the settlers wanted to keep in touch with the people they left behind. They wanted to read newspapers from back home. That did not prove easy, but the settlers were so eager for news from the East that one San Francisco sharpie boarded incoming steamers to gather up all the newspapers the passengers had brought aboard, paying up to three dollars each for penny newspapers when he had to. He resold them for up to eight dollars each.

"Can somebody tell us what has become of the U.S. mail for this section of the world? Some four weeks since it has arrived here. The mail rider comes and goes regularly enough but the mail bags do not. One time he says the mail is not landed in San Diego; another time there was so much of it the donkey could not bring it, and he sent it to San Pedro on the steamer, which carried it up to San Francisco. Thus it goes wandering up and down the ocean..."

— Letter to the
Los Angeles Star

Discovery of silver in Colorado and gold in California added to the numbers of pioneers heading west. The census of 1860 recorded nearly a half million U.S. citizens in territories west of the Rockies. That did not include Native Americans, the many Chinese immigrants brought in as labor, or African–Americans. To provide service for the prospectors and assorted fortune seekers in the California gold rush, the U.S. Post Office contracted with the Pacific Mail Steamship Company. Ships carried letters and packages from New York to Panama, where they were loaded aboard wagons pulled by mules or stagecoaches or loaded onto canoes to cross the Isthmus, then onto another ship bound for San Francisco. The promised three–to–four–week delivery schedule was just that, a promise. Until a railroad crossing the Isthmus of Panama was completed in 1855, delays were more likely to be the rule. When California was admitted to the Union in 1850, Los Angeles did not learn of it for six weeks.

PONY EXPRESS

The Pony Express advertised that it could get telegraph messages from San Francisco to New York in eight days and letters in twelve days. Riders galloped through alkali deserts, mountain passes deep in snow, and rocky ravines where a stumbling horse could mean death. "Road agents" lay in wait to snatch money. Native American war parties lay in wait. Hungry riders sometimes ate wolf meat. It was no job for the faint of heart. The Pony Express lasted only 18 months during 1860 and 1861. It carried a total of nearly 35,000 letters written on thin paper and wrapped in oiled silk for weather protection. Costs began at five dollars per half ounce and eventually dropped to one dollar per half ounce, but even at that rate, few personal letters were sent. Business correspondence and condensed news dispatches filled the rider's pouch.

Financially, the Pony Express failed for reasons not of its own making, but it set a path across the plains and through the Rocky Mountains that the railroad would follow. It showed that a central route could be used for a transcontinental railroad, summer and winter. Less than a decade later, such a line, once thought impossible, was running. The Pony Express kept a communication link open between California and the rest of the nation during the crucial early days of the Civil War, when some men dreamed of separating California from the Union. Above all, it added a chapter of American lore that will not soon be forgotten. It was said that only one mailbag was ever lost.

While certainly the most colorful, the Pony Express was not the only express mail service in the rapidly expanding United States. Throughout the nineteenth century, except for these expresses, information flowed at the speed of the postal service until work gangs raised the telegraph poles and strung the wire. The added speed of news transmission created by the expresses and the railroads gave some competitive advantage to both city and small town newspapers. Railroads carrying newspapers from the large cities meant that metropolitan newspapers could attract distant readers, possibly at the expense of small town newspapers. On the other hand, expresses gave news quickly to the smaller newspapers, so important stories and business news could be published locally before metropolitan dailies arrived.

NOT THE ONLY EXPRESS SERVICE

Let us cross the Atlantic to look inside the General Post Office in London in the 1830s, the years before postal reform introduced postage stamps. A postman, who collected letters by walking through the streets ringing his bell, arrives. The room he enters is dark and windowless, so that postal clerks working in the gloom must hold each envelope up to a candle to see how many items are enclosed. If there is one enclosure besides a single sheet, double postage is charged. Two enclosures, triple postage.

THE LONDON POST OFFICE

Is money in the envelope? A mistake by someone too trusting. The letter may be furtively slipped into a trouser pocket. The clerks keep busy weighing letters and writing information. They record each letter onto a form so that the cost of sending it can be debited against the postmaster of the town it will be sent to.

Across Great Britain, forty rates are in use. When it is time to send out the letters, they are loaded onto mail coaches. Next to each driver sits a guard armed with a cutlass, two flintlock pistols, and a blunderbuss. Highwaymen are one reason the postal service operates deeply in the red. Cities and larger towns in Britain have enjoyed free home delivery of local mail since 1774, but a letter arriving from beyond the town can be ruinously costly to a poor addressee. Letters go to local post offices, but not every town has one, let alone every village. Towns with as many

Mothers yearning to to hear from absent children would pawn clothing or household necessaries rather than be deprived of the letters which, but for that sacrifice, must be carried back to the nearest post office to await payment.[20]

— Recollection by Rowland Hill's Daughter

as 12,000 residents probably have no post office at all. There just isn't enough business.

When a letter finally is delivered to a cottage in the country, the postman will knock at the door. Whoever answers will be asked to pay for the letter before it is handed over. That may lead to an argument because the postage will not be cheap. Although methods vary from country to country, it has long remained the custom for recipients to pay for receiving mail, just as the buyer of potatoes pays for the potatoes.

But what if the recipient refuses? One postman complained that it took him more than five minutes to deliver a single letter. Sometimes the addressee can't afford to pay. Sometimes the addressee is unwilling to pay, unwilling to receive what may be bad news. Before paying, the addressee has no way of knowing if the letter contains something worthwhile. People complained that when they paid for a letter marked "Due" (instead of "Paid"), what they got was often just a nuisance. The novelist Sir Walter Scott said he paid large sums for mail that turned out to be manuscripts from aspiring writers, until he finally got sick of it and refused all mail addressed to him. When he did so, the Post Office was stuck with the mail.

Some Britons managed a ruse to get a mailed message without paying for it. According to a frequently told tale, a man was walking among the hills of the Lake District one day when he saw the postman stop outside a mean cottage. An elderly woman came out, took a letter from the postman, turned it over in her hands, and then gave it back. It was from her son, she said, but she did not have the money to pay for it. The observer was moved with pity and offered to pay the fee himself, but the woman refused his offer with warm thanks. When the postman had gone, she confessed that the letter would have contained no writing. Her son regularly sent her such letters; the way in which he spaced and wrote the address told her essential things about how he was getting on. It seems likely that the postman knew all about the little ruse but sympathized with his poor client. Such use of codes in addressing letters grew common.[19] Had she paid, the Post Office would not have known about it unless the postman told them. It was not unusual for postmen to pocket the money.

"SMUGGLING" LETTERS

The public had a good idea of what was going on. One Manchester merchant estimated that four of every five letters written in his city were sent privately, yet to do so was illegal. Charging a penny to deliver a letter was regarded as smuggling, but the typical English man and woman did not consider it sinful to defraud the Post Office by not using their shaky, high-priced service. A Glasgow book publisher admitted "smuggling" 20,000 letters to his customers before he was caught. Even the family of postal reformer Rowland Hill sent letters to relatives by private "smugglers."

Many attempts were made to find a solution that would guarantee that postal service providers would receive the tax that was their due. In France, a Monsieur De Velayer, owner of a local post office, began in 1653 to offer customers small pieces of paper mentioning "receipt for the payment of transport." The French system lasted only a short time, but it may have inspired a working class Londoner to try his luck. Private delivery of mail had been attempted before, but did not last long before the authorities cracked down. Customs officer William Dockwra lacked government approval for his private venture and, unfortunately, he stepped on some highly placed toes. In 1681 Dockwra began a prepaid penny post in London. To him goes the credit for introducing prepaid postage. He used a handstruck stamp that read "PENNY POST PAID". He charged twopence to send a letter to the London outskirts. He set up 450 collection boxes, offered hourly collection, and six to ten deliveries a day in the London area. Moreover, his carriers knew their way around a city with no numbers on shops, no identification of houses, and a lot of places called the Red Lion or the Blue Boar.

As soon as the business showed success, the Duke of York complained that it infringed on his monopoly. City porters also complained that their interests were ignored, and tore down Dockwra's placards. The courts stepped in with heavy fines and took over his business. Dockwra died in poverty. His brilliant idea of a cheap, prepaid, fixed charge to deliver a letter died with him, not to be reborn for more than 150 years, although versions of the penny post survived in a number of English cities and towns. The Duke of York fared better. He became King James II.

One reason the Post Office lost money was that members of Parliament and certain state officials had franking privileges, which meant they sent mail postage free. The word "frank" or "free" next to a seal with a unique mark was all that was needed. Over the years the marks grew more imaginative, such as crosses or scallops. Sometimes the fortunate officials signed their names. And their idea of "mail" included:

> *Thirty dogs sent to Rome;*
>
> *two laundresses sent to an ambassador;*
>
> *a cow that accompanied a doctor on a trip;*
>
> *a parcel of lace sent to a duke's regiment.*[21]

Bales of stockings and entire wardrobes of clothes were also sent free under frank. The government tried to limit the worst misuses, but the members of Parliament and the lords — often the same people — used

**DOCKWRA'S
PRIVATE POST**

FRANKING PRIVILEGES

every loophole they could to keep this privilege. When Britain was fighting Napoleon, money was needed to pursue the war. Postal income would help. The prime minister, Pitt the Younger, managed to limit franking to ten letters sent and fifteen received daily. The aristocrats cheerfully ignored the law. Newspapers, which in those days were seldom seen by the poor and were not intended for them, paid a stamp duty for the right to publish, but went postage–free. That was a major expense to the Post Office. The British Post Office in the nineteenth century, a victim of so many abuses, faced bankruptcy.

ROWLAND HILL

It was saved by postal reformer Rowland Hill. He calculated that the cost to the Post Office of delivering a letter bore no relation to the distance it traveled within Britain. With letters starting to move along the new railroad lines, change was in the air. The real cost, said Hill, was in the complex handling of a letter so that it would be paid by the recipient. He said this in one of the most famous pamphlets ever written, *Post Office Reform: Its Importance and Practicability*. Instead of raising postage once again, Hill recommended lowering it sharply so that even poor people could afford letters. At the time it was estimated that the postage on an ordinary letter cost half a day's wages for a factory worker or shop clerk. Obviously, working class people wrote few letters.

PROPOSING A UNIFORM RATE

Hill proposed a uniform rate based on the weight of a letter regardless of distance within Great Britain or the number of sheets of paper, with a one–penny minimum for a half–ounce letter irrespective of the distance the letter traveled within Britain. Increasing the weight of the letter, not the number of enclosures, would increase the postage. He suggested that senders should be required to mail letters in wrappers or "little bags called envelopes" with markings showing that postage had been paid. Hill also proposed abolishing the franking privilege and charging newspapers postage.

Most important, he proposed that all postal charges should be collected in advance from the sender of the letter, which would just be left at the address. That the letter was prepaid by the sender would be noted by "a bit of paper just large enough to bear the stamp and covered at the back with a glutinous wash."[22] And so, in 1840, after the government recovered from the shock of these radical proposals, was born the postage stamp.

PAYING IN ADVANCE

Merchants supported the plan. So did a number of newspapers and a public–spirited citizenry. Reform supporters argued that, to increase revenue, the Post Office should charge less, so that more people would use the mails without worrying about the cost of postage. Yet even such a slight blurring of class distinctions as postal reform offered had its opponents among the upper classes. Needless to say, a postal reform law that limited or eliminated franking would run into opponents. They responded with a zero sum argument, concluding that to increase postal revenue, charge more. In class–conscious England, the notion that the poor would write letters if mailing costs were reduced to a penny not only failed to move the opposition to reform, it was an argument against reform. How many aristocrats were opposed to a penny post precisely because they did not want the poor to take this step toward literacy and democracy?

Said one aristocrat, "Prepaid postage! Preposterous! I prepay my letters to my groom but, bless my soul, the fellow hasn't got the money to pay for that sort of thing. And I give him good wages. Ten shillings sixpence a week."[23] One opponent argued that the Post Office would be overrun with mail if this reform took effect. Another declared it "entirely repugnant to reason." A few of the rich expressed snobbish displeasure that just anyone could now use the mails. They also debated the propriety of mailing personal letters. It seemed so impersonal compared to delivery by a footman, who stood and waited until given a reply to an invitation to tea.

This attitude would crop up again later in the century in opposition to the use of the telephone by people who could not afford to rent one. Lord Lichfield, the Postmaster General called postal reform "the most extravagant of all the wild and visionary schemes" he ever heard of. "The walls of the Post Office would burst," he said.[25] Of course, that was the idea.

Fear may have lain behind the opposition by the well–to–do. Hill came up with another idea that infuriated the aristocrats. He wanted a slot cut in front doors where letters could be dropped. At heart, like the postage stamp, it was a democratic idea, with everyone from the lord of the manor to the humble cottager being treated equally by the arriving mailman. Some aristocrats refused this assault on their doors, remembering the saying, "An Englishman's home is his castle." They were not about to lower the drawbridge by sawing through their mahogany doors. On the other hand, more than one quarter of a million Britons signed petitions demanding reform.

Objections by the powerful and influential to losing their free franking were somewhat muted when young Queen Victoria stepped forward to say that she was willing to give up her own franking privilege. It was said that she was displeased that the high postal rates kept her poorest subjects from using the mails.

The adhesive on the back was a glue made from potato flour. A rumor spread that the glue contained poison. Another rumor spread that licking the stamp could bring a contagious disease. It was also said that licking a stamp holding a portrait of the queen dishonored the monarchy. So

At their evening affairs they smiled politely at "the nonsense of penny postage"...

Actually they were frightened, for those were days of lively radicalism and riotous agitation, and the polite world was horrified to think that the Hill plan might put a cheap and easy means of communication at the disposition of the poorer classes.

Some of the braver of them frankly admitted in the columns of the Quarterly Review and other learned journals that they were opposed to penny postage because it would make mischief among the poor and promote sedition.[24]

— Mauritz Hallgren

THE POSTAGE STAMP

was the process of canceling the stamp because it meant putting black ink on the queen's portrait. Not everyone knew where the stamp should be stuck. Some senders put this piece of "government sticking plaster" on the back of the envelope. One local landowner asked the postmaster if he thought "this penny post scheme" would last. Assured that it probably would, the landowner ordered three of the penny stamps. Taking his scissors in this period before perforation, the postmaster carefully cut three stamps — the now famous penny blacks — from a sheet.

THE POOR BENEFIT

As Hill predicted, letter writing rose sharply, and the poor benefited. Within twenty years most of the world had adopted Hill's reforms. Postcards at a halfpenny each were particularly popular with the poor of England, where the reforms began. Hill received many proofs of what his work had meant to the poor and humble. On a journey in Scotland, he once gave his coat for mending to a journeyman tailor in a little village. On learning who Hill was, the man refused payment. A friend working in a poor district wrote to tell him of the joy the people there felt now that they could "at last write to one another as if they were all Members of Parliament."[26]

Letter carriers must have enjoyed some easing of their stressful lives. Payment for mail was now severed from delivery of mail. The postman no longer had to seek out someone at each home, no longer had to cajole someone into buying a letter, no longer had to wait, and no longer had to trudge back to the station with unwanted letters. The middle class was the early beneficiary of the postage stamp because it aided business, but the poor were not far behind. The flow of information through this means of mediated communication soared. In 1838, 75 million pieces of mail went through the British Post Office. In 1841, the number jumped to 208 million and continued to climb. People who had never received a letter were now sending and receiving them even if the reading was slow and writing was difficult. Many letters still had to be written by others and read aloud when they arrived, but the literacy rate climbed.

Mass communication was beginning to transform the perception of family... Now almost the same level of intercourse could be maintained with an aunt in the next county as an uncle in the next street. News, gossip, small services, tokens of affection, could be exchanged with little effort and less expense. The subsequent arrival of the telephone and cheap road transport merely completed the transition which was set in motion not by the Penny Post but by the halfpenny postcard.[27]

— DAVID VINCENT

The postman became the partner of the schoolteacher. Literacy was promoted not only as a political goal but also as a moral good. Public letterboxes went up on street corners. Private home letterboxes went up next to front doors, sparing both expensive mahogany and cheap pine; postmen would not have to knock and wait.

At first, the new penny post did not pay its way. The loss to the postal revenue the first year was about one million pounds sterling, a substantial sum. Hill predicted that this loss would be made up and then some, but it would take time. Continued opposition to postal reform after its adoption led to deliberate mismanagement by postal bureaucrats. They managed to get Hill fired from his position as supervisor of the penny post process. The public howled for Hill's return. In 1854, with Hill back and firmly in charge, the total number of letters mailed in Britain rose to 443 million a year; in 1859, 545 million.

Rowland Hill died in 1879, filled with honors. His system of cheap pre-paid postage had spread across the world. Nations everywhere adopted his reforms because they produced a service that was at once profitable to the government and a delight to people all over the world who were getting dependable and speedy delivery of personal letters and public information at modest cost. It was all based on a tiny bit of gummed paper stuck on the outside of a letter dropped into any corner mailbox day or night. This was truly a revolution.[28]

Brazil beat the United States in becoming the first nation in the Western Hemisphere to print postage stamps. The United States had a cheap postage movement of its own, arguing as the British did that cutting rates would increase the amount of mail to the point that it would run a profit. In 1847, the United States followed Britain's lead in selling adhesive–backed postage stamps, followed five years later by stamped envelopes. For eight more years the use of prepaid postage stamps was voluntary and most mail went collect–on–delivery; after all, the recipient, not the sender, was getting something. Nevertheless, as it was in Britain, the postage stamp and other reforms led to a huge increase in the volume of mail sent.

Here is a list of nations, including regions that are now parts of other countries, and the years they began issuing postage stamps:

STAMPS IN OTHER NATIONS

1840:	Great Britain
1843:	Brazil
1847:	U.S.A., Mauritius
1849:	France, Bavaria, Belgium
1850:	Victoria, Spain, Schleswig–Holstein, Saxony, British Guiana, Switzerland, New South Wales, Austria, Austrian Italy
1851:	Canada, Sardinia, Wurtemberg, Baden, Tuscany, Trinidad, Denmark
1852:	Holland, Brunswick, Luxembourg, India, Reunion
1853:	Cape of Good Hope, Chile, Portugal, Nova Scotia, Tasmania
1854:	Western Australia, Philippines
1855:	Norway, Sweden, Cuba, South Australia, New Zealand
1856:	Finland, Mexico, Uruguay, St. Helena
1857:	Ceylon, Natal, Newfoundland
1858:	Argentina, Colombia, Peru, Romania, Russia, Naples
1859:	Roman States, Sicily, Lubeck, Venezuela
1860:	Egypt, Malta, Liberia, Sierra Leone, Jamaica, St. Lucia, Poland, Queensland

In 1879, Belgium became the first nation to use a parcel post stamp.

In 1898, Turkey introduced the first military stamps to frank mail sent by soldiers.

1861:	Prince Edward Island, St. Vincent, Grenada, Greece
1862:	Costa Rica, Nicaragua, Italy, Hong Kong
1863:	Wenden, Turkey
1865:	Ecuador
1866:	Bolivia, Honduras, Virgin Islands, Serbia
1867:	Salvador, Straits Settlements, Turks Islands
1868:	Orange Free State, North German Confederation
1869:	Sarawak, Transvaal
1870:	Afghanistan, Persia, Paraguay, Fiji
1871:	Guatemala, Japan, Hungary
1872:	Germany
1873:	Iceland, Puerto Rico, Suriname
1874:	Montenegro
1876:	Montserrat
1877:	Mozambique, Samoa, San Marino
1878:	China, Falkland Islands, Panama
1879:	Tobago, Bulgaria

CHEAP RATES FOR NEWSPAPERS

The United States postal service was being described in speeches as the nation's great educator not only in political affairs, but also in improving general knowledge such as the liberal arts and science. Two ways that the Post Office contributed were the handling of newspapers and the distribution of public information by the government itself. Low mailing costs for newspapers contributed to the spread of political knowledge. At the same time that a one–page letter cost at least six cents postage, a newspaper in the United States could be sent one hundred miles for a penny. The post riders who delivered the mail were also allowed to carry newspapers outside the mail system under their own private arrangements.

The generosity accorded to newspapers did not extend at first to magazines or pamphlets. Publishers of this printed matter fumed as newspapers thrived. Between 1801 and 1830 the number of newspapers in the new nation jumped from 200 to 1,200. The weekly rural press was especially favored. After the War of 1812, the low rate gradually was allowed to all periodicals. Just as the number of newspapers rose sixfold in a little more than a quarter century, so did the number of periodicals between 1825 and 1850, from about 100 to 600.

Congress voted low postal rates for newspapers because they carried political news. But, on this basis, why shouldn't a magazine that carried political information be equally entitled? Was it content that determined the lower rate, or format? The one–sided advantage to newspapers led to a new kind of magazine, one that was more like an advertising flier or a newspaper than a real magazine. The Post Office had the task of deciding what was or was not a newspaper, based on appearance and content. Because they faced abuse from magazine publishers for a contrary decision, postal officials quickly wearied of making such choices, although they created such distinctions as daily or weekly issues versus monthly issues. In 1863 the second–class mail category was established for both newspapers and magazines. It set a single category for all periodicals.

Nothing was easy. Although the law gave periodicals cheap second–class rates, advertising publications fell into the more expensive third–class category. After all, periodicals carried ads. The publishers of ad fliers wanted the cheap rates, so they designed their output to look like magazines, creating an early version of "advertorials," and flooded the mails with them. It took decades for postal authorities to separate the periodical sheep from the advertising goats.

Books were another matter. They were heavy, and there was no urgency about them, unlike time–dated periodicals. However, pressure on Congress and the spreading of the railroad network, where weight hardly mattered, led in 1852 to special postal rates for books. Adopting a policy of "if you can't beat 'em, join 'em," a couple of book publishers also adopted newspaper–like formats to qualify for the newspaper postal rates, reprinting novels as a cross between a book and a newspaper in appearance.

MAILING BOOKS

This change helped bring novels to a mass readership. Congress let it go at first, but soon blocked the effort to treat books like periodicals. Nevertheless, thanks to this attempt to take advantage of cheap newspaper rates, many Americans were introduced to novels. They liked them. Books did not get the favorable treatment granted to newspapers and magazines until President Franklin D. Roosevelt in 1938 set up a book rate category.

Lower postal rates introduced a wide American audience to a variety of magazines and books. This would in time lead to the dime novel and the nickel magazine. Published as "libraries" and "serials" on the cheapest paper with gaudy covers, the sensational dime novels did little to elevate the public taste, and some of the magazines were not much better. All this was not what the Post Office Department had in mind for its second class mailing, but postmasters general hesitated to deny them the privilege at the risk of being accused of censorship.

LOWERING POSTAL RATES

Matching the British system, an 1825 U.S. law allowed unpaid postmen to deliver letters, their income derived from the penny or two they could collect from the addressee. The American system operated in the larger cities, but it had all the ills of the British system. People were not home, they did not have the pennies, they were not willing to part with them, or some other reason existed for not completing the transfer. The postman had few alternatives. Sometimes he handed over the letter upon a promise to pay later; then he had to go through the awkward and sometimes difficult task of collecting.

FREE HOME DELIVERY

The U.S. Post Office Department was not tasked with putting letters into mailboxes. For many years it just had the responsibility of hauling mail from one post office to another. No further. Before free home delivery, a resident of city or town normally took a letter to the post office. The addressee went to another post office to get it, saving the penny or two for voluntary delivery. The sender could prepay the postage; if not, the recipient had to pay. Even after postage stamps were introduced in 1847, this arrangement of recipient payment continued.

MAILBOXES

In 1855, the law in the United States was altered so that the sender had no choice but to buy a stamp, and still had to go to the post office to mail the letter. That began to change in 1858 with the appearance on New York City streets of mailboxes. Those proved so popular that mailboxes were installed in most cities. At the other end, the addressee still had to pay extra to have a postman deliver the letter to the home. Otherwise, to get their mail, residents went to the local post office. In 1863 the assistant postmaster in Cleveland, Joseph Briggs, adopted the idea of free city home delivery because he "was appalled at the sight of anxious wives, children, and relatives waiting in long lines at the local post office for letters from soldiers off fighting the Civil War."[29] By coincidence, on the first day of the Battle of Gettysburg, July 1, free home delivery began in forty–nine cities. Before the century ended, post offices were offering free delivery to homes in cities throughout the nation.

WEEKLY NEWSPAPERS

If you lived in the country, you still went to town for your mail and your weekly newspaper. Of course, you combined that trip in your buggy with shopping in the general store for supplies and, as needed, to the doctor and the blacksmith. That could occupy most of your day. Actually, the post office was likely to be located in the general store. Because of this weekly schedule, the idea of weekly newspapers took hold in small towns. When a weekly trip to the village post office was the farmer's only way of receiving mail, there was little reason for him to subscribe to a daily newspaper. The country weeklies best served his needs.[30]

RURAL FREE DELIVERY

Country folks, who outnumbered their city cousins in 1890 by four to one, might envy their city cousin's free home delivery, but it wasn't until that year that anything was done. Postmaster General John Wanamaker had been pushing for rural free delivery. Opposition came from small–town postmasters who correctly saw that rural free delivery would shut down the smaller post offices. The small town tavern owner was especially upset. So was the owner of the country general store where the fourth–class rural post office had been located until postal routes came along. Storekeepers knew that when the farmer and his wife came to town for mail, they often stopped to buy something. If they didn't have to come to town, they might prefer to order from the catalogue that Mr. Montgomery and Mr. Ward had sent them. Not only did the storekeeper lose the postmaster's salary, but also the extra business generated by people coming in for their mail.

Wanamaker had his supporters for rural free delivery, notably the urban newspapers. They saw the possibility of getting a daily newspaper into farmers' hands. The effect on advertising rates could be substantial. Farmers wanted daily newspapers not only for the news and the general pleasures found in the pages, but also in these pre–radio days for the weather and crop market reports; and, very important, by having mail delivered, the farmer would save the time it took to ride into town to the post office. Shopping was not always on the farmer's mind.

Congress did vote funds for a test of rural free delivery just before Wanamaker left office in 1893. When RFD finally arrived, entire villages were affected because those whose post offices got the rural routes would be much better off than those whose fourth–class post offices were eliminated. Opponents in Washington called RFD a foolish expenditure to send a postman out summer and winter traipsing over bad roads, or no roads at all, to every home in every hollow. That was not the opinion of people who lived in the country. They loved it, for in the years before radio and rural telephones, a chance to read the latest happenings in letters and newspapers eased their isolation. The new rural delivery service, made permanent nationwide in 1902, was so welcome that after a few months one farmer commented that it would take away part of his life to give it up. An old Missouri farmer would look back over his life and estimate that he must have journeyed 12,000 miles to get his mail from the post office. Now he no longer had to make that trip. Men, women, and children who lived along rural roads waited patiently beside their mailboxes for the postman.

Rural Free Delivery helped to expand the American network of roads and bridges. The postman who trundled down the road stopping at the rural mailboxes needed a better road to trundle down, or at least a road without deep ruts that would be under water in the spring and under ice in the winter. The U.S. Post Office Department rejected hundreds of applications for RFD service after inspecting the roads. It required that roads be passable summer and winter, spring and fall. It also required that, to get RFD, at least one hundred families must live along a twenty–five–mile route. Heeding the frustrations of farmers, local governments raised the revenue needed to gravel roads, repair bridges, and construct culverts. As the years went by, the gray, tunnel–shaped rural letterbox with its red flag went up on fences and posts along every dirt road in

EXPANDING ROAD NETWORK

place of the lard pails and soap boxes. Circulation of daily newspapers skyrocketed.

Mail and parcel post bringing newspapers and magazines as well as goods are two means of mediated communication that have made country living less isolated and more desirable. In a curious way, the Internet has joined RFD in encouraging a return to village and rural life. The Internet has made it possible for many professions to function from anywhere, including deep in the countryside. Various jobs are performed via high speed connections. Education is available through the Internet, and so, of course, by means of television, DVD, and the Internet, is entertainment.

At the turn of the twentieth century, more than half of the American population lived in the countryside. Now that letters were deposited in their letterboxes sitting on posts beside their roads, country people wanted packages delivered the same way. If their city cousins could get medicine and shoes delivered to their doors, why couldn't they? Direct mail enabled advertisers to reach the public in their homes at rates below the cost of ordinary first class mail.

Mailings could be huge; fat catalogues sent to millions of households by Montgomery Ward and by Sears Roebuck were a principal means of shopping, thanks to RFD. The 540–page catalogue mailed out by Montgomery Ward in 1887 listed 24,000 items for sale. Sears Roebuck in 1897 said it was selling one watch and four suits every minute. Unhappy local merchants put pressure on their newspapers to fight the "Mail Order Trust" by refusing their newspaper ads.

The triumph of mail order, and its new literature, brought visions of new ways of living which were a triumph of a larger over a smaller community. It was a victory of the market over the marketplace. And it spelled the defeat of the salesman by advertising. In a word, it was a defeat of the seen, the nearby, the familiar by the everywhere community.[31]

— Daniel Boorstin

PARCEL POST

Parcel post was a political minefield issue that brought the federal government into competition with private express services and small town shopkeepers. Like rural free delivery it was a boon to farm families but a bane to the fellow who ran the general store in town. It brought the farmers useful products and material comforts, although it did not achieve one promised goal: shipping their produce to market, "farm–to–table" through the mails. Coupled with catalogues, parcel post doomed the businesses of many country storekeepers. The general store, which once thrived, survives mostly as American folklore.

"WISH BOOKS"

Even before federal legislation established parcel post, it was possible to mail a package of up to four pounds. Because of international agreements a package going overseas could weigh up to eleven pounds. In addition, it was cheaper to send a package to a foreign country — twelve cents per pound — than within the borders of the United States — sixteen cents per pound. Besides this illogic, it cost no more to send a parcel from New York to San Francisco than from New York to Newark, New Jersey. One rate for the whole country.

Parcel post service in the United States began on New Year's Day, 1913. Sears Roebuck and Montgomery Ward were big winners. Their fat, well–thumbed catalogues, known as "wish books," were proudly displayed in rural homes. After five years of parcel post, Sears Roebuck reported that its income had tripled. Looking back, it seems worth noting that small town stores were indeed hurt by the catalogues, a new means of mediated communication. Today, Internet online shopping, based on an even newer means of communication, has, in its turn, badly hurt catalogue sales.

The Sears catalogue and parcel post together were the Wal–Mart of their day, forcing village general stores out of business. But the general store was an essential part of its community, and without it the village was changed.

The Post Office Department was also expected to keep pornography out of the mails and to catch thieves and con artists. Paying a bill or sending some financial help to a needy relative would be, as we know, less bother if we simply put the cash into an envelope; as we also know, it is the most dangerous method. The envelope passes through many hands, and it only takes one hand to make it disappear. To deal with this light–fingered problem and with nasty folks like Jesse James, an Office of Inspection was created during the 1830s, staffed by employees called special agents.

Con artists were another problem. Lotteries were popular even during colonial times, but because of accusations that they were both dishonest and immoral, most states outlawed them before the Civil War. After the war, they resumed their popularity in the states where they were legal, especially in Louisiana, where the lottery ticket sellers took advantage of the improved postal system, now restored to serve the reunited Union. Using the mails, the Louisiana Lottery Company fleeced Americans on a national scale, collecting millions and paying little out.

As for pornography, a law against importing obscene materials, words, and pictures from foreign countries was passed in 1842. There was no law against domestic pornography until the end of the Civil War, and that law was weak. A political activist, Anthony Comstock, took it upon himself to clean up the mails. He founded the New York Society for the Suppression of Vice and convinced Congress to pass what was known as the Comstock Law, outlawing the transportation or delivery of pornography. That included birth control information and anatomy textbooks for medical students.

Wangling an appointment as an unpaid postal inspector with the right to carry a weapon, he began a one–man, anti–porn crusade. Using a New York anti–obscenity law as his weapon, Comstock seized not

PROTECTING THE PUBLIC

ANTHONY COMSTOCK

DESTROYING BOOKS

only masses of printed matter but also many pounds of the recently invented condoms. In addition, he also cracked down on medical and sociological articles that offended his sensibility, regarding anything he disapproved of as filth. He claimed that he was responsible for three thousand arrests, the destroying of fifteen tons of books, plus printing plates and nearly four million pictures.

As a result of public pressure to clean up the mails in a move toward Victorian purity, Congress passed several laws in the last half of the nineteenth century to ban anything smacking of fraud or obscenity. Getting clues from magazine ads for a variety of products promising contraception and abortion medicine, the postal inspectors seized material and arrested the senders. Patent medicine ads in magazines, which required mailing in money to receive the medicine, were eventually curtailed by the Pure Food and Drug Act.

"SUBVERSIVE" PUBLICATIONS

Based on the Espionage Act voted by Congress during World War I, the Post Office suppressed newspapers, magazines, and other printed matter that it considered subversive. The publications came from socialists, pacifists, and labor unions, plus some whose offense was that they were written in German, the language of the enemy. Postal authorities backed away from this suppression during World War II and later.

Meanwhile, the argument of advertising matter did not go away. Newspapers invented the term "junk mail" to refer to them; that was one way for newspaper publishers to stick it to the competition for local ads.

Meanwhile, the Post Office's money problems did not go away. Postal policies changed over the years, sometimes to save money, sometimes to be more efficient. During World War II, V–mail ("V" for "Victory") became the way to correspond with soldiers and others overseas. The lightweight pale blue sheets were photographed, reduced in size and weight, flown overseas, the recreated. V–mail arrived quicker and took up less space on cargo planes.

HOME DELIVERY ONCE A DAY

In 1950, home delivery was cut from twice daily to once. When President Dwight Eisenhower's choice for postmaster general, businessman Arthur Summerfield, began his new job in 1952, unpleasant surprises greeted him. Summerfield's inspections uncovered a massive, creaking, nineteenth century bureaucracy. Equipment and facilities were badly outdated. Shopworn equpment was housed in run–down, overcrowded, poorly lighted postal buildings. Wages were low. Despite all this, the postal service was bleeding the U.S. Treasury of millions of dollars a day. Summerfield began a modernization program that successive postmasters general have carried on.

MORE MAIL THAN EVER

The 1960s witnessed a steep rise in the amount of mail, especially business mail. That convinced the Post Office Department that its operations had to be mechanized. Increasingly, computers at banks, utility companies, insurance companies, credit card issuers, department stores, and other firms were sending bills, receipts, notices, and advertising to their millions of customers. The government mailed truckloads of Social Security checks each month. Yet at post offices, thousands of clerks still sorted the mail by hand, throwing letters into bins or sacks, moving them to central locations, then unsacking and further sorting. Some automation had been accomplished. Businesses used postage meters, which were invented in New Zealand in 1905 and introduced in the United States in 1920, but much more was needed.

A major improvement was the Zoning Improvement Plan (ZIP) code. In 1963, five–digit ZIP codes were added to addresses. The system, built around eighty–five big city hubs, reduced the congestion on busy downtown streets. These hubs became the core of 552 sectional centers. Each center managed from 40 to 150 local post offices. For the next step, each sectional center got a code number. Beyond this, numerical codes were issued to neighborhood post offices. The result was a five–digit code that covered the entire United States. Every home and business address had its five–digit code. The first digit represents a region, from 0 in the Northeast to 9 in the Far West. The next two digits identify cities and sectional centers that fit the USPS transportation plan. The last two digits identify individual post offices or urban postal zones.

ZIP CODES

As it modernized, postal service automated. More and more, machines took over. Pigeonhole boxes were thrown out when machines sorted the mail, including parcels. Envelope addresses were read by optical character readers. Conveyer belts moved letters along. Vending machines sold stamps, including the popular self–sticking type. Other machines canceled them (canceling machines go back to the 1890s). Computer scales at the postal clerks' window not only weighed but calculated costs for various classes of mail. Bar codes stamped by mass mailers of national newspapers, magazines, and catalogues moved them rapidly through the system.

The newest generation of automated equipment can read an entire address optically and convert it into a bar code sprayed on the envelope that is read by an electronic sorter that processes nine envelopes a second. Even some hand–written envelopes can be moved along like this. The combination of regional printing plants and bar code addresses put newspapers and magazines in home mailboxes often within hours of printing.

AUTOMATION

Mass mailings have continued. In 1988 a government brochure, "Understanding AIDS," was sent to 107 million addresses. In 1990 approximately the same number of census forms were mailed. By 1996 close to

600 million pieces of mail were handled daily; that works out to about 700 letters per person per year.

THE U.S. POSTAL SERVICE

As the national mood swung toward privatization of industry, eyes turned toward the postal service. After lengthy negotiations and a strike by postal workers, Congress in 1970 passed the Postal Reorganization Act; President Richard Nixon signed it. By its provisions, a year later the Post Office Department became the U.S. Postal Service, an independent organization. The postmaster general left the president's cabinet. The U.S. Postal Service would become a self–supporting business corporation wholly owned by the federal government, run by an independent Board of Governors who were appointed by the president for nine–year terms with approval by the Senate. A separate five–person Rate Commission would determine what the public paid for postage stamps, and the postal service would be fully independent of Congress. Even the postal emblem changed — from a post rider to the national bald–headed eagle standing on a block labeled U.S. Mail. In 1977, to compete with Federal Express and UPS, the Postal Service introduced Express Mail.[32]

In much of the world, postal systems were erratic, offering the sender of a parcel or letter no reasonable assurance that it would actually reach its destination. By the nineteenth century the postal service in several nations was a mess. Efforts at reform ranged from uneven to non–existent. Rates were so high that poor people could not afford to receive letters. The rates were kept up as a means of government revenue, not merely to support the national postal service. Unpaid letter carriers in many nations collected money for every letter they delivered, and kept it, which meant that the letter could not simply be dropped at a destination. In effect, in addition to postal charges to the person sending a letter, the letter carrier sold the letter to the addressee.

INTERNATIONAL MAIL PROBLEMS

If postal regulations within each nation were confusing, the problem was compounded and compounded again between countries. Each nation had its own rules, its own rate scales, its own suspicions of mail from other nations, all adding up to a maze of conflicting regulations. A letter crossing several borders added charges by each country it traveled through.

Cooperation between nations was sometimes willing, sometimes grudging. The wonder was not that a letter mailed to an address beyond a frontier would be delayed, but that it would ever arrive. According to the British Postal Guide of 1856, a half ounce letter from the United States to Brazil cost sixty–six cents or thirty–four cents to mail, depending upon whether it went by French or British mail. From the U.S. to Japan, a letter could cost anywhere from a dime to sixty cents, based upon five routes and five rates. Nations signed bilateral treaties to get their letters delivered. A separate treaty had to be negotiated with each country.

Strong nations served as transit points to weaker nations not only for the postage income but to exert influence over their neighbor. Nor did possibilities for spying escape notice.

With the growing commercial trade between countries, it was time to end the rickety system of frontiers that blocked the free flow of mail. Pointing in a fresh direction was the German–Austrian Postal Union founded in 1850. It removed all frontier barriers to the flow of mail. Of course, it helped that Germany and Austria shared a language and had a history of strong diplomatic relations.

Could such an agreement expand to encompass all nations? The need for a regular American transatlantic packet service led the U.S. Post Office Department to begin bilateral discussions with postal officials of major European countries. These talks led to better mail service across the Atlantic not only for diplomats and businessmen but also for the growing number of recent immigrants to America who were eager to retain contacts with their loved ones back home.

In 1863, in the midst of the American Civil War, the United States Postmaster General Montgomery Blair called for an international conference. Delegates from 15 nations meeting in Paris agreed on general principles, but had no power to establish much. The nations did, however, agree to use the metric system to measure distance and grams to calculate weight. Eleven years later, twenty–two nations met in Berne, Switzerland, for the first International Postal Congress. A German postal official, Heinrich von Stephan, drew up a plan for an international postal union. The conference created the General Postal Union.

THE UNIVERSAL POSTAL UNION

The Treaty of Berne, signed on October 9, 1874, is now observed as World Post Day. The old postal conventions between nations were now obsolete. At the second International Postal Congress in 1878, because membership grew so fast, the name of the General Postal Union was amended to the Universal Postal Union, the world's first truly international organization. A dozen years later the only major country outside the UPU was China, and that was because of special circumstances. UPU members agreed that there would be a single rate for foreign mail, there would be no difference in the treatment of domestic and foreign mail, each nation would keep the money from its sale of stamps, but it would not charge to deliver foreign mail. Arbitration would settle disputes.

INTERNATIONAL ACTION AT LAST

As a result of the treaty, the delivery of letters would not be part of international scheming for power. It was no longer necessary to add postage stamps of every country that a letter or package passed through. However, some payments to the receiving countries still exist. For example, the U.S. Postal Service pays developing countries about $4 per kilogram for a local post office to take letters the "last mile" to a mailbox. Nations keep records of the amount of incoming mail from other countries and how much is sent out to those same countries. If there is an imbalance, the nation that received more than it sent can make a claim for some payment.

The International Bureau of the UPU was housed in Berne, and there it remains. The Universal Postal Congress meets every five years. It has added to the international postal network such services as money orders, registered mail, parcel post, and reply cards. Each country, of course, issues its own stamps, but there is an agreement on uniformity of international rates and units of weight.

The original agreement applied only to letter mail. Today, in addition to money orders, newspapers and magazines routinely cross frontiers along with millions of letters. The U.S. Post Office Department became a messenger carrying the tidings of the new, expanding, democratic nation to people everywhere who were eager to learn as much as they could.

PIGEON POST

The first known use of pigeons as postal messengers was in ancient Egypt. In 2900 B.C.E. in Egypt, incoming ships released pigeons as an announcement of important visitors. Around the time of Moses, the Egyptian army used carrier pigeons to deliver messages. In 2350 B.C.E. King Sargon of Akkadia — the present Iraq — ordered each messenger to carry a homing pigeon. If the messenger was about to be captured, he released the pigeon, which flew back to the palace. Its arrival meant another messenger should be sent. Pigeons also bore messages in ancient China, Persia, India, and Greece, where the names of Olympic victors were carried back to their cities.

During the Dark Ages the Arabs established regular airmail pigeon courier services. According to one tale, a caliph in North Africa satisfied his taste for Lebanese cherries by having pigeons fly them in. Each carried one cherry inside a silk bag. It was the first parcel post. Reportedly, a prize pair of carrier pigeons in the Arab empire could fetch one thousand gold pieces.

During the Crusades Richard the Lion Heart's men captured a pigeon that carried a message reporting that a Moslem army would arrive in three days to break the Christian siege of Ptolemais. A forged message was substituted, saying that no help would be coming. The besieged town surrendered. The Moslem relief army arrived to find the Christians solidly entrenched.

Pigeon post was the world's fastest communication system for all the centuries of the Dark and Middle Ages, and remained so until Samuel Morse's invention of the telegraph in 1844 and Guglielmo Marconi's invention of radio in 1895. Stockbrokers and bankers relied on pigeons through much of the nineteenth century. London banker Nathan Roth-schild made a killing when a pigeon brought early news of Napoleon's defeat at Waterloo. In 1840 the European news agency Havas ran a London–to–Paris pigeon news service with the promised flying time of six hours. In the Franco–Prussian War of 1870–71, a gap existed in telegraph lines between France and Germany. Julius Reuter bridged it with pigeons and made the fortune he used as the basis of what is now Reuters, one of the world's great news agencies.

During World War I, The American army kept several thousand homing pigeons. The fledgling British Air Force kept more than 20,000 for an unusual mission — intelligence gathering. Each pigeon, with a message holder attached, was placed inside a basket that was attached to both a parachute and a rigged balloon. When the wind was right, the balloons would be released. The rigging freed the basket over enemy territory, and the parachute gave the pigeon inside the basket a gentle landing. A message asked anyone who found the basket to supply intelligence information, put it in the message holder, and, for a promised future reward, free the pigeon to fly home. The Germans caught some of the birds and responded by shooting anyone they caught who sent a pigeon aloft with information.

Even in modern times, pigeons have been postal couriers. In 1981, Lock-heed engineers in California needed to send negatives on a regular basis to a test station. The birds covered the distance in half the time and less than one percent of the cost of a car. Other means of communication have replaced the cooing messengers, but here and there they can still be found doing the useful work that made them the email of the Middle Ages. And they work for… pigeon feed.

THE POSTMAN THROUGH HISTORY followed two trails, the path of the government and the path of the private citizen. Only in the past few centuries, a fraction of postal history, have they merged. For most of recorded time communication included transportation, with postal service serving as a common carrier of writing and, later, of mass communication printing. Although their origins are lost, it is probable that postal communication preceded writing. Rulers would have sent messengers with oral instructions.

The Bible refers to postal service. A postal runner delivered the mes-sage — "Nike!" — to the waiting Greeks, Pheidippides. A postal service kept the vast Roman Empire functioning. Like most early postal services, the Roman service was only for government use, though it quite likely carried private messages as well. Postal service fell victim to the barba-rism of the Dark Ages, but new services arose. Monasteries stayed in

Unquestionably, the most unusual aerial camera ever made was Dr. Julius Neubronner's Doppelsport. The little camera, patented in Germany in 1903, …was designed to be mounted on the breast of a car-rier pigeon. (It) took only single exposures, and had timing devices to delay that moment on exposure until the pigeon — one hoped — was above its target. Homing pigeons were trained to carry these cameras. The German military was interested in the panoramic model prior to World War I.[33]

— S.F. SPIRA

CONCLUSION

touch with each other. The University of Paris developed a service with royal support. As mercantile cities grew, business mail was needed.

Carrying news has always been an important part of postal service, including the Pony Express. Until the telegraph, sending most information required physically carrying the written page; this meant that communication remained a function of the available transportation. The means of conveyance was always an important part of the postal story, from the horse rider to the stagecoach to the railroad to the airplane. The need for better postal service led to building better roads.

When what was being mailed was a newspaper, magazine, book, or a Montgomery Ward catalogue, the mails were transmitting forms of mediated mass communication, just as they were when the parcel being mailed was a news story, a manuscript, or photographs destined for publication. Only by improving transportation did the information get out more quickly to more people at greater distances and at less cost.

William Dockwra's attempt to set up a penny post in London was knocked down. Postal reform was opposed by aristocrats, who did not welcome Rowland Hill's argument that the poor would write more letters, but the reformers won. The postage stamp was born. Prepaid postage would be adopted by every nation. It may be no coincidence that the decade of the postage stamp also saw the invention of an electric telegraph, and Charles Babbage's vision that led to the computer. It is not surprising that Hill and Babbage knew one another, or that Babbage, the "father" of the computer, spoke out in support of postal reform. Both men belonged to the Society for the Diffusion of Useful Knowledge.

The postage stamp belongs in the category of media that changed the world. The simple bit of printed and glued paper and accompanying postal reforms added to the rise of both democracy and literacy. They are among a series of nineteenth century changes in mediated communication that left their mark on society through photography, phonograph records, and advances in printing and paper technologies, plus the electric inventions of the telegraph, telephone, movies, and radio.

They are the key elements of the democratization, the standardization, and the affordability of communication, and the repeatability of experience. Because of them, we all live in a much different and more egalitarian world.

5 TELEGRAPH AND TELEPHONE WIRES: REMOVING DISTANCE

"WE ARE IN GREAT haste to construct a magnetic telegraph from Maine to Texas," Henry David Thoreau wrote, "but Maine and Texas, it may be, have nothing important to communicate." Actually, Maine, Texas, and everyone in between had plenty to say to one another. Even more, as anyone discovers who overhears a cell phone conversation in an elevator, even when there is nothing important to say. Just to be connected matters to us all. For years comedians joked about phone use at inappropriate times, and were rewarded with laughter about recognized behavior.

THE TELEGRAPH

The telegraph sped information through society at speeds the Pony Express could only dream of, and overnight put that colorful enterprise out of business. Previously, no communication could exist without transportation, with the exception of the limited capability of semaphore flags, smoke signals, or the flash of an ancient Greek bronze shield in the sun. The telegraph was the first device to use electricity for a practical purpose, even though it was a scientific tool in a day when no one was quite sure what kind of "fluid" electricity really was or how it worked.

The telegraph brought about standard time zones and it altered the nation's economy by smoothing out the variation in prices among different regions. It allowed the branch offices of major industries to communicate with their head offices for the first time on a daily basis. It sharply reduced the time between an event and the public awareness of the event. It gave news an urgency previously absent, and it altered the appearance of news and, to a degree, its very nature.

Telegraph wires ran alongside railroad tracks, the nerve path beside the spine, each benefiting the other. Each brought business to the other. Freight trains hauled the heavy poles and wire that stood beside the tracks. The railroad had so much need of the telegraph to dispatch trains and carry messages that the jobs of railroad station agent and telegrapher were combined into the same person. Dots and dashes alerted switchmen when a train was highballing along a single railroad track, so that they could send to a siding any train heading in the opposite direction; the train engineer no longer had to wonder if the "9:05" was on schedule.

With less fear of collisions, railroad operations were more efficient, and that lowered freight charges and brought more goods, including the much–welcomed daily newspapers and magazines that too often had been abandoned near a stagecoach stop to end up as soggy piles. The uncertainties of stagecoach delivery of information were quickly forgotten in the age of the railroad and telegraph. Their paired growth aided another means of communication, the mail system, which needed dependable transportation. A new era in postal communication began when U.S. stamps went on sale in 1847, three years after telegraph companies began stringing wire.

ANCIENT ROOTS

"Tele" comes from the Greek word for "distant"; "graph" comes from the Greek word for "writing." The telegraph had ancient roots. Homer's *Iliad* speaks of beacon fires that heralded a ship's arrival. Greek ships flew signal flags to distinguish themselves from enemy ships. Signals for the start of the battle, for the change of course, stopping, surrounding the enemy fleet, and disembarking troops were, no doubt, signaled with flags.[1] Both Greeks and Romans used signal fires to warn of attacks. Greek and Roman bronze shields glinting in the sunlight carried messages. Scythians carried identifying flags into battle. Native Americans used smoke to signal.

SEMAPHORE

Obviously, shields, smoke, and flags were of limited use. The demand to forward more information more quickly surged during the Industrial Revolution. French cities communicated much better than ancient warriors when they were connected by semaphore towers in the nineteenth century. Two signaling arms, serving as a visual telegraph, were moved according to a codebook of 8,400 words and phrases. Semaphore was used for several decades, especially to pass along military communiques, but it was blind at night and on foggy days. But because nothing better was at hand, a similar system was planned along the East Coast of the United States. Meanwhile, a pair of semaphore flags, with each letter of a message identified by the position of the flags, was a common way for naval ships to signal each other. The telegraph would render such signaling systems obsolete.

The idea of electricity as a means of sending messages was considered well before Samuel F.B. Morse thought of it. No one really invented the telegraph, just as there was no single inventor of the photograph, the motion picture, or the computer. Several inventors contributed ideas as far back as 1727, three–quarters of a century before electricity came out of the laboratory. A Danish scientist, Hans Christian Oersted, discovered electromagnetism in 1820. In 1830, an American scientist, Joseph Henry, rang a bell more than 1,000 feet down an iron wire circuit from an electromagnet hooked to a series of small batteries. Morse, an artist not a scientist, may not have known of most of the previous experiments with this invisible "fluid."

An electric telegraph was working along the Great Western Railway in England in 1839. A renowned physicist, Charles Wheatstone, and a businessman, William Cooke, built it based on an alphabetic system that required five needles and five wires; the needles pointed to the correct letter. Two years later the inventors came up with the first printing telegraph; it could manage as much as fifteen words a minute. The British public and the government paid little attention until they learned of the capture of a murderer, John Tawell, and the pickpocketing gang of Fiddler Dick. All of them had tried to escape by train, but ran into bobbies who had been alerted by telegraph messages. If such anecdotes seem trivial in the long history of communication, they are not, for the resultant news reports helped to establish the telegraph in the minds of government officials as well as newspaper readers. That led to official support, and from the telegraph much of modern communication has evolved.[2]

SAMUEL MORSE

However, the fame as the inventor of the telegraph went to Morse, an American portrait painter of considerable talent who developed an interest in electricity after listening to a lecture on its properties when he was a student at Yale. According to a frequently told tale, Morse was a passenger on a ship taking him back to America after three years in Europe trying to make a living as an artist. A dinner conversation with other passengers about electromagnetism led him to conclude that an electric telegraph was feasible, saying, "I see no reason why intelligence might not be instantaneously transmitted by electricity to any distance."[3]

Morse went on to become a professor of art in a New York university, but he hired a machinist, Alfred Vail, and began experimenting with the transmission of signals over a wire hooked to a battery. Vail has been called the true inventor of the Morse Code and the telegraphic apparatus that carries Morse's name.

SUPPORT, RIDICULE

At the time that Wheatstone and Cooke were improving their multi–wire telegraph in England, Morse and Vail were following a different, single–wire design in the United States, hoping to get government support. They managed to demonstrate their device before President Martin Van Buren, his cabinet, and a congressional committee. Although several officials showed interest, others ridiculed the contraption that relied on a pen attached to one end of a pivoted arm, with an electromagnet and a windup clockwork motor that drew a paper tape under the pen, leaving marks on the paper tape according to the current flowing through the electromagnet. Vail improved the device with a click key at the transmitter, and a receiver that indented a pattern of dots and dashes on the tape. When they realized that the operator could figure out the clicked message by listening to the clicks, Morse and Vail discarded the paper tape.

SUCCESSFUL EXPERIMENT

Congress finally provided $30,000 to construct an experimental line that ran from Annapolis to Washington, although seventy congressmen did not bother to vote on what they thought was a trick and a waste of money. In 1844 the Whig Party convening in Baltimore chose its presidential candidate. A Morse associate who was present joined newspaper reporters on the train to Washington to report the news, but got off at Annapolis, one end point of the telegraph wire, to report the results to Vail, who telegraphed them to Morse in Washington at the other end point. Reporters on the train later confirmed the political news, but the newspapers at first overlooked the implications of this first public demonstration of the Morse telegraph. The carrier pigeon and the semaphore flags had competition.

KEEPING IT PRIVATE

On May 24, 1844, after the wire reached Baltimore, Morse chose as his first message a quotation from the Book of Numbers: "What hath God wrought?" The pious artist and inventor was convinced that God had chosen him to improve communication on Earth. Morse had hoped to sell his telegraph patent to the government. That did not happen, but the Post Office put Morse in charge of a sub–department tasked with developing his invention. In 1847, Congress chose not to buy the patent rights to it, and to sell the experimental line to Morse business interests. Private express companies came forward eagerly because they saw the business possibilities of a privately owned telegraph system. Once Morse had shown the way, the technology was simple to copy, and within a few years more than 50 telegraph companies were active. The American telegraph, unlike most of the world's telegraph systems, would be managed as a commercial venture, followed by private industry development of the telephone, radio, and television. Most governments chose the path of public ownership of all these wired forms of mediated communication.

In its first four days of operation, the telegraph brought in a total of one penny. Despite the slow start of business, private capital jumped into the telegraphy business, although in a disorganized, non–cooperative way, so that, until the wires were connected, it still could take several days for a message to reach its destination. The telegraph line did not reach San Francisco until October of 1861, spanning the continent a year after the Civil War started; the Pony Express between St. Joseph, Missouri, and San Francisco quickly faded into lore when the telegraph replaced it as the conduit of time–sensitive mail between the nation's interior and the Pacific coast for those willing to pay the heavy charges. "Intelligence" could now cross from California to Missouri and points east in minutes.

Normal non–urgent mail, such as letters from loved ones, however, still took weeks to travel from coast to coast via the Isthmus of Panama.

The main use of the telegraph was for business, just as the main use of the Internet today is dot.com. Speculators thrived on early information. The messenger who arrived first with news that led to a rise or fall in cotton prices promised large profits for his quick–witted employer. Manufacturers could bypass wholesalers, saving on commissions, and deal directly with retailers, sometimes undercutting the prices of competitors. Retailers able to order quickly could keep smaller inventories. With the telegraph, dealers in fish and other perishable foods could gauge market demand more accurately.[4]

The Crimean War saw the first military use of the telegraph. During the American Civil War both armies relied on telegraph communications, but the South suffered from a lack of wire and other supplies needed to operate a telegraph system. Wires radiating from General Grant's headquarters enabled him to coordinate troop movements across a wide front.[5] At the start of the Civil War, six fiercely competitive telegraph companies, each dominating a region of the United States, formed a cartel to crush smaller rivals. The war proved ruinous for those whose lines ran north to south. Three companies remained after the war. Western Union bought out its two rivals. It was the first company of any kind in the United States to have a business monopoly.

The telegraph removed the barrier of time in transmitting news. When information could be transmitted instantly from distant places, the value of news dispatches as a commodity increased, because fresh reports are always preferable to old news. Independent "telegraph reporters" tried to participate, but newspapers preferred their own system.

To save money, several newspapers in different Eastern cities combined their resources to create something new, the news gathering cooperative. In some cases, competitive newspapers shared the services of the same reporter. During the U.S. war with Mexico, 1846–48, several major northeastern dailies shared the costs of horseback riders, fast boats, railroads, carrier pigeons, and telegraph lines to beat the U.S. mail. This combination of an eastern version of the pony express and the infant telegraph system regularly beat the government mails between New Orleans and New York during the Mexican War. This express system was so efficient that President James Polk learned of the American victory at Vera Cruz from the publisher of the Baltimore Sun.

The public could not get enough of war news dispatches. The telegraph ran for only 130 miles when the Mexican War began, the line from Washington running no further south than Richmond, but it fit in well with news delivery. The Associated Press arose out of these combines in

Although it has now faded from view, the telegraph lives on within the communication technologies that have subsequently built upon its foundations: the telephone, the fax machine, and more recently, the Internet. And, ironically, it is the Internet — despite being regarded as a quintessentially modern means of communication — that has the most in common with its telegraphic ancestor....

Time–traveling Victorians arriving in the late twentieth century would, no doubt, be unimpressed by the Internet. They would surely find space flight and routine intercontinental air travel far more impressive technological achievements than our much–trumpeted global communications network. Heavier–than–air flying machines were, after all, thought by the Victorians to be totally impossible. But as for the Internet — well, they had one of their own.[6]

— Tom Standage

Insofar as the invention and spread of the telegraph provided the crucial catalyst and means for regular cooperative news gathering, it supplied the technological underpinning of the modern press; that is, it transformed the newspaper from a personal journal and party organ into primarily a disseminator of news.[9]

— DANIEL CZITROM

1848, formed by six New York dailies that otherwise competed furiously with each other.[7]

With the telegraph a new concept took hold on what news was and how it was to be delivered to the mass audiences who read the penny press newspapers that took root a few years before the telegraph was invented.[8] The concept was *objective reporting*. A wire service made money according to how many newspapers it could sign up. Because newspapers did not agree on political issues, a wire service saw a greater value in impartial reports that irritated the fewest number of editors. And so, *objectivity* was born, defined as providing information that contains only verifiable assertions and avoids statements of value that lack clear attribution to source. As one test of objective reporting, the knowledgeable reader should not be able to determine the opinion of the writer. Overt opinions were confined to the editorial page, and there they have remained. The frequently voiced argument that a truly dispassionate objectivity does not exist, particularly in political news, has some validity, however.

In the delivery of important political and military reports, small town newspapers had no chance to compete against large dailies until the telegraph leveled the playing field. Newspapers that were able to receive a telegraph news service could now offer the significant national news of the day along with the local news that its readers cherished, and could put its papers out on the street before the city papers arrived in the mail. Readers no longer had to subscribe to a large city newspaper to learn what was happening beyond their community.

Obviously, the publishers of the large city newspapers did not greet the equalizing effect of the telegraph with unalloyed joy. In fact, the manager of the London *Times* wished the telegraph had never been invented.[10] When telegraph news became widely available, city newspapers in the interior of the country could compete on the same footing with the eastern press. Equal access to news encouraged the growth of dozens of new provincial dailies.[11]

CROSSING SEAS

News of the assassination of Abraham Lincoln was transmitted instantaneously by telegraph across the nation, but lacking a cable, the news took twelve days to cross the Atlantic. Laying cables underwater proved a challenge, as unsheathed iron did no more than stun fish. Rubber failed because it rotted in water. When the answer was discovered, Brittania would rule not only the waves, but also the ocean floors where cables were laid, because its Malayan colony grew the gutta–percha trees whose gum sheathed the cables as nothing else could.

A cable was laid in 1851 under the English Channel to connect England to France. Other cables connected England to Ireland, and Denmark to

Sweden. A cable across the Mediterranean tied Europe and Africa. After several failures, the first transatlantic cable was laid in 1866 between England and Canada by the *Great Eastern*, a vessel five times the size of any other ship afloat.[12] Australia was connected to the telegraph network in 1902. Shanghai became the first connection to China in 1906.

To please its readers, the New York *Tribune* began a column of telegraph bulletins two years after Morse invented the telegraph, acquiring speed at the cost of story detail. Newspapers and telegraph companies, in a stormy relationship over costs, got into a battle of wits concerning what a word was. Because the telegraph companies charged by the word, as much as fifty cents for ten words between New York and Boston, editors grew creative in their instructions to reporters filing dispatches. On the assumption that a word could be any grouping of letters between two spaces, news stories combined verbs and prepositions into single words that Noah Webster had not identified. They also used codes to transmit information, never mind that occasional blunders resulted. Telegraph companies retaliated by charging every five letters or even every three letters as a word. Not to be outdone, telegraph operators developed shorthand codes for phrases, such as "GM" ("good morning") and "SFD" ("stop for dinner"), just as teenagers sending email or instant messages on BlackBerries use "LOL" ("laughing out loud"). Email and computer chat lines today pour old wine into new bottles.

When the dust finally settled, and because telegraph signals might fail while news was being transmitted, American news writing was well on its way to the new style of the 5–W lead (who? what? when? where? why?), and the inverted pyramid (as the story progressed, the writer added less important information). In addition, there was objectivity, resulting in reports that were less likely to offend anyone than European newspaper reports were, but lacked the pungent flavor of the European press news essays. All in all, the new American news style produced stories that were more structured, more predictable, and less like the work of individuals.

As the telegraph wires spread across the United States, they also spread across Europe, Canada, and parts of South America. However, the nations of Europe continued to deflate Morse's dream that the telegraph would provide understanding and goodwill that could unite the world. For example, the reality was that Austria and Prussia built their national services, but there was no direct connection between their political and commercial centers in Vienna and Berlin. Instead, at a shared border office a telegraph clerk from one country physically handed a message to a clerk from the other country for retransmission. In time, interconnection agreements would be signed, but the telegraph made diplomats nervous. Diplomacy required patience, not the instantaneous aware-

WHAT IS A WORD?

A NEW STYLE FOR NEWS

ness brought by the electric wire. If a message could make its way to a national capital in no time at all, troops could be ordered to the frontier just as quickly.

REUTER'S NEWS AGENCY

Europeans had entered the news service business even before the Associated Press. In Paris in 1833, the year the penny press began in New York, Charles Havas began a news agency using the mails and carrier pigeons. In exchange for his news reports, newspapers gave him advertising space that he could sell. The enterprising idea led two of his workers, Bernard Wolff and Paul Julius Reuter, to start their own news agencies. When the telegraph lines went up in Germany and France, Reuter observed that the lines of the two nations were unconnected. Seeing a business opportunity, he covered the gap with carrier pigeons, which he had already employed to report the latest market prices. In time, after a telegraph line filled the gap, Reuter moved to England, where he founded the news agency, now known as Reuters, one of the world's largest.[13]

LATER INVENTIONS

Thomas Edison invented improvements that could send two messages at a time in each direction. He was working on improvements to this "harmonic telegraph" when he stumbled onto a way to record sound and invented the phonograph. Another inventor trying improve the telegraph, Alexander Graham Bell, invented the telephone instead. Other inventions that grew out of the telegraph include the telex, the teletype, and the teleprinter, which are combinations of printers, typewriters, and telephones used by newspapers, government offices, and businesses; the tieline, a direct private line between a telegraph office and a business office; and the Telequote and Quotron machines, also derived from the telegraph, that give instant reports on stock market prices.

Decades later, after the telephone was invented and a national network was in place, when it was cheaper to send a telegram than to place a long distance phone call, telegrams were more popular than ever. They reached a peak of sorts between the two World Wars. Radio comedians joked about using the word "stop" in place of periods; punctuation cost extra, but the four–letter words usually were sent free. And there were jokes about Western Union messengers delivering off–key versions of "Happy Birthday" singing telegrams. But during World War II, families feared the sight of a Western Union messenger because the telegram might be from the Department of War reporting that a soldier had been killed. Today, the telephone medium it gave birth to has replaced the telegraph. So have fax and email. In 2006, the newer technologies finally proved too much; Western Union got out of the telegram business. It is still used to transfer money from country to country, allowing foreign workers in Europe and the United States to send wages home.

To succeed, an invention must find a social use. It must improve some aspect of life in the society of its time. The telephone was originally seen as an aid to business, such as a doctor being able to contact a pharmacist directly. That it would become so much more took time to evolve, but not a lot of time relative to many inventions, because the value of being able to speak directly with someone without meeting face–to–face quickly became apparent to Victorian America.

THE TELEPHONE

Before the telephone, to communicate with someone meant to go to that person or write a letter, but with an estimated average of one letter written every three weeks, communication with a distant friend or loved one was simply less frequent than it would become in the future. Even rumors took longer to reach ears.

Before the telephone, if you were sick, you went to the doctor or sent someone to ask the doctor to make a house call, which may have been a more pleasant use of the doctor's time but was certainly less efficient. If you needed a policeman in a hurry, you were in some difficulty. If you needed a fire wagon in a hurry, too bad. If you lived alone, how would you manage during a sudden illness or after an accident? If you were elderly, to live alone was an invitation to trouble. If you lived in the countryside, as most people did, you took a risk to live alone no matter how old you were. When a son or daughter married or moved out of the house to enter college or start a career, your tears may not have been only of joy, for the child's familiar voice might never again be heard in your home.

LIFE BEFORE THE TELEPHONE

At the time the telephone was invented, at the height of the Industrial Revolution, business and industry moved at a slower and more cautious pace than it would in the years to come. If, say, you were a wholesaler of fruits and vegetables, how would you know what to load onto a wagon for the grocers whom you served? Or if, say, you wanted to build a skyscraper, how would the workers at the top communicate with those on the ground? The answer: before the telephone (a time that also preceded the safety elevator and cheap steel), there were no skyscrapers. If you worked in a mine, how would you call for help after a cave–in? Mine safety is imperfect today, so you can imagine what it was then.

All in all, compared to what they would be after the telephone became a common household fixture, the good–old–days of the late nineteenth century were lonely for many, uncertain for most, and pinched for everyone, The Victorian head of a household may have harrumphed with displeasure at the ringing telephone that interrupted the well–regulated family dinner, but the farmer's wife regarded the telephone as a godsend.[14] The telephone has been — and still is — both irritant and blessing, and it is likely to be the last means of communication you would willingly part with.[15]

MORE LONELY, LESS CERTAIN

"KEEP IN TOUCH"

For some people, the telephone is a way to keep a distance from others, but it is surely more than happenstance that the word "touch" is employed, even though the telephone advertising slogan, "Reach out and touch someone," involves no touching, nor does the offhanded "Keep in touch." Yet, for most people, the telephone is a way to connect to others, and it is a factor in the way people choose to live their lives. It allows just a confined intimacy, but for the infirm and those who live alone, it can be a life saver. For others, the telephone is a way to do business, to send family news, to make or break a date, to express love or anger in preference to face–to–face contact, or just to pass the time.

Bell and his assistant, Thomas Watson, in working with tonal frequencies to develop a harmonic, multiplexed telegraph signal, recognized that the on–and–off signaling of the telegraph would have to be replaced by a continuous current whose frequency must be modified. The human voice could be transmitted if a current could be varied to reflect the variations in air pressure as words are spoken, and the voice might be heard with better fidelity if a telephone instrument received the arriving sounds the way an ear does. That moment famously came on March 10, 1876, when Bell called out from an adjoining room, "Mr. Watson, come here. I want to see you." And the telephone was born.

"MY GOD, IT TALKS!"

Another famous moment enshrined in telephone lore occurred at the 1876 Philadelphia exposition held to commemorate the centennial of the signing of the Declaration of Independence. Bell went there to demonstrate his telephone, but he attracted little attention until the visiting emperor of Brazil, Dom Pedro II, recognized the professor who had given a lecture in Boston that Dom Pedro had attended. When Bell demonstrated his device to Dom Pedro, the emperor exclaimed, "My God, it talks!" As a result of the publicity that followed, Bell's telephone was the hit of the exposition.[16]

The dream of speaking at a distance did not originate with Alexander Graham Bell; "lovers' telephones" consisting of two cans attached by a wire could carry a voice the length of a football gridiron. Other inventors than Bell had tried to create an electric version. On the same day that Bell got his patent, a well–known inventor, Elisha Gray, informed the U.S. Patent Office that he had invented "the art of transmitting vocal sounds or conversations telegraphically through an electric current." Like Bell, he had started out to improve the telegraph with harmonic tones, and he also decided to shift his focus to assembling a device to carry a voice over a wire.

BELL WINS PATENT FIGHT

The outcome of a lengthy court battle between them ended in Bell's favor, but the apparatus designed by the twenty–nine–year–old Scottish–born teacher of the deaf and professor of vocal physiology at Boston University did not inspire universal confidence. In London his demonstration was ridiculed as something of a toy. James Clerk Maxwell, the Scottish scientist whose theory of invisible waves would underlie the invention of radio, concluded that Bell's apparatus could have been "put together by an amateur."[17] The chief engineer of the British Post Office, William Preece, reported to a committee of the House of Commons that Bell's invention might be more useful in America than in Britain, which enjoyed "a superabundance of messengers, errand boys and things of that kind."[18] In the United States, when Cole Younger, a member of Jesse James' outlaw gang, emerged from prison, he told a reporter that "it was all I could do to keep my face straight at the spectacle of a fellow jabbering into a dumbbell."

Bell and his financial backers initially conceived a business model for the telephone, but were delighted when the doctors and merchants who were the first customers ordered an additional telephone for their residences. That led the Bell System to try to rent out their phones as an addition to the home. Its newspaper advertisements soon stressed the telephone not only as a valuable instrument in an emergency, but also as a social tool, offering up such slogans as "Friendship's path often follows the trail of the telephone wire," "No girl wants to be a wallflower," and "Call the folks now!"

Telephones were for rent, not for sale. They were considered part of an integrated system that included the wires that connected them to a switching network and to the phone operators needed to make the connections. Improvements in equipment were convincing potential users that what Bell had invented was a tool, not a toy. Within two years of the awarding of Bell's patent, some 10,000 Bell telephones were in use.

At first, a single megaphone was used for both speaking and listening, with the user alternately pressing his ear to it and turning his head to shout into it. This device yielded to a separate transmitter and receiver; the transmitter took a bell shape to focus the sound of the voice, and a metal disk substituted for the original skin diaphragm at the receiver. To add to conductivity, copper wire replaced telegraph iron wire. It was evident from the start that each telephone could not be connected directly to every other telephone; a central switching system was needed. Following the logic of a switching system in each city, Bell envisioned a central switching system to connect distant cities so that long distance calling might be possible, even though the existing equipment was not yet up to the task of sending a clear vocal signal between cities. Subscribers who had to shout into Bell's equipment might have given up except that another inventor, Emile Berliner, who was also improving the phonograph, developed a more sensitive transmitter.[20]

Western Union executives came to a different and ultimately short–sighted conclusion when a Bell partner offered to sell the Bell Telephone

Telephones are rented only to persons of good breeding and refinement. A householder becomes morally responsible for its proper use by all members of his family. There is nothing to be feared from your conversation being overheard. Our subscribers are too well bred to listen to other people's business.[19]

— EARLY TELEPHONE
ADVERTISEMENT

Company to them for $100,000. Western Union turned down the offer, but in 1878 Western Union decided to compete in the telephone business itself using a receiver designed by Gray and a transmitter designed by Thomas Edison, both superior to Bell instruments. Western Union had the additional advantage of thousands of miles of telegraph wire already strung along poles.

The newly formed National Bell Telephone Company sued Western Union over patent infringement, and won. Western Union gave up its telephone business. National Bell became American Bell and later the American Telephone and Telegraph Company, with the goal of establishing phone service around the world. By the end of the century, upon the expiration of the first Bell patent, a number of entrepreneurs went into the telephone business. Subscribers frequently had to sign up for both Bell and a competing service. The Bell company expanded to create a phone equipment manufacturing company, Western Electric, and a research unit that would become Bell Laboratories. In the future, Bell Labs would be the source of many communications ideas and inventions, including information theory, motion picture sound, transistors, laser beams, optical fibers, the communications satellite, and advances in computers and television.

EXCHANGES, NUMBERS

In 1878, the first commercial telephone exchange was opened in New Haven, Connecticut, with a switchboard of eight lines and twenty–one telephones. A year later saw the introduction of telephone numbers in place of a subscriber asking the operator to place a call based on the operator recognizing a name. That reportedly came about during a measles epidemic when a physician in Lowell, Massachusetts, feared that if the city's four trained operators came down with the illness, inexperienced substitute operators would throw the phone system into disarray without the simpler use of numbers instead of names. Lowell telephone managers were concerned that the subscribers might bridle at being assigned numbers, but the common sense of the numbering operation prevailed.

All this occurred before the automatic dial telephone invented by Almon Strowger came into use. A Kansas City undertaker, Strowger believed that another undertaker had bribed a telephone operator to tell callers that Strowger's line was busy. To protect his business, he invented the forerunners of the dial telephone and the automatic telephone exchange.

The need for several telephones in one location led to the private switchboard, called a Private Branch Exchange, or PBX. Although many are still in use, they have been replaced at large companies by a "local area network," or LAN, to link their telephone systems and computers.

The telephone was one of those communication technologies, like magazines and the postal service prior to the postage stamp, that some wealthy subscribers regarded as a status symbol not to be shared by the lower classes. Snobbish objection was expressed to any widening of access to the Bell system by such devices as coin–operated public telephones or telephone directories available to the general public. One Washington, D.C. hotel proprietor had to go to court to keep his service after he allowed guests to use the phone in the lobby. In Leicester, England, a subscriber was criticized for calling the fire brigade about a fire that was not on his property; it took a ruling from the postmaster general to establish that a telephone could be employed in the event of fires and riots.[22] In time, as telephones became as common in homes as the refrigerator that replaced the icebox, the telephone took on an egalitarian hue.

Under the leadership of Theodore Vail, a distant relative of Alfred Vail, Morse's assistant in inventing the telegraph, AT&T grew to be a communications giant, standardizing everything possible, even the shape of the black — only black — telephone in every office and home. AT&T bought up all the small telephone companies it could. AT&T's control of the industry was absolute until government rulings during the late twentieth century forced division and diversity.

The original telephone operators, teenage boys, who did well as telegraph messengers, proved too rowdy in the confined space of a telephone switchboard room. But who could take their place? It represented a significant social change to replace them with young women, because in starchy Victorian times, it was unusual and a bit daring for a young woman to take employment outside the home and thereby jeopardize her marriage prospects. Nevertheless, the chance to get out of the house and earn money of her own to spend as she pleased won out, never mind that the pay packet was light and the headsets weighed as much as six pounds. Telephone engineers discovered that the frequency range of a typical woman's voice more closely matched the early frequency transmission band than a man's voice did, so women speaking on the phone were easier to understand.

Telephone operators were part of the social revolution that allowed women to take employment outside the home. Others were hired as store clerks, typists, and, thanks to stories about Florence Nightingale and Clara Barton, as nurses. Middle–class subscribers regarded telephone operators — "hello girls" — as an extension of household servants. On the other hand, the Chicago Telephone Company found it necessary to instruct operators to query, "Number, please," instead of saying "Hello" or even "What do you want?"[23]

**NOT FOR THE
LOWER CLASSES?**

It is conceivable that cables of telephone wires could be laid under ground or suspended overhead, communicating by branch wires with private dwellings, country houses, shops, manufacturers, etc., uniting them through the main cable with a central office where the wires could be connected as desired, establishing direct communication between any two places in the city. Not only so, but I believe that in the future, wires will unite the head offices of the Telephone Company in different cities, and a man in one part of the country may communicate by word of mouth with another in a distant place.[21]

— ALEXANDER
GRAHAM BELL

"Before the great switchboard the girls seem like weavers at some gigantic loom, the numerous cords crossing and recrossing as if in the execution of some wondrous fabric. Indeed, a wondrous fabric of speech is here woven into the record of each day."[24]

— A VISITOR TO A
TELEPHONE EXCHANGE

Bell's dream of a nationwide and even an international service was not fully realized until technology caught up with these visions. M.I. Pupin's invention in 1900 of the loading coil, Lee de Forest's invention in 1906 of the three–element vacuum tube, and H.D. Arnold's vacuum tube amplifier in 1914 added clarity to phone calls and changed a local service into an operation that could comfortably replace the dots and dashes of the telegraph with the human voice. In 1915, AT&T had a transcontinental line running from New York to San Francisco. That year also saw successful testing of the wireless telephone, a boon to the U.S. Navy; it had been trying for years to improve military communication. The government took over all telephone and radio service for a brief time during World War I.

A few years later, AT&T began laying deep sea cable and providing trans–oceanic radio phone service. Radiotelephony between the New York and London financial centers started in 1927 during the boom of the Roaring Twenties.[25] It was extended to other large European cities and to South America. In 1947, the transistor, an invention out of the Bell Telephone Laboratories, replaced the vacuum tube. Microchips would follow. A transatlantic telephone cable was laid in 1956. High speed computer data phone service followed. A fiber optic cable link between California and Japan was laid in 1989. Meanwhile, communication satellites able to carry thousands of calls simultaneously were placed in orbit. How a phone call or an email message reaches its destination is no longer of concern except to engineers. The remark, "You sound as if you are next door," can be heard halfway around the world.

MCI RULING

The 1956 Supreme Court Hush–a–Phone decision opened the telephone network to non–Bell equipment. Further changes came with the Supreme Court's MCI ruling that opened up the long distance market, and the breakup in 1983 of AT&T into seven regional operating companies. Small companies bought line capacity wholesale, then retailed it through telephone cards and special phone numbers. The days of POTS (Plain Old Telephone Service) disappeared as the public snapped up their own telephones in colors and shapes far removed from the AT&T black phone.

Improvements in voice communication were joined by improvements in sending *data* anywhere in the world, from the printing telegraph to the teletypewriter to the teletype to the digital computer data stream, all used by governments, by global business, and by wire news services. In addition to text, images have been transformed into digital data streams that flow effortlessly along telephone pathways to be reconstructed as still and motion pictures.

Thousands of inventions have improved the telephone system. Among them have been the introduction in 1963 of the Touch Tone, the coaxial cable, the means to transmit computer data, the conversion from analog to digital signals to improve clarity, microwave, satellite communication, and fiber optics. Integrated Services Digital Network (ISDN), a technology of the '90s, converted analog to digital signals for more efficient transmission of telephone calls, fax, computer, and video. With Digital Subscriber Line (DSL) technology, the skinny telephone line converts its capacity to broadband and can transmit a movie.

These changes and many, many more tumble out of a hundred locations around the world. They help to change that world into what Thomas Friedman has labeled a "flat Earth" that is now in the process of restructuring societies and realigning the international economic and power structures. The telephone network with a fiber–optic "backbone" is an essential element of our flat Earth.

However, progress is not always positive, and certainly the telephone has not always been employed to benefit the social order. *Telemarketing*, the organized selling by telephone, is a case in point. Telemarketers buzz in, especially at dinner time. In some cases their "boiler rooms" are located as far away from the United States as India, whose native English speakers are trained to use American accents and to become familiar with American sports news. In the U.S. their unwanted presence was curtailed by legislation in 2003. Adding to a general sense of social disorder is pornography in the form of "adult" lines for which per–minute fees are levied. On the other hand, such features as unlisted numbers Caller ID, anonymous call rejection, voice messaging, and the answering machine, have given the subscriber at least a measure of control over unwanted intrusions.

Well before a point–to–point Morse Code radio business operation changed into a mass communication voice and music business, there was *wired broadcasting*. Several European capitals had a service that allowed customers, for a fee, to listen to operas, plays, and concerts picked up by microphones in theaters and fed along telephone wires to earphones. In Buckingham Palace Queen Victoria could hear the opera coming from Covent Garden or the Royal Theater in Drury Lane, while in Paris the Theatrophone Company offered coin–operated headsets at holiday resorts. Several American cities had church services available. One Canadian tavern owner found a judge willing to set a microphone on his bench during a murder trial; a wire carried the testimony to customers who could listen in on one of twenty earphones at twenty–five cents an hour.

The best known wired broadcasting service was the Telefon Hirmondo in Budapest put together by a Hungarian engineer who once worked at an Edison lab. Thousands of subscribers listened on earphones. The service, published in a printed schedule of programs, began in 1893 and

And the lever that is enabling individuals and groups to go global so easily and so seamlessly is not horsepower, and not hardware, but software — all sorts of new applications — in conjunction with the creation of a global fiber–optic network that has made us all next–door neighbors. Individuals must, and can, now ask, Where do I fit into the global competition and opportunities of the day, and how can I, on my own, collaborate with others globally?[26]

— THOMAS FRIEDMAN

WIRED BROADCASTING

continued until radio broadcasting replaced it. It was heard not only in the homes of the well–to–do, but also in hotels, hospitals, restaurants, and dentists' waiting rooms. Programs included music, a calendar of events around Budapest, a children's concert on Thursday evenings, and even commercials, all presented a full generation before regular programming by radio.[27] Telefon Hirmondo had tapped into people's desire for information and entertainment on a regular basis, piped into their homes and public spaces. That desire would be more fully met when technology came along in the form of radio broadcasting, and all the entertainment media that followed.

As for wired broadcasting, it continued in countries ruled by dictators. Radios consisting of one preset station blaring from atop a pole in a village square or on a train to a captive audience, with no competitive broadcasts, was perfect.

FACSIMILE

Because so many technologies have improved the way a message is sent, the place of facsimile in communication history can easily be overlooked. The best argument that *facsimile* (from the Latin "to make similar") has embedded itself in our lives is in the use of the word as a noun, *facsimile*, that was shortened into *fax*, referring either to the machine or its output; then it became an adjective *fax* ("a fax message") and a verb ("Fax it to me." or "How about faxing it?") with a past tense ("I just faxed it to you."). The word *telephone* has the same variations.

Facsimile breaks a bit–mapped image into a pattern of dots for transmission over the telephone network. The message can be on paper or in a computer file, but fax does not require a computer. A fax message carries graphics as easily as text, which was wonderful news for Chinese and Japanese users, whose written languages rely on complex ideographs. The Japanese, the largest manufacturers of fax machines, have also been its best customers.

SENDING PHOTOGRAPHS

In 1842, with excitement about the Wheatstone–Cooke telegraph in the air, Scottish inventor Alexander Bain sent a signal over an electric wire that transmitted a letter of the alphabet and recorded it on a sheet of paper. Next, F.C. Bakewell in London invented a copying telegraph that could send handwriting and sketches over a wire. An Italian inventor, the Abbe Jean Caselli, in 1865 sent a photograph over a wire, recording it on treated paper. The American inventor Elisha Gray, who came within a few hours of patenting an invention for the telephone before Alexander Graham Bell patented it, also invented a device to record train reservations, a facsimile–like system that sent handwriting over telegraph lines.

The first photoelectric scanner was invented in 1902, just before Lee deForest's vacuum tube began electronics. By 1934, the Associated

Press was using photoelectric scanners to transmit news photographs to newspapers. They were called wirephotos. AT&T and RCA figured out how to send photographs along radio beams. The reading public quickly grew accustomed to seeing news photographs next to news stories that they read with their morning coffee.

One recent experiment that did not prove a financial success was the facsimile newspaper. The idea was to send it directly to homes and businesses. The costly machines were slow and the output was poor.[28] However, there was a demand for the service itself. It is now met by CNN and hundreds of other news outlets on the Internet.

The first commercial facsimile machine, the Telecopier, introduced by Xerox in 1966 and manufactured by Magnavox, produced poor quality faxes, but replaced many telex machines, an electric typewriter hooked to a telephone. Because a facsimile machine must be connected to a telephone line, fax growth would not have been possible without the Supreme Court's Carterphone Decision in 1968 that allowed customers to connect non–Western Electric devices to the Bell System. Japanese fax machines took over in 1984, and have not let go of the dominant market share. The market for facsimile machines has been huge, first in business offices, then in homes, a pattern begun by the telephone and continued by video recorders, computers, copiers, and other communication devices.

Time–conscious newspapers and news magazines seeking to reach a national and even an international readership combined a facsimile service with a satellite hookup that sped pages from the head editorial offices to regional printing plants, where the pages were printed for same–day or next–day delivery. To cite just two other changes in communication due to facsimile, maps go from the U.S. National Weather Service to television stations, and layouts go to clients from advertising agencies. The dark side is junk fax that uses the machine's paper to send unwanted ads, including ads for the fax paper that the ads are using up!

Today, sending pictures through telephone equipment means much more than facsimile. It can mean Internet downloads. It is now a simple matter for a young father to point a camera phone at a brand new baby, snap a picture, and instantly email it to relatives. Or for a mother to send a child's picture to a soldier father halfway around the world. And when soldiers and their families see each other by webcam during their conversations, it is easy to forget the years of efforts, not all successful, to send pictures by phone.

The Bell Laboratories in 1924 experimentally sent pictures over telephone wires. Public excitement initially greeted the Picturephone at the

1964 World's Fair, but the reception was fuzzy, and it was a commercial failure. The service was continued at Disneyland and world's fairs, but only as a peek into the future. High operating costs, poor pictures, and doubts about who would want to see or be seen by someone on the telephone kept it from public acceptance. With improved technology and lower transmission costs it returned as video teleconferencing. As a business tool, the teleconference allowed face–to–face communication without the trouble and expense of travel.[29]

The cell phone has its own history. The walkie–talkie hand–held, two–way radio transceiver, designed for military use, saw extensive service during World War II. After the war it became a tool for police, emergency crews, and industrial workers. Low–powered versions were sold as toys.

Mobile radio systems connected to the telephone network, known as radiophones, started in Sweden after World War II, expanded to the United States, and gradually shifted from calls placed through an operator to direct dial. Among the users were police cars, fire trucks, and television crews who raced to where the police and firemen were headed.

CELL PHONES

The cellular telephone, a version of two–way radio, was invented in 1973 by Motorola's Martin Cooper. Calls are transferred from base station to base station as a user travels, for a cell phone is a kind of two–way radio. Engineers looking at mobile car service realized that a network of small cells in a city could sharply increase the number of mobile phones that could be served. Cells are low–powered receiver–transmitters scattered throughout cities, connected to the telephone system through switching centers. AT&T started testing cell phone service in Chicago in 1978, but a full system had to await FCC approval. A year later the first cell phones went into cars. Portable fax machines with attached acoustic couplers could be dialed into the cellular network.

Cell phones found a ready market in Japan, where early adopters of communication gear thrive and where much of the technology emerges. By 1979 the Japanese had the first cell phone network running. The FCC did not authorize full commercial cell phone service in the United States until 1982.

BRAIN CANCER?

As the equipment shrank with every new model, a rumor, started in 1993, flew that, by sending radio waves into and out of devices pressed against the ear, cell phones were causing brain cancer. The accusation was never either confirmed or fully refuted, but sales have continued to soar. The handy little units soon offered email text messaging, access to the Internet, and other computer functions. Cell phones quickly became the cool must-have ornament of well–off teenagers. Carried around all day, they were bound to be identified as "statements" of their owners. Manufacturers, quick to seize upon this vanity, turned them out in a variety of styles. An example, a Samsung model for women, featured rich colors, a ring of synthetic diamonds, a biorhythm calculator, a calorie counter, and a calendar to track menstrual cycles. The wristwatch telephone of the Dick Tracy comic strip decades ago, was almost at hand.

New products have continued to tumble out. In 2007 the iPhone created excitement with a cell phone that combined with an iPod music player, email, Web access, and clever touch-screen features. The telephone, the camera, and wireless technology came together in the camera phone, a pocket digital cellular phone that took and emailed pictures or posted them on a website. This Japanese invention reached the Western market in 2002.

THE CAMERA PHONE

What the camera phone snaps and sends in moments may be priceless to a soldier or traveler. It can also generate anger. A camera phone used to take unapproved photos of the hanging of Saddam Hussein, and transmitted on the Internet, loosed a furious response by Sunni Arabs. The small, unobtrusive digital cell phones have been used surreptitiously and inappropriately to take and send pictures of celebrities and unaware women. School administrators have raised concerns that they could be employed to cheat on tests. Some American schools and the nation of Saudi Arabia responded by banning camera phones altogether.

On the other hand, the little devices have created millions of potential instant citizen photojournalists around the world, with the rare opportunity to record history, and some encouragement from established media willing to buy newsworthy photographs. Women have used their camera phones to take pictures of strangers who have harassed them, then posted the pictures on websites. It was also a camera phone in the hands of an audience member that captured the racist comments of actor Michael Richards in 2006, followed by postings to websites, damaging his career.

Cell phone technology has made life freer for many people, particularly teenagers who get, from their parents or themselves, greater permission to stay out later because they now have a lifeline for emergencies. It hardly seems to matter that drivers and pedestrians on cell phones intent on their distant communications are less aware of their surroundings than is safe. A survey of American roads in 2006 reported that one driver in ten used a cell phone daily. At the same time, the cell phone has made life easier for organizers of political demonstrations, who can use the cells, the BlackBerries, and the Internet to whistle up an angry crowd in short order.

CHANGING LIFESTYLES

ALWAYS "HOME"

The cell phone has altered the very nature of the telephone call. Before the cell phone and its predecessor mobile phones, a telephone call was directed toward a phone at a fixed location where, the caller hoped, a specific person would be present. A daughter phoning her mother over a "landline," for example, is actually calling her mother's telephone in the expectation that her mother will be nearby. With an active cell phone in her handbag, her mother will always be nearby, always "home."

Cell phone users are likely to keep their phones within reach all day and all night, as much a part of themselves as their shoes. Some people relish being connected 24/7, but not everyone does. For the employee whose boss wants to reach him at any time, there is no certain time off. The cell phone has been compared to a slave bracelet and the ringing to a dog whistle. Calls are routinely received or initiated on freeways, in restaurants, cinemas, public rest rooms, on buses, even on skateboards. A ringing backpack on campus is not unusual. In an eyeblink of history, the cell phone has gone from novelty to necessity. For drivers, it has moved into the danger zone.

The United States is not in the wireless forefront. Americans have been slower than others to "cut the cord." Look to Europe and East Asia for that. In many of their cities young people were quick to abandon fixed–lines for mobility in phone calls, chat lines, messaging, and email. Europe and Asia are far ahead of the United States in cell phone use for two reasons. First, most cell phone systems were begun by a government–owned and subsidized telephone monopoly that could set standards and run matters as they wished. That could save years of regulatory hearings and competitive wrangling. Second, developing countries had a relatively small — even meager — telephone infrastructure in place, coupled with a huge backlog of requests for telephones. A wait of ten years for a telephone was not unheard of. The market for the cell phone alternative was ready and waiting. In poverty–stricken Cambodia, nine of ten phones are cell phones.[30] The low cost of wireless technology was a dream come true, and it has spread like a gasoline fire.

"NEGROPONTE FLIP"

Nicholas Negroponte, director of the Massachusetts Institute of Technology's Media Lab, predicted in the mid–nineties that media depending on hard wires would become wireless. He also predicted that wireless media would be wired. Negroponte argued that it was a historical accident that simple telephone calls were wired while more complex television signals went wireless. The "Negroponte Flip" is taking form today. Owners of wired telephones are going wireless. Over–the–air radio and television are being cabled.

WI-FI

Radio and television broadcasts have long been dependent on a limited frequency spectrum, first in the AM band and then extending upward to the FM band. The arrival of cable has multiplied the available channels, no longer spectrum dependent. Digitizing the radio and television signals further increases their number. The technology, if not yet the economics, of the so–called 500–channel universe has arrived. At the same time, the home telephone line is yielding to the cell phone. In addition, the wired computer and its wired modem are giving way to the wireless laptop and its wi–fi (wireless fidelity) path to the Internet. Entire cities are turning themselves into wi–fi hot spots to give their residents broadband access.

Negroponte pinpointed three causes, over little more than a generation, for the wire–wireless flip. First, in the 1970s, digital technology gave us the precise transmission lacking in analog technology, allowing such developments as multimedia. Second, packet switching gave us 24/7 asynchronous connections that brought email and faster data transmission. Third, mobile communication has stretched the "Information Highway" to every corner of the globe.

Meanwhile, technology is improving that can chop voice traffic into digital bits and ship it around the world via the Internet the way that email travels. Cheap Internet telephony, known as VOIP (Voice Over Internet Protocol), is already available with reasonable voice quality from Skype and competitors like Google Talk and iChat. Inventive and admittedly brash users from non–English speaking countries like China are using the VOIP service to contact VOIP users in English–speaking countries at random just to practice their English skills; it is an audio version of finding a pen pal.

JAPAN LEADS

As it has often done with telecommunications in recent decades, Japan has led in using the Internet for voice calling. But cell phones now do more. In a McDonald's in Japan, customers point their cell phones at the wrapping around their cheeseburgers to get nutrition data. They point their phones at a certain magazine to get insurance quotes. If, on the way to the airport, they pass a billboard advertising a movie, pointing their cell phone downloads a trailer. At the airport, pointing their handy cell phone substitutes for a ticket. In short, microchips have been chatting with microchips.

FINLAND FLIPS

Italy's Telecom Italia rebuilt its network around Internet equipment. In Finland, a long–time leader in cell phone technology and manufacture, the national telephone company, TeliaSonera, ran radio and newspaper ads in 2002 urging customers to give up their wired telephones for the mobile cell phone. What will happen to the 3.2 million copper lines that are the "last mile" to Finland's homes and businesses? They will do the "Negroponte flip" and be used for broadband; TeliaSonera operates DSL connections to the Internet, which can make better use of those copper wires.

In country after country, new companies are offering alternate communication services. Established companies, of course, are not accepting these losses quietly but are adapting new technologies themselves. It is much cheaper to set up a cell phone network than to erect telephone poles. More than half of all telephones in the world today are cell phones. That percentage is rising rapidly.

FLASH MOBS

We live in an era of "flash mobs." The French urban riots of 2006 were strung together by cell phones, texting, and the Internet. The combination of organization and street technology proved so efficient that the French government and police hardly knew what hit them or how to stop it, although by that time they should have known.

During the global disputes about the Iraq War that started in 2003, armies of antiwar protesters were summoned to the streets of Western capitals by email and cell phone instant messaging. One day, at a command, 400,000 American antiwar protesters created a "virtual demonstration" by tying up the White House and Congressional switchboards with emails, telephone calls, and faxes. In Rio de Janeiro, on the same day, an imprisoned Brazilian druglord used a smuggled cell phone to organize bombings, bus burnings, and street riots.

The flash mobs' tool of choice is the cell phone. The transmission of brief text messages, known as "texting," has been especially popular among the youth of developing countries, who are now always connected. Cell phone use has spread quickly in developing countries. A coded message of a few words can send cell phone owners not only to a political protest but also to chase down a celebrity discovered shopping. In Nigeria, texting summoned rioters to the Miss World contest and shut it down. Hundreds were killed. Other examples of the use of communication devices to stir up feelings are not hard to find. Even in rural China, unrest of peasants has been growing despite efforts to silence it.

The telephone has had an egalitarian effect on its users in their ability to communicate, but today — despite cell phone growth — most of the world's six billion people still have no phone. In Bangladesh, a micro–finance program has allowed "telephone ladies" to go into business by purchasing solar–powered cell phones for villages without electricity; they sell phone time to other villagers. There is now at least one telephone, plus radio and television sets, in most of the 68,000 villages of Bangladesh.[32] A researcher in India estimated that a single new phone line in a developing country adds an average of $3,700 to its national wealth.

When full mobile satellite service is realized, a portable phone call could be placed between any two spots on Earth. The ultimate goal is to allow any two people anywhere with cell phones to talk to one another

The current crop of Communist leaders is aware that rural unrest could spark political mayhem, especially when cell phones and the Internet can connect citizens with the click of a button.[31]

— TIME REPORT ON RURAL CHINA

with the clarity that attends digital communication. With the camera phone rapidly being diffused into society, those conversations across continents might someday be routinely accompanied by letting the people who are speaking look at each other, and also see what the other is seeing. When that happens, humankind will have taken another step in the ongoing effort to shrink the globe.

THE WISH TO SEND messages quickly at a distance has ancient roots, but before the telegraph every communication device had limited value. The telegraph allowed people for the first time to communicate instantly with each other beyond the reach of a human voice. The last telegraph pole became the new information frontier. By giving businesses the ability to learn what customers wanted to buy, the telegraph helped to reduce the prices of goods and to expand the delivery of perishable foods. It made the railroads safer.

CONCLUSION

The telegraph changed much of the nature of news. News organizations like the Associated Press were formed, dependent upon telegraph dispatches. News writing was altered to reflect the realities of telegraph transmission. Objective reporting took hold. Newspaper success was influenced by access to telegraph reports.

Like so many communication technologies, the telegraph was expected, at least in some quarters, to change the world by bringing understanding to all mankind of a shared humanity, and world peace. It did, and it did not. The telegraph is part of what has demonstrably changed the world. The telephone, the phonograph, the radio, television, and the Internet followed. The telegraph helped to connect the scattered communities of the vast American nation. In this way, the telegraph helped to unite the United States. However, the hope that the telegraph would bring world peace was never realized. World peace is still out there somewhere.

The telephone went beyond the telegraph in its effects. It changed the pattern of daily life. Before its invention, emergency access, such as to the fire or police departments, was slow and often too late. The telephone went much further than the telegraph in connecting people to each other. By doing so it has made life safer and more pleasant. It has erased some of the loneliness of living remotely from other people and some of the sadness of being far from loved ones, yet it also allows people to erect a wall of separation from others if that is their wish. Like most mediated communication, a degree of isolation accompanies the telephone, the opposite of the advertising claim, "Reach out and touch someone."

The arrival of the telephone in the nineteenth century home brought connection to the outside, but it did so at the expense of the domestic tranquility of the pre–telephone home. Something in life was lost that

The BlackBerry device alone makes it seem as though we're living in a '50s futuristic film. The paradox is that all this nominal communication has led to enormous isolation, with people hunched over their handhelds or staring into the screen of the computer. There is the illusion of keeping in touch, but always at arm's length.

Sometimes it seems that what people want most is the one thing they no longer have: human contact.[33]

— ANNA QUINDLEN

had value, or else it would not have been established in the first place. There was also a thinning of the wall of class separation. Some effort was made to restrict its use to those who could afford to rent a telephone. Just as with postal reform, a split between haves and have–nots manifested itself.

Before the telephone, getting married or finding a job did not often mean leaving the area where you grew up, partly because such a departure might be as complete as a death. Today, with phone calls, emails, total messaging, and blogs, physical separation is no longer complete separation, and therefore is apt to be taken without trembling.

Modern telephone service that we now take for granted was created step by step through dozens of inventions, experiments, and business decisions. One of the more interesting, wired broadcasting in Budapest, was a forerunner of radio broadcasting and television cable service. Another was facsimile, particularly sending photographs line by line over a telephone connection.

The cellular telephone industry grew out of World War II walkie–talkies and postwar mobile radio. Cell phones and camera phones have had an astonishing degree of public acceptance, but they have also had social problems, such as accidents caused by inattentive drivers. Nor do all owners of cell phones like being permanently connected to their jobs.

Among the notable changes being brought about by cell phones has been the "flash mobs" that can be quickly assembled, particularly by the urban young and poor. The telephone has had an egalitarian effect on its users in their ability to communicate.

The telephone is such a part of our lives that we use it when we have no need to, and answer a ring even when it intrudes on what is immediately going on around us, including matters of some importance.

6 PHOTOGRAPHY: CAPTURING THE EYE

PHOTOGRAPHS DO MANY THINGS for each of us. They preserve the memories of what matters to us, capturing time and affirming our past. As we see our youth, they remind us of our mortality. We put them on our walls and on our furniture. Fleeing a burning house, we may leave everything but a photo album. Our wallets hold the thumbworn images of loved ones, the edges cracked from handling. A wedding seems incomplete without new photographs, or a memorial service without old photographs. No significant occasion in life is without a camera to record it. How many snapshots have been taken of children and picnics, of dogs and cats? Of all the effects that photography has had on civilization, this personal effect may be the greatest.

The art and the science of photography bring us the startling scene on the newspaper front page, on the magazine cover. As a tool of journalism, photographs accomplish what words alone cannot. The eyes of starving African children with flies hovering at their edges have launched cargo planes. The pained eyes of brutalized women in Rwanda, Bosnia, and Darfur have shaken Western nations into at least belated action. The Abu Ghraib prison photos have embarrassed a nation that prided itself on being above such acts, and stirred hostility around the world. The noted photographer Gordon Parks said such photographs change those who see them.

> …one should not grow tired of witnessing these things — corpses stacked, awaiting the fire of a Holocaust oven; two young black lynch victims, dead before a cheerful white mob; a Viet Cong guerilla, his eyes tightly shut, grimacing as a policeman fires a bullet into his head — for that is the photographer's charge to us, that we never forget. Recalling such shocking tragedies makes our thoughts burn as if doused with oil, and we no longer walk around forgetful. We remember the black hours with fury and shame, and we are changed. The cameras keep watch as mankind goes on filling the universe with its behavior, and they change us.[1]

There is much, much more. The eyes of baby harp seals just before the fur hunter's club crashed down led to a limit on the slaughter, just one of many examples of how photographs of animals being killed or abused has generated anger, humiliation, and change. Yet, on the next page, the advertising photograph and the fashion photograph generate quite opposite emotions.

…at some point in the second half of the twentieth century — for perhaps the first time in human history — it began to seem as if images would gain the upper hand on words.[2]

—MITCHELL STEPHENS

Every branch of science has been enriched by photography, from electron microscope photos of the almost invisible world around us and even within us to men walking on the moon. What is there that has not been seen through a lens and captured?

Still photography is less than two centuries old, and motion photography a little more than a century old, but the technology of photography has ancient roots. Imagine a sunny street in an old city, a house with a dark room, and a tiny hole in the wall facing the street. If you sit inside the room and look at the wall opposite the hole, you might see an image of people walking by upside down. Because the world is full of dark rooms with holes in the walls, this phenomenon has been known for centuries. Aristotle mentioned it in the fourth century B.C.E. The Arab scholar Alhazen described it at some length in the eleventh century. Later, so did Leonardo da Vinci.

During the sixteenth century in Italy, the *camera obscura* — still a room — aided drafting and painting. The name comes from the Latin "camera" ("room") and "obscura" ("dark"). To sharpen the image, artists placed a lens over the pinhole. To preserve the image, they traced it onto a sheet of paper.

The problem with a room in a house is that you can see only what is opposite the room, but if the room were portable, you could take it to any location. By the seventeenth century portable rooms were built, usually a kind of tent. When the users — mostly painters and landscape architects — realized that they did not actually have to stand inside the room to get their image, the camera obscura shrank to a box carried under the arm, a herald of our own cameras.[3] Each had a peephole, a lens and sometimes a mirror, plus a pane of glass on which a thin sheet of paper could rest for tracing an image. An even smaller portable device, the *camera lucida*, consisted of a glass prism suspended by a brass rod over a piece of paper. Looking through the prism, the artist traced an image. No other way existed to save an image.

THE SECRET IS LIGHT

Chemical discoveries eventually provided the way. For thousands of years it has been known that colors change outdoors, such as colored cloth fading in the sunshine. It was also known that certain salts of silver darkened in the open air, but it was not known if this was due to the air itself or the heat of the sun. German scientist Johann Schulze in 1727 noticed that a bottle filled with a silver compound turned violet black on the side that was accidentally exposed to sunshine; experiments confirmed that *light* was responsible.

Thomas Wedgewood, of the family of pottery makers, produced photographic contact prints by placing a tree leaf against chemically treated paper, which he then exposed to light. To show his photographs to visitors he was compelled to display them for moments by dim candlelight before they blackened.

In 1827, one century after Schulze's publication of his discovery, and following a decade of experimentation, French inventor Joseph Niépce used a camera obscura to produce what until recently was considered the world's first true photograph, the courtyard outside his window. In 2002, the French National Library paid about $500,000 for a photograph believed taken a year earlier than Niépce's courtyard view, a photo of a Dutch engraving showing a man leading a horse. The photographer is unknown.

Niépce became partners with Louis Daguerre, a painter and theatrical producer, who was also trying to capture a camera image. After Niépce's death, Daguerre improved the process, and in 1837 he produced a photograph of surprising quality on a copper plate coated with silver and exposed to iodine fumes. Daguerre named his result after himself, a daguerreotype. The exposed plate was the final picture; there was no negative. In 1839 he delivered an important paper to France's Royal Society describing his process. Why a century had gone by between Schulze's discovery and the experiments of Niépce and Daguerre and even more centuries since the camera obscura was designed has been described as one of the mysteries of history.[4]

While Daguerre was experimenting in France, amateur English scientist William Fox Talbot, frustrated by the difficulties of drawing with the camera lucida, achieved some success in taking contact photographs by laying such objects as a leaf, a feather, and a piece of lace directly on sheets of translucent paper that had been treated with silver chloride. This method created a negative image, the dark and light areas reversed. The translucent paper allowed Fox Talbot to make any number of contact positives, something that Daguerre could not do.

The problem of the darkening image was solved in 1839 with sodium thiosulfate (still used today, commonly called "hypo") followed by washing with water. Its discoverer, Sir John Herschel, a well–known English scientist and a friend of Fox Talbot, also devised the words "photography" to replace Fox Talbot's phrase "photogenic drawing," and "positive" and "negative" to replace the terms "reversed copy" and "re–reversed copy."

Fox Talbot was soon taking pictures of buildings, rooftops, and chimneys, choices of subject dictated by the need for a great deal of light and immovable objects. Only after years of chemical and optical improvements in photography was he able to take pictures of people, whom he posed stiffly with orders not to move because his pictures required long exposure.

Both Daguerre, the French artist, and Fox Talbot, the wealthy English botanist, had been working independently and unknown to each other, yet they were producing similar pictures with similar chemicals and equipment. One difference was that the quality of Daguerre's work was far superior. Another was that Fox Talbot could make copies from his negatives.

A photography hobby spread across Europe and into North America as the technology improved. The daguerreotype process received an enthusiastic welcome in the United States even though the nation was beginning one of its economic depressions just as photography was being introduced in Paris in 1839. The early 1850s produced three million prints each year.

POSING STIFFLY

Smaller cameras reduced the size of photographic plates that were also made more light sensitive, reducing the time that a subject would have to sit with a fixed expression. With the aid of a portrait lens the time needed to pose dropped to a manageable fifteen to thirty seconds. That still required subjects to sit still, which explains the stiff expressions on the faces staring at us in old photographs. Yet the subject eagerly posed, aided by iron supporting stands that stiffened the spine and held the head in place.

Photographs could be taken not only outdoors in the sunlight but also in the new portrait studios by photographers known as daguerreotypists, whose brisk trade took business away from portrait painters such as the artist Samuel Morse, one of the earliest American experimenters in daguerreotype photography, who would soon become famous for a different means of communication.

Anyone who knows what the worth of family affection is among the lower classes, and who has seen the array of little portraits stuck over a labourer's fireplace ...the boy that has 'gone to Canada,' the 'girl out at service,' the little one with the golden hair that sleeps under the daisies, the old grandfather in the country — will perhaps feel with me that... the sixpenny photograph is doing more for the poor than all the philanthropists in the world.[5]

— AN OBSERVER
OF THE DAY

By the 1850s in the United States, the cost of a photograph had dropped enough to make it available to most Americans. Miniature portrait paintings were available only to those wealthy enough to afford them. But, as photographs, they became common to middle class families by the mid–nineteenth century. That the upper crust of society disdained the portrait photograph as vulgar and cheap was not unexpected.

Family pictures were popular, especially pictures of children, partly because of their high mortality rate, for many children died of epidemics like measles. One advertising line for postmortem photographs, based on an old saying, was: "Secure the shadow 'ere the substance fade." Photographers in the mid–nineteenth century advertised their readiness to take pictures of the dead in their coffins or, for a child, in a mother's lap. A photograph of the deceased would also be mounted in a headstone. They were called "memento mori" (reminder of mortality). We may consider the practice macabre, but in the nineteenth century, the practice held therapeutic value for the survivors.

The two known methods of taking photographs had severe limitations. *Daguerreotypes* were one–of–a–kind positives, usually on copper plates. They were fragile and had to be kept under glass. They were expensive. They were hard to copy and required a number of chemicals, including the dangerous mercury. The term "mad as a hatter," familiar to readers of *Alice in Wonderland*, could have been matched with "mad as a photographer," because mercury fumes affected the brain. The daguerreotype produced a sharper image and was better suited to portraiture than the *calotype*, which was Fox Talbot's improvement on his original grainy and blotchy paper prints. Unfortunately, the calotype prints faded in the light over time. Because daguerreotypes produced only positive prints, the prints were used as the source for engraving.

In 1851, Frederick Archer introduced wet–plate photography. Within a decade, daguerreotype and calotype methods were gone. Wet–plate provided greater sensitivity and a shorter exposure time, with multiple prints possible from one glass plate, but it was complicated and untidy. Because photographs had to be developed immediately or the emulsion would dry, chemicals had to be applied in fairly rapid succession in darkness.

WET–PLATE PHOTOGRAPHY

A photographer on the road carried a darkroom. For a negative, a glass plate was coated with collodion, a clear, thick, sticky liquid that had found an application as a surgical dressing. Then a layer of light sensitive silver iodide was applied before the plate was inserted into the camera. After exposure, the glass plate, still wet, was developed, fixed and washed on the spot before the negatives could be printed on paper. Photographers needed wagons to haul around hundreds of pounds of bottled chemicals, plus the glass plates, dishes, measures, funnels and a water pail, to say nothing of the heavy camera, lenses, and tripod.[6]

One version of wet–plate photography was the ambrotype, offered by photo studios. Ambrotypes lacked the brilliance of daguerreotypes, but they were cheap, easy to produce, and best of all, prepared while you wait.

If printed on iron sheets instead of paper, *tintypes* were sturdy enough to be mailed or carried in a shirt pocket, yet thin enough to cut with scissors to fit a brooch or locket. During the Civil War, soldiers mailed them to the families they left behind and received tintypes in return of parents, brothers, sisters, wives, and children. (They were shown in the film *Cold Mountain*.) Besides the familiar stiff portraits, photographers took pictures of groups in a variety of activities and settings, with their imagination limited only by the technology of the day. Many tintypes survive. So do mass–produced prints that were collected like modern–day baseball cards.

TINTYPES

Realizing that they had in their hands a new way to record life, travelers using the new wet–plate system could hardly wait to haul their heavy cameras and darkroom equipment to distant corners of the world. When they returned, their photographs were featured in popular lantern–slide shows.

In 1854, an album of photographs of ancient Egyptian monuments was published, actual prints sewn into books, the first time that people could see, let alone own, such images. The *printing* of photos on regular book pages along with text would have to wait until the art of *photoengraving* advanced sufficiently toward the end of the nineteenth century. After that, newspapers and magazines blossomed with photographs.

Roger Fenton traveled with fellow Englishman James Robertson and a darkroom in a covered wagon to the Crimean War. What Fenton saw appalled him, but he took no pictures of the horrors of war. Partly because he had been commissioned to shoot only portraits of officers and scenes of the Crimea, partly because collodion was a tricky chemical in the Crimea's summer heat, and partly because he was suffering from cholera and several broken ribs as a result of an accident, Fenton spent little film on unpleasantness. To sense what battlefield carnage was really like, civilians would have to wait for Mathew Brady and the American Civil War.

Felice Beato, an Italian, and Robertson recorded the aftermath of an uprising against the British in India. For the first time in history people safe at home saw a little of what went on in a war. Beato went to China to take pictures of the Opium Wars, then on to fascinating Japan, newly opened to the outside world.

A picture can win or lose a war.

— LINE FROM THE FILM *FLAGS OF OUR FATHERS*

The public would soon see the aftermath of American Civil War battles. A well–known New York portrait photographer, Mathew Brady, hired other photographers to join him at some risk. They traveled to the battlefields with their clumsy, clattering wagons. Before the Civil War ended, hundreds of photographers had followed Brady's lead to record the scars of battle. Brady himself nearly died at Bull Run. When Brady at a New York gallery displayed photos of the dead of Antietam, the *New York Times* commented:

If he has not brought bodies and laid them in our dooryards and among our streets, he has done something very like it.

By the end of the Civil War photographers had taken more than seven thousand pictures of battlefields and encampments, soldiers living and soldiers dead, officers and men, weapons and equipment. They revealed war stripped of glory — a brutal, wearying misery, no matter how noble its purpose. Studying pictures of how people walk, a physician designed artificial legs for maimed soldiers.

Photographs were a source of propaganda by the French government in the uprising of the Paris Commune in 1871 in opposition to the Franco–Prussian War. After soldiers killed an estimated 40,000 Communards, photographers were summoned to take pictures of the dead in the streets and the revolutionaries who were executed. One photographer did not stop there. He produced fakes to display what seemed to be atrocities committed by the revolutionaries. Truth and photography were now separated.

After the American Civil War, photographers headed West to continue what, in a few years, had evolved into a tradition of visual documentary. Lugging 300 to 400 pounds of wet–plate equipment and chemicals on the backs of mules, they left to posterity a permanent record of the American Indian, of great vistas without a trace of human habitation, of the coming of the railroads, of the miners, the settlers, and the cowboys. William Henry Jackson's photographs helped in the political effort to establish Yellowstone as the first national park. This may have been the first time in the United States that photography influenced political change. It would not be the last.

It had already happened in England. As well as the splendors of the Taj Mahal, photographers in distant climes captured ordinary life to give visual support to what would be called *ethnography*. The English traveler John Thomson recorded the life of the people he encountered in Asia. On returning to London he published a four–volume illustrated anthropology. While in London he continued his documentation by photographing the daily life of the London poor, publishing the results along with written text in 1877 as *Street Life in London*. In doing so, Thomson opened a new door for photography: social documentary.

To a comfortably wealthy, conservative Londoner, scenes of poverty in far–off China were quaint. Scenes at one's doorstep were something else again, especially if you were in a position to do something about it. Thomson usually photographed reasonably pleasant views in working class neighborhoods, but not always. An earlier photographer, Richard Beard, had taken daguerreotypes in London streets; none survive, but they were used for illustrations in a sociological study.[7] Eventually an embankment was built to prevent the Thames from periodically spilling over into the slums of London.

Journalists soon recognized photography as a means not only to present information but to stir emotion. Jacob Riis, a Danish immigrant hired as a New York City police reporter, was determined to reveal the humanity of the poor that the better–off ignored. One of the first journalists to recognize that photographs could help to bring about social change, Riis used both words and pictures to expose conditions in the slums. He went about his personal mission even when he panicked a roomful of

We learn that the group he photographed in front of a shop represent people who had been grievously affected by the flooding of the Thames in Lambeth. The shop's stock had been badly damaged, its owner's health ruined. Only the vigilance of the shop boy had enabled them to salvage something from the flooding…

The popularity of the book among the wealthy governing classes made such images and the stories behind them important politically. They played a part in getting better flood protection for the poor low–lying areas next to the river.[8]

— Peter Marshall

sleepers or actually set fire to himself and to a house by using flash powder, a recent invention that for the first time permitted photography in darkness. (The flashbulb would not be invented until 1925.)

Riis' books, *How the Other Half Lives and Children of the Poor*, became an important part of *muckraking*, dredging up awful conditions for the public gaze. Theodore Roosevelt coined the term "muckrakers," an insult that the objects of his derision wore as a badge of pride. The polite term today is "investigative journalist."

Among Riis' successors, sociologist Lewis Hine recorded the miserable lives of immigrants who were pouring out of Europe into Ellis Island. From there they went to fetid homes and sweatshops where they barely eked out enough to put bread on the table. Hine followed. He drew the attention of his contemporaries to their condition, and for the generations that followed, he built an unforgettable record of documentary photography.

Perhaps you are weary of child labor pictures. Well, so are the rest of us, but we propose to make you and the whole country so sick and tired of the whole business that when the time for action comes, child labor pictures will be records of the past.[10]

— LEWIS HINE

In 1908 the National Child Labor Committee hired Hine as an investigator. "I wanted to show the things that had to be corrected," he said, and focused especially on children sent to work in food processing plants, factories, and mines. He found them at every turn, but he had to disguise his picture taking and fact gathering to avoid beatings, or worse. He sometimes pretended to be a fire inspector. Hine showed his photos in public presentations as he carried his message about the need for child labor laws. He considered himself a social photographer.

Publication of his photos in magazines, books, slide shows for lectures, and traveling exhibits stirred efforts to pass child labor laws that took children out of the mines and factories, and into schools.[9]

During the Depression of the 1930s, the Resettlement Administration (the RA) was created as part of the New Deal to help small farmers. Crop failures were all too common, topsoil disappeared down rivers, the Dust Bowl drove families off the land that their families had plowed for generations, and banks foreclosed. The RA came to help with low–interest loans and land management guidance, but such government intrusion was resisted and damned as "socialism." To help argue its case, the RA turned to social documentary photography, with both still and motion pictures to show how bad things were and how government aid would make a difference. Dorothea Lange, Walker Evans, Carl Mydans, and Ben Shahn were among those whose photographs have endured through the decades. The most unforgettable of these is Dorothea Lange's 1936 photo of a migrant worker in a ragged dress, a thin woman sitting pensively as her two daughters hide their faces from the camera.

From the wellspring of feeling for the downtrodden and anger at social injustice sprang the social documentary motion picture, notably in Great Britain and the United States, but increasingly a rewarding expression throughout the world. The tradition continues today in both still and motion pictures with images of life on the streets of Baghdad, in the desert of Darfur in the Sudan, and in other pain–racked corners of the world.

Some documentary photographs found their way into picture magazines. The most outstanding, *Life*, was first published in 1936, but the picture press itself had started much earlier. In fact, it is just about as old as photography itself. The weekly *Illustrated London News* began to publish in 1842 with engravings, usually carved from daguerreotype photographs or artists' sketches into wooden blocks.

At first, engravers laid tissue paper over a photograph to trace the image, which they then transferred to a wooden block. Just before the Civil War, the engravers learned how to coat the surface of a wood block with light–sensitive silver nitrate. Placed in a camera pointed at a photograph, the wood block captured an image good enough to guide the engraver's knife.

PHOTOS IN NEWSPAPERS

Real publication of photographs would not be possible without a technology that could convert an ordinary photograph into a picture that could hold ink and be printed on the same page as type. *Photoengraving* started in England, but results were poor until Frederick Ives at Cornell University created a *halftone* process that broke a photograph into tiny dots that could pick up ink, giving the appearance of a continuous tone from light to dark. The *halftone* set pictures next to words, leading to one of the great advances in the history of mediated communication: *photojournalism*.

Although they could be seen in the pages of weekly journals and magazines, photographs would not become common in newspapers until the quality of newsprint — the paper itself — improved toward the end of the nineteenth century. The first newspaper photograph, entitled "Shanty–Town," appeared in the New York *Daily Graphic* on March 4, 1880. By the end of the century photographs were regularly printed. Innovations continued as technology opened opportunities for photography in the realms of science.

OFFSET LITHOGRAPHY

Based on nineteenth century inventions, *offset lithography* became the basis of most photo publication. In the twenty–first century, the process has become entirely digital from the photographer's camera until a page plate containing photographs and printed matter is mounted on a press.

As a tool of the artist, photography pleased the public. Alfred Stieglitz and Edward Steichen built reputations rivaling painters who used brush and palette. Henri Cartier–Bresson, Ansel Adams, and Edward Weston followed them. Stieglitz led a movement devoted to the idea of photography as an art form and a means of personal expression, creating the "one–man show" and founding *Camera Work*, a magazine for fine photographic art. More than anyone, he saw photography as a form of art and he raised it to a new level.

SHORTER EXPOSURES

From the beginning photographers fretted about the time it took to expose a picture. At first, people could not be captured on film at all. Even when exposure time shortened, the subjects had to hold still; one reason subjects in early photos look grim is that it was too hard to freeze a smile for so long. Because the early cameras lacked shutters, the photographer simply took the lens cap off for the number of seconds required to expose the plate.

As film improved, inventors formulated ideas for exposing the film for shorter and shorter time periods. The demand for stop–action pictures pushed the inventors of optical and mechanical equipment and photochemistry to bring new products to the marketplace. By the end of the nineteenth century, focal plane shutters, located between the lens and the film, could limit exposures to $1/5000^{th}$ of a second.

DRY–PLATE PROCESS

The wet–plate process gave way to a gelatin silver bromide dry–plate process that provided even greater sensitivity and shorter exposure. It also freed the photographer from carrying a darkroom wherever he went. As long as glass plates served as the recording medium base, cameras would remain bulky. The glass plates themselves had the limitations of weight and fragility, requiring special chemicals and special handling.

These difficulties led to a search for a substitute material, something lightweight but flexible enough to be rolled around a spool, yet tough, transparent, and impervious to photographic chemicals. Inventors turned to nitrocellulose, the source of collodion, an important chemical in glass plate photography. Simply put, they threw away the glass and kept a version of the sticky stuff that stuck to the glass. At first, flexible film on a roll holder was fitted to the back of a folding–bellows camera. Later, cameras small enough to hold in the hand removed the requirement of a tripod.

AFFORDABLE HOBBY

Changing technology has consistently enabled tens of millions of people all over the world to own cameras and participate in the making and acquiring of photographs of better and better quality, and with them, to create memories. As the twentieth century dawned, the hobby of photography, not just the price of a single photograph, was becoming affordable for average people. Some fifty different camera models were being manufactured.

Determined to make the camera "as convenient as the pencil," George Eastman introduced the Kodak with a fixed focus, fixed aperture, and one speed; it further simplified the somewhat complex process of taking a picture to the three steps of pulling a cord, turning a key, and pressing a button. The first Kodak was a wooden box encased in leather; it sold for twenty–five dollars. Owners returned the camera to the company, where the film was unloaded, processed by transferring negatives to glass plates for printing, and returned to the owner with paper prints and a fresh roll installed. Eastman's slogan was, "You Press the Button, We Do the Rest." His ten dollar charge wasn't cheap, but if you could afford the hobby of photography, it was certainly convenient.

CONVENIENT AS A PENCIL

Almost overnight, everyone who could afford to do it wanted to take pictures. The photographer did not need to understand chemistry when, for the first time, anyone could take a picture. As prices came down, millions of people soon did. Camera clubs sprang up everywhere. Eastman said his cameras brought photography "within the reach of every human being who desires to preserve a record of what he sees."

CAMERA CLUBS

When Eastman's Brownie camera in 1900 sold for a dollar with a six–exposure roll of film that cost fifteen cents, photography was truly available for "the man in the street." Eastman had designed the Brownie for children, but adults used it, too. Eastman's slogan was, "Plant the Brownie acorn and the Kodak oak will grow." He also sold a developing and printing kit for seventy–five cents. Pictures that could be taken easily came to be known by the way that hunters described shooting a rifle from the hip without aiming: a snapshot.

During the nineteenth century it was common to color prints with paint. Retouching by hand was an important feature of studio work, although the delicate daguerreotypes needed extra care. By the turn of the twentieth century, color film and color filters had become the basis of attractive color photographs.

In 1947, Edwin Land's Polaroid camera process allowed film development and printing inside the camera. The back of the camera carried separate negative and positive film rolls; the act of tugging the film out of the camera pulled it between two rollers that broke small pods of developing fluid, spreading them evenly across the film surface. One minute later the positive print was ready to peel away. This "instant print" process was available in color by 1963, which combined the negative and positive materials in a single unit, thanks to fourteen separate coatings.

"INSTANT PRINTS"

The years following the end of World War II saw Americans flush with cash, soldiers returning to civilian life, and ready to buy homes, cars, television sets, appliances, and whatever else they could afford, often with little or no money down. Into this happy situation came new models of the 35 mm camera from Germany and Japan, the former enemies benefiting from American government policies encouraging them to get back on their feet politically and economically. The 35 mm camera was just the thing to take along on that long delayed vacation. Some models were single–lens reflex. Others had rangefinders. Leica, Minolta, and Nikon were praised for their quality. They competed vigorously with Kodak models.

From Japan a couple of decades later came the point–and–shoot, automatic–everything camera with coated lenses and synchronized internal flash. The focus adjusted instantly to whatever stood in front of the lens. Like so many inventions, the camera itself grew more complicated in order to make its operation simpler.

In the days of the daguerreotype and wet–plate photography, the camera was little more than a box with a lens, but getting pictures took training, practice and skill. Cameras now are crammed with microcircuitry and intricate mechanical and optical parts, but a child can press a button. Eastman's old advertising slogan, "You Press the Button, We Do the Rest," could hardly be truer for the automated single–lens reflex camera controlled by computer chips and infrared sensors.

The filmless camera arrived from Japan in 1981 with Sony's Mavica, but only as a prototype that did not go into full production because of its poor images. Five years later another Japanese firm, Canon, marketed a better camera. The SVC — still–video camera — recorded images onto a small magnetic disk that, without chemical processing and after transmission over ordinary telephone lines or by satellite, was immediately available for viewing on television screens around the world.

Another device, the photo CD player, used photographs encoded digitally on compact discs. The photographs could be displayed in color on a home television set, accompanied by any functions the owner wished to add, such as pans and zooms, skip selection, audio narration or music, text and graphics. Kodak and Japanese camera and film manufacturers joined to introduce the Advanced Photo System in 1996. Moving even more "buttons" inside, it featured drop–in, no–threading film canisters. Users could choose standard or wide framing for each shot, and on the back of a print could identify the date, location, and subject.

Meanwhile, Microsoft's Corbis Corporation gathered what may be the world's largest depository of images. Its customers literally have millions

Welcome to the age of the crowd…

Technological advances in everything from product design software to digital video cameras are breaking down the cost barriers that once separated amateurs from professionals. Hobbyists, part–timers, and dabblers suddenly have a market for their efforts, as smart companies in industries as disparate as pharmaceuticals and television discover ways to tap the latent talent of the crowd. The labor isn't always free, but it costs a lot less than paying traditional employees. It's not outsourcing; it's crowdsourcing.[11]

— Jeff Howe

of photographs to choose from, all digitized, catalogued, and ready for use.

Early in the twenty–first century, more buyers were choosing digital cameras than those with film, and the number of pixels approached the quality of film. Cameras were also combined with telephones, so that (*as noted in the previous chapter*) a picture could be instantly transmitted anywhere and posted on websites. A considerable advantage to journalists and a convenience to most users, the camera phone, however, in the hands of a sexual predator, could create such an invasion of privacy that it was banned in a number of places.

One of the social effects of the digital revolution in mediated communication has been to enable average people to do what only professionals using expensive equipment have been able to do in the past. Nowhere is this more true than in photography. Great numbers of people — tens of millions — throughout the world feel free to express themselves and to share those feelings with everyone else through photographs. Websites like YouTube, MySpace, and Flickr display images that both friends and strangers click on, no matter how amateurish.

The company iStockphoto, which grew out of a free image–sharing service, offered a large database of still and video pictures without royalty costs. Like those other websites, users were also contributors. They provided the content. The successful companies behind them managed what the users provided.

After 1989, photos could be digitally manipulated on a home computer. Now the tampering could not be detected. Digital imaging converted images into dots — pixels — that could be moved or removed. Electronic changes eliminated any evidence of tampering. Customers came to the shops of expert digital imagers who scanned old photographs that had seen better days, cleaned up the damaged areas using Photoshop or other software, and reproduced them.

Actually, it is no longer necessary to go to the experts for much of this. With off–the–shelf software like Smart Erase, unwanted people can be replaced by whatever color and pattern is in the background. Another feature allows the combining of images from more than one photograph into a seamless whole. Changes have included taking unidentified people out of a photograph; removing a divorced spouse from a family scene, adding missing relatives to a family reunion; bringing grandmother, mother, and daughter together for a three–generation portrait, closing gaps in a photograph of relatives to make the scene cozier, and eliminating braces from teeth before the orthodontist does it.

In professional hands, retouching can lead to public embarrassment. Computer software for digital retouching shifted the pyramids at Giza

Certainly the identity of a photographic image no longer has to do with its support or its chemical composition, or with its authorship, place of origin, or pictorial appearance. It instead comprises... a pliable sequence of digital data and electronic impulses.[12]

— GEOFFREY BATCHEN

With the new technology we can enhance colors or change them, eliminate details, add or delete figures, alter the composition and lighting effects, combine any number of images, and literally move mountains, or at least the Eiffel Tower, as one magazine did to improve a cover design. TV Guide *didn't even stop at decapitation — it placed Oprah Winfrey's head on Ann–Margret's body!*[13]

— ARTHUR GOLDSMITH

for a *National Geographic* cover in 1982. That improved the framing, but did nothing for the magazine's reputation for authenticity. In 2005, *Newsweek* not only placed Martha Stewart's head on a model's body for a cover, but in the accompanying article freely admitted doing so and saw nothing wrong with such a "photo illustration."

The old saw that pictures never lied had been suspect from the start. In the 1920s a few newspaper editors combined pictures into "composographs," which brought images of people from different photographs together in close proximity. Publishers justified using them because they sold newspapers, but such distortions also had political value. Enough voters were deceived during the McCarthy "Red Scare" era of the 1950s to defeat liberal Senator Millard Tydings for re–election after he was shown standing beside Communist leader Earl Browder, an event that never happened.

During the 2004 election campaign, a fake photograph circulated on the Internet showing John Kerry on a podium with Jane Fonda to demonstrate against the Vietnam War. They never shared a podium, but the toxic effect of this digital imagery may have affected a presidential election.

STEREOSCOPE

The scientific roots of seeing in three dimensions also go back to ancient times. Two Greek scientists, Euclid in the third century B.C.E. and Galen in the second century C.E. described stereoscopic vision, or stereopsis. Each eye sees a two–dimensional world. Together, they signal depth to the brain. Leonardo Da Vinci and Johannes Kepler wrote about it at length, but each apparently missed a true understanding of why we see depth.

In England, one of the telegraph's inventors, Charles Wheatstone, built a mirror–based stereoscope. Invented at the dawn of photography, it displayed hand–drawn images, but it had too many faults to succeed. Nevertheless, Wheatstone was the first to recognize just what happens when the image of an object strikes the retina of each eye at a very slightly different angle, giving us our sense of depth. His 1838 lectures on three–dimensional vision stirred the interest of other scientist–inventors. David Brewster built a successful stereoscope that stirred public excitement when it was shown at a London exhibition. In 1854, a British company began manufacturing the hand–held devices that showed pairs of photographs, one for each eye; in two years it reported sales of a half million stereoscopes and a million stereographic cards, each holding two photos. Other stereoviewers were manufactured, but the public craze ebbed by the end of the century.

3–D MOVIES

The excitement led to the Kinematoscope in 1861, a three–dimensional version of the devices like the Thaumatrope and Phenakistiscope that preceded motion pictures (*see next chapter*). With the coming of movies, other inventors, including Thomas Edison, tried to combine motion photography with stereoscopes. Nothing worked well until 1952, when spectacles with one red and one green cellophane lens were issued to ticket holders to see a B–movie in 3–D. A total of 65 cheaply made films were shot quickly and rushed to the theaters, with titles like *Bwana Devil*, *It Came from Outer Space*, *Creature from the Black Lagoon*, and *House of Wax*. Most of them featured arrows or fists or other unpleasant things flying at the viewers, who predictably screamed each time, but soon grew tired of doing so.

Digital photography is reawakening interest in 3–D through experiments that eliminate the need for special glasses or stereoscopic devices. For example, in 2004 the Rover mission sent 3–D images from Mars. In 2005, *Chicken Little* was released as a digital 3–D movie that was filmed at 144 frames per second instead of the usual 24 fps. The frames alternated right–eye and left–eye images to produce the effect. Also in 2005, two iPod photo players were combined as a 3–D "stereopod," and an episode of NBC's *Medium* was shot in 3–D. A frame-by-frame conversion produced a 3-D rendering of *Superman Returns* and the ending of a *Harry Potter* movie in 2007.

Meanwhile, work has continued on practical, affordable holography, a two–dimensional photographic system that produces three–dimensional photographs using laser beams. A hologram can appear to extend deep into the wall on which the picture is hanging or it can seem to extend outward into a room so that viewers carefully walk around what is not there.

HOLOGRAPHY

In addition to a number of scientific uses, holograms can be found on magazine covers and on museum walls. The first of the *Star Wars* films contained a hologram appearance by "Princess Leia," who delivered a "mailed" message to a spaceship. If, one day, motion holography reaches the home as television pictures, there is little doubt about its acceptance. To view a video hologram would be more like looking through a window at the street outside than like watching TV.

The office copier belongs to this list of innovations that provides what Daniel J. Boorstin has called "the repeatability of experience," a further step toward an open and egalitarian society.[14] To copy a document or pages of a book was, before the twentieth century, a discouraging chore. To make multiple copies multiplied the work. The typewriter and the mimeograph eased the burden somewhat, but at the expense of appearance. To produce many copies of a document in a form as attractive as the original was a dream, but it was a dream worth pursuing.

THE COPIER

Ancient Greeks experimented with static electricity by rubbing amber with silk to attract bits of hair. Systematic observations began in the nineteenth century with the chemical generation of electricity. Related research was being done in television.

Trained as both a physicist and a patent attorney, Chester Carlson continued the trail of experiments with the specific goal of finding a better means than carbon paper or mimeograph machines to copy documents. Working mostly in the kitchen of his Queens, New York, apartment with the assistance of a German refugee scientist, he produced his first fixed image from an electric charge. His breakthrough combined rabbit fur, India ink, a handkerchief, wax paper, a light bulb, sulfur, mossy powder, a microscope glass slide, and a small metal plate. He called his invention xerography, from the Greek for "dry writing."

Carlson took it to one major corporation after another, but each showed what he termed "enthusiastic lack of interest." A small company eventually manufactured the first useful model in 1950, a copier using plain paper, the Xerox 914 (referring to copies up to 9 x 14 inches). Within six years 65,000 machines had been sold. Today some twenty companies worldwide sell more than $50 billion of copiers and supplies annually. The laser printer, the facsimile machine, and the light pen, which transmits information along a beam of light, depend upon some of the same principles of photo–electricity.

CARTOONS Photography was not the only way to communicate messages by images. Sketches that originated with political cartoons and the sharp drawings of the eighteenth century English artist William Hogarth have given birth to a worldwide phenomenon of comic books, newspaper comic strips, magazine cartoons, Internet drawings, and, of course, the ever popular political cartoons.

In 1896, a few years after photographs started to appear in newspapers, the technology supporting color in newspaper improved enough for William Randolph Hearst to bring out a comic strip supplement in the *New York American*. Yellow ink was added to an outlandish skirt worn by a little boy in one strip, "Hogan's Alley." Renamed the *Yellow Kid*, it was a hit with readers and opened the way for a major industry with dozens upon dozens of comic strips.

Some comics were intended to be comical. Others were intended to be serious adventures, but the term comics has stuck to them all. Italians call them "fumetti," meaning "smoke." In Portuguese they are "história em quadradinhos" (a story in little squares). The French prefer the no–nonsense "bande dessiné" (drawn strip). Whatever they are called, they are a staple of the modern newspaper, sometimes the first place a reader goes to.

For many newspaper readers, the comic strips are the one part of the newspaper that they would never do without. Reading *Dilbert* or *Doonesbury* is as much a part of their morning routine as a cup of coffee. The effects on society of single cartoon panels, comic strips and comic books have been disputed, but little doubt remains that cartoons stir something in many readers. Politicians pilloried by cartoons have condemned them in harsher terms than they used for written criticism. Psychologist Fredric Wertham's accusatory book, *Seduction of the Innocent*, argued that comic books corrupted youngsters with pornographic images and excessive violence. Untold numbers of adults have complained that comics rot the brains of youngsters. The youngsters themselves just keep on scanning these durable media.

Some comics have a stronger appeal to adults than to children. Art Spiegelman's *Maus* won a Pulitzer Prize. Another increasingly popular genre with adults has been the graphic novel, combining text and drawings in stories that are more complex and frequently darker than comic book tales. *V for Vendetta* and *Sin City* became films not only drawn from graphic novels, but produced to look like them. Purists may scoff at the notion that what appears in comic books can be considered art, but when a museum hangs a Roy Lichtenstein painting of a single comic book panel, admiring visitors gather.

CONCLUSION

ONLY A FEW CENTURIES before people saw the first photographs, their forebears lived on a flat Earth patrolled at its edges by dragons and gryphons. If you wanted to know about the world, you could see graphic representations in a cathedral, where stained glass windows told Biblical and other religious stories in pictures.

Photography gave different images. Ordinary people could see with their own eyes for the first time in history those who actually lived beyond the horizon — people who did not look like they did in features or dress, but still human beings going about their lives. Photography made the world less strange and more interesting.

In time, those who did no more than view photographs could buy the cameras with which they caught images of family members. They captured facial features that they could look upon all their lives to remember those who no longer appeared as they once did and those who were gone. They could also be reminded of themselves when life was more full of promise. Of all the effects that photography has had on civilization, the personal effect may be the greatest. No significant occasion in life is without a camera to record it.

George Eastman was instrumental in making photography affordable and simple. The twentieth century saw continued improvement in all phases of photography and camera technology. It was the century of art

Do a YouTube search today on the term police brutality, and you get more than 780 videos from Houston, Hungary, Egypt and beyond. This is just one sign of how much YouTube — and similar video–sharing sites — has changed the flow of information. People have had cameras for decades and Web access for years. It's the combination of two simple things — easy, cheap recording and easy, free distribution — that makes YouTube so potent and its impact so complex. It's not just a new medium; it's several in one…

It's a Surveillance System… a spotlight…a micro-scope… a soapbox. [15]

— TIME

photography, the Polaroid instant camera, the fully automatic point–and–shoot cameras, and the digital cameras that replaced film entirely.

The camera became about as common in the American household as those other communication devices: the telephone, the radio, and the television. Early in the twenty–first century, devices like the digital camera phone combined the features of several mediated communication devices. By the push of a few buttons, a young mother took pictures of her children and transmitted them instantly to her soldier husband on the other side of the world.

Photography today is a tool of every branch of science and almost every occupation, every kind of business, every hobby. It is an important tool of journalists, scientists, and artists. As a tool of journalists, photography has generated anger, humiliation, pride, and, above all, change. As a tool of medicine, photography has helped to improve our health. From the Mars pictures taken by the Spirit and Opportunity rovers to the searches for the origin of the universe, digital imagery has transformed astronomy.

Documentary and travel photography have enriched our culture and our awareness of other cultures. Through pictures posted on Internet sites like YouTube and Facebook devoted to personal sharing and video sharing, the digital age has enhanced our awareness of ourselves and the ordinary individuals around us. Photography has become so much a part of our lives that it is difficult to imagine modern life without it.

As for the movies, the photography of motion, they have been called the most important cultural phenomenon of our times, an invention possibly exceeding the atom bomb in their political impact and certainly in their cultural impact.

7 MOTION PICTURES: SHARING EMOTIONS

WHAT MANY OF US KNOW ABOUT CULTURES other than our own we either know through the movies, or our knowledge has been influenced by movies. They are part of our lives. Director Steven Spielberg called the motion picture "the most powerful weapon in the world."[1]

Even films that do not set out to leave a message still do so in a dozen subtle ways. The condition of the streets and buildings, the cars and clothes, the food, what the actresses wear and their attitudes, the role of the police and politicians all convey the message to an audience that this is the way things are in other places. If life is much different where you live, that should tell you something, and maybe you will want changes where you live. President Sukarno of Indonesia, a socialist and revolutionary, said that Hollywood, in effect, preached revolution because it showed a society in which ordinary people had houses with several rooms, and possessed automobiles.[2]

And as the movies have accomplished all this, they have sweetly encouraged us to sit back and let the skillful people who make them for us, usually working far from our homes, entertain us so that we forget how to entertain ourselves.

A few matters about motion picture history stand out:

FIRST, as with most mediated communication, no one person invented the motion picture. It evolved in a series of small steps. Thomas Edison is often credited as its inventor, but he had less to do with its invention than others.

SECOND, no indication has been found that anyone involved in its early growth showed any concept of how important it would become—a means of story telling that would entertain, enthrall, and influence billions of people around the world.

THIRD, the public played an important part in what the movies, both an art and an industry, became. By ticket purchases, the public influenced the course of its growth.

FOURTH, like all mediated communication, motion pictures have substituted for direct contact with other people. The time that is spent watching a film is time away from other pursuits, including direct activities with family and friends. Watching a film with someone provides some—but only some—degree of contact.

The American press is read only where English is read; the American radio is heard only where English is comprehended; but the American movie is an international carrier which triumphs over differences in age or language, nationality or custom. Even the Sumatran native who cannot spell is able to grasp the meaning of pictures which move, and he can love, hate, or identify himself with those who appear in them…[4]

— Leo Rosten

FIFTH, as the years have gone by, more and more people are making movies at every level. Production and distribution are decentralized as never before. The motion picture today contributes to an egalitarian world trend not only by its content, but also by the fact that the making of movies exists in many hands.

SIXTH, motion pictures have sometimes been a force for knocking down barriers among races, religions, and nationalities. They can help to turn our focus from local and parochial matters to broader perspectives. However, in a few hands, they have done just the opposite; they have been used as propaganda to foster hostility.

SEVENTH, no cultural force of such power settles in without opposition. Almost from its onset the motion picture had its enemies. Middle class reformers who attacked working class drinking went after the nickelodeon. Representatives of the clergy managed to close some movie theaters.[3] A variety of city, state, and national censorship boards took root. Today's rating system is Hollywood's self-regulation in a constant hope of keeping outside censors away. In addition, many nations have their own board of censors. It is common knowledge and accepted practice that films are kept from audiences for political reasons. Motion pictures are never considered purely on their merits. Their impact on society is far too great.

ROOTS OF MOTION PHOTOGRAPHY

Motion picture technology has three roots that go back for centuries. The *chemistry* of film has its roots in still photography. The other two roots are *projection*, which had its origin in the magic lantern, and *stills-in-motion*, which began as toys that depended on *persistence of vision*.

Because it takes the eye and the brain a fraction of a second to lose an image, a series of still pictures presented in quick succession will appear as a single moving image. An examination of the flickering images of the persistence-of-vision devices built throughout the nineteenth century may lead to the conclusion that the invention of the motion picture was inevitable. From the Thaumatrope, invented before photography, to devices with with complex names like the Phenakistoscope, the Praxinoscope, the Zoetrope, the Zoopraxiscope, the Omniscope, and the Stereofantascope, inventors strove to fool the eye. The Thaumatrope was a disk at the end of a string with different images on each side of the disk, such as a cage and a canary. Spinning the disk placed the canary inside the cage. The inventor was probably influenced by a scientific paper on persistence of vision by the remarkable Peter Roget, creator of Roget's *Thesaurus* of English synonyms, and the inventor of the log log slide rule. Roget was also a respected physician.

In 1878, railroad baron Leland Stanford, ex-governor of California and founder of Stanford University, wanted to settle a bet on whether a trotting horse lifted all four hooves off the ground at the same time. He hired professional photographer Eadweard Muybridge, who, after several trials, set a row of twenty-four cameras along a racetrack. Strings that stretched across the track tripped the camera shutters as the horse trotted by. That resulted in a series of stills. Flipped in rapid succession, they displayed the horse in motion. (Stanford won his bet; all four feet lifted off the ground.)

Muybridge continued his experiments by photographing the movements of a variety of animals. Exhibiting his work in Paris, he met physician Etienne Jules Marey, who was doing research in such animal locomotion as the flapping of a bird's wings. That meeting led Marey to take an important step forward in the invention of motion pictures. Adapting a "photographic revolver" designed by astronomer Pierre Janssen to record the transit of Venus across the sun, Marey built a single camera that rapidly shot a series of pictures on a single plate. It did not require strings, which would have interfered with the fluttering wings. Inventors in several countries solved other mechanical difficulties standing in the way of motion pictures; among them were William Friese-Greene in England and the brothers Louis and Auguste Lumière in France.

Thomas Edison assigned assistant W.K.L. Dickson to build a motion picture system, based on the French "photographic revolver." Edison originally thought of motion pictures as something to accompany the sound in his phonograph parlors. Working in Edison's laboratory in New Jersey with strips of celluloid film manufactured by George Eastman for his Kodak still cameras, Dickson invented the Kinetograph camera and the motor-driven "peep show" Kinetoscope, which ran 50 feet of film in about 30 seconds for one viewer at a time. Sprockets guided the film's perforated edges past the lens with a controlled, intermittent movement like the ticking second hand of a watch.

To produce something to display, Dickson erected a studio building that could be turned to take advantage of sunlight; workers referred to the studio building as the "Black Maria," because with its tarpaper covering it vaguely bore the shape of a police wagon with that nickname. Trained animal acts, circus entertainers, and the like performed there.

Kinetoscopes for viewing the films went into parlors modeled after Edison's successful phonograph parlors, with the difference that admission was not free; customers paid one quarter for tickets allowing them to peep into five machines. Start the electric motor, gaze into the peephole, and there was magic! The viewer stared into a box to see the frames of film flicker by. The inventive Dickson later built the Mutoscope peephole machine, with a series of cards that were flipped by a handle; Dickson made the Mutoscope different enough from his early Kinetoscope

**EADWEARD
MUYBRIDGE**

EDISON AND DICKSON

**KINETOSCOPE AND
MUTOSCOPE**

to get around Edison's patent. (Mutoscopes can occasionally be found in old-fashioned penny arcades.)

LUMIÈRE CINEMATOGRAPHE

Yet it was not *projection*, which appeared first in France. The Lumière brothers, Louis and Auguste, owners of a photographic products manufacturing business, set about to improve a Kinetoscope they saw on display in Paris. This they did with their Cinematographe, a combined camera, film printer, and projector. Substituting a hand crank for Edison's electric motor, the Lumières reduced the machine's weight so that they could carry it to any location. Edison's bulky Kinetograph required performers to appear in the studio. Where Edison's films gave the view of a stage, the Lumière films were like a view through a window. In addition, the Lumières were able to project their films onto a screen for an audience, whereas Edison's Kinetoscope accommodated only one viewer at a time.

Their first film, of workers leaving their factory, shot in March 1895, was shown at a special exhibit for photographers. On December 28, 1895, in the basement of a Paris cafe, the Lumières projected the first motion pictures presented before a paying audience. For one franc apiece the audience saw a twenty-minute program consisting of ten films, accompanied by a piano, commentary by the Lumière's father, and their own gasps of amazement.[5] In no time at all long lines formed outside the cafe to see the show. The movies were born!

One excited Parisian newspaper exulted: With this new invention, death will no longer be absolute, final. The people we have seen on the screen will be with us, moving and alive after their deaths[6]

— DAVID SHIPMAN

Two months later, projected films were shown in London. Two months after that, they appeared in New York. Once the early excitement had died down, the audiences were not drawn primarily from the wealthy or the middle class. Movie audiences came from the multitudes of the industrial working class and the poor, who had no opportunity to dress up for a night at the theater, the concert hall, or the music hall. The wealthy had the opera, the symphony, and a variety of private amusements to occupy their leisure.

When members of the wealthier classes went to the early cinema, there was a sense of social mixing that was out of the ordinary. The middle class frequented music halls, which normally presented vaudeville on stage, but not all members of the middle class went to any theatrical amusement.

A strong sense of "middle class morality," based on scruples set during the age of Queen Victoria, kept many Americans out of all theaters. The working class was unlikely to afford the price of admission to vaudeville shows, which were a succession of actors, singers, dancers, jugglers, and trained dogs. For entertainment in the evening, the sober urban poor, except for a special occasion, could afford not much more than to go for walks.

However, a few entrepreneurs foresaw that customers who so eagerly parted with their hard earned coins to look at moving pictures in a box might, even more willingly, spend those coins if the pictures were projected against a screen. One way or another they acquired projectors, buying them or assembling copies.

FOUNDERS OF HOLLYWOOD

In the cities they converted stores, restaurants and dance-halls to look like vaudeville houses, or they cordoned off a section of a parlor or penny arcade and placed wooden chairs in front of a screen, even if it was no more than a white wall or a bed sheet. At county fairs a tent would do. Lecturers who illustrated their talks with slides adopted the new medium when they recognized the improvement that moving pictures would bring to their presentations.

The entrepreneurs themselves arose from the masses of the poor. Some of the more successful were immigrants, mostly Jewish, born into the poverty and the anti-Semitism of Russia and Eastern Europe, not fully comfortable with the English language or the dominant Protestant culture of their new country. Yet they were totally at home with the Protestant work ethic that has infused the lives of so many immigrants: work hard and success will follow.

ENTERTAINMENT FOR THE WORKING CLASS

They had an instinctive sense of the simple narratives that would appeal to the poor, working class families who crowded into nickelodeons. Marcus Loew, who started as a furrier, would one day see his name identifying a large national chain of cinemas. Louis B. Mayer started out as a scrap dealer who switched over to nickelodeons. Samuel Goldwyn and Mayer started MGM. William Fox gave his name to 20th Century Fox; his name now identifies the Fox media empire. Adolph Zukor began Paramount. Out of a clothing store in Oshkosh, Wisconsin, Carl Laemmle came to run Universal. The four Warner brothers began in Manhattan by borrowing chairs from a nearby funeral parlor; when the chairs were needed for a funeral, movie patrons stood.

Albert E. Smith and a partner bought a projector and a supply of movies from Edison, who sold projectors but refused to sell cameras in an effort to control movie production. As they showed films, it dawned on Smith that he could make more money producing films, and that a camera was a kind of backwards projector. Converting one into the other, he and two partners created the Vitagraph Company in 1899 and went into competition with the powerful Biograph Company.

THE TRUST

Battles over patent infringements were fought in the courts as a trust of bankers and businessmen sought to acquire enough patents to monopolize the motion picture industry despite anti-trust laws. They fought the newcomers hard. The trust, the Motion Picture Patents Company, provided cinema owners with a projector, a projectionist, and films.

The owners paid a fee to run these authorized projectors and could not show unauthorized, "outlaw" movies. Eastman, whose company manufactured much of the still and motion picture film, at first contracted to sell raw film stock only to members of the trust.

Of course, the trust did not care that their heavy-fisted methods choked efforts to produce more imaginative pictures, especially the fiction stories that audiences by this time wanted to see. Business was business. The legal warfare lasted for seven years until a federal court ruled the motion picture trust illegal.

D.W. Griffith and actors from the Biograph Company, including Lillian Gish, Mary Pickford, and Lionel Barrymore, went to Southern California in 1910, as far away from the heart of film making in the New York-New Jersey area as possible. In Los Angeles they could escape the subpoenas and the heavy hand of the Pinkerton detectives hired by the trust, and at the same time find cheap labor and adequate sunshine for their filming. Nearby ocean, mountains, lakes, desert, woodlands, pasture, Spanish architecture, and town settings held the prospect of outdoor locations. If they heard word of the Pinkertons, the film makers could load their cameras into cars and head for the Mexican border. In a friendly village near Los Angeles called Hollywood, they began filming.

Soon, the motion picture companies started by Laemmle, Jesse Lasky, and a few others joined them. They rented barns or hammered a stage together. The first movie studio occupied a converted saloon. For the United States, New York would remain the distribution center for films, but Hollywood would become the production center. These breakaway moviemakers would become the Hollywood studio establishment, and one day the studios themselves would battle television and independent movie makers just as hard as the trust had once battled them.

The idea of the nickelodeon—a nickel admission—started in Pittsburgh in 1904; within a year 2,500 were in business. Sitting in a room with strangers to watch mediated communication as a shared experience was a new way to get entertainment. Reading a magazine or book was mediated communication, but it was a solitary pursuit. Attending a lecture, a circus, or a concert was a direct experience, not mediated, and these events took place in lighted halls or outdoors. In any case, many in the audience were illiterate and probably unfamiliar with lectures. Here was something entirely different: sitting in the dark among strangers to share the laughter and tears and thrills of an unfolding story that was easy to understand.

The poor of the day included large immigrant groups for whom the English language was difficult, who lived in crowded slums and worked in unheated, badly lit, unventilated and often dangerous factories, long

By the turn of the century, moving pictures had survived their infancy and outgrown their "novelty" stage. They were no longer a plaything or a cheap novelty to be seen once and abandoned. . . . Moving pictures had not yet assembled their own audience, but they were beginning to draw on every other kind of entertainment audience, accelerating the promiscuous mixing of disparate social groupings that would come to characterize commercial amusements in the early twentieth century.[7]

— DAVID NASAW

hours for mean wages. Or they labored at home doing subcontracted piecework for even meaner wages. They had little money to spend on entertainment, but a young man or young woman who earned a dollar a day might be willing on a Saturday night to spend a nickel or two amid blazing lights and cheerful crowds. A nickel could seat you in a room with your friends and neighbors to share the experience of watching a program of motion pictures projected against a wall.

To keep up with demand for new movies, exhibitors changed the bill daily or even twice a day. Customers packed in from morning to night, one show after another, seven days a week. They streamed out of one nickelodeon into another, beguiled by the barkers, the flashing lights, and the colorful posters outside until their endurance or their pockets were drained.

Between shows the nickelodeon owners sent their relatives up and down the aisle selling snacks and soda pop. In some theaters the attendants squirted the air with a solution to mask the foulness, which did nothing about the pestilential germs that worried city inspectors.

Attracted by their gaudy lights, phonograph music piped outside, and shouting barkers, the public poured in by the hundreds of thousands daily. But this was likely to be a whites-only audience because, at many nickelodeons, African-Americans were barred. When the nickelodeons were replaced by large, permanent cinemas, African-Americans were often directed by ushers to the balcony or along the sides. As for women, who had limited options for entertainment, the nickelodeon was safe, affordable, and interesting.

The appeal of the movies expanded beyond the poorer classes to be embraced by middle-class Americans. As movie venues, the nickelodeons, the storefronts, the backs of the arcades, and the circus tents were joined by cinemas built specifically for watching films. The architecture became gaudier and grander with the construction of movie "palaces" in the downtown sections of large cities, featuring orchestra pits, pipe organs, and plaster Byzantine architecture. Some advertised "Air Conditioning" in marquee letters as big as the names of the stars.

The palaces were designed to attract those middle-class patrons who wanted to see motion pictures but did not want to sit in dingy, crowded nickelodeons. The largest movie palaces could seat several thousand patrons, with uniformed ushers to guide them down the aisles.

The bill of fare changed, too. Instead of a series of one or two-reelers, the cinemas showed the longer feature films the public had already come to love. Film exchanges, instead of *selling* films to exhibitors, rented them. In time, as the industry matured, distribution centers and chain owners would dominate the mom-and-pop beginnings of film exhibition. Movie

In the slums of the great Eastern and Middle Western cities there were herded vast immigrant populations. Largely unfamiliar with the English language, they could not read the newspapers, magazines, or books. But the living pictures communicated their meanings directly and eloquently. To enjoy them, no command of a new language was essential. They made illiteracy, and ignorance of American customs, seem less shameful; they broke down a painful sense of isolation and ostracism.

Dwellers in tenements, workers in sweatshops, could escape the drabness of their environment for a little while, at a price within their means. They could learn about their adopted country, see the water come tumbling over Niagara Falls...

In the penny arcades, moving pictures took a deep root, both as an agency for information and as a cheap form of entertainment for the masses. In the small rural communities to which they were taken by traveling showmen, they met equally responsive audiences. A broad popular foundation was being laid for a major industry, as well as a social instrument of incalculable power.[8]

— Lloyd Morris

theater chains with hundreds of outlets either contracted with studios or had the same corporate ownership, guaranteeing both a steady supply of product and dependable distribution. Warner Bros. films opened in a Warner Bros. theater, Paramount films at a Paramount, MGM films at a Loew's theater.

The sight of ocean waves coming toward the camera elicited squeals from the first patrons, who were sure they would be soaked. The earliest Lumière and Edison films were actualities, scenes from real life: people in a park, workers leaving a factory, a man playing a fiddle, a baby being fed, a parade. In time, audiences tired of this.

Motion pictures might have ended as just another novelty. What made the difference was *fiction*. In the division between the planned films that led to fictional narrative and the realistic films that led to newsreels and documentaries, the movie-going public by their ticket purchases made its choice clear. They had enough troubles at home; reality in the form of actuality film was not what they entered the darkened theater for.

The documentary would come to be respected more than it would be watched. It is little wonder that, by crafting fantasy, Hollywood came to be known as "the dream factory." In time the public would also express its preference for color and sound; these added even more escapist pleasure to an evening of going out to the movies.

For audiences that loved stories, French magician George Méliès produced the first openly fictional films. Even today, audiences enjoy his *A Trip to the Moon*, which is shown as a whimsical introduction to the history of space flight. Méliès was among the first to stretch the film from less than one minute to an entire reel of ten to fifteen minutes.

Méliès' humorous moon fraud was innocent, unlike a number of serious efforts to deceive the naïve patron. The run-up to the Spanish-American War was the first to be influenced by mediated communication. Shown in cinemas, purported Spanish atrocities in Cuba were filmed in New Jersey. The famous charge up San Juan Hill went up another hill considerably later. The Boer War was filmed on a golf course. Mount Vesuvius erupted far from that mountain. A safari into the heart of Africa featured two elderly zoo lions who politely allowed themselves to be shot on camera.

Movie makers knew that, like everything else for sale, the yardstick of money — in the form of box office receipts — would identify the movies that they should produce. Hollywood production was measured by that yardstick, not critical judgment or classical theatrical artistry. In short, Hollywood gave the public the movies that it bought tickets for. A lot of their customers had little formal education and many were immigrants who were illiterate, at least in the English language; they wanted to see

More than any other entertainment form, the cinema opened up a space — a social space as well as a perceptual experiential horizon — in women's lives.... Married women would drop into a movie theater on their way home from a shopping trip, a pleasure indulged in just as much by women of the more affluent classes. Schoolgirls filled the theaters during much of the afternoon, before returning to the folds of familial discipline. And young working women would find in the cinema an hour of diversion after work, as well as an opportunity to meet men.[9]

— Miriam Hansen

what they could understand. The burlesque tradition, particularly prat-fall comedy, filled the bill nicely, and so did simple stories of adventure and romance.

In 1903, director-photographer Edwin Porter made *The Great Train Robbery*, the first memorable story film and the first to utilize film editing to establish relationships. In eight minutes, bandits hold up a mail train, a posse is formed to chase after the bandits, a shoot-out follows, and the bandits are wiped out. For the first time, too, the camera moved with the action, indoors and out. Excited audiences lined up to get in.

Audiences wanted more than excitement and romance. They wanted to laugh. *Fred Ott's Sneeze* (1893), an early Edison film for the Kineto-scopes, began a long tradition of film comedy. Under the guiding hand of Mack Sennett, slapstick grew from its limited roots in burlesque to an art form. The Keystone Kops' nonsensical appearance and incompetence allowed people to laugh at a social institution that anywhere in the world was anything but funny. For immigrants from many countries, regarding the policeman as a figure of ridicule must have been strange indeed. They loved it! In the slapstick comedies, danger was constant and hairbreadth escapes were common, but no one died and no one was even seriously hurt.

Realism was exaggerated to absurdity by fast-motion film, ridiculous props, split-second timing, and incongruous film cutting. When the screen comic hero's automobile missed the oncoming locomotive by inches, the audience suspended belief and laughed. Sennett, the director, was followed by silent film actors who took the comic art to yet greater heights. Harold Lloyd, Buster Keaton, and, above the rest, Charlie Chaplin, blended slapstick with pathos. His meld of mirth, romance and sadness created one of the classic characters of any age and culture, the little tramp, in such films as *The Kid*, *The Gold Rush*, and *City Lights*. Humor came in other forms, not all of them tolerable by today's more sensitive standards of what is offensive.

People willingly plunked down their nickels for visual comedy and stories, especially when they featured actors they had learned to adore. The first screen actors were people who appeared in front of the camera only because they were not busy working behind it. Wives, friends, and visitors took a turn. When stage actors rode the trains west heading to the new movie studios to look for work, they were given acting jobs but not the publicity they expected, because studio owners were afraid this would lead to demands for better pay.

This situation changed after theater owners reported to producers that audiences looked forward to seeing familiar faces. Word raced through every town that the actor or actress who had appeared in such-and-

The nickels rattled down like hailstones as working-men and their families crowded into the lobbies, overflowed in long patient lines on the street. Inside, the program lasted from twenty minutes to an hour: a brief melodrama or chase; a comedy; a news picture or travel picture; a glimpse of dancers or acrobats…

.Far too often, in the middle of a picture, the projection-ist inserted a slide reading, "One Minute, Please!" This indicated a break in the film, or trouble with the machine… The audience, impatient for a renewal of illusion, whistled and shouted.

Youngsters carrying trays piled with peanuts, candy, popcorn and soda pop rushed up and down the aisles, crying their wares. Presently the machine resumed its sputtering, and the screen came alive again. There was a ripple of applause, a fluttering sigh of contentment. Then silence, broken by the crackling of peanut shells and popcorn, the whimper-ing of a frightened child. In the fetid darkness, tired men and women forgot the hardships of poverty. For this was happiness. This was the Promised Land.[10]

—LLOYD MORRIS

Most of the early comedies borrowed their characters, if not their plots, from vaudeville skits. As in vaudeville, ethnic and racial parodies were prevalent, with dim-witted Irish servants blowing themselves up trying to light the stove or taking off their clothes when asked to serve the salad "undressed," unscrupulous Jewish merchants in full beards and long black coats cheating their customers, and blacks behaving like children — cakewalking, grinning, shooting craps, stealing chickens, and eating watermelon...[11]

— DAVID NASAW

such a role could be seen again at the Bijou in a new motion picture. That resulted in ticket sales and the start of the movie star system. In 1914 Charlie Chaplin was being paid $125 a week. By 1915 he was getting $10,000 a week plus $150,000 for signing the contract. By 1916 Mary Pickford was getting $10,000 a week plus half the profits of her pictures.

An early survey of audience preferences for film plots received, in response, questions instead about the actors and actresses. What was he like? Was she married? The fiction film itself was only a few years old when the first movie fan magazine, *Photoplay*, was published.

As the familiar faces loomed over them in close-ups on the big screen, patrons could feel a closer identity with the stars than with members of their own families. The mediated pleasure sprouting from this connection has continued to displace flesh-and-blood connections from generation to generation. It has spawned its own world of press agents, fan magazines, Hollywood reporters intent on the smallest private details, paparazzi, bodyguards, and millions of viewers watching the Academy Awards and other events honoring these luminaries.

The star system was one of several ways in which the public determined the direction that movies would take. The love affair between movie fans and the objects of their desire on the silver screen deepened with the passing decades as the movie studios and actors themselves turned out to be expert at churning out publicity.

The star system reached its zenith when the big studios reached their peaks in the 1930s, '40s and '50s. Household names over the decades have included John Barrymore, Greta Garbo, Jeanette MacDonald, James Cagney, Gary Cooper, Katherine Hepburn, Cary Grant, John Wayne, Bob Hope, Bing Crosby, Judy Garland, Fred Astaire, Humphrey Bogart, Gene Kelly, Ingrid Bergman, Danny Kaye, Marilyn Monroe, Errol Flynn, Bette Davis, Paul Newman, Elizabeth Taylor, Frank Sinatra, Sophia Loren, Henry Fonda, Audrey Hepburn, Marlon Brando, Goldie Hawn, Clint Eastwood, Sean Connery, Harrison Ford, Mel Gibson, Denzel Washington, Julia Roberts, Tom Hanks, Halle Berry, Meg Ryan. Politicians counted themselves fortunate when a movie star agreed to a joint appearance at a rally. Arnold Schwarzenegger was twice elected governor. Ronald Reagan was not only elected governor but was twice elected president and is an iconic figure in American history.

Silent movie theaters were anything but silent, for the audience kept up a cheerful racket; slides carried the message, "Please Do Not Stamp. The Floor May Cave In." That seemed to young patrons like an invitation to stamp. Some movie palaces boasted orchestras, organs, or sound effects machines like the Noiseograph, the Dramagraph, and the Soundograph, whose keyboards imitated crashing glass and galloping horses. Professional actors working in the movie houses interpreted the dialogue behind the screen.

In Japan, a unique occupation arose from the Japanese oral tradition. A benshi, a kind of story teller, narrated the films, altering his voice to speak for each of the characters. More popular than movie stars, benshi could order directors to alter scenes so that they, the benshi, could talk for a long time. When sound films finally arrived in Japan, the benshi were able to delay their widespread distribution for a few years.

The efforts to produce sound on film began with sound on a separate medium, phonograph records synchronized mechanically to the projectors. This system worked passably well when the film was new. Unfortunately, the record started to wear out after about twenty plays, and after a projectionist spliced a few film breaks, removing a few frames here and there, the soundtrack was totally out of sync with the picture.

In Hollywood, the only real interest in sound films materialized at Warner Bros., desperate and nearly bankrupt. Using Vitaphone, a system that synchronized phonograph disc recordings with a film projector, Warner in 1926 presented some sound shorts and a silent film, *Don Juan*, to which the studio added a music score plus the clash of swords for a duel, but made no effort to lip-sync words. A year later the troubled studio tried again with a silent feature film that had music accompaniment and four singing or talking sequences. *The Jazz Singer* starred Al Jolson, who belted out "Mammy" and, in the second reel, uttered those prophetic words, "Wait a minute! Wait a minute, I tell ya! You ain't heard nothin' yet."

Hollywood executives wanted to leave well enough alone and stay with silent film. They saw no reason to pay for sound-proofing studios, "blimping" noisy cameras, or figuring ways to position microphones so they would not show up on camera. Efforts to hide mikes can be seen in films of the early 1930s when actors huddle over "props," like a vase of flowers, to deliver their lines. Unfortunately for them, some of the best known actors had thick foreign accents or squeaky voices, in sharp contrast to their all-American, matinee idol looks. Changes were inevitable.

Most studios and stars, notably Chaplin, preferred the silent screen with the dialogue printed on cards that appeared after the words were spoken. The public again, by their ticket purchases, forced the switch to sound. In so doing, the public again determined the direction that films would take. Lines at the box offices swept aside the argument that "talkies" were for lowbrows while the more sensitive, intelligent audiences wanted silent films. Hollywood executives should have known better

Opposite the barren school yard was the arcaded entrance to the Nickelodeon, finished in white stucco, with the ticket seller throned in a chariot drawn by an elephant trimmed with red, white and blue lights. …Here were groups of working girls—now happy "summer girls"—because they had left the grime, ugliness, and dejection of their factories behind them, and were freshened and revived by doing what they liked to do.[12]

— SIMON PATTEN

Never in history has the public been so avid for information about mortals who earn a living by posturing.… The sheer magnitude of this adoration invites awe. Each day millions of men, women, and children sit in the windowless temples of the screen to commune with their vicarious friends and lovers.[13]

— LEO ROSTEN

The systematic use of... live performers during motion picture presentations began at least as early as 1897... and during the first decade of the century a number of professional actors companies were founded to provide such services to theaters on a regular basis.... In fact, then, the "silent film" is a myth. It never existed. Furthermore, the term was rarely used prior to 1926 — only afterwards.[14]

— Raymond Fielding

(Most producers) were annoyed with Warner for rocking the industrial boat. Box office was down slightly and competition from the new sound entertainment of radio seemed one possible cause, but it was by no means certain that the addition of recorded sound to movies would bring larger audiences into the theaters.[15]

— Jack Ellis

because talkies followed right behind broadcasting, which was spreading as fast as people could afford to buy radio sets. Ticket sales rose sharply for the talkies that soon poured out of the Hollywood studios. Two years after *The Jazz Singer*, the Academy Award for best picture went to *Broadway Melody*.

Sound increased the information content of films, heightened their entertainment, and gave the movies a cultural value akin to books and plays. That seems plenty, but the talkie did much more. The sound motion picture in the United States, along with the radio, helped to standardize American speech. By bringing forth a shared cultural experience, the movies and the radio tightened the bonds that held a large and diverse country together. Like the telegraph and the telephone before them, the talkies helped to unite the United States.

The first patent for a color process was issued in 1897, shortly after movies began. At first, a few films were hand painted, frame by frame, clearly an impractical solution. In another process, scenes were tinted; segments of black-and-white film were simply dipped into dye so that scenes showing a lot of sky might be blue, scenes of a burning building might be tinted red. An improved method chemically toned the darker areas and shadows, leaving the highlighted areas clear.

These attempts tried to heighten the mood of the film rather than to add realism. Several optical color processes used colored filters or dyes with less than spectacular results. Only Technicolor, invented by Herbert Kalmus, was successful, emerging in 1922 as a two-tone process, but changing over the years to a much better three-tone process. The complicated method involved not only printing images on film containing layers of emulsion, but shooting with camera lenses that split the light beam, sending the split images through different colored filters. Technicolor gradually took over Hollywood films, although most of the Hollywood establishment did not seem to care about it one way or the other.

The public did care and, as usual, prevailed. Long lines for *Gone With the Wind* in 1939 should have convinced any doubters that the public loved romantic stories in lush Technicolor. During the 1980s, when old black-and-white films were colorized for television, the establishment did come out firmly, but this time against color, arguing that computer-generated colors ruined the directors' original visions. Once again, the public preferred color; once again, the public prevailed.

To colorize a black-and-white film, technicians using computer graphics software choose a color for each field in a frame. For example, the technician might assign light blue for a woman's dress or a man's shirt, unconcerned about the original colors. A few classics, including *Citizen Kane* and *Casablanca*, escaped the improving hand.

Adolph Zukor spent $35,000 to bring to the United States in 1912 a film made in France, Sarah Bernhardt's portrayal of Queen Elizabeth. In the era of nickelodeons he charged a dollar a ticket, an unheard of price, and rented a major theater. Its success gave him the funding to start his own production company, Famous Players, which later merged into Paramount Pictures. Called the "father" of the feature film, Zukor once said, "The public is never wrong."

Movie-goers wanted formula films that did not vary much from one comedy to the next, one cowboy western to the next. Most of all, they wanted happy endings. The hero dashed up at the last minute to save the tied-down heroine from the oncoming train, then turned to thrash the villain. Film cuts kept the pacing and mood. Fades that marked a change of time and location surpassed the theatrical practice of raising and lowering a stage curtain. Real locomotives and spinning circular lumber saws enhanced the sense of reality more than the cardboard imitations of the stage.

The popular melodrama easily made the transition from stage to screen. Melodrama and outdoor filming were clearly made for each other. The melodrama evolved into the romantic drama with *The Birth of a Nation* (1915), a feature film nearly three hours long. Director D.W. Griffith's manipulation of long, medium and close-up shots, pacing, cross-cutting, and optical effects, plus his choice of locations and his attention to actors' movements set new standards for the motion picture. He insisted on close-ups of actors despite protests from studio executives that audiences wanted to see the actors from head to toe and would not accept "half an actor."

Starting with *The Birth of a Nation*, the movies would have a visual language that the public understood, a language to which it responded. Although a silent film, *The Birth of a Nation* had the accompaniment of live music, anything from a seventy-piece symphony orchestra to a single piano playing a musical score written for the film.

Griffith has been lauded as the single most important individual in the development of the motion picture as an art form, but *The Birth of a Nation* was also a racially biased movie, fostering stereotypes of African-Americans as vicious and inferior. The Ku Klux Klan was portrayed as noble, galloping up on horses to save the heroine. Griffith was a Southerner, the son of a Confederate veteran, raised with post-Civil War sensibilities as a member of a conquered people. He had not finished high school.

The improvement in the Technicolor system was unquestionably the most important technical advance of the decade (of the 1930s), but was regarded with almost total indifference by most people in the industry.[16]

— DAVID SHIPMAN

The new possibilities of the movie camera (especially in the early days before sound) tempted movie makers to exploit the peculiar capacity of the movie screen to depict what could not have been physically represented on the stage. The first great box-office success...was D.W. Griffith's Birth of a Nation, *which attracted millions by its expansive battle scenes, its torrential action, and its close-ups of the faces of leering villains and of dead soldiers. This was the first movie ever shown in the White House. After seeing it, President Wilson is said to have remarked, "It is like writing history with lightning."*[17]

— DANIEL BOORSTIN

For all its artistry, *The Birth of a Nation* brought out protest marches. The NAACP tried unsuccessfully to have the film banned or at least to have certain scenes removed. Griffith tried to make amends with an even more ambitious film, *Intolerance*, which spanned much of history, but it was a failure at the box office.

The major studios that dominated Hollywood during its Golden Age, starting about 1930, developed genres, and kept stars identified with a particular genre under contract. For MGM, it was the musical and the light comedy. 20th Century Fox specialized in musicals and biographies. Columbia became known for romantic comedies and for the populist films of director Frank Capra. Paramount had European sophistication. Warner Bros. had cowboys, gangsters, and swashbucklers. Universal did well with horror films.[18]

MUSICALS

The musicals from the 1930s onward were Hollywood at its brightest. If audiences loved fantasies mixed with glitter, the "dream factories" were only too happy to turn them out on the production lines. Several studios produced musicals, but none with such success as MGM, which had a "stable" of gifted performers. That the plots were absurd and always predictable only added to their charm. The audiences wanted to escape into a singing, dancing, Technicolor fantasy, and the studios gave them what they wanted.

WESTERNS

If any type of Hollywood movie was even better known around the world than the musical, it was the western. Ever since *The Great Train Robbery* put movies firmly on the track of narrative fiction, Hollywood produced "horse operas" and created the myth of the lone cowboy doing what was right, no matter what the odds. Westerns could be turned out cheaply and quickly, with familiar plots, pedestrian dialogue, heroes in white hats, villains in black hats, and Indians who said little more than "How!" and were shot off their horses on cue, perpetuating the stereotype. Generations of small boys, dreaming of growing up to be cowboys, attacked their little brothers, assigned to be the Indians.

As for historical epics, to put it simply, audiences loved them. Ticket buyers filled the theaters at premium prices for big budget films with the biggest stars, the most lavish costumes, the grandest sets, and a cast of thousands.

Audiences have loved action adventures since the very first fiction film, *The Great Train Robbery*. Violence travels well, requiring of audiences neither much thought nor competence in the language of the country where they were made. Hollywood and Hong Kong have developed specialties of widely appreciated mayhem, with actors now supported by computer augmentation.

In the early years of the motion picture, a few movie-makers, in a throw-back to nineteenth century pre-motion picture devices like the Thau-matrope, drew a series of pictures, each a little different from the last. The first animated cartoon short may have been *Gertie the Dinosaur* (1914), but audience enthusiasm began with Walt Disney's *Steamboat Willie* (1928), one of the first animated cartoons with synchronized audio. The first color cartoon reached cinemas in 1932. During the Depression, audiences expected that a night out at the movies would include — in addition to one or two feature films — a newsreel, previews of coming attractions, and a color cartoon. Mickey Mouse was more famous around the world than any actor. Tom and Jerry from MGM and Bugs Bunny from Warner Bros. offered him competition.

The popularity of the shorts led Disney to risk a feature-length animated film based on a popular fairy tale. *Snow White and the Seven Dwarfs* (1937) combined the story with song. The public, old and young, was enchanted. A long string of feature-length animated films followed, notably *Fantasia* (1940), which introduced stereophonic music to the public, and *Beauty and the Beast* (1991), which earned an Academy Award nomination as the best picture of the year. The cost of frame-by-frame cel animation prompted shortcuts, starting in the 1960s by the Hollywood company Hanna-Barbera and in the 1970s by Japanese animators, at the expense of quality.

ANIMATION

In the 1990s, computer-based animation restored and lifted animation standards. In the decade of the 2000s, advanced digital animation from Pixar, Dreamworks, and other studios pulled in audiences with stories and dialogue that allowed both adults and children to enjoy films like *Shrek* and *Ratatouille* at different levels of understanding. In 2001, a computer-generated feature film, *Final Fantasy*, tried to make its characters look and move like real people, not cartoons. From England, ignoring computers, the "Wallace and Gromit" films, patiently animated with clay figures, built a loyal fan base.

Computers enhanced movies in ways other than cartoon animation. In live action movies, morphing, or shape shifting, starting with *Terminator 2* (1991), could smoothly change one character into another before our eyes. *Jurassic Park* shocked us with hungry dinosaurs (1993). *Titanic* brought us a realistic ship sinking in 1997. *Troy* (2004) was one of several historical epics using computers to transform a relatively small number of extras into vast armies.

At the same time, television news adopted computerized non-linear editing such as the Avid system; Hollywood feature films also adopted non-linear editing in place of Moviola and flat-bed film editing systems. The result was quicker, more precise, more complex editing at lower cost.

During the Depression, audiences had continued to express their preference for light comedy and adventure films that gave them escape from their difficult lives. The quarter that paid for an average cinema admission could have bought a pound of beef, a gallon and a half of gasoline, or enough postage stamps to mail eight letters with a penny left over for a postcard. By 1939 an average of 85 million movie tickets were sold each week.

MESSAGE FILMS

For the most part, audiences would not pay to see sad or serious films, so the Hollywood studios stayed away from them. Although a few films like *The Grapes of Wrath* and *Mission to Moscow* were produced, the studios avoided message films that might provoke trouble for them. Producer Samuel Goldwyn is supposed to have said, "If you've got a message, send it by Western Union."

That changed sharply with American entry into World War II. The war years were filled with movies bearing patriotic messages. Besides war-themed films, Hollywood turned out films of home front patriotism, documentaries like the *March of Time* series, weekly newsreels, and a variety of training films. All the belligerents, notably Britain, Japan, and especially Nazi Germany, recognized the power of the motion picture in their own productions.

After the war a few Hollywood producers summoned up their courage. The film industry tackled social issues like racism and anti-Semitism with such films as *Home of the Brave* (1949), *Pinky* (1949), and *Gentleman's Agreement* (1947). *The Lost Weekend* (1945) dealt with alcoholism, *Brute Force* (1947) with prison brutality, *The Snake Pit* (1948) with horrid conditions in insane asylums, *The Man with the Golden Arm* (1955) with drug addiction, and *Blackboard Jungle* (1955) with juvenile delinquency.

THE RED SCARE

However, the Cold War, which closely followed World War II, brought with it the "Red Scare." A deep political division tore Hollywood apart. Actors, writers and directors suspected of Communist leanings were blacklisted and denied work. They could not be nominated for Oscars. Following hearings by the House of Representatives Committee on Un-American Activities, a few went to prison. Frightened studios put a temporary end to films that advocated social change. Escapism was more popular and less worrisome.

It took years, but over time this pain went away, though its scars persist to this day. Social problems reappeared in movies, which gradually became more frank than ever as they attracted the interest of Main Street as well as the critics. At one time such themes as hostile race relations, homosexuality, police brutality, and political corruption lay beyond the pale. No longer. Spike Lee won critical applause and lines at the box office with motion pictures like *Do the Right Thing* (1988), which examined, with no holds barred, black-white race relations, and the controversial *Malcolm X* (1992).

The best picture Oscar for *Midnight Cowboy* (1969) and the nomination of *Brokeback Mountain* (2005) for an Academy Award indicate that little lies beyond the boundaries of what mainstream moviemakers will examine. In fact, for the first time, each of the other films nominated for a best picture Oscar in 2005 dealt with a controversial theme: race relations, homosexuality, McCarthyism, and deceit in the oil industry. They marked a considerable departure from the usual production of films, but though the critics praised them, none was a huge box office success.

More commonly, movies compete nationally and internationally for the audience's dollars, marks and yen with explicit sex and considerable violence. The audience obviously is willing to pay to see all this and more. And, as we have seen, the audience usually gets — sooner or later — what it is willing to pay for.

The history of motion pictures began at the end of the nineteenth century with scenes from real life, both true and faked. Fiction films soon dominated the public's interest, but reality did not disappear from the screen. Broadly, it took two forms, the newsreel and the documentary.

Independent companies and studios supplied newsreels to the cinemas. The major companies were Pathé, Fox Movietone, Paramount, Universal, MGM, Telenews, and Gaumont, plus the newsreel-like *March of Time*. Because governments were quick to recognize their propaganda value, a number of countries had their own government-sanctioned newsreels, such as Nazi Germany's *Deutsche Wochenschau* and Japan's *Yomiuri*. A network of cameramen and film processing laboratories was set up in major world cities to churn out thousands of feet of film each week, but the limits of the technology of the day hampered the newsreel companies. The same 35 mm film equipment that studios used for features slowed cameramen in reaching a news scene and getting the film to a processing lab, with further delays in sending prints to thousands of cinemas. Most news items were shot by hand-held 16 mm silent cameras, with narration and music added in postproduction, but this process was also slow.

As a result, a typical cinema newsreel began with a hard news story a week or two old, followed by several light features whose timeliness barely mattered. Because New York City was a major processing and distributing point, many stories, such as socialites leaving aboard an ocean liner or a New York dog show, were newsreel staples. Newsreels often deserved the reputation of being frivolous, even if audiences enjoyed

PUSHING BOUNDARIES

NEWSREELS

them, or at least did not seem to mind when they were pointless. When commercial television began in the late 1940s and early 1950s, newsreels moved to the new medium. They were kept separate from non-visual newscasts that had been transferred from radio. In time, the two were melded into the timely and visual newscasts we see today.

DEFINING DOCUMENTARIES

The word *documentary* takes in a great deal of territory, from Michael Moore's filmed political tracts to nature movies for children. "Documentary" should not be equated with "truth," but may be defined as *the creative interpretation of reality*, with variations in the degree of creativity. The first well-known documentary was Robert Flaherty's *Nanook of the North* (1922), a look at the life of an Inuit hunter, his family, and his village. In truth, Flaherty portrayed the more primitive life that Nanook's grandfather had lived.

As with newsreels, governments realized the value of the documentary as a political tool. All nations with film industries made some documentaries under government supervision.

The hand-held Bell & Howell silent camera gave newsreel combat photographers a front line view during World War II; their footage can still frequently be seen in retrospective war documentaries. Combining a silent camera with an audio tape recorder gave the next generation of photographers a more flexible tool than the heavier 16 mm sound camera. Today, the digital video camcorder may look like a toy, but it enables documentary photographers to be the much desired fly-on-the-wall, recording images in some situations without being observed doing so.

CENSORSHIP

The boundaries of new forms of mediated communication are inevitably tested by content that exceeds the limits of what has gone before. Just as inevitably, the content brings cries for censorship in its wake. That was as true for private mail in ancient Rome as it is for the Internet, and it has certainly been true of the movies. If the motion picture had not achieved such a central position in public life, it would not have generated such controversy. Its very success is the reason it has been shadowed by censorship, accusations of bias and distortion, and hostility that sometimes has a basis in religion and sometimes explodes into violence. The mob scenes in *The Day of the Locust*, a film about Hollywood, tried to show the thin line between adoration and hostility.

Although the upper classes did not generally go to nickelodeons, they were concerned that the lower classes might be getting revolutionary ideas from the films showing at the nickelodeons. Starting in the early years of the twentieth century, there were calls for regulating, censoring, or even suppressing the growing number of nickelodeons, limitations cheered by saloon owners who saw business dwindling because of this alternative form of enjoyment. In 1909, the National Board of Censorship of Motion Pictures was created, independent of Hollywood. In that year the New York Society for the Prevention of Cruelty to Children stated in its annual report, "God alone knows how many (girls) are leading dissolute lives begun at the 'moving pictures.'"

The motion picture industry responded to threats by devising various means of self-censorship to ward off tougher government standards. Hollywood in 1922 created what came to be known as the Hays Office, named for its first president, Will Hays; the organization was established to protect audiences from indecency or violence. A code of acceptable on-screen behavior was adopted in 1934 to serve as guidelines for what could be shown, and a Production Code Administration enforced the code. These guidelines were softened over the years as moviemakers challenged the limits.

THE HAYS OFFICE

Protestant and Catholic leaders argued that Hollywood's self-censorship code was too weak and that Hays himself was nothing more than an employee of the industry; they led an attack on movies that went on for decades. The focus on sex and violence was soon expanded by self-appointed critics to include political views that they opposed. Disputes between labor and management were frowned on, and so were stories featuring government or police corruption, and official injustice. The motion picture medium itself, in the view of these critics, should be for entertainment; it was an improper vehicle for political controversy. Films that failed to meet strict standards were blacklisted and boycotted.

A number of states and cities set up their own censorship boards to examine movies, but the standards varied from one board to another, creating a difficult situation for a national industry. The Kansas board, for example, banned scenes of smoking or drinking and limited kissing scenes to a few seconds. A series of United States Supreme Court decisions from the late 1940s to the 1970s overturned state obscenity laws and resulted in more leeway for moviemakers.

LOCAL BOARDS OF CENSORS

The import of foreign films and the rise of television also influenced an easing of censorship restrictions. European nations themselves restricted what could be shown. While generally more open in regard to sex content, they could be stricter about uncomfortable political ideas. For example, *All Quiet on the Western Front* (1930), denounced for its pacifism, was banned by a number of European governments. Pressured from all sides, the motion picture industry in the United States decided on new standards based on age. In 1968, modeled on a government system used in Britain, a self-censorship code was adopted that we know by the G, PG, R, and NC-17 (formerly X) designations. It has

G, PG, R, NC-17

been modified, but remains firmly in place as a barrier to government censoring.

MAKING FILMS IN MANY COUNTRIES

The United States, of course, was not alone in developing a movie industry. All large nations and many small nations did so even if a limited national language base gave little promise of financial success. Like a national airline, a film industry was a source of pride. While American motion picture production was shifting to Hollywood and surrounding communities in Southern California at the dawn of the last century, other nations constructed their own film industries. Germany and Denmark each claimed to have built the first motion picture studio.

World War I gave a boost to Hollywood because almost all the European studios shut down. Among their wartime shortages was cellulose, the film base, needed to make explosives. Lacking their own films, Europeans began to import American product. After the war, their national production resumed, but European audiences had developed a taste for American films, especially westerns. What followed in subsequent decades has been a melding of influences, ideas, and talents in what has truly become an international industry. Its products now often cannot be assigned to a single nation. It would be difficult to identify another industry as globally integrated as motion pictures in the twenty-first century.

"AUTEUR" TRADITION

France, the early leader, fell behind in building a strong film industry after World War I, but led experiments into unusual forms of expression, notably the avant-garde movement in film as well as in poetry, painting, and music, looking at the world in new, symbolic ways. Expressions of art that had a shock value were prized, "decadent" or not. After World War II a new tradition swept a revived French motion picture industry. "New Wave" rebelled against accepted morality and normal codes of behavior. With it grew the *auteur* tradition, which saw movies as the product of a single mind, that of the director, rather than as a collaboration of the talents of writers, actors, and dozens of others. That tradition now influences movie making around the world.

"AGITPROP"

In Russia after the Bolshevik revolution of 1917, a Soviet film industry and the world's first film school fostered Marxist-Leninist ideology. Recognizing the political power of mass communication, Lenin said, "The cinema for us is the most important of the arts." To build support, "agitprop" (agitation and propaganda) trains fanned out across the countryside lauding Communist ideals for an illiterate proletariat. Meanwhile, radio sent the message across the vast reaches of the new Soviet Union. In rural areas where few radios existed, loudspeakers went up on poles in village squares. The film industry was led by such brilliant directors as Sergei Eisenstein, whose theory of montage — the relationship of one scene to another — influenced later film makers.

His *Battleship Potemkin* has been called the most important film ever made because it showed the broad possibilities of film editing based on rhythm and the connecting of visual images.

GERMAN FILMS

In Germany a sturdy film industry grew in the fifteen years following World War I, with films that were more psychological than the lightweight American product. They explored darker visions of the soul, reflecting the despair of a once proud nation bitter and defeated, when a barrel of money bought one loaf of bread. It was said that the low point of the nation was the high point of its silent film. Here the techniques of the moving camera expanded. When the Nazis took power in Germany, directors, actors, and technicians, many of them Jewish, escaped to Hollywood. The Nazi takeover transformed German cinema into a propaganda arm of the state. In *Triumph of the Will* (1934) and *Olympia* (1938), their most brilliant director, Leni Riefenstahl, demonstrated the sheer political power of film even in a hateful cause. After World War II a revived German film industry emphasized strong and unusual dramatic themes.

BRITISH AND ITALIAN FILMS

In Britain a social documentary tradition grew during the Depression and World War II that identified problems confronting the nation and suggested governmental solutions. Its leading figure, film maker John Grierson, called it "the drama of the doorstep." The British were also able to enjoy a good laugh at themselves. A string of postwar British films like *Passport to Pimlico* and *Tight Little Island* tapped a vein of gentle self-humor. They drew appreciative audiences in the United States and the British Commonwealth. Monty Python humor evolved from earlier examples of dry British wit.

Italy after World War II originated a school of neorealism, the exact opposite of Hollywood glitter. Films like *Open City*, *Shoeshine*, and *The Bicycle Thief* had the gritty look of documentary as they chronicled the bleak lives of poor people in distress.

JAPAN, CHINA, AND INDIA

Japan's film industry sparkled because of its great directors. Akira Kurosawa is the director best known to Western audiences. His *Rashomon* (1950), a costume drama set in Japan's long feudal era, is a classic that someone mentions in ordinary conversation to make the point that people who go through the same experience may have different memories of it. Critics list *Rashomon* among the great films of all time.

India and China have also developed notable film industries. India's Bollywood produces more films than Hollywood. From China in recent years have come award-winning dramas and fantasy films that have captivated audiences with their ethereal action. Iran is among smaller nations that have recognized the influence and goodwill that can follow the distribution of strong film stories of ordinary people dealing with ordinary problems. They reveal a shared humanity that all mankind can recognize existing beyond cultures, languages, and frontiers.

DIVESTITURE

The Supreme Court, in a 1948 anti-trust decision, *U.S. v. Paramount*, ordered the studios to divest themselves of theater chains. It took Hollywood several years to recover from the triple blows of divestiture, an influx of foreign films from the postwar European film studios, and competition from the newly emerging television industry. Box office receipts plummeted.

Hollywood at first tried to ignore television as just a fad, denying the new medium access to its actors, directors, scripts, studio back lots, and film libraries. Little by little, television chipped away at each of these barriers. None stand today. With their heavy overhead and expensive talent on contract, the big studios were losing millions of dollars. To protect themselves they cut their staffs, ended contracts with their stars and other high priced talent, and began renting out their studio facilities to television production companies.

INDEPENDENT PRODUCTION

This weakness allowed independent producers to step in, make smaller films, take artistic chances with new approaches to subject matter, and distribute their films to theaters that were no longer in the tight grip of the major studios. Some of the independent films tested the limits that censors would allow. A fresh breeze was blowing through studios whose practices had become stiff and stale. Efforts to compete by expanding the screen with new projection systems like 3-D, Cinerama, and CinemaScope had mixed success. Greater use by the studios of color and stereo, especially in musicals, showed favorably in comparison with the monaural, black-and-white of the television screen. But the 1950s also saw movie stars break away to make independent deals, starting with James Stewart in 1952. The era of the big studios was coming to an end. Movies continued to thrive.

DRIVE-INS

Downtown cinema palaces and single neighborhood theaters shut down as television reached across the land in the post-World War II generation, and as middle and working class people migrated outward to the suburbs, but one kind of movie theater thrived during the 1950s and 1960s. In an era of suburban, outdoor living, of gardening, boating, and barbecuing, the drive-in theater, where the movie stars competed with the real stars, was a natural. A salesman, Richard Hollingshead, opened the first drive-in in Camden, New Jersey, in 1933, during the depths of the Depression. By 1958 nearly one theater in every three was a drive-in, nearly 5,000 across the nation, even though the weather closed them for months in the northern states.

More families had automobiles, gas was cheap, and so was an evening at the drive-in, with free admission for kids and no problem about bringing your own sandwiches, even the whole dinner. This was family time, an evening with friends, or a date, and no strangers to shush you if you talked. It was not unlike an evening with the television of the day, except that the movies were more fun than most of the available live TV fare and the screen was bigger. The image was certainly a lot clearer than on a round, gray television tube.

You didn't have to dress up or pay for parking or a baby sitter, no small consideration in the baby-boom postwar years. The drive-in's fast-food island did a brisk business. Some drive-ins provided playgrounds, laundromats, picnic spots, and even miniature golf courses. All provided a hangout for teens away from their parents, a favorite place to "neck." The double feature was usual, the triple feature not unknown. No "B" picture was so bad that it could not be found at some drive-in.

For all these reasons, the drive-in theatre was a harbinger of television and video rentals. Those entrepreneurs with foresight recognized a change that the public wanted: on an average night it was better to stay in than go out. After two generations, the downtown movie palace was a tottering white elephant. It would take another generation for the technologies to catch up with the desire, in Faith Popcorn's phrase, to "cocoon.[19]

Rising real estate values along with better choices on television eventually shut down the "ozoner." The adoption of Daylight Savings Time also hurt drive-ins because it pushed show starting times too close to bedtime. Teenagers found their escape from the family at the new shopping center's air-conditioned multiplex. The rest of the family would do their eating, talking, and baby minding in front of the tube, maybe with a tape in the VCR.

We can watch a movie at home today without any worry about what friends will say or neighbors will think. There is no need to dress up, or get dressed at all, or pay parking fees, or be quiet, or even sit up. The viewer can phone a pal, leaf through a magazine, eat a snack or a seven-course dinner, stop the DVD or the tape to go to the kitchen, the bathroom, or the baby's crib, watch a scene over, or set the machine to record a TV program while the viewer is away. The viewer does not have to miss a syllable.

TiVo, recordable DVD, and videotape allow the "time-shift" of television programs, so prime time is any time. Fast forwarding through taped commercials gave advertising agencies heartburn before TiVo did so. But for the viewer at home, did Cecil B. DeMille have it any better than this?

A pattern has developed of staying home to watch movies instead of visiting relatives and friends or going to dances, sports events, club meet-

FORETASTE OF TV, VIDEO RENTALS

Cocooning is the act of insulating or hiding oneself from the normal social environment, which may be perceived as distracting, unfriendly, dangerous, or otherwise unwelcome, at least for the present. Technology has made cocooning easier than ever before. The telephone and the Internet are inventions that made possible a kind of socialized cocooning in which one can live in physical isolation while maintaining contact with others through telecommunication.[20]

ings, or bowling alleys, activities that television and stored media have to some extent displaced.[21] Most movie theater tickets today are sold to young people going on dates or spending an evening out with friends, glad for the chance to leave the house where the older generation is settling in to watch their movies on television screens.

The drive-in has not totally disappeared. In fact, it has seen a slight resurgence, with some new drive-ins using DVD players, digital projectors, iPods, and FM transmitters.[22] New York City even has outdoor rooftop showings. Hip New Yorkers in summertime are now enjoying movies under the stars, catching up to what poor people in tropical countries have been doing for decades.

MULTIPLEXES

Despite fears about the new medium, television certainly did not kill the motion picture. Nor did it kill the motion picture theater, although changes followed. Gone were most of the ornate downtown picture palaces, the mom-and-pop single neighborhood theaters, and the suburban drive-ins, replaced by the more efficient, unadorned multiplexes in shopping malls, where they shared parking spaces with supermarkets and clothing shops. Multiplexes started in 1963 in Kansas City with two cinemas side by side. The landscape would in time be dotted by mega-multiplexes with fifteen to twenty screens sharing a lobby redolent of popcorn in an effort to make going out to the movies an event more enjoyable than just watching the same movie at home. Facing economic pressures on all sides, cinemas derived most of their income from the snack bar.

With the arrival of television, movie-goers stayed home to watch their favorites on their television screens instead of going out to a cinema, but the content of much of television and almost all of rented DVDs and videotape is movies. To put it accurately, only the delivery media have changed. Movies are still movies.

MORE MOVIES THAN EVER

It is a mistake to think of motion pictures as an industry that begins with production and ends in a motion picture theater. Considered that way, the old medium certainly suffered with the advance of the new medium, television, just as the television industry later suffered with the popularity of the newer medium, videotape, which suffered with the advance of the even newer medium, DVD, which at this writing is competing with downloading. Seen purely from the production standpoint, however, the motion picture medium has expanded. Around the world more motion pictures are being made on a variety of media than ever before, and they are distributed through an increasing number of outlets to an increasing number of viewers. The Sundance Film Festival is an annual reminder of how things have changed in the cinema world.

We "go" to the movies in different ways, using new hardware for the software we love to watch. We may travel no further than our comfortable living room sofa, fortifying ourselves with a bowlful of freshly microwaved popcorn before we tune in or pop in a promising film.

HOW MOVIES GET AROUND

In the changing "software" distribution pattern of the first decade of the twenty-first century, a feature motion picture usually started its life in first-run mall theaters in the United States and large cities in other countries. From there the more popular films went to cheaper second-run discount theaters. A few months after their introduction, while the public still remembered the newspaper ads and reviews, films reached cable pay-per-view, video shops like Blockbuster for sales and rental, and mailing services like Netflix. (Films that looked less than promising went straight to the video shops.) After that came HBO, Cinemax, other premium cable channels, and any channels willing to pay a fee for early release. Next, network television. Several years after they were first issued, the films were syndicated to local television stations and free cable channel "superstations." Along the way there was an extensive network of foreign distribution and such specialty outlets as airlines.

DISTRIBUTION PATTERNS CHANGE

A new release strategy in 2006 sent some films to several outlets at once: cinemas, DVD, and television. The spreading technology of DBS (Direct Broadcast Satellites) and the various choices of ordering films from home by downloading, mail, or pay-per-view has reformed the old movie business model. So has viewing a television program with the commercials stripped out. Tossing in the popularity of home theater audio/video systems, "going" to the movies without going anywhere has become part of the mediated communication landscape.

"Home movies" have been around at least since 1923, when the Cine-Kodak film camera and the Kodascope projector went on sale. They, too, form part of the story of motion pictures. Today, in homes far from Hollywood, more "movies" are being made than ever before as a result of the availability of inexpensive easy-to-use desktop video hardware and software. After the video camera-recorder—camcorder—was introduced, millions were sold each year, the digital camcorder gradually supplanting the analog version. Many a mother took home videos of her two-year-old's birthday party, and many a father recorded his daughter's wedding with enough pans and zooms to make a sailor seasick. The output, edited on a computer, is inflicted on guests as after-dinner entertainment.

Technology that supported motion picture production during the decades of the golden age of Hollywood required enormous sums of money. Although that helped to concentrate, in just a few hands, the ability to make films (and still does in the rarefied world of high budget film making), more recent technology has pushed in the opposite

User-generated content — turning the audience into the auteur — isn't exactly an online innovation… The difference is that in past eras most self-expression stayed close to home. Users generated traditional cultures and honed regional styles concentrated by geographical isolation. In the 20th century recording and broad-casting broke down that isolation. Yet those same technologies came to reinforce a different kind of separation: between professional artist and audience. A successful artist needed not only creativity and skill, but also access to the tools of production — studios, recorders, cameras — and outlets for mass distribution…

Independent types could, and did, release their own work, but they couldn't match the scale of the established entertainment business.

They still are at a disadvantage. But they are gaining.[23]

—Jon Parales

direction — outward to many hands. Production and distribution of motion pictures have been broader than ever. While big budget movies were still being turned out, so were movies of quite good quality that were shot on a shoestring. The phrase *desktop video* has found its way into the language next to *desktop publishing*.

In 1999, two college students in Florida, Dan Myrick and Eduardo Sanchez, made a feature film, *The Blair Witch Project*, for $31,000, with early marketing done mostly on the Internet. It reportedly brought in about $150 million, although the two young film makers sold their interests long before that stratospheric sum was realized. *The Blair Witch Project*, admittedly a remarkable example, showed that low cost video production could produce a motion picture of technically acceptable quality at a price that would have brought derision just a few years ago.

In 2003 the technology market research firm IDC estimated that as many as one million camera owners were making movies intended for a wider audience than family and friends. Amateur filmmakers posted their movies on such websites as AtomFilms.com and Undergroundfilm.com; the website imdb.com listed films. Some filmmakers rented theaters and advertised, and numerous film festivals existed for these hopefuls, who dream of finding a willing distributor.

From *A Trip to the Moon* (1902), to *King Kong* (1933), to *Who Framed Roger Rabbit?* (1988), to *Jurassic Park* (1993), to the latest comic book derivation, special effects have intrigued the audience. With digital video postproduction software, little lies beyond a would-be moviemaker's capacity to deliver magic.

Computer-based technology brought — within reach of the average family — non-linear editing processes with such effects as morphing that only recently were limited to machines costing hundreds of thousands of dollars if they were available at all. Production facilities to shoot and edit digital motion pictures, and off-the-shelf software for inexpensive digital animation, were going into schools, offices, and businesses that once would not have considered doing such a thing as making a movie.[24] In addition to editing software like Final Cut Pro and Premiere, even simpler online editing programs such as Jumpcut and Eyespot could be used to string video clips together and add soundtracks, titles, and effects. The arcane art of editing a movie was becoming almost as easy as updating a file or sending an email.

Attempts at recording television are nearly as old as television itself. John Baird, who led Britain down the blind alley of mechanical television in the 1920s and '30s, tried without success to record a picture signal on phonograph records. American radio pioneer Lee de Forest built an apparatus that included a revolving wheel and needles that etched a moving film coated with silver, but it too failed. Two Englishmen, R.V.L. Hartley and H.E. Ives, finally devised a way to record a television image on film, but the quality of the *kinescope* left much to be wished for. The explosive growth of television in the 1950s sharpened the demand for recorded programs. Until wide-band telephone or microwave links could be established for live feeds, a blurry kinescope was the only means by which a network program could be played on a local station.

RECORDING TELEVISION

In 1951, seeking an electronic solution, engineers at Bing Crosby Enterprises demonstrated a black-and-white videotape recorder that used one-inch tape running at 100 inches per second. At that rate, a reel of tape three feet in diameter held about fifteen minutes of video. Ten heads recorded video, plus an eleventh head for audio and a twelfth head for a control track to synchronize the recording with the tape speed. With all of that, the picture had lots of problems. Crosby continued to fund the research, driven not only by a sense of its business possibilities, but by his wish to record his television programs so that he could play golf without being tied down to live performances. Two years later, RCA engineers fabricated their own recorder, which turned out not only black-and-white, but color pictures. However, tape ran past the heads at 360 inches per second, which is more than twenty miles per hour. Neither machine produced pictures of adequate quality for broadcast. It was just not possible to produce a stable picture at such a high tape speed.

At the same time, a California electronics firm built a machine on a different principle. Instead of sending the tape racing past a stationary recording head, its engineers spun the recording head. They succeeded in 1956 with a recorder the size of two washing machines. Four video heads rotated at 14,400 revolutions per minute, each head recording one part of a tape that was two inches wide. One of the engineers on the project, Ray M. Dolby, began work on audiotape just after he left high school and later grew famous for his tape noise reduction process.

The breakthrough company was named after the initials of its founder, Alexander M. Poniatoff: A-M-P, plus E-X for excellence: Ampex. Another company, 3M, worked with Ampex to make high-quality recording tape. The quality of the video recordings was a tremendous improvement over fuzzy kinescope images. Broadcasters and engineers who saw the first demonstration at a national convention actually jumped to their feet to cheer and applaud. Television programs could now be recorded for playback at any time. Stations on the West Coast could, without sacrificing picture quality, delay live East Coast network news and entertainment broadcasts for three hours to evening prime time, when most viewers were home after work and had eaten dinner.

AMPEX

A few years later, sports fans could watch instant replay. By 1958, the networks recorded video in color. A machine was built that was synchronized with a television signal, so a director could not only *cut* to tape, but could employ the familiar film editing techniques of the *dissolve* and *wipe* into and out of tape. These two-inch reel-to-reel Ampex and RCA machines (the size refers to tape width) survived for a generation before they were replaced by more compact and efficient one-inch reel-to-reel *helical scan* machines and three-quarter-inch cassette machines. The first videotape recorders, large monochrome-only consoles, were sold to television stations for $50,000 each. Today, small VCRs and DVDs showing far superior images in color sell for $50 in cheaper dollars.

FOR NETWORK NEWS REPORTS

A portable video camera plus an Ampex portable two-inch recorder that could be worn with considerable effort as a backpack was used by television networks for news coverage in 1968. From Japan in 1971, Sony introduced the U-matic three-quarter-inch cassette tape recorder; JVC followed. From now on, there would be no more physical handling of tape. Television news *film* cameras were discarded. Videotape needed no developing time, was reusable, and was more suited to the television medium than film. As the technology improved further, television news editors stopped cutting tape with razor blades and began editing electronically, the start of ENG — electronic news gathering. Portable machines in the field covered news stories that were microwaved back to the station for taping or live feeds.

For the television news audience, this meant more pictures at the scene of news events, more coverage of late breaking news, and reports of events as they happened, frequently combining a reporter at the scene and videotape of earlier activities. Television news has advanced a long way from the newsreels. Whether the public is better served by the immediacy of reports is not always clear, but like all advances in mediated communication, once it arrived, no one wanted to go back.

HOME VIDEO MACHINES

With broadcasting, educational, and industrial markets in hand, Japanese video companies turned their attention to the potentially vast home market. Hobbyists who modified portable reel-to-reel machines were already taping television programs at home to play again later and were building movie libraries. Sony had considered the home market from the start. Recognizing that not only television stations, but viewers ought to be able to time-shift programs, Sony president Akio Morita said, "People do not have to read a book when it's delivered. Why should they have to see a TV program when it's delivered?"[25] Sony introduced its half-inch Betamax machine in 1975. A year later, rival Japanese companies led by JVC brought out VHS (Video Home System) machines, a format incompatible with Betamax. Sony lost the competition as VHS gradually captured the home market.

The motion picture industry and the manufacturers of recording/playback machines quarreled in boardrooms and courtrooms over their recording capabilities. Put simply, owners of machines that recorded movies could copy without paying; machines that could not record were of less interest to buyers. The motion picture industry considered the *videodisc* a better way to bring a movie into the home, pointing out that it had a sharper image, stereo sound, and a lower cost. Best of all, the videodisc was playback only; no record button, so no free copying. But the public wanted to record, not so much to copy rented films illegally as to record for later playback movies and television program favorites off the air while the owner was away. If tape could not quite equal laser discs for image quality, it was good enough, and tapes soon added stereo sound and lower costs. Thanks to the head start that Betamax and VHS tape players had, more movies were available in this format.

QUARRELS OVER COPYING

To add to the problems of videodiscs, Selectavision and DiscoVision, among a number of systems that tried to improve on videotape, were incompatible with each other and with a third format, high density discs. In the battle over competing formats, VHS tapes emerged the clear winner, at least until the arrival of DVD (Digital Versatile Disc) players using digital compression techniques.

After DVD players pushed them aside, it was easy to forget that videocassette recorders had been the fastest-selling domestic appliance in history. DVD players would sell even faster. *A Wall Street Journal* poll reported, unsurprisingly, that people most desired those inventions that yielded convenience and control.[26]

LIBRARIES OF VIDEOS

The video store dazzles with its DVD and VCR variety. In addition to the new releases, far more choices sit on every shelf than all the theaters in town advertise. The big stores are stuffed with shelf after shelf of movies. A personal home library of movies has become quite common. Many immigrants to the United States from countries whose primary language is not English keep a shelf of films in their native language. Centuries ago a book was a precious possession that only the rich could own. Now, of course, anyone can own a book. Today it is almost as easy to own a movie, and it is by no means unusual for a home "library" to contain many more movies than books.

Businessman Andre Blay made a deal in 1977 to buy cassette production rights to fifty 20th Century Fox movies, but Blay discovered that few customers wanted to buy his tapes at his prices, although everyone wanted to rent them at a lower price. Rental shops soon sprouted like corner groceries. In fact, sometimes the corner grocery itself devoted a shelf to videotapes, making it simple to stop by after work to pick up the fixings for the evening's dinner and entertainment, maybe to be consumed together.

RENTING VIDEOS

In time, these video shops would be joined by video supermarkets that displayed tens of thousands of titles stored on both videotape and DVD discs in sections labeled *new releases, comedy, adventure, horror, science fiction, romance, children, family, inspirational, exercise, travel, concert, foreign, classics, documentary*, and, in a separate room, *adults only*. Music videos and games got their own sections and so did "how-to's" on everything from losing weight to cooking. Candy bars, ice cream, and bags of popcorn for microwaving at home mimicked the cinema.

There is one thing that home viewing is not. It is not an *event*. Being surrounded in a darkened theater by lots of strangers who are sharing the moment, seeing the action on a big screen, and hearing the sound all around adds to the sense of escapism that cinemas offer. And needless to say, some scenes look better on a large screen. Although that sense, along with the heavily advertised first run movies, can pull patrons to the box office line, it is not enough on a blustery evening to coax most people out of their homes. We "cocoon."

As a result of the appeal of this easygoing lifestyle, we as a society are less social. Our pattern of life has been marked by less reading of books, a drop-off in church and lecture attendance, and fewer visits to friends and family.[27] When adult friends or relatives drop by for an evening, it does not presage an evening of conversation as it once did, but perhaps a little conversation and a lot of movie watching. When the friends of a child visit the home, the social activity may be a videogame accompanied by a minimum of conversation as each participant is glued to what is unfolding on the television screen.

Camcorders and phone cameras are everywhere, as common as the Kodak Brownie once was. Like so much of mediated communication, videotape and its successor technologies have been egalitarian, enabling ordinary users to do what once could be done only by those in power. A few examples illustrate the point:

- The Rodney King beating, taped by an amateur from an apartment window, has reverberated nationwide, and arguably has affected the way police behave during arrests; it played again and again on television, fueling the African-American anger behind the Los Angeles riots.

- The riots in their turn were taped, fueling white and Asian-American resentment. "Video vigilantism" by "visualantes," who barge in wherever they think news is happening, is of concern to law officials and the public, with its effects not only on journalism but on law enforcement itself.

- The scene of the slayings on the Virginia Tech campus was recorded on a camera phone by a student crouched for safety,

We have just entered from the impersonal streets, and suddenly we are alone but not alone, the sighing and shifting all around hitting us like the pressures of the weather in an open field.

The movie theatre is a public space that encourages private pleasures: as we watch, everything we are — our senses, our past, our unconscious — reaches out to the screen. The experience is the opposite of escape; it is more like absolute engagement.

…even people who like going to movies alone don't necessarily go to be alone. In a marvellous paradox, the people around us both relieve us of isolation and drive us deeper into our own responses.[28]

— DAVID DENBY

and uploaded to CNN for the world to see. Recognizing the reach that camera owners give, television stations have invited them to contact the station if they shoot events suitable for a newscast.

- Two remote population groups, seemingly helpless against outside intruders, the Kayapo of the Brazilian rain forest and the Inuit of northern Canada, have shot video to argue for political justice.

- Several developing countries that could not have afforded the cost of making such films by the older methods have set up exchanges for tapes on such subjects as farming, nutrition, health, and population control.

Video technology has changed education as the noisy 8 mm and 16 mm projectors went into storage closets next to slide projectors. Television and movies stored on tape were deplored by educators as a poor substitute for books, but the school library has been renamed "the media center." In high schools, the video yearbook has joined or even replaced the printed version; the DVD sells for much less. Even in grade schools, curious little fingers push the camera buttons.

WHAT MANY OF US know about other cultures we either know through the movies, or our knowledge has been influenced by movies. Even films that do not set out to leave a message still do so in subtle ways. They show how other people live, their cars, clothes, food, and behavior.

Motion pictures have influenced audiences in many directions, sometimes firming up flabby sympathies into the sinews of active commitment. Evidence can be found in the history of efforts to suppress them by governments, public and private institutions, and local censors. Censorship is a constant companion. No means of communication of such power can escape the wish to control what can be seen or known by the public. To avoid censorship by civic and religious groups, the Hollywood motion picture industry has created its own censorship boards and rules. The PG rating system is an example.

It should not be hard to find an adult who has never read a book or a magazine or a newspaper. Where can you find an adult who never saw a movie? From childhood, movies have been part of our lives. If the world were deprived of the fiction film, life for most of us would be less knowledgeable, less pleasant. The skill of moviemaking is one of the reasons we do not create our own entertainment. Watching movies has substituted for other activities and for direct contact with other people.

The poor, particularly the immigrants who crowded American cities, found inexpensive pleasure for their families in the silent films showing

CONCLUSION

"This is called a camcorder," she says. "Can you say cam-corder?"

"Cam-corder," her pupils respond in singing unison.

"Good," she says. "And what do you think 'camcorder' stands for? That's right. It's a video camera and a video recorder. Now, can you say 'battery pack'?"

"Battery pack," the students sing out in fascination. Their eyes are as wide as CBS' famous optical trademark.

Welcome to TV 101…. At North Star Primary School in Minneapolis, where Sue Krueger is a media specialist, and at other schools in Minneapolis and St. Paul, teachers are turning students on to video at an early age.[29]

in the neighborhood nickelodeons. The immigrants' difficulty with the English language was no barrier. The silent film helped in the effort to assimilate them into the American culture.

The cinema is a fixture at the shopping mall. For couples, it is the place to go on a date. For youths, it is a place to meet friends, to hang out, to escape the family for an evening. For kids, it is a Saturday afternoon treat. It continues, but the studio system has largely collapsed with the growth of cable subscribers and cable channels.

More channels mean more choice, and choice is a fundamental driver of mediated communication. As a result, more production sources are turning out more films and television programs at lower costs to smaller audiences. A few big budget spectaculars may buck the trend, but the trend itself seems unstoppable. Inevitably, the star system must give way to more journeymen actors who work for smaller wages than stars command. The star system seems destined to decay in the face of the inexorable mathematics of expanding choice.

In the home, entertainment is often scheduled around the DVD or the VCR. Movies are played that were picked up on shopping trips that included a stop at the neighborhood video rental store. The reasons are obvious: choice, convenience, and control.

That more people than ever before are producing movies is due in part to digital technology. Making a film that looks relatively professional has become affordable for many people. It was not possible during the golden age of the studios. The phrase *desktop video* has found its way into the language next to *desktop publishing*.

All leading nations of the world and many of the smaller nations have their own motion picture industries. They are a point of national pride, like a national airline. Some have had notable histories and an influence on all motion picture production. Today, the motion picture industry is more international than any industry in the world.

The social effects of films have been extensive, including knocking down misunderstandings among different cultures. However, films have also been used in the opposite direction, to foster hate. As has happened so many times with mediated communication, the moving picture has had a significant impact on the lives of ordinary people, but ordinary people who have developed a lifelong attachment to movies have also had a significant impact on the direction that movies have taken. In sum, motion pictures are more than occasional diversions.

8 RECORDING: CAPTURING THE EAR

HOLD AN IPOD IN your hand, and any of your thousands of stored music selections comes flooding into your ears. How many thousands is a movable number that increases exponentially with newer models and is joined by photos whose numbers also grow. All of this is improbably stored in a shiny device the size of a flapjack.

Such questions as whether anyone needs thousands of songs at the push of a button falter at the feet of the technology that makes them available. The clever marketing and immense popularity of the iPod, its competitors, and the iTunes library of music have tapped into a deep root in the human spirit, for every tribe on Earth responds to music. The melodies coming from a voice or a musical instrument lie at the heart of every culture.

Yet, mediated communication has changed the age-old desire to listen to the expressions of our own culture, which we traditionally created ourselves; we were indifferent to a rasp in a voice or a slip of a finger. Instead, unlike the custom of centuries of forebears, our current, revised culture has chosen to be entertained by the refined and packaged expressions of many cultures. Do you like classical symphonies? You have them, along with new age music, rock, jazz, reggae, Latin, Christian music, country music, hip-hop, movie soundtracks, grand opera, melodies of any nation, or whatever else your favorite is. Just turn the dial or push the button.

Except for group singing at church or school, we as societies in the twenty-first century are less likely to make our own music because so much other music with professional audio fidelity is at our fingertips. After all, the Black Eyed Peas and the Dixie Chicks do it so much better than our friends and relatives. The old-fashioned pleasures can still be found, if we make the effort, in the karaoke, the electronic keyboard, the piano, and the guitar that are sometimes put to use when friends and strangers gather, but recordings by professionals set our standards.

Nothing comes into our lives without replacing something else, and a price must be paid beyond the ninety-nine cents to download a song. We listen in place of asking a sister to sing or a brother to sit down and strum. It is the price of a loss of self-expression and perhaps of family closeness. This is nothing new. By choosing recorded music over the enthusiastic music we make ourselves, we extend our choices well beyond those of our own narrow culture. We may spend less time making our own music, but the music of other cultures that we hear is of our own choosing, not dictated as it once was by what was suitable for our own culture.

Music has achieved onrushing omnipresence in our world: millions of hours of its history are available on disk; rivers of digital melody flow on the Internet; MP3 players with ten thousand songs can be tucked in a back pocket or a purse. Yet, for most of us, music is no longer something we do ourselves, or even watch other people doing in front of us. It has become a radically virtual medium, an art without a face. . . .

The fact that their records played a crucial role in the advancement of civil rights puts into proper perspective the aesthetic debate about whether or not technology has been "good" for music.[1]

– ALEX ROSS

Recording began when age-old dreams of capturing the human voice were realized during the last quarter of the nineteenth century. As a result, music, an essential form of human expression, has broken the old boundaries and has moved in new directions. Recording brought jazz out of the confines of the African-American milieu, just as it carried Irish folk songs beyond their Irish roots, and we have learned to appreciate gypsy tunes, Latin tunes, Arab music, Indian music, Chinese music, and several dozen others.

In addition to music, recording has stored and sent out the sounds of nature and of the man-made environment, and the sound of voices presenting news, opinion, advice, literature, and lessons.

The first device to deliver recorded sound, the phonograph, was invented about the time its sister invention, the telephone, was invented, extending – for the first time since humans began to speak – the sound of the voice beyond the distance someone could shout. By capturing the voice, recording caught some of the unique personality of the individual.

Both the phonograph and the telephone were offshoots of research into improving the telegraph, with the difference that the telephone was an intended invention. The phonograph came out of an accidental discovery, so unusual that the U.S. Patent Office, looking for connections to other inventions, could find nothing like it. The first invention remotely like the phonograph was Thomas Young's device, built in England in 1807, to trace the amplitude of sound vibrations by means of a stylus on a cylinder blackened with smoke. In France, a half century later, Leon Scott's "phonautograph" used a similar stylus to record the sound of a voice, but could not reproduce it.

Again in France, twenty years later, the impoverished poet Charles Cros, in a sealed letter left at the Académie des Sciences in Paris, described a device that reproduced the voice so that the deaf could read what was said. This was the country where braille was invented as an aid to the blind. In the same year, 1877, Thomas Edison designed a voice recording device, one year after Alexander Graham Bell and Elisha Gray invented competing voice transmitting devices.

Trying to adjust the rate of telegraph transmission, Edison heard a musical note at a certain speed. Curious, he pursued the sound by putting a new piece of paper in the revolving disc he was working with and, as he described it, shouted "Whooooo". Sending the paper back through the machine, he heard his voice faintly. He tried it again with some words from a nursery rhyme: "Mary had a little lamb. Its fleece was white as snow." He listened with amazement as the first words ever recorded came back to him.

Ever the businessman, Edison could not think immediately of a practical application. He made several improvements, but the quality of the tinfoil phonograph he constructed gave no promise of commercial success, so he put it aside to concentrate on the electric light bulb.[2] However, other inventors took up the talking machine, leading Edison a decade later to rethink his dismissal of its commercial possibilities. Increasingly deaf, he did not at first focus on music, but instead considered the potential for dictation, books for the blind, talking dolls, and even a record of the dying words that relatives might want to preserve. Edison took out patents for an improved microphone, a phonograph that played cylinders, and a battery-operated motor. For its potential as a court recording device, two Supreme Court stenographers were franchised to sell it in Washington, D.C. and Maryland. The product did not sell as a business tool, but their company, the Columbia Phonograph Company, would one day become CBS, the Columbia Broadcasting System. Edison took several of his inventions to an exposition in Paris, where he set up listening booths for the phonograph.

When his phonograph cylinders were improved enough to provide entertainment that could return income, although still a long way from audio fidelity, Edison placed his "automatic phonograph parlors" in stores all over the nation. For a penny or a nickel listeners could put a sound tube against their ears to listen to singers, whistlers, instrument soloists, and humorists, or the most popular choice, marching band music. The well-lit phonograph parlors, with rugs and potted plants to provide a homey touch, attracted families, couples who shared listening tubes, and young women whose entertainment choices were limited by Victorian propriety.

There were also home versions of machines on which their owners could record. Columbia's advertising slogan was, "That Baby's Voice in a Columbia Record." Attractive as this feature might be, buyers really wanted the phonograph to play records by professional singers and musicians. The recording industry was still quite young when the public indicated its preference for packaged music.

Further improvements came from Emile Berliner, who had invented a microphone and improved Bell's telephone, For his Gramophone, Berliner used records with lateral grooves instead of the up-and-down "hill and dale" tracks, a coating of fat as its wax, and most important of all, a flat disc instead of a cylinder. The disc was part of a master system that stamped out records, an efficient and cheap way to produce them.

Berliner took his hand-cranked Gramophone to the New Jersey machine shop of Eldridge Johnson, who became so intrigued with the notion of recorded music that he went into the business for himself, founding the successful Victor Talking Machine Company. Johnson not only mended

I had built a toy which included a funnel (and a diaphragm). . . . A string . . . was connected to a little cardboard figure of a man sawing wood. When someone sang "Mary had a little lamb" into the funnel, the little man started sawing. I thus reached the conclusion that if I could find a way of recording the movements of the diaphragm I could make the recorder reproduce the original movements imparted to the diaphragm by the person singing, and thus reproduce the human voice.[3]

– THOMAS EDISON

The public queued eagerly at the listening booths. The phonographs stood on tables, with an attendant to change the cylinders, and rubber tubes with earpieces led to listening booths around each table. People awaiting their turn looked in astonishment at listeners' faces, unable to explain the rapt expressions and sudden outbursts of mirth.[4]

– DANIEL MARTY

During the model-making days of the business one of the very early types of talking machines was brought to the shop for alterations. The little instrument was badly designed. It sounded much like a partially-educated parrot with a sore throat and a cold in the head, but the little wheezy instrument caught my attention and held it fast and hard. I became interested in it as I have never been interested before in anything.[5]

– ELDRIDGE JOHNSON

The home wears a vanishing aspect. Public amusements increase in splendor and frequency, but private joys grow rare and difficult, and even the capacity for them seems to be withering.[6]

– OBSERVER IN 1893

The phonograph provided a focus for concern about cultural stability in an era of rapid change. More, it offered a chance to lay the foundation for an ideal future culture based on a chosen past. The past of choice was European high culture.[7]

– CAROLYN MARVIN

some of the audio problems, but also created the Victrola cabinet that heightened its social use as a home entertainment device. In addition, his Victor Red Seal records put operatic music onto records, a far cry from the turkey-in-the-straw tunes for common people that Edison preferred.

The phonograph player, equipped with a large horn, went into lecture halls. A smaller version was sold for the home, where the device joined two other machines in the family parlor that produced sound, the piano and the telephone. When the competing Victor Company encased its machine in a wooden cabinet and replaced the large external horn with an internal horn, its "Victrola" looked like furniture and truly belonged in the family parlor. Millions would be sold. Record playing machines in handsome wood cabinets remained popular for decades until audio high fidelity led buyers to favor machines that looked like machines.

Interest in music boomed during the late nineteenth and early twentieth centuries. It was the heyday of band concerts and the popularity of John Philip Sousa, whose band recorded many of his tunes for the Victor label. His most famous marches included "The Stars and Stripes Forever" (1897), the Marine Corps anthem "Semper Fidelis" (1888), and the "Washington Post March" (1889). It was also the period that Scott Joplin produced some of his best ragtime music, like The Maple Leaf Rag (1899), which found a market among white listeners that continued when jazz took center stage. Increases in sheet music sales reflected a public enthusiasm for playing the music.

The excitement fueled by recorded music sparked a strong interest in new dances like the one-step, the turkey trot, and the tango around the time of World War I. To an older generation accustomed to decades of Victorian stability, the American dance craze and the rising popularity of jazz were part of a disturbing pattern of things changing too fast, an accelerated pace of national and cultural development.

The choice of music has always been influenced by such social distinctions as economic class and ethnic background. Most people a century ago preferred the lively melodies that reflected their own roots, as people traditionally do, but the wealthy patrons of the arts supported classical music in the grand European tradition, the staid music of drawing rooms, symphony halls, and opera houses. All were accommodated by the expanding music industry. The growth of recorded music and of music in motion pictures, radio, and television have given the music of traditional roots a much broader audience and a new-found respectability. Discovering new types of music and entertainment, the public bought what it liked, paid at the box office for what it liked, and tuned in to what it liked. Recorded music, like other mediated communication, has offered new and enriching choices to multitudes of listeners, perhaps the true meaning of going platinum.

The *fin de siècle* and the early years of the new century were also the time of the most famous advertising painting ever done, misnamed "His Master's Voice," of the dog Nipper listening to a phonograph record of a voice that was actually not his master's.

The popularity of recorded music of all genres attracted competitors from Europe, including Pathé, better known for its newsreels, and another French manufacturer, Henri Lioret, who put record players inside dolls long before Chatty Cathy. In addition, record players went into toys, fake cameras, fake books, lamp shades, and hat boxes. The "phono-fiddle" preceded the electric guitar and the talking Peter Pan Clock preceded the radio alarm clock.

Phonographs with coin box attachments foreshadowed the jukebox. Gaudy, neon-lit jukeboxes made by Wurlitzer and other manufacturers later were featured attractions in bars and restaurants. A nickel offered a popular song from a menu of up to several dozen choices; the patron watched as a mechanical arm plucked the desired record from its berth, then returned it at the end of play. Still later, smaller versions were installed at every table and all along the bar. Patrons danced to the music, listened, or talked over it, but seldom were able to ignore it totally.

Another form of recorded music was actually intended to be ignored by the conscious mind while it worked to soothe the mood of shoppers. The Muzak company hired arrangers who reworked passages to create melodies that were heard as background music, a pastel environment that would relax shoppers. Critics derided Muzak and called it "elevator music," but its omnipresence indicated that it did its job. There were even reports of its success in the farmer's barn to soothe cows and chickens as a means to produce more milk and eggs.

Music recorded electrically went on sale in 1925 during the "flapper" era. It was the start of high fidelity and of public interest in the technology of "hi-fi." Engineers improved every audio element between the microphone and the speaker. They replaced mechanical systems with electronics and added pre-amps and amplifiers. Vacuum tubes would remain in wide use until transistors replaced them after World War II. Bell Labs created stereophonic sound; the public was introduced to "stereo" in Walt Disney's *Fantasia*. First adopters who could afford it could now listen to music of concert hall quality in their living rooms.[9]

Recorded music was banned by the radio networks before World War II, but following the war and the arrival of television, radio needed a new format to survive. Recordings and the disc jockeys who played them

Nipper the dog was born in Bristol in Gloucester, England in 1884 and so named because of his tendency to nip the backs of visitors' legs. When his first master, Mark Barraud, died destitute in Bristol in 1887, Nipper was taken to Liverpool in Lancashire, England by Mark's younger brother Francis, a painter.

In Liverpool Nipper discovered the Phonograph, a cylinder recording and playing machine and Francis Barraud "often noticed how puzzled he was to make out where the voice came from". This scene must have been indelibly printed in Barraud's brain, for it was three years after Nipper died that he committed it to canvas.[8]

— ERIK ØSTERGAARD

would dominate the radio industry. One public change that emerged from this was that life became noisier. Once played only because people actively listened to it, music was now heard as background music to accompany other activities.

The large segment of the public that had bought phonographs provided a ready market for a radio broadcasting service and gave radio broadcasters a preconditioned audience. The network of retail stores established to sell phonographs and records was available to perform the same function for radios. At first, radio broadcasting was considered to be a competitor of the record industry. In time, however, the industries developed a symbiotic relationship. Radio needed records as a source of programming, and records needed radio for sales promotion.[10]

– ANDREW INGLIS

When the public was being introduced to high fidelity, the prevailing wisdom in the boardrooms of the radio and recording industries was that the public would not pay for hi-fi. That was challenged by a number of audio engineers whose speakers for the home market set new standards. They included such names as James Lansing, Henry Kloss, Paul Klipsch, and Rudolph Bozak. Sapphire-tipped needles instead of steel needles, condenser microphones instead of ribbon mikes, and turntables without rumble made a difference, but the scratchy clay-and-shellac 78 rpm recordings with their five minutes of playing time were still a barrier to listening purists. Peter Goldmark of CBS alleviated the problem in 1948 with the better sound and longer wear of the LP ("long playing") record made of plastic, thinner, lighter material that was played at a slower 33 1/3 rpm and provided twenty-three minutes of music per side. RCA sold the small, cheap 45 rpm disk in a variety of colors, just right for an exciting and controversial new kind of music, one song per side. Teenagers loved it.

In Cleveland, the disc jockey Alan Freed discovered that white teenagers in large numbers were dancing to the African-American music known as "rhythm and blues." He renamed it "rock 'n' roll" and led the effort to bring this music into the mainstream culture. He rejected accusations that he was corrupting a generation. Because of racial prejudices, it took white performers, notably Elvis Presley, to broaden the appeal of "rock." It has been followed by "hip-hop" and other musical styles, leading to a general acceptance of African-American performers by the mainstream community. They have become a fully visible part of American music culture.[11]

The white teenagers of the 1950s and '60s who fervently embraced the new music over the objection of their parents would themselves be disturbed a generation later when their own children followed the growing trend of using a recorded music genre to identify themselves and distinguish themselves from their parents. Each generation establishes its own identity, and recorded music is now one of the banners it raises.

Recordings of patriotic songs stirred emotions during wartime, and so did songs with other political themes. During World War I, when Americans sang "Over There" and "I'm a Yankee Doodle Dandy," Germans sang "Lili Marlene." Tin Pan Alley churned out many songs during World War II, such as "The White Cliffs of Dover" and "Coming in on a Wing and a Prayer." Emotions were also stirred by "We Are the World," which raised $50 million to buy food and medicine for drought-stricken regions of East Africa.

Quite different emotions were touched by rap music accused of demeaning women and spreading hate. There were arguments that some recordings should be labeled "dangerous," like cigarettes. During the controversial Iraq War, the patriotic song, "The Bumper of My SUV," was at the center of a home-grown propaganda campaign to convince radio disc jockeys to play the song.

Audiotape and the later CD technology did more than improve the quality of recorded sound. They have affected human interaction in two important but totally contradictory ways. First, taped music pouring out of car radios and hand-carried "boombox" players at volumes much louder than is necessary for personal enjoyment is an aggressive expansion of personal space, a challenge to anyone in the listening vicinity who dislikes this kind of music, and at the same time it is an invitation for a friendly response from those who share those musical tastes. In short, recorded music has become a social weapon.

Second, the opposite effect surrounds the Walkman and similar personal music devices that are unheard by anyone but the earphoned listener who, while jogging, walking or skating, prefers music to communion with anyone, including us. Like Stepford Wives with ear attachments, the listener of a portable player or telephone creates an acoustic environment that tunes out the surrounding environment of sound, which may include both traffic noises and birdsong. Not paying attention adds to danger because part of the user's attention has been diverted, and it is a potential irritant to others.[13] To offset the problem, earphones have gone on sale that reduce the music volume and pick up street sounds at the touch of a button without actually requiring the wearer to remove the earphones.

In an 1888 experiment, Oberlin Smith noted that iron filings on a piece of paper rearranged themselves into arcs when a magnet was passed under them. He theorized that magnetic impulses were put into them and could be extracted, but he did not build a device to do that. Danish inventor Valdemar Poulsen did build one in an experiment with steel wire wound on a drum. Poulsen thought his "Telegraphone" could become a telephone answering machine or a music recorder and playback device; however, he lacked the funding to accomplish this, and his efforts failed. In 1928 in Germany, Fritz Pfleumer built a prototype of a tape recorder, and the I.G. Farben chemical firm began its long history of manufacturing audiotape.

Magnetophon audiotape recorders that delivered better sound quality than phonograph records were one of the best-kept German secrets of

Is the user of the Walkman more considerate than the master of the "monster box"? Each moves in a portable acoustical bubble, and while the effect of the miniaturized unit is less political than the box (certainly an important distinction), each of the users displays some attempted mastery of his or her own movable turf.[12]

– GARY GUMPERT

Just walk down Main Street. Look at the numbers of people with earphones listening to their own music, oblivious to the world about them. The proliferation of the Sony Walkman and similar sound devices is strikingly symbolic. Look at the faces. They are blank. With earphones on, the individual closes out all outside stimuli. He is his own captive audience.[14]

-RICHARD HOLLANDER

World War II. Allied shortwave listeners who heard music with excellent fidelity from the Berlin Philharmonic in the middle of the night finally realized that the Germans had moved far ahead in sound recording.[15] The Allies had nothing better than steel bands and steel wire as magnetic recording media. American radio journalists using portable wire recorders not only had to endure poor audio quality, but a break in the taut hair-thin steel wire caused a snarl worse than a fishing line tangle.

AUDIOTAPE RECORDERS

As World War II ground to an end, U.S. Army Signal Corps engineer John Mullin discovered audiotape recorder/players at a German radio station. "Liberating" two of them, he returned to the United States. Mullin was hired by singer Bing Crosby, who did not like live broadcasts, to tape his radio shows for later playback. Mullin would later help to invent videotape.[16]

As portable recorders accompanied the reporters, audiotape changed radio news reports because listeners could hear interviews and ambient sound, everything from artillery to crying babies. When audiotape came along after World War II, reporters were able to edit it with a snip of the scissors and a bit of adhesive tape. The superior sound of audiotape replaced phonograph turntables, first in radio studios, then in the home. The early tape players were reel-to-reel, but that gave way to the endless loop cartridge player, first four-channel, later eight-channel. They in turn were replaced by the simpler cassette, introduced in 1963.

HEARING LOSSES

The Sony Walkman, the personal stereo tape player introduced in 1981, was the first of an enormously popular line of listening devices that was expanded to include cassette tapes, radio, compact discs, and even television. The unpleasant news that earpiece devices from the Walkman to the iPod have led to hearing losses has not seemed to deter sales. The portable cocooning they offer, a bubble of privacy amid the urban hubbub, apparently trumps hearing worries.

The closing decades of the twentieth century saw rapid changes in audio technology and public acceptance that waxed and waned with each introduction of home audio equipment. The number of users who wanted to be early adopters sharply increased, spurred by clever marketing.

But not every innovation was snapped up. Quadraphonic sound systems and recordings did not catch on. The compact disc (CD) player, introduced in 1982, was not an immediate hit because of competing, non-compatible formats, but ultimately the CD won out over the competitive technologies. Its optical pickup head did not make physical contact with the record, a huge advantage, but it suffered the disadvantage that the home user was not able to record.

However, the advantages of the CD steadily became apparent and led to the CD taking over from audiotape, including the new digital audiotape (DAT), a technology that angered and frightened the music industry because it could copy music without any derogation of audio quality.

In a precursor to the Napster court battles, music industry spokesmen lobbied for federal legislation to force Japanese manufacturers of DAT players to modify these machines to prevent illegal copying. To no one's surprise, the manufacturers resisted; the ability to copy was, after all, one reason why people bought such machines. Other formats popular in the 1990s included the digital compact cassette (DCC) and the Mini-Disc (MD), but they were not compatible with anything else or with each other.[17] The MiniDisc, unlike the CD, was also recordable.

At the end of the century, the MP3 format was welcomed because of the ease of downloading its music files from the Internet. The music-downloading Napster was born, was silenced by court order because of its advocacy of illegal downloads, and was reborn to sell downloads legally. In 2001, Apple's iPod MP3 player, which legally downloaded songs for 99 cents each from its iTunes online music store, was immediately and extraordinarily successful. It perfectly met the desire for choice. By 2006 it had sold more than one billion music downloads. Meanwhile, the video iPod was being used to view movies and television programs downloaded on computer hard drives, then easily transferred. It was one more process to worry entertainment moguls.

At the same time, owners of CD collections were transferring them to iPods. In less than a lifetime, the technology had gone from standard 78s to LPs and 45s to reel tape to cartridges to cassettes to CDs to digital storage. Where the original Walkman tape player was based on an analog audio format, the iPod was a digital player that could hold several thousand songs. The shuffle feature of random play added to the pleasure of iPod listeners. Attics groaned with the weight of still shiny but already obsolescent audio devices and recordings.

Music has been the dominant product of these digital audio technologies for the home market, but it was not alone. The public also bought audiotapes and compact discs of spoken content, particularly for long commutes to work. Audio renditions of novels were sold through video stores, groceries, gas stations, and stop-and-shops. The growing popularity of audio books met the public's wish for choices beyond music. The visually impaired have been appreciative users. For many people, here was an opportunity to improve the mind with a how-to book or a good novel during a long, humdrum daily commute. It put being stuck in traffic to an educational use.

"Although I originally thought it would be considered rude for one person to be listening to his music in isolation, buyers began to see their little portable stereo sets as very personal," (Sony co-founder Akio) Morita admitted. "And while I expected people to share their Walkmans, we found that everybody seemed to want his or her own"...

The Walkman was not about sharing, it was about not sharing. It was a me machine, an object of empowerment and liberation.[18]

– STEVEN LEVY

Defining "multimedia":

First, there must be a computer to coordinate what you see and hear, and to interact with. Second, there must be links that connect the information. Third, there must be navigational tools that let you traverse the web of connected information. Finally, since multimedia is not a spectator sport, there must be ways for you to gather, process, and communicate your own information and ideas.

If one of these components is missing, you do not have multimedia. For example, if you have no computer to provide interactivity, you have mixed media, not multimedia. If there are no links to provide a sense of structure and dimension, you have a bookshelf, not multimedia. If there are no navigational tools to let you decide the course of action, you have a movie, not multimedia. If you cannot create and contribute your own ideas, you have a television, not multimedia.[20]

—Fred Hofstetter

Language and how-to books on audiotape or CD could be rented or checked out free. Public libraries filled more and more of their shelves not with books, but with CDs and movies on DVD. Libraries featured rows of computer desks for patrons who wanted to access the Internet. Public and school libraries renamed themselves "media centers."

Increasingly, audio books were downloaded from catalogues with, again, thousands of choices. When downloading became available in a home computer hooked to the Internet, a trip to the bookstore or the library was no longer necessary. Change was arriving at warp speed.

For many years, each new season has brought new media and has introduced so many new terms for equipment and for systemic changes that a glossary is needed to keep up. Each new term identifies an additional choice in the welter of mediated communication. The combination of content across categories is sometimes called multimedia, but that requires explanation. "Multimedia" is a term that identifies a variety of both content and process; i.e., it is not merely text, but it links text, graphics, animation, video, and audio.

The World Wide Web combines all this through hypertext-enabled multimedia linkages that let the user click effortlessly from anyplace to anywhere, page after page, choice after choice. Some connections lead to moving or still images and to sound. If instead of the Internet we were clicking our way through a CD-ROM, we might encounter enough text and pictures to fill several fat books. Requests with the words "sex," "God," or "professional wrestling" are the most popular.[19] These choices speak volumes about our world.

If hypertext and multimedia can dazzle us with their capacity for variety and complexity and impress us with their potential for teaching pre-literate children and illiterate adults, they may also disturb us for the same reason. If learning can occur with just the most meager literacy, then the labor to become fully literate has diminished value. This is painful for teachers, whose efforts are challenged by the popularity of television, video games, movies, and recorded music.

Listeners have been venturing well beyond downloading in their quest for choice. Software and MP3 technology allows them not only to assemble their own CDs from individual songs but to mix vocals and instrumentals within a song. Listeners can even insert their own voices. During the 1980s, Philips, Warner Bros., Sony, and Toshiba worked on competing DVD technology (DVD=Digital Versatile Disc; V for "versatile," but the "V" is widely regarded as meaning "video"). They agreed in 1995, under prodding from IBM, to a universal format that could store both movies and computer data.

Hollywood studios, fearing digital pirates, balked at first. The engineers avoided the non-compatibility problems that plagued analog television, early videotape recording, and cell phones. However, they built in regional limitations, so that a pirated DVD movie sold in Thailand could not be played in the United States unless the purchaser owned a "region-free" player. Piracy continued as a problem for all content.

The DVD format has had an astonishing degree of acceptance. At the start of the new century, DVD players were sold at a faster rate than any other electronic device. DVD movies could also be played on computers. They were carried aboard planes and hauled to vacation spots to be played on laptops and the Sony PlayStation 2.

DVDs not only had better video and audio quality than VHS tapes, but their greater storage capacity and non-linearity included such features as commentary by directors and actors, deleted scenes, and jumps to segments of the movie. Tape rewinding was gone. In 2002, Americans spent $4.2 billion buying or renting DVDs. A karaoke insertion of the viewer's voice on a cartoon track was available in 2003 with the release of *Shrek*.

We live in a world where user preferences strongly influence technology. In retrospect, it seems inevitable that the advances of digital storage media would lead to the personal video recorder (PVR), such as TiVo, that allows a viewer to pause or rewind live programs. The PVR owner can also record a selection of programs over a period of days on a hard drive and fast-forward through commercials. Leaving for work or even for vacation, the owner returns home to find a selection of favorite programs waiting.

It should be obvious that TiVo owners watched a lot of television. As with any recorder, TiVo could be paused for a baby's cry, a ringing phone, or a bathroom break. When TiVo staffers could send along new fare based on their judgment of a viewer's tastes, this "choice without choosing" comes at the expense of some privacy, but added choice wins out for many viewers.

According to one prediction, the number of U.S. households with a digital video recorder would expand from 1.7 million in 2002 to 39 million in 2007.[22] Television executives fumed over their loss of "eyeballs" for the commercials that drove their business, but have been stymied by the PVR. Advertisers have turned to product placement as one alternative, but that does not ring cash registers in the television industry.

Does any doubt linger that the Internet and accompanying digital technology are a watershed in the long history of communication, equivalent to Gutenberg's invention of movable type? Consider that information in both verbal and pictorial form are being transmitted instantly to all

But while multimedia may appeal to the MTV-fueled rhythms of a hot-wired generation, some critics believe that all that hot-linking is an educational detriment. Considering the sorry state of literacy, there's real danger in even a partial abandonment of narrative forms and rigorous modes of thought associated with logical arguments; where A leads to B. Multimedia's forte is not reason, but hot emotional impact — the same ingredients that make local TV news compelling, yet less filling.[21]

— NEWSWEEK

TiVo might be called the ultimate tool for choices, at least until something cooler comes along. . . . The recorder can also record additional programs based on TiVo staff members' judgments of the viewer's tastes. One viewer commented, "I walk through the door, put down the mail, see what TiVo taped and then I plan my evening from there."[23]

— NEW YORK TIMES

corners of the world and can be stored by anyone who receives this information in devices other than writing on a physical surface.

The book has been the principal information storage container for thousands of years. It has been joined and, to an extent, is being upstaged by successive containers: phonograph discs, film, audiotape, videotape, and digital CD-ROM and DVD discs. But nothing lasts forever.

At another level, the physical level, all storage materials slowly deteriorate. Silverfish chew paper, film chemicals leach, tape signals fade, and so on. None of the currently used material is likely to withstand slow erosion over a period of centuries as well as the clay tablets of the Babylonians. That technology awaits discovery. When modern materials have turned to dust, the clay tablets will still be here.

Download, Play, & Burn Unlimited Music and Movies...

for FREE!

This was the promise of an ad on the Internet, all for 97 cents a month. The ad promised that this was "100% safe, 100% legal, 100% fun." The downloaders who paid nothing or just pennies per point-and-click were often students who felt no guilt or, at most, a guilty pleasure at acquiring libraries of hit songs and films. Artists and media executives called it thievery, a naked grab of other people's work.

Unmindful of commercial possibilities, owners of music collections offered them at no cost to their friends or to anyone who wanted to be a friend. Why not, they argued. They had bought the music. Why not share it with everyone everywhere?

The distinction between inviting a friend or stranger to their home to listen to a song and sending the song to them via download was no big deal, they argued. Having come into their possession, the music and videos were theirs to do with as they wished. Their opinion, not shared by the courts, was reminiscent of the argument that cable signals that crossed your yard should be free for the taking.

Several technologies make file sharing possible, starting when one person acquires mediated content, never mind how, and sets it up on a home computer for others to copy using file-sharing software. Plenty of content exists because broadband Internet service allows huge quantities of visual and audio material to flow through wires at speeds undreamed of a few years ago. Computer storage has grown like Jack's beanstalk, and cheap home computers come with CD and DVD burners.

Legal action has been difficult because the global nature of communication limits governments from taking prompt action across frontiers, further evidence of a weakening of nation-states in confrontation with a global community, no matter how transitory that community may be.

These establishments, which are sprouting up along ancient trade routes in North Africa, Southeast Asia, and the Indian subcontinent, are an important element of everyday life in much of the world. The proliferation of piracy bazaars and shops that sell unauthorized copies of Indian films has left Bollywood frustrated. Revenues were down more than $30 million in 2002, compared to 2001. While some blamed a worldwide economic slump and a dearth of hits, others blamed piracy. Regardless of the source of losses, Bollywood (as well as Hollywood) is alarmed about the normalized distribution and consumption of pirated material in much of the world.[24]

—Siva Vaidhyanathan

Time Warner CEO Richard Parsons protested, "This isn't about a bunch of kids stealing music. It's about an assault on everything that constitutes the cultural expression of our society… Worst case scenario: The country will end up in sort of a cultural Dark Ages."[25]

At the time that Napster, a music sharing system designed by Shawn Fanning, an eighteen-year-old college freshman, was stopped by a court decision, it claimed seventy-seven million users. Any song was available from someone. It was an unimaginable amount of choice. Napster's business was based on a simple program that permitted downloading digital files in the common MP3 format from a hard drive. The downloaded files could be played either on a computer or, with inexpensive software, burned onto a CD that played in a stereo system. Before it was stopped, Napster occupied about half the bandwidth of college computer networks.

Sharman Networks, owners of Kazaa Media Desktop, proved harder to control than Napster. It placed its corporate identity on the tiny South Pacific island of Vanuatu but involved addresses in Sweden, Denmark, Britain, Australia, Holland, and Estonia in a strand that defied legal tracking. Sharman claimed 230 million music downloads by May of 2003.

The total number of all free downloads, including television shows, video games, and computer software, may have been more than ten times that number. One estimate of movie piracy was of between 400,000 and 600,000 downloads daily. Besides Kazaa there were peer-to-peer (P2P) networks such as BitTorrent and Gnutella, a worldwide distribution system set up to be virtually impregnable to being shut down. They connected millions of computers whose anonymous owners exchanged digital music files free.

In 2003, in an effort to rein in free downloading of music and harness it to a profitable business, Steve Jobs of Apple computers created the iTunes Music Store, a low-cost online record shop. Meanwhile, the sellers of music recordings and also the sellers of movies, software, books and other digital content festooned their products with DRM (Digital Rights Management) software to block their unauthorized use.

The placing of radio-style programs on the Internet for easy downloading to iPod and other MP3 players, known as "podcasting," proved to be another huge hit when it was introduced in 2004. A year later, downloading became even easier and more popular when podcasts were available from iTunes.

In a number of countries, particularly in Asia, piracy is an established, technically sophisticated, almost respectable industry. Pakistan alone had five optical disc factories in 2003. Street sellers can be found in

Since its inception, the entire premise of the Internet centered on file sharing. Many people don't realize that fact, but if you think about it you realize that the Internet has always existed to promote the sharing of information. Gnutella arms the Internet community with a tool that goes back to the basics of the Internet…

However, what the technology really accomplishes is not a threat to any industry; rather, it creates a revamped atmosphere on the Internet, enabling users to share information like never before. To put it simply, Gnutella puts the personal interaction back into the Internet. When you run Gnutella software and connect to the Gnutella Network, you bring with you the information you wanted to make public. And you choose what information to share. You can choose to share nothing; you can choose to share one file, a directory, or your entire hard drive.[26]

— ANGELO SOTIRA

most cities of most countries of the world, with goods openly on display. Underground networks feed millions of illegal copies of videotape and DVD movies throughout the world. New motion pictures turn up in shops from Cairo to Singapore, sometimes within days of their release in first-run American movie theaters; sometimes, before their release.

Pirated movies have even been shown on television stations, whose owners argue that they cannot afford the dollars charged for Western programming. Arriving as they did without the intrusive hand of a censor, the pirated versions gave purchasers in the developing world their only opportunity to see a film as its makers intended.

Media companies desperate to protect their copyrighted products devised blockages, only to see them circumvented. In Norway, Jon Johansen, age 15, broke the copy protection system of DVD films. Despite his wizardry, *Harry Potter* did not escape young Johansen's magic. The irrepressible Norwegian teenager also broke a key iTunes proprietary program in 2004.

While media piracy injured the large media companies of Hollywood and elsewhere, it had a murderous effect on the struggling film and music industries of the developing countries where piracy flourished. Media carry much of their culture.

Unless a way can be found to stop piracy, damage to national cultures is inevitable. Viewers who prefer American films are watching them instead of programs approved by their governments. Indonesian officials complained that fewer people watched their newscasts because they would rather watch entertainment programs on their VCRs.

CONCLUSION

EVERY TRIBE ON EARTH responds to music. The melodies coming from a voice or a musical instrument lie at the heart of every culture. Recorded music taps into a deep root in the human spirit. Yet mediated communication has changed the age-old desire to listen to the expressions of our own culture, which we traditionally created ourselves. We are less likely to make our own music now because so much other music with professional audio fidelity is at our fingertips.

Today's listeners may know more *types* of music than their great grandparents knew *tunes*. From childhood the listener is introduced to this pleasant and unthreatening aspect of other cultures, although it is no longer true, as John Erskine once observed, that music is the only language in which you cannot say a mean or sarcastic thing. Some lyrics can be quite mean or sarcastic, but the listener learns to appreciate the songs or to ignore the lyrics.

Until the phonograph was invented, there was no means, except for books, to bring mediated professional entertainment into the home.

The phonograph led the way that radio, television, cable, audiotape players, VCRs, and DVD recorders would follow. As Marshall McLuhan put it, the phonograph broke down the walls of the music hall.[27] The others would break down the walls of sports arenas, auditoriums, and cinemas.

Each machine in turn, like the piano, would find a central place in the home, although some of these assemblies of steel, copper, plastic, and glass would have to be disguised as a kind of furniture to civilize them. They would multiply in different rooms of the home and spread to the family car. In miniature form they would find a place on the body during walks and bike rides. When the devices were turned on, meals would be eaten near them and conversation would either stop or focus on them, no matter who came to visit. The notion that people could take them or leave them alone seems quaint.

Music stored on a medium that traveled became more than personal entertainment. It developed into both a weapon that intruded into the private space of others and a shield that blocked the outside world from intruding into the user's own private space. As a car or boombox stereo played loudly, it was a poking sword. As a Walkman, it was an isolating shield. Both were uses that their inventors probably had not considered.

The now familiar vacant stare into mid-space of contented listeners would continue with the users of the MP3 players, the iPod, and the iPhone. Add drivers with cell phones and you have a community of isolated people occasionally bumping into each other with consequences. A Washington Post critic wrote about "the look and sound of the Walkman dead: the head cocked at a slight angle, the mouth gently lolling... The eyes flicker with consciousness but they don't see. They're somewhere else."

Digital storage media have gone further than anything previously available in giving users choices of what to hear and see. They have also raised the nagging problems of copyright thievery. The advertising and television industries, based as they have been since inception on the delivery of viewers' attention to commercials, have at this writing devised no certain means of combating what the personal video recorder has undone. Nor have the music, motion picture, or computer software industries been able to prevent illegal copying of their products. The combination of easy access and difficult prosecution has presented challenges that have yet to be overcome.

The broader questions of intellectual property and copyright protection continue to bedevil bilateral relationships between nations, nowhere more keenly than between China and the United States. Sino-American

Obviously, exalted status comes from cool music libraries. Such libraries distinguish one as a thinking person, a discerning individual, a lover of fun, a blender of high and low culture, and a bird dog in unearthing undiscovered gems. So valuable is a great collection that some people fret whether the iPod's ease of use, combined with the Internet (on which all fruits hang lower), allows one to concoct a plagiarized personality from an undeservedly spicy playlist.[28]

– STEVEN LEVY

relations have festered over illegal audiotapes, videotapes, DVDs, CDs, and computer software that were being sold at fractions of their retail price with no regard for copyright. The weight given to this issue in diplomacy has offered still another proof of the centrality of mediated communication in modern life.

9 RADIO:
HEARING VOICES

DURING THE DEPRESSION OF the 1930s, radio broadcasting brought hope to a dispirited populace. It brought the entertainment of comedy, drama, and music, plus news and information. It brought inspiring words from the president of the United States that life would get better; we would get through this. In a nation too large for a national press — based on the available technology of the day — radio commentators provided national voices.

If you already owned a radio set, it delivered all this and more at no cost to you except a minute or two of your time every so often to listen to a commercial, and some of these were just as entertaining as the programming. Illiteracy did not matter, nor foreignness, as announcers chosen for their lack of regional accents spoke to all Americans. Radio was an ideal medium for a poor society with millions of immigrants eager to learn the new language and to fit in. More than any other medium in history, the radio gave people everywhere a sense of sharing what the day held for them.

This was *broadcasting*, a word that did not exist when radio began, except to describe what a farmer did when he sowed his field with seed. The U.S. Navy had appropriated the word during World War I to describe messages sent to a number of ships at once; the wireless industry derived its use of the word from this. Based on the idea that rays of electromagnetic waves radiated from a transmitter, the word *radio* itself came into general use only after the vacuum tube sent voices into the air. The term most used was wireless. Once wireless was perfected, no part of the Earth's surface or the sky above it would be out of range, no point beyond instant communication.

People involved with radio at its beginning did not consider broadcasting, and were not concerned with connecting with the public; in fact, they did not want intruders tuning in. They thought instead of what the telegraph could not do.

As the decades passed, each stage of radio had its own purpose, its own technology, and its own business basis. Radio was invented as *wireless telegraphy*, a point – to – point service. Its main business was to exchange Morse Code messages between ships at sea and shore stations. With the invention of the vacuum tube, radio began to move into the era of *wireless telephony*, replacing the dots and dashes with voices, but still a point – to – point service. When its potential as a point – to – multiple – point service was recognized, when technology opened a path, and when advertising provided an economic underpinning, radio found a new social use as *broadcasting*. Out of radio broadcasting has come television broadcasting, and out of television broadcasting has come cable television, a non – broadcast service, but one that will be considered along with television because it is an outgrowth of broadcasting. Finally, out of broadcasting, with its effort to reach the broadest possible nationwide radio audience, has come *narrowcasting*, reaching a closely defined audience.

THE PUZZLE OF ELECTRICITY

During the nineteenth century, scientists puzzled over the nature of electricity and what it might be capable of doing, sharing their discoveries in papers and lectures. Michael Faraday in England and Joseph Henry in the United States published papers on electromagnetism. Scottish physicist James Clerk Maxwell added to what was known with a theory of the existence of invisible waves. It was widely believed that light waves and electro – magnetic waves could not simply travel through "nothing." Scientists imagined a substance like a thin, colorless, odorless jelly in the air that they named "ether" (not to be confused with the gas used as an anesthetic). The theory has long since vanished, but the word stuck around to refer to radio transmission.[1]

HERTZ

Heinrich Hertz, a German physicist, supported Maxwell's theory by experiments that sent electrical current through the air. French scientist Édouard Branly put iron filings in a glass tube; when he sent an electric current through the air, the filings packed together, or cohered, around metal rods at the ends of the tube. This action in his *coherer* completed a circuit so that electricity passed through the tube. English physicist Oliver Lodge went a step further by tuning the transmitter and the receiver of the current to the same frequency. He wanted to send a Morse Code message through the air, but his coherer could do no more than identify brief bursts of electric energy.[2] In Moscow, Alexander Popov in 1895 demonstrated to fellow scientists a practical application of radio waves, but he did not seek a patent.

MARCONI

These researchers were scientists, not businessmen, but it was obvious that a practical potential existed. Guglielmo Marconi, the teenage son of a well – to – do Italian landowner, fascinated by reports of the research, began his own radio experiments at home in the hope of creating a business with wireless telegraphy. He received some guidance from a physics professor, Auguste Righi, who was a neighbor to the Marconi family.[3] In 1894, young Marconi sent a current through a coherer to sound a buzzer ten yards away. Soon he was able to send Morse Code dots and dashes for miles across the hills around his home. Marconi's mother, Anne Jameson Marconi, a member of an Irish family famed for its whiskey, foresaw the possibilities of a method for ships at sea to signal for help if they were in distress and to receive messages from coastal stations. However, according to Marconi family lore, a short – sighted official in the Italian Ministry of Posts and Telegraphs turned the invention down as having no value.

She and her son took the radio equipment to England, the nation with the world's greatest navy, where their well – connected relatives arranged meetings with telegraph officials of the British Post Office, including William Preece, who once was dismissive of Alexander Graham Bell's telephone invention. Preece's support put Britain firmly behind the young Marconi, whose successful demonstrations led to financial offers as well as to claims that others had already sent such signals. Marconi held firm; his family arranged to sell equipment to the British army and navy and to train the radio operators. They also provided equipment for commercial shipping companies, along with operators aboard ships and at shore stations. With this, wireless communication emerged from the laboratory and strode firmly into the world of commerce.

Extending the radio signal's reach, in 1901 Marconi transmitted the three dots of the Morse Code letter "S" faintly across the Atlantic from Cornwall, England to Newfoundland in Canada. He formed an American subsidiary, the Marconi Wireless Telegraph Company of America that would eventually become RCA, the Radio Corporation of America.

Competition and new inventions came from several quarters, because Marconi's radio transmission was not too complex to imitate. His efforts to monopolize radio by refusing communication with non – Marconi operators except in emergencies raised a storm of protest. The German government was furious. Its navy was operating its own system, originally based on copying Marconi's experiments. A rising militant nationalism among the great powers of Europe that would culminate in World War I hardly softened mutual suspicions. A conference in Berlin in 1906 resulted in the world's first international agreement on radio, mandating that international coastal stations must handle all messages, no matter who sent them, and that the letters "SOS" should be used for distress. Marconi operators generally ignored the decision and continued to use "CQD" ("seek you, distress").

Besides German contributions, improvements were made by other scientists and inventors who saw the business possibilities in radio. These radio pioneers included Oliver Lodge in England and Reginald Fessenden, Lee de Forest, John Stone, and E. Howard Armstrong in the United States. The quarrels that resulted among them would end years later in lengthy court battles fought over by corporations.

Radio not only affected the lives of ordinary citizens dwelling peacefully in every nook and cranny, it also changed the way wars are fought. Military communication from the platoon level up is today as essential as any weapon, to say nothing of global propaganda as a means of warfare.

RADIO GOES TO WAR

Radio first went into combat in the Russo – Japanese war in 1904. Both the Russian and Japanese fleets had installed the new signaling devices, but the Russian admiral chose wireless silence in hopes of eluding the waiting Japanese fleet. Meanwhile, warned by shore radio at lookout points of the impending arrival of the Russian "great white fleet" into Asian waters after a journey halfway around the world, the Japanese navy set a trap that sank most of the imperial Russian ships at the battle of Tsushima Strait.[4] The Japanese fleet suffered almost no losses, achieving the most one – sided naval victory in history. Russia sued for peace. Radio had already played a small but vital part in affecting the course of history. News of the Japanese victory in the Russo – Japanese War was hailed all across Asia and Africa. At last, a non – European country had defeated a European imperialist. The news brought hope. Japan was now firmly entrenched on the Asian mainland, remaining there and expanding its territory until the turn of fortunes of World War II.

Within a few years, the major powers had equipped their fleets with radio, although some ship captains regretted the loss of absolute control that they commanded at sea. Radio's military possibilities took to the skies in 1911 with the first air – to – ground transmission; World War I airplanes used Morse Code when they served as artillery spotters.

THE *TITANIC*

Commercial shipping added radio equipment, nudged by new laws. Two sinking merchant ships radioed successfully for help, signaling CQD. The rescues led Congress in 1910 to require most passenger ships to carry radio equipment. The law did not require operators to be on duty around the clock, an oversight it regretted two years later after the *Titanic* hit an iceberg and went down with 1,522 passengers and crew on its maiden voyage. The *Titanic* was on a well – traveled sea lane and a ship, the *Californian*, that might have come to the rescue was only nineteen miles away, but its radio operator had gone to bed, and the ship sailed on.

RADIO ACT OF 1912

Congress changed the law, and also passed the Radio Act of 1912, notable for requiring that a federal license was needed for radio transmission. Unlike the right of print publishing guaranteed by the First Amendment, broadcasting would be a privilege the government could grant or take away. This was an effort to bring some order to an otherwise uncontrolled but growing activity. Getting a license was as simple as sending a postcard to the Department of Commerce. At the time, no sense emerged of the chaos that would arrive a decade later with the arrival of commercial broadcasting.

If one purpose of the Radio Act of 1912 was to limit the number of amateur broadcasters, it failed. Most licenses went to hobbyists who used spark transmitters to send Morse Code. By 1917 there were 13,581 of them, plus uncounted thousands of other hobbyists who broadcast without a license. Alone among the large industrialized nations, the United States would allow all three forms of mediated point – to – point communication — telegraph, telephone, radio — to remain predominantly in private hands.

At the start of World War I, radio meant dots and dashes for military and commercial purposes. The main business of radio was in part the manufacturing of wireless equipment for ships, shore stations, and military communication, and in part the selling or leasing of communication services to the shipping industry and the government.

THE BUSINESS OF RADIO

That would change, because inventors who were busy improving telephone service wanted to apply the results to radio. Studying the so – called "Edison effect" of electrical "leakage" that Thomas Edison had noted during the course of improving telegraph transmission, John Ambrose Fleming built a two – element vacuum tube, or "diode." It sent electrons flowing from a wire filament to a plate. It was the first electronic device, and it carried speech on radio waves to earphones.

While tinkering, and not quite sure of what he had accomplished, American inventor Lee de Forest in 1906 added a third element between the filament and the plate, a piece of wire bent into a zigzag grid. His "audi-on" tube regulated the flow of electrons and amplified them, controlling sound volume. A more competent inventor, E. Howard Armstrong, figured out how to use the audion tube as an oscillator that transmitted radio waves as well as receiving them. Reginald Fessenden, a Canadian who had once worked in the Edison laboratory, and Swedish immigrant E.F.W. Alexanderson, a General Electric engineer, designed a high frequency alternator that could send a radio signal thousands of miles.

AUDION TUBE

Fessenden was the first inventor to send a human voice over a radio frequency. He did so on Christmas Eve, 1906, from his laboratory at Brant Rock, Massachusetts, to an audience of some amazed Marconi operators on duty at their posts on ships and at coastal stations listening for dots and dashes. He also reached some New England fishermen, a few naval officers, and reporters whom Fessenden had notified a few days earlier by radiotelegraph messages. He read from the Bible, sang, played the violin, broadcast phonograph music, and gave a short speech.[5]

VOICE, MUSIC THROUGH THE AIR

Two years later de Forest went to the top of the Eiffel Tower in Paris to broadcast opera music that could be faintly heard 550 miles away. De Forest saw the possibility of bringing music and voices into people's homes on a schedule, telling a *New York Times* reporter, "I look forward to the day when opera may be brought into every home. Someday the news and even advertising will be sent out over the wireless telephone."[6] By 1909, Charles "Doc" Herrold, who operated an engineering college in San Jose, California, broadcast news and music on a regular schedule. In 1915, de Forest manufactured equipment that was tuned to his occasional music and news broadcasts plus the commercials he aired to advertise his equipment. He had stumbled onto the vacuum tube by chance, but his vision of the potential of broadcasting was clear long before broadcasting became a reality. Also in 1915, from a transmitter in Virginia, AT&T sent an audio signal that was picked up in both Paris and Pearl Harbor.

CRYSTAL AND CATWHISKER

Because a single vacuum tube easily cost a week's wages, listening to distant radio signals might have been an expensive hobby out of the range of most purses, except that the "crystal and catwhisker" detector, easy to fashion and cheap, was the poor hobbyist's answer. A quartz crystal or a galena rock, by admitting electricity in only one direction, can detect radio waves if the crystal is touched at a certain spot with a fine wire, dubbed a "catwhisker." This discovery opened radio to thousands of hobbyists, many of whom would become the cadre of the broadcasting industry. They wrapped a copper wire to fabricate a tuning coil around a round, sturdy Quaker Oats cardboard box, the kind you still find in grocery stores. The catwhisker radio could detect a wireless signal and feed it into earphones, although it could not amplify the signal.

HOBBYISTS

The hobbyist's pleasure came from picking up call letters from a distant city. That would change when entertainment programs were created in the 1920s to attract listeners to commercial advertisements. Meanwhile, the hobbyists, many of whom were teenage boys and young men, formed wireless clubs that met by wireless. Their enthusiasm and stubbornness kept them at it day and night, but it proved to be a problem for U.S. Navy and commercial operators trying to transmit on the same frequency; they complained that children hogged the ether and would not give way. Adding an additional wavelength helped somewhat, but the mutual rancor continued. Preachers and educators who wanted to use the airwaves joined the fray,

Armstrong, while he was still a graduate student, did more than convert de Forest's audion tube into an oscillator. He reworked it so that sound came booming out of earphones. When radio sets with these redesigned vacuum tubes went on sale, all the earlier equipment was instantly outdated, and radio had the start of the technology necessary to change from a hobby for teenage boys in basements and garages to an instrument of family entertainment that was fit for the parlor.

It would take more than this technology, however. Even when manufacturers after World War I began to manufacture radio receivers, they were large, clunky, temperamental metal boxes with expensive tubes, lots of knobs that were tricky to adjust to wandering signals, a mess of wires, and a large, smelly battery filled with acid, not unlike the storage battery in an automobile. A radio was hardly a fit thing to put on a good parlor rug or a polished mahogany table. When the batteries and the maze of wires that accompanied them were replaced by plugs that went into sockets for 110 – volt AC current available in the wall, and the earphones were replaced by a loudspeaker that the entire family could listen to at the same time, the radio was ready for its new social use of broadcast entertainment. More than one set of earphones could be hooked up, but a loudspeaker secured a better sense of family togetherness. Housed inside a wooden cabinet to match the furniture, the radio would take its place in the family parlor beside two other machines disguised as furniture that delivered enjoyable sounds, the piano and the phonograph.

Some controversy now exists over the accuracy of a claim made by David Sarnoff, who arrived in America at the age of nine, a Russian immigrant who rose from poverty to become the head of RCA. He said that when he was an employee of the American Marconi Wireless Telegraph Company in 1916, he sent a memo to the company president about something very different from the point – to – point Morse Code that was at the heart of company operations. Sarnoff said that he proposed that the company build a "Radio Music Box" for the public. According to Sarnoff, the company president ignored the memo. (A broadcast history scholar, Louise Benjamin, has questioned whether Sarnoff accurately reported the date of his memo.[7])

At the end of World War I, the business of radio was still largely the manufacture of ship – to – ship and ship – to – shore radiotelegraph (Morse Code) and radiotelephone (voice) communication equipment, the transmission of messages, plus the manufacture of spark transmitters bought by hobbyists. Some inventors and engineers tinkered with improvements, and hobbyists built their own receivers, but they acted outside the small wireless industry. That a vast market existed for radio was hardly credible, but in the years immediately after the war, there were hints of its future beyond a hobby. Hobbyists by the thousands had become radio operators for the Army and Navy. With the war over, they wanted to start new stations to broadcast voice and music.

Frank Conrad, a Westinghouse Corporation engineer who had manufactured portable equipment for the Signal Corps, was one of them. Setting up a transmitter in the garage of his home in Pittsburgh, he was an amateur who broadcast to other amateurs for the pleasure of doing it. He broadcast music by placing his microphone next to a Victrola, requesting postcards from listeners so that he could determine the range

I have in mind a plan of development that would make radio a household utility in the same sense as the piano or phonograph. The idea is to bring music into the house by wireless.

While this has been tried in the past by wires, it has been a failure. . . . With radio, however, it would seem to be entirely feasible. . . . The problem of transmitting music has already been solved in principle, and therefore all the receivers attuned to the transmitting wave length should be capable of receiving such music.

The receiver can be designed in the form of a "Radio Music Box" and arranged for several different wavelengths, which should be changeable with the throwing of a single switch or the pressing of a single button.

The "Radio Music Box" can be supplied with amplifying tubes and a loudspeaking telephone, all of which can be neatly mounted in one box. The box can be placed on a table in the parlor or living room. . . . There should be no difficulty in receiving music perfectly when transmitted within a radius of 25 to 50 miles.

— David Sarnoff
"Music Box Memo"

of his signals. So many listeners replied to ask for a particular song that Conrad started transmitting the broadcasts according to a schedule, adding sports scores and some singing and instrument playing by his children. A Pittsburgh newspaper printed a feature story about it, which further broadened his audience.

KDKA, PITTSBURGH

To meet requests for music that Conrad did not possess, the owner of a phonograph record shop agreed to lend him records in return for identifying the store on the air. The records that Conrad played increased the store owner's sales of those titles. All this interest led a local department store to offer assembled wireless sets for sale. That led Conrad's employer, Westinghouse, the first major corporation to consider a market beyond point – to – point transmission, to manufacture radio receivers for voice and music. Conrad's garage broadcasting equipment was brought onto the Westinghouse lot, a transmitter went up, and broadcasting began on November 2, 1920, with the call letters KDKA. The date was chosen so that the first broadcast would be of the Harding – Cox presidential election. Following Conrad's idea, Westinghouse offered a regular program schedule. A few thousand people tuned in.

The business of broadcasting became the sale of equipment to transmit or receive broadcasts, not the broadcasts themselves. Radio clubs were formed by eager high school and university students. Universities erected transmitters, through which professors lectured. Newspapers also set up transmitters to enhance their reputations and attract new subscribers, not to make money.[8] Some department stores set up low – powered broadcast operations in a corner of the store to attract curious shoppers, but they did not advertise their goods. Nothing was advertised. No one spent much money on radio broadcasting or expected much money back. The quality of the sound was poor; it was not helped by scratchy phonograph records. Even so, spontaneous groups got together to listen in stores, hotel lobbies, or speakeasies, legal saloons being outlawed by Prohibition.

Evangelists set up stations to attract worshippers; Billy Sunday and Aimee Semple McPherson grew rich and famous as they built large, devoted national followings. McPherson in particular sensed that the "wireless telephone" in the home carried a degree of intimacy and connection to the lonely. She employed it effectively to bring listeners together to share moments of silent prayer, an oddly brilliant use of the talking medium. McPherson lost her license because she would not stick to her assigned frequency, arguing that she needed to operate on "God's frequency."

THE FIRST COMMERCIAL

Both before and after the introduction of commercials, the purpose of programming was to attract listeners to buy something, radio sets at first, then advertised products. The AT&T radio station in New York, WEAF, opened the floodgates to commercial broadcasting when it rented time to a real estate company, the Queensboro Corporation, to talk about its new apartments on Long Island. For its $300 investment in purchases of time for a repeated ten – minute, soft – sell sales pitch during one evening and four afternoons, the real estate company sold $127,000 worth of apartments.[9] AT&T, which was normally in the business of renting its equipment by the minute to telephone callers, had treated its station like a telephone, initiating what it called "toll broadcasting,"

AT&T considered itself to be the sole proprietor of this idea, but other transmitting stations saw the possibility to make money. It took four more years of almost no "toll broadcasts," many arguments between corporations, and a final agreement between the Telephone Group headed by AT&T and the Radio Group headed by RCA, but broadcasting in the United States now was constructing a strong financial base and a new social use, even if not everyone warmed to the idea.

A number of listeners were offended that commercials were broadcast over a radio station that depended on a government license. Secretary of Commerce Herbert Hoover told broadcasters, "I believe that the quickest way to kill broadcasting would be to use it for direct advertising. The reader of the newspaper has an option whether he will read an ad or not, but if a speech by the president is to be used as the meat in a sandwich of two patent medicine advertisements, there will be no radio left."[10] The advertising industry itself, with a nervous eye on the print media, chimed in with editorial comment in *Printers' Ink*, "Any attempt to make the radio an advertising medium... would, we think, prove positively offensive to great numbers of people. The family circle is not a public place, and advertising has no business intruding there unless it is invited."[11] The National Association of Broadcasters used similar language in its first Radio Code in 1929, but soon changed its mind.

Broadcasting stayed in private hands, but the United States government was not totally divorced from it because radio stations needed licenses to transmit. Radio station owners needed the support of government officials to pursue what they sensed would become a lucrative commercial business. To avoid giving verbal ammunition to opponents, radio stations were cautious about what they advertised; they worried at first, for example, that toothpaste might be too intimate a product to advertise. But the potential of the new medium was just too great to do nothing. Toothpaste found its way into messages.

None of the corporations who had taken over the patents from individual owners had total control of the medium, ranging from the manufacture of radio sets and station equipment to broadcasting rights. Bitter court battles lasted for years and ended with either hard – fought victories or compromises in the form of cross – licensing agreements

As a medium for those who hoped to control mass behavior, radio offered numerous advantages over print media. Like graphics but unlike the printed word, radio could influence illiterates (6 percent of U.S. adults in 1920) and preliterate children, so that Ipana toothpaste, for example, could make its radio pitch for "the one in the red and yellow tube." Unlike newspaper and magazine ads, radio commercials could not be skipped over — they interrupted desired programming and could follow listeners from room to room.... Not only could one listen to radio while engaged in other activities, including reading, one could continue to listen long after becoming too tired to do anything else — so that broadcasting promised (or threatened) to fill every waking moment of the day.[12]

—James Beniger

for companies to use each other's patents. The leading corporations in the broadcasting industry were General Electric, Westinghouse, RCA, AT&T, and Western Electric. Initially, RCA, General Electric and Westinghouse, the "radio group," concentrated on the receivers of messages, the audience; they regarded broadcast programs as a service to create public demand for their radio sets. AT&T and Western Electric were known as the "telephone group"; their concern was with the senders of messages, later called "sponsors." Eventually, an amalgam of these approaches produced present day broadcasting, combining programming and commercials.

BBC MODEL

Other nations chose a different direction. Governments controlled all aspects of broadcasting. They would have no commercials for decades. The British Broadcasting Corporation, solidly pro – establishment in its programming policy, followed the principle of presenting what those in charge believed listeners should hear for their own good, not the American policy of broadcasting what listeners wanted to hear. Funds to support the BBC came from annual user license fees on radio sets. Years later, it would be licenses on television sets. In the mid – 1950s, as television replaced radio, the British government finally licensed an independent commercial service, ITV, to operate. Most other industrialized nations preferred a version of the BBC model, often with direct government operation, although Canada and Mexico were among countries that permitted a mix of government and privately owned radio stations.

Some countries were much more controlling. To a dictatorship, the propaganda potential of radio was all – important, an adjunct in retaining power. Totalitarian governments funded radio stations the way they funded all their departments, with annual taxpayer – supported budgets, a sure way to treat broadcasters like government employees and to keep them firmly under the thumb. Radio programming and the television programs that would follow had as their mission citizen loyalty, the promotion of national policies, support for the government and the security forces, and opposition to the enemy, internal and external.

OUTSHOUTING EACH OTHER

The United States after World War I provided only one frequency for all radio transmission, with a second frequency added later for crop and weather reports and later a third frequency for music, based on the maritime communication model, where sender and receiver exchange brief messages, then go silent. But broadcast stations are not silent. In fact, the broadcast stations were trying to be heard by boosting their transmission power to outshout each other. They were drowning each other out. A new system was plainly needed. Government efforts to alleviate the clamor by opening up more frequencies were overwhelmed by the new stations coming in to take advantage of radio's commercial possibilities. Shortwave, previously used only by amateurs, was taken over for commercial and government purposes.

Congress preferred not to upset anyone, yet some action was clearly needed. The only solution was regulation, but the four conferences called by the government in the 1920s had various groups at each other's throats. Owners of large stations wanted stronger controls on who could broadcast, small station owners wanted to be under the broadcasting tent, and so did hobbyists. Educators found themselves being squeezed out of the tent by commercial broadcasters. The result of somewhat hesitant government intervention was the Radio Act of 1927, expanded by the Communication Act of 1934, and not substantially changed again until the Communication Act of 1996. An example of the reluctance of government to involve itself in broadcast content, coupled with contradiction, concerned obscene language. In the 1927 Act, repeated in the 1934 Act, the government said, "Nothing… shall interfere with the right of free speech by means of radio communication." It was followed by, "No person within the jurisdiction of the United States shall utter any obscene, indecent, or profane language by means of radio communication."

Under the theory that airwaves belong to the public, all the laws were based on the government's right to regulate broadcasting and determine who can hold a license. Stations pledged to operate "in the public interest, convenience, or necessity," but neither Congress nor the regulatory agencies have ever specified what this means. By these laws, the government is not permitted to determine what is broadcast, and it is forbidden to act as a censor, although it can fine stations heavily for broadcasts it considers indecent. However, its power to issue or retrieve the extremely valuable licenses is great, although almost never enforced. The history of broadcast regulation in the United States has been one of competing influences, intense lobbying, power structures, and the advantage that comes with owning stations that can help or hurt political candidates.[13]

Not everyone waited for the AC power that began to replace radio batteries in 1926; in that year, one house in six already had a radio, many of them equipped with loudspeakers, so that listening took on the pleasure of family conversations at dinner. Nearly half the population lived out in the countryside, far from telephones or newspapers. If they were also far from electricity, the battery – operated radio became their connection to the world. They may have bought the radio for entertainment, but it also delivered information. A rural public that might have been uninterested and uninformed about the economic and social turmoil elsewhere in the nation and the world was now learning to care about what was going on elsewhere.

I lived through the day when the Victor Talking Machine Company — and they did a great job in their day — could not understand how people would sit at home and listen to music that someone else decided they should hear. And so they felt that the "radio music box" and radio broadcasting were a toy and would be a passing fancy.[14]

— DAVID SARNOFF

"IN THE PUBLIC INTEREST"

Radios were being installed in automobiles. In 1930, a battery elimi-nator for cars was a marked improvement; cars and radios have gone together ever since like ham and eggs.[15] Listeners wrote warm letters to radio stations. Magazine articles described the joys of sitting at home alone or with family members to listen to their radios.[16] People went out to the movies, but stayed in to listen to the radio, as they would later with television.

De Forest, who insisted on calling himself the "father of radio," would attack broadcasting for presenting commercial "spots," which de Forest called "stains," and he asked the industry, "What have you done with my child?" But he expressed pride in positive changes.

Audience surveys had not yet come into existence. They would be started by Archibald Crossley in 1929, and increase in size and sophistication as audience growth and network demands for higher ad rates led adver-tising agencies to insist on better information about who was listening. Surveys revealed that even low income homes had at least one radio, and the average home had a radio turned on more than five hours a day. In fact, low – income homes listened to the free entertainment even more than middle – income homes, just as low income homes today watch more free television. During the Depression, when Americans cut back on going to the movies and buying subscriptions to newspapers, they spent even more time with free radio. Advertisers paid attention.

Radio has kept the wanderer home at nights, it has brightened the gloom of separation and shortened the long hours of loneliness. It is a comfort-ing companion to the shut–in; it soothes the pain of the suffering. It brings counsel to the housewife, information to the farmer, entertainment and gaiety to the young. On silent wings it flies to the forgotten corners where mails are uncertain and few, where the cheer of kindly voices comes only through the head–phones, where music is never heard.[17]

— LEE DE FOREST

The tying together of stations, first as temporary "hookups" in a "chain" and later as permanent networks, solved a problem for broadcasters: how to pay for better programs. When stations in several cities broad-cast the same program, its cost could be shared. Better programs also drew listeners away from competing stations. The larger total audience meant higher advertising charges, so there were other advantages to joining a network. National advertisers who saw no benefit in dealing with individual stations were interested when a network audience could be measured in the millions. RCA in 1926 assembled a number of sta-tions into two permanent networks, the "Red" and the "Blue." One year later the competitive CBS (Columbia Broadcasting System) network was formed. A fourth national network, the Mutual Broadcasting Sys-tem, was put together in 1934. In New England, the Midwest, and the Far West, regional networks formed.

When broadcasting began, the broadcasters programmed what they themselves liked or what their friends suggested. Vaudeville was popular, so some ideas came from there. In time, radio — and the movies — took so much from vaudeville that there was little reason to pay good money for tickets. It has been said that movies killed vaudeville. Radio wielded a knife, too.

In the 1920s, the networks were less likely to do their own programming than to sell blocks of time to advertisers or their agencies to create the programs. Many were named for the advertised products, such as "The Eveready Hour" advertising batteries, "The Gold Dust Twins" advertising a household cleanser, and "The A&P Gypsies" advertising the grocery chain. Because newspapers carried program logs as a public service, the newspapers were really giving free publicity to a competing medium. As the newspapers themselves were carrying advertising for what the radio programs advertised, that did not sit well at publishers conferences.

Another cause of anger was that during the Depression radio profits grew while newspaper profits stagnated. To add insult to injury, for the two or three cents it cost to buy a daily newspaper, those radio stations that presented newscasts had access to all the news that a newspaper had labored to assemble. The stations could present that news over the air long before a delivery boy threw a copy of the newspaper onto the front porch. Newspapers struck back weakly. Some newspapers eliminated the free listings of daily radio programs, or they identified a program only as "Music" instead of "A&P Gypsies." That did not last long. Irate letters from readers and canceled subscriptions forced those newspapers to abandon such tactics.

Radio coverage of the 1932 election that swept Franklin Delano Roosevelt into office and the intense coverage of the Lindbergh baby kidnapping opened the eyes of newspaper publishers to the potential of radio to shove newspapers aside as the public's preferred way to get the day's news. All this led to the "Press – Radio War" of 1933 – 35, when members of the powerful newspaper industry demanded that all newspapers stop the free daily radio logs. They pressured the wire services to deny their feeds to radio stations, except for a restricted feed by the new Press – Radio Bureau that was available only for non – sponsored newscasts.

Radio stations rebelled and started their own newsgathering units. Newspapers that owned radio stations joined independent radio stations and networks to oppose controls; to some extent the "Press – Radio War" was a "Newspaper – Newspaper War."[18] In a short time, newspapers who tried to limit radio news gave up the fight. As war clouds gathered in Europe, listeners sought more news from both newspapers and radio.

The increase of broadcast news went on for decades. It was not long before radio's coverage of national and international news made it the medium that the public went to first for news, ending the long dominance of newspapers. Today, wire services are all too happy to sell their

NAMING PROGRAMS FOR PRODUCTS

PRESS – RADIO WAR

feeds, including a special broadcast wire, to radio and television stations. Newspaper listings of programs are still free.

During radio's golden age, families everywhere gathered in the evening around the radio to listen to dramas, comedies, music, quizzes, and variety shows. In the morning, melodramas, dubbed "soap operas" to reflect their sponsors, captured an audience made up largely of housewives. The message from day to day through convoluted plots that were never resolved was: stay tuned. After school and on Saturday mornings dramatic children's adventure serials delivered the same tune – in – to-morrow message, followed around the weekday dinner hour by news and commentary programs. (In Great Britain, the BBC mandated that the after school "children's hour" meant silence.) Sunday mornings offered church services, and Sunday afternoons featured classical music and operas. Live reporting of baseball and football games, boxing matches, and horse racing drew large audiences. The schedule made the radio in the parlor the place for the family to come together, listening to their favorite programs broadcast on a daily or weekly schedule.

With all this free, attractive programming, a change in people's lives passed largely unnoticed. Families were spending less time entertaining themselves with such active behavior as reading, pursuing hobbies, strolling in the evening, or visiting neighbors. The passive pleasure of sitting in front of the pridefully dusted Philco console or Atwater Kent to hear distant entertainment pouring into the parlor gradually took hold in the home. Being alone could seem less lonely. For listeners who disliked silences, here was an alternative that could keep at bay stray thoughts or any thinking at all. As the quality of broadcast entertainment and technology improved, this shift in behavior strengthened until it has become the norm to sit passively at home in the evening to be entertained.

Evidence of the influence of radio in the 1930s became plain when "Doctor" John Brinkley, who hawked goat gland remedies — the Viagra of its day — to a trustful audience, nearly won the Kansas gubernatorial election by write – in votes on the basis of a three – week broadcast campaign and no political experience or any other support whatever. Those who opposed all radio commercials said Brinkley's goat gland scam fulfilled their predictions of what radio would become. For persuasive radio speakers, anything seemed possible.

THE WAR OF THE WORLDS

No single entertainment program delivered a stronger punch than Orson Welles' production of H.G. Wells' novel, *The War of the Worlds*. Approximately six million listeners were told that Martians had invaded Earth and were slaughtering everyone with death rays. It was done in the form of a news broadcast, which radio listeners had learned to trust in the years leading up to World War II. That a twist of the dial to another

How easy it is to close the eyes and imagine the other listeners in little back rooms, in kitchens, din-ing–rooms, sitting–rooms, attics; in garages, offices, cabins, engine rooms, bungalows, cottages, man-sions, hotels, apartments; one here, two there, a little company around a table away off yonder.[19]

— ORANGE MCMEANS

station might bring sanity, or that the narrator said this was a fictional tale, did not stop some listeners from running into the streets screaming that the world was coming to an end. The play was broadcast one month after the Munich conference that would elicit Neville Chamberlain's wistful phrase, "peace in our time"; millions of newspaper readers and radio commentary listeners still thought war was on the way. Later rebroadcasts of *The War of the Worlds* to other countries also resulted in public panic. In South America, several people died in a riot caused by anger at having been tricked by a radio station.

The most popular comedies, dramas, and variety programs brought listeners of different backgrounds together in a shared experience. Everyone who had listened to Jack Benny or Fred Allen the night before could talk about them the next day at the factory lunch break, at the office water cooler, or on the telephone.

Radio executives had not set out to alter fundamental human behavior. They did not consider themselves a catalyst for bringing Americans together as a nation in order to continue at a deeper level what the telegraph and the telephone had done. Yet here was another marker of mediated communication. With announcers chosen for their neutral, non – regional speech pattern, and with strong Southern, New England, and Brooklyn accents used for humor, along with exaggerated foreign and ethnic accents, it was made clear that the best accent was a non – accented American way of speaking. By modern standards, those programs were — beyond question — racist or ethnically stereotyping. The foreign, ethnic, and regional characters were never presented as evil. They were funny. However, they conformed to negative public images, notably Amos 'n' Andy, whose white actors portrayed the African – American characters as lazy, irresponsible, not very bright schemers.[21] Sadly, because of segregated housing and schools, many whites knew of blacks only through these caricatures.

Radio did its part to heat the "melting pot" of the American immigrant experience. There was little room on the dial for intentional efforts to separate or segregate groups. The Ku Klux Klan, so popular in the South and Midwest during the 1920s, did not take hold on American networks. Father Charles Coughlin, the firebrand anti – British, anti – Semitic, and increasingly pro – Nazi priest, had a huge radio following for a time but, as his attacks intensified, stations unplugged from his hookup. Under pressure from Roman Catholic Church leaders and the government, Coughlin finally left the airwaves. At the height of his popularity, a plea from him could pile 100,000 telegrams on senators' desks.

With factories turning out inexpensive radio sets that could be plugged into household current and tuned with ease, with government regulation in place, with programming created by a growing cadre of talented

For the first time, history has been made in the hearing of its pawns. Radio has given them not only the words but the voices of the protagonists: Hitler, Benes, Chamberlain, Daladier, Mussolini. The radio has our ears. It is scarcely too much to say that the future of civilization will be determined to a considerable degree by who rules radio and how.[21]

— JAMES RORTY

HEATING THE "MELTING POT"

Radio helped tie the country together during the dark years of 1942–1943, when we "hung on" while our war machine geared for maximum effort, and the brighter 1944–1945 period, when we knew the enemy had to give in. Radio news reported the war at home and abroad, delivering more news to more citizens than any other combination of film and print media.[23]

—Christopher Sterling
and John Kittross

directors, writers, musicians, and actors, with distribution funneled through networks, and with commercials to pay the bills, radio broadcasting entered its "golden age," lasting from about 1930 to about 1950, when television replaced it as the center of family entertainment.[22] That its only cost to listeners was the time to listen to commercials was accounted as no cost at all, especially during the Depression, when any expense, even a dime or quarter for a movie ticket, was too much to the millions of families "on relief," as welfare was then called. A laugh, a song, or a story lifted the day's burden.

Arguably the radio dramas by Norman Corwin and a few other writers and directors were the highlight of radio's golden age. Radio has not produced their equal since then. From the start of the Depression through World War II, the most popular entertainment media were radio and motion pictures, enjoying their golden ages at the same time, and providing information as well as entertainment.

One of the functions of mediated communication has been to bring choice to the public. That should have happened in 1933 when Armstrong's invention of FM (frequency modulation) radio held the promise not only of a clearer audio signal than AM (amplitude modulation), but also a bandwidth that could accommodate many new stations. That FM was not diffused until after World War II, more than a dozen years later, was due to the machinations of David Sarnoff, who understood its potential all too well, but considered FM as a hindrance to television, which RCA was then spending a fortune to develop. Armstrong tried without success to convince the FCC to rescind its decision to shift FM to a different bandwidth, which left 400,000 prewar FM receivers useless. Armstrong's frustration led to his suicide.

After the war, new FM stations did arrive, slowly at first, most of them devoted to music to take advantage of the FM clarity. Also arriving in the postwar years were stereophonic transmission, high fidelity audiotape, LP (long playing) records, and tape cassettes, all promising better sound. America shifted slightly from being a nation of just radio listeners to a nation of audio appreciators. Even without FM, the quality of radio sound improved year by year as audio engineers, replacing vacuum tubes with transistors, labored over every part of the sound's path from the microphone in the studio to the speaker in the home radio set. In 1971, AM–FM radios were being installed by car manufacturers.

Without transistors, radio sets would be the size of sewing machines and computers the size of houses. Personal computing as we know it simply wouldn't exist, nor would the World Wide Web.[24]

—James Gillies and
Robert Cailliau

Tuners, turntables, pre–amps, amplifiers, and their connections were improved for the amateur audiophiles who insisted on perfect tones and were willing to pay for them. Perhaps you can recall being invited to someone's home to listen to a new "rig," only to have the host interrupt the music after a few bars to laud the quality of the sound and the precise placing of the speakers. The owner's praise of his new equipment blocked any serious effort to actually hear the music. This was not the first time that a form of mediated communication was the subject of attention as well as the means of delivering content. It certainly would not be the last time.

Postwar radio seemed headed for trouble as television arrived, gobbling up radio's best programs, staff, talent, funding, and energy. Families forming and expanding through the postwar boom years moved their radio consoles out of their new tract homes to give pride of place to the round screen 7 – inch or 12 – inch television set.

Contrary to general expectations, radio did not die. It was reinvented, so that today there are more radio stations than ever, and 99% of all U.S. homes have at least one radio.[25] Prime time each evening would in the near future be taken over by television, but radio shifted its attention to drive time, the morning and afternoon work commute. Listeners carried portable radios to the beach and placed them near the kitchen sink and the factory work bench. Some radio stations shifted their programming focus to ethnic minorities. Adding to the day's radio listening were the clock radios to wake up to or fall asleep to, the automobile radio for the twice – daily commute, background radio to accompany a meal, and music pouring through Walkman earphones to accompany a jog. It was clear that radio broadcasting would be different, but it was far from finished.

One significant difference was that people no longer looked at their radio sets. In the days when the radio sat in the parlor, the family that gathered around for their favorite programs looked at the radio, which — after all — was talking to them. Postwar radio was largely heard as an accompaniment to driving, working, starting the morning, and so forth. Listeners were too occupied to stare at their radios.

Postwar radio programming changed totally. Networks got out of the radio business except for newscasts and sports, splitting into multiple news networks to broaden their appeal to independent, competitive stations. The networks left programming to the individual stations and, in larger cities, to an increasing role for public radio. The concept of identifiable, prewar – style programs of fixed length, usually fifteen or thirty minutes, was transferred to television, where the fixed length was 30 minutes or an hour. In its place on radio were longer segments of recorded music guided by a disc jockey, a new marriage of the audio recording and radio.

Before the war, with the exception of *The Make Believe Ballroom*, most of the music heard on radio had been live, due to poor phonograph recording quality and pressure from the musician's union. The network ban on recordings during the 1930s was lifted briefly to play the frantic

ENTER TELEVISION

LOOKING AT RADIO SETS

RECORDED MUSIC

reaction of a Chicago program producer, Herbert Morrison, who was recording the arrival of the German dirigible Hindenburg at Lakehurst, New Jersey, when it burst into flames. For the most part, the American Federation of Musicians was able to enforce a ban of broadcast recordings to protect musicians' jobs. That ban crumbled when ABC lured Bing Crosby from NBC by promising to allow him to record his programs.

RADIO COMMENTATORS

Another change has been talk radio, eventually dominated by conservative political commentary from talk show speakers like Rush Limbaugh, who frequently referred with pride to their large audiences, yet insisted that they themselves were not part of "media" and were not journalists. They identified themselves as "antidotes" to "the media," by which they meant newspapers, news magazines, and television news, but not radio.

The music and the talk programs marked another change of radio programming. With the doubling and redoubling of the number of radio stations since World War II, programs were no longer designed to reach the largest possible general audience. Instead, stations sought to develop a particular type of "sound" in their choice of music, commercials, disc jockey patter, and even news. Several "all news" stations went on the air and, for a little while, even an "all ads" station.

A STATION'S "SOUND"

With a distinctive sound, stations tried to reach a niche market, an identifiable segment of the radio market, such as listeners between eighteen and thirty – five, or an audience that enjoyed country western music. Where broadcasting during the golden age of radio acted to bring people together, a new era of narrowcasting now evolved. To the best of the ability of the fourteen thousand radio stations in the United States to do so, listeners were channeled into separate markets. Musical tastes were the stations' most effective tool; a playlist stayed within a range that could be identified as rock 'n' roll, jazz, MOR (middle – of – the – road), country western, mariachi, rhythm and blues, classical, big band, hip hop, and so on. Record companies eagerly participated because it increased music sales.

SATELLITE RADIO

The future promises to continue to chop up the audience; and to give them more content choices. The first decade of the twenty – first century saw rapid growth in several types of radio programing. Except for the networks and shortwave broadcasts, radio had once been local. Network programs had always been fed through local stations, and only a handful of "clear channel" stations sent signals more than a few dozen miles. In the new century, satellite radio services like Sirius and XM carried music with CD – quality sound, plus news and talk, all without commercials. Because the signal arrived from a satellite, it remained constant as a car crossed the nation, compared to the limited range of local stations. Distance no longer implied static and loss of quality.

Another change was AM stereo radio.[26] Still another change has been the conversion of analog radio to non – satellite digital transmission of both AM and FM stations, known as HD Radio. To owners of HD radio sets, the new service offered CD – quality sound without the subscription fees of satellite radio. Like standard AM and FM radio, it is supported by commercials. By 2007, more than 700 U.S. radio stations had converted to HD.

At the same time, thousands of Internet radio stations came online. An Internet station could specialize in, say, Broadway show tunes or, for that matter, Albanian folk music, reaching an international audience of a few dozen if someone was willing to program for them. The website www.radiolocator.com listed more than ten thousand radio signals streaming audio over the Web.

INTERNET STATIONS

Established radio broadcasting stations also sent their news, weather, sports, and traffic reports to the World Wide Web and to wireless receivers in PDAs (personal digital assistants) and telephones. It all added up to a huge increase in choices. That, of course, extended both our connections to media sources and our mediated separation from other individuals.

Separate from broadcasting, radio has continued to serve point – to – point functions. Guardians of the public welfare, such as police, sheriff's deputies, fire dispatchers, Forest Service personnel, air controllers, and the Coast Guard have their own radio frequencies. Radio astronomy has fought for its bandwidth. Mobile phones, beeper pagers, and cell phones have all needed frequencies for wireless transmission. Citizen's band radio, a continuation of the old pre – broadcasting hobbyists' radio service, at one time counted participants in the millions, most famously the long haul truck drivers who warned each other of the "smokies" who lay in wait behind highway billboards. To some extent, cell phones have replaced their transmitting rigs, but CB radios, still sending out a sense of what radio was like before broadcasting, refuse to disappear.

RADIO WAS NOT ONE thing, not one invention. It did not have one effect on the world. As point – to – point wireless Morse Code communication, it extended the effects of the telegraph to the places where wires could not run. As a point – to – point voice carrier, it extended the telephone. Industry leaders at the start of radio did not think of broadcasting, and did not want listeners tuning in. Radio's dots and dashes were primarily for ship – to – shore point – to – point communication. As broadcasting, radio did not have "one audience." You would be more correct to invert that phrase to "an audience of one" millions of times over. Broadcasting

CONCLUSION

gave a degree of uniformity to a diverse population, contact for the lonely, comfort to scattered listeners. As it did so, it created a landscape of those who depended on the company of unseen others for information and entertainment.

The business of broadcasting was just the sale of radio receiving sets and transmission equipment until commercials began in 1922. During the Depression and World War II, considered the "Golden Age of Radio," the radio set in the family parlor brought entertainment, information, and hope to an American population in need of all three. In the midst of the widespread Depression misery, the public was grateful for the "free" entertainment provided by radio and did not regard listening to commercials as a "cost." Comedians became household names. In a nation too large for a national press based on available technology, radio commentators provided national voices.

Importantly but generally unnoticed, people's habits changed because of the time spent each day listening to radio programs. This has continued into the age of television. Broadcasting has helped both to push its listeners together and pull them apart. People in any situation may push themselves together by efforts to find commonalities in humor and ordinary daily life. The golden age of radio, when three networks dominated, brought people together to talk about what was on last night. Radio broadcasting disseminated national culture and, at its best, informed and taught its listeners, and sometimes influenced government leadership. Listeners were also pushed together by hearing a common language spoken with a standard national accent.

When postwar business constraints led to narrowcasting, the opposite occurred. Combined with all the other choices people now have for mediated communication, there is less commonality to share at the water cooler. Communication by radio exists, but more and more it is with those who share our interests, no matter where in the world they are, and much less face–to–face with someone who heard the same radio program. We live in a virtual water cooler world.

One overlooked difference of radio today is that people no longer look at their radios, a sign that radio is an accompaniment to other activities, like waking up, driving, eating, working, jogging. People sit together to watch television, not radio, as they once did.

The power of radio to influence the public was exemplified by "Doctor" John Brinkley and by the reaction to *The War of the Worlds*. If comedies and dramas during the golden age of radio pushed people together, the news explainers pulled them apart. Unlike radio news today but like talk radio, the best known newscasts of the 1930s, '40s, and '50s were delivered by commentators who used a news item of the day as a hook to deliver a partisan monologue. There were both liberal and conservative commentators during radio's golden age. Listeners generally tuned to the commentator whose views made the most sense, which meant the commentator they agreed with.

Radio broadcasting also changed the way that people chose to be entertained and informed. Reading requires active participation. Sitting in a theater or concert hall, while passive, at least requires dressing up before going out and sharing the event with others in the auditorium, making such a trip a social experience. Radio broadcasting has required none of this. The listener can sit quietly at home and let the newscast, comedy, drama, or music do all the work. Once a radio station is chosen, listening is essentially a passive activity. The medium has been quite a success.

Our history will be what we make of it. And if there are any historians about fifty or a hundred years from now, and there should be preserved kinescopes for one week of all three networks, they will find recorded in black and white, or color, evidence of decadence, escapism, and insulation from the realities of the world in which we live.

— Edward R. Murrow
Speech to Broadcast Executives
15 October, 1958

10 TELEVISION: LEANING BACK

"**Television has been called** a fatal attraction, a sort of cultural death wish," blamed for social ills ranging from illiteracy to obesity to childhood hyperactivity to crime. Yet television was adopted by the public with a speed unmatched in history until then. Even today, with all the competition from other media and despite all these critical insults, television continues to be watched, and watched, and watched. The average American home now has more television sets than people, including babies.

The influence of television has extended to every facet of life, including judgments about desirable careers, desirable life styles, what and how much to buy, ethical standards, relationships, conversations, behavior, how we should spend our discretionary time, and everything in between. To dismiss television viewing as something we can take or let alone ignores its addictive nature, as study after study has shown. This is not just an American phenomenon. Research reported that the Japanese were even more addicted.[1] Marshall McLuhan was thinking of television, plus radio and movies, when he wrote about popular culture, or "pop kulch." Today, with television programs available on TV screens, computer screens, telephone screens, and video iPod screens, arriving wired, wireless, downloaded, stored on tape or disc, bought or rented at thousands of neighborhood video shops, watched for hours daily, in all its manifestations, television is, in a word, *us*.

TELEVISION'S ROOTS

Television, meaning "seeing at a distance," came to mean "seeing by electricity." Its roots go back to 1817, a time of excitement about the properties of electricity, when Sweden's Jon Berzelius shone various amounts of light on selenium, a sulfur–like byproduct of copper refining, and noticed variations in how well it conducted electric current. Scotland's Alexander Bain, in 1842 sent a current that caused a metal brush to duplicate alphabet letters onto paper. In 1847, the Abbé Caselli, an Italian researcher in France, sent drawings between two cities electrically. In 1873, Ireland's Joseph May, by varying the amount of light on selenium, sent a signal across the ocean on the Atlantic telegraph cable. That led an American engineer, Philip Carey, to envision a television matrix based on an array of selenium cells in a camera, each wired to a light bulb in a matching array in a receiver. English, Italian, German, French, Russian and American inventors added their efforts during the nineteenth century, leading in time to wirephotos, facsimile, and the flashing lights at Times Square.

In 1830, experimenting in a different direction, England's Michael Faraday sent electricity through a vacuum in a glass bottle. Sir William Crookes followed this path in 1878 by shooting electrons from the cathode terminal to the anode terminal of an evacuated tube. Sir J.J. Thomson added to this experiment with a magnet that moved the stream of electrons across the tube face. Germany's Karl Ferdinand Braun, in 1897 coated the inner face of a tube with fluorescence so that it glowed when struck by the cathode rays. All these experiments led to the television tube.

What was missing was an image on the face of the tube. In 1884, German student Paul Nipkow introduced this by using two disks with matching patterns of holes that scanned and reproduced a scene fast enough to reach the human eye's persistence of vision. England's John Logie Baird experimented with Nipkow disks into the 1930s, but this mechanical system proved to be a dead end, even though Baird managed to send a murky image across the Atlantic Ocean in 1928. The future lay with an electronic system.

EXPERIMENTS

Russia's Boris Rosing had a workable system by 1907, partly electronic and partly mechanical, using a cathode ray tube. Others continued electronic experiments. One was Rosing's assistant, Vladimir Zworykin. England's A.A. Campbell Swinton pursued the same electronic trail. Another, improbably, was an Idaho high school student, Philo Farnsworth, who had read about such experiments in a popular science magazine.

While still a teenager, Farnsworth acquired a patent for what he called an "image dissector." Zworykin, an immigrant to the United States, in 1923 sent a still image from a camera tube that he called an "iconoscope" to the face of a cathode ray display tube that he called a "kinescope." True television is dated from this 1923 demonstration. Zworykin's fellow Russian immigrant, RCA executive David Sarnoff, assembled a team from Westinghouse, General Electric, and RCA under Zworykin to develop electronic television.

In 1925, American inventor Charles Francis Jenkins sent the first transmission of a moving object, windmills, to a receiver five miles away. In 1926, a Bell Telephone Labs team under Herbert Ives transmitted a motion picture. AT&T used a mechanical scanning system to send a black–and–white still photo from Washington to New York in 1927, and color photos in 1929. The quality was poor, an experiment of no possible commercial use, but from AT&T also came co–axial cables and microwave transmission. Everything that anyone did was quickly followed by patent applications. Because no one held all the patents, cross – licensing agreements would be necessary, just as progress in radio required them.

In 1928, an experimental General Electric station in Schenectady, New York, transmitted programs three times a week, mostly to its own engineers. RCA had its own NBC experimental television station in New York that would become WNBC – TV. CBS set up WCBS – TV in New York. As the Depression years leading to World War II went by and the world's attention focused on life – and – death political and economic issues, teams of dogged engineers, scientists, and communication executives in the United States, Britain, Germany, Russia, and Japan pursued the experiments that would lead to television. In England, the BBC started the world's first regular television service in 1936, testing both mechanical and electronic methods until it became clear which was the better system. Germany began its own electronic television service in Berlin.

Where to present television was a matter of dispute. The cinema was a likely venue because movies on celluloid already appeared there, and television might be considered another technology for distributing the moving image. Instead, DuMont Laboratories decided to go after the home market, and sold its first electronic sets to wealthy individuals in 1938 during the depths of the Depression. Much of the public was introduced to television in 1939 through magazine and newspaper articles, and also at the RCA Pavilion in the New York World's Fair, whose theme was "The World of Tomorrow."

The Federal Communications Commission gave CBS and NBC television broadcasting licenses, but the technology was not ready and World War II loomed. Even the small percentage of people in the New York area who could afford the bulky sets with tiny screens that sold for the price of a new car had almost nothing to see. The prewar home market for television did not exist. Some sets were sold to taverns that bought them for the occasional telecasts of sports events. World War I had blocked commercial radio; now World War II was blocking commercial television, because electronic research was required for such military needs as radar. The government froze commercial television development. Of the ten experimental stations in existence, six fed occasional programs to an estimated 10,000 sets, some of them belonging to station executives and engineers. The Dumont station alone tried to provide service throughout the war.

If Television Past was only experimental and Television Present was dormant, Television Future bustled with energy and promise as the war ground to an end and the public permitted itself dreams of a postwar future of reunited families and newly married couples moving into single

Each day, from a primitive studio at Radio City, RCA beams to the fairgrounds a vintage cartoon ("Donald's Cousin Gus") or a travelogue ("Jasper National Park, Washington — Shrine of Patriotism") or a culinary lesson (usually a simple salad, since the heat in the studio is almost enough to roast a cook). . . . Yet to many among the millions of fairgoers who come to gape (at the New York World's Fair in 1939), the video image that lingers longest isn't anything on the screen; it is the sight of the set itself. A clunky, all – wooden set housing a glass rectangle exactly five inches high. A miniature looking glass.[3]

— Newsweek

family homes with an automobile in the garage and, in the living room, one of those new–fangled radios with pictures that the newspapers and magazines were writing about. By war's end, a huge market for television was ready and waiting, savings in hand because very little had been for sale during the war years marked by rationing and self–denial. The public demand was more than matched by manufacturers ready to produce sets, radio broadcasters and newspaper publishers eager for television licenses, and a potential army of workers and entertainers waiting for an industry to come into being. Sets in use jumped from 5,000 in 1946 to about one million in 1948 to almost 10 million in 1950.

BATTLE OVER COLOR

At first, the pictures were black–and–white, because RCA and CBS could not agree on a color system. As applicants quarreled over who would get the potentially valuable licenses, another battle was shaping up over expanding the VHF (very–high frequency) spectrum to allow for more television stations, something that RCA resisted, not wanting more competition. With the additional concern that the narrow space between VHF frequencies was causing signal interference, the FCC ordered a freeze on new stations that lasted from 1948 to 1952. This was to the advantage of CBS and NBC because most local stations had already affiliated with one or the other, rather than with ABC or Dumont. The technology continued to improve despite the FCC freeze, and, by 1951, network programs reached from coast to coast. As sales of new television sets soared and pictures became clearer on larger screens, prices of sets plummeted.

NO UHF DIALS

By extending the VHF frequency spectrum, channels 2 to 13, to a new UHF (ultra–high frequency) band, channels 14 to 69, and later expanding it still further, the FCC dealt with the limited number of channels, assigning local channel licenses in more than 1,200 communities. Many UHF stations failed. Their signals did not transmit as far or with as clean a picture as VHF stations. Early sets were sold without any UHF dials, or lacked click dials. Hunting for signals, inexact tuning, ghosts, and interference reduced audiences, and without audiences, the stations could not attract advertising to pay for network programs, thus further reducing the audiences. Several years would pass before manufacturers were required to equip UHF dials with the precise clicking feature of VHF dials. UHF stations struggled, but for VHF stations, "A license to broadcast is a license to print money," the Canadian media mogul Lord Thomson said.

NTSC, SECAM, PAL

The battle over color standards ended in 1953 with an RCA victory. Its proposal had been for an all–electronic system, compared with a partly mechanical CBS system, and its "compatible color" system could be seen on existing black–and–white sets. Another FCC decision resulted in the NTSC system of a picture made up of 525 lines which are "refreshed" 60 times a second, interlacing the even – numbered lines and the odd – numbered lines that are transmitted alternately. Europeans delayed adopting a technical system for a time, then adopted two slightly better systems, the French SECAM and the British – German PAL.

Based on colonial, cultural, and trade ties, other nations chose one or another of the three. Because the systems were non – compatible, the choice determined many of the programs that these nations would receive.

HDTV

HDTV ("high definition television") emerged in the 1990s as a replacement for all three systems, offering a sharper and brighter digital image in place of the standard analog pictures. It also offered a cinema screen – like 16x9 width – to – height ratio instead of the standard television 4x3 ratio, and more than twice the number of scanning lines of NTSC pictures, and, therefore, at least twice the sharpness. It offered ten times as much color information and CD – quality sound.

The possibility that had been raised in the 1930s for cinema distribution arose again with HDTV; that is, distribution to movie theaters. Most movies still arrived in cinemas as cans of film. A proposal imagined a scrambled HDTV signal sent by satellite at a specific time to cinemas where audiences were waiting. This would not only reduce the cost of distribution but would also allow for films of limited appeal to find their potential audiences. As to the question of abandoning cinemas entirely and simply making all films available as DVDs for home viewing, the answer might well be that going out to a movie is a social event, but sitting at home is not. It is an argument that carries a little weight, but the counter argument for home viewing alone has never carried the day. It ignores the market of teenagers and young lovers who want to get out of the house at any cost.

THE REMOTE

A less impressive technology associated with television has also changed over the decades, and has taken its place as an artifact of modern civilization. Like the telephone answering machine, the television remote control is a small, humble gadget attached to a more important device. We use it but pay little attention to its influence on our behavior. Family members frequently fight over its possession. It confers status on the holder, although less so in the era of PlayStation and Xbox. In more traditional families, the husband and father may regard the remote as his by right. No doubt the remote has contributed to divorce. Its effectiveness at muting commercials has influenced broadcast industry decisions to reduce or even eliminate commercials between programs and to make commercials funnier and more interesting.

In its half – century of existence, the remote control has changed almost everything about television: the way people watch it, the way networks package their shows, the way advertisers make commercials.... The surfing instinct is so ingrained — the majority of American homes have had remote – controlled televisions since about 1986 — that it's easy to overlook its unintended consequences.[4]

— Bob Baker

Remotes predate commercial television. During World War I Germany used remote controls for motorboats. After World War II, remote – controlled automatic garage door openers helped sell new houses. Requiring a wire connection, Zenith in 1950 introduced "Lazy Bone," the first television remote control; unfortunately, people tripped over it. Five years later Zenith came out with the "Flash – matic," a wireless version; unfortunately again, because this remote depended on photocells, television sets might change channels by themselves on sunny days. The following year, Zenith did it better with the "Space Command," a remote control based on ultrasonics. However, their need for extra vacuum tubes raised the price and the size of a television set. The arrival of transistors reduced both. In the early 1980s, the technology changed once again when infrared remote control units replaced ultrasound.

Viewers sat transfixed at their sets as the phrase "couch potato" entered the lexicon, and happy advertisers poured money into the broadcasters' coffers. While television in the U.S. continued down the private path begun by the telegraph, most of the rest of the world saw government controls retained in the expansion from radio to television.

EDUCATIONAL BROADCASTING

Not all U.S. broadcasting was for profit. A few educational radio stations had hung on during the early years of commercial television despite poor funding that translated into weak programming. Educators had learned some hard lessons in competing for radio licenses with take – no – prisoners commercial broadcasters. The educators did much better in securing non – profit television licenses from the FCC, thanks in part to help from major organizations, especially the Ford Foundation. Federal grants also helped, leading over the decades of the last half century to a national public television network, the Public Broadcasting System, plus such public radio networks and distributors as National Public Radio, American Public Media, and Public Radio International. As money arrived through federal and private grants and from pledge drives, programming improved.

Although television remained popular as the new century began, audiences for the entire television industry declined in the competition with new forms of media. What was true in the United States was at least as true elsewhere. European public television networks, complacent and overstaffed, suffered far worse than ABC, CBS, and NBC. Wracked by commercial competition that was permitted in the later decades of the twentieth century, plus the growth of cable channels, the use of satellites, and the expansion of videotape rentals, Italy's RAI, Spain's RTVE and Germany's ARD and ZDF faced financial ruin.[5] State – run Asian television networks were also hurting as viewer choices increased. In France, Russia, the nations of Eastern Europe, and Mexico, among others, state owned stations were sold to private interests. To keep viewers in the huge and tumultuous Indian market, the government service Doordarshan reduced its educational fare and added more commercial programs. As the twenty – first century unfolded, the television industry everywhere was undergoing significant change.

Of the various ways to support the television industry everywhere and pay for programs, commercials won the greatest favor as being the least painful and the least subject to government involvement. Television commercials were also the principal means of political campaigning, notably in the United States. Political managers remained convinced of the efficacy of spending tens or even hundreds of thousands of dollars for a few seconds of commercial time. The money that a candidate raised became one of the surest ways to predict the probability of victory.

The British Broadcasting Corporation's (BBC) dependence upon annual license fees on television sets to fund public broadcasting remained the policy in several countries, but all of them had stations that broadcast commercials as well. Even American public television gradually shifted from total rejection of commercials to sponsorship announcements that identified and even promoted a company or product. As for totalitarian governments, they still preferred direct government subsidies, but nevertheless allowed some commercials.

Once again, the views of critics of a commercial – based system were not shared by millions of viewers who liked looking at a favorite commercial, no matter how often they saw it. Children seemed to enjoy them more than the programs themselves, a situation perhaps explained by the fact that far more thought and expense goes into a thirty – second commercial than into thirty seconds of any program.

When radio broadcasting was new in the late 1920s, it was not uncommon, at those times when a popular show such as *Amos 'n' Andy* was on, for neighbors to seek out neighbors who owned a radio set. The first television programs had the same effect. They went out over existing stations to viewers who crowded into the homes of neighbors who owned sets, or who gathered in front of stores that sold sets; store owners put a working television in the window and piped the sound outside.

Marshall McLuhan observed that a new medium chooses for its content the medium it displaces. Television displaced, among other entertainments, novels and movies, both of which became television content. The radio variety show, born out of stage vaudeville, was reborn to be presented to national audiences as the television variety show. The crowds outside the stores were largest for such popular fare as the variety shows hosted by Milton Berle and Ed Sullivan, and "B" movie westerns owned by their cowboy stars.

FUNDING TELEVISION

The child is right in not regarding commercials as interruptions. For the only time anyone smiles on TV is in commercials. The rest of life, in news broadcasts and soap operas, is presented as so horrible that the only way to get through life is to buy this product: then you'll smile. Aesop never wrote a clearer fable.[6]

—Edmund Carpenter

Television is different because it encompasses all forms of discourse. No one goes to a movie to find out about government policy or the latest scientific advances. No one buys a record to find out the baseball scores or the weather or the latest murder. No one turns on radio anymore for soap operas or a presidential address (if a television set is at hand). But everyone goes to television for all these things and more, which is why television resonates so powerfully throughout the culture.[7]

— NEIL POSTMAN

Variety shows traveled well from radio to television, as did the quiz shows, such as radio's *$64 Question* that became television's *$64,000 Question*. When it was discovered that some of the quiz shows had been rigged to favor certain contestants whom the audience had taken a liking to, congressional inquiries followed. The public, at least as the headlines told it, felt betrayed. Fearing government sanctions, the networks embarked on a period of documentary production; documentaries did not draw the large audiences beloved of networks, but their purity of purpose made them worthwhile.

Did television hurt the movies? In reality, it was not films themselves, but the cinemas that were even partially displaced by people who preferred to view movies in the comforts of home. The success of drive – in theaters should have served as a wake – up call to cinema owners. The inevitable close alliances between the television industry and the motion picture industry was delayed due to Hollywood executives' concerns that television would erode their profitable business. Their fears were justified insofar as the Hollywood studios were linked financially to theater chains. The 1948 U.S. Supreme Court decision, U.S. v. Paramount, had ordered those links severed. In time, a revived, restructured, and thriving motion picture industry came to see television as a valuable distribution channel. The studios had the talents both in front of and behind the camera, the equipment, and the back lots on which scenes were shot; the television networks had the audiences and cash. It was a natural fit, so the live dramas that marked the "golden age" of television of the 1950s were replaced by filmed dramas and comedies that could be shot on location, edited, and kept on a shelf until used and reused.

As the audience stared at their television sets, television stared back with even more intensity. With advertising rates spiking, the advertisers and the ad agencies wanted better information about just who was watching what. What ages, gender, income, and other factors were involved? These demographic data would later be augmented by focus groups and by psychographic data that considered social class, lifestyle and personality characteristics. In time, marketing decisions based on such data would do their part in converting television broadcasting into narrowcasting, removing certain groups from marketing considerations, notably the elderly, who became almost a shadow audience for programs aimed at a younger demographic. Network newscasts were an exception, as the commercials for medicine and dentifrices showed. (A satellite radio service, Companion Radio, would one day be specifically programmed for people living in senior housing.)

CRITICISM AND RESPONSE

Many critics have hammered at the sex and violence of American television programming, yet the content has not measurably improved. Quite the opposite. The evidence is all too plain that more blatant sex and more gory violence are now visible, and that children's programs are of as little value as ever. To the industry's standard answer that the unhappy viewer should hit the "off" button comes the complainer's equally standard answer that the family did not buy a television set to turn it off. To the industry's justifiable argument that the complainant wants to impose her or his personal tastes and morality upon everyone, comes the equally justifiable argument that the airwaves belong to the public, and the industry is giving back next to nothing in return for the public's gift of valuable licenses. To the industry's accurate argument that television is a business, not an educational institution, comes the equally accurate argument that, like it or not, television is an important educational institution. And so the arguments go, around and around, without closure.

What neither side to the endless quarrel talks about much is the time spent daily with television (8.2 hoours a day in the average American home). Neither side is campaigning to reduce the substantial amount of the public's discretionary time spent each day staring at the phosphor dots. For the industry it is a bread – and – butter issue. For those who complain, a campaign to limit viewing would be hopeless.

It has been said that viewers do not watch programs; they watch television, flipping the dial until they find what is least objectionable to them. If this theory, once prevalent in television network circles, still affects programming decisions, it would lead to bland, copycat programs not likely to offend viewers. In fact, the "L.O.P" theory (Least Objectionable Program) reportedly once guided programmers, and to some extent perhaps still does. Other means of mediated communication, notably radio and motion pictures, have influenced society, particularly youth. Because television has absorbed radio programs and movies, presenting both as its content, this alone would be reason enough to recognize its influence.

WATCHING TELEVISION, NOT PROGRAMS

Before the diffusion of television, the public neither listened to the radio or went to the cinema for many hours each day. Television has drawn families together, but not necessarily to communicate with each other. Too often, they sit silently. Another change brought about by television is that a visitor to a home with the television on frequently feels like an intruder. Visitors to a home have been aware that their arrival, while welcome, does not result in the television set being turned off or the sound volume lowered. They are welcome to join the watching.

THE TV SET STAYS ON

Because non – cable television is free — beyond the time given over to commercials — and because most programs require little if any education, television has been called a consolation prize for the powerless.[8] In the age of the Internet, it remains the medium of choice for the poor, the uneducated, children, and the elderly.

"A Vast Wasteland"

In 1961, the chairman of the FCC, Newton Minow, challenged television executives to watch a single day of their own station's programs from start to finish. "I can assure you that you will see a vast wasteland," he said.[9] In defense of television programming practices at the time, columnist and program host Ed Sullivan said the three networks (ABC, CBS, NBC) had to "produce 10,950 hours of entertainment a year, in contrast to only 600 hours demanded of the entire motion picture industry of our country and the 125 hours per year demanded of the Broadway theater."[10] "Hell, there isn't even enough mediocrity to go around," one television executive grumbled in agreement. That is no longer true.

Cause – effect connections are seldom clear. No agreement exists about the general effects of television programs. A never – ending drumbeat of criticism has come from community and religious leaders, educators, and parents about televised violence begetting street violence, and televised sexual imagery lowering societal standards of decency. A half century ago, a study by the National Association for Better Broadcasting concluded that the average child was likely, between the ages of five and fifteen, to see more than 13,000 characters destroyed violently; characters were attacked by such a variety of methods as fire, rape, poison, acid, spiders, snakes, crocodiles, pitchforks, knives, time bombs, live steam, poison gas, hypodermic needles, and an assortment of blunt instruments. Season after season, the inventive mayhem continued.

Does TV Violence Cause Violence?

Events such as the Virginia Tech and the Columbine High School massacres by students notwithstanding, the response of the entertainment industry — movies, television, gaming — has been to deny media influence, and to argue that television does not lead to aberrant behavior except perhaps for a handful of already disturbed individuals. Furthermore, it is argued that programs do no more than reflect what is already happening. Studies showed that televised violence has led to adolescent violence, but only among children predisposed to aggressive behavior.

That many millions of viewers enjoy the programs without altering their personal behavior has been a strong argument. The industry argued further that normal viewers will not be influenced by a mere television program, although this is a position that flies in the face of the billions spent on television advertising based on the opposite conviction that what appears on television can indeed influence behavior.

A Sisyphus quality has attended the complaints and industry responses. Using fresh evidence of effects, those who want change push the rock of reform up the hill, only to be met by sufficient resistance and indifference to require a new effort. Congressional committees have held hearings, starting with the Kefauver hearings in 1952 into the causes of juvenile delinquency. Some reform was put in place by the Telecommunication Reform Act of 1996; a "V – Chip" was mandated for each new television set so that parents could block violent and explicit sexual programs. Networks and cable channels reluctantly accepted an accompanying rating system. Hollywood and the comic book industries also instituted ratings.

In 2007, the Federal Communications Commission asked the Congress for legislation that would allow the FCC to regulate violence on TV. For decades the FCC has fined stations for stepping over the line regarding sexual material or language, but has lacked the authority where violence was broadcast.

The angry dialogue over television programs that children might see has been sharpened over programming *intended* for children. On the major broadcast networks and local television stations, children's programs were never strong. However, good children's fare could be found on PBS, and frequently on cable channels that were striving for a young audience, such as Animal Planet, Discovery, Nickelodeon, and Disney. The overall total of children's programs has increased over the years, despite the abdication of true concern by the networks and the local stations, although some of the cable programming leaned toward cheaply made cartoon adventures from Japan.

Reformers led by the grassroots group Action for Children's Television (ACT), pointed out that some cartoons were advertisements for toys, and other cartoons were filled with commercials for sugared cereals and candy. Calling for changes in commercialism and violence, and supported by local community groups, ACT went before Congress and the FCC with complaints that the general level of programming for children was a national disgrace. The passage of the Children's Television Act of 1990 required local stations to program at least three hours of educational programming weekly. Among the better programs at this writing were *Sesame Street, Blues Clues, Dora the Explorer, Dragon Tales, Recess*, and *Sagwa*.

Proposals for a Family Viewing Hour, the first hour of prime time, were defeated, and plans for voluntary compliance gradually dissolved into standard evening fare.

With television on in an average American home for above eight hours a day, and not much less in other industrialized nations, the content of programming may be a nation's primary educator and standard setter, and, according to some critics, too often more influential than school, church, community, and even parents.

It sounds like mass hypnotism on a scale unequaled in human history. Roman gladiators in the Circus Maximus could not begin to compare in popularity. Did anyone inside or outside the television industry think

The average young child in this country watches about four hours of television a day and each year sees tens of thousands of commercials, often for high – fat, high – sugar, high – salt foods; thousands of episodes of violence, and countless instances of alcohol use and inappropriate sexual activity. By the time U.S. children finish high school, they have spent nearly twice as many hours in front of TV sets as they have in the classroom.[11]

—JANE BRODY

FAMILY VIEWING HOUR

The debate on mass culture lines up on one side those who say that TV educates and amuses people, democratically opens up the range of possibilities available to them, puts them in touch with the whole society or even the whole global village, helps them to improve their material lives, and so keeps the economy going; and on the other, those who say TV creates illusions, corrupts morality and taste, promotes rape and murder, destroys literacy and the English language, isolates people from one another, puts them in debt by making them want things they don't really need, and turns them into political zombies. The optimists and the worriers both see mass culture as a profound force in our society.[13]

— RICHARD OHMANN

If the ultimate goal stops being about capturing an audience's attention once, and becomes more about keeping their attention through repeat viewings, that shift is bound to have an effect on the content.[14]

— STEVEN JOHNSON

this was a good idea? There were reports of changes in family life – styles, sleeping habits, children's entertainment and activity preferences. It was a lot more fun and easier just to tune to *Dora the Explorer* than to go outside and actually explore. And Dora was regarded as one of the better programs for children. A nationwide study as early as 1960, funded by CBS, concluded that television had replaced other means of socialization for all but people of high education and income. Of all household items, television was the one non – essential item in the home that nearly everyone regarded as essential.[12]

Effects of television programs could also be seen in the popular morning and afternoon soap opera melodramas. Along with newscasts, they have been the most consistent and enduring of all programs. Soap operas moved seamlessly from radio to television and from daytime to prime time. Their appeal, once primarily to housewives, has spread to the work place, retirement homes and college campuses. Viewers spend hours each day with "their soaps." For some viewers, the anticipation of the coming day's episode made a dull or difficult life endurable.

The major change over the decades has been the sexual content. Today's soaps are a far cry from radio's *The Romance of Helen Trent*, whose announcer daily asked, in his rich baritone, if a woman over the age of thirty – five could still find romance. The melodramatic formula of a soap opera is to keep several subplots running within a program, which meant that while one favorite character had finally solved an emotional problem, another was in the midst of a crisis or just beginning one. The formula was so effective in delivering its real message — stay tuned — that it also became central to evening prime time dramas.

All the soap operas, like all television programs, had target audiences, and the targeting appeared to be effective to the degree to which the viewers became emotionally snarled. The conviction that the afternoon soap operas could keep their huge audiences enthralled in the ongoing plots was supported by the letters, birthday and anniversary cards, and even gifts that arrived at the networks when one of the characters gave birth. These were real gifts for an imaginary infant. When a character was in financial trouble, the postman brought offers of loans.

The United States was not alone in enjoying soap operas. Many countries produced and distributed them. Mexican and Brazilian "telenovellas" were especially popular. From England, *Coronation Street* became an international hit. A South Korean soap opera, *The Jewel in the Palace*, was hugely popular with Chinese viewers, as well as generating a national interest in a nation against whom China had gone to war at the time that television was new. Chinese fascinated by the melodrama were buying Korean goods, tasting Korean dishes, listening to Korean pop star music, and visiting South Korea.

As the years have rolled by, television dramas and comedies have grown more complex, with several story lines threaded through a typical program, and carried from episode to episode. Besides the increase in sex and violence, an increase in the number of characters and problems marks a clear difference between now and a generation ago, let alone the story lines during the golden age of radio. The complexities often include a "back story" that is not part of the main plots, or references to previous episodes that only fans of a program will understand. Invariably, those complexities involve social or romantic entanglements that serve as side stories to the main narrative thread.

Why the change from the straightforward, self–contained story plots? The obvious answer is that the audience gets what it wants. Audiences heavily composed of people living isolated lives with time on their hands can find connections with fictional characters, the syndrome that leads soap opera viewers to send baby gifts for fictional newborns. Yet there is a less obvious reason for the preference for complexity over simplicity. It is the phenomenal rise in DVD sales. A customer willing to pay the added cost of owning instead of renting a DVD is likely to watch it more than once. A program full of complications, plot twists, and subtlety may yield fresh insights each time the viewer sees it.

The ability to choose to watch something already seen rather than something new is itself a new choice on the day's menu. The flexibility of ownership adds the further choice of watching something whenever you want.

The hour–long police or medical drama and the half–hour situation comedy, or "sitcom," have changed over the lifetime of television in two important ways. First, like all of mediated entertainment, notably movies and popular music, the dramas and sitcoms have been coarsened by crude behavior and sexuality that could not have been dreamed of at the start of televised entertainment; the change began in the 1970s with the "jiggle" of *Charlie's Angels*. Second, they have been vehicles for delivering social messages.

Also starting in the 1970s with *All in the Family* and its comically racist character, Archie Bunker, some prime time television programs have moved to the cutting edge of social change, particularly regarding African–Americans, who were almost invisible at the start of television in the 1940s and 1950s, and barely appeared in the motion pictures of the day except in minor and often demeaning roles. Today, African–Americans appear regularly, almost always as positive role models, often in leadership roles. Other social issues that are regularly treated on television, with characters who are regarded with sympathy, include HIV/AIDS, homosexuality, and the abortion issue. Those issues were simply not discussed at the dawning of television programs.

The listener's sense of security was enhanced by emphasis placed in the serials upon such matters of special interest as marriage ties, the problems encountered by career women (a role the listener had avoided), the importance attached to the role of the wife and homemaker, and, in all things, the triumph of good over evil. It was not by chance that nearly all of the moral, emotional, and spiritual strength was invested in the female characters.

At a more widely shared level of appreciation, the serials were enjoyed simply for the companionship provided by characters who became familiar to the listener over a period of months and years. The punctuality and dependability of the daily visits doubtlessly lent a sense or order to many a pointless day.[15]

— GEORGE WILEY

In 2007, the radio and television talk show personality Don Imus was fired for a slur against African – American women, members of a college sports team. The national uproar that followed what Imus had intended as an off – handed remark demonstrated not only a significant shift in what would be tolerated — consider *Amos 'n' Andy* in the 1930s — but also the power of broadcasting to affect the nation.

A different social matter that produced headlines and national derision was a speech by Vice President Dan Quayle criticizing a sitcom, *Murphy Brown*, for its positive attitude toward the central character having a baby out of wedlock. The speech itself was thoughtful, if controversial, but the uproar about the vice president of the United States making a fuss about a fictional baby in a television comedy was thought to be a large factor in destroying his political career. Without doubt, the views on social issues presented in television programs have influenced the national dialogue.

REALITY SHOWS

Non – fiction has had as great a role in television as fiction, and is even more varied, ranging from newscasts and news specials to violence – flecked police chases and sex – drenched "reality shows." Contestants in the new millennium competed against one another in challenges ranging from enduring discomfort, as in *Survivor* and *Fear Factor*, or risking public humiliation, as in the old *Gong Show* and *American Idol*, to marrying someone introduced to them on camera, as in *The Bachelor*. Social critics carped that such programs must spell the end of Western civilization, but large audiences found them diverting, which guaranteed their on – air health.

As in dramas and comedies, complexities found their way into reality shows. No topic was taboo on afternoon talk shows like *Oprah*, whose host became a national icon for tolerance, fairness, and honesty as she dealt with topics that, a few years ago, many people did not know even existed, let alone were fit for exposure to millions of viewers. In the new century, somewhere in the world of television, almost no topic had been ignored. That, of course, meant that many topics were laid bare on the national table at the same time, a condition that weakened efforts to focus on any single concern. It was easy to change the subject.

TELEVISION NEWS

Television news began at the birth of commercial television as two kinds of programs. From radio came what was soon derisively called the "talking head." The listener who enjoyed *hearing* radio reporters and commentators quickly tired of *looking at* them reading a newscast. From movies came the other kind: the newsreel, a collection of stale news and fluff. Years would pass and technology would improve before they were put together in what would grow into the public's preferred way to learn of the day's events. Television news would become a fixture in millions of homes, serious national and world news delivered by serious men and, later, serious women, and a mixture of serious and light – hearted local news delivered by chatty men and women who laughed frequently.

The power of mediated communication to influence the public and move the nation showed itself in both the rise and the fall of Sen. Joseph McCarthy. His unsupported announcements that he had lists of the names of communists in the State Department and elsewhere in government generated headlines and television coverage. It led to the "Red Scare" that traumatized the nation during the 1950s. It was also on television that Edward R. Murrow's devastating attack on McCarthy and the coverage of the Army – McCarthy hearings brought him down.

The televised debates between John F. Kennedy and Richard Nixon further changed the political landscape of the nation, shifting away from locally – based ward politics and party loyalties. The young and relatively inexperienced senator from Massachusetts was not expected to hold his own against the man who was twice elected vice president after serving in Congress and the Senate. Yet Kennedy dominated the debates, especially the first debate, which showed a pale and sweating vice president facing a tanned and confident young senator. Curiously, radio listeners believed Nixon had won the debates, but those radio listeners would not be enough when the votes were counted. One clear winner: image. Political campaigns would be forever changed. The focus in future would be on television.

It has frequently been said that television news came of age in its four days of coverage of President Kennedy's assassination and the subsequent events in November, 1963. In some nations, street riots might have followed the somewhat mysterious assassination of a popular president. In the United States, viewers were glued to their television sets. At one point, 9 out of 10 Americans were watching.

Among the many changes of the turbulent 1960s was an awareness of the reach of television. The medium went on to bring the country the story of the struggle for racial equality in the South and in major cities across the nation. By affecting public sensibilities with scenes of snarling police dogs, high – pressure water hoses, and little girls marching off in their Sunday best to be arrested, television news willy – nilly aided the civil rights movement. In television entertainment, the color bar that kept out most racial minority members, especially African – Americans, was broken by the 1970s. With comedy shows about African – American families, and with actors regularly appearing in dramas and variety shows, television moved to the forefront of efforts to improve racial relations. The civil rights movement for African – Americans and women would have progressed much more slowly without the constant broadcast coverage of recent decades.[17]

Americans who depend on local television news get little meaningful information — much less in – depth explanations or exposés — on what is going on in the world around them. Instead, they get a distorted caricature of their communities, a daily drama of crime, accidents, traffic tie – ups, stormy weather and other calamities, leavened by cheerful video of photogenic events like parades, charity walks, and county fairs.[16]

— LEONARD DOWNIE JR. AND ROBERT KAISER

FOUR DAYS IN NOVEMBER

CIVIL RIGHTS COVERAGE

SPACE COVERAGE

The space effort, also covered intensely by television, enthralled all mankind, culminating in the live pictures of Neil Armstrong setting foot on the moon. This historic event provided one of those rare occasions when the whole world looked at something together. Marshall McLuhan's image of a "global village" was realized, however briefly.

VIETNAM WAR COVERAGE

Another major television news effort of the turbulent 1960s and '70s was coverage of the Vietnam War, now filmed in color, with images reaching television screens only one or two days after the battlefield film was shot. The war in Vietnam was called the first television war, and "the living room war." It brought the reality of bloodshed, pain, and frustration home. Such intimate contact with warfare had never been experienced by a whole nation. Television coverage was credited — or blamed — for sparking the student demonstrations that led the anti – war movement. War planning would change in the future to take into account home front reaction to instant coverage of battle. The movements of reporters and, especially, television photographers would be more closely monitored by the military during the Gulf War of 1991 and the Iraq War of the 2000s, when the "embedded" journalist system would be initiated.

ANCHORS

More than radio commentary and far more than impersonal newspaper stories, television newscasts added a human dimension to the daily reports of events. Network news anchors, particularly Walter Cronkite at CBS and the team of Chet Huntley and David Brinkley at NBC, were welcomed each evening into millions of homes almost like members of the family. The anchor brought a recognized voice, a familiar face, and a sense of personality to the recounting of the day's events. One survey voted Cronkite the most trusted man in America.

Television newscasts grew in length, with major cities having news blocks of two hours or more. In addition, morning programs would not be complete without news reports. News interview programs were matched in popularity by prime – time news magazine programs like the iconic *60 Minutes*, although documentaries were usually left to public television and cable stations. Editors were given the authority to break into entertainment programs to report momentous events, and could take over completely, as they did to report the assassination of President John Kennedy and the 9/11 attacks. Less important breaking news was reported as crawls of text along the bottom of the television screen.

MAGAZINE PROGRAMS

Magazine programs, led by *60 Minutes*, consisted of extended news reports of ten to fifteen minutes, and were less susceptible to accusations of bias. Through much of the last half of the twentieth century, *60 Minutes* was among the most watched programs of any kind on television. Its combination of hard news, exposés, feature news, and interviews resonated strongly with viewers. Its success spawned other magazine shows, such as *20/20, Dateline*, and *Primetime*.

From morning network programs like the daily *Today* and the weekly *Meet the Press* to evening programs like *Nightline*, programs dealing with current events have been an important part of television schedules, with individual stations matching locally what networks do nationally. Politicians who agree to be interviewed use these programs to garner support for themselves and for their views on controversial issues.

Once again, when something was added, something else was lost. Television news gained power and influence when news anchors and some reporters became household names and political leaders bent their efforts to appear on newscasts and interview programs. But as television rose, the old power of political parties declined. The ward captains, the city aldermen, and the favors they could dole out were forgotten. The power of labor unions to deliver the vote was reduced. Unions and corporations provided money to pay for televised political ads.

HOUSEHOLD NAMES

Like the Asian proverb that the nail that sticks up gets hammered, the new visibility of television news had its price. Vice President Spiro Agnew attacked network news in a speech denouncing network news "liberal bias" by a "small, unelected elite." Tens of thousands of angry letters, phone calls, and telegrams to the networks quickly reinforced the message. Stung by the threats to station licenses, television news started out slowly and nervously in covering the Watergate story. Newspapers did the heavy lifting, but no newspaper could match television's ability to reach a mass audience, to convey the tension of the Senate hearings on impeachment in 1974, and the presidential speeches that showed viewers a tired and troubled Richard Nixon slowly losing his grip on the reins of power.

"UNELECTED ELITE"

The question of fairness roiled both radio and television for more than two decades until President Ronald Reagan led the effort to get rid of the FCC's Fairness Doctrine (*see Chapter 13, "Being Persuasive"*). Before that happened, the Fairness Doctrine was a catalyst in ending tobacco advertising on television. A successful petition to allow anti – smoking commercials as a counter to the ubiquitous cigarette commercials, along with Congressional pressure, frightened the tobacco industry into calling for a law that banned all broadcast advertising related to tobacco. The broadcasters opposed the law to end the profitable commercials; understandably, they bridled at the hypocrisy of the law's support by the print media, which continued to reap millions from tobacco ads.

FAIRNESS DOCTRINE

Mass audiences, surveys show, tune in for major news stories, but drift away at quiet times. Viewership spiked at news reports of the 9/11 attack, the Iraq invasion, and hurricane Katrina. On most days, Americans tuned in and out of television news, radio news, and the Internet news services. When many average American adults awoke, at dinner time, and when they went to bed, they checked to see if the world had

9/11, KATRINA

changed. Satisfied that it had not, they went about their lives or used the media for diversion, or for learning facts that they could act upon. That is why weather reports occupied so much of local newscasts each day. A weather forecast can lead you to take an umbrella to work or stuff a child into a heavier jacket. Entertaining news was — and is — part of the diversion, which explains much of what else we see on local newscasts. The boast that "We're number one in this market" is always based on the quantity of viewers, often to measure specific demographic groups, nothing else.

INTERNET BLOG COMPETITION

The arrival of the Internet as a news venue, the growing popularity of blogs for news and opinions, and the 24 – hour news cycle of CNN and other cable channels sharply cut into the audiences of the major network newscasts, just as the newscasts had cut into the readership of newspapers one or two generations earlier. Increasingly, the audience for television network news and the readership for newspapers were skewing toward the elderly, with young people going elsewhere for news, or going nowhere. To counter the threat of the Internet, network and local television news organizations, following the dictum of "if you can't beat 'em, join 'em," have placed their news stories on it. So have newspapers. Each news organization maintains a website where text and — often — video reports are available, sometimes in greater depth than an on – air newscast will permit, and sometimes before they are presented on the evening newscasts. Network news has also been made available to established venues like AOL. Like entertainment programs, newscasts could be downloaded for viewing anytime on a variety of devices.

SKYPE

Janus Friis of Denmark and Niklas Zennström of Sweden, the creators of the music file sharing service Kazaa and the Internet telephone service Skype, created a new file sharing service named the Venice Project to download television programs to computers. It called upon the television content that users have stored, an endless library in total. Advertisers who could reach a targeted market were obviously pleased.

What was occurring has been a significant national shift toward increased choices, especially among the most desired segment of viewers, the better educated younger viewers who prefer to get their news at the time of their choosing and know how to surf online for the topics that interest them; impatient, they no longer need to wait. There is also a greater suspicion of traditional journalism, and a greater preference than in the past for opinions with which the reader agrees, even outrageous opinions. (*See the discussion about blogs in Chapter 11, "Computers and the Internet: Leaning Forward."*)

Let us back up more than a half century. The story of cable television is as American as a Horatio Alger tale. Unlike cultural changes that begin in major cities and find their way to rural villages and towns, cable was the country boy who went to the big city. Born in humble circumstances in rural Pennsylvania to help folks living out in the countryside to enjoy something that only city folks had, it eventually went to cities, where it challenged a major industry and succeeded beyond all expectations in affecting part of our way of life. When cable began in 1948 as community antennas, it was just a means to bring television signals to towns too far from a large city station for good reception. The broadcast industry, if it thought about the matter at all, welcomed community antennas because they added viewers at no cost to the stations. That would change when signals began to compete with what the stations were broadcasting.

The roots of cable can be traced back to Telefon Hirmondo in Budapest, the service that began in 1893 to bring radio – style information and entertainment to subscribers over telephone lines. After radio broadcasting began in the early 1920s, community antennas were set up at a number of places in the United States and Europe to improve reception; a number of families in an apartment house shared an antenna, with the wires running to their apartments.

The same sharing of an antenna began in 1948 as television broadcasting increased, but did not spread uniformly. In the towns of Lansford and Mahanoy City, Pennsylvania, hills blocked reception from Philadelphia. The owners of radio repair shops, who were trying to sell television sets, erected antennas on hilltops, ran wires to their shops, and feeder wires to homes that had purchased a set from them, charging about two dollars monthly for the service. Placing a television in the shop window with the sound audible outside brought large crowds to the shops and increased sales. The owner of a radio station in Astoria, Oregon, followed a similar path, but went a step further by receiving permission from a Seattle television station to retransmit its signal. That brought the matter to the attention of the FCC, which took no action.

As newspapers wrote feature stories about these small town ventures, the number of communities with CATV (Community Antenna Television) grew. Because the equipment they used had spare capacity, the owners of CATV operations were able to attract additional customers by bringing in signals from more distant cities, a feature that city dwellers did not enjoy. That caused local television stations to protest because of the competition for the viewers' attention and because the unregulated CATV owners profited from the broadcasters' programs. Competition sharpened when the CATV stations started to run their own commercials. CATV was moving beyond simple master antennas by technology that amplified the arriving signals and sent them to homes over sheathed

CATV IS BORN

TELEFON HIRMONDO

DISTANT SIGNALS

co – axial cables. It was also a profit – making business using a product, television programs, that it was snatching off the air and not paying for. In addition, because CATV ran along public streets and used telephone or electric poles to hang its wires, the private CATV companies were signing contracts with communities and utilities.

BROADCASTERS COMPLAIN

Complaints from broadcasters grew louder when the CATV owners added programming of their own, such as a locally produced variety show and coverage of city hall meetings and local high school sports. This began in 1951 in the town of Pottsville, Pennsylvania, when a CATV owner used a small, personal television camera to pull together a 30 – minute variety show with Pottsville residents as entertainers. Neighbors were delighted with local origination.

BECOMING CABLE TV

With this addition, CATV became what is now called cable television. All this was taking place in the midst of the FCC freeze on new television licenses, when only 108 stations were on the air. Some broadcasters observing this fast growing business invested in it themselves; in time, media conglomerates would own cable systems as well as stations in their communication empires. Others were convinced that once the FCC freeze ended and new licenses led to new stations, the cable business would wither. Instead, cable continued to grow, aided by continually improving equipment. Even after the four – year freeze ended in 1952, many communities too small to support a television station could support cable. The television industry was troubled that the presence of a cable system that could bring in a half – dozen or more stations would discourage thoughts of starting a television station in the same community.

FCC PAYS ATTENTION

Committed to encouraging local broadcasting, the FCC was now paying full attention to the upstart cable industry. Should support be given to a single television station that would broadcast to everyone in a community or to a cable operation that would send many television signals to the part of the community that lay where the wires ran and that would pay for the service?

What was happening was little different from what always happens as mediated communication grows. Viewers who are offered the opportunity for making choices will always choose to have them. The proliferation of radio stations after World War II brought so many choices that stations, for their own survival, opted to focus on a specific market segment, such as youth. The proliferation of cable channels would follow the same narrowcasting path, just as magazines had done.

Critics have argued that a sameness exists in television, and that offering more channels does not really offer more choices. Based on the popularity of services with large numbers of channels, the majority of the public does not appear to agree with that assertion.

When they sought exclusive city franchises, cable systems promised to do what local stations were tasked to do; they pledged to provide local information. Cable systems did this in their own way by setting aside local access channels, allocating equipment, and in some communities providing free training and equipment to community residents who wanted to make documentaries. Some cable operations added local newscasts; in fact, local cable newscasts became the fastest growing segment of all types of newscasts, meeting the FCC's policy of encouraging localism. What had begun as a way to improve television broadcast signals for small communities far from a television station, had expanded to bring in more distant signals and a few local attractions.

Cable underwent an important change in 1975 with a test in Wilkes – Barre, Pennsylvania, that delivered programming unavailable anywhere until then. It was called Home Box Office, a pay channel that for three years had been feeding videotape recordings of recent movies and some sports coverage to nearby cable systems. More and more cable systems wanted to add the popular channel to their service, so many, in fact, that HBO decided to take the financial risk to sell the service across the nation by bouncing a signal off RCA's domestic communications satellite, SATCOM. To attract a large audience, HBO chose as its first offering a boxing match in the Philippines between Muhammed Ali and Joe Frazier. What Ali dubbed the "thrilla from Manila" went to cable systems that had installed a satellite receiving dish 10 meters in diameter at a cost of $150,000. The experiment was a success.

As the technology for acquiring a satellite feed improved, the dish size and the costs shrank. One cable system after another signed up for the twenty – four – hour service of recent movies shown uncut and sports events. The monthly fee to residents who took HBO was shared between the cable systems and HBO.

Seeing the success of HBO, Atlanta UHF station owner Ted Turner decided to provide a similar service via the same SATCOM satellite, but with a different financing method. Instead of charging individual subscribers, Turner offered an extra channel of movies and sports that the cable systems themselves would pay for, on the basis of a few cents per subscriber. Each cable system would be using the same dish it had installed for HBO. The extra channel gave viewers still more choices, so it was attractive to cable systems in their efforts to win customers. Turner's WTBS became the first "superstation."[18] His ownership of a UHF station on which he showed the ball games of the baseball team, the Atlanta Braves, that he also owned, not only gave Turner program-

MOVING INTO CITIES

THE "THRILLA FROM MANILA"

TED TURNER

ming, but also a national audience that he parlayed into much higher fees for commercials.

SUPERSTATIONS, NEWS 24/7

Chicago's WGN, New York's WOR, and several other new superstations followed. HBO was followed by pay channels Cinemax, Showtime, and The Movie Channel. Several dozen cable channels have since been created on the way to what futurists predicted would become "a 500 – channel universe," actually meaning a universe of channels limited only by audience demand. Most of the channels would specialize in a certain content area or would target an age group, an ethnic group, a gender, or an interest area. To compete with network newscasts, Turner began CNN (Cable News Network) in 1980, distributed via satellite. Once again, success bred competition and imitation. The ABC – Westinghouse all – news Satellite New Channel failed, but CNN was joined in the 24/7 cable news list by CNN Headline News, CNN International Edition, Fox News, and MSNBC.

The opinion that you are entitled to any signals crossing your property has been soundly rejected by the courts, but some people still try. They may also tap into a neighbor's feed. As a result of this theft of service, HBO and other pay channels, unwilling to drag citizens into court, have scrambled their feeds so they cannot be seen by non – subscribers. Manufacturing descrambling devices is considered a criminal act.

NARROWCASTING

With so many choices, it was inevitable that the industry would fracture into narrowcasting, with programmers shifting away from trying to reach a general audience. On occasion the audiences coalesced around a single program or event, such as the coverage of the Olympics or a truly major worldwide news story, but for the most part, viewers went their separate ways to their channels of choice.

As the programming choices increased, the technology of cable television itself was given competition by DBS (Direct Broadcast Satellite), also known as DTH (Direct – to – Home). In some communities a non – satellite wireless service that uses microwave also competed with cable. DBS suffered in competition with cable until a 1999 law allowed it to retransmit local signals back to the local community. In the first decade of the new century, more than two – thirds of all the households in the United States received a cable or DBS service. Said one cable executive, cable television was like air conditioning, "You don't need it, but once you live with it you can't live without it."[19]

In 2005, the average American home was able to receive 96.4 cable channels but actually watched 15.4 channels, according to a Nielsen survey. The average household watched fifty – seven hours and seventeen minutes of programs a week. The average American during the 1996 season watched four hours and thirty – five minutes of television daily, a record. A large proportion of the population had much to see on the television screen from regular television fare, plus the addition of VHS tapes and DVDs. It flew in the face of reality to harbor any thought that television was still the unifying medium it might have been in its early years.

Talk show host Larry King noted a danger in channels that fractured voters, "In some ways this will be good for politicians and their media consultants because it will be easier to target niche audiences with specific messages."[20] The media consultants obviously knew about these divisions. It would not be necessary for political candidates to send contrary messages over the different channels. It would be enough to shift emphasis. For example, a channel that appealed to the elderly could hear of a candidate's concern for Social Security. At the same time, a channel with an appeal to a young voter demographic could hear of the same candidate's concern for more jobs and more elementary schools.

NICHE AUDIENCES

Among the channels created for cable systems were those specifically devoted to shopping at home and those channels that were given over at night to infomercials (program – length commercials). These added a kind of choice that competed with the catalogues sent by Sears and Montgomery Ward: the opportunity to shop without leaving home. As watching television and shopping were two of the favorite activities of millions of people, "electronic retailing" seemed a sure bet for success. Selling goods this way was done at the expense of the mailed catalogues, just as those catalogues had once prospered at the expense of the small town general store. Communication technology was again forcing change.

SHOPPING CHANNELS

Still more choice was available to those willing to pay for it. Known variously as PPV (Pay – per – View), STV (Subscription Television), or pay – TV, it delivered recent first – run movies, plus original entertainment and sports events to homes and hotel rooms. Since each cable location has an addressable converter, each cable subscriber has an identifiable location as unique as a telephone number. Pay – TV was a service that had begun long before HBO as Zenith's Phonevision experiment in Schenectady, New York, in 1951, and later expanded to Hartford, Connecticut, where three movies a day were available. The programs were broadcast electronically scrambled. When a subscriber telephoned the service to order a film, the service activated an unscrambling device attached to the subscriber's set. A second firm, Skiatron, sent its scrambled signals by wire, not broadcast. STV was tried in Los Angeles and San Francisco in 1964, with a mixture of sports, movies, children's programs, and theatrical performances.

PAY – PER – VIEW

The owners of cinemas and broadcast stations feared this competition and launched what would prove to be a successful campaign in the courts and at the ballot box to block it. However, the industry never forgot about charging for individual programs, and with better technology and a different economic structure, STV in the form of pay – per – view returned.

VIDEO – ON DEMAND

The new century has seen popular television programs sold as video – on – demand (VOD) for downloading without commercials. For fans who missed a favorite episode, such a piecemeal purchase — quickly available — was a desirable alternative to waiting for reruns or acquiring a DVD of an entire season. Viewing would happen when it was more convenient for the viewer, and over other media than the TV set, including laptops, tiny iPods, and cell phone screens. A program could be watched anywhere that a cell phone could be carried. A couple lying side by side in bed at night, instead of each reading a book, could each separately be watching and hearing a favorite program.

TIVO

The new century brought the personal video recorder TiVo that stored television programs, paused live programs, and skipped over commercials. Because of its widespread adoption, the television industry and the advertising industry have scrambled to find new ways to reach those "eyeballs," such as product placement. Firms that do television viewer research are also being compelled by fast – changing communication technology to rethink the basic broadcasting model, which is that viewers are given free entertainment in return for minutes of their time to watch commercials.

TV CLOTHING?

The new century has also seen the growing popularity of alternatives to the cathode ray tube home television and the rear projection set; the liquid crystal display (LCD) and the plasma tube offer large screens and panels that may be thin and flat enough to hang on a wall. Problems of cost and image quality are being addressed.

Among the experimental technologies that are likely to bring a new type of choice is optical transmission, based on digital light pulses, not electrical signals. A single hair – thin optical fiber is able to transmit 167 television channels, while a bundle of six strands can feed out more than 1,000 video signals. This broadband opens the possibility of interactive cable television. In 2007, Sony introduced a TV screen as thin and flexible as paper, opening the possibility of TV wallpaper and even TV clothing.

(Television) permits millions of people to listen to the same joke at the same time, and yet remain lonesome.

— T.S. ELIOT

Steven Jobs of Apple distinguished between passive listening or viewing and the interactivity offered by computer screens, video games, and cable experiments as the difference between modes of leaning back and leaning forward. As an example of the possibilities of interactive television, viewers in one test chose among camera angles in baseball and hockey games, choices currently reserved for television directors. It has been proposed that game shows could include questions for contestants at home. Experiments with interactive television have drawn mixed results, however, because a lot of the television audience is content to remain passive.

Alternate branching points have been suggested for a televised drama, so that the hero could take the path to the left, leading to the village, or the path to the right, leading to the mountain. In other words, the television drama would take on the elements of a video game. Viewers would be given the opportunity to make choices within a program.

TELEVISION HAS CONTINUED AND EXPANDED upon what radio began. It gave a face to radio and longer legs to the motion picture. As an oral version of a written culture, television programming, like radio programming before it, is positioned to take the best of both oral and written cultures. As an oral culture, television programs reach audiences who, while watching, receive entertainment or information passively instead of through more active experiences, such as reading. Television also calls upon the breadth of written culture with its infinite resources.

Augmented by cable and other technologies, television has given us an astonishing number of choices at any hour of the day or night. The poet and dramatist Norman Corwin wrote of "Sofa – sitters taken by kilocycle to the ball park, the concert hall, the scene of the crime..."[21] Yet thoughtful observers who acknowledge what television does *for* us never stop asking what television does *to* us. Nor should they.

The survey of broadcasting in the previous chapter and this one began with the point – to – point wireless transmission that preceded broadcasting. It has concluded with wired cable, which is technically not broadcasting. The survey also identified what is sometimes called narrowcasting, a distinction based on an effort by the broadcasting and cable industries to break away from attempts to reach the entire television audience and instead try to attract a specific audience based on age, gender, ethnic, and interest factors.

Despite all the criticism and all the blame for so many social problems, television has been and continues to be enormously popular all over the world; this, even in the face of competition from the Internet and video games. The influence of television has extended to every facet of life, including judgments about desirable careers, desirable life styles, what and how much to buy, ethical standards, relationships, conversations, daily behavior, and how we should spend our discretionary time.

A principal criticism of television centers on its depictions of sex and violence, especially its sexual content. However, there is more of both than ever. The increased sex content in daily soap operas is a case in

CONCLUSION

This instrument can teach. It can illuminate. Yes, and it can even inspire. But it can do so only to the extent that humans are determined to use it to those ends. Otherwise, it is merely wires and lights in a box.[22]

— EDWARD R. MURROW

point. The public is apparently getting what it wants. Except for the time that children spend watching, little attention is paid to the amount of time spent staring at phosphor dots, and that has been growing. There have been few organized efforts to reduce viewing time despite Newton Minow's calling the TV schedule "a vast wasteland."

Programming has changed over time, however. In recent years television has taken on social issues that the networks once avoided. Almost no topic is taboo today. Notable among other programming changes has been the growth of "reality" shows and the placing of contestants in seemingly dangerous and clearly humiliating positions. Again, the public appears to be getting what it wants.

The Internet has cut into television news viewing along with newspaper reading. Both are "skewing" older. Many younger viewers prefer the opinions in blogs. All in all, this is a further example of the movement in mediated communication to a greater number of choices and to dividing the audience along familiar fault lines. The day of three principal daily network newscasts is gone.

Cable news is now a tough competitor. Cable began after World War II as a way for people far from a television station to receive a signal. It extended its operations to cities and it increased its offerings. Several hundred channels are available in large markets, supported by user fees and commercials. A greater number of choices with consequent audience fractioning has been an ongoing pattern.

In 1938, when it began to attract public notice for its future potential, television drew the attention of a leading American essayist, E.B. White:

> *I believe television is going to be the test of the modern world and that in this new opportunity to see beyond the range of our vision, we shall discover either a new and unbearable disturbance of the general peace, or a saving radiance in the sky. We shall stand or fall by television — of that I am quite sure.*[23]

**COMPUTERS
AND THE INTERNET:
LEANING FORWARD**

WHAT IS A REVOLUTION? Look it up in the dictionary and you will find such words and phrases as "an overthrow," "a radical change in society or the social structure," "a sudden, complete, or marked change," "a drastic and far – reaching change in ways of thinking and behaving," and so on.

The Internet — especially the World Wide Web — has brought about a revolution, and almost all of us are affected. The more educated we are, the greater the effect. But educated or not, this touches us. "Web 2.0," comprising the newest additions to the Web, has in the blink of time's eye brought about a second revolution. The main difference between "Web 1.0" and "Web 2.0" is that the former consists of pages provided by those with something to sell or tell to the rest of us. Web 2.0 is provided *by* the rest of us *for* the rest of us. *Time*'s "Person of the Year" ("You") for 2006 celebrated this revolution.

A survey in 2005 of Internet use reported that men are heavier consumers of news, stocks, sports and pornography, while more women look for health and religious guidance. Men use the Internet more often, listen more often to music, and are more likely to bid in online auctions. Women email more, write longer emails, and reach out to a wider circle of friends and relatives. More girls than boys start personal blogs.[1]

None of these uses has anything to do with what computers were created for. Yet when average people realized how the computer could extend life's choices, they could hardly wait to get one. Attitudes shifted markedly starting in 1995, a watershed year for the Internet. It was the year that the National Science Foundation, which ran the Internet backbone, allowed commercial intrusion into a nonprofit online network, and it was the year of the Netscape browser. Netscape revealed the shared world of hypertext connected by hyperlinks that lie at the heart of the World Wide Web.

That changed everything. It allowed almost anyone to find almost anything, learn almost anything, say anything, and buy or sell anything. It opened a world that was, in William James' phrase of another era, "a blooming, buzzing, confusion" that holds more than 100 million websites with domain names and content. The total number of Web pages is, of course, much larger. It is a world dominated for the most part by ordinary folks, not by governments that try with

The Internet has morphed what we used to think of as a fancy calculator into a fancy telephone with email, chat groups, IM, and blogs. It turns out that we don't use computers to enhance our math skills — we use them to expand our people skills.[4]

— WILL WRIGHT

incomplete success to control what goes on within their own borders, and not by large corporations.[2]

In addition to the Internet, this brief survey of computer usage will be restricted to identifying its roles in the storage and communication of information and entertainment. We should recognize that "while the Internet may be subjected to criticism on a variety of fronts, it is unlikely that going online will ever suffer from the same type of scorn that television has received over the years ('the idiot box,' 'the boob tube,' 'the vast wasteland')."[3]

The story begins centuries earlier than 1995.

Pick up a current computer magazine. Its articles and ads will describe devices that have nothing at all to do with what computers were invented to do. They were not invented to hold words or do anything with language. They were not invented to communicate from one place to another. They certainly were not invented to play games or entertain in any way. Computers were invented solely to calculate.

THE ABACUS

The need for a device to calculate started with counting boards on which pebbles were moved around ("calculus" is Latin for "pebble," used for counting), and led to the invention of the abacus in the Mediterranean or the Near East about 5,000 years ago. Partitioned by fives and tens to match the fingers, it aided merchants and tax collectors across the ancient world to add, subtract, multiply, and divide. Today, here and there, even in our current age of cheap, hand–held calculators, the abacus is used.

Calculating all day long is weary work. The counting tables of the Middle Ages helped, but there was an impetus to build a better machine. Leonardo da Vinci designed one. In the seventeenth century German professor Wilhelm Schickard constructed a "calculating clock." In France, at age nineteen, the future philosopher Blaise Pascal built a shoebox–size device to help his father, a tax collector.

In Germany, at about age twenty–six, the philosopher Gottfried Leibniz designed a decimal calculator because "It is unworthy of excellent men to lose hours like slaves." Leibniz also conceived of binary calculation, but found no practical use for it. Efforts in England and Scotland resulted in the slide rule and logarithms. The first widely marketed mechanical calculator, the "Arithmometer," was built in France in 1720.

CHARLES BABBAGE

The foundations for a true computer were laid in the nineteenth century by a 20–year–old math student at Cambridge University. Charles Babbage grew frustrated at reading newspaper accounts of English ships foundering on rocks because published navigation tables were calculated in error. He set out to build an "engine" to figure the tables accurately.

He imagined that the machine could also help in banking, surveying, mathematics, and the sciences.

Part way through the construction of his "difference engine," and after being appointed as a professor of mathematics at Cambridge, Babbage had a better idea, an "analytical engine" that could solve any arithmetic problem. It would grind out the answers in a "mill" and place them in a "store." Punch cards would feed the problems into the machine; a new set of cards meant a new problem. When a certain point was reached, for example at a tally of 200, a different sequence of steps would begin.

With these ideas, Babbage invented programming and the computer. He derived his notion of punch cards from their use in the weaving industry, where cards guided threads into complex patterns on a loom. Babbage's idea for using cards came from Joseph – Marie Jacquard, owner of a French weaving factory, who used thousands of wooden cards in series with holes punched to weave the intricate designs.

ORIGIN OF PUNCH CARDS

Babbage did not complete his analytical engine, but he explained his ideas to a family friend, Ada, Lady Lovelace, the daughter of the poet Byron. She published them in a series of *Notes*, writing that the engine would weave algebraic patterns the way the punch card loom weaves flowers and leaves. A few years ago, the programming language Ada was named to honor her contribution.

Cards were at the heart of a different effort in 1890 by a U.S. Patent Office employee, Herman Hollerith, to cross – tabulate census data, such as determining the number of Minnesota bachelor farmers born in Norway. This was data processing.

The pattern of holes in each card allowed for electrical contacts so that counting registers for each variable could advance one digit. This would be the basis of binary calculation. Hollerith left the Census Bureau to start a company that would one day become IBM.

Boolean logic (with symbols for AND, OR, and NOT) and binary arithmetic (base – 2 — 0's and 1's — not the base – 10 decimal system) set researchers on the digital path used today. In a flash of insight, Bell Telephone Lab engineer George Stibitz combined Boolean logic with binary arithmetic at home one evening in 1937. Working at his kitchen table, he wired some flashlight batteries and bulbs together with strips of metal cut from a tobacco can to create a crude electrical digital calculator, the world's first.

AN ELECTRIC CALCULATOR

That led to calculators to solve telephone engineering problems. In 1940 he hooked two modified typewriters into a telephone circuit between New York and New Hampshire to begin the world of telecommunications.

World War II and the postwar years saw considerable advances in both computer theory and construction. A British computing effort joined by Alan Turing, one of the geniuses in the history of computing, cracked the German secret Enigma military code and helped to win the war. Nazi Germany could have been aided by a genius in their own country, Konrad Zuse, who built the first computer guided by software, but he received much less support from authorities.

FIRST RESEARCH COMPUTERS

In the United States, ENIAC, a digital computer built at the University of Pennsylvania, was completed too late for its objective of calculating the trajectory of artillery shells, but it managed to examine a postwar plan to build the hydrogen bomb.

Ideas from mathematicians Norbert Weiner and John von Neumann charted the path taken by postwar computers. Meanwhile, Bell engineers Claude Shannon and Warren Weaver raised communication theory from a kind of guesswork to science. Universities set up research computers with acronym names: ENIAC, EDSAC, ILLIAC, JOHNNIAC, MADM, SWAC, BINAC, MANIAC, and the Air Force's Whirlwind. Each of these advanced knowledge of what computers could do.

In 1952 the UNIVAC introduced the public to computers when it helped the CBS network forecast an Eisenhower landslide on the night of the presidential election, instead of the close results the experts expected. In 1957 a computer figured in the Spencer Tracy – Katherine Hepburn film, *Desk Set*.

Most people had never heard of the computer when British scientist Charles Percy Snow told an MIT audience, "We happen to be living at a time of a major scientific revolution, probably more important in its consequences than the first Industrial Revolution, a revolution which we shall see in full force in the very near future."[5]

"MAN OF THE YEAR"

The end of the decade of the 1950s saw the end of the hand – built, one – of – a – kind computers; commercial firms assembled the new computers on assembly lines. The first were the large mainframe computers. Then came the mini – computers, and in the 1970s came the micro – computer. The computer became *Time's* "Man of the Year" for 1982.

The computer was meant to be a serious tool for scientific, government, and business use. Could anyone imagine that children would use computers? Absurd!

HOBBYISTS

The notion that it would ever be a common household device like a washing machine would have been considered ridiculous as recently as 1974, when the Altair 8800, a kit for hobbyists to assemble, started the move to the personal computer. The hobbyists had to write their own binary code and flip a switch on the front panel for each binary digit.

Three years later the already assembled Apple II, Commodore Pet, and TRS – 80 opened the floodgates. The Apple II was the first PC with color, high – resolution graphics, sound, and a way to control games. The Atari video games were in arcades, and the first Osborne portable would soon be at the fingertips of reporters on assignment.

The history of the computer is also the history of its internal products, like the transistor, integrated circuits, core memory, and microchips, plus input devices like the card reader, tape drives, disk drives, the mouse, the joystick, and the scanner. It is also the story of such output devices as printers, synthesizers, and routers, plus wireless technology like Bluetooth to connect them.

INPUT, OUTPUT CHANGES

And it is the story of software, from the 1's and 0's of the era of vacuum tubes to assembly languages, compilers, programming languages, and eventually software available off the shelf to do hundreds of tasks. A four – year – old child at the start of the twenty – first century playing a game has more computer power at her fingertips than the geniuses at the dawn of the computer era could have imagined.

The computer made other forms of communication easier. All medium and large newspapers, magazines, radio and television stations, plus thousands of small ones now have computer – based online versions. Computers assist the newspaper publishing process at each step from the reporter's laptop to the delivery trucks.

AIDING NEWS DELIVERY

News has been transmitted by computers since 1970, when the Associated Press switched over to them. Magazine publishers use computers to separate subscribers by targeting advertising. Book publishers require authors to submit their work in electronic form; typed manuscripts have now joined handwritten manuscripts and dodo birds.

 For research the information age has added electronic archives; Lexis-Nexis is among the better known of more than four thousand databases available for retrieving information. Archive.org has archived more than fifty – five billion pages of text and audio that appeared at one time or another on the Web.

For what once was considered laughable sums of money for such enterprises, someone working out of a garage can publish a newspaper, magazine, or book, or even produce a movie. Inexpensive microcomputers and easy to learn desktop publishing software today create output of a quality that only a skilled printer had been producing with bulky machinery.

DESKTOP PUBLISHING

WORD PROCESSING

Desktop publishing began with word processing, and that began with a wish to duplicate what was typed. Early attempts to do this consisted of attachments to an electric typewriter. The M. Schultz machine used rolls of paper much like player piano rolls to record typing. Form letters could be turned out, one after the other, with only the address and salutation changed. Paper rolls were succeeded by the paper tape of the Flexowriter, which allowed for correcting mistakes and the physical cutting and pasting of text, a precursor to what word processing would do electronically. An IBM Selectric typewriter with a magnetic tape drive began true word processing, but at a basic level, in 1964.

The term "word processing" came from IBM to encompass writing, editing, printing, and storing text. Text could also be punched on standard 80 – column punch cards. In 1969, IBM's MagCards increased what could be stored on a single card from 80 characters to a pageful of characters. Three years later came video screens for display and tape cassettes for storage. In the early '70s, floppy disks permitted the storage of one hundred pages of text on each disk.

A Chinese immigrant to the United States, Dr. An Wang, designed an automatic typewriter with limited editing functions. Word processing spread rapidly when it became software that could run on a general purpose computer. The Electric Pencil program in 1976 was followed by WordStar and WordPerfect. At present, Microsoft Word dominates the field.

Xerox Corporation researchers conceived of a graphics – based computer that not only could be controlled by a mouse, but also displayed typefaces on a screen and sent the displayed output to a laser printer, beginning what would become known as WYSIWYG: "What you see is what you get."

Although Xerox did not take advantage of the ideas flowing from its research division, Steven Jobs of Apple did with the introduction in 1984 of the Macintosh computer. The PostScript page description program and the Hewlett – Packard low – cost laser printer brought to the public the reality of "desktop publishing," a term coined the following year by Paul Brainerd, developer of PageMaker, which became the leading page layout program.

PDAs

Later, the hand – held personal digital assistant, or PDA, recognized handwriting and acted like a memo pad that connected to a computer. Apple introduced the first of these, the Newton, in 1993. Like all electronic devices, it was superseded by more advanced devices; in Newton's case, by the smaller, cheaper, easier – to – use, feature – filled Palm Pilot. PDAs were pulled from briefcases, purses, and even pockets everywhere from business meetings to supermarkets.

Engineers have labored to add more features, including voice recognition software. Other engineers combined features of the PDA and the cell phone into such units as the BlackBerry, which is also a handheld emailer and Web access device. Owners could blog, send instant messages, and pay bills at any convenient opportunity, including sitting in a car while waiting for a red light to change.

By themselves, computers and laser printers, the principal equipment in desktop publishing, have not created the first opportunity for people of moderate means to publish. After all, typewriters and mimeograph machines were around for decades. What computers and printers have provided is much more egalitarian, the means at low cost to offer an attractive and professional looking product.

PROFESSIONAL QUALITY

Tens of thousands of people now do what only a relatively few people could do in the past: they package their writing attractively without having to turn to others for help. In a real sense, desktop publishing puts the ability to disseminate information into many hands. Businesses, schools, government offices, clubs and organizations of every sort turn out innumerable newspapers, newsletters, magazines, and flyers. Restaurants print menus, theaters print programs, and students, who do their research by browsing the Internet instead of browsing through library shelves, hand in slick looking term papers.

In a historical sense, desktop publishing is as old as the start of printing in Europe; Gutenberg and those who followed him a half millennium ago were printer – publishers. So was Benjamin Franklin, for that matter. Things changed with the introduction of big and costly machinery two centuries ago as part of the Industrial Revolution. Desktop publishing has, in the sense of personal empowerment, turned the clock back. Going a step further, with the Internet, even the computer printer is no longer needed to publish.

ONLINE PUBLISHING

Newspapers, magazines, radio stations, television stations, and news networks all publish online sources of information. So do individuals and small groups who produce online products like *The Drudge Report* and *The Huffington Post*. So do tens of thousands of bloggers. They have undercut A,J. Liebling's ironic statement, "Freedom of the press belongs to the man who owns one."

If you have expressed concern that entire sections of the newspaper delivered each day at your front door go straight to the recycle bin, you are not alone. The waste of resources in printing and delivery of newspapers and magazines that are unread has led to several proposals for electronic substitutes to replace the printed page.

TELETEXT, VIDEOTEX

Prior to Internet online news and advertising, there were teletext and videotex. Teletext was transmitted via a television signal's unused scanning lines, or vertical blanking interval (the visible horizontal bar on a television screen when the set isn't tuned perfectly). Teletext was a one – way broadcast transmission, but videotex, using telephone lines, had an interactive feature; the user requested information from a computer data bank, the precursor of current online news retrieval. Neither service was successful.

Videotex, originally called "viewdata," had a run as the British Post Office's Prestel and the Canadian government's Telidon. With a television set, a keypad, and a telephone equipped with a modem, a user accessed computers loaded with information ranging from the stock market to horoscope readings. However, not enough British households were interested to keep the service alive in the face of newer technology like the videotape recorder, the personal computer, and two teletext services, Ceefax and Oracle, that offered such choices as puzzles and fiction as well as news, plus a cheaper decoder.

FRANCE'S MINITEL

A success around the same time occurred across the English Channel. The French PTT (Post Telephone and Telegraph) handed out free Minitel video terminals (monitors and keyboards) that replaced telephone directories. Charging businesses for listings, Minitel was so popular and profitable that in the years ahead France would lag in adopting the Internet. The public used the Minitels to both shop and pay for the goods they bought, check airplane and train schedules, make hotel reservations, learn the latest news, the weather or what their horoscope advised, play computer games, and chat with fellow hobbyists. Subscribers also used it for email. Despite criticism about permitting access to pornography, the French government limited its own role to managing the system. It kept its hands off content.

That was too much freedom for the government of Singapore, which tried to interest its people in a similar system, Singapore One, but without free terminals and certainly without a hands – off approach to content. The government, like a nanny, looked at everything, which limited the available content. Singaporeans stayed away.

INTERACTIVITY EXPERIMENTS

Before the Internet, experiments in interactive television were attempted in the widely held conviction that viewers sometimes wanted to do more than lean back and "veg out"; sometimes those viewers wanted to lean forward and get involved in what appeared on the screen.

In a humorous *Saturday Night Live* experiment, comic Eddie Murphy held up a live lobster he had named Larry, and asked viewers to vote, at fifty cents per phone call, on whether Larry should live or be cooked. This test of interactivity drew 240,000 phone calls. (Larry narrowly was allowed to live, although it was rumored that the results were "cooked" in his favor.)

The quiz show *Jeopardy* experimented with choosing contestants through an online quiz. More recently, a popular television program that introduced amateur singers, *American Idol*, allowed viewers to vote on contestants in a successful effort to involve the public in entertainment decisions. An Internet – only program, *Gold Rush*, attracted more than ten million players to a quiz show and national treasure hunt. Like television quiz shows, products were on display and could be won.

Online shopping has continued to grow both in the number of shoppers and the volume of purchases, with many customers initially going to stores to browse the merchandise, then, despite concerns about loss of privacy, fraud, and credit card information theft, buying their selections over the Internet, where it was cheaper.

In limited tests of interactivity in the Chicago suburb of Deerfield and the Los Angeles suburb of Cerritos, viewers could order from several dozen local stores by punching into the phones the catalog numbers of the items displayed on the screen.

A larger test of interactivity, Qube, in Columbus, Ohio, continued for seven years before it was ended. Disappointment also attended a Time – Warner digital video – on – demand and shopping service, plus games and news, in Orlando, Florida, for four thousand homes, that started in 1994. In an early, experimental version of TiVo, viewers could pause or rewind a movie as if they had a tape, combining the bandwidth of fiber optic cable with the flexibility and storage of computers; the experiment lasted three years.

QUBE

Interactive experiments called ACTV allowed television viewers to participate in a game show, and to choose camera angles in a music show and sports events. The Massachusetts Institute of Technology Media Lab also tested audience interactivity for a soap opera and a television newscast. Although these experiments were terminated, their functions would become part of what the Internet and new communication technologies would offer a few years later.

The Internet itself began quietly when some science researchers at universities and in industry wanted a better way to contact each other through their mainframe computers that were connected by telephone lines. In 1969, they sought a grant from the Advanced Research Projects Agency of the Department of Defense, which had been organized in 1958 as a government think tank in response to the Soviet launching of Sputnik. With the grant the scientists set up the ARPANET, the Advanced Research Projects Agency Network.

ARPANET was to be a test area for computer networks, a link – up of time – sharing systems. Because of the heavy cost of constructing and operating mainframe computers, sharing made sense. A principal goal

ARPANET

of the ARPANET was to share data and programs in the days when data existed on punch cards and programs were not sold at the computer store (there were none), but had to be written by individual researchers for their own projects. Computers then were employed mostly as mathematics tools, although by the '60s some non–mathematical research was done, such as language analysis (including one study by the author of this book).

A TOOL FOR COMMUNICATING

The ARPANET was seen as something more than a *research* tool. It was also a *communication* tool, an important distinction. No one had ever used a computer for ordinary communication the way people made a telephone call or sent a telegram.

The ARPANET was not intended to connect computers but rather to connect the researchers who used the computers, another important distinction. To accomplish that goal, it was necessary to establish protocols — agreed–upon ways of communicating — such as a file transfer protocol (FTP) and a remote login (Telnet). These signals would open up channels to allow data to pass through, and then close the channels.

J.C.R. Licklider, first head of ARPA's Information Processing Techniques Office, envisioned a network that could spread everywhere, an "intergalactic network," as he put it. The idea caught on. Licklider also moved ARPANET thinking away from a military focus to talking about basic computer research.

WHO SHOULD USE IT?

One question that arose early was access. Who should be allowed to use the network? If access was to be limited to certain universities, certain industries, and certain government and military offices, it would not be "intergalactic." To be that, to be universal so that the network's potential benefit could reach all of mankind, access could not be limited, nor could control of the network.

It was decided early that the network would not have a single central command and control point. Each node — each point of connection — would be able to connect with any other node. In the event of an atomic bomb attack, the network would not be brought down by the destruction of a headquarters site.

That concept grew out of a 1962 Rand Corporation study, "On Distributed Communications Networks," by Paul Baran. He called for what amounted to a new kind of public utility. In describing such a utility, Baran created the concept of packet switching and store–and–forward technology, which now lie at the heart of email data transmission.

By the end of 1969 ARPANET had connected computer nodes at four universities: UCLA, Stanford, the University of California at Santa Barbara, and the University of Utah. Four years later forty nodes existed, including a satellite link to Hawaii and low speed links to England and Norway. Ten years after that, there were four thousand nodes, but it was no longer the original ARPANET.

In 1975, as messages flew from node to node, ARPANET was declassified as a research project. Responsibility for it was given to the Defense Communications Agency. That same year the Xerox Corporation started an experimental internet. The ARPANET was eventually split in two, into a civilian internet and the military network, MILNET.

Because humans are social animals, the researchers were also using their new pathways to create interest groups. Are there other lovers of homemade beer or wine out there? How about science fiction fans? How about gardeners? Messages on these subjects took momentary time to travel but the transmisson time was not delaying real work. The computers and the telephone lines had enough capacity for all of it, and if they did not, more could be provided.

These private groups and personal emails lay outside the formal research – purposed structure of ARPANET, so casual social messages could be troublesome if officials found out how their expensive equipment was being used, but everyone who was using the connected computers enjoyed the extra social benefit. No one complained.

A few years later, Usenet was created. In 1979, two Duke University students, Tom Truscott and Jim Ellis, created a separate online network, a kind of computerized bulletin board that they called Usenet. Anyone could offer news or information articles in the form of files. The network began at two sites, Duke and the University of North Carolina. Other universities soon signed on.

The University of California at Berkeley provided a gateway between the mailing lists of ARPANET and the more open Usenet. Where ARPANET tried — not too successfully — to limit its discussions to research issues, any topic was fair game for Usenet bulletin boards: find a few like – minded souls and set up a newsgroup! The question of distasteful postings came up. It was decided that peer pressure via emails should nip offensive postings. Repeat offenders would be removed from the Usenet.

By 1983 Usenet had leaped the Atlantic Ocean, as European sites connected to the growing network. It wasn't cheap. With the standard 300 – baud modems, the transfer of data was slow enough to run up considerable phone charges, especially for always impoverished college students. The arrival of the 1200 – baud modem helped somewhat. So did an organized network of *backbones* — main trunk lines — in different countries to connect UNIX user groups.

Inherent in most mass media is central control of content. Many people are influenced by the decisions of a few. Television programming, for example, is controlled by a small group of people compared to the size of the audience. In this way, the audience has very little choice over what is emphasized by most mass media. However, Usenet is controlled by its audience. Usenet should be seen as a promising successor to other people's presses, such as broadsides at the time of the American Revolution.[7]

— MICHAEL HAUBEN

CONNECTING EUROPE

The Internet was up and running by the 1970s, but transferring information was too much of a hassle for a non – computer expert. One would run one program to connect to another computer, and then in conversation (in a different language) with the other computer, run a different program to access the information. Even when data had been transferred back to one's own computer, decoding it might be impossible.[7]

— TIM BERNERS – LEE

Eventually Usenet spread across the world. Thousands of newsgroups discussed everything from philosophy to recipes and movies. Anyone could post. Everyone could read. The free, even anarchic nature of the Internet was never clearer.

The U.S. Department of Defense had originally provided the money to set up the Internet in order to improve communications with the private sector. The National Science Foundation ran it, but soon realized that the Internet had grown into much more than an accompaniment to research. In 1994, the Internet was turned over to private enterprise.

Famously, the Internet is "a network of networks." From the beginning it was as complicated as it sounds.

In 1990, Tim Berners – Lee wrote a point – and – click browser – editor program that he called WorldWideWeb, a combination of hypertext — non – sequential texts — and computer networking. Hypertext linked directly from one website to another. In addition to text it also featured graphics, sound, and video. Importantly, it was much less scientific than it was commercial and personal.

At a time of incompatible computers run by idiosyncratic operating systems, Berners – Lee's browser became a means to scan networks of computers to see what was out there and to summarize their contents. It started as a tool to enable researchers to browse other research, with the goal of linking anything to anything else. Later the browser was distinguished from the virtual space filled with websites. The virtual space itself retained the name with word separation: the World Wide Web.

Over the years the World Wide Web, or "Web," has become synonymous with the Internet, but it shouldn't be. The Internet is a broader designation that includes email, Usenet, and other systems and networks. Each quickly swelled to enormous size. The Web's virtually uncountable number of sites would be of little use if not for browsers to organize and read them, and search engines to locate what the "netizen" is looking for.

BROWSERS

At first, college students wrote most of the browsers and search engines in their spare time. The name "Archie" for a Web navigator was originally intended to conjure up "archive," not the comic book character (an association that its designers detested). An improved search engine called "Gopher" took the user from directory to directory. That was followed by a new search engine called "Veronica," named just to tease the "Archie" team. Among other browsers were Erwise, Viola, Lynx, Arena, Amaya, and Midas.

In 1993, college students Marc Andreesen and Eric Bina designed Mosaic, a more efficient browser than any at the time. To overcome its weaknesses, two years later they wrote Netscape. Unlike Mosaic, it worked almost identically with the Windows, Macintosh, and UNIX platforms. It was modem friendly, enabling the user to act on the quickly available text and hyperlinks while it more slowly downloaded graphics.

In addition, service providers came along to improve and extend access for a fee: America Online (AOL) and CompuServe were leaders. AOL tried to look hip for a young, with–it clientele. The Dow Jones News Retrieval began as a business information service before reaching out to the general public. Prodigy hired women to help design and market its product; its goal was a family–oriented service, but it captured only a small fraction of the market.

A variety of search engines that came along included AltaVista, Dog-pile, Hotbot, Lycos, and Yahoo, plus hundreds more that specialized in specific information areas. At this writing the most popular browser is Microsoft's Internet Explorer. For Macintosh users, it is Safari.

The dominant search engine, Google, almost instantly replies to any topic request by identifying websites that relate to the topic. According to a 2005 survey, Google handled requests for information from 380 million separate users each month in ninety languages. Google offered several searches. The best known was for text websites. Another was for images. Still another was for topic groups such as recreation or science, each of which were divided and subdivided into special topics. Another topic grouping could be found in its "directory," which also was divided and subdivided and subdivided again. There were also a news search and a finance search keeping up with current events across a broad range of topics. News editions by 2005 were available for ten different countries, and there were editions in French, German, Italian, and Spanish, as well as English.

It was only a matter of time, after broadband replaced narrow band-widths with their low baud numbers, before the capacity to make phone calls would bypass local phone companies. One difficulty of Internet phone calls lay in the difference between email transmission that lasts fractions of a second and the voice transmission of a phone call that lasts as long as the call itself. Early efforts resulted in poor transmission, but the quality improved and the cost was hard to beat. Skype was a leading provider of VOIP (Voice Over Internet Protocol). Calls by a Skype user to any other Skype user were free anywhere in the world.

The astonishing proliferation of websites spawned industries that have included books and consultants on website design, software to assist production, and courses in high schools, technical colleges, and universities. Entire libraries of books were online. Gutenberg.org was a free

It has already provided us with a gigantic Information Marketplace, where individuals and organizations buy, sell, and freely exchange information and information services among one another. The press, radio, and television never got close; all they can do is spray the same information out from one source toward many destinations. Nor can the letter or the telephone approach the Web's power, because even though those media enable one–on–one exchanges, they are slow and devoid of the computer's ability to display, search, automate, and mediate. Remarkably—compared with Gutenberg's press, Bell's telephone, and Marconi's radio—and well before reaching its ultimate form, Berners–Lee's Web has already established its uniqueness.[8]

– Michael Dertouzos

website that had archived thousands of books in the public domain; they were available in their entirety for downloading or reading online.

In 2003, Amazon.com created a mini–revolution by scanning 120,000 books and promising to scan many more. Google topped that by setting out to scan 20 million books, digitizing the collections of five top libraries: Stanford, Harvard, Oxford, the University of Michigan, and the New York Public Library. The project eventually may allow any Internet user anywhere in the world to search inside millions of volumes, seeing the pages exactly as they appeared in the originals, complete with illustrations, charts and photos.[9]

The British Broadcasting Corporation planned to gather the largest archive of films, photographs, and personal accounts from every human group on the planet, and put it all online in electronic form. It called on universities and other organizations to contribute to its "Dictionary of Man."

The effect (of Wikipedia) was explosive. That simple button turned readers into contributors and contributors into evangelists. . . . And most extraordinary, the site has not been defaced by vandals or hijacked by zealots. Or more precisely, it is vandalized every day but it is usually repaired within minutes by any one of the millions of users who are motivated to protect and nurture the site.

Today Wales is celebrated as a champion of Internet–enabled egalitarianism. . Everyone predicted that mob rule would lead to chaos. Instead it has led to what may prove to be the most powerful industrial model of the 21st century: peer production.[10]

— Time

The egalitarian nature of the Internet has no better example than *Wikipedia*, the online encyclopedia for which anyone can write an article. It also allows anyone to edit what someone else has written. Clearly, here is room for propaganda and distortion, and some constraints have been necessary, but somehow it all works.

More people use it than the online *Encyclopædia Britannica* and it already contains ten times as many articles as the *Britannica*. In 2006 *Wikipedia* had more than one million entries in English and hundreds of thousands of entries in 50 other languages. Its founder, Jimmy Wales, noted that few articles had been contributed until he decided to allow any reader to contribute or edit an article.

One result has been the constant changing, and changing the changes, of comments about politics and other topics that stir readers to revise, tweak, or distort the encyclopedia text. In a few cases, a person who is the subject of a *Wikipedia* article has quietly altered it to improve his image.

For folks with the urge to be the first to pass along the latest news, or to dish some gossip, Wiki (from the Hawaiian word for "quick") is the way to go. Breaking news can find its way there before journalists can post it online.

Impoverished countries and countries ruled by a dictator or an oligarchy — usually the same — have used parts of mediated communication in ways superior to their use in Western nations. Cell phones are one example. Another may prove to be a curious version of *Wikipedia*. Located at wikileak.org, *Wikileak* is a place to deposit government documents. Where governments control access to newspapers and broadcast outlets, here is an outlet for whistle blowers. The site relies on volunteers to vet the information. Potential for abuse is great, as it is with *Wikipedia*, and the temptation is probably greater, but over time it may succeed.

Copyright in the matter of e – books was thrown wide open in 2002 when a court ruled that because e – books are made of changing digital signals rather than fixed texts on printed pages, they were not books in the normal sense. Unless the decision is reversed, authors can negotiate for electronic publishing rights and bypass the publishers of their printed books.

Of all aspects of the Internet, the most powerful and transformative for most people has been email. Connecting distant lives is the feature that changes non – users of computers into daily users. (Surveys of students taken by the author of this book year after year shows that of all the tools of communication at their disposal, the one that they would least want to give up is email.)

ARPANET founders saw that not only could universities send messages, so could individuals. Electronic mail was born. Its popularity came as a surprise. By 1973, almost everyone who helped develop the ARPANET discovered the convenience of the new message service. Email resembled a telephone network in connecting one node with another in seconds, and it resembled the postal service in handling written information. Unlike locations on the Web and Usenet, email messages did not have websites.

With email communication dropping messages into electronic mailboxes, the recipient received and replied easily at convenient times, bypassing the postal system and "telephone tag." For anyone reading this who still does not know, email — electronic mail — bypasses not only the post office but the telephone as well.

Email is total communication without transportation, a point – to – point system that puts a mailbox in the home, inside any computer or hand – held device with a modem and communication software. The sender can email, attaching documents and photographs, to one or many persons down the hall or halfway around the world. It is estimated that the USPS is losing about one – third of its business to email. In 2005, an estimated 35 billion emails were sent daily somewhere in the world.[12] Emails sit unannounced until summoned, but a variation, "push email," delivers messages to a computer as soon as they are sent.

Instant messaging — IM or "IMing" — is a cell phone service, also called SMS (Short Message Service) that uses text. It was created as part of the GSM (Global System for Mobile Communication). The system alerts you when someone is trying to reach you with a text message. Because

In 1994, most people had to call the bank to check their balances. Or inquire in person, or wait for a paper statement to arrive in the mail. Baseball box scores were found in the newspaper. Weather forecasts came over the phone from the weather bureau, or on TV. Back then, most Americans still had to lick a stamp to send mail.

According to the Pew Internet & American Life Project, fewer than one in seven Americans were online in 1995. Today, the majority of Americans are surfing the Web, exchanging e – mail, reading bank statements and ball scores, checking the weather. Today, Pew says, two out of every three Americans spend time online. . .

Want to know how to grow cannabis? What are the ingredients for a Molotov cocktail? What's the best strategy to successfully shoplift? Web surfers can get just about any kind of information, including bomb – making manuals, recipes for illegal drugs and even a step – by – step guide to becoming anorexic.[11]

— CNN REPORT

We have serious problems with spam, phishing, scams, electronic identity theft. It's ironic that a system originally designed to make us more secure has resulted in a tremendous amount of personal vulnerability.[14]

— Don Brazeal

The issues involving children and the Internet are countless: Does the Internet help my children with their schoolwork? (Children say yes.) But, does the Internet improve grades? (Adults say no.) Do my children spend too much time online? Should I actively monitor online access by my children? Should I use filtering software? Are my children potential victims of online predators? How do I know my children's friends when they contact so many of them mainly by e–mail? And, how can I keep track of what my children do online when they know more about computers and the Internet than I do?[15]

— Digital Futures Report

cell phone use spread rapidly in parts of the world where phone lines were scarce, IM got an early foothold. Teenagers and pre–teenagers grabbed their cell phones to IM friends the instant the closing school bell rang. Cell phone and PDA (personal digital assistant) texting joined online chat rooms in public favor. IM could connect two people as well as a group for business or personal exchanges in real time.

If IM is not casual enough, Twitter may do it. This service lets "twitterers" send out "tweets," or brief messages to let anyone in the Twitter network know that the sender is at the mall, and others may show up for fun and shopping.

Another outgrowth of email, the LISTSERV is a discussion forum on a particular topic. Subscribe to one and you get an email any time someone posts a comment. If you ask a question or reply to one, your message is posted to each LISTSERV subscriber. A stock market message board, such as the one run by Yahoo, allows a similar group contact.

If email eased communication for millions of people, it also eased the way for the unscrupulous and the criminal. A lot of problems about email defied easy solution. Email could be addressed to hundreds of thousands of people at once, but the source of the email could be untraceable, a nightmare that created computer junk mailers.

With the discovery that messages could be mailed to huge numbers of people at virtually no cost, spam grew so fast that it choked the Internet. In 2003 the research firm IDC estimated that 4.9 trillion unwanted messages were sent to addresses in the United States alone.[13] Efforts to stop the spammers or, in extreme cases, to throw them in jail foundered on clever ruses used by the spammers to disguise their addresses. Adding to the problem, *botnets* install themselves on millions of computers, creating a crime network unknown to the owners of those computers.

Malicious hackers spread viruses, which infect computers when someone clicks on an email attachment, and worms, which race across the Internet without human intervention. Motives for writing and spreading these destructive programs varied, but none were pleasant. Pedophiles located the email addresses of children to whom they sent pornographic letters and pictures, or arranged meetings. They joined chat rooms set up for youngsters and used instant messaging to talk directly to the young victims. Sending a youngster a webcam to attach to a computer in the child's room as a "gift" was a favored trick. Finding a way to stop them has not proved easy.

Con artists were also busy sending email to the gullible, promising fortunes in exchange for bank account information, but children remained the larger concern.

A more benign change was the effect of email on letter writing. Email messages have developed a life of their own, different from ordinary letters. People who hate to write letters may feel fine about the informality of tapping out a few words on a keyboard. It is easier and more fun for distant friends and relatives to stay in touch by making a comment or forwarding a joke.

Emails seem to have revived the art of writing letters, even if they are not as graceful as letters written with pen and ink or even on a typewriter. Writer's block may dissolve when the medium seems so transitory and informal. Messages tend to be shorter and more informal. In terms of emotional investment, an email is more like a telephone conversation. Sentences tend to be shorter, spelling and grammar are often ignored. There is less of a sense that each word matters and must be weighed. After all, a message disappears at the tap of a finger. Words can so easily be changed, added to, eliminated, and moved around.

Emails were meant to lack permanence, but people, as it turned out, like to keep letters. No matter how sloppy, they were saved in files. And many were sloppy. Some observers bemoaned the sloppiness and thought the new technology doomed the art of letter writing, but philosophy professor David Glidden saw a return to gentler days:

> *With every new technology the art of writing changes. When Henry James switched from writing successive drafts on paper to dictation to a typist, his sentences grew longer and his fiction more diffuse. His writing became more like the way he talked. Composing by computer has had somewhat the opposite effect, making prose more focused and finessed, enabling — even encouraging — an endless series of revisions that would have strained the hand or forced the typist to quit.*[16]

Email and word processing did not bring the "paperless office," a promise that always seems a decade away, but never arrives. The world continues to convert forests into sheets of paper. One change seems to be a shift from the practice of first printing, then distributing, to first distributing (electronically), then printing.[18]

A special kind of letter writing, the greeting card, has been available for all occasions online as an ecard at no cost with little more than a few button clicks. The Electric Postcard, established by the MIT Media Lab, allowed a sender to select an image, such as the Mona Lisa, and write a message. It was delivered at no charge by email. A number of commercial firms, like Hallmark and Blue Mountain, offered similar services, both free and paid, transmitting greeting cards with moving graphics and accompanying music. To cite just two other examples, the Albany, NY, *Times Union* offered postcards with local photos, and the

About email

One could write tersely and type imperfectly, even to an older person in a superior position and even to a person one did not know very well, and the recipient took no offense. There was none of the formality and perfection that were required in a typed letter… Among the advantages of the network message services over the telephone were the fact that one could proceed immediately to the point without having to engage in small talk first, that the message services produced a preservable record, and that the sender and receiver did not have to be available at the same time.[17]

— MICHAEL HAUBEN

Islamic Information and News Network offered postcards with mosque images.

BLOGS

When one person controls a website for the purpose of expressing herself or himself, either through opinions or a diary, the product is a "blog," short for "weblog," and the user is a "blogger" engaged in "blogging." By 2006 millions of blogs filled the Web, another astonishing estimate. These open – to – the – public diaries and opinion sites were originally limited to text, but audio crept in as "podcasts" and video crept in as "vlogs."

To cite two recent examples of its immediacy, the Israeli war against Hezbollah in Lebanon in 2006 was presented at its most personal level on video blogs. Safe at home, viewers saw live video of people huddled in air raid shelters as bombs dropped near them, and they saw soldiers in firefights because one soldier was carrying a small camera phone.

In 2007, while a crazed student at Virginia Tech University was massacring teachers and fellow students, other students were calling 911 on their cell phones, and some students were sending out emails and actually blogging on myspace.com and facebook.com. One student, crouching to avoid bullets, was uploading video from his camera phone to cnn.com. The interplay of mass and personal communication had never been clearer.

Vlogs — video blogs — compete against television networks and cable channels. They add immeasurably to the totals of producers and their content with a growing array of fare that is often sophomoric and usually amateurish. Only now and then does it yield a clip — they offer brief clips, not programs — worth the trouble. Yet they manage to attract hundreds of thousands of viewers who might otherwise still be in that desired youth segment of the television audience. That has brought about changes at the television networks, with more changes in the offing.

I prefer email, because it's such an effective way of getting information to somebody without running the risk of becoming involved in human conversation.

— DAVE BARRY

Costs to blog can be extremely low. One site, Rocketboom.com, which had sponsors for its not – too – serious daily newscasts, estimated a cost of $25 a day and was reaching 50,000 viewers.[19]

Well written blogs that were focused on a narrow range of topics have become a genuine alternative to mainstream media. In an echo of the "Never trust anyone over thirty" slogan of the 1960s, many college students and other youths trust bloggers of their own age more than they trust established news media. Bloggers have broken significant stories. Topics ignored by journalists or dropped after a day or two were kept alive and pushed to the point that politicians felt forced to respond. As a source of news independent of newspapers and television, blogs in 2003 kept attention on the public naming of an undercover CIA agent, a felony possibly committed by someone connected to the White House. Blogs that were riveted on a CBS News error regarding President George W. Bush's military service led to the resignation of its anchor, Dan Rather.

With an inexpensive digital camera and an MP3 recorder – player, a self – appointed journalist can set up a news website and, at least in theory, attract an international readership to daily news and opinions. With this equipment, photo interviews can be done. The Internet offers a wealth of source material on almost every topic.

Suspicion about the objectivity and honesty of established news media has become endemic, so it is understandable that some news consumers, particularly young adults who have grown up with the Internet, will seek out a Web news site or a blog they trust. That, of course, means a site whose opinions they agree with.

On blog sites, references to other bloggers have seemed less incendiary than chatroom comments. The lack of anonymity and the greater effort that goes into running a blog compared to making comments in a chatroom may explain the greater civility.

Quick to pick up a new means of communication, marketers have used blogs to peddle products, such as Raging Cow milk – based drinks, to youths. Young entertainers drew attention to their performances by posting them on a blog. It cost little to try; occasionally it worked. A popular skit might be downloaded and passed along millions of times from friend to friend, another example of the egalitarian nature of the Web that bypasses the walls erected by corporate television and corporate Hollywood. "It's the dawn of the democratization of the TV and film business," wrote a *Newsweek* reporter.[20]

All over the world, blogs have been started by young people who want to express themselves. They are particularly popular in China, where they test the limit of what authorities will allow. The idea that their thoughts and their performances can reach an international audience is hugely exciting to youth whose efforts at self – expression have been limited.

With thousands of new blog sites coming on line, the Chinese government has been hard pressed to keep track of content. They have attempted to do so indirectly by holding Internet service providers responsible for policing the blogs to make sure pornography and political messages hostile to the government do not appear. The ISPs were given lists of forbidden words; filtering software either replaced the words with asterisks or blocked the message altogether.

This is not solely a Chinese practice. Westerners, including Americans, frequently replaced letters of obscene words with asterisks. Chinese bloggers, too, found creative ways around forbidden words, such as

There's no denying that the content of your average online diary can be juvenile. These diaries are, after all, frequently created by juveniles. But thirty years ago those juveniles weren't writing novels or composing sonnets in their spare time; they were watching Laverne & Shirley. Better to have minds actively composing the soap opera of their own lives than zoning out in front of someone else's.[21]

— STEVEN JOHNSON

Don't touch my Internet. Keep the government out, and let us cyberjunkies regulate ourselves! The Internet stands for liberty and open expression. It is pure freedom of speech— the good, the bad and the ugly. And you don't have to get past magazine editors to be heard.[22]

—LETTER TO *TIME*

A Hollywood movie is understood to be fictional. Vlogging on YouTube is not. Plus, to fully harness the medium, they (the two producers of Lonelygirl15, an actress who pretended to be a teenager named Bree) intended to carry on email correspodence with YouTubers while posing as Bree. In short, they were planning to exploit the anonymity of the Internet to pull off a new kind of storytelling…

On YouTube, a video can be streamed at any time. The good ones are watched again and again, sending a clear message about what works and what doesn't…

Beckett (one of the producers) tried to explain to the executive that the central theme of online entertainment was interactivity, as opposed to the passivity of television… in which the line between reality and fiction is blurred, where viewers can correspond with the characters and actually become involved in the story by posting their own videos…

Beckett is clearly frustrated. "The Web isn't just a support system for hit TV shows," he says. "It's a new medium. It requires new storytelling techniques."[24]

—JOSHUA DAVIS

using Chinese characters that sound like banned words when spoken aloud, but have totally different meanings. When the management of the search engine Google agreed to filter sites that the Chinese government wanted to keep out of the country, a small uproar of criticism in the United States followed.

Nations that did not allow journalists to speak freely did not give bloggers a free pass. In 2007, for example, an Egyptian court sent one blogger to jail for four years for expressing his opinions.

Other means of personal communication via the Internet have grown so quickly that the verb "exploded" does not seem extreme to describe what is broadly identified as "Web 2.0." Chatrooms are virtual spaces where ideas can be exchanged and where strangers can "meet." The result could be what is termed a "virtual community," although some chatrooms degenerated into testosterone – laden cursing sessions.

Organized under a little control, they could attract tens of millions of members, as YouTube, MySpace and Facebook do. Paul Roberts, who runs an online service, said of these sites, "People will always have egos and want to project their images and tell their stories for posterity. The founders of the Internet knew this and made that dream come true."[23]

As it has turned out, contributors to MySpace and Facebook projected their political views as well as their images and stories, another example of the egalitarian nature of the Internet as they offered news about themselves, opinions, or just gossip.

The wish by users for greater choice in variety and quantity has driven the expansion. Users provided the content, much as Tom Sawyer's friends paid to whitewash his fence. Flickr is another massive website where users provide and control the content, in this case photos they have taken, plus information about themselves. At prosper.com users who want to borrow or lend money directly from or to one another provide the content. None of the founders of these sites could possibly supply the enormous amount of content — choices — that users happily donated. And if they did, the sites would not be so popular. Each site is actually a worldwide community, fulfilling Marshall McLuhan's prediction of a global village.

Computer users in high schools were once called "geeks" and "nerds." No longer. Something else is going on. People who provide content are naturally curious to learn if anyone is paying attention. Someone who proudly displays a series of photos on Flickr or a poem on MySpace or a political opinion in a blog wants to know how many passersby clicked on the personal page. Tracking hits can be as obsessive as stopping to look each time you pass the hallway mirror, one more example of how mediated communication intrudes in our lives.

When disaster strikes, one of the greatest needs both inside and beyond the disaster zone is for information. Within twenty minutes of the Los Angeles earthquake of 1994 an Internet bulletin board was set up to get messages in and out. Within one day 12,000 messages had been filed.

At the time the tsunami hit South and Southeast Asia in 2005, the Internet use was even more organized and responsive. In just a few hours, while the governments of Thailand, Indonesia, Sri Lanka, and India tried to get on top of the situation, websites were set up as information clearinghouses for friends and relatives of the missing. Donations soon flowed into the websites of aid agencies.

The story was repeated after Katrina struck the Gulf Coast. For months, as federal, state, and local government agencies scrambled to deal with its aftermath, the Hurricane Katrina Information website pumped out information. Notices of people looking for missing relatives, where to call for help, photographs, and a place to post messages and gripes were all online.

OneWebDay is now observed annually on September 22, but nothing so immense or so much a part of so many lives as the World Wide Web exists without controversy. To discuss any of these controversies could — and has — generated books and countless articles. The list of issues includes freedom of expression, pornography, child pornography, hate websites, the right of privacy, copyright, plagiarism, the lack of accountability or dependability of the information, and laws to govern the Internet.

No medium of communication of such power can exist without challenges from those who wish to change it to something that it presently is not. Those changes, at this writing, range from Chinese censors to American telephone executives seeking to exchange "net neutrality" for a two-tier broadband system that would advantage large users. The telcos argue that they could provide better service under a new arrangement. Supporters of the existing system argue that such a change would stifle innovation.

Controversy has also continued between traditionalists who argue that the social standards and laws that govern conduct should fully apply to the Internet, and the anarchic view that anyone should have access to anything, including copyrighted material, movies, music, pornography, even recipes for making hydrogen bombs.

In the unfolding third millennium, it seemed that nothing lay beyond the scope of the Internet. Churches put sermons on the Internet and sent songs and prayers by email that could be downloaded to iPods. The rapidly rising number of religious websites included both discussion groups and prayer groups. The cyberchurches were a blessing to

Where I live, just outside Washington, Facebook.com is both noun and verb, the unchallenged colossus of adolescent communication that works like the telephone, the back fence, the class bulletin board (and, at times, the locker room), all rolled into one virtual mosh pit. In other towns, myspace.com plays the same starring role. In both cases, they have legions of parents pulling out their hair. Here's why: those online social networks have become, almost overnight, booming teen magnets exerting an almost irresistible pull on kids' time and attention. [25]

— Michael Duffy

It's bad enough when professors point an accusing finger at the Internet for the increase of student copying of essays, but when pastors blame the Internet for tempting other pastors to steal sermons, clearly there is much to discuss. [26]

— Terry Mattingly

Within two decades, most of the world's knowledge will be digitized and available, one hopes for free reading on the Internet, just as there is free reading in libraries today.[27]

— STANFORD UNIVERSITY LIBRARIAN MICHAEL KELLER

individuals who found themselves in communities where almost no one else shared their faith.

Private corporations established intranet networks within the Internet to provide internal communication and technical support for their customers. Support groups used newsgroups to deal with problems relating to physical disabilities, eating disorders, drug use, AIDS, cancer, diabetes, and mental illness. It was more convenient and decidedly less embarrassing to type in: "Hello, my name is Susan, and I'm an alcoholic," than to face others at a meeting. Sympathetic and understanding replies came flying back from online members all over the world.

Politicians have used the Internet as a cheap way to get their messages to voters. So have the extreme fringes; it has not been possible to stop certain militant groups from setting up websites to pour out their messages of hate. The United States, with its First Amendment protection, has long been hospitable to printing thoughts, no matter how vicious, but not all nations are so sanguine about what should be printed on the websites of the global Internet. Countries unaccustomed to anyone printing anything they liked had little choice but to get used to it.

Government censors in some nations probably did not know what was being sent and, even if they did, could scarcely halt the exchange of information across their borders short of seizing all computer modems or tracking down all international phone calls.

As for pornography, an international NGO (non–governmental organization) Internet group proposed a rating label for content, possibly like the movies' PG system and the E to M system for videogames. Software would block unrated content and any content with the equivalent of an X rating. A current, widely accepted labeling system considers four matters: the levels of violence, sex, nudity, and language (including hate language). It may rate a site a 2 for violence, a 1 for sex, and so on. A proposal for a .xxx domain designation was rejected by ICANN, the Internet Corporation for Assigned Names and Numbers.

INTERNET ADDICTION

Internet addiction has become a problem. The South Korean, Vietnamese, and Thai governments tried to limit the hours that teens spent online, such as kicking them off network games after five hours. China went further, treating heavy Internet use as a mental disorder and locking teens up in rehabilitation clinics. In the United States, the equivalent of Alcoholics Anonymous groups for cyber addiction have been formed online (despite the irony of such a venue). It has been called Internet Addiction (IA), Internet Addiction Disorder (IAD), and Pathological Internet Use (PIU), accompanied by estimates that as many as one Internet user in ten has an addiction potentially as destructive as alcoholism.

Like television, excessive time in front of an Internet screen is time not spent at other activities, including direct contact with other human beings. Seductive, the Internet coaxes otherwise busy people to wile away hours, detoured by websites that catch their attention. Lost hours and lost sleep can lead to dysfunctional behavior that costs marriages and careers. Users admit being online for eighteen hours a day or more, racking up hundreds of dollars in monthly phone bills, addicted to chat lines, porn sites, or game sites. Internet addictions have been compared to addiction to other forms of mediated communication, particularly television and telephone use.

According to a study covering sixteen nations, online time seems to be taken mainly from television viewing rather than time with family and friends. A study of heavy Internet usage reported unsuccessful attempts to cut down, anxiety when not online, and significant relationship discord because of use, although some respondents admitted to pre – existing psychiatric problems, such as bipolar disorder, depression, or alcohol abuse.[28] Internet addiction has also been characterized as a fad that is easily corrected, and not an addiction at all.[29]

For several centuries, news has been a commodity, available through a physical medium. The printed newssheet led to the newspaper. The telegraph and the telephone fed news first to newspapers, then to radio, then to television. In the course of these changes in the delivery mechanism, the style of writing changed. What constituted news also changed. Timeliness became an important factor; so did the separation of facts from the obvious presence of opinion. Distance became less of a factor. Altered by the demands of the telegraph, writing style was further altered when news facts were heard rather than read.

The Internet has presented news in several new ways, a clear example of a narrowcast system offering the choices that the public always prefers:

• A news report can be any length. Websites such as CNN employ editors who limit the length of news stories, as editors must, but much more complete versions can be found somewhere on the Internet. The nagging problem of too little space for newspaper story detail and too little time in a radio or television newscast are gone. Online space for written details and photos is endless. So is online time for video news stories.

• News appears as soon as it can be processed. The hours of waiting for a scheduled newscast or the next printed edition do not exist online.

• The online reader can look at headlines and choose among stories. The sequential structure of broadcast news does not exist.

The telegraph, telephone, radio, and especially the computer have put everyone on the globe within earshot — at the price of our privacy. It may feel like we're performing an intimate act when, sequestered in our rooms and cubicles, we casually use our cell phones and computers to transmit our thoughts, confidences, business plans, and even our money. But clever eavesdroppers, and sometimes even not – so – clever ones, can hear it all. We think we're whispering, but we're really broadcasting.[30]

— STEVEN LEVY

It took two centuries to fill the shelves of the Library of Congress with more than 57 million manuscripts, 29 million books and periodicals, 12 million photographs, and more. Now, the world generates an equivalent amount of digital information nearly 100 times each day.[31]

— BRUCE MEHLMAN
AND LARRY IRVING

• News packages can be set up in an on – demand form, feeding readers news items only on specified topics. The reader can be alerted by email to fresh news on those topics.

• In addition to text and still pictures, reports of some news events are accompanied by motion pictures with sound.

• The reader can choose among thousands of online news agencies, newspapers, radio stations, television stations, and news channels all over the world, often at no cost.

• For readers who prefer news heavily seasoned with opinion, thousands of blogs and special interest websites are just a few fingertip clicks away.

• The shift to paperless news in the first decade of the new millennium reaches each of us asynchronously at the time of our choosing with the subject matter of our choosing. That fits environmental concerns about the wasteful practices usually associated with news delivery on paper.

Will the Internet replace newspapers and newscasts? It is obviously too soon to tell, but for some people, especially educated people living in dictatorships, it already has.

The traditional way to get an education, now referred to as "bricks and mortar," has been augmented by what once were called "open universities" and "correspondence courses." The old system depended on the mail to move lessons and teacher evaluations back and forth. Today the technology of mediated communication goes beyond correspondence courses in breaking down the classroom walls. With email, instant messaging, newsgroups, and video teleconferencing, the correspondence course has come a long way from its roots, and allows high schools, trade schools, and universities to offer rigorous study courses up to the Ph.D.

Dozens of universities have developed online courses. Some schools award degrees almost solely from online coursework. In the "flat earth" of the twenty – first century, education is much less restricted by distance. Lectures, assignments, questions, and answers flow at electric speed. Books and journal articles are downloaded. Students do not have to scribble notes as the teacher speaks. Students who want to understand a poem do not need a trip to the library; with a click they are hyperlinked to a literary review along with a biography of the author. Study sessions with other students may be separated by continents, but can be just as intense as late night cram sessions in a dorm.

Available subjects include business, public administration, accounting, information technology, nursing, education, criminal justice, history, geography, biology, communication, literature, mathematics, psychology, astronomy, sociology, health care, foreign languages, computer programming, law, graphic design, geology, engineering, anthropology, and art. Consider some examples:

• An American middle school teacher at an international school in China worked toward a Ph.D. from an American university. This education would be denied to her if not for a distance learning program.

• Students in developing countries were being trained by teachers in (not from) Japan and Western nations.

• A student appointed by her company to head its telemarketing department in a distant city said, "Invariably, whatever course I was taking applied to whatever job I was doing."

• A Spanish language teacher in Spokane lectured by satellite across the Pacific to 1,300 students as far away as Guam.

• Severely injured and chronically ill children participated in daily classroom activity by means of equipment at their bedside that showed them the teacher and their classmates.

• Software let law students remain anonymous when they asked a cantankerous "Paper Chase" professor about legal points that puzzled them. They were less afraid to ask "dumb" questions. Lecture notes, assignments, and a legal database were online.

• A rural school system in Houston, Minnesota, facing consolidation due to declining enrollment, added online learning and tripled its student numbers.

Thousands of servicemen and women enroll in online courses. Students deployed overseas must leave their classrooms, but not their education. Online educators have recognized that military duty can pull a soldier away from completing an assignment, so they have made allowances for time constraints. Recognizing that outside education as well as military training can produce a better soldier, the Department of Defense has established a tuition assistance program.

Universities that do not offer online formal courses for credit nevertheless use mediated communication in such areas as agricultural extension services. Nursing is another field where keeping up to date is essential, but where practitioners in distant locations lack the opportunity to return to a university for that information.

With the aid of the Internet, students can do their research from anywhere that will let them plug in. For most research, students no longer need to live near a large library. The infinite number of informational websites and the astounding speed of Google to identify them combine to make the Internet a sufficiently powerful research tool. Information

In the 21ˢᵗ century, the ability to be a lifelong learner will, for many people, be dependent on their ability to access and benefit from online learning.[34]

— Michael Flanagan

(Houston, MN teacher) Dan Odenbach settles in at the computer for a lesson with Zoe Betts, a 5 – year – old kindergartner…

He pulls up a screen with today's subject, coins, and talks to Zoe through a headset microphone. A "blackboard" program on the computer shows Zoe's written answers on Odenbach's screen.

"OK, Zoe, can you tell me which one of these coins is the penny? Can you circle it?" Odenbach asks, flashing pictures of a penny, a nickel, and a dime.

Within seconds, a scrawled circle appears around the penny on Odenbach's screen.

"That's great!" Odenbach says, hitting a key that sends a pair of clapping hands to Zoe's screen.[35]

Karen Frederick used to drop her children off at day care at 6 a.m., drive about 50 miles south into the Twin Cities to work, and then hope to be home again around 5 p.m.

Now 6 a.m. has Frederick making a "two – second" commute to her basement office, taking a break at about 7:30 to get Tanner, 7, and Cody, 5, off to the school bus. Then it's back to work until about 4:30 p.m., when the bus brings her boys back home.

Frederick is a claims specialist for Midwest Family Mutual Insurance Co. in Plymouth, which has transformed itself over the summer into a virtual company. The 50 – plus men and women workers now do their billing, underwriting and policy reviews on computers and phones in ergonomically correct workstations in their homes, all provided by the company.

"The more we talked about it, the more we said, 'Well, why not?' "President Ron Boyd said.[36]

— H.J. Cummins

found in online sources is not always accurate, but neither is information found in books.

The Internet has also shaken the traditional merchant – customer relationship. Millions of dollars in transactions are made between people who never face one another. Unnumbered thousands of websites provide online shopping accompanied by online means of paying that is — to paraphrase Marshall McLuhan — knocking down the walls of the general store. Electronic merchandise may be downloaded, so the entire process never departs from a computer screen. Other merchandise sold online can be shipped in more conventional ways, just as catalog merchandise has been sold since the late nineteenth century, when Mr. Sears and Mr. Roebuck shipped pocket watches by parcel post.

In Pierre Omidyar's San Jose, California living room, eBay was created in 1995. From its start, eBay was a market and an auction for the sale of all manner of goods. With the reach of the Web, Omidyar and co – founder Jeff Skoll turned auctioning into an international activity that everyone could observe as the minutes ticked down to the close of a sale. Tens of thousands of sellers were making a living on eBay and tens of millions of buyers made purchases in what has become a significant change in an important part of life.

As always, when something is gained, what it replaces is lost. The handshake and smile that concluded a sale is gone, exchanged for a global reach for goods and customers.

Medicine is a field where specialists in distant hospitals used telecommunications to guide medical emergencies or even routine procedures. From at least one major hospital in Iowa, cardiologists checked cardiograms and X – rays of heart patients in rural clinics dozens of miles away. Images, sounds, and data crisscrossed as digital pulses over fiber optic lines.

Television journalism is, of course, itself mediated communication. And no field has made more use of other kinds of mediated communication. Replacing filmed coverage in the '70s, electronic news gathering — ENG — was supplanted a decade later by satellite news gathering — SNG. At the network level, reporters "embedded" with troops in the field beamed live reports in the midst of battle. If a camera is mounted on a truck or tank, the audience senses the bumps. When bullets fly during a firefight, it is not only the reporter who winces. The viewer may be horrified or elated by being electronically placed in the center of danger and carnage, but in either case has been affected by what is happening, and may be spurred to action as a citizen and voter.

TELEJUSTICE

"Telejustice" defines interactive video for judicial proceedings. It cuts legal costs. Defense attorneys at jails, victims who did not want to travel to parole hearings, parole judges, someone seeking a protection order on a weekend from a "duty video" judge, and expert witnesses have all participated. Consider that the arraignment in New Jersey federal court of Theodore J. Kaczynski, the Unabomber, was held in Sacramento, California. Estimated cost of transporting Kaczynski was $30,000. Using TeleJustice the court conducted the arraignment on murder charges for about $45.[37]

Not all mediated communication change is positive. The middle management employee who is issued a cell phone to wear off duty has no certain escape time in his work week, and that week now contains seven days, not five. Doctors are easier to call morning, noon, or night. On the positive side, many white collar workers are now able to spend at least part of each work week telecommuting.

Among the work–at–home occupations are accountants, architects, bankers, bookkeepers, clerical workers, computer operators, programmers, systems analysts, counselors, data entry clerks, engineers, journalists, lawyers, real estate agents, secretaries, brokers, travel agents, and, of course, writers.[38] A broadcast journalist who must file a story or update one in a hurry can do so from a mini–studio at home instead of driving to the studio in the hour that the news breaks. Some doctors are e–visiting patients, and medical insurers are covering the activity.

Telecommuting holds advantages for both employer and employee. Employers may need less office space; more significantly — or ominously — in many cases they have eliminated full–time staff members, substituting part–time contract workers or consultants, not only saving health care and other costs but changing the employer–employee dynamic. For the employee, the time and expense of the daily commute is eliminated along with a contribution to pollution. Caring for small children may determine whether the employee is even able to hold a job outside the home.

The isolation of being apart from other adults during the workday is offset for parents by the pleasure of spending time with children, other family members, and neighbors. In fact, with the telephone and email, colleagues are not truly apart. Alvin Toffler used the metaphor of "the electronic cottage" for the increasing shift of work from office and factory to the home.[39] "The communication toolshed" is another metaphor.[40]

The Industrial Revolution led to a population exodus from villages and farms into cities. After World War II, many young American families reversed that centripetal migration with a centrifugal flow from cities to suburbs. The past decades in the United States have also seen small towns shrink as young people moved to cities and suburbs. If telecom-

TETHERED TO THE JOB

When transportation meant ships, people built Venice. When it meant trains, they built Chicago. When it meant cars, they built Los Angeles. Cities have always been fundamentally shaped by the dominant transportation of their time. It's one of the givens of urban planning. But today, planners are beginning to see that society is on the verge of building a new kind of city in an era driven not by transportation but by telecommunications…[42]

— PETER LEYDEN

munications succeeds in pulling people out of cities, the exodus will be primarily of the middle and upper income groups, those who most easily travel the electronic pathways, leaving the poor and the elderly behind. Such a movement often erodes a city tax base, with potentially dire consequences.[41] Peter Leyden of Global Business Network, who predicts that telecommunications may change our cities, points out that it would not be the first time that technology has done so.

Mediated communication allows some self–employed workers, such as consultants, to settle wherever their work takes them, no matter how temporary, carrying their homes with them, turtle–like. The home, filled with communication and computation equipment, may be a van or a boat. Their home address may be a website and an email address. As for anyone whose work requires neither a daily commute nor travel to where a job is, the choices of where to live are almost infinite, like those of a successful novelist, limited only by imagination.

OUTSOURCING

Telecommuting has also led to outsourcing, as white collar jobs followed factory jobs to low wage countries, still another change that mediated communication makes possible. While it has resulted in white collar layoffs in developed nations, outsourcing has made life better in developing countries for quite a few skilled workers, especially in India. In Bangalore and other Indian cities with a cadre of educated, English–speaking workers, entire industries have sprung up to do computer programming, telemarketing, banking, plus a variety of different jobs that can be handled through global communications at lower costs. American software engineers who were paid $150,000 a year have been replaced by Indian engineers who earn an average of $20,000. The same change is happening to radiologists.[43]

CONCLUSION

RATHER THAN ASK WHERE computers can be found today, including the fingernail–size microprocessors that control so many mundane devices, it is better to ask where they cannot be found. The ultimate fate of the computer seems to be to fade into the background—to be everywhere.[44]

Like the phonograph and the telephone, the computer and the Internet were conceived for different purposes than what they are today. The computer was never intended for anything but arithmetic calculation. When ordinary people realized how a computer could extend life's choices, they could hardly wait to get one.

Along with so many communication media technologies, the Internet has become more of what their users wanted, and less of what their inventors intended. Its inventors did not contemplate its use for a myriad of private purposes by the folks who lived down the street. They certainly did not envision the Internet as a means of entertainment.

That is what today has brought. What will tomorrow bring? Just as the Industrial Revolution in the nineteenth century and the move to the suburbs after World War II in the twentieth century changed population patterns, economic shifts brought about by the Internet in the twenty – first century may have their own effect on population patterns.

In the hands of the Greeks, writing combined the alphabet and papyrus. It eliminated time and space in the sense that thoughts could be stored for future generations and could be sent to like – minded thinkers (e.g., a mathematician to a mathematician) in a distant place. Writing connected thinkers. It now connects everyone. The Internet can be described in much the same way.

This creation of computer networks has produced a change in human communication that can compare with the invention of writing, the printing press, or any other medium. Especially by its World Wide Web and email, the Internet has brought about a revolution, and almost all of us are affected, even non – users. The more educated we are, the greater the effect on us.

The Internet defies description. Instead of asking what is it, one might well ask, what isn't it? Thinking of just what the Internet is recalls the fable of the blind men describing an elephant. Touching a different part of the elephant, each man variously identifies it as being like a snake, a spear, a tree, a wall, a rope. Depending upon how it is used, the Internet is like a telephone, radio, television, a newspaper, the postal service, magazines, a library, or a soapbox.

To cite one example of unexpected use, myspace.com, principally a way for teens to express themselves, helped to organize demonstrations for immigrants. And, in 2007, as noted, myspace.com and facebook. com hosted blogs describing the Virginia Tech massacre while it was happening. Such personal expression in the shift known as Web 2.0 is expected to expand, and no doubt will benefit if Internet broadband speeds available in the United States catch up to Japan and South Korea, which have access rates ten to fifteen times faster.

By allowing anyone to garner information and, even more, to post information, the Internet has had an egalitarian effect in society. The potential for individuals to challenge governments and even dictatorships almost with impunity, far beyond anything ever known throughout history, has enormous importance for society.

Yet there is more to the story. "Power to the people" holds both positive and negative elements; positive, for example, in opposition to tyrannical governments; negative when child pornographers and sexual predators, con men and drug dealers elude justice. Nor can we forget the hackers,

The great thing about broadcast is that it can bring one show to millions of people with unmatchable efficiency. But it can't do the opposite — bring a million shows to one person each. Yet that is exactly what the Internet does so well…

Before the Industrial Revolution, most culture was local… But in the early nineteenth century, the era of modern industry and the growth of the railroad system led to massive waves of urbanization and the rise of the great cities of Europe. These new hives of commerce and hubs of transportation mixed people like never before, creating a powerful engine of new culture. All it needed was mass media to give it wing.[46]

— Chris Anderson

who derive pleasure from destructive behavior. Dealing with them has not been easy.

Who controls this digital hydra? Internet headquarters are in Reston, Virginia, but as one observer put it, "asking who is in charge of Internet is like asking who is in charge of the national sidewalk system."[45]

The Internet houses a wish list of choices. If you want it, you'll probably find it somewhere, from the most professional to the most personal. Who could have predicted an international matchmaker? News and opinion no longer come only from newspapers and broadcast stations that exist because of expensive investments. A teenager sitting at home in pajamas has powerful effects if his or her blog attracts attention.

Online education has grown into an important part of the education industry. Retail sales are an important part of the World Wide Web. Thanks in part to the Internet and email, many white collar and professional jobs can be done at least partially at home. The personal impact has been substantial for those who do it, and there is a potential for a positive environmental impact through telecommunication instead of commuting.

As you are reading these words, in ways undreamed of not long ago, vast amounts of data are being transmitted to distant places, multiplying the choices for acquiring information, education, and entertainment. As did writing in the days of Pythagoras and Aristotle, the Internet connects thinkers. It also connects fools and criminals.

12 PLAYING VIDEO GAMES

IF IT IS TRUE THAT OUR STORYTELLERS determine our culture, we must pay attention to video games. Move over, movies. Move over, television. Most people like to compete, and there is no society on earth that does not play games. It is doubtful that a school or community exists anywhere without them. Did cave dwellers play games to sharpen their skills at bringing down hoofed food? Did quieter games in every century help pass the evening hours and long stormy days?

We also enjoy watching games of every sort, and we like to engage in all manner of personal competition from cards and chess to running and wrestling, just as we like team competition ranging from debates and tug–of–war to paintball. The list is endless. Or we can play by ourselves against a machine, setting a level of difficulty as a challenge. Think about the phrase "personal best."

Inserted into this world of games is modern mediated communication in the form of video games. (Distinctions between online games, platform games like Playstation, computer games run by software, usually on a CD, and arcade games have become blurred and can be confusing. All these games will be identified here as video games, unless noted.) In 1982, when the computer was *Time*'s "Machine of the Year," the January 18 issue featured video games as its cover story under the headline: "GRONK! FLASH! ZAP! Video Games Are Blitzing the World."

Video games are all about choice. *The Oregon Trail* blazer must choose the longer river path or the shorter but more dangerous mountain path. *Ms. Pac–Man* must instantly go left or right to evade the gobbling monsters. The making of decisions never ends until the game does. The challenge is addicting, and doubly so against human opponents who face the same choices. We can play video games against relatives, friends, or strangers on the other side of every ocean. We can carry on conversations as we try to "kill" them, without knowing who they are except what they tell us, and that may be as false as what we tell them. Video games are played all across every continent, even in places no one might expect to find electronic games. Would you be willing to bet that they have never been played at stations in Antarctica or in Mongolian yurts? You would probably lose. They are played in arcades, on game consoles, on cell phones, on television sets, and on home and office computers. They are played quietly using software sold in stores or downloaded from the Internet. They are played noisily in clubs and tournaments, just as they are played online against unseen opponents.

NOT JUST CHILD'S PLAY

American children average about an hour a day of video games. One invented name for the typical player is a "screenager." But video games are not just child's play. In 2004, more than half of all Americans played video games. The age of the average player was twenty–nine.

From their early days, video games sold computers. It has been argued that video games were the first electronic interactive devices and that games can be credited with drawing the general public into the world of computers.[1] Until they heard about games, a lot of people saw no need to buy a computer. A small calculator was enough for budgets and taxes, and a typewriter for letters. Only when they saw how much fun video games were did they decide to splurge on a computer. Today, it is not research that drives microcomputer development to be bigger and faster. It is games. Their speed of play, their graphics, and the amount of data needed for the different paths their story line can take is what pushes the demand for better computers.

No other pop–cultural form directly engages the brain's decision–making apparatus in the same way.[2]

— STEVEN JOHNSON

Parents have used video games as bargaining chips to motivate their children:

"Keep your room clean and I'll buy you…"

"Clean this mess or I'll turn off…"

"Do your homework before you…"

Parents worried that kids spent too much time and too much money on arcade video games. Campaigns to ban video games scored victories as some towns banned arcades altogether. That once troubled game maker Nolan Bushnell. He wanted to create a place that parents and kids could visit together, and the kids could play video games. His solution was a pizza parlor that included video games. He called it Chuck E. Cheese. The first restaurant in San Jose, California, has been copied, as of 2006, by 500 outlets all over the United States.

ADDICTION

The goal of the game maker is to keep the player at it; for arcade games, to keep dropping coins in the slot. The psychologist B.F. Skinner famously devised the "Skinner box" to show how rats can be conditioned to keep at a task for the reward of a crunchy food pellet; the smart rat learned to keep pressing the lever. A nice reinforcement, but it did not go on like this forever. After a while it no longer handed out a pellet with each press, only an occasional pellet. This "partial reinforcement" kept the rats at it. Now consider the game player who is rewarded by higher and higher scores for hitting a button. The player discovers that the game grows harder with time and success. This partial reinforcement makes the activity even more addictive. The player has to try harder to build up a score. The goal — the pellet equivalent — is the higher score. The computer makes it easy to program a game to be addictive. The rat doesn't know it is being manipulated. If game players know, they may relish it.

Have you ever been so caught up in a game that you did not want to stop? Have you ever thought about getting back to the game while you were doing homework, having lunch, or traveling somewhere? It means the game maker has done a good job. Game makers know that their products must appeal to emotions. Games that don't are "boring," "dumb," and "for babies."[3]

Excessive playing of video games is not unusual, with players logging on for twenty–four hours straight or longer at a session. For some online game players it becomes the most important activity in their lives. Game playing has led to the occasional marriage and the occasional suicide. It is the most important social life some teenagers and young adults have, and, when they are alone at the computer, exchanging messages with other players is their only social interaction. However, the American Medical Association decided at its annual meeting in 2007 not to label excessive game play as an addiction pending more study.

Parents and teachers have complained that game players are so much into their game that they move with little awareness of what is immediately around them. That might raise an interesting, practical question: what can society learn from an activity that is so attractive? That question was raised years ago about television programs. Now it is video games. What can teachers learn from game designers?[5]

For example, it is known that adults are nervous when they go into surgery, but a youngster can be terrified. In San Francisco, anesthesiologist Anu Patel noticed that a friend's seven–year–old son was so busy playing his Game Boy that he wouldn't eat or talk to anyone. Dr. Patel did an experiment with seventy–two children, ages four to twelve. He found that those children who were given a Game Boy to play before their surgery showed the least anxiety. In fact, often no anxiety at all, and they did much better than children who were given tranquilizers or children whose only comfort was the presence of their parents.[6]

Other positive outcomes have been observed. Players are not always alone when they play. Particularly in Asia, teenagers like to play video games in crowded rooms while carrying on conversations with old friends and new acquaintances. Some youths have developed such dexterity that they earn substantial purses in sponsored competition. Las Vegas sponsors an annual world championship. In South Korea, the best video gamers are treated like rock stars.

Hikikomori refers to the state of anomie into which an increasing number of young Japanese seem to fall these days. Socially withdrawn kids typically lock themselves in their bedrooms and refuse to have any contact with the outside world. They live in reverse: they sleep all day, wake up in the evening and stay up all night watching television or playing video games. Some own computers or mobile phones, but most have few or no friends. Their funk can last for months, even years in extreme cases. No official statistics are available, but it is estimated that more than one million young Japanese suffer from the affliction.[4]

— Ryu Murakami

CREATING RELATIONSHIPS

American teens will carry a laptop or Game Boy to a friend's house for an evening of games. Video games have been a way to create relationships, a middle ground for people to meet, a means to encourage cooperative behavior and social skills. They have provided a way to reduce aggressive behavior and have taken the emotional heat out of a situation by attacking aliens on screen rather than anything in real life. Video games can encourage fantasy lives, where we do dangerous or illegal things that we may daydream about but that no reasonable person would actually do, such as murdering people, or cannot possibly do, such as killing aliens. In a fantasy game, these reservations do not matter, and playing well raises self–esteem for a task well done. Get a high score, surpass your personal best, or reach a goal, and you feel good about what you have accomplished.

Obviously, excessive game play limits physical movement. While the heroes or monsters run and jump, the players do not. They sit still, except for busy fingers making repetitive movements. Staring at screens doesn't help their bodies either, nor do sudden spurts of game–infused adrenaline. In terms of health, the best thing that can be said about video games is they are a step up from passively watching TV; admittedly, that is not saying much. A 1989 research study reported that video games were partly to blame for a decrease in the physical fitness of American schoolchildren, including cardiovascular fitness. Physical problems have been blamed on heavy video game play. Joints, skin, thumbs, and muscles have suffered from repeatedly hitting buttons. Players have complained of neck stiffness, wrist pain, finger numbness, blisters, calluses, sore tendons (that some doctors have jokingly called "Nintendinitis"), and sore elbows (sometimes called "*Pac–Man*'s elbow"). In rare cases, epileptic seizures were reported among players who are photosensitive.

On the other hand, Dr. James Rosser, director of the Advanced Medical Technologies Institute at Beth Israel Medical Center in New York, headed a study showing that surgeons who played video games three hours weekly have thirty–seven percent fewer errors and accomplish tasks twenty–seven percent faster in doing laparoscopic surgery. Laparoscopy involves manipulating instruments where the surgeon's movements are guided by watching a television screen.[7] However, as one of the study's authors commented, spending more than an hour a day playing video games is not going to help the chances of getting into medical school. For the game player who thinks otherwise, there is *Trauma Center: Second Opinion* for the Nintendo Wii.

As for "Nintendinitis," Nintendo's newest remote, for the Wii console, doubles as a wand that gets players up and moving. Depending on the game, the player swings it like a baseball bat, a tennis racquet, a golf

(In Sim City) it's easy to slide into a routine with absolutely no down time, no interruptions from complete communion with the computer. The game can grow so absorbing, in fact, your subjective sense of time is distorted… You look up, and all of a sudden it's morning.

It's very hard to describe what it feels like when you're "lost" inside a computer game, precisely because at that moment your sense of self has been fundamentally transformed.[8]

— TED FRIEDMAN

club, a bowling ball, a fishing pole, a sword, or a fist. Despite its value as a spur to exercise, it has caused some injuries and property damage in the hands — and flying out of the hands — of overzealous players.

In EyeToy games for PlayStation2, a camera pointed at the player converts body movements into movements onscreen. Crouch and your character starts to move. Lean to the right and your character moves right. Roll your arms in circles and your character does a back flip. If you want to stop, hold your arms out to the side. And so on. Your body moves. After doing this for awhile, the player has acquired a day's ration of exercise, but can still get sore, or may even dislocate something. The remedy prescribed for these symptoms and ailments: hit the pause button and go somewhere else for a while.

Chairs are sold with built–in vibrators and sound systems, plus light systems to enhance a game's effects; to accompany a storm on screen, the player's room goes dark, the floor rumbles underfoot, and the wind howls. For travelers, a special pair of glasses will bring on the desired unease.

Adults and children tend to approach new games in different ways. The cautious parent is more likely to read the manual first; the child is more likely to start by pushing buttons, learning by trial and error. Prof. James Paul Gee of Stanford argued, "When people learn to play video games, they are learning a new literacy."[9] It is not a waste of time. Among thirty–six "learning principles" he cited:

Having active and critical, not passive, learning.

Learning about design.

Learning about the connections among images, words, actions, and symbols.

Taking risks without real–world consequences.

Participating in an identity you are committed to and find compelling.

Learning more about yourself and what you have the potential to do.

Getting a lot of response for a little effort.

Acquiring rewards at all skill levels.

Doing non–boring tasks and getting practice.

Finding challenges to improve yourself.

Discovering ways to make progress and solve problems.

Learning basic skills in context with their usefulness.

More games now include features that let players invent some aspect of their virtual world, from characters to cars. And more games entice players to become creative partners in world building, letting them mod (modify) its overall look and feel. The online communities that form around these imaginative activities are some of the most vibrant on the Web. For these players, games are not just entertainment but a vehicle for self–expression.[10]

— Will Wright

Getting new information just when you need it.

Learning that when a strategy doesn't work, you switch to another.

Using what you have learned to solve new problems.

Sharing what you have learned with others.

Sharing based on goals and practices, not race, gender, or ethnic background.[11]

EDUCATIONAL GAMES

An advantage is that students learn at their own pace. Parents can look for educational games. For example, game makers added Nintendo excitement to algebra in *Dimenxian*; navigating with grid coordinates is needed to survive.

Yet an hour playing a video game is an hour that the player is not at another activity. Something is gained at the cost of something lost. Among the activities that players give up are studying, time with friends, time with family, helping around the house, and sleeping. Quite often, what players do less of is watch television; they prefer the sense of control that a video game gives them. One nine–year–old girl said, "In TV, if you want to make someone die, you can't. In *Pac–Man*, if you want to run into a ghost, you can." Another girl of the same age said, "On TV you can't say 'Shoot now' or, with Popeye, 'Eat your spinach now.'" She went on to say she would get frustrated sometimes watching Popeye and wanting him to eat his spinach at a certain time when he didn't.[12] Playing a video game, she is in control. As watchers, we can do nothing about what goes on in a television show or a movie. In a video game we interact. We still stare at the screen, but we are no longer passive. By taking action, we change what we see, and that makes all the difference.[13]

Tetris… is more popular with women than any other game and notoriously addictive among female professionals…

It's about detritus raining down on your head, trash falling into messy piles and piling up until it finally suffocates you…

The psychological payoff for the player is a state of rapturous relief. "Yes," she thinks. "Yes! The mess is vanishing! I can make the mess disappear." It's not about blowing things up.[14]

— J.C. HERZ

Both video game playing and TV watching are usually done while sitting indoors, and both attract by means of pictures and sounds on a screen. Both entertain and tell us stories. Yet consider the differences. Video games require active participation and making choices moment to moment. They develop certain skills. They promote competition and sometimes cooperation among players. They may require strategic or tactical thinking to reach a goal. While TV watchers may "veg out" with programs that don't challenge their minds, video game players prefer challenges.

Males designed most video games for males. Console manufacturers and game makers put a lot of thought into how to hang on to customers as they grow older. Teenage boys remain the most important market for most games, especially the first–person shooters, known also as "twitch" games. But teenagers are a shifting market. Yesterday's child is today's teenager and tomorrow's adult. Boys who discover that girls are not so annoying after all become less concerned about laser blasting.

An important reinforcement to the play/performance comes from friends and strangers who watch the player. At the arcades what the observer usually saw were teenage boys playing the games and teenage girls cheering them on and admiring their skills instead of playing themselves. Girls may have played video games all along, but not in arcades, which seemed to be dominated by boys making noise. Most video games were boy–oriented until video game makers discovered that girls were interested in playing video games too. They began making games like the *Nancy Drew* mysteries for this half of the population that they had neglected. Studies showed that boys liked aggressive games more than girls did, so the game makers took that difference into consideration. A study of heart rates while playing video games showed that girls' heart rates increased more than boys' rates. That was true for both playing and just watching.[15]

Nintendo introduced Game Girl to match its successful Game Boy players, but it did not catch on. *Pac–Man*, on the other hand, has been described as cute, with an appeal to women. Recognizing that a market for women and girls was being ignored, its manufacturer, Namco, introduced *Ms. Pac–Man*, who wore lipstick and a red bow on her yellow head. Namco then discovered that both boys and girls liked it even better than *Pac–Man*. Patricia Greenfield, author of many books about how children learn, was pleasantly surprised when she tried *Pac–Man*.

Pac–Man proved to be a "cross–over" game. People who had no interest whatever in shoot–em–ups or spaceships or monsters "crossed over" into video games to play it. They could not seem to get enough of the dot–eating little creature. (*Pac–Man*'s name comes from the Japanese term "paku paku," meaning "gobble, gobble." Game designer Toru Iwatani said its shape came to him after he ate one slice from a pizza, then stared at what remained.)

A 2007 study by the Entertainment Software Association reported that thirty percent of all video game players were adult women compared to twenty–three percent of players who were boys under 18. As expected, women tend to avoid violent games. They prefer to solve puzzles, test their dexterity (Nintendo's Wii system is popular), help their comrades put dragons in their place, and heal their fallen friends. The online *Second Life* is a big favorite. Women and younger girls particularly liked non–lethal games needing sharp eye–hand coordination, sometimes called "muscle memory." You needed quick reflexes to play *Pac–Man*, *Donkey Kong*, *Frogger*, and *Prince of Persia*. Women liked these games. Researchers also noted that women preferred to take their leisure time in short segments, rather than to sit for hours at a game.

Pac–Man was the first video game to transcend the demographic of hard-core teenage arcade rats and computer engineering geeks. The game appealed to an audience far broader than industry pundits had ever dreamed possible. Everybody loved Pac–Man. Kids, teens, college students, moms, dads, doctors, lawyers, even Wall Street executives.[16]

— VAN BURNHAM

Pac–Man is more like life than like chess. The player must not only overcome the obstacles but must also perform the inductive task of figuring out the nature of the obstacles… Rick Sinatra, a computer programmer, …remarked, "Video games are revolutionary; they are the beginnings of human interaction with artificial intelligence"[17]

–PATRICIA GREENFIELD

(Ideal game choices of Japanese women)

…a simulation game of being a housewife, giving experience of leading a happy married life, including housework, having/raising children… a simulation of buying a house, a game in which the user raises a human baby, a job simulation game, a game in which the user can date actors/singers, a simulation game of overseas travel, a game of cooking in which the user finds ingredients, cooks, and becomes a master chef, a climbing game in which the user tries to reach the summit. On the way, rivers, valleys, birds, and little animals appear.[19]

— STEVEN POOLE

Another favorite of women, the *Sims,* are games about ordinary people living ordinary lives. The player controls the characters and must navigate them through human situations. *SimCity* has been used as a training tool in college management classes. A survey of Japanese adult women who like the games expressed several wishes for new simulations. This is a long way from shooter games. The *Sim* series, the *Civilization* series, and the *Tycoon* series (e.g., Zoo Tycoon) crossed gender lines. These "god games" allowed the player to play a god in a variety of situations, such as a war or managing a city.

Testosterone continued to get the game designers' attention. In 1996, from Britain came *Lara Croft, Tomb Raider.* Despite being a female hero, her busty, leggy appearance was designed to appeal to young males. The original script called for the main character to be a man, but the designers feared that the game looked like an Indiana Jones ripoff. Instead, Lara was born. By *Tomb Raider III*, the player who reached a higher level sent Lara into a new virtual reality in some exotic corner of the world. What seemed just a game provided a geography lesson with a male fantasy.

A study of how players referred to games reported that most people referred to a game as "it," as in "It hates me." Next most common was "he," as in, "He's trying to get me." Also common was "you" ("You dumb machine!") and "they" ("They think they're so smart; I'll show them"). No one referred to a game as "she." One player called the game "Fred."[18]

Games are divided into types, but some games fit into more than one category. Here is one of several lists:

adventure: reach a goal by solving puzzles.

god games (also called "simulation"): manage a community, an empire, or a war.

scroll: run and jump and avoid the nasties.

sports: play tennis, golf, hockey, race cars.

first–person shooters: kill the enemy.

one–on–one: hit, kick, do whatever it takes to put an opponent down.

brain and finger busters: hone your skills against the machine.

learning: solve math, language, and other school subject problems.

role–playing: adopt an identity, wander through other worlds.

As my fourteen–year–old niece exclaimed recently, when I asked her what she liked about playing The Sims, "You've got one Sim who you've got to get to school, and another who needs to get to his job, and their kid has been up all night and is in a bad mood, and the house is dirty — I guess there's a ton of things to do!"[20]

— JOHN SEABROOK

In the role–playing, god game *Black & White* (2000), the player is considered a god. You decide the kind of god you want to be: either cruel or gentle. You will be worshipped, you can uproot trees with your bare hands, and you can raise fierce animals to enforce your will and expand the empire you control. What you get is up to you. If you pet an animal each time it eats a villager, guess what kind of animal you will have?

Among the best–selling games are those that appeal to the worst of human impulses. They can be acquired one way or another by youngsters. Despite a rating system, it is not so difficult for a ten–year–old to buy a game in which scantily dressed prostitutes, begging the player to kill them, are murdered by chain saws. Filthy language spews from cartoon mouths, and cannibalism is a choice.

Nor is it difficult for children to acquire *Grand Theft Auto*, which presents drive–by shootings and drug dealing as desirable, and awards points for killing innocent people and for having sex with prostitutes.

In the horror game *Clocktower 3* a little girl has her head smashed with a sledgehammer and a screaming old woman is lowered into a vat of acid. In *Carmageddon* and *Twisted Metal* the player scores points for running over pedestrians. Similar brutality runs through other games as game designers vie for viciousness. *Quake* lets the player digitally superimpose images of people and places they know to customize the game. As video games become the storytellers for the younger generation, the cry for regulation has grown louder.

In 1999, the Columbine High School killings led to public attacks on video games. News reports from Littleton, Colorado, noted that the two young killers were obsessed with the ultra violent games *Doom* and *Duke Nukem*, which combine violence with sexy images. The boys apparently tried to replicate *Doom* and the film *Matrix* in real life. News reports recalled other instances of high school shootings in Pearl, Mississippi; Paducah, Kentucky; Jonesboro, Arkansas; Springfield, Oregon; and Tabart in the Canadian province of Alberta. Studies have shown that angry youths are more stimulated by violent video games than are easy–going kids. One study of players of the first–person shooter game *Medal of Honor: Frontline* had greater activation than players of a non–violent game in the amygdala, the portion of the brain involved in emotional arousal, and less activity in the prefrontal portions of the brain involved with control, focus, and concentration.[21]

The first successful video game, *Pong*, was nonviolent. Destruction started in the second generation with *Breakout*, which involved knocking a wall down, but no human aggression. The next generation of popular games, such as *Star Wars*, involved human aggression, and became more personal, with hand–to–hand combat, in such games as *Mortal Kombat*. Violence continues with *Grand Theft Auto, Half–Life, Halo, Mace*, and dozens more.

Many parents continue unaware. For example, a survey found that while 80% of junior high students said they were familiar with *Duke Nukem*,

The ratings differ by outlet (video arcade versus console and home computer), are not well understood, are not reliably followed by retail outlets, and apparently have little impact on the marketing efforts of the companies that produce them.[22]

— Craig Anderson

(John) Romero designed the graphics and game play for an ultra–violent game, which called on his own love of 1950s horror comics… The result was Doom…

Everything about the game was designed to inflame a teenage boy's fantasies of power while causing grave distress to his parents.[23]

— John Seabrook

Video games, because they are active rather than passive, can… actually encourage violence… by rewarding participants for killing one's opponents in the most grisly way imaginable.[24]

— Robert Chase

At the time the research was conducted, the popular game genre among the male subjects was side–view fighters. The popular genres among the female subjects were role–playing games and puzzle games. To someone unfamiliar with video game genres, it would seem that the male preferences required much more ability than the female choices. This, however, is very incorrect.

Side–view fighters, for example, are typically very rigorous games that require fast reflexes and contain battles that are over in minutes…

Role–playing games, on the other hand, are enormous quests requiring patience, memorization, critical thinking, and strategy…

Therefore, the games that "women prefer" are not "less demanding games" than those that men prefer. They are simply demanding in different ways.[27]

— SAM HART

rated "mature," a survey of more than 500 parents found that fewer than 5% had ever heard of it.[25]

Until the mid–1970s all the games could be called family fun, all of them suitable for children to play. That would change in 1976 with *Death Race*. The arcade game, housed in a cabinet showing skeletons driving race cars, was based on the film *Death Race 2000*, with Sylvester Stallone as a racing car driver in a futuristic world. The driver got extra points for striking pedestrians. In the video game, the "pedestrians" were shown as "monsters," but the public was not fooled. For some players, running over pedestrians was sick fun.

Complaints against offensive games led eventually to a self–protective, industry–designed rating system. Hollywood had taken the same step with its G, PG, R, and X ratings in hopes of avoiding government censorship. The AAMA (American Amusement Machine Association), representing the video game industry, created this ratings system in the hope that its own controls would avoid government laws:

C: for children

E: for everyone

T: for teens

M: for mature

AO: for adults only

Ratings don't mean much if any youngster can buy any game. The National Institute on Media and the Family sent young boys and girls to stores to see if they could buy M–rated games. Girls were able to buy the games about once in 12 tries. Boys could buy the games half the time.[26]

Some adults objected to even the tame arcade games because they ate up lots of quarters and lots of time. The Pittsburgh, Pennsylvania, City Council passed an ordinance that threatened the license of any arcade that let kids in during school hours.

Comparisons of video games with comic books are a reminder of the public campaign to end the amount of sex and violence in comic books that even pre–teen children were reading. Hearings by a U.S. Senate committee in the 1950s were led by Sen. Estes Kefauver (D, TN), who twice ran for president. No laws were passed, but the comic book industry grew more careful about what it published. In 1982, long before the present generation of games, the U.S. Surgeon General, Dr. C. Edward Koop, said video games were evil and produced "aberrations in childhood behavior."

Again, in the current generation, there have been Senate hearings on video game violence. Sen. Sam Brownback (R, KS) led a hearing in 2000 that industry executives chose to avoid. According to one witness, the more time spent playing electronic games, the lower the school performance. Teens who play violent games do worse in school than teens who do not. Youth who prefer violent video games are more likely to get into arguments with their teachers, and are more likely to get into physical fist fights, whether they are boys or girls.[28] Video games featuring slaughter and gore are marketed primarily but not exclusively to American teenage boys and young men. Eugene Provenzo, University of Kentucky professor of education, called video games "a teaching machine."

Doom and *Grand Theft Auto* (especially *Grand Theft Auto 3* with its glorification of delinquent behavior) have been denounced again and again for glorifying acts that in real life earn long prison sentences. It has not mattered. In 2004, adding to more than 30 million copies in the series already sold, *Grand Theft Auto: San Andreas* sold more than two million copies in its first week. Criticized as lacking morals and being "ethically reprehensible," the games nevertheless won praise for the quality of their graphics and game play. The anger reminded some observers of the uproar that greeted the making of the films *Birth of a Nation* and *Triumph of the Will*. These movies were also praised for artistry but condemned for evil subject matter. Said one critic, "No matter how artistic this game might be, I do not welcome it."[30]

Sen. Joseph Lieberman, who later became the Democratic candidate for vice–president, also led hearings. He was supported by such groups as Mothers Against Violence in America. While not yet as widespread as video game violence, the amount of sexual material in video games increased year by year, including obvious pornography.

It was argued that video games could lead to real–life aggression, to a lack of human feelings and sensitivity, and to an increase in fear, all behavior harmful to social relations and our culture. Some games were damned as sexist and racist. One group published a game in which points are awarded for "killing" anyone who isn't white or is Jewish; another game awarded points for "killing" pregnant Mexican women. Critics pointed out that physical assault cases increased sharply not only in the United States but across Europe, Canada, Australia, and New Zealand, countries where violent video games were widely played.

Brazil was among countries that banned violent games. Illinois Governor Rod Blogojevich wanted his state to ban violent games for everyone under eighteen. A legal effort to require parental consent for purchase by anyone under seventeen was struck down in 2003 as unconstitutional.

Now, defenders of these games say that they are mere fantasy and harmless role–playing, but is it really the best thing for our children to play the role of a murderous psychopath? Is it all just good fun to positively reinforce virtual slaughter? Is it truly harmless to simulate mass murder?[29]

–Sen. Sam Brownback

When violence is stylized, romanticized and choreographed, it can be stunningly beautiful and seductive. At the same time, it encourages children and adolescents to assume a rhetorical stance that equates violence with style and personal empowerment.[31]

— Eugene Provenzo

Each gore zone gets a different reaction to keep you from getting bored… Now the only question is where your next target gets it first.

— Soldier of Fortune Ad

An age–old question has been raised frequently: does fictional violence lead to real violence? Also, is it the violence that attracts young players? Defenders of violent games have argued that it is not the violence that is so exciting, but the challenge of learning how to advance in the game, overcoming obstacles, solving problems, and relishing competition either against an opponent or against one's own personal best. Critics respond that in real life, even when someone is angry, showing violence is rare; however, in these games, violence scores. The more harm the player does, the more points accumulate.

Military games, such as the World War II *Call of Duty 2*, with intense, realistic and brutal action, were best sellers. So was *Battlefield 2: Special Forces*, about a futuristic war in which the player can choose to fight for the United States, China, or the "Middle East Coalition." The Army has used video games as training material for recruits; for example, *Full–Spectrum Warrior* teaches maneuvers in an urban environment along with hand–eye coordination and "muscle memory."

A dilemma exists. Games are supposed to be fun, but the Pentagon will be the first to point out that a real battle lacks fun. Dilemma or not, *America's Army*, a training and recruiting game supported by the U.S. Army, had more than six million registered players in 2006. Referring to the potential of this cross between The *Sims* and *Doom*, *Time* called it a "killer app."[32] The British army trained troops with a version of another military game, *Half–Life*. One of its developers noted that the commercial version of the game had to be altered for military use to remove some of its fantasy. In combat, the soldier who is shot doesn't simply get up and continue to fight. Opponents of video game violence have challenged game designers by asking how they could say their games were harmless when military trainers used them as teaching tools for soldiers heading for combat.

How did all this begin? Video game inventors could have had no more idea than Gutenberg or Niépce of the transformative nature of their inventions. In fact, a game was played a few years after the first computers were built, assembled by hand, usually in the engineering department of a university. Scientists who patiently programmed them with codes made up of the digits "1" and "0" were engaged in serious business. They might have been shocked at the thought that anyone could have fun using a computer, obviously an expensive waste of time. In 1952, the room–sized EDSAC at Harvard, depending on thousands of vacuum tubes, was programmed to play tic–tac–toe. A.S. Douglas wrote the program as part of his doctoral dissertation, just to show that it was possible. Douglas and his professors may have been the only players.

In 1958, when computers still filled entire rooms, William Higinbotham, at the Brookhaven National Laboratory in New York, a nuclear research lab, created "Tennis for Two" using an analog computer and two hand–held control boxes. The screen was a 5–inch oscilloscope. He wrote the game program to entertain visitors to the National Laboratory. Lab staffers waited for hours to play, but Higinbotham did not think enough of his little invention, the first interactive video game, to bother getting a patent.

"TENNIS FOR TWO"

One day in 1962 at the Massachusetts Institute of Technology, a PDP–1 "mini" digital computer arrived in the electrical engineering lab. It was the first computer with a keyboard for input and a screen for output instead of the usual punchcards and the large sheets of printer paper with green stripes and sprocket holes along the sides. On this new computer, having some fun, student Steve Russell and some friends created *Spacewar*. Guided by four toggle switches, two "spaceships" moved around the circular screen, jumped through hyperspace, and shot torpedoes at each other while avoiding the gravity pull of a central sun. Russell assumed that no one would pay to play a game on a computer, so he left the program for anyone to copy. In this way *Spacewar* became the first video game that could be played on a number of different computers; it was soon played at several universities. Students may have picked up the idea to program games of their own. *Empire* was the popular game at Cal Tech. To get around a no–nonsense systems operator, one student changed the name of his game to "Test." No one objected to a student running a program test. With millions of government dollars being spent on equipment and research time, IBM tried to ban games from their buildings, but so many employees complained that IBM executives backed off.

SPACEWAR

Electrical engineering student Nolan Bushnell could not stop playing *Spacewar*. In 1971, after he graduated, he got together with a pinball company to design the first coin–operated video game, the first plan for video games to make money, and the first arcade video game. Because entire computers were too expensive to house in arcades, Bushnell built *Computer Space* out of parts to create a game that maneuvered a rocket ship. Put into arcades, supermarkets, college student union rooms, bowling alleys, pizza parlors, and taverns, where it competed with pinball machines, *Computer Space* was a commercial failure. It was too complicated. Pinball machines were simpler.

PINBALL WAS SIMPLER

The following year, Bushnell had more success with his next effort, consisting of two moving paddles and a ball. He called it *Pong*. The day after the first machine was installed in a tavern, a line of people waited for a chance to play it. A few days later the tavern manager called to complain that the machine had stopped working. The problem, as it turned out, was that it was jammed with quarters.

PONG

Atari made a home game console in 1974 with just one game, *Pong*, the first interactive video game played on a home device. Like the arcade version, it was a big hit. *Pong* soon had millions of players twirling a dial to smack a ball across the TV screen. Sold through Sears, it beat out Adidas sneakers as the product of the year.

PLAYING IN MALLS

Stand–alone games in their colorful cabinets would have little future next to jukeboxes and pinball machines in taverns, because few high school students went to taverns. Teenagers would be the primary customers for video games, and the future lay in arcades located in something new being built across America: the shopping mall. Scientists considered the notion of putting a computer inside a box to receive quarters as outlandish. But realizing how many quarters could be collected, several entrepreneurs jumped in with *Space Race, Asteroids, Rally, Gotcha, Gran Trak 10,* and *Tank.* In *Gotcha,* a two–player game, a box chases an X through a maze.

The games got better. Atari's *Battlezone* used ROM (read only memory) chips and vector graphics to create figures more detailed than the simple blocks of *Pong*. Year after year, improved games brought players into arcades and pizza parlors located in shopping malls. Teenagers ignored the familiar pinball machines to plunk quarters into the colorful noisy video game machines.

Today, far more *home* games are played than *arcade* games, but in the early video game years most games were played on stand–alone machines. The most popular games were fighting and blaster games. Action games like *Death Race* were played on machines found in bowling alleys, movie theater lobbies, taverns, student unions, and other places where people went to have fun. By 1975, 100,000 coin–operated video games were played in the United States alone.

INTO THE HOME

Parents were not likely to spend their afternoons or evenings at arcades, but a home video game provided a reason for family quality time. Manufacturers moved to bring the arcade game, without the flashing lights and huge cabinets of the arcade version, into the living room. Ralph Baer, an engineer working on a military project, got the idea in 1968 that the millions of TV sets in people's homes could also be used for game play. He started the chain reaction that evolved into today's multi–billion dollar interactive entertainment industry.[34]

"FOX" AND "HOUNDS"

The play was primitive compared to today's video games because Baer could not do more than move two or three spots around a screen. The designer's most difficult task was to invent games with this technical limitation. Baer and a friend, Bill Harrison, started the "TV Game Project," putting together a boxful of transistors, switches, and diodes that eventually could play about a dozen simple games and let the player aim at targets with a rifle that detected a light beam from the TV set. That was the start of shooting games. As for the two spots, they called one a "fox" and the other a "hound." The hound would chase the fox. When it caught the fox, the hound won. With three spots, Baer created tennis and ping–pong games of two paddles and a ball.

Most television channels were, of course, broadcasting television programs, but the Federal Communications Commission required alternate channels in each city to remain unused to avoid signal interference. In New York, nothing was broadcast on channel 3. In cities where channel 3 was broadcasting programs, channel 4 would be available under the FCC regulations. Baer, who was not broadcasting anything, just wanted an unused channel, so he decided that game players would use channels 3 or 4; those channels are still used for video game consoles hooked to a television set. The Magnavox television company agreed to manufacture Baer's games as the Odyssey 100 game console. It was sold with Magnavox TV sets, along with six plug–in game cartridges and a lot of extras, like poker chips, play money, playing cards, a playing board, a map, and clear plastic game overlay sheets with game layouts to place over the TV screen. Because of national advertising, the Odyssey introduced home video games to millions of people who had never heard of them.

USING AN EMPTY TV CHANNEL

Competition followed. Atari soon brought out its 2600 video game console. In 1979 the Milton Bradley Company, famous for Monopoly, introduced a hand–held game played on a two–inch square screen. Mattel manufactured the Intellivision console, which played dozens of cartridge games and could also deliver games through a home's television cable. The large media company Philips sold the Videopac system complete with a game board. Coleco's Telstar was followed by Coleco-Vision, with the popular *Donkey Kong*. It sold millions of game consoles and cartridges; computer keyboards, joysticks, game pads, and track balls guided the action.

ARCADE GAMES VS. CARTRIDGES

An important difference between arcade games and cartridge games is based on how their manufacturers make money. Arcade games make money when people plunk in quarters, so the most successful games have no endings. The aliens keep coming as long as you have quarters. Cartridge game manufacturers make money when buyers finish a game and head to the store for another. So the popular cartridge and CD games have stories that end. You can win a cartridge game.

As home games caught on, arcades tried to lure young customers out of the house with large screen games requiring equipment not duplicated in the home, such as games needing complicated foot controls, and cars with steering wheels and pedals to negotiate obstacle courses. *Dance Dance Revolution* is a recent example; it sends four arrows in different combinations floating to the bottom of the screen. The player must match this combination with steps on a floor mat. The best players show off not only their footwork to watching friends, but also their rhythm. The game hits the right notes for teenagers: social activity and physical challenge with fast music, flashing lights, and a score that rose. Its popularity led to other games, such as XaviXPORT and three from Eye Toy: Kinetic, Anti–Grav, and Groove. The players got a physical workout by ducking moving objects or negotiating an obstacle course on a screen.

IMPROVING THE GAMES

As the years went by and the games rolled out, everything improved: the graphics, the sound, the color, and the game play. Because the early arcade video games competed against pinball machines, the pinball culture influenced them. The games were fast and demanded fast responses by the player. At home, by contrast, the early cartridge games played on a computer were slower and required more thinking. As the computer and storage technology improved, such distinctions gradually disappeared. The computer games of today demand lightning fast wrist action or thoughtful analysis, based on the kind of games they are.

HAND–HELD GAME BOXES

In the 1990s, CD–ROM discs started to replace game cartridges. CDs were not only cheaper to manufacture, but they also stored much more data, including video, animation, music, and more detail in game play. Video games took on the look of movies as hundreds of titles followed hundreds of other titles onto the store shelves. Most were quickly forgotten, pushed aside by new titles, like paperback books at the drugstore. Because so much money could be made from a popular game, advertising and public relations budgets soared as the titles nudged each other for the customer's attention, especially the attention of the teenagers who bought most of them. The first hand–held game box, the Microvision in 1979, sold so well that it led to an entire sub–industry of game consoles by Sony, Sega, Microsoft, and the leading game maker of the time, Nintendo. The newest versions of PlayStation, GameCube, and Xbox led Christmas wish lists, and, when new models went on sale, buyers lined up all night long to be the first in the department store for consoles and the promised games that fit only those consoles.

Like *Frogger*, the frog that is smashed flat and is reborn, the video industry itself was smashed in the early 1980s, then reborn. Too many companies were competing. With hundreds of different arcade and home console games for sale, with too many console "systems" in competition, facing a poor national economy, the video game industry ran into problems. Game prices collapsed. The "video game crash" of 1982, 1983, and 1984 sent a lot of companies out of business, at least out of the video game business. The industry revived with the improved Japanese game consoles and has roared upward ever since.

Video games became an even bigger business through media convergence, as movies expanded into games and games were remade as movies. In 1982, the year of *Time*'s "Machine of the Year," Disney Studios released *Tron*, a science fiction feature film that took the audiences inside a video game. Audiences saw computer–generated imagery for the first time in a feature film. It would not be the last. When Disney released *Tron*, it also created a *Tron* arcade game that more or less followed the film's plot. The game was just hard enough to keep teenagers dropping in the quarters. As it turned out, the game brought Disney more money than the movie.

Matrix, the movie, became *Matrix*, the video game. *Lara Croft*, the video game, became *Lara Croft*, the movie. *Family Guy*, the animated TV series, became a video game. Toys and dolls (called "action figures") were spun off. *Star Wars*, *Star Trek*, the James Bond films, and others followed.

Games derived from hit films include *The Da Vinci Code*, *Monster House*, *The Godfather*, *Lord of the Rings*, *Raiders of the Lost Ark*, *E.T.*, *Aliens*, *Toy Story*, *Rambo*, *Batman*, and *King Kong*. *Lara Croft*, *Mortal Kombat*, *Wing Commander*, and *Super Mario Bros.* went in the other direction. They began as video games. The *Matrix*, *Star Wars*, *Blade Runner*, *Sin City*, and *V for Vendetta* are films designed to look like video games or comic books. Video games from time to time turn up as props in movies. In *Airplane*, one of the tower controllers who should be directing air traffic is playing Atari *Basketball*. In *The Princess Bride*, *Hardball III* is seen in the opening, owned by a boy whose grandfather arrives to read him a story out of a book. The grandfather takes for granted the superiority of a fairy tale in a book to an interactive game, with the grandfather, not the child, doing the reading. The audience is expected to agree that, at least in this instance, passive listening is better.

The average hot new game costs five times as much as the average first–run movie ticket. Video games have earned more money than movie theaters since 1999. This is a multi–billion dollar business. A different convergence of movies and games can also be seen — the arcade game in the multiplex lobby.

Movies and video games have a lot in common besides the obvious fact that they both present entertainment on a screen. In both media, some of the characters now have familiar voices, well–known actors playing the roles. In 1999, David Bowie not only wrote and performed an album for the soundtrack to *Omnikrom: the Nomad Soul*, he was also a digitized character in the game. Add much improved graphics and

Video games are a new form of art. They will not replace books, they will sit beside them, interact with them, and change them and their role in society in various ways, as, indeed, they are already doing strongly with movies.[35]

— JAMES PAUL GEE

GAMES DERIVED FROM MOVIES

music to this, and the result is a product with appeal for adults as well as teenagers. Original music scores are written for the most expensive games. Special effects companies do animation and motion–capture for both media.

In addition to actors and directors, writers also work for both games and movies. Tom Clancy, author of blockbuster military novels, wrote scenarios for video games that his own company produced. Best selling novelists Michael Crichton (*Jurassic Park* and many others) and Douglas Adams (*The Hitch–Hiker's Guide to the Galaxy*) did much the same, and so did George Lucas, director of the *Star Wars* series.

We can reanimate footage from the past… We could put Marilyn Monroe alongside Jack Nicholson or Jack Black or Jack White… If we want John Wayne to act alongside Angelina Jolie, we can do that. We can directly mimic the performance of a human being on a model. We can create new scenes for old films, or old scenes for new films.[36]

— Andy Wood,
animation company
Image Metrics

Starting with basic circles and squares, improvements in visual imagery have astonished those who do not follow changes year to year, and continue to astonish. Grass in a field and hair on an arm can move in a breeze. 3–D adds depth. The animation of the British virtual "newscaster" Ananova in 2000 was improved by the motion capture in 2004 of the movements and appearance of the "avatar" of actor Tom Hanks in *The Polar Express*. Two years later, new technology by the company Image Metrics provided animated avatar faces whose expressions closely matched those of live actors. The computer game *24*, based on the television series, took advantage of it. In 2001, *Waking Life* was shot as a live action film, then was given the look of animation by a computerized technique called rotoscope. Actually, rotoscope, which enables animators to trace live action frame by frame, has been around for decades. It was used in *Snow White and the Seven Dwarfs* (1937). *Machinima*, also known as machine animation or cinema animation, is a way to use video game software such as first–person shooter CGI (computer–generated imagery) to create films. Write your own script and add your own voices. Add your own music or help yourself to what is out there. You control what is going on.

The *Decisive Battles* series on the History Channel used video game graphics "to make the past come alive," its producer, Margaret Kim, said. She particularly hoped to reach young males who spend more time playing video games than they do watching television.[32]

With TiVo stripping commercials from programs, advertisers have sought other venues. Product placement in movies has been one way to get attention. Another is product placement in games, with ads that can be updated appearing in online games.

Movies are linear; that is, like most novels, one element follows another from the start to the end of the narrative. Video games can also tell a story with a beginning and an ending, although they are non–linear. They can jump around and take a number of paths. Another important difference between a movie and a game is that the characters in a movie determine the path of the plot; in a game the player — the "audience" — determines what happens.

Modern video games have plots. The best tell a good story, but only as the player uncovers it. When the player doesn't know which way to turn and gets killed, that is not the end of the story. Death is never final in a video game. Even if you have run out of lives, you just reload the game and start over again, smarter this time. Now you know how to avoid the swamp, the ax, the ogre.

It has been said, as noted at the start of this chapter, that our storytellers determine our culture. Radio once had its dramas, soap operas, and sitcoms; television still has programs talked about at the office water cooler and over the phone the next day. Movies have given us stories for a century. If the story tellers do indeed determine our culture, we must look beyond radio, television, movies, and books to video games with a story line, especially the multi–player, role–playing online games. If anyone wonders why we should pay any heed to online fantasy games, it is because millions of people around the world play them each day.

Online games began with the PLATO educational system, first created in 1960 to find ways to use computers to teach. The first MUD (Multi–User Dimension) game for a computer was written in England and was shared first with players at all universities involved in PLATO research, and later with players in many parts of the world. In time, MUDs were replaced by MMOGs (Massive Multi–User Online Games) and then by MMORPGs (Massive Multiplayer Online Role–Playing Games). By this time, it was big business for Sony, Microsoft, and other game makers who first sold the games, then charged a monthly fee for playing.

In 1974, multi–player role–playing was introduced with a pencil–and–paper–and–dice, role–playing and story telling game. *Dungeons & Dragons* (sometimes called "D&D") grew out of a 1971 simulation game, *Chainmail*. Shy high school boys were especially attracted to the role–playing game because it helped them talk to other players. The games were social; they brought people together who formed bonds with each other in a new and comfortable community.

The D&D game opened up an industry of books, maps, and small figurines. It led to video fantasy games. Rules for D&D changed; one basic structure required a dungeon master and several players in a fantasy medieval setting. Wizards, dwarves and all manner of characters and magic spells were part of the fantasy. The first MUD video game for arcades, *Gauntlet*, released in 1986, allowed up to four players at once, each with an identity. One role was that of a female warrior. The other three were a male warrior, a wizard, and an elf.

VIDEO GAMES ARE NON–LINEAR

Most players in MUD went there to converse and play with other players. The game itself was quite good, but it was the multiplayer angle that made it addictive and compelling. The unpredictability of having real human opponents, as well as AI (artificial intelligence) ones, made it incredibly enjoyable.[37]

— Jeremy, age 15

In the physical world we vainly scrounge for glory. Bin Laden still taunts us, the bus doors close before we reach them and leave us standing in the rain. But in the fantasy world of Azeroth, the virtual geography of World of WarCraft, the physical pain comes only from hitting a keyboard too hard, camaraderie is the norm and heroism is never far away...

For millions it is more than a game — it's an escape, an obsession and a home...

"Ninety percent of what I do is never finished — parenting, teaching, doing the laundry," says Elizabeth Lawley (Level 60, Troll Priest), a Rochester, N.Y. college professor. "In WOW (World of WarCraft), I can cross things off a list — I've finished a quest, I've reached a new level."[38]

— Steven Levy

The online players of such games choose from a variety of identities, each with its own set of skills. From these, each player creates an avatar. Some players create their own ideal of strength or beauty or interesting occupation. Others prefer to create a quirky character for themselves, even an animal. Occasionally a player will select the opposite gender for a character. Females pretend to be males; males pretend to be females. Sometimes it is done with evil intentions, such as gaining someone's trust. Sometimes it is done just to see how other players will react, or just to sense what it feels like.

High school student Richard Garriott loved to play *Dungeons & Dragons*. He convinced his school to let him link the school's teletype machine to a distant computer so he could write his own D&D games. It was part of a one–student (himself) course with no teacher and no curriculum. The result was an astonishing twenty–eight games, one of which became *Akalabeth*. When California Pacific published it. Garriott was assigned royalties that would total $150,000. *Akalabeth* eventually became part of the famous game *Ultima*, which has gone through at least ten versions, including *Ultima Online*.

Major corporations are now behind the addictive games. (Players have called *The World of WarCraft* "Warcrack.") In 2007, eight million players worldwide surrounded themselves with reference books, maps, and one or two computers for daily or all–night adventures in a medieval fantasy world where the player/avatar can make friends or slay enemies. It combined sexy images of fighting women plus dragons and sword fights with player teamwork. Each player paid about $15 a month. In return, friendships have been cemented, plus relationship that bloom into marriages, at least in the virtual world.

A survey reported that the average age of *EverQuest* players was twenty–five. About one in six players was a woman, two out of three were single, one player in five had children, and one person in three said making friends was the most important reason for playing.[39] Microsoft offered *Asheron's Call*. Mythic Entertainment designed *Dark Age of Camelot*. From Korea, NC Soft designed *Lineage*.

Not everyone has been happy about online games. Conservative Christian groups have said that Dungeons & Dragons games encourage worship of the occult, violent behavior, and suicides.[40] At least one American player did commit suicide because of an online game. One Christian–themed game was sold. *Left Behind: Eternal Forces* was in the genre of the *Left Behind* books that imagine a world in which the elect are lifted into Heaven, and the rest suffer the eternal penalties of the damned.

A different complaint came from social scientists who think that it is not healthy for a nation that so many of its citizens — and voters — are so wrapped up in an ideal but artificial environment that they neglect our messy, real world.

Yet there were positive elements; for example, in at least one of the *Ultima* games, honesty was promoted. In this game, a blind woman merchant holds out a cup for money when something is bought from her. Players who shortchange her in order to save their money for weapons discover at the end of the game that they need her help, and she refuses with bitter words.

Players have sent text or voice messages to each other while they battled assorted demons, battled other players, or tried to avoid battle altogether. Friends and fellow workers have joined together so they could take supporting roles in team play. For them, cooperation was more important than conflict, and that has attracted many women to the game. A lot of players have enjoyed the game as a means to a social get–together. If your character meets another character in the game, you can just sit around and chat. Other players prefer to look for players to slaughter.

Social get–togethers online have expanded to get–togethers in real life. People in the same community have established clubs and luncheon groups. Some players have met for dates. A few who met in game play have married. It has been said that the players have taken the game over from the designers.[42]

Sometimes real money changes hands. Players have advertised on game websites that they own certain virtual (not real) game items that are hard to win in the game, and these are for sale for real dollars; in some cases, thousands of dollars. A *Project Entropia* player paid $100,000 in real U.S. dollars for a virtual space resort in the multiplayer game. His goal was to sell condos, floor space in a mall, and tickets to shows, all imaginary, to other players for game dollars that the game's developer promised to convert into real U.S. currency.[43] Someone else reportedly paid $30,000 (real money) for an imaginary castle in the game *Lineage*. Other examples have been reported. *EverQuest* hosts a site, "Station Exchange," where players can buy or sell — for real money — weapons, play money, or entire characters.

Why would people pay real money for imaginary property, items, and money? One reason is that it takes many hours of game play to accumulate the virtual goods or dollars, and for some people, paying real dollars is a worthwhile shortcut. As for how much something is truly worth, the old law of supply and demand operates.

Are these games? If you think of a game as a contest that has an ending, a winner and a loser, probably the online virtual worlds are not games.

As a former WarCraft player, I don't think your article did enough to examine the addictive qualities of the game. Maybe most players are not adversely affecting their futures, but those who are tend to be in high school or college and just starting to find their way in the real world. Many experience a precipitous fall in their academic standing. Games like WarCraft are designed to never end…

The effects of games like this on today's youth will surely be felt for years to come.[41]

— Nadir Dalal

Online Internet inter–actions, in which players pretend to be someone else or at least stretch their own self–presentations, are common experiences of adolescents. Online inter–actions allow adolescents to experiment with facets of themselves that they are not always comfortable expressing in real life.[44]

— Sandra Calvert

One game designer said the modern online D&D games are "chatrooms with a game attached."

SECOND LIFE

Second Life may be as close to heaven as you can get on Earth. It is less a game than a parallel universe that by 2007 had drawn in more than six million players from all over the world. "Residents" find a plot of land, build a house, start a business, socialize with other residents, and generally live a "second life," just as the title promises. That avatar life can be a person of a different age, race, gender, physical attributes, whatever. Thousands of residents "attend" church; different faiths and denominations are a click away. Real auto manufacturers, including Toyota, Nissan, and Pontiac, have opened virtual dealerships to offer virtual cars for sale for "linden dollars" to residents who want to express their tastes but don't need a car for transportation on a world where they can teletransport their avatar from place to place. Researchers in several dozen schools and educational organizations, including the Harvard Law School, can be found there; a number of them are studying how *Second Life* can be used to advance education. The news agency Reuters has a correspondent there. You can watch full-length feature films on the Sundance Channel inside *Second Life*. And quarrels over imaginary real estate have led to real life lawsuits.

USERS PROVIDE THE CONTENT

This imaginary world was set up by a San Francisco firm, Linden Lab, but its users provide the content, just as do the users of YouTube and the other websites that have had phenomenal growth in just a few years. To help you move around in this virtual world, other residents will be happy to exchange your real money for the "linden dollars" of *Second Life*. Residents spend real money for virtual furniture and virtual clothes. Millions of real dollars change hands. Some residents make real money from wheeling and dealing in this virtual world. Starting with an investment of $9.95, Ailin Graef, born in China and living in Germany, earned more than $1 million U.S. dollars buying, building, selling, and trading virtual property.[45] After learning that the game generates several million dollars each month — real dollars — in game economic activity, a Congressional subcommittee met to consider taxing the more fortunate.

Second Life has one of the online multiplayer universes in 3–D. While imagining a 3–D world has challenged programmers, offering the real world in 3–D has been even more challenging. But Microsoft and Google have set out to do just that. At the present writing, they have not ventured much beyond San Francisco, but the potential to create a virtual world holds intriguing possibilities in a number of directions, including future video games.

CHEAT SHEETS

An industry has sprung up to help frustrated players negotiate their way through games. The player who cannot figure out how to cross a bridge, enter a room, or get past a troll can find the answer in books that supply either hints, which many players prefer, or actual directions. These guidebooks are known as "hint books," "walk throughs," or "cheat sheets." They are the *SparkNotes* and *CliffsNotes* of the video game world. Some games also contain "cheats," built–in codes that give the players a boost. They can be found on the Internet.

Video games are a new means of mediated communication that changes and grows. Perhaps more than any other medium in the early years of the new millennium, response to it has been generational. Older people, if they have more than a hazy awareness of video games, are likely to be indifferent to most games and disapproving of the more extreme. It is the children, the teenagers, and the young adults who have responded to them. Memories of boys inventing their own games with sticks and balls have dimmed. Many stores sell video games. It is no longer easy to find a store that sells a bag of marbles.

TODAY, IT IS NOT ACADEMIC RESEARCH or business needs that drive microcomputer development to be bigger and faster. It is games.

The public has been both enthralled and appalled by video games. The excitement and pleasure that games provide, plus their power as teaching tools, have been rightly recognized. But the sex and violence featured in some games, where they reveal the seamier sides of human nature, have been too readily available to children despite age–based ratings.

Complaints, of course, are nothing new. They have been directed against the content of books, magazines, recorded music, television, the Internet, and anywhere else that human beings can see, hear, and express what they want.

However, the impact of violent games on the young may be much greater than the influence of violence in other media because video games are interactive, and therefore more involving. In some games the player identifies with the aggressor, participates in violent acts, is rewarded for violent acts, and learns by repeating violent acts. The player is rewarded for taking inappropriate action by any social standard. The Columbine High School killings were by two students obsessed with the ultra violent games *Doom* and *Duke Nukem*. There have been other reports of violence connected to violent games.

The industry response has been disingenuous, but that is nothing new. It is not difficult to find in most industries the argument that customers should get whatever their purchases show that they want, not what is best for them or for the society as a whole. As usual in the world of mediated communication, the users determine its direction.

CONCLUSION

…they also actually teach these kids how to be sharpshooters. The repetitive training of eye to joystick means that if these kids ever do snap and pick up a gun, they are in every sense highly skilled killers.[46]

— DIANE BURLEY MCGLUE

REFLECTING OUR CULTURE

As noted at the start of the chapter, video games tell stories that to some degree both influence and reflect our culture. They are played by young and, to a much lesser extent, by old, creating a generational disconnect. Some games have a stronger appeal to one gender or the other, just as some games appeal to certain age groups. Teenage boys are the primary market for first–person shooters. Girls generally prefer non–lethal games requiring sharp hand–eye coordination. Adult women are major participants in some games, such as the online *Second Life*.

In many families an ambivalence exists in parents' attitudes toward video games. They may worry about the time the kids spend and about violent content, but they may also recognize that many games have positive learning aspects, that the games are task–oriented and require useful dexterity. A game may teach strategic thinking and dealing with frustration. Parents may be pleased that their children are so enthralled by a game. Actually, "enthralled" may be too gentle a word for some players' behavior. "Obsessed" may be more accurate for both adults and children. That has obvious negative consequences.

Video games follow Marshall McLuhan's dictum that each new medium uses as content the medium it displaces. The first games were like pinball machines; scores rose as the equivalent of balls bounced off objects. The newest generation of teenagers and young adults are playing games that incorporate movies. The titles and plots of movies, the music, voices, and the very faces of the actors are there, but the medium is interactive, not passive.

Some of the newest games allow modification by the players, building choice into expressions of individual imagination. The same is true for video games of professional sports and the assembling of dream teams. Once again, by their choices, the users dictate the direction the medium takes.

As for online role–playing games, especially *Second Life*, what better example can there be of how mediated communication distances its users? Divorcing themselves totally from the reality of their lives, players enjoy a fantasy world of their own creation. Their connections are only with people far away who have also separated themselves from their own lives. Video games are not the first time that mediated communication has been the path that its users walk to escape reality. Nor will it be the last. So far, it is the most effective.

13 BEING PERSUASIVE

TRAVELING ACROSS THE CENTURIES on a parallel track with *informing* others has been the effort to *convince* others through essays, drawings, photos, slogans, advertising, public relations, government propaganda, blogs, you name it. This chapter will touch briefly on a few of the many ways that this has been done and continues to be done. If nothing else is consistent in human history, you can count on the desire of almost everyone to try to convince almost everyone else of something.

Expressing political opinions via mediated communication in the hope of swaying opinion has an ancient history. The first broadsheets, newsbooks, and newspapers in Europe did not differentiate between news and opinion, but most did not stray from what the government would approve, for the printer's freedom and perhaps his neck were at risk. Printers were forbidden to publish without permission, evidence that even in the age of the divine right of kings those in power were aware of the potential for mischief of political expression in print. Yet, a few printers dared to defy authorities. At least one printer in Protestant–controlled Elizabethan England, William Carter, was hanged, drawn, and quartered for printing pamphlets that supported the Catholic cause. Where the Inquisition prevailed, the Catholics returned the favor.

In 1644 the poet John Milton published the *Aereopagitica*, with its famous plea for freedom of expression, "Let her (truth) and falsehood grapple; who ever knew truth put to the worse in a free and open encounter?" His words made no strong impression at the time. More than a century would pass before his peculiar notion would be picked up again an ocean away, and would lead to the First Amendment to the U.S. Constitution.

British government controls eased with the end of licensing of printers, but authorities remained wary of letting anyone speak his mind, especially in print. Stamp taxes replaced licensing. Laws against treason and penalties for seditious libel sat firmly in place. Truth was no defense. Simply reporting news of Parliament was enough to raise the threat of seditious libel. The Tories, representing the old aristocracy and the Anglican Church, pressed for maintaining controls. The Whigs, representing the emerging middle class, published the newspapers and magazines that slowly chipped away at entrenched power. It was the day of such brilliant, rebellious writers as Daniel Defoe and the satirist Jonathan Swift.

Let her (truth) and falsehood grapple; who ever knew truth put to the worse in a free and open encounter?

—John Milton

Controls, including licensing, extended to Britain's colonies in the New World. That led to the demise after one issue of a newspaper by Benjamin Harris, who had previously been jailed in London for possessing seditious literature. In the early decades of settlement in the New World, colonists who had emigrated from England got most of their printed news from the mother country. The few colonial newspapers that were started made sure to announce that they were printed "by authority."

The first decades of the 18th century saw a few bold publishers, led in Boston by James Franklin, Benjamin's older brother, try to tweak the noses of authority. James was jailed for it, but Ben, who took over a newspaper in Philadelphia, got away with taking a stand on issues. As immigrants poured in from Europe, other newspapers started up, and with them came the seeds of revolt.

NEWSPAPERS IN AMERICA

At this time the courts followed the principle that the greater the truth, the greater the libel. The reasoning was that exposing truth could upset the public and undermine the authority that kept the peace. In this judicial climate a German immigrant printer in New York, John Peter Zenger, was arrested on the charge of sedition for printing attacks on the colonial governor and bureaucracy. His attorney, Andrew Hamilton, defied the judge's order not to argue truth in the matter of libel. Hamilton told the jury to follow their consciences, uphold liberty, and support "exposing and opposing arbitrary power . . . by speaking and writing truth." The jury also defied the judge and found Zenger not guilty. At first the verdict did not seem to matter much beyond this courtroom. A half century would pass before any law accepted truth as a defense against the charge of libel, but its effect has echoed through the history of press freedom.

As sentiment against British rule gradually grew, the political divisions of the home country carried over into the colonies. The Tories clung to Britain. The Whigs were torn between support for stability and opposition to the Crown. A third group, radicals, ineffective at home, began to make their mark in the colonies. The radical movement spread, using newspapers and pamphlets to foment rebellion. Leading the radical—patriot—cause was the Boston journalist and propagandist Samuel Adams and the movement he led, called the Sons of Liberty. Among the writers who followed was Thomas Paine, whose pamphlet *Common Sense*, copied, reprinted, and widely distributed throughout the colonies, energized the movement toward complete independence from Britain. Six months after its publication, Thomas Jefferson and a committee wrote the Declaration of Independence.

This daring document made its way to several other countries, where it was hailed as a cry to end oppression. The Declaration of Independence was not allowed to see the light of day in authoritarian nations of Europe such as Spain and Russia. Its biggest impact was in France, where it was used as propaganda against Britain, the hated enemy across the English Channel, but also influenced the revolution that would consume France.

As the American Revolution dragged on from one military defeat to another, Paine continued to write to rally enthusiasm for the flagging rebellion led by General George Washington. The first of Paine's widely read *Crisis* papers began with the now famous sentence, "These are the times that try men's souls." Tired men inspired by his words trudged on.

Printing supply problems also bedeviled the colonists' efforts. The newspapers that supported the revolution, like all colonial newspapers, had relied on England for their paper stock, which was superior to anything from colonial paper mills. Washington himself sent a plea to women to save rags as the raw material for making paper.

After the war ended and the new nation was created, political quarrels harried the shaping of the emerging government structure. Newspapers stayed in the forefront of policy advocacy. One of the compromises reached among Federalists and Anti–Federalists in drafting the Constitution was a Bill of Rights. The first of its ten amendments called for freedom of the press, along with freedom of religion, freedom of speech, the right to assemble, and the right to petition the government. New York City newspapers printed a series of 85 articles explaining and supporting the Constitution in simple language. They have come down to us as the Federalist Papers.

The years that followed were marked by agitated newspaper attacks against opposing politicians, as the press and its news columns were used as the principal tool of persuasion in the many issues that confronted the vigorous new nation. In 1798 a polarized Congress passed the Alien and Sedition Acts, threatening two years imprisonment and a then hefty $2,000 fine for anyone who would "write, print, utter, or publish . . . any false, scandalous, and malicious writing" against the government, the president, or Congress. A partial reversal of the First Amendment, it did allow truth as a defense, an echo of the John Peter Zenger trial, and it did not forbid criticism of government, only false and malicious criticism. The Sedition Act stood for two years, generally supported by the Federalists and opposed by Jeffersonian Anti–Federalists, before it expired.

Jefferson never abandoned the principle of a free press, although in the years to come, he clearly grew sick of the "lying and calumniating" of the Federalist press that opposed him.[2] The press continued to serve as a vigorous partner to the growth and political development of the nation

The great development of the press during the first half of the eighteenth century was its victory over the forces that would have restricted that liberty. This victory made the press the most powerful weapon of the American revolutionaries.[1]

—The Press and America

The basis of our government being the opinion of the people, the very first object should be to keep that right; and were it left to me to decide whether we should have a government without newspapers, or newspapers without a government, I should not hesitate a moment to prefer the latter.[3]

— Thomas Jefferson

as it expanded westward across the continent, built up its industry, and divided into two bitter, warring camps, North and South. But the press itself was changing as technology, literacy, and the thrust of democracy resonated across political life.

The penny press that began in New York City in 1833 was far different from the much more expensive commercial newspapers then sold mostly by subscription, not on the street. The established commercial press reflected the conservative, property–owning, business sentiments of its middle–class readers. By their choice of stories as well as their expressed opinions, the commercial press advocated steady, sensible growth, unmindful of, or hostile to, any rebellious winds of change sweeping the nation. They largely supported the politics of New England, not the Jacksonian democracy of the West and South.

THE PENNY PRESS

The raffish penny press reached readers who enjoyed the scandal and crime news that filled its columns and were not at first particularly interested in political opinions. That did not last long. Because of the volume of newspapers sold, the persuasive clout of penny press newspapers could not be ignored. Most notable for political commentary was the *New York Tribune* of Horace Greeley. He supported the working man and the formation of unions, equal pay and full civil rights for women, temperance, agrarian reform, a greater share of material wealth for common people, the abolition of imprisonment for debt, and the abolition of slavery. In practice, he was a cross between a socialist and a Whig, not quite either.

A more outspoken abolitionist, Elijah Lovejoy, saw his printing presses in St. Louis and nearby Alton, Illinois, wrecked by mobs. When he set up a third time, he was killed by the mob. On both sides of the Mason–Dixon Line, mobs smashed the presses, yelling "Copperhead!" and "Secesh (secessionist) paper!" in the North, or "Yankee!" and "Abolitionist!" in the South.

Of all the newspapers of the day, the most outspoken and influential against slavery was *The Liberator*, a small circulation newspaper published by a leading abolitionist, William Lloyd Garrison. He aroused consciences and caused the most violent public reaction since the much praised and much reviled Thomas Paine.[4] It should be noted that newspapers in the South could be just as vehement in attacking the North.

AFRICAN–AMERICAN NEWSPAPERS

A number of African–Americans were able to start newspapers in the North and speak for themselves. One of the first of these stated in its first issue, "We wish to plead our own cause. Too long have others spoken for us."[5]

After the Civil War, a division between news and opinion gradually prevailed. The objectivity of the Associated Press dispatches was based in part on saving telegraph costs by reporting facts and eliminating opinion, and based in part on not wanting to annoy editors or publishers who were the customers. During the twentieth century, objectivity became a standard for local news as well. The notion of fairness in presenting information took hold as a standard that was important to build circulation among readers who held a variety of viewpoints, and also to leave those readers with a sense that the news they were reading had not been colored to encourage a conclusion. The goal was to trust newspaper reporters not to stray beyond the facts.

The decades following the Civil War saw the emergence of major newspapers led by powerful publishers who held strong convictions on social and political issues, and were not shy about putting their stamp on their publications. The leading publishers of the late nineteenth century were William Randoph Hearst, whose chain of newspapers ran from New York to California, and Joseph Pulitzer of the *St. Louis Post–Dispatch* and the *New York World*. They were deservedly accused of sensationalizing the news by their choices of stories, the writing, headlines, and layout, but the public kept buying their newspapers.

Their product was labeled "yellow journalism," for the yellow color of the skirt of the little boy in the "Hogan's Alley" comic strip who was identified in the public mind as "the yellow kid." This first comic strip, drawn by different artists, appeared simultaneously in Hearst's *New York Journal American* and Pulitzer's *New York World*. Pandering to low class tastes, yellow journalism undercut the moral tone the newspapers tried to reach on their editorial pages.

This is not to imply that newspapers did not crusade on important issues. Hearst, in particular, was accused of pulling all stops in both news reporting and opinions to involve the United States in what became the Spanish–American War. Seeing European nations reaching out to grab colonial territories around the world, Americans pushed by newspapers pursued the notion of "manifest destiny": it was the Anglo–Saxon's destiny, thanks to his racial and cultural superiority, to extend the benefits of his civilization over the dark–skinned, lesser inhabitants of the planet, and by, doing so, take charge of the natural resources of their lands. This "Social Darwinism" easily ripped Cuba and the Philippines from the weakened grip of Spain and would lead the United States to dominate the economies of Central and South American nations.

The Spanish–American War was quickly over. World War I proved to be a different story, excepially for the European belligerents who would endure four years of massive casualties in the trenches and deprivations at home. At first, little propaganda was needed, but that changed as the war dragged on. It became essential for both the Allies and the Central Powers to convince the home front as well as other nations of

In all the belligerent countries (World War I), the most developed of them especially, industrialization had drawn millions of people from traditional, predominantly rural ways of life into fast–growing urban centers. It created a need for the education of these people — for a literate workforce — while slashing the cost of producing newspapers. Both an enormous new reading public and new means of reaching that public came into existence...

The war's first propaganda fell into place almost effortlessly. As invariably happens at the start of a war, people everywhere were swept up into ecstasies of patriotism. Almost everything they heard and read assured them that their glorious armies would soon be victorious, that their cause was a noble one, and that the enemy was wicked in ways rarely seen in history. Formal censorship of the press was scarcely necessary...

Many (newspaper publishers) saw it as their mission not to inform the public (which long remained ignorant of the realities of the war) but to do their bit to keep morale high.[6]

—G.J. MEYER

the purity of their cause and of the evil acts being committed by the enemy. Perhaps more than in previous wars, truth during World War I was a casualty.

BROADCAST JOURNALISM

The wish to persuade readers to a point of view that would make itself felt at the ballot box continued to be a part of newspaper journalism throughout the twentieth century. It was joined during the 1930s by radio journalism and commentary, later by television journalism and even television situation comedies, and now, in the new century, by Internet blogs. In their endless sniping, conservatives and liberals continued to decry the influence of media to push voters away from the writers' own points of view, angered by the mote in the eye of the political opposition while ignoring the beam in their own. Most preached to echoing choirs.

A Martian visiting the United States during a modern election campaign might be forgiven for concluding that one of the candidates was "the media." From the major parties came the constant complaint that the media were biased against them. From the minor parties the complaint was that the media ignored them.

CARICATURES

Drawing and sculpting figures for the purpose of lampooning, which led to political cartooning, can arguably be traced to the ancient Chinese, Egyptians, Greeks, and Romans. It is not clear if the pot–bellied, homely Chinese gentlemen who survive in carvings represent persons worthy of ridicule. Nor is it clear that the foxes, lions, dogs and monkeys behaving like humans in Egyptian carvings represented actual people. Nevertheless, the comic touches are undeniable.

The Greek caricaturists who poked fun at the gods risked divine wrath when they left their images on pottery. Graffiti artists drew and carved satirical sketches on a variety of media that survive in Rome and Pompeii. During the Middle Ages, when cathedral windows told Biblical stories to the illiterate faithful, sketch artists chose religious themes such as the devil and the grim reaper. Some of their work displayed in prayer books show a high degree of artistic skill.[7]

The late Middle Ages, the Age of Enlightenment, and the Victorian Age brought out artists willing to risk official displeasure. In England, the brilliant William Hogarth's sketches showed the moral decay of the city. George Cruikshank exposed the foibles of society and, in a pamphlet that went through forty printings in six months, attacked government corruption. James Gilray did not hesitate to caricature leading political figures. In France, Honoré Daumier took aim at government incompetence; he went to prison for six months for his caricature of the king.

THOMAS NAST

In the United States, Thomas Nast's cartoons helped to bring down the corrupt Tweed Ring in New York. One cartoon that found its way to

Spain led to the recognition and arrest of Boss Tweed, who would die in prison. Nast used his artist's pen to support the abolition of slavery and the plight of Native Americans and Chinese immigrants, but he also employed it to show bias against Irish Americans. One of Nast's cartoons was credited with the reelection of Abraham Lincoln. He has been called the father of American political cartooning, although historians might prefer giving that credit to Benjamin Franklin, whose pre–Revolutionary War sketches stirred patriotic fervor. Cartooning represented still another facet of one of the most versatile figures in world history.

On the shoulders of these giants, a vigorous art and industry of political cartooning has evolved. In the twentieth century David Low in England, and Herbert Block and Bill Mauldin in the United States were just three of a long list of important cartoonists. Their biting wit has been blamed — or praised, if you prefer — for influencing a lot of what has happened in the world. Today, there may be no nation that does not have newspaper editorial cartoons. The reprinting in 2006 of the Danish cartoons mocking extremist Muslims, followed by riots and killings, are just a recent example of their power. (*More about this in Chapter 14.*)

POLITICAL CARTOONING

During the "golden age" of radio in the 1930s and 1940s, listeners could look forward each evening to hearing news and opinion from a favorite commentator, a span of fifteen minutes that put an exclamation point on the day! These were the troubled times of the Depression, the gathering war clouds, and World War II. The commentators brought explanations tinged with their opinions, sometimes along with the day's news. The best of them had a folksy manner, taking advantage of the apparent intimacy of the radio medium. One of them, Quincy Howe, referred to fellow commentators as "excess prophets."

In Washington, legislation was introduced, passed, or killed, investigations were launched, and more than once or twice officials left government service in disgrace after a newspaper columnist doubling as a radio commentator spoke out. Some identified officials went to jail and some seemingly died before their time. A voice amplified by radio had proven persuasive power. The influence of the national commentators with large followings was understandable, for if manufacturers spent millions of dollars in the conviction that audiences would buy their soup and soap, why not opinions? Why not scandal? For example, a single appeal by the rabble rousing priest Charles Coughlin, a powerful broadcast commentator of the 1930s, piled 100,000 telegrams on the desks of senators.

RADIO COMMENTARY

President Franklin Delano Roosevelt recognized the medium of radio as a way to bring his economic and international policies directly to the American public without having them filtered and distorted through

As he (President Franklin Delano Roosevelt) talked his head would nod and his hands would move in simple, natural, comfortable gestures. His face would smile and light up as though he were actually sitting on the front porch or in the parlor with them.[8]

— LABOR SECRETARY
FRANCES PERKINS

American newspapers that opposed his New Deal and were isolationist during the years before the war. A superb orator, he realized that radio was not a lecture hall, but a quiet parlor where he could chat with one or two people at a time.

Radio commentators dominated the informational side of radio broadcasting. Most of them understood that their opinions were best served up with a quiet, one–to–one conversational tone. Lowell Thomas, H.V. Kaltenborn, Raymond Gram Swing, Elmer Davis, Fulton Lewis Jr., Gabriel Heatter, and Edward R. Murrow were household names during World War II. None of them shouted.

As an exception to this rule, the popular Walter Winchell was a shouter, but was probably appreciated more for being interesting than for being convincing. It was said that on a warm Sunday evening, with the windows thrown open to catch the breeze, you could walk down the street during a Winchell broadcast and never miss a word. He was also the world's most widely read columnist, appearing in 800 newspapers. Stridently anti–Nazi and a supporter of Roosevelt during the 1930s, he probably had some effect in America's nervous shift from neutrality to intervention on Great Britain's side.

Of the journalists in the past century whose work stands out for their persuasive gifts, no one stands taller than Edward R. Murrow. He employed the relatively new medium of radio broadcasting not only to provide information, but also to convey an urgent message. He did so indirectly, in part because his employers did not allow him a more direct option. Murrow's familiar voice spanned the Atlantic Ocean night after night to describe something of great importance, but spoke like the neighbor next door. For his listeners, the world shrank. Arguably, no voice other than those of Roosevelt and Winston Churchill did so much to bring the ordinary American people into sympathy with the ordinary British people. Murrow was a reporter who, following a CBS directive, did not openly advocate national policy. He nevertheless helped to move American opinion by applying oratory of a rather high order of skill. Archibald MacLeish, well–known poet and the Librarian of Congress, explained how this was done at a dinner honoring Murrow one week before Pearl Harbor took the United States into war.

Benito Mussolini once credited his own strident radio speeches with allowing him to gain control in Italy. It is worth noting that Adolf Hitler, who chose an even more strident, rabble rousing tone, had recognized the force of oral communication, but overlooked the intimate nature of the radio medium. In *Mein Kampf,* he argued that the spoken word was much better able to change the world than "the goose quill."

Both the Allies and the Axis used radio to distribute propaganda during World War II. From those beginnings a sub–genre of radio and now televised government programming has taken hold. Today, the American Armed Forces Radio and Television Service reports Pentagon policies and delivers "a touch of home" to military forces. Voice of America, the official broadcast service of the United States to people beyond its borders, is joined by Radio Free Europe/Radio Liberty, Radio Free Asia, and others. The United States government also has clandestine services, notably exile groups from hostile nations who are sending their voices back into into their home countries. What they accomplish is impossible to track with any accuracy, but hope springs eternal.

If any single thread runs through the tapestry of television, it may be that persuasion has been at its most effective, at least in the United States, when it entertains. The metaphor of medicine inside a candy coating comes to mind, despite such occasional exceptions as Murrow's indictment of the condition of migrant workers, *Harvest of Shame*, and several documentaries about Senator Joseph McCarthy. As a function of television news departments, persuasion has been limited to documentaries, news specials, magazine shows, and editorials. Otherwise, news departments tended to follow newspapers in striving for objectivity in their news reports.

In each of these types of television reports, photography and other graphical elements have played a significant role both to inform and to engage viewers. Decisions in television newsrooms on what stories to cover always considered visual elements, and that is particularly true in longer–form news reports with a persuasive focus.

Film documentaries that began in cinema moved easily to the television medium. However, although documentaries were generally less expensive to make than other types of programs, networks and stations tended to be leery of them because they were not as popular as entertainment programs and because a documentary intended to persuade had, by definition, a political point of view. That meant some audience opposition might rear its head in complaints to the Federal Communications Commission. Documentaries reached a peak of popularity in the 1960s, when the quiz show scandals sent networks scrambling to prove they were keeping their promise to operate in the public interest. Documentaries with a persuasive focus in the early years of the twenty–first century have been seen mostly on public broadcasting stations and cable channels, where small but appreciative audiences watched such series as *Frontline.*

Built around major news events, news specials have been done infrequently, and often do not promote a controversial viewpoint, As for editorials, these were relatively brief (two minutes or so) persuasive

I am talking to you, Ed Murrow. And what I have to say to you is this… that you have accomplished one of the great miracles of the world… How you did this, I do not know. But that you did was evident to anyone. You spoke, you said, in London…. But it was not in London really that you spoke. It was in the back kitchens and the front living rooms and the moving automobiles and the hot dog stands and the observation cars of another country that your voice was truly speaking. And what you did was this: You made real and urgent and present to the men and women of those comfortable rooms, those safe enclosures, what these men and women had not known was present there or real. You burned the city of London in our houses and we felt the flames that burned it. You laid the dead of London at our doors and we knew the dead were our dead — were all men's dead — were mankind's dead — and ours. Without rhetoric, without dramatics, without more emotion than needed be, you destroyed the superstition of distance and of time — of difference and of time.[9]

—Archibald MacLeish

statements that reflected the view of the station owner on a particular topic, although it might be prepared and presented by a member of the news department, much as a newspaper editorial prepared by a journalist reflects the views of the publisher. A 1972 survey reported that two–thirds of television stations presented editorial commentary, but many did not do so daily. A few editorials were accompanied by political cartoons that a camera showed with zooms and pans. In any event, the television editorial briefly had its day. Televised editorials offered as a newscast feature like weather forecasting and sports reporting may no longer exist in the United States. Political opinion continued in interview programs, such as *Meet the Press*, where the views were expressed by the guests, and *The O'Reilly Factor*, where the dominant views were expressed by the host.

A truly free radio cannot be used to advocate the causes of the licensee. It cannot be used to support the candidacies of his friends. It cannot be devoted to the support of principles he happens to regard most favorably. In brief, the broadcaster cannot be an advocate.

— Mayflower Decision

Expressing a station's political opinions during broadcasting's first two decades was routine. In fact, the right to air opinions was not given much thought until a challenge to a station's license, which included the charge that it editorialized, led to the FCC's Mayflower Decision in 1941 that broadcasts must not take political positions.

Broadcasters who wanted a newspaper's freedom of choice to say anything, as embodied in the First Amendment, rebelled. They pressed the FCC to reverse the ruling. Eight years later, the FCC did just that, but went further than the broadcasters intended. In 1949, in its Fairness Doctrine, the FCC said not only that stations may offer political opinions, but that they *must* do so, seeking out matters of importance to a community.

This hardly satisfied broadcasters. They did not want the government to instruct them in what to do beyond conforming to technical specifications. Broadcasters certainly did not want the government to be involved in the content of what they were broadcasting. They did not want to be required to seek out public issues and devote time to present both sides. They wanted the free choice of newspapers.

Was the Fairness Doctrine even constitutional? This question bubbled for the next eighteen years, until the Supreme Court ruled on a Fairness Doctrine case, Red Lion Broadcasting Co. v. Federal Communications Commission. The Court ruled in favor of the Fairness Doctrine and of what was called "Section 315," a federal law that required "equal opportunity" for all candidates for public office to broadcast. Also upheld was the Personal Attack Rule, which required that a station that had broadcast an attack upon an individual must allow equal opportunity for a response at no cost. The Court argued that the decision was needed because of the scarcity of broadcast stations. Section 315 exempted newscasts and documentaries, but the Fairness Doctrine did not.

Feeling hobbled and denied full First Amendment rights, broadcasters mounted an attack on the Fairness Doctrine and the Personal Attack Rule, arguing that even though these rulings were rarely enforced, they had a "chilling effect" on broadcasts. Rather than presenting contrasting viewpoints on many issues, some stations simply avoided those issues entirely. That was the opposite of what the FCC intended. With the passage of time, the scarcity argument could not be supported because most areas of the country were getting more radio and television stations and fewer newspapers. The FCC repealed the Fairness Doctrine in 1987 and the Personal Attack Rule plus a corollary Political Editorial Rule in 2000. Section 315 remained.

Efforts to revive the Fairness Doctrine have not succeeded. It became a polarizing political issue, with liberals favoring its revival and conservatives opposing it, but it was not a major issue that resonated strongly with the general public amid so many other issues. The broadcast community, for whom the Fairness Doctrine was a major issue, prevailed.

The practice of convincing by advertising is the economic engine that powers modern newspapers, magazines, radio, and television, to say nothing of the direct mail industry. Advertising, along with public relations, expressed through media have dominated political activity. Candidates make decisions about running for office based on the funds they can raise that will largely be spent on communication media. The advantage to candidates who can afford to advertise is frequently commented upon, overshadowing fitness for office. Many candidates are rich. Few who win are poor.

The relation of advertising to news delivery media — newspapers, magazines, radio, television — has offered a striking example of how gain in mediated communication is accompanied by loss. In the case of advertising, the gain is of money that allows media to stay in business, to continue delivering information and entertainment at a price acceptable to its receivers, and for no cash price at all in the case of most radio and television. Advertising obviously also benefits potential buyers who seek information. The loss is in the independence of the news department. It has varied from place to place. It comes when the desire for advertising revenue determines what appears — or does not appear — in a publication or broadcast.

More subtle influences of advertising over non–advertising content have affected news choices, but to what extent is not always clear. The motivations behind daily editing decisions are so complex as to be impossible to tease out. Much of the income of a newspaper or a magazine and all of the income of a commercial radio station, television station, and broadcast network come from advertising. Publishers and editors often will censor themselves to provide an advertising–friendly climate.

Broadcast licensees have an affirmative duty generally to encourage and implement the broadcast of all sides of controversial issues over their facilities . . .a conscious and positive role in bringing about a balanced presentation of the opposing viewpoints. . . .This requires that licensees devote a reasonable percentage of their broadcasting time to the discussion of public issues of interest in the community. . .

— FAIRNESS DOCTRINE

ADVERTISING

The man–slave Shem, having run away from his good master, Hapu the Weaver, all good citizens of Thebes are enjoined to help return him. He is a Hittite, 5'2" tall, of ruddy complexion and brown eyes. For news of his whereabouts half a gold coin is offered. And for his return to the shop of Hapu the Weaver, where the best cloth is woven to your desires, a whole gold coin is offered.

— FIRST KNOWN POSTED AD, EGYPTIAN, 3000 B.C.E.

Despite what some viewers may think, the customer of a television station is not the viewer; it is the advertiser. The viewer's attention is what is *sold*. In the trade it is known as "selling eyeballs."

Until the start of the Industrial Revolution, advertising had hardly advanced past market criers in Greece, where a whitewashed board announced a gladiatorial contest, or the sandwich–board men who displayed pictures on the front and back of their shirts in Carthage. The ruins of Pompeii reveal a terra cotta image taking the place of words for an illiterate population; in the Roman world, a goat signified a dairy. A boy being whipped signified a school.

Signs and street criers grew more common as town populations increased during the Middle Ages and the early modern period. Like the ancient ads, these fall in the category of information, not persuasion. The spread of printing in Europe brought the posting of printed handbill listing books for sale, a logical activity because the printers of handbills were also the printers of books. A few sixteenth century posters survive, again basically informational. The seventeenth century saw the start in England and France of public registers, where buyers and sellers could post notices. It was also the century of the first newspapers and the first newspaper ads.

The term "siquis" from the Latin si quis ("if anyone"…desires, knows) meant a notice. They were replaced when the words "advices" and then "advert' and "advertising" gained currency during the seventeenth century. Shakespeare and the King James Bible had used the word "advertisement" to mean "warning" or "notification." Also used were the pejorative terms "puff" and "puffers," from which 'puffery' derives.[10] By now, handbills were fancier, with woodcut illustrations, hand lettering, and border designs. The eighteenth century introduced the billboard.

The governments that controlled newspapers also controlled advertising. The censors were ever present to look for anything smelling of sedition or blasphemy, and the powerful trade guilds were watchful for any sales effort that might encroach on their control of trade. In Britain, the government imposed a tax on each page of a newspaper and a heavier tax on each newspaper advertisement. Nevertheless, as trade grew, so did notices of goods for sale. In Paris, *Les Petites Affiches* (*Little Notices*) reported the sale of property and goods, currency exchange rates, and new books. Germany, England and the American colonies developed their own newspapers devoted to commerce and notices, such as auctions, houses for rent, spices for sale, and other merchandise just arrived by ship, plus rewards for runaway horses or runaway apprentices. In the United States before the Civil War, notices of slaves for sale were common.

Persuasion crept more forcefully into advertising with notices of patent medicines guaranteed to cure a long list of ailments. They followed what advertising leader Rosser Reeves argued was a basis of advertising: if you buy this product, you will get that specific benefit.[11] Since patent medicines failed to cure anything except the thickness of wallets, a certain skepticism arose. The conjoined twins of advertising claims and public skepticism have been together ever since.

Mass advertising began during the Industrial Revolution. Factories turned out goods and needed customers. Workers received cash wages. As mass production of a variety of goods and mass distribution grew, it was inevitable that mass marketing would follow, for the goods had to be sold, and that meant advertising beyond simple notices. Advertising was needed to create demand.

Entrepreneurs, first in France and then in the United States, spied an opportunity in the need for factories to advertise their goods in newspapers. They created the first advertising agencies. Based on bargaining, not on fixed rates, the entrepreneurs bought space in bulk from the publications and sold it piecemeal to the producers of goods. They found a typical niche as middleman in a wholesale–retail operation, where they dispensed advice as needed, but offered no extra service.

Their role as space brokers took on added value when they could offer cut rates to national businesses to advertise in several dozen newspapers at a time with the same ad. They also revealed actual circulation figures, which differed from the puffed up numbers of publishers who were reluctant to disclose the true numbers. Some publishers regarded the acceptance of ads directly from advertisers as beneath their dignity. They sold ad space as a kind of *noblesse oblige*, the moral obligation of powerful people to treat weaker people with kindness. Asked by an advertising agent for circulation figures, *Harper's Magazine* executives responded by rejecting his advertising. This attitude certainly did not stand the test of time.

Gradually the space brokers became full–service advertising agencies. They created the ads, wrote the copy, designed the illustrations, and handled ad budgets. Advertising expanded into campaigns managed by agencies. Out of this came slogans, branding, trademarks, and, in the early twentieth century, the Audit Bureau of Circulation that produced verifiable circulation figures instead of publishers' myths. At the beginning of the twentieth century, the national magazine was the natural vehicle for national advertising of factory goods, starting with a campaign for the Columbia brand of a new means of transportation, the bicycle. Its success led the way to national ads for a newer wheeled conveyance, the automobile.

Mass production and distribution cannot be completely controlled, however, without control of a third area of the economy: demand and consumption…The mechanism for communicating information to a national audience of consumers developed with the first truly mass medium: power–driven, multiple–rotary printing and mass mailing by rail.[12]

— James Beniger

The crowd is now in the saddle. The people now rule. We have substituted for the divine right of kings the divine right of the multitude.

— Ivy Lee

Advertising brought another social change as well as providing entertaining reading. That was the personal ad, a breaking away from arranged marriages, introductions by friends, and other means to meet prospective mates. Starting in the nineteenth century, potential suitors advertised themselves. Most frequently, a man regarded as an "adventurer" wrote that he wanted to meet a younger woman with property. Today's lovelorn ads continue that tradition of longing for romance, and receiving unblushing exaggeration. In the most personal way, mediated communication replaced the traditions of centuries of family involvement in marriage selection.

Competition to newspaper and magazine advertising came from direct–mail catalogues that contained nothing but ads, especially those of Montgomery Ward and Sears Roebuck. Most Americans lived out in the country, far from stores. These "wish books" were treasured, despite their reputation of being the wherewithal of outhouses.

The primary argument of the salesman was personal and private: this hat is perfect for you (singular). . . . The primary argument of the advertisement was public and general: this hat is perfect for you (plural)... The advertisement succeeded when it discovered, defined, and persuaded a new community of consumers.[13]

— DANIEL BOORSTIN

The combination of mail order catalogues and brand names led to the decline of an American tradition, the traveling salesman, or "drummer," who carried his battered case to small towns around the country, giving a personal touch and a human face to selling. A writer for the Lord & Thomas agency said that ad agencies were not selling space or slogans, but salesmanship in print.

As advertising agency pioneer J. Walter Thompson noted, "The purpose of advertising is to sell goods to people living at a distance." That raised issues of trust, for buyer and seller could not look each other in the eye or shake hands in the time–honored way of closing a deal. Historian Richard Ohmann observed that no one could say, "'My word is my bond.' The seller is a stranger; buyers are masses; anonymity prevails."[14]

To create the human face in printed ads, agencies invented icons to go with products, such as the Morton Salt girl with an umbrella, the sleepy boy holding a Fisk tire, Aunt Jemima, Betty Crocker, and Nipper, the dog listening to a Victor record. Today it is a gecko, a pair of squirrels, a monkey galloping on a dog, and the ageless Betty Crocker. Testimonials were once sought from opera stars, boxers, and explorers. Advertisers tried to build "brand loyalty" in consumer purchase decisions. With its jingles, slogans, theme songs, comedians' jokes, and the natural appeal of a voice, radio further humanized the products that were advertised. The commercials were often the target of radio humor, but never the product. Television commercials would join the effort.

Printers' Ink, published for the advertising industry, said in an 1895 editorial that the ad writers would have to study psychology because, "The advertising writer and the teacher have one great object in common — to influence the human mind."[15] Research grew in scope and included studies of human behavior managed by psychologists with Ph.D. degrees who examined subtle differences in motivation and consumer activity. For instance, pursuing the psychology of fear, advertisers created campaigns that ran for years against such ignored bodily demons as halitosis, gingivitis, and "B.O." (body odor).

Advertising and the agencies earned respect as the business community recognized their skills and the role they played in the grand scheme of economic activity. The growing advertising industry managed to survive a reputation for fraudulent practices during scandals over rigged lottery schemes and worthless patent medicines. *The Ladies' Home Journal* took the lead in publishing chemical analyses of widely advertised nostrums, revealing that alcohol and cocaine were being used, and morphine was an ingredient in a widely advertised soothing syrup for babies. The government stepped in by passing the Federal Food and Drugs Act in 1906. Truth in advertising was codified into law, starting with New York State. The industry itself tried with mixed success to set ethical standards.

The early twentieth century brought ads based less on information than on psychological attack, a naked appeal to emotions. For example, at the start of World War I, the British government needed soldiers for the brutal trench warfare that would take so many lives. Its advertising included such questions as, "What will you answer when your children grow up, and say, 'Father, why weren't you a soldier, too?'"

Through mediated communication, shopping for the home changed, and so did the packaging of goods. Before advertising campaigns in magazines and newspapers, soap flakes were ladled out of a grocer's barrel; customers did not ask for a brand. To sell a pickle, the grocer rolled up his sleeve and plunged his arm into a barrel of brine. Butter and lard were scooped from tubs. The druggist squirted soft–drink syrup from a bottle and mixed it with carbonated water for a refreshing drink. Customers bought what the grocer had in stock without wondering about who had manufactured it.

Advertising of brand names changed all that and introduced packaging for food and other household staples. Flour was just flour until it became Gold Medal Flour or Pillsbury Flour. Tea and coffee were just that until it mattered that they were Lipton's and Maxwell House. The iconic cracker barrel around which men sat around to talk really existed until the National Biscuit Company began its advertising campaign for Uneeda Biscuits. This campaign convinced housewives that crackers were better for their families if they arrived wrapped in wax paper inside a cardboard box than if they were pulled out by the grocer's unwashed hand from a barrel or a bin.

Tobacco companies prevent publication of reports on the dangers of smoking by threatening to withdraw advertising. Revlon retaliates against Ms. for publishing a front–cover picture of Soviet feminists who were not wearing makeup. Proctor & Gamble announces a threat to retaliate against broadcasts criticizing its purchase of El Salvadoran coffee, withdrawing ads from stations that break ranks.

This censorship by advertisers accomplishes little other than to reduce the perspectives and information available to the public while increasing the media's slant toward commercial values.[16]

—C. Edwin Baker

PACKAGING, BRANDING

By informing the public about goods they had barely heard of, advertising changed public attitudes. They made people want what they did not have—and may not have needed—and made them dissatisfied with what they already had. Advertising created awareness and appetite. Winston Churchill once wrote of advertising, "It sets before a man the goal of a better home, better clothing, better food for himself and his family. It spurs individual exertion and greater production. It brings together in fertile union those things which otherwise would never have met."[17]

Pre–Civil War newspapers had placed ads on their front pages, a practice that still exists in several countries, but in the United States the Civil War news dispatches crowded the ads into inside pages, where they have remained.

Newspapers and magazines were not the only printed media that carried advertisements. In the cities and along the sides of the roads, billboards appeared. Signs advertising tobacco and patent medicine went up on fences, barns, bridges, large rocks, and even curbstones. Vacation destinations, roads, and railroad pathways have been favored locations for billboards, to the point that a few communities have passed laws limiting such signage; later, some laws faced First Amendment challenges. Serial signs along highways, notably the Burma Shave rhymes, became part of the American culture, changing the look of the landscape. Broadway got its first electric sign in 1891, and later became so illuminated that it was called "The Great White Way." Advertising took to the air soon after the Wright brothers flew. Decorating the clouds were skywriting, banner towing, ads on the sides of blimps, and even a magic lantern throwing an image.

Outdoor (renamed out–of–home) advertising today has spread to placards on the sides of buses, bus shelters, taxi roofs, and gasoline nozzles. The billboard industry adopted digital technology, so that signs switch messages every few seconds, and it is experimenting with voice messages.

Advertising…not only sold goods, kept factories running, supplied the home with staples, and kept men and women with luxuries undreamed of a few years earlier, but also affected morals, manners, customs, and the very spirit of the times.[18]

— James P. Wood

BROADCAST ADVERTISING

When point–to–point radio communication was transformed into multipoint broadcasting, it was supported in the United States by advertising, which sharply increased advertising's reach. Instead of the hundreds of thousands who read a magazine, radio was heard by the tens of millions, and its commercials could not be skipped by flipping a page. The extension of advertising into broadcasting was by no means without worry. Having discovered a goose that would lay golden eggs, the industry worried about what the government might permit on the government–licensed stations. In the 1920s, no merchandise samples could be offered or prices revealed. Description of a container, even its color, was left out at first by broadcasters who were nervous about how

Congress might react. Actually, there were no commercials. Instead, a program would be named for a product, such as 'The Gold Dust Twins" or "The A&P Gypsies." A decade would pass before prices were mentioned on the air. In time, radio advertising would be so deeply ingrained in American culture that a jingle for a product was as likely to be hummed casually by radio listeners as any hit song.

Franklin Delano Roosevelt, confronted by William Randolph Hearst, Robert McCormick and other hostile newspaper barons, took to the airwaves with his "fireside chats" to sell his New Deal and his interventionist foreign policies directly to the American voters. Ever since, the way that presidents have used media has been a hallmark of their administrations. The quadrennial presidential and vice–presidential debates, the subtle manipulations of presidential press conferences, the daily press briefings, official news releases, and the back–channel leaking of information are now taken for granted as part of the political landscape. These are elements of mediated communication radiating from a president to the world. They are part of the way a president conducts the nation's business. And much of what the president does, governors, senators, and city mayors also do.

A generation after the uneasy start of commercial radio, as television began in the years following World War II, there was no question in the United States about it having a commercial basis dependent upon advertising. On the other hand, cable television began independent of the advertising that is now a major funding source of cable channels. Shopping channels and many late night programs are, as viewers know, now totally devoted to selling products.

Many Internet websites, still struggling to determine an economic basis, depend upon advertising as a funding source. The World Wide Web appears to be a natural venue for specialized ads, including banner ads and the much maligned "pop–ups." But the Internet is also a source of something new, the viral ad, so clever that friends buzz to friends to click on it. Virus–like, it spreads from person to person, and website to website. What the actual product is may not immediately become clear. Part of the attraction may be guessing what is being peddled. At this writing, examples could be found at theviralfactory.com.

Advertising not only provides an economic base, but also is itself a significant source of both information and entertainment. Today, more planning goes into television commercials than into programs, which may explain why viewers may be delighted to look at and listen once again to a commercial they have already seen two dozen times. Most radio and television commercials seek to capture attention in enjoyable ways so that viewers will remember the product, but the commercials do not provide information that will lead to rational decisions. No one

Change the way you count, for instance, and you can change where the advertising dollars go, which in turn determines what shows are made and what shows then are renewed. Change the way you count, and potentially you change the comparative value of entire genres (news versus sports, dramas versus comedies) as well as entire demographic segments (young versus old, men versus women, Hispanic versus black). Change the way you count, and you might revalue the worth of sitcom stars, news anchors and — when a single ratings point can mean millions of dollars — the revenue of local affiliates and networks alike. Counting differently can even alter the economics of entire industries, should advertisers… discover that radio or the Web is a better way to get people to know their brand or buy their products or even vote for their political candidates. Change the way you measure America's culture consumption, in other words, and you change America's culture business. And maybe even the culture itself.[19]

—JON GERTNER

expects a commercial for a hamburger or a soda to list ingredients or benefits. However, ads that warn of the dangers of certain activities, like taking drugs or ignoring seat belts, may be quite informative.

PEOPLE METERS

The programs that most people choose to watch today will determine to a considerable extent tomorrow's programs. The numbers distributed by Nielsen, Arbitron, and other rating services guide the way advertisers spend their money and the amount they spend. This user–choice system assumes precise measurements, but complaints about accuracy have churned for decades as the rating services have tried one method after another, and one device, such as the P.P.M. (portable people meter), after another to gauge what viewers are actually watching. In a real sense, the ratings accuracy affects not only the movement of millions of dollars but a significant part of a modern nation's culture.

During the Depression of the '30s, part of the golden age of radio, advertising in all media was attacked as a tool of big business for making promises that could not be kept. By its nature, advertising was out in front, an obvious target for a nation's discontent. Yet it survived, expanded, and embedded itself not only in the United States but in every country of the world, including those that had nothing good to say about capitalism. Advertising today is everywhere.

500 ADS A DAY?
3,000 A DAY?

One researcher estimated that the average American receives an ad, on average, every three minutes of the waking day, or five hundred ads a day. Another put the daily figure at three thousand.[20]

The inevitable result is a numbness to ads that advertisers try to break through. Another result, critics allege, is that an increasingly materialistic public has learned to define happiness in terms of ownership, never satisfied with what they have, but always wanting to own more. Mountains of credit card debt and the notorious American paucity of saving for old age may indicate that this form of mediated communication, advertising, has been more successful than is healthy for the nation.[21] Not all change brings progress to a desired goal.

The Federal Trade Commission regulates "false and misleading" commercial advertising. "Carter's Little Liver Pills" became "Carter's Little Pills." Campbell's Soup was required to remove the clear marbles that supported a pile of vegetables and made them visible in a pot of bubbling soup.

However, when the "product" is a politician, the government regulatory agencies must be mute in the face of misleading claims and wrongful accusations because of the First Amendment guarantee of free speech.[22] Such mischief by and about candidates has done much more harm than any soup promotion.

The conscious and intelligent manipulation of the organized habits and opinions of the masses is an important element in democratic society. Those who manipulate this unseen mechanism of society constitute an invisible government which is the true ruling power of our country. . . . It is they who pull the wires which control the public mind.[23]

— EDWARD L. BERNAYS

To each of us, advertising is the price we pay for reading the daily news or watching a television sitcom, for without advertising, we would have to pay in some other way, such as a subscription charge or taxes. Advertising has given the public values, but these values, such as a standardization of judgment and taste or the belief that purchasing certain goods will bring happiness, are not always in accord with the values taught in the home, in the school, or in the pulpit. When something is gained, such as a hankering for a certain advertised product, it replaces something else, such as a hankering for simplicity.

In a perfect world, advertising would be a perfect example of how mediated communication is a signpost along the way to a democratic, egalitarian society, for everyone could advertise to everyone else. A kind of yearning results from recognizing that we live in an imperfect world, where some people are more able than others to send out their opinions.

Nevertheless, advertising is embedded into our lives to such an extent that we, especially those of us who live in industrialized societies, find mediated persuasion to be as much a part of our world as trees and grass. By the end of the twentieth century, the leading advertising agencies operated worldwide.

The art of *public relations* can be traced to the circus showman P.T. Barnum in the mid–nineteenth century. His skill at generating news stories and public excitement about such minor talents as "Buffalo Bill" Cody and "Jenny Lind, the Swedish nightingale," spawned imitators. Political parties came to call. Public relations grew to be an important element in what ad agencies offered.

If the business of "scientific" public relations had a "father," it was Edward L. Bernays. In his book *Propaganda*, he laid out the goal in frank terms. It was "manipulation." Even more than advertising, public relations via mediated communication has been used to persuade the public on political issues, the merits of candidates, and the demerits of the opposition.

With the strategies of promoting government policies and defending business corporations both under fire, public relations became more organized and focused. In a seminal book, *Public Opinion* (1922), political columnist Walter Lippmann wrote about "the pictures in our heads." To tune those "pictures" in support of government policies and large business corporations, public relations practitioners developed specific strategies to influence the public.

Exposés by muckrakers and, later, investigative journalists were countered by skillful "PR." Ivy Lee, a publicist in the early decades of the twentieth century, convinced his clients to act against their personal

(Bob Schieffer of CBS News) made a good point.... He said that successful presidents have all skillfully exploited the dominant medium of their times. The Founders were eloquent writers in the age of pamphleteering. Franklin D. Roowvelt restored hope in 1933 by mastering radio. And John F. Kennedy was the first president elected because of his understanding of television.

Will 2008 bring the first Internet president?...

In a country where more than 40 percent of voters now self–identify as independents, it's no longer a question of whether the Internet will revolutionize American politics, but when.[24]

— JONATHAN ALTER

It is frequently asserted that global information technology and instant communications have promoted democratic ideals, as in the case of CNN's worldwide broadcasting of the occupation of Tiananmen Square in 1989, or of the revolutions in Eastern Europe later that year. But communications technology itself is value–neutral. Ayatollah Khomeini's reactionary ideas were imported into Iran prior to the 1978 revolution on cassette tape recorders that the Shah's economic modernization of the country had made widely available. If television and instant global communications had existed in the 1930s, they would have been used to great effect by Nazi propagandists like Leni Riefenstahl and Joseph Goebbels to promote fascist rather than democratic ideas.[25]

— Francis Fukuyama

instincts to hide or gloss over unpleasant accusations by a policy of openness. By the time of World War I, public relations techniques were used by government agencies, politicians, corporations, and celebrities to persuade the public of this or that, to tune "the pictures in our heads."

Both the 1991 Gulf War and the initial invasion portion of the Iraq War a dozen years later were accompanied by a public glued to their television sets watching the effects of the newest weapons technology reported through the newest media technology. General Norman Schwarzkopf, in charge of the coalition forces during the Gulf War, felt it necessary to remind everyone that real blood was being shed. He said, "War is not a Nintendo game." Yet that is how it appeared to hundreds of millions of people around the globe who saw the bridges and buildings blown up at the push of a button from remote sources. Viewers sitting comfortably at home traveled down with the missiles that struck the approaching targets. A Nintendo game or even Buck Rogers could easily come to mind, at least before the Iraq War settled into the grim grind of urban guerilla warfare.

Arguments in support of the American position during the Iraq War were aided by the "embedding" of reporters in the midst of military units. They brought with them the tools of mediated communication that allowed reporting from tanks on the move. The embedded reporter expressed sympathy for the soldiers who shared his daily life and shared the danger of bullets pinging audibly around them. The sympathy that he also expressed would be reflected back home at the ballot box.

In *The End of History and the Last Man*, Francis Fukuyama argued not that media are unimportant, but that they are neutral. Large and small media will serve every hand. This is a viewpoint hotly debated. Mediated communication with a political effect had appeared in dribs and drabs as early as the American Civil War and was more evident in both World Wars, but really came into its own on both sides of the arguments that raged during the Vietnam War, the "living room war" that brought daily battle footage in color and close–up to television sets. The cameras that showed the brave American troops also showed the body bags and the pitiable Vietnamese children and grandmothers. Other cameras showed the American street protests. The public anger on both sides of the Vietnam War issue, fueled by the mediated images, still resonates in America, and probably will continue to do so for many years.

Controversies over the New World Information Order marked an effort by Third World and non–aligned nations to alter the direction of the worldwide flow of information, and with it, the worldwide flow of opinion and culture. The argument in the decades after World War II centered at UNESCO, the United Nations Educational, Scientific and Cultural Organization.

Third World nations complained that the uneven flow of news, from north to south and west to east, emphasized disasters, dictatorship, corruption, and general backwardness instead of progress. This, they contended, harmed the developing nations and impeded efforts at improvement. It was further argued that Western–based media poured their Western attitudes into countries unable to control or censor what was coming in.

What they wanted was a New World Information Order of international agreements about communication, including licensing journalists. In response, Western media argued that the NWIO was an effort at censorship to perpetuate corrupt governments and hide the misery of most of their populations. The NWIO effort failed. The New World Information Order was never created despite bickering that lasted for years.

In China, what happened in Tiananmen Square in 1989 had a lot to do with communication media. The demonstration was called by students in Beijing to coincide with an influx of foreign journalists to cover a state visit by Soviet President Mikhail Gorbachev. To students under the yoke of a heavy–handed dictatorship, this was an opportunity to force change by daring to call for democracy.

Stunned at first and embarrassed by this public revelation that all was not well, the Chinese government's response to the demonstrators was dictated by efforts to contain the outflow of news. Various big and small media sent the stories around the world and, importantly, to other Chinese cities. The government cracked down at night, when the camera's eye was at its dimmest.

At the extreme end of political communication is unapologetic hate propaganda using whatever mediated communication is available. Nazi propaganda minister Joseph Goebbels boasted, "We have made the Reich by propaganda."

In the twenty–first century, the hot wars of the Middle East are fought sporadically, but the media wars never cease. Through books, magazines, pamphlets, Internet blogs, radio and television broadcasts, the enemy is demonized to audiences of both children and adults.

As one example of many, the Hezbullah television station Al–Manar in Beirut broadcast a drama about Jews slitting the throats of Arab children to use their blood in holiday baked goods, and it encouraged youths to go to Iraq on suicide missions. The broadcasts were just one

The students (in universities outside China) collected about 1,500 fax numbers in China from anyone who knew them. They posted the numbers on their computer bulletin boards and sent their messages without any idea who was at the other end — the electronic equivalent of a note in a bottle. In China, students, hotel waiters or office workers retrieved the messages; then they were reproduced by the hundreds in photocopiers and put on public display.[26]

— NEWSWEEK

The streets are in play. The theater is for those wealthy and comfortable enough to be distracted from the real battles over Egypt's future. Cairo resembles like–size cities around the world more than it does the rest of Egypt. The dramas that play themselves out daily on its streets presage conflicts likely to spread to every corner of the Earth: teeming crowds of disgruntled citizens watched by armed guards.

The press is remarkably free and mildly criticizes the government occasionally, yet illegal religious sermons by outlawed clerics pass from hand to hand on home–copied cassettes and compact discs.[28]

–Siva Vaidhyanathan

more instance of how far mediated information has been able to depart from reality in favor of persuasion at any cost.

The secretive use of small media in the Middle East did not die with the Ayatollah Khomeini, who from exile had used audiotape recordings to spread his message in opposition to the controlled press and broadcasts supporting the Shah of Iran. It pitted small media against big media. During the next generation, Osama bin Laden would accomplish much the same by using videotape and audiotape made in hidden caves and spread by the Internet and Arab news outlets.

The attacks using hijacked airlines on September 11, 2001 were done not to kill enemy soldiers but to send a message through mass media. The 9/11 suicide bombers intended to reach a global audience with a truly horrific act that would resonate around the world.

Years earlier, Beirut and Iranian hostage takers sporadically issued photographs and videotapes of their American and European victims that American and European journalists eagerly featured on the front pages of their newspapers, and played and replayed on television newscasts.

British Prime Minister Margaret Thatcher said, "Democratic nations must try to find ways to starve the terrorist and the hijacker of the oxygen of publicity on which they depend."[27] That has not happened.

Another war, another example, if more are needed, of the reach of mediated communication. Russian television carried the images from Chechnya of wild, starving dogs circling corpses of people killed in the war. Television also carried the terrorist reprisal takeover and killings at a school in North Ossetia and the attack on a Moscow theater. For all the decades when Russia was at the heart of the Soviet Union, such scenes of brutality and government weakness were neither photographed nor reported.

The post–Soviet Russian government has tried to control what could be broadcast by taking over television stations, and by the order issued to radio news staffs in 2007 that at least half of its news about Russia must be positive, and that the United States must be portrayed as an enemy. Meanwhile, CNN and Western European news services beam their signals all the way to Vladivostok.

In the twenty–first century, the old practice of jamming radio signals is pointless. A satellite TV signal is not so easy to jam. And even if all television signals could be controlled and all radio signals hushed, the Internet would bubble with media channels.

We live in what is increasingly a borderless world, opened notably by 24–hour–a–day financial transactions through the tools of communication and the penetration of global news agencies. The Russian government may try to control what its citizens learn by shaping the news and eliminating opposition news organizations inside Russia itself. But, unlike the old Soviet Union, Russia is unlikely to isolate itself from worldwide communication. More to the point, it no longer can.

CONCLUSION

THAT WE LIVE IN THE MIDST of new communication tools is not a cause for celebration. It is a cause for awareness that life is now different. Mediated communication at several levels is one reason why life is different. The most significant level may be that of persuasion.

It is important to recognize the extent of persuasion through mediated communication, if only because recognition can lead to better personal understanding of why we hold the views we hold. The wish to inform and the wish to entertain are joined and often overshadowed by the wish to convince. It would take an effort of thought to find anything in human interaction so ubiquitous as the wish to convince. Mediated communication in all its forms has provided new means for that.

It has an old history. During the long era of the divine right of kings, persuasion of the public was unnecessary beyond liberal use of the lash. That changed with the scattered emergence of democracy in the seventeenth century. The need for persuasion through mediated communication grew as democracy grew. It is today a many–headed activity that reaches deeply into the facets of organized activity. Persuasion is less an industry than a way of life.

The growth of the Associated Press, due to a great extent to the telegraph, led to newspaper publication of more timely news received by wire, and consequently rising interest in national and foreign news. It also led to the concept of objectivity. Political persuasion, at least in theory, was confined to the editorial page, but it has never truly remained there. And, of course, persuasion by advertising was never confined anywhere.

Advertising has changed public attitudes. It has made people want what they do not have and dissatisfied with what they have. Advertising created awareness and appetite. It not only has provided an economic base for media outlets, but has itself been a significant source of both information and entertainment as it has tried to persuade. It is also the price we pay for reading the daily news or watching a television sitcom, for without advertising, we would have to pay in some other way.

Advertising has given the public values, but these values, such as a standardization of judgment and taste, or the belief that purchasing certain goods will bring happiness, are not always in accord with the values taught in the home, in the school, or in the pulpit.

Another means of mediated persuasion, public relations, has become an integrated part not only of business but of politics. Convincing the general public of policy decisions, especially regarding war and foreign policy, is an ongoing effort. It is more central to a democracy than to a dictatorship.

Although it is pursued everywhere by all available means, persuading others is not the easiest of tasks, nor the most welcome. In a world inundated with messages, a high degree of skill is needed to convince people to buy this product or vote for that candidate.

Where politics are involved, venturesome souls in past centuries risked personal freedom, savings, reputation, and all too often life and limb to publish a cause or even to distribute reports of what was happening. In the present generation, in an increasing number of places, the effort to persuade or just to inform can still be life–threatening, as the world's roll calls of kidnapped and slain journalists will attest.

14 CROSSING BOUNDARIES

IT IS THE NATURE of any society to regard its own culture as superior. Every society, nationality, religion, ethnicity, and tribe believes this delusion, or its culture will not long survive. If another culture has a clear material advantage, why that must be due to circumstances that can be explained and, in any case, is only temporary, is it not?

Yet in today's global political climate, a question arises. What happens to us when a distant culture with a material advantage intrudes into our own, when we believe that alien culture to be an invasion, an effort to change us into something *worse* than we are?

Mediated communication is the pathway for that intrusion, that invasion into established, traditional cultures. If what it brings may influence others, it will be regarded as dangerous. If the content brought by this mediated communication comes from people we cannot see or know or do much about, that can lead to a feeling of helplessness, and that can lead to rage. Aspects of the present turmoil may be considered in this light, including the matter of the Danish cartoons. It is part of what is being described today as an *information war*. And a war of ideas fuels a war of bullets.

THE DANISH CARTOON CONTROVERSY

In 2006, European newspapers reprinted a dozen cartoons from a Danish newspaper that showed Arab Muslims and the prophet Mohammed in a negative way, such as wearing a bomb in place of a turban. To the democratic West, these political cartoons were expressions of free speech. To the Islamic world, any depiction of the prophet is an insult and an invitation to idolatry. Islam rejects idol worship in any form, and caricatures of the prophet are considered a sacrilege. Pursuing their anger over the cartoons, the Muslim imams in Copenhagen circulated not only the published cartoons—including several old drawings from the cartoonists' archives—but cartoons they called "even more offending" from another Danish newspaper, plus several additional offensive cartoons never published anywhere, but sent anonymously to further stir up feelings.[1]

The news of the cartoons raced through the Muslim world, releasing a pent–up fury against the West. Crowds took to the streets shouting "Death to Denmark," and "Death" to specific other nations whose newspapers reprinted the cartoons. Danish flags were burned and Danish dairy

The religious believer assigns dignity to whatever his religion holds sacred — a set of moral laws, a way of life, or particular objects of worship. He grows angry when the dignity of what he holds sacred is violated. The nationalist believes in the dignity of his national or ethnic group, and therefore in his own dignity qua member of that group. He seeks to have this particular dignity recognized by others, and like the religious believer, grows angry if that dignity is slighted.[4]

— FRANCIS FUKUYAMA

products disappeared from store shelves in some Islamic countries. Acts of violence included the burning of embassies, stone throwing, hate messages, and death threats against editors. Demonstrators demanded that the cartoonists' hands be chopped off. It did not matter that political cartoons in their own newspapers were at least as demeaning in their depictions of the West. As police moved in, some actual deaths and injuries among the demonstrators were reported. Demonstrations over the cartoons, which had nothing to do with the United States or Israel, took on an additional anti–American and anti–Israeli dimension.[2] In Nigeria, what began as an anti–cartoon demonstration became all–too familiar religious killings between rampaging young Muslims and Christians.

Why was the response so strong? Both religion and politics came into play among the demonstrators. Religious and nationalist factors surfaced as extremist imams goaded the populace to further violence in Islamic countries ruled by secular law. Moderate Muslims in Europe and the United States tried to distance themselves from the shouting mobs, but extremist fervor controlled the Middle East streets. Even to express moderation carried risks. Muslim leaders demanded apologies from European nations plus limits on what could appear in a newspaper. European government spokesmen responded that a government cannot apologize for what appears in a newspaper.

Deeply held cultural values had confronted each other in fury: the principle of free speech and the principle of respect for faith. One of the Copenhagen imams, where it all began, gave both sides their due, "In the West, freedom of speech is sacred; to us, the prophet is sacred."[3]

No clearer example could be given of a clash of cultures brought through mediated communication, or the effort to wield those tools of communication as weapons in an ongoing struggle of good and evil, with each side convinced of its own goodness. Those who might have thought the reaction to the Danish cartoons was a singular, "one–off" event would have their opinion shattered a few months later by the furious reaction to the publication of a speech by Pope Benedict in which he quoted a medieval ruler critical of Mohammed.

While the matter of the cartoons, and other examples given in this chapter, have definite political dimensions, the division is too deep to be limited to a political explanation, nor is it limited to a religious explanation. The overarching term *culture* may be more appropriate.

An Arab–American psychologist, Wafa Sultan, painted the struggle in Manichaean black and white when she was interviewed on the pan–Arabic television channel Al–Jazeera.

We are in a battle. And more than half of this battle is taking place in the battlefield of the media.[5]

— AYMAN AL–ZAWAHIRI
AL QAEDA LEADER

An argument can be made that this viewpoint, although from an Arab, is too extreme, utterly one–sided, and that it ignores the local political objectives that drive insurgent action, including suicide bombers. It is also about the people characterized as "hard–liners," not the moderates in the society. Others saw a much stronger domestic political element behind the demonstrations against the Danish cartoons.

The clash of cultures that disturbs much of the world today is not new, for clashes of cultures have formed much of history. They go back beyond the attitudes of cultural and racial superiority that drove German and Japanese armies during World War II, beyond the nineteenth century opening of Japan and the savaging of China, beyond the European colonizing of Asia, Africa, and the Western Hemisphere since the fifteenth century, beyond the Crusades since the end of the eleventh century, beyond the invasions of the Vikings, the Mongols, the Muslims, the Roman Empire, and no doubt beyond the spread of the Egyptian, Sumerian, and Chinese empires at the expense of the lesser tribes around them. The invading army threatened or clashed until it dominated the field and introduced its culture.

Unlike previous clashes of cultures involving nations, the present one is not limited by infantry front lines. With notable exceptions, foot soldiers are not invading traditional cultures. Western media are. In terms of societal change, the results are little different than in those centuries when Roman culture or Chinese culture or Arab culture or British culture or French culture was imposed by the conqueror. Sometimes it was accepted grudgingly by the conquered. Sometimes it was resisted with bloody results, as when the Hebrews refused Roman religion or the Hindu and Muslim sepoys in the Bengal army rose in 1857 to slaughter the British who were trying to impose Christian values.

The Arab regions of which Wafa Sultan was speaking had once led the civilized world. They fell backward during the periods of the Enlightenment and the Industrial Revolution, after the West broke its own medieval shackles and moved ahead in education, political equality, personal freedoms, and economic opportunities. Yet there was also some progress in Turkey and Arab lands, accelerated by three major developments in communication. According to Middle East historian Bernard Lewis, they were:

1. Printing. The establishment and spread of printing presses.

2. Translation. Books, primarily on useful topics, but also some literary works, were translated into Turkish, Arabic, and Persian.

3. Newspapers. The first were produced by foreigners. Then came locally produced business newspapers, then general

The clash we are witnessing around the world is not a clash of religions, or a clash of civilizations. It is a clash between two opposites, between two eras. It is a clash between a mentality that belongs to the Middle Ages and another mentality that belongs to the 21st century. It is a clash between civilization and backwardness, between the civilized and the primitive, between barbarity and rationality. It is a clash between freedom and oppression, between democracy and dictatorship. It is a clash between human rights on the one hand, and the violation of these rights on the other hand.[6]

— WAFA SULTAN

(The telegraph) was a change of immense significance, and transformed Middle –Eastern peoples' perception both of themselves and of the world of which they were part.[8]

— Bernard Lewis

The symbolism involved in the Danish cartoons is important precisely because of the implications for political stability around the globe, and for the question of "Who shall govern?" in individual states. The uproar occurred not because every Muslim who saw it was necessarily offended, but because the publication was taken up by leaders and organizations who exploited the cartoons for political purposes. The stated target of the riots was either the "West" or "America," but the unstated (and darkly implied) target is the existing governments in Muslim states that are seen as adopting too many westernized traits.[11]

— Philip Tichenor

newspapers. The telegraph spread news and other information through public and private channels throughout the Middle East in unprecedented ways. According to historian Bernard Lewis, the coming of the telegraph to the Middle East was a watershed event. In modern times, television and satellite, fax, and Internet have brought a new openness, and are beginning to undermine the closed society and closed minds that sustain autocracy.[7]

The role of mediated communication in all the recent uproar cannot be ignored. Cartoons in newspapers provided the initial goad, reprinting extended it, and media reports set the streets ablaze in several countries. If there were no communication media, two geographically separated cultures with opposing values might have continued to coexist without open conflict, as they did in so many places for centuries.

What is new and more dangerous now? A century ago most people had never seen a movie and no one had ever heard a radio or TV broadcast. Most people in the world were illiterate. Some were unaware even of the existence of newspapers, magazines, or books. It is unlikely that most people who lived in what are now called developing countries had ever seen a visitor from Europe or North America, let alone Japan. They were born, lived, and died as they had always lived, unaware that people unlike themselves existed. Wealthy merchants, government officials, and scholars knew of the differences, and were not troubled by them. Now, because of mediated communication, poorly educated ordinary people see the cultural divide, and many *are* troubled.

Today's social change will be familiar to anyone who has lived in countries filled with the advertising, products, sights, and sounds of America, Western Europe, and Japan delivered by media. Advertising tempts even those who do not buy, but simply notice — cannot help noticing — the brand names, the pictures, the proffered delights, the sharp reflections of life as it is being lived by the fortunate.[9]

That the developing, non–Western world continues to come to the West either to seek a better life, as the poor do, or to send their sons for education, as the wealthy do, does not mean acceptance of Western culture. Many non–Westerners regard Westerners "as rich, technologically sophisticated, economically and politically dominant, morally contemptible barbarians."[10] Fathers who send their sons to Europe or the United States for an education may in fact try to limit Internet use at home, limit the teaching of English, and generally control communication with the West.

What is barbarism? For those non–Westerners to whom poor living conditions are a fact of life, although unpleasant, amputation for crime and female circumcision are age–old means toward social stability, and they are not barbarous. That exists in what they see as the Western absence of regard for honor and for family values.

In educated Western society, ethical matters, like religion and choice of career, are likely to be regarded as subjects of personal preference. Not so in non–Western cultures. If shamelessness is extended to sexual matters in films, on magazine covers, and in person, if women are permitted to display themselves, then in traditional non–Western thinking the presence of shamelessness can more or less be taken for granted everywhere else.[12] Western media show that people in the West pay lip service to family matters, but not at the expense of freedom of personal action. Certainly, many Americans have complained of the coarsening of culture in movies, television, and tabloid magazines, but the complaints are not accompanied by violence or street demonstrations.

In addition to displaying its women, Hollywood, whose villains are often evil government officials and business leaders, grinds out massive amounts of anti–establishment propaganda. The screen images that Hollywood sends of nasty non–Westerners and corrupt foreign government and religious figures do not sit well in the non–Western hierarchical world of leaders and followers.

The relative lack of respect for parents and authority figures in Western entertainment, the tolerance for uncomfortable ideas, the equality or even the superiority of women over men, and, above all, blatant sexual imagery and behavior are an affront to many cultures. They blame movies and television if moral slippage is perceived at home, say a boy seeing a girl outside the strict confines of a traditional society.[14] The Hollywood product that is sought for its sex and violence is also bitterly attacked for undermining tradition, decency, and social cohesion. The hypocrisy seems to be unnoticed.

In Islamabad, Pakistan, in 2007, Muslim seminary students threatened shopkeepers selling films and music. Maulana Abdul Azi, the cleric who led them, threatened suicide bombings if the government tried to stop his activities against "centers of vulgarity."

With income from foreign box offices now well ahead of domestic box office, Hollywood is not about to change formulas, especially for the blockbusters that include a minimum of conversation and a maximum of car crashes and cleavage. After all, even in traditional societies, a considerable market exists for such films. At times, where it may profit, Hollywood modernism joins traditional values, such as in its growing web of connections with Bollywood, where the culture of India hews to older standards of morality.

My contention, however, is that the primary cause of most present conflicts in which the West is now engaged is neither religion nor foreign policy, but culture....

Mere interests can "cut a deal"; cultures, however, cannot compromise their key characteristics without ceasing to exist.[13]

— MEIC PEARSE

Evil TV Ban

A Muslim cleric has reportedly issued a diktat against watching television or even owning a TV set in the northern Indian state of Uttar Pradesh. Mufti Raees Ahmed, the 24–year–old religious leader of Jogiakheda village, told people to "surrender the evil TV set — or else." TVs would be "smashed to pieces" if found in any home.[15]

— STORY IN THE *BANGKOK POST*

*For most Westerners…
charges of barbarism
… generally refer to
material conditions.
Westerners might refer to
dirty living accommoda-
tions, or eating or washing
facilities, as 'barbarous.'
Even more commonly, they
might designate cruel treatment of people as 'barbaric.'
e.g., hand amputation or
female circumcision…*

*(Westerners) can afford
to live with division and
ambiguity in ways that the
vast majority of humanity
who lived — and still live
— close to the margins
of existence, cannot. For
them, all links of obedience
and loyalty have to be kept
strong or else anarchy will
follow… Most people have
needed real meaning, and
outside the West, they still
do. They understand that
an affront to piety is an
assault upon an entire society and the bonds that hold
it together. It is a central
aspect of their deep unease
about Western influences
on their societies.[20]*

— MEIC PEARSE

For financial and other reasons, smaller nations cannot compete with the endless and overwhelming flow of popular American, Western European, and Japanese content. But what the rest of the world sees of American films and television programs is not the full range of enter-tainment available at home. Much of the world sees an emphasis on sex and violence that requires little translation and is in demand. So are hor-ror films. They travel better than culturally bound humor and thought-ful drama. The result is that too often the available fare in much of the world is the tawdry and puerile stuff that many educated Westerners would not themselves choose to watch. The world sees an industrialized West peopled by gangsters, prostitutes, monsters, and morons.

There is no denying that what non–Westerners see of Western imports is tempting, but that is precisely what makes these exports a problem. That *Baywatch* is widely watched in the Third World not only fails to convince the upholders of traditional values, it proves to them that Western entertainment, particularly American, bearing its message of a looser and wealthier lifestyle, is a conscious effort to undermine the values held by billions in the rest of the world. An Iranian Hezbul-lah leader [in Iran] said that seeing people dressed in American–style clothes is "seeing the bullets of the West."[16] Armed attacks become a justified defense against this Western aggression.

Images and articles about the role of women in society and how they dress, including the arguments in Western Europe over the burkas worn by Muslim women and the hijabs that some students wear, have been sore points. According to Lewis, the emancipation of women is a mark of Westernization, but, both for traditional conservatives and radical fundamentalists, such emancipation is neither necessary nor useful. It is noxious, a betrayal of true Islamic values.[17] The Ayatollah Khomeini gave it a prominent place in his indictment of the misdeeds of the Shah and the crimes of his regime.[18]

Again quoting Pearse, non–Western people "cannot exist without real meaning, without religion anchored in something deeper than existen-tialism and bland niceness, without a culture rooted deep in the soil of the place where they live. Yet it is these things that globalization threat-ens to demolish. And we wonder that they are angry?"[19] In Somalia, after radical militiamen banned TV, they killed two people who were in a group of teenagers watching televised World Cup football.

By communication satellites and by CDs and iPods in student back-packs, American and other Western influences have been spreading to every corner of the globe. The mufti in India who threatened to smash all television sets in his village correctly identified his village's televi-sion sets as the carriers of values different from those traditional values he espoused. His Luddite response was to destroy, without apparent awareness that a television set can carry a range of ideas. But others are fully aware.

Among those who object to the intrusion of Western media in their society are people who are quite skilled at using mediated communication themselves. Not all supporters of traditional values are modern–day Luddites. Even extreme anti–Western fundamentalists recognize the need to modernize, especially the technologies of propaganda, harnessing mediated communication to their own traditions. Jihadist websites have offered videos that were widely viewed; those showing attacks on Americans reportedly got the strongest responses.

David Kilcullen, an Australian expert on insurgent behavior, said that insurgents do not blow up a Humvee "because they want to reduce the number of Humvees we have in Iraq by one. They're doing it because they want spectacular media footage of a burning Humvee." Kilcullen regarded the wars in Iraq and Afghanistan as, in part, information wars that the United States and its allies were not only not winning, but were barely competing in.[21]

In virtually every society, people today use email. Learning to use the tools does not mean adopting the culture. Apparently operating from remote caves in Afghanistan and Pakistan, the leaders of Al Qaeda produced videotapes. Just as supporters of the Ayatollah Khomeini a generation ago used audiotapes with considerable success, it would be no stretch at all for Al Qaeda to use Wi–Fi, Google, and IM. Their messages appear on websites and on Al Jazeera. As Robert Wright said, that makes it "much easier for small groups to rally like–minded people, crystallize diffuse hatreds and mobilize lethal force. And wait until the whole world goes broadband."[22] Jihadis use the Internet extensively and effectively to spread radical Islam. The asymmetrical and global nature of the Internet has changed warfare. What the machine gun, the tank, and the atom bomb did, the Internet now does. There are no front lines.

Former Secretary of Defense Donald Rumsfeld admitted that those he regarded as enemies have done this well: "Our enemies have skillfully adapted to fighting wars in today's media age, but for the most part we — our country, our government — (have) not adapted." Internet websites and television newscasts have shown hostages begging for life and hostages being decapitated. Some viewers were horrified. Others might be energized. Gilles Kepel, a prominent Arabist and a professor at the Institut d'Études Politiques in Paris, commented, "One can say that this war against the West started on television."[23]

The programming available in a number of nations tends to reflect in some degree the traditional religious values predominant in those

...while it once appeared that the new media would enhance the power of governments (as, for example, Orwell argued in 1984), their effect recently has been the opposite: breaking state monopolies of information, permeating national boundaries, allowing peoples to hear and see how others do things differently. It has also made richer and poorer countries more aware of the gap between them than was possible a half century ago, and stimulated legal and illegal migration.[24]

— PAUL KENNEDY

In the United States, Homer Simpson is a unique character, interesting for how he deviates from American behavioral norms. In Europe, he is a typical American — fat, rude, stupid, and provincial.[25]

— Siva Vaidhyanathan

"A lot of us really admire Americans' way of living: better houses, better education. I want CNN," Muhammad Ishgi, a Chamber of Commerce official in the Red Sea port of Jidda said. "But there is what you might call an American cultural danger to us, because they show us another way to look at things. They tell us we might do things differently. You must know that education is a weapons system. It can go either way."[26]

nations. In the United States, both traditional and secular voices speak out. Traditionalists could be found in every religion. American fundamentalist Christian leaders, such as Pat Robertson and the late Reverend Jerry Falwell, attacked much of what can be seen on television, and appeared regularly on television to say it. Yielding to pressure from Orthodox rabbis, Israel imposed restrictions on television broadcasting for cultural reasons.

Cultural differences extend to news as well as entertainment. Like the unbalanced flow of entertainment programs from West to East and North to South, news flows daily from Western developed countries to the non–Western, less developed. AP, BBC, Reuters, CNN, Deutsche Welle, and Agence France–Presse are the major news suppliers to the world. Many countries have complained that Western values distort the news they get from these agencies and the news that other countries get about them. Most of what Kenyans and Bolivians learn about each other is fed through Western news services and their Western–educated editors.

What difference can this make? In much of the world, news is primarily of government leadership, national economic growth, and police activity in a positive light. In the United States, news, especially local television news, is quite often of violent crimes, the sexier and gorier the better. "If it bleeds, it leads" is a saying familiar to American journalists. Those standards influence the American news product.

To Western journalists the news of the Yangtze River flooding was about villages swept away and people killed or homeless. There was no political malice in this, for the the aftermath of the Katrina hurricane that ravaged New Orleans was treated the same way. To Chinese journalists, tragedy is all too familiar. The real news of the Yangtze flooding was about the heroic efforts of soldiers to stem the flood and to save lives. Government pressure certainly influenced the coverage, but the news judgment remains valid.

Many other examples are available of the way that mediated communication pokes at cultural sensitivities. Western and particularly American producers of popular entertainment for export might be forgiven for thinking that the sale of movies, TV programs, and music to other countries is just business, as in: Asia sells television sets and the industrial West sells the programs for them. Hardware for content. Chinese–made DVD players for American DVD movies. Films starring Will Smith or Julia Roberts in return for Saudi oil to drive us to the cinema and Nigerian cocoa and peanuts for the chocolate bars.

Obviously, it is not that simple. We in the West do not regard the hardware and other goods connected with mediated communication as cultural imperialism, a threat to our culture, an effort to homogenize all cultures to look like theirs, but, if anything, an enhancement. By contrast, other parts of the world do not consider the mediated content coming from Western Europe, Japan, and especially the United States to be benign.

It should be noted that China, South Korea, Japan, and India are among Asian nations now exporting content, but their relevant cultural standards are not so different from those nations receiving them. The United States is different. Government and religious leaders in non–Western countries nervously observe the video shops and Internet cafes on their city streets. Looking at exports of communication content, Americans may see, officially at least, global economic policy — globalization — at work. Others see an overt nationalistic, cultural invasion.

All over the world, movies have left a lot of people with the sense that others enjoy better lives than they do. It stands to reason that those who see richness beyond their grasp can grow more dissatisfied with their own lot. That is fuel for revolution. That awareness has also created in the minds of many a sure and sometimes terrible resolve to improve their own lives, no matter what it takes to do so.

To what extent are television and movies instrumental in the mass migrations of the past half–century from have–not parts of the world into more developed regions? Thousands of Mauritanians on the west coast of Africa, joined by desperate families from Senegal and Mali and Nigeria, find their way onto small, leaky fishing boats to embark on perilous Atlantic Ocean journeys of five hundred miles from Mauritania to reach the Spanish–owned Canary Islands as a first step to entering Europe. What has led them to risk so much, knowing that so many have drowned? Why do desperate people from other places try to climb the barbed wire fences built specifically to keep them out? Families in Mexico and Central America sell what they have to scrape together the sums that the "coyotes" demand to move them across the Rio Grande. Families from Turkey to Afghanistan pay out life savings, borrow more, and may even risk their lives to reach Germany. Families from the former Soviet Union and Eastern Europe head west. An international sex trade, with young women chasing a Western dream and others knowingly sold by complicit parents, has become a global scandal.

The mass migration that has roiled the governments of a dozen countries is one of the most significant political stories of the new millennium. But why now? After all, poverty and misery, disease and famine have stalked many of these lands for centuries. What has changed now? In one form or another, the answer is exacerbated by mediated communication that has brought information about a better life lying over the horizon. The émigrés have received cell phone calls from relatives

Aalo Maity barely remembers life before her tiny Indian village got its first television set. She only remembers that after, life seemed unbearable. Every night she would gather with other villagers in a hut to watch soap operas that showed people in pressed clothes strolling while savoring ice cream from pretty cups. "In my hut we ate soggy rice and lentils and I wore darned saris," Maity recalls, "I wanted a better life." So she and her husband, Gaurang, leased out their land and found jobs in New Delhi.[27]

— *Newsweek*

Every time an Indian villager watches the community TV and sees an ad for soap or shampoo, what they notice are not the soap and shampoo but the lifestyle of the people using them, the kind of motorbikes they ride, their dress and their homes.[28]

— Nayan Chanda
Indian editor

who went. They have seen the newspapers, the magazines, and the letters with reports of salaries beyond belief for the same work they now do for a pittance. When they watch Western movies, they look past the actors and the stories to the cars on the streets, the houses, the clothes, the food, the unimaginably rich way of life.

The enticements lie within national borders as well as beyond them. Poor Chinese have seen not only Western films but films from Hong Kong and Shanghai; the Chinese government must deal with the unusual problem of mass internal migration. Similar stories of internal population shifts are common in India, the Philippines, Indonesia, other countries. The division between haves and have–nots has always existed within countries. What media do is expose that difference, setting up Industrial Revolution–like population shifts.

In most Arab countries, women generally do not go to movie theaters. Because of the rapid spread of VCRs, Arab women are among the fastest growing group of movie watchers. After the Israeli army invaded Lebanon, the first ship to arrive at the Lebanese port of Sidon was loaded with videocassette recorders. The city had suffered heavy damage in the fighting, people were desperately in need of cement, housing materials, and other staples, but what came steaming into the port were VCRs from Japan. First things first.[31]

— THOMAS FRIEDMAN

The lucky ones who arrive in European or North American cities where the welcome is less than cordial, where the streets are not paved with gold, and where the work is menial and the wages mean, have brought with them not only the language of their home country, but their religion, culture, and customs. These they do not shed as easily as the sand in their shoes. Confined by necessity or choice in a Little India or a Little Istanbul, unable to find adequate salaries, or pleasant working conditions, or even any work at all, and with their media–fueled dreams vanished, they or their sons or grandsons can become a sullen, aggrieved proletariat. Recall the thousands of rock–throwing, car–burning protestors who took to the Paris streets in 2006. When sons perceive their immigrant fathers as failures, they often look for other authority figures, including rabble rousers.

Deprived people see a living standard they want access to. When they can manage it, one of their first goals is to acquire the tools of mediated communication for themselves. When Saddam Hussein fell in 2003, thousands of Iraqis rushed to buy satellite dishes, some primarily for entertainment programming, others for news.[29]

Direct broadcast satellites (DBS), which are not routed through a control point but go directly into people's homes, have clearly not been greeted as an unalloyed joy by dictatorships. These communication satellites rekindled old quarrels about cultural imperialism. Unlike incoming radio signals, satellite television transmission is difficult to block. Media magnate Rupert Murdoch, owner of Star TV, declared that technologies such as satellite television "proved an unambiguous threat to totalitarian regimes everywhere."[30]

In Saudi Arabia, a younger generation has access to the Internet and satellite dishes, through which they receive a far different picture of the world than their government–controlled media allow them. Affordable pizza–sized satellite dishes on rooftops have given millions of Egyptians a new outlook on a world previously blocked from their view by their government, by tradition, and by their own illiteracy. They can see Western entertainment and news programs that are informed by Western values, and even programs from neighboring Israel. Of course, hard–liners are infuriated that ordinary Egyptians can now hear and see directly what has hitherto been fed to them filtered, if at all.

As if in response, from its Qatar studios Al Jazeera began to broadcast not only news in Arabic, but also its own English–language version, offering a view of world events with an Arab perspective. The video service supplemented its text service available online. To those who believe in the free flow of information, the Al Jazeera newscasts have been a healthy development. However, when the service began, not a single cable provider in the United States would carry it. It was seen by Americans only on the Internet. Worldwide, it had, in 2007, more than fifty million viewers for its Arabic and English–language services.

Its success has led to hundreds of competitive Arabic channels, including the U.S.–sponsored Al Hurra. For the first time, Arab journalists had the power to interpret events. Once, only government officials could do that.

Governments everywhere act to insure retention of power, so the appearance of satellite dishes on modest houses is not without political undertones. Home dishes at one time or another have been banned in Iran, Syria, Saudi Arabia, Lebanon, Qatar, Iraq (under Saddam), Vietnam, and Singapore, though the bans have not always been enforced. The military junta ruling Myanmar (Burma), which dealt with unwanted programming by a prohibitive license fee on dishes, went further when it declared that just watching a certain BBC soap opera was a treasonable offense; in theory, tuning in could be lethal.

China officially limited its satellite dishes to luxury hotels and some businesses, although an estimated one million illegal dishes were pointed to receive programs from the West and other Asian nations. Malaysia had restrictions similar to China's. Former Indonesian President Suharto had even banned advertising on his own country's Palapa satellite, apparently out of fear that rural people would see how much better some urbanites lived; the ban remained in effect for eight years. Indonesian viewers were later permitted to watch programs, but their dishes had to be pointed only at the Palapa satellite.

The demand for media choice is overtaking old feuds. With hesitation, Japan—of all countries—agreed to permit pointing home dishes at foreign satellites. On the other hand, when the DBS footprint, or reception area, of a Japanese television signal spilled over into part of South

Hundreds of people clamoring to buy imported VCRs surrounded stores in a Soviet city for five days, and some even staged a hunger strike and protests demanding the chance to buy the devices … The newspaper Sovietskaya Rossiya described the incident in Yaroslavl as a "video uprising"… Finally, after five days of turmoil, a happy buyer walked out of the store with the first VCR, called the local TV station and declared, "Victory! The Panasonic is in my hands!"[32]

—AP Moscow report as the Soviet Union collapsed

Korea, it did not please that government. Circumstances change. Korea now beams programs to Japan and elsewhere.

On any given day, hundreds of radio broadcasts cross national borders for the purpose of bringing down governments. As an example, radio broadcasts from Los Angeles were beamed into Iran nightly by Iranians opposed to its theocracy. When students in Tehran took to the streets in 2003 to protest against the government, the broadcasts spread the word throughout Iran in real time. In 2006, with Iran rattling a nuclear saber, the Voice of America sharply increased its Farsi television programming starring Iranian exiles.

The Soviet Union is gone, but in the new Russia the belief that government must be vigilant about what information its citizens get remains very much alive, a polar opposite to the First Amendment philosophy that has informed — if not completely influenced — the United States and, in some form, much of the West.

When Western values find root in other societies, they do not settle where nothing existed before. Democracy replaces something else. So does free enterprise. So do Judeo–Christian moral values. So does consumerism. So do attitudes toward governmental leadership, family structure, individual rights vs. family and societal responsibilities, sexual standards, and so forth. The same holds true if new values take hold in the United States. All new values that take root do so at the expense of existing values, for no society since the dawn of time has existed without values.

At a national level in wealthier nations, prosperity has gone hand in hand with freedom of the press, mostly unfettered broadcasting, and Internet access. Almost everywhere, repressive societies are poor. Poor societies are repressive either because of government policy or deeply entrenched traditions, and literacy rates are low. In countries of vast poverty plus wealth at the top and a small middle class, leaders operate on the sound but cynical conviction that open communication may threaten their political and economic control. However, governments cannot fully stop modern media, although they may try. As media content spreads, Western culture spreads, good and bad. Democracy and capitalism spread, as do images of sex and violence, all part of globalization and mediated communication in a shrinking world.

The anti–government riots in Thailand in 1992, during which soldiers fired directly into crowds of peaceful demonstrators, were never shown on Thai television news, but were seen in other parts of the world. Yet, videotapes taken from American news programs, brought secretly to Bangkok, reportedly became the most popular rental item in videotape stores. Such Western films as *Gandhi* (India), *Sadat* (Egypt), and *Miss-*

Not everyone welcomes the array of choices. The X and R–rated shows, in particular, generate fiery opposition in a region where many people are shocked to see a woman's upper arm in public, let alone cleavage. Some critics also lament a loss of traditional culture.…

"Those who are really proud of the Arab culture and the legacy of Islam are saying it is wrong to watch these kinds of programs," (American University in Cairo Journalism Department Chairman Hussein) Amin said.

Amin predicted that the most profound transformations will come as illiterate viewers in conservative and highly traditional rural villages gain vast knowledge about the outside world.[33]

— Minneapolis
Star Tribune

ing (Chile) were banned in the countries where their stories unfolded, but nevertheless have been widely seen there on tape. Disputes that their own newspapers declined to publish because of political pressure have circulated widely on the decentralized Internet. They are sent by dissidents ranging from Ecuadorians to the Tibetan Information Network out of London distributing information to Tibetan exiles. Websites have supported separatists in Chechnya and Nigeria. Citizens of Arab countries have swapped curses and sometimes conversation with Israelis in chat rooms and online forums when face–to–face contact was impossible.

It took the telephone seventy–five years and television thirteen years to acquire fifty million users. It took the Internet five years. By 2006, more than 500 million people around the world were connected to the Internet, an impressive number even allowing for world population growth. Its development is a historical prime mover like the alphabet and the printing press. The Internet has no borders and is unregulated as it crosses frontiers, but it uses phone lines that are national and regulated by each government, so Internet regulation is possible but difficult. It can be bypassed by determined "netizens," even at some personal risk.

Laws in different countries govern the Internet. Some countries assign departments the responsibility for what it brings, although the Internet has proven harder to keep in check than any other means of communication. Governments are aware of its threat to provide unrestricted news and opinion originating both outside and inside the country, and to serve as a communication alternative to controllable media. Britain, France, Belgium, Germany, and Singapore proposed setting up regulations for ISPs, the Internet service providers. China held ISP managers responsible for what flowed through their systems.

A dilemma can exist for all governments, for they know that what enters their country without their power to stop undercuts the impressions of stability and public satisfaction that they seek to establish. At the same time, all governments need information technology and the Internet as gateways to economic progress. To ignore the Internet is to risk stagnation.

It is not just pornography that troubles bureaucratic sleep. One of the most irritating capacities of the Internet is its ability to connect dissidents beyond the borders of a country with unhappy people at home. The interconnectivity offered by the Internet has enabled minority groups to share their struggles with the rest of the world.

Beyond the cells of plotters who intend sabotage, rebel groups everywhere have turned to the Internet. Websites are accessible and email is hard to monitor. Instant messaging, usergroups, and chatlines can

What's wrong with our young people these days? The parents of families living in the country's bigger cities are complaining more and more that their children are becoming addicted to computer games and fast food.

In addition, Thai children are paying less attention to their family affairs and social problems. They are increasingly pursuing activities for nothing more than their own pleasure…

Young Thais are no different from their foreign counterparts in this respect. They chat on the Internet, eat fast food, talk on their mobile phones and listen to the same kind of music as youngsters living overseas. They also see the same violence in video games, and react violently when being faced with problems in their daily lives…

It is high time that government agencies concerned with youth policies look closely into the changing behavior of young Thais. If globalization is partly to blame for this problem, then corrective and preventive measures must be taken to enable our young people to cope with the changes.[34]

—Editorial in Thai newspaper *Matichon*

be insidious. It is virtually impossible to identify and block all the sites and pathways. New sites crop up faster than old sites can be identified. Proxy servers offer ways around censorship blockages, and, on the other side of a border, a government has no legal power to shut down a site.

All any government can hope to do is block reception within its own borders. Denied access by dictators who strictly controlled newspapers and broadcasting, rebels relied on satellite phones to bring their causes into cyberspace. Sometimes they were transmitting news via their blogs faster than journalists did. Even in the horrific struggle over Darfur, where life has been reduced to a primitive level, conflicting rebel groups maintained competing blogs in other countries.

In 1995 Mexican President Ernesto Zedillo announced the start of a military offensive aimed at capturing the Zapatista leader, Subcommandante Marcos, and to bring the rebellion in Chiapas state to a decisive close. Within hours the president's words were on the Internet via the rebels' fax machines and laptop computers. The Zapatistas also faxed out a communique that the *federales* were "killing children, beating and raping women." That brought a global reaction. Many thousands of faxes from around the world opposing the Mexican military action were sent directly to the president's office. Faced with this pressure, the government ordered its troops to halt, and reporters were allowed into the area. They found no evidence of atrocities. Meanwhile, the Zapatistas had melted away into the rain forests, lugging their guns and laptops. As Marcos pointed out, what governments should really fear are not rebels in the jungle but a communications expert.

The Iraq War generated massive antiwar protests around the world, but when these demonstrations received less television news coverage in the United States than their sizes suggested, the Internet picked up what the stations ignored. Each day thousands of blogs have been devoted to political opinions, filled with links to other opinions and news stories supporting the sundry viewpoints of the bloggers.

Like it or not, the media have become part of the arsenal of the political conflicts that define many aspects of U.S.–Arab relations. This is not incitement; this is digitized combat.

— EDITOR OF A LEADING MIDDLE EASTERN NEWSPAPER

GOVERNMENTS SELL THEMSELVES

Governments now employ the Internet to sell themselves. This is not a new response to the introduction of mediated communication technology. Almost as soon as the printing press was invented, governments and churches tried both to regulate it and to use it. Radio and television, which can be controlled, are arms of government in most countries and regulated in all others. They are centralized and dependent on the assignment of frequencies. That uneasy governments would ignore the Internet defies bureaucratic logic, but they must wrestle with the best way to do it.

In addition to the anti–government propaganda that outrages dictatorships, Internet violations of national laws everywhere include distribution of pornography and child pornography, hate propaganda, defamation, invasion of privacy, copyright and trademark infringement, deception, and thievery. One problem that governments face is the shortage of skilled staffs to combat Internet violations or even to recognize them. The law–breakers live at the cutting edges of fast changing technology and some are now being aided by encryption that, for example, can allow drug money to flow across the Internet to be laundered. For the most part the governments are far behind. They cannot afford the kind of counter–measures needed, and many government leaders do not fully understand what is needed. In any case, their priorities lie elsewhere.

The United States created the Internet and handles half of all its traffic, but should the United States lay down laws for everyone? Few people could want that, even in the United States. Within its own borders, should each nation's laws dominate the Internet? That seems logical but unlikely. With the erosion of borders, nation–states have been losing authority to multinational business, non–government organizations, and to media, including the Internet. Parallels can be drawn to Europe in the Middle Ages, when power passed from feudal barons to commercial interests, a change helped by the spread of another means of communication, printing. In time, the map of Europe would be redrawn. This is not to say that today's nation–state will soon be on history's dust heap. Resistance to change is more than strong; it is formidable. For example, while the nations of the European Union have made changes in the direction of mutual cooperation, core concerns like control of national armies remain under firm national control. Voters in France and the Netherlands led resistance to further cooperation by voting against the EU constitution.

WHOSE LAWS FOR THE INTERNET?

For poorer countries, the Internet is virtually beyond control. For the poor in most nations the demands of daily survival and dealing with natural disasters make the Internet little more than a curiosity or a distraction, if they are aware of it at all. The world Internet map resembles a medieval mariner's chart filled with dark areas in much of Africa, Asia, and South America. In large regions of such countries as Mozambique, Madagascar, Sudan, Rwanda, Zaire, and Indonesia most life is too basic to consider the argument that a telecommunication infrastructure plus computers and modems will make a difference in their lives. The Internet is there, but telecommunication has a low priority compared to basic needs for safety, food, clothing, shelter, clean water, and health care.

INTERNET BEYOND CONTROL?

The problem is that modern health care, education, industry, and agriculture all require information, and that now means telecommunication and the Internet. Industries that are especially dependent on the Internet and other telecommunications include banking, health care, journalism, transportation, and education. Some countries — notably India — have used their English language skills and the global communication network to great advantage, and that is leading change for a vast nation.

COMMUNICATION IS A LUXURY

Today, despite astonishing cell phone growth, most people have no phone, let alone Internet access. A lot of the world's population has never made a phone call. A researcher in India estimated that a single added phone line in a developing country adds an average of $3,700 to its national wealth. But in some countries, even when a family can afford a telephone, five or even ten years can go by before a dial tone reaches them via a "land line." That is why cell phone technology is so important. In Bangladesh, the cost of a modem is reported to be the cost of a cow. Nevertheless, hand–cranked radios have been used in villages where electricity was absent. In 2006 a hand–cranked computer costing $100 was developed by MIT's Media Lab.

In India, from their legions of otherwise unemployed college graduates, have come computer programmers, data entry clerks, help–line technicians, and even telemarketers, who are trained to use American accents and know baseball team standings when they interrupt American dinners with telemarketing spiels. Using British accents, they can discuss a cricket test match, or with excellent French, German, or Italian, they can commiserate over World Cup scores. This is a testament not only to their skills and determination but also to their global reach through the tools of communication.

CONCLUSION

AN INSEPARABLE CONNECTION HAS always existed between the communication web and the social fabric. Throughout history they have developed together in an intertwined, mutual cause–and–effect relationship. A boundary between culture and communication cannot be drawn, for each fastens to the other. This argument, that communication cannot be separated from culture or from ideology, has been made strongly by thinkers as diverse as Martin Heidegger, Jacques Ellul, and Marshall McLuhan. It should be as obvious as being aware that a writer who communicates his thoughts through publication draws from his culture, adds to the culture of his time, and seeks a wide audience by using tools of communication.

We live in a world of mediated communication. That will not change except to increase the world's sum of mediated communication. The genie will not go back into the bottle. As the new millennium unfolds, mediated communication is regarded as a weapon that opposing cultures both feel threatened by and wield to spread their own messages.

The newest means of communication, the Internet, is — so far — the hardest to control or even to grasp. Its potential to support or to undermine a political position or an entire culture is still being worked out, but few who understand it underestimate it. In the era of the Internet it is harder than ever for the government of a nation that holds traditional values to defend itself against the intrusion of new values introduced via the Internet. For poorer countries, the Internet is virtually beyond control.

With the Internet, as well as with satellites, cell phones, and the rest of the arsenal, it can no longer be argued that information will not get through. The tools of communication have been weaponized as never before. Governments also use the Internet to sell themselves to their own citizens. They cannot shut the Internet off completely because modern health care, education, industry, and agriculture all require information. In this age, that means telecommunication and the Internet.

Mediated communication allows pathways for one culture to invade another. Sometimes, but not always, the invasion is intended. At other times, what is happening may just be business as usual, but that invasion can lead to a feeling of helplessness, and that can lead to rage. Cultural invasion is central to what is described today as an information war. Films and other media displaying cultural differences are seen as attacks on traditional culture. Armed attacks become a justified defense against this Western aggression. In 2007, when a hit film, *300*, depicted the Greek–Persian battle of Thermopylae 2,500 years ago, the government of Iran expressed outrage, and an Iranian newspaper headlined, "Hollywood Declares War on Iranians."

Separate cultures have formed much of the world's history, but the differences have often existed without causing conflict, when relatively few people knew about the differences or found them offensive. In previous centuries, those who came into regular contact with the "other" were likely to be in business or government, educated enough to be accepting of other cultures. Today, mediated communication has brought those other cultures to the forefront of the lives of ordinary people.

Political and religious leaders who find an advantage in framing "otherness" in hostile terms have sharpened the differences. Hostile news organizations are all too ready to retransmit the worst aspects of news stories and accompanying images to serve an agenda.

Westerners may think their culture radiates such desirable values as freedom from fear, freedom to choose, and hopes for the future, and in some ways it does. But when Westerners are also seen as self–absorbed hedonists with no real family values, the question of why these different perceptions arise begs to be asked. How mediated communication participates begs to be understood.

Al Qaeda may have seventh-century ideas, but they have 21st-century acumen for communication.[35]

— Bruce Hoffman

PATHWAYS FOR INVASION

Not all cultural differences that are displayed through media are negative, especially when they show economic and political benefits. Many are enviable. Movies have left a lot of people with the sense that others enjoy better lives than they do. Deprived people have seen living standards they wanted access to. That is fuel for revolution or the basis for personal migrations by people who seek better lives for themselves.

Mass migration is one of the most significant political stories of the new millennium, brought about in part by mediated communication. Some of this migration is not across borders but within countries from have–not regions to those with more promise. The rural–to–urban migrations within China and India are examples.

Mediated communication can hardly be blamed for current world conflicts, but there should be no doubt that it is a catalyst. Is there a remedy for what has been worsened by mediated communication? If it exists at all, it may lie in communication itself. For those who believe with John Milton that the grappling of truth and error will see truth rise triumphant, the advance of mediated communication should bring hope of a better world.

As U.S. Supreme Court Justice Louis Brandeis famously said. "The remedy to be applied [for false speech] is more speech, not enforced silence." This type of change will necessarily work slowly because thoughtful logical argument must overcome the cognitive dissonance lurking in entrenched values. It must also overcome the opposition of powerful, deadly forces.

The optimist may hope that the same tools of mediated communication that reveal the gulf between cultures will also reveal the better path. This thought may comfort those on each side of the current controversies who are convinced that their culture is superior and will prevail, if others would only open their eyes to the truth.

15 ON MEDIATED COMMUNICATION

SINCE ANCIENT TIMES, MEDIATED communication has had an effect everywhere it has been used, and the effect has been profound. It began with the insertion of writing into oral cultures. An oral culture bases itself upon a two–way, limited scale of information. It has a human dimension, a human limitation. Knowledge in an oral culture is handed down to the next generation by parents and storytellers.

Our written culture is so extensive that no human being can absorb its totality. Who can, for example, recall every scrap of information in an encyclopedia or, for that matter, in a textbook for a college introductory course? No one is expected to, because the book is there.

To point up how much we rely on mediated communication not only for knowledge but for the basics of daily life, we need not go back a thousand years to the illiterate medieval peasant who knew nothing of what dwelled beyond his hamlet except dragons, and lacked the curiosity to inquire. We can look back less than one and a half centuries to the introduction of the telephone into a world without tall buildings, deep mines, or ready access to the fire department in the event of a fire, the policeman in the event of a crime, the doctor in the event of an injury, fresh news of distant events or a distant loved one, and on and on. Most children quit school after a few years, and many never started. Illiteracy was common. Except perhaps for a Bible, many homes had no books, newspapers, magazines, or even a photograph. No one heard a voice on the radio or went to a movie. No one heard a tune that was not performed then and there. People once lived in a narrower world.

Many still do, as any traveler to a remote village or a poor city neighborhood can attest. Yet Western travelers cheerfully visit those remote villages, not in any sense to feel superior but to share for a brief time an existence now denied to the travelers by their own choice. It is an existence almost parched of media, filled instead with streets teeming with the friendly life of direct, face–to–face communication, greeting neighbors, chatting with strangers, enjoying the day, "living in the moment."

Without thinking about it, we as a society have made a trade. To live as we choose to do in a media–rich environment, we cannot live as they are forced to do. For example, spending an hour with a favorite television program or a book is an hour not strolling through the neighborhood. There is always a trade–off. The yearning for "the simple life" may send us to the countryside for

Today 82% of kids are online by the seventh grade, according to the Pew Internet and American Life Project. And what they love about the computer, of course, is that it offers the radio/CD thing and so much more—games, movies, e–mail, IM, Google, MySpace. The big finding of a 2005 survey of Americans ages 8 to 18 . . . is not that kids were spending a larger chunk of time using electronic media—that was holding steady at 6.5 hours a day (could it possibly get any bigger?)—but that they were packing more media exposure into that time: 8.5 hours' worth, thanks to "media multitasking"—listening to iTunes, watching a DVD and IMing friends all at the same time. Increasingly, the media–hungry members of Generation M, as (the Kaiser Family Foundation) dubbed them, don't just sit down to watch a TV show with their friends or family. From a quarter to a third of them, according to the survey, say they simultaneously absorb some other medium "most of the time" while watching TV, listening to music, using the computer or even while reading.[3]

— Time

a two–week holiday with the resolve to "get away from it all," but even if we manage to leave a cell phone, a laptop, or a BlackBerry behind, we will still pack a book or two. Our dependence upon mediated communication is just too strong.

The baby in the crib of a modern home may now hear recorded or broadcast sounds and may watch televised moving pictures for hours each day. A 2007 University of Washington study reported that forty percent of three–month–old American infants watch TV regularly. By age two, it's ninety percent. Conditioning begins early in life to consider mediated communication as a reward. In return for certain behavior, the older child is promised a film, a favorite TV program, or a video game. A few decades ago, it was the promise of a radio program. A few decades before that, a book. Like the unruly convict who is denied access to television or reading material, the child discovers that mediated communication—almost independent of whatever content it carries—plays a role in being happy. A few years later, that child, now grown, lives more fully each day in the world of mediated communication.

A *Time* cover story reported that parents returning home at the end of the day are likely to be ignored by their children, who are so absorbed in multitasking with communication devices that they are oblivious to the parents' arrival.[1] In day–to–day living, the fully plugged–in family shares a roof, but not much else. It has been argued that attention spans suffer. It can also be argued that multitasking mediated communication has made the family dysfunctional.

Of an average 6.5 hours with all media, the average American child spends more than 4.5 hours daily in front of a screen watching television, playing video games, or surfing the Internet.[2] That is more time than is spent with parents or listening to a teacher. An expert on attention deficit disorder sees the hours with electronic media as a possible source of the disorder: "Raised on a diet of sound bites and electronic stimulation, children can lose the ability to carry on an extended conversation or listen to one, whether or not they have ADD."[4] How much mediated communication actually contributes to ADD or ADHD (Attention Deficit Hyperactivity Disorder) among the "video game generation" has not been established, but it is a topic of inquiry. In Japan, concentration on mediated communication has a name, "hikikomori." It means social withdrawal.

A study of teenagers found that between junior and senior high school, both girls and boys were spending less time being physically active and more time on the computer, not counting schoolwork. They were also watching more television than spending time at exercise and computers combined.[5] Once again, something was gained and something was lost.

Comparing surveys in 1985 and 2004, a team of sociologists reported a one–third drop in the number of people with whom the average American could discuss "important matters." The average number of close friends had dropped to two. One in four said they had no close friends. Isolation assumes many shapes. The current generation of youths is referred to as "the ME generation."

Mediated communication brings routine and predictability into our lives, and we desire that. Such predictability is comforting. Think of the newspaper that is savored each morning, the favorite sections read in a specific order. Or the blogs that are visited daily. Or the magazines expected from the mail carrier on a particular day each week or each month. Think of the schedule of radio programs or television programs in our lives. Some viewers will not be deterred from watching "my soaps" or "my programs" even when visitors show up. A comfortable predictability prompts viewers to react with more letters and phone calls to disparage a news anchor's new hairdo than to any news that she reports.

If real life is too upsetting or out of control, mediated communication comes to the rescue there, too, with fantasy choices, such as *Second Life*, where players can live out perfectly regulated dream lives.

As part of a modern, forward looking civilization, we are not satisfied with just the media that we have, let alone the media that we inherited from the previous generation. Yet, to switch to any new means of mediated communication — say, to adopt writing or the printing press or the cell phone — has always been an exchange, giving up the way that we have managed our affairs for the promised improvement that the new tool or method will deliver. At times, not everyone thought that the change was a good idea. Socrates was quite correct in warning that the adoption of writing would come at the expense of memory. It has. Nevertheless, writing offered too much benefit to be ignored once it had been taken up as a tool.

Acquiring the elements of our present culture has never been pure gain. Each new means of mediated communication replaces what currently exists, whether it is a piece of familiar equipment that we will discard or a method we know well. What presently exists once had value. This was understood by Socrates when he opposed the teaching of writing, and it is understood by mullahs in the Middle East who regard Western movies as an invasion of their traditional culture.

It is an old story that we adopt new means of communication because others do. While the Protestant Reformation used the printing press to

Hikikomori refers to the state of anomie into which an increasing number of young Japanese seem to fall these days. Socially withdrawn kids typically lock themselves in their bedrooms and refuse to have any contact with the outside world. They live in reverse: they sleep all day, wake up in the evening and stay up all night watching television or playing video games. Some own computers or mobile phones, but most have few or no friends. Their funk can last for months, even years in extreme cases. No official statistics are available, but it is estimated that more than one million young Japanese suffer from the affliction.[6]

—Ryu Murakami

INVADING CULTURES

great effect to disseminate the reformers' beliefs, the Counter–Reformation saw the Roman Catholic Church employing printing to present its own best face in the religious schism that was tearing Europe apart. Not every prelate had welcomed printing, for it weakened the dominance of the Church over books, but the Church allowed printing — and used it — for its obvious advantages.

MEDIA CHANGES US

In our haste to adapt to the new, few of us have paused to think, as Socrates did, about what we must exchange and how that may affect how we live. Each means of mediated communication in its own way alters us as a society or as individuals, whether we like it or not. The phonograph, the movies, and radio broadcasting eroded our desire to amuse ourselves and, over time, even our capacity to do so. Television changed the way we spent our discretionary time. Lots of people have wished television would just go away. It will not, unless it is replaced by another communication medium. Again, our mediated communication is just too strong.

The Internet is changing us. It has already affected dozens of occupations. There may be few people who wish it had never been born, but there are certainly those who don't like it the way it is. It will not go away unless it is replaced by other mediated communication.

OPPOSITION TO CHANGE

Some new means of mediated communication have entered our lives over considerable opposition from those who anticipated a threat to their comfortable existence. Opposition by some churchmen to printing is not the sole example of this. The introduction of postage stamps, an important addition to mediated communication, was bitterly fought by English aristocrats who correctly foresaw an erosion of one of their privileges in society from those bits of gummed paper. Some gentry on both sides of the Atlantic wanted to limit the use of the telephone for the same desire for exclusivity. Not all captains of ships were pleased by the early ship–to–shore radios because these devices undercut their absolute mastery of their ships at sea. And so on.

Universal literacy was never universally accepted, even if its nineteenth century aristocratic opponents did not resort to the violence today that the Taliban in Afghanistan display to block female literacy and access to books.

CAUSE–EFFECT

Identifying cause–effect connections can be as elusive in mediated communication as they are anywhere else. We are informed that, since the invention of printing, communication media have been an element in all wars.[7] But to what result? The role that propaganda or simple unpurposed information plays has by no means been apparent in war or peace. Sometimes a cause–effect line can be drawn, such as the increased interest in travel after the foreign forays by early photographers. But a concurrent opposition to the Civil War cannot be credited to Mathew Brady's photographs, however tempting it would be to do so. Cause–effect was certainly evident later in that century as one factor in the run–up to the Spanish–American War, when William Randolph Hearst led a full–throated cry by leading American newspapers for military intervention in Cuba and the Philippines.

On a more peaceful note, we can be equally sure that innovations that simplified photography led to a demand for family pictures and later to a rush to own simple cameras that required only the push of a button. Headline grabbing, visual camcorders have spread the producer base in dramatic ways from the Rodney King beating response to the daily flood of video uploading to YouTube. The camera phone/website combination, which recorded and published racist comments by Virginia Senator George Allen and actor Michael Richards helped to turn an election, and has made a lot of people more wary when they are out in public.

Mediated communiction began as long as ten thousand years ago with the tokens that preceded writing. The millennia of recorded history that followed reveal some common personal effects:

- Because of mediated communication, everyone's potential knowledge base has expanded from what one person can be expected to know. It is now boundless.

- If we can store information, we can reflect upon the past and build upon the information. We can share it systematically. That happens every day.

- The more educated we are, the more we rely on mediated communication. The content that we choose is, of course, a determining factor in what we know.

- We use mediated communication to separate ourselves from the here to connect to the there. The there is now anywhere on Earth, or even beyond.

- Information comes from unknown others. Interest grows in what is distant.

- A significant part of each day is spent mentally, and probably physically, isolated from other people. The more time spent with mediated communication, the less time remains for a traditional social dynamic.

- As new inventions and new methods diffuse into a society, the number and variety of our choices of information and entertainment rise. Life becomes more complex.

We're not saying people are completely isolated. They may have 600 friends on Facebook.com and email 25 people a day, but they are not discussing matters that are personally important.[8]

— Lynn Smith–Lovin

After I arrived at my hotel, I reflected on our trip: The driver and I had been together for an hour, and between the two of us we had been doing six different things. He was driving, talking on his phone, and watching a video. I was riding, working on my laptop and listening to my iPod.

There was only one thing we never did: talk to each other.

It's a pity. He probably had a lot to tell me.[9]

— Thomas Friedman

• Mass comunication has expanded to include personal communication. The truly descriptive term is mediated communication. That is good news for supporters of democracy.

• As mediated communication spreads, it has an equalizing effect.

• The number of producers of communication in free societies expands along with the number of receivers.

• Expansion stirs opposition from those who would control or limit the number of producers and the type of content.

TELEVISION TAKES OVER

Consider the loss of time to do other things or to have ordinary conversations when an entire evening is given over to watching television. The television in the living room has reduced book reading, another form of mediated communication. It has also reduced physical activity, participation in social groups, and family communication. Or, a different example: the Walkman on the jogger's ears in the park reduces the sense of harmony with nature, and on urban streets increases the danger from cars. (On the other hand, in a gym, it reduces boredom.) Something gained, something lost, but what is gained is regarded as more valuable.

Do new communication systems and devices alter long–held opinions, tastes, and behavior, or is it simply a matter of pouring old wine into new bottles? Change sometimes occurs in obvious and superficial ways, not in the fundamental ways that alter a society. Arguments can be marshaled to show that, for example, movable type printing changed everything, and also that little or nothing changed for most people.

As for today, the current metaphor of the "information highway" implies direction, a destination, and change. The telephone companies, cable companies, and broadcasting companies lay down the electrons for a virtual highway, but while the information highway offers cheap and easy access to unlimited stores of information, its direction is less to the public library or the news office than to the cinema, the shopping mall, and the video arcade. So what has changed? The society might wish it otherwise, but tastes and behavior have proven stubborn attributes. Inventions are easier.

Another factor of changes in mediated communication is their unplanned effects. Among the hardest things to predict with accuracy is how new communication methods will be used. Inventions by themselves have scant value until they acquire a social use. That social use sometimes was neither intended nor anticipated by the inventors. Gutenberg would not have considered how his invention of movable type would affect Europe within a century. Those French tinkerers, Niépce and Daguerre,

Fifty years ago, the length of a pop single was influenced by what would fit on a forty–five–r.p.m., seven–inch desk. The length and the episodic structure of the Victorian novel — Dicken's novels, especially — were at least partly created by writers and editors working on deadline for monthly periodicals. Television, for a variety of commercial and spatial reasons, developed the single–set or two–set sitcom. Format always affects form, and the exhibition space changes what's exhibited.[10]

— DAVID DENBY

could hardly have imagined what still photography would accomplish, let alone movies, within a century. Nor did the university researchers who first sent email messages back and forth guess its future.

Some communication media began their public existence beyond anyone's understanding of how they could have any meaning to ordinary daily life, yet as they were diffused into society, the public found that meaning. Some communication media were intended for government and business, not for personal use. The computer, a means to process numbers quickly, was one device that went through periods of government support and little public awareness. The telegraph was another. It took years before the copier was considered by those who heard about it to be anything more than a complicated, expensive, and unnecessary substitute for a perfectly adequate sheet of carbon paper. The typewriter, the telephone, the phonograph, the radio, audiotape, videotape and, of course, the computer, were initially considered for their military or commercial applications. Few thought that millions of ordinary people would sooner or later want to take them into their homes. The fax machine and the copier have joined the communication devices in the home.

MEANINGS FOR ORDINARY LIFE

A few decades ago, who would have dreamed of publishing a book at home, let alone producing a motion picture there? Today, more movies are being shot than ever, as desktop video brings a budget version of Hollywood to Main Street. Home computers expand information use in ways only recently unimaginable. When technology has merged the home computer and connective media like cable and satellite with the end–user media of cell phones, digital photographs, books, and television, we are hard put to find its like anywhere at any time. Perhaps a comparison can be stretched to the fifteenth century, when printing began in Europe, joined with the paper technology brought from the East, and was midwife to the modern age.

WHO WOULD HAVE DREAMED OF IT?

Another mark of the connected attributes of our mediated communication has been their political pattern of growth from their origins. They may take root in absolute and settled autocracies, but they do not blossom there. Mediated communication grows best where there is ferment, not where life is controlled. The reason should be obvious. A communication invention finds a wide social use where it improves upon what exists. That means change, and change is frequently egalitarian, spreading knowledge, encouraging democracy, and opening economic opportunities.

GROWING IN FERMENT

Writing blossomed in the troubled, independent ancient Greek cities, not in the controlled empires of Babylonia, Persia, and Egypt. Printing with movable type did not spread across China, where it was invented, for several reasons, not the least of which was a controlled society where

For this current trip down memory highway (driving from New Jersey to Florida), *I looked forward to enjoying some of these experiences with my children. I thought this trip would be a chance to relive a simpler time, but those 1,200 miles aren't what they used to be.*

Companionship and shared experience have been replaced by individual desires and personal technology. I knew I'd have to combine the old with the new. I made speeches about library books, but also borrowed a two-screen DVD player. What I didn't realize was just how much technology was packed already.

Aside from the DVD player, we had two computers, three MP3 players and three cell phones, which meant we connected to a lot more than scenery. Gone are the days of marveling at a new bridge…

In our quest to be tuned in at all times, I hope we don't tune out some of the basic things that have kept us going for generations—things like simple tools, a Sunday drive, everyone singing the same song in the car.[11]

—Lisa Segelman

literacy continued to be limited to those with a measure of power. Yet it thrived in Western Europe in the midst of political, economic, and religious turmoil. Today, the breathless emergence of one communication device and method after another comes out of the free, competitive, and frequently turbulent industrial belt stretching in the Northern Hemisphere from Finland west across two continents and two oceans to Japan and South Korea. Autocratic regimes that try to stifle turbulence use some of the products but contribute nothing to their improvement.

The fertile ground of a society where people are free to experiment with communication lends itself to improvements in the technology and to fresh uses. But one hand washes the other, for better and freer media contribute to a freer society. Again, the reason is obvious. As more people are able to communicate ever more freely to wider and wider audiences, they will take advantage of all the available means to do so and seek new means.

Where societies are not free, the yearning to communicate is no less strong. People have willingly risked their lives to express themselves through media. It is not necessary to go back to the burning of printers along with their books. Instead, look along the margins of controlled societies during recent history for examples. Underground "samizdat" media were a factor in overthrowing the Soviet Union, risking arrest. A growing film industry has been nudging China toward a more open society. "Small media" like smuggled pamphlets and audiotapes assisted risk takers in shaking off the dictatorship of the shah in Iran, and new media may yet contribute to shaking off the theocracy that has replaced it. At one time, revolutionaries seized railroad terminals and factories. Today they would seize television stations or, unable to do that, produce videos of acts that television stations will show. The world has in recent years been treated to horrific examples of this.

Open expression is often crushed, but, inevitably, the introduction of new means of mediated communication leads not only to a greater dispersal of information over more and more channels, but to considerably greater quantities of information. Content broadens. Today, little remains that is not openly discussed and openly available to anyone who takes the trouble to read or hear or watch. As for the accusation that news reports and opinions emphasize conflicts, it is obviously true. News has always done so, reflecting what interests and concerns people, and it is no less true in an era of Internet blogs. That a political element is involved in decisions of what to report is also obvious; for example, victimization in Darfur will be news to the extent that it suits a blogger in his pajamas or an editor in a large studio newsroom. This reality is not new. What is new is the capacity of mediated communication in anyone's hands to send this information to the furthest reaches of the world, including places that block free expression, to add pictures and sound, and to edit that information to show what is most inflammatory.

Mediated communication demonstrates its greatest effects at the nexus where new technologies are combined with other new, or relatively new, technologies. Thus, movable type printing with the new paper, not the old papyrus or parchment. Thus, recorded sound with recorded motion photography. Thus, computers with telephone lines and television. Text messaging, resulting from combining cell phones and computer technology, is hugely popular with American youth, and is even a bigger communication factor in Asia and Europe. At this writing, the full effects of merging cell phones and cameras in the cameraphone are yet to come, but the potential is making itself felt in many ways, including news reporting by ordinary citizens.

COMBINING TECHNOLOGIES

As the quantity of communication and the variety of topics grow each year, so do the size of the audience and the choices of delivery. No end is in sight. In free industrial nations, bookstores and magazine stands are overflowing. So are public libraries. We are drowning in email. Industrial societies are awash in mediated content contained in videotapes and DVDs clogging store shelves, the outpouring of desktop publishing newsletters, self–published books, magazines, and multimedia presentations. New video games emerge every day. In the United States, the announced goal in cable television is of five hundred channels, which is shorthand for an unlimited number of channels, constrained only by demand. More than two hundred channels are already available in some markets. In addition to cable, the Internet is being used as a delivery route for movies and television programs. Video news stories and video podcasts flow through thousands of openings. Even children express themselves by blogging on their own websites for the world to take notice.

NO LIMIT TO CHANNELS

YouTube alone absorbs tens upon tens of thousands of uploaded videos *each day*. The average was 79,000 daily by 2006, although many contained programming lifted from sources under copyright. In industrial societies it has been true for some time that anyone can own a book. Now, anyone can own a movie. Almost anyone can make a movie. This overload of information includes — to say it politely — much of dubious value. Misinformation is always a click away. The familiar cry, "Them lying newspapers" also applies to cable, the Internet, digital photographs, advertising in any form, and all other types of content. As communication has improved, so has the ability to manipulate it and to bury us under its flow. The trade–off to having so much to choose from is having fewer choices in common. It is no coincidence that movie box

EASY TO BE MISINFORMED

As the number of choices keeps growing, negative aspects of having a multitude of options begin to appear. As the number of choices grows further, the negatives escalate until we become overloaded. At this point, choice no longer liberates, but debilitates. It might even be said to tyrannize. . . . We do ourselves no favor when we equate liberty too directly with choice, as if we necessarily increase freedom by increasing the number of options available.[12]

—Barry Schwartz

CHOICE IS PREFERRED

office receipts, newspaper circulation, and magazine store sales are all declining.

The availability of information to everyone has brought inevitable changes to the social structure. When more people can be more informed — or misinformed — on more topics than ever before, the old rigid limitations on social status and income, the walls that separate one group from another, weaken under the force of those who are able to use information to better their lives. The Horatio Alger–like tales of media–aided success are not a fiction, and they extend far beyond the financial valuations of Google and YouTube. Many immigrants to the United States have been storied for taking advantage of opportunities to acquire knowledge that were denied them where they or their parents came from, and to use what they learned to break through social barriers that had excluded them.

Occasionally, we hear of traditional parents who oppose advanced education for a daughter or, in fewer cases, a son. The parents fear that books will take their children away from them. They may be right. If you fear change, books are not the only media you should fear. All media change us. They inform, educate, entertain, channel, and isolate us, separating us from what is near, connecting us to what is distant, different, and strange.

The right to choose among the means of communication and the content they deliver has an egalitarian thrust that carries the seeds of democracy, but also of separation from one another. A 2007 Nielsen Research television study reported that rich people and poor people watch different programs. Allowed to choose, they choose what appeals to them based on education, culture, experience, whatever. Where free choice is ample, it is the users — much more than the rulers of a society or even the owners of the communication tools — who eventually determine the direction that mediated communication takes. And as mediated communication goes, so goes civil society.

Sending or getting a communication is a fundamental element of being free to choose how we live our lives. The more choice that we have, the greater our sense of freedom, whether justified or not. Those who are limited by illiteracy, poverty, or laws are not always aware that they are restricted in what they can do, but those who are able to constrain the communication of others own a jealously guarded authority.

In 1991, during the dissolution of the Soviet Union, I was sent by the United States Information Agency to the newly liberated Baltic countries to talk to broadcast journalists about American practices. After I returned, a Lithuanian government broadcast official I had met, a holdover from the former Soviet regime and one of the overseers of a controlled and limited broadcast service, came to Minneapolis on a State Department tour. During his brief stopover he asked to go shopping. When we arrived at the first mall he had ever seen in a Western country, he expressed astonishment at the variety of goods, then said firmly, "It is too much. People have too many choices. They should not have so many." He sounded quite serious about this, but it was plain, as he moved from one shop window to the next, that "people" did not include a man accustomed to preferential treatment. My visitor was an apparatchik from a society still mired in severely limited choices in many facets of civil life, especially media, but eager to break free. Reflecting on his comment, I thought about how the desire for choice and the freedom to choose have been driving forces in the history of mediated communication, yet some of those with power and influence who want choice for themselves also want—with considerable vehemence—to deny it to others.

Can we have too many choices? People living in an age of plenty may suffer what Gregg Easterbrook calls "choice anxiety," when they have so many options that choice becomes a source of anguish.[13] Certainly, given a choice between more channels or fewer channels to watch, more magazines or fewer to choose from, one community newspaper or three, we would vote for more every time.

Yet some questions arise. Would more always be the wiser course, considering the fractioning of community that goes with it? What if the choices are among equally dreadful alternatives? Is this really choice at all? Referring to mediated communication, columnist George Will expressed the view of critics who dismiss such choices as providing no real choice.

Concerning that popular metaphor of our era, the "global village," Marshall McLuhan foresaw technology that would permit most of humankind to share information.[14] (McLuhan wrote before the Internet arrived in home computers.) His vision of a village on a global scale presumes that radio and television are returning us to an oral culture. Yet, written culture includes the one–way communication of radio and television, plus their content of recordings and motion pictures. They are all oral versions of the limitless quantity of information that identifies a written culture, not an oral culture with knowledge on a human scale. Nor do users of broadcasting routinely share the same experiences, as villagers would. The culprit undermining the conceit of a global village is, once again, the quantity of communication available in industrialized societies, translated into the variety of choices of reading, viewing, and listening. On rare occasions, such as a lunar walk, the Olympic games, or the Iraq War, the world ventures together into the shared space of a global village. For the most part, people go their separate ways, reveling in

Ours is an age besotted with graphic entertainments. And in an increasingly infantilized society, whose moral philosophy is reducible to a celebration of "choice," adults are decreasingly distinguishable from children in their absorption in entertainments and the kinds of entertainments they are absorbed in—video games, computer games, hand–held games, movies on their computers and so on. This is progress: more sophisticated delivery of stupidity. An optimistic premise of our society, in which "choice" is the ideal that trumps all others, is that competition improves things, burning away the dross and leaving the gold. This often works with commodities like cars but not with mass culture. There competition corrupts.[15]

—GEORGE WILL

the offered choices. Certainly aware of this are newspapers besieged by Internet and cable competition, and television networks observing how their audiences have dwindled under the onslaught of new choices.

At a personal level, going our separate ways sometimes means choosing to go alone. Social scientists report a noticeable shift toward a more isolated life. Robert Putnam found that Americans are no longer participating in group activities as they once did.[16] Another study found "a remarkable drop in the size of core discussion networks, with a shift away from ties formed in neighborhood and community contexts."[17]

CONCLUSION Mediated communication has altered the human experience. It was not long ago that people lived in a narrower world. Many still do, but the benefits of mediated communication have a down side. They are exchanged for a simpler life. Something is surrendered, although few of us since Henry David Thoreau would truly prefer the simpler life. What is lost in the shift to new media has value, or else it would not have been established in the first place.

Our dependence upon mediated communication has become almost as basic as breathing and eating. Our attachment is, in many ways, a reward for labor, and it is more central to human lives today than ever before. How a particular kind of mediated communication has made a difference in life is not always clear. We know for sure that new means of mediated communication add to our choices. They disperse greater quantities of information over more channels. Content broadens. Today it overflows industrial societies. Little remains that is not openly discussed. As for the number of our choices, questions have been raised about whether a great increase is good for society as a whole.

Mediated communication has been entwined in human life for many centuries and is now entangled more than ever. The media matter to us every day, and the more educated we are, the more media matter. Mediated communication is not something we can easily take or leave alone. Leaving media alone is not really an option in a modern world. We will not allow ourselves to be deprived of mediated communication, and we will resist any attempt to reduce what we have. If nothing else, that is worthy of our attention.

Notes

INTRODUCTION

1. *Minneapolis Star Tribune*, 26 November 2006: A1.

2. *Time*, 25 December 2006: 40.

3. Francis Fukuyama, *The End of History and the Last Man*, 2nd ed. (New York: Free Press), 88.

4. S.F. Spira, *The History of Photography: As Seen Through the Spira Collection.* (New York: Aperture Foundation, 2001) 217.

CHAPTER 1 — WRITING: HOLDING THOUGHT IN OUR HANDS

1. Denise Schmandt-Besserat, *Before Writing.* (Austin: University of Texas Press, 1992), 1.

2. Schmandt-Besserat, *Before Writing.* 178ff.

3. Schmandt-Besserat, *Before Writing.* 128.

4. Stephen Houston, ed., *The First Writing: Script Invention as History and Process.* (Cambridge University Press, 2004) 94.

5. Steven Roger Fischer, *A History of Writing.* (London: Reaktion Books, Ltd., 2001) 69.

6. Will Durant, *Our Oriental Heritage.* (New York: Simon & Schuster, 1936), 129.

7. Adolf Erman, *Life in Ancient Egypt.* (London, 1894), 328, in Durant, 170.

8. Steven Shubert, "The Oriental Origins of the Alexandrian Library," *Libri* 1993, vol. 43 no. 2: 163.

9. Peter T. Daniels and William Bright, eds., *The World's Writing Systems.* (New York: Oxford University Press, 1996) 1.

10. Louis Delaporte, *Mesopotamia: The Babylonian and Assyrian Civilization.* (New York: Columbia University Press, 2004), 199.

11. Robert K. Logan, *The Alphabet Effect: The Impact of the Phonetic Alphabet on the Development of Western Civilization.* (William Morrow and Co., 1986).

11. Durant, *Our Oriental Heritage*, 131.

12. Ibid.

13. G.R. Driver, *Semitic Writing: From Pictograph to Alphabet.* (London: Oxford University Press, 1948), 196.

14. Logan, *The Alphabet Effect*, 73.

15. Leonard Cottrell, T*he Quest for Sumer.* (New York: G.P. Putnam's Sons, 1965), 86.

16. Durant, *Our Oriental Heritage*, 171.

17. Harold A. Innis, *The Bias of Communication.* (University of Toronto Press, rev. ed., 1972), 16.

18. Innis, *The Bias of Communication*, 7.

19. Innis' arguments on communication, dense with historical references, are not always easy to follow, but *The Bias of Communication* and *Empire of Communication* reward the patient reader. For a lucid exposition of Innis' main points, as well as those of Marshall McLuhan, see James Carey, "Harold Adams Innis and Marshall McLuhan," *The Antioch Review*, vol. 27, 1967, 5-39.

20. Fischer, *A History of Writing*, 121.

21. Daniels, *The World's Writing Systems*, 25.

22. Logan, *The Alphabet Effect*, 33-36.

23. Logan, *The Alphabet Effect*, 82.

24. Ibid.

25. Jack Goody, *Literacy in Traditional Societies.* (Cambridge: Cambridge University Press, 1968), 3.

26. W.M. Flinders Petrie, *The Formation of the Alphabet.* (London: MacMillan & Co., 1912), 5.

27. Durant, *Our Oriental Heritage*, 106.

28. Leonard Shlain, *The Alphabet Versus the Goddess.* (New York: Viking, 1998) 65.

29. John A. Crow, *Greece: The Magic Spring.* (New York: Harper & Row, 1970), 16.

30. Herodotus, *The History*, 5:58.

31. See Herodotus, 5:57ff.

32. William A. Mason, *A History of the Art of Writing.* (New York: Macmillan Co., 1920), 343.

33. Eric A. Havelock, *Preface to Plato.* (Cambridge, Mass.: Belknap Press, 1963), 42.

34. See Plato, *Phaedrus*, 275, trans. C.J. Rowe, 2nd. (corrected) ed. (Warminster, England: Aris & Rowe, 1988).

35. Henri-Jean Martin, *The History and Power of Writing.* (Chicago: University of Chicago Press, 1994), 46.

36. Logan, *The Alphabet Effect*, 107.

37. Gaston Maspero, *The Dawn of Civilization: Egypt and Chaldæa, trans. M.L. McClure.* (London: Society for Promoting Christian Knowledge, 1922), 220.

38. *Phaedrus*, 123.

39. Walter S. Ong, *The Presence of the Word: Some Prolegomena for Cultural and Religious History.* (New Haven: Yale University Press, 1967), 23.

40. Daniels, *The World's Writing Systems*, 5.

41. Arnaldo Momigliano, "History and Biography," in M.I. Finley, ed., *The Legacy of Greece.* (New York: Oxford University Press, 1984), 160.

42. Finley, *The Legacy of Greece,* 16.

43. Innis, *The Bias of Communication*, 7.

44. Marti Lu Allen, *The Beginning of Understanding: Writing in the Ancient World.* (Ann Arbor: Kelsey Museum of Archaeology), 4.

45. Finley, *The Legacy of Greece*, 3.

46. Albertine Gaur, *A History of Writing.* (London: The British Library, 1987), 156.

47. Robert Pattison, *On Literacy.* (New York: Oxford University Press, 1982), 57.

48. G.E.R. Lloyd, "Science and Mathematics," in Finley, *The Legacy of Greece,* 262.

49. William V. Harris, *Ancient Literacy.* (Cambridge: Harvard University Press, 1989), 56.

50. For example: "Herodotus' *Histories* were composed in written form to be read in public." Kathryn Payne, "Information Collection and Transmission in Classical Greece," *Libri* 1993, vol. 43 no. 4: 278.

51. C.B.F. Walker, "Cuneiform," in J.T. Hooker, ed., *Reading the Past: Ancient Writings from Cuneiform to the Alphabet.* (Berkeley: University of California Press, 1990), 49.

52. Durant, *Our Oriental Heritage*, 161.

53. Samuel Kramer, *From the Tablets of Sumer.* (Indian Hills, CO: Falcon's Wing Press, 1956), 254.

54. Alfred Hessel, *A History of Libraries.* Trans. Reuben Peiss. (New Brunswick, N.J.: The ScarecrowPress,1955), 2.

55. Shubert, "The Oriental Origins of the Alexandrian Library," 163.

56. James W. Thompson, *Ancient Libraries.* (Berkeley: University of California Press, 1940), 2.

57. Thompson, *Ancient Libraries*, 15.

58. Thompson, *Ancient Libraries*, 17.

59. Goody, *Literacy in Traditional Societies*, 55.

60. Ibid.

61. Durant, *The Life of Greece.* (New York: Simon & Schuster, 1939), 600.

62. Thompson, *Ancient Libraries*, 23.

63. Shubert, "The Oriental Origins of the Alexandrian Library," 143.

64. Innis, *The Bias of Communication*, 7.

65. Marshall McLuhan and Bruce Powers, T*he Global Village.* (New York: Oxford University Press, 1989), 137.

66. Durant, *The Age of Faith.* (New York: Simon & Schuster, 1950), 910-12.

67. Durant, *Our Oriental Heritage*, 357.

68. Daniels, *The World's Writing Systems*, 2.

69. Durant, *Our Oriental Heritage*, 675-76.

70. Durant, *Our Oriental Heritage*, 652.

71. Steven Fischer, *A History of Writing*, 101.

72. Diego de Landa, of the Monastery of Izamal, Yucatan. Reported in Dard Hunter, *Papermaking: The History and Technique of an Ancient Craft.* (New York: Dover Publications, 1978), 26.

CHAPTER 2 — PRINTING: REPRODUCING INFORMATION

1. Robert Pattison, *On Literacy.* (Oxford University Press, 1982), 88.

2. Thomas F. Carter, *The Invention of Printing in China and Its Spread Westward*, 2nd ed. (New York: Ronald Press, 1955), 32.

3. T. Tsien, "Why Paper and Printing Were Invented First in China and Used Later in Europe," in Li Guohao et al., *Explorations in the History of Science and Technology in China.* (Shanghai Chinese Publishing House, 1982), 459.

4. W. Kim, *A Brief History of Metal Type Printing in the Lee dynasty.* (Seoul: Hyangtoseoul, 1958), 7.

5. Ibid.

6. William A. Mason, *A History of the Art of Writing.* (New York: The MacMillan Co., 1920), 456.

7. Nicolas de Clamanges in his tract *De Ruina et Reparatione Ecclesia.* (*The Ruin and Reform of the Church*), reported in Barbara W. Tuchman, *A Distant Mirror: The Calamitous 14th Century.* (Alfred A. Knopf, 1978), 485.

8. Carter, *The Invention of Printing in China and Its Spread Westward*, 157.

9. Carter, *The Invention of Printing in China and Its Spread Westward*, 112.

10. Jixing, Pan, *History of Chinese Science and Technology: Papermaking and Printing.* (Beijing: Kexue, 1998), 22-23.

11. Carter, *The Invention of Printing in China and Its Spread Westward*, x.

12. Carter, *The Invention of Printing in China and Its Spread Westward* , 174.

13. Siva Vaidhyanathan, *The Anarchist in the Library.* (New York: Basic Books, 2004), 107.

14. Kenneth Clark, *Civilization.* (New York: Harper & Row, 1969), 17.

15. Lucien Febvre and Henri-Jean Martin, *The Coming of the Book: The Impact of Printing, 1450-1800.* Trans. French edition, 1958. (London: Verso Editions, 1984), 20.

16. Natalie Davis, "Printing and the People: Early Modern France," in *Literacy and Social Development in the West: A Reader*, ed. Harvey J. Graff. (Cambridge University Press, 1981), 85.

17. Barbara Tuchman, *A Distant Mirror: The Calamitous 14th Century.* (Alfred A. Knopf, 1978), 581.

18. Herbert J. Altschull, *Agents of Power.* (New York: Longman, 1984), 4.

19. Tuchman, *A Distant Mirror*, 594.

20. Frank J. Krompak, "Communication Before America," in T*he Media in America*, William Sloan, et. al., eds. (Worthington, OH: Publishing Horizons, 1989), 16.

21. Albert Kapr, *Johann Gutenberg: The Man and His Invention*, tr. by Douglas Martin,. (Aldershot, England: Scolar Press, 1996), 15.

22. Mason, *A History of the Art of Writing*, 468-69.

23. David Vincent, *Literacy and Popular Culture.* (Cambridge: Cambridge University Press, 1989), 9.

24. Elizabeth Eisenstein, "Some Conjectures about the Impact of Printing on Western Society and Thought: A Preliminary Report," *The Journal of Modern History*, March, 1968: 40.

25. Tuchman, *A Distant Mirror*, 453.

26. Will Durant, *The Reformation, Vol 5. of The Story of Civilization.* (Simon and Schuster, 1957), 784.

27. Ithiel de Sola Pool, *Technologies of Freedom.* (Harvard University Press, 1983), 14.

28. Febvre and Martin, *The Coming of the Book*, 60.

29. Elizabeth Eisenstein, "Some Conjectures about the Impact of Printing on Western Society and Thought." 7.

30. Tuchman, *A Distant Mirror*, 60.

31. Kenneth Clark, *Civilization.* (New York: Harper & Row, 1969), 159-60.

32. Durant, *The Reformation*, 123.

33. Elizabeth L. Eisenstein, *The Printing Revolution in Early Modern Europe.* (Cambridge University Press, 1983), 274.

34. Will Durant, *The Age of Napoleon. Vol 11. of The Story of Civilization.* (Simon and Schuster, 1980), 137-38.

35. Febvre and Martin, *The Coming of the Book*, 242.

36. Ibid.

37. A study of social groups in the diocese of Norwich, England, 1580-1700, estimates 89% illiteracy among women of all classes. See David Cressy, "Levels of Illiteracy in England, 1530-1730," *Historical Journal*, Cambridge University Press, 1977: 1-23.

38. Durant, *The Reformation*, 157.

39. Lawrence Stone, "The Thirst for Learning," in Norman Cantor and Michael Werthman, *The History of Popular Culture*. (Macmillan, 1968), 279.

40. William Manchester, *A World Lit Only by Fire: The Medieval Mind and the Renaissance*. (Boston: Little, Brown and Company, 1992), 98.

41. Benedict Anderson, *Imagined Communities: Reflections on the Origin and Spread of Nationalism*. (London: Verso, 1991), 44.

42. C.D. Selwyn-Jones, "The Origins of English Orthography." http://www.lit-notes.co.uk/spelling.htm.

43. Eisenstein, "Some Conjectures about the Impact of Printing on Western Society and Thought," 5.

44. Durant, *The Reformation*, 849.

45. Manchester, *A World Lit Only by Fire*, 106.

46. Durant, *The Reformation*, 320.

47. Pattison, *On Literacy*, 113.

48. Durant, *The Reformation*, 160.

49. Durant, *The Reformation*, 425-6.

50. Henri-Jean Martin, *The History and Power of Writing*. Trans. Lydia G. Cochrane. (Chicago: University of Chicago Press, 1994), 266.

51. William A. Mason, *A History of the Art of Writing*, 454

52. Febvre and Martin, *The Coming of the Book*, 153.

53. Adam Nicolson, *God's Secretaries: The Making of the King James Bible.* (New York: HarperCollins, 2003) 247.

54. Durant, *The Age of Faith*. (New York: Simon & Schuster, 1949), 907.

55. *Leonard Shlain, The Alphabet Versus the Goddess. (New York: Viking, 1998)* 342, 354, 361.

56. Carter, *The Invention of Printing in China and Its Spread Westward*, 3.

57. Carter, *The Invention of Printing in China and Its Spread Westward*, 136.

58. Harold A. Innis, *The Bias of Communication*. (University of Toronto Press, 1951), 24-9.

59. Albertine Gaur, *A History of Writing*. (London: The British Library, 1987), 46.

60. James Burke, "Communication in the Middle Ages," in David Crowley and Paul Heyer, *Communication in History*. (New York: Longman, 1991), 75-76.

61. Douglas C. McMurtrie, *The Book*. (New York: Dorset Press, 1989), 67.

62. Morse Peckham, *Beyond the Tragic Vision*. (New York: George Braziller, 1962), 25-27.

63. Febvre and Martin, 39-40.

64. R.R. Bolgar, "The Greek Legacy," in M.I. Finley, ed., *The Legacy of Greece*. (Oxford University Press, 1984), 452.

65. Steven Roger Fischer, *A History of Writing*. (London: Reaktion Books, Ltd., 2001) 264.

1. Mitchell Stephens, *A History of News*. (Viking, 1986), 153.

2. Alvin W. Gouldner, *The Dialectic of Ideology and Technology*. (Oxford University Press, 1976), 92.

3. Lucien Febvre and Henri-Jean Martin, *The Coming of the Book: The Impact of Printing 1450-1800*. Trans. French edition, 1958. (London: Verso Editions, 1984), 208-11.

4. Febvre and Martin, *The Coming of the Book*, 210-11.

5. Elizabeth Eisenstein, *The Printing Revolution in Early Modern Europe*. (Cambridge University Press, 1983), 93.

6. Anthony Smith, "Technology and Control: The Interactive Dimensions of Journalism," in James Curran, et. al., eds., *Mass Communication and Society*. (London: Edward Arnold, Ltd., 1977), 176.

7. Wayne E. Fuller, *The American Mail*. (Chicago: University of Chicago Press, 1972), 116.

8. Michael Schudson, *Discovering the News*. (Basic Books, Inc., 1978), 46.

9. Schudson, *Discovering the News*, 19.

10. Theodore Glasser, "The Role of the Press and the Value of Journalism," *Focus*, University of Minnesota, Fall, 1988: 8.

11. It was first called: *A Weekly Review of the Affairs of France*.

12. *Worcester Magazine*, III, 181. (first week, July 1787).

13. Carl Bode, "Popular Magazines," in Norman Cantor and Michael Werthman, *The History of Popular Culture*. (New York: Macmillan, 1968), 485.

14. James P. Wood, *The Story of Advertising*. (New York: Ronald Press, 1958), 444.

15. Richard B. Kielbowicz, *News in the Mail: The Press, Post Office, and Public Information, 1700-1860s*. (New York: Greenwood Press, 1989), 121.

16. Adam Nicolson, *God's Secretaries: The Making of the King James Bible*. (New York: HarperCollins, 2003), 236-37.

17. Reverend Enos Hitchcock, *Memoirs of the Bloomsgrove Family*. (Boston: Thomas and Andrews, 1790).

**CHAPTER 3 —
EXTENDING
READING**

18. Ann Haugland, "Edward L. Bernay's 1930 Campaign Against Dollar Books," in Ezra Greenspan and Jonathan Rose, eds., *Book History*, vol. 3. (University Park: Pennsylvania State University Press, 2000), 233.

19. William Gray and Ruth Munroe, *The Reading Interests and Habits of Adults.* (New York: Macmillan, 1929), 149.

20. B.S. NeDaniel Radosh, "The Good Book Business," *The New Yorker*, 18 December 2006: 54-57.

21. Marshall McLuhan, *Understanding Media: The Extensions of Man. (*New York: McGraw-Hill Book Co., 1964), 259.

22. CBS News, 10 March 2006.

CHAPTER 4 — MAIL: HAULING INFORMATION

1. For some opinion, see Alvin F. Harlow, *Old Post Bags.* (D. Appleton, 1938), 7.

2. The Silk Road Foundation website, http://www.silk-road.com/artl/marco-polo.shtml.

3. Herodotus, *The History* 8:98.

4. Wayne E. Fuller, *The American Mail.* (Chicago: University of Chicago Press, 1972), 4.

5. Richard R. John, *Spreading the News: The American Postal System from Franklin to Morse.* (Cambridge, MA: Harvard University Press, 1995), 14.

6. Marshall McLuhan, *Understanding Media: The Extensions of Man.* (New York: McGraw Hill, 1964), 100.

7. William Manchester, *A World Lit Only by Fire: the Medieval Mind.* (Boston: Little, Brown, 1992), 61.

8. Laurin Zilliacus, *Mail for the World.* (New York: John Day Co., 1953), 18.

9. George Walker, *Haste, Post, Haste.* (New York: Dodd, Mead & Co., 1939), 34.

10. Clyde Kelley, *United States Postal Policy.* (New York: D. Appleton and Co., 1932), 9-10.

11. Richard B. Kielbowicz, *News in the Mail: The Press, Post Office, and Public Information, 1700-1860s.* (New York: Greenwood Press, 1989), 21.

12. Carl H. Scheele, *A Short History of the Mail Service.* (Smithsonian Institution Press, 1970).

13. John, *Spreading the News*, 25.

14. Fuller, *The American Mail*, 90.

15. Richard B. Kielbowicz, "Post Office and the Media," in Margaret Blanchard, ed., *History of Mass Media in the United States.* (Chicago: Fitzroy Dearborn Publishers, 1998) 525.

16. Siva Vaidhyanathan, *The Anarchist in the Library.* (New York: Basic Books, 2004), 102.

17. Richard K. Craille, ed., *Speeches of John C. Calhoun.* (New York, 1864), 190.

18. Kielbowicz, *News in the Mail,* 57.

19. Zilliacus, *Mail for the World,* 147.

20. http://www.scholars.nus.edu.sg/landow/victorian/history/letters/crowdy.html

21. Mauritz Hallgren, *All About Stamps.* (New York: Alfred A. Knopf, 1940), 47.

22. Rowland Hill, "Post Office Reform: Its Importance and Practicability," pamphlet, 1836.

23. H.W. Hill, *Rowland Hill and the Fight for Penny Post.* (London: Frederick Warne & Co., 1940), 13.

24. Hallgren, *All About Stamps,* 56-57.

25. Hill, *Rowland Hill and the Fight for Penny Post,* 20.

26. Zilliacus, *Mail for the World,* 163.

27. David Vincent, *Literacy and Popular Culture.* (Cambridge: Cambridge University Press, 1989), 52.

28. Vincent, *Literacy and Popular Culture,* 37.

29. James H. Bruns, *Mail on the Move.* (Polo, IL: Transportation Trails, 1992), 89.

30. Daniel J. Boorstin, *The Americans: The Democratic Experience.* (New York: Random House, 1973), 135.

31. Ibid.

32. Gerald Cullinan, *The United States Postal Service.* (New York: Praeger Publishers, 1968), 192-93.

33. S.F. Spira, *The History of Photography: As Seen Through the Spira Collection.* (New York: Aperture Foundation, 2001) 124.

CHAPTER 5 — TELEGRAPH AND TELEPHONE WIRES: REMOVING DISTANCE

1. Grga Novak, "The Adriatic sea in conflicts and battles through centuries," http://www.crwflags.com/fotw/flags/gr_ancgr.html.

2. For details, see Tom Standage, *The Victorian Internet: The Remarkable Story of the Telegraph and the Nineteenth Century's On-line Pioneers.* (New York: Walker Publishing Co., 1998), 50-56.

3. George P. Oslin, *The Story of Telecommunications.* (Macon, GA: Mercer University Press, 1992), 16.

4. Standage, *The Victorian Internet,* 166-69.

5. Oslin, *The Story of Telecommunications,* 127.

6. Standage, *The Victorian Internet*, 205, 213.

7. Oslin, *The Story of Telecommunications*, 161.

8. Edward Cornish, "The Coming of an Information Society," *The Futurist*, April 1981: 14.

9. Daniel J. Czitrom, *Media and the American Mind*. (University of North Carolina Press, 1982), 18.

10. Francis Williams, *Transmitting World News*. (UNESCO, 1953), 19.

11. William Sloan, James Stovall and James Startt, *The Media in America*. (Worthington, OH: Publishing Horizons, 1989), 204.

12. James R. Beniger, *The Control Revolution*. (Cambridge: Harvard University Press, 1986), 253.

13. In the United States, it is known as Reuters, not Reuter, due to the erroneous title of a popular Hollywood movie, *A Disptach from Reuters*. Life sometimes imitates art.

14. John Brooks, *Telephone: The First Hundred Years*. (New York: Harper & Row, 1976), 94.

15. Before email became so widely used, the author periodically asked students to identify the one communication device in the home they would be most reluctant to lose; invariably it was the telephone.

16. Oslin, *The Story of Telecommunications*, 220.

17. George Basalla, *The Evolution of Technology*. (Cambridge University Press, 1988), 98.

18. Marion May Dilts, *The Telephone in a Changing World*. (New York: Longman's Green, 1941), 11.

19. Dilts, *The Telephone in a Changing World*, 15.

20. Oslin, *The Story of Telecommunications*, 227.

21. Dilts, *The Telephone in a Changing World*, 10.

22. A few years ago the fire department of the upper income Los Angeles suburb of Bel Air for a time had an unlisted number.

23. http://www.webbconsult.com/1800.html.

24. Sylvester Baxter, "The Telephone Girl," *The Outlook*, 26 May 1906: 235.

25. Oslin, *The Story of Telecommunications*, 281.

26. Thomas L. Friedman, *The World Is Flat*. (New York: Farrar, Straus, and Giroux, 2005), 10.

27. Beniger, *The Control Revolution*, 285.

28. Eli Wathne and Carlos Reos, "Facsimile Machines," in Grant, August E., and Kenton T. Wilkinson, eds., *Communication Technology Update*, 1993-1994. (Austin: Technology Futures, Inc., 1993), 286.

29. Kimberly Ann Vavrek, "Videophone," in Grant, et. al. 321-23.

30. CNN, 4 August 2003.

31. *Time*, 13 March 2006: 29.

32. Private communication from Kenneth Doyle, University of Minnesota School of Journalism and Mass Communication.

33. *Newsweek*, 20 March 2006: 80.

1. *100 Photographs That Changed the World.* (New York: Life Books, 2003), 7.

2. Mitchell Stephens, *The Rise of the Image, the Fall of the Word.* (New York: Oxford University Press, 1998).

3. Richard G. Tansey and Horst de la Croix, *Art Through the Ages.* (Harcourt Brace Jovanovich, 1986)

4. See Geoffrey Batchen, *Each Wild Idea.* (Cambridge: MIT Press, 2001), 4.

5. *MacMillan Magazine*, September 1871, quoted in Gus Macdonald, *Camera: A Victorian Eyewitness.* (London: Bastford, 1979), 5.

6. Daniel J. Boorstin, *The Americans: The Democratic Experience.* (New York: Random House, 1973), 398.

7. Henry Mayhew, *London Labour and the London Poor*, 1851-62.

8. Peter Marshall, http://photography.about.com/cs/documentary/a/a041504_4.htm.

9. Richard Hofstadter, *The Progressive Movement*, 1900-1915. (Simon & Schuster, 1963).

10. Found at http://www.spartacus.schoolnet.co.uk/IRhine.htm.

11. Jeff Howe, "The Rise of Crowdsourcing," *Wired*, June 2006:177-83.

12. Batchen, *Each Wild Idea,* 179.

13. Arthur Goldsmith, "Reinventing the Image," *Popular Photography*, March 1990: 49.

14. Boorstin, 371.

15. *Time*, 25 December 2006: 63-64.

**CHAPTER 6 —
PHOTOGRAPHY:
CAPTURING THE EYE**

1. Speech at the American Museum of the Moving Image, 24 February, 1994.

2. Ian C. Jarvie, *Hollywood's Overseas Campaign: The North Atlantic Movie Trade, 1920-1950.* (Cambridge University Press, 1992), 299.

3. Miriam Hansen, *Babel and Babylon: Spectatorship in American Silent Film.* (Cambridge: Harvard University Press, 1991), 63.

4. Leo Rosten, *Hollywood, the Movie Colony and the Movie Makers.* (Harcourt Brace & Co., 1941), 7-12.

5. Harry M. Geldud, *The Birth of the Talkies: From Edison to Jolson.* (Indiana University Press, 1975), 28.

**CHAPTER 7 —
MOTION PICTURES:
SHARING EMOTIONS**

6. David Shipman, *The Story of Cinema*. (Englewood Cliffs: Prentice-Hall, 1982), 18.

7. David Nasaw, *Going Out: The Rise and Fall of Public Amusements*. (New York: Basic Books, 1993), 152-3.

8. Lloyd R. Morris, *Not So Long Ago*. (New York: Random House, 1949), 29.

9. Hansen, *Babel and Babylon*, 117.

10. Morris, *Not So Long Ago*, 34-35.

11. Nasaw, *Going Out: The Rise and Fall of Public Amusements*, 167.

12. Simon Patten, *Product and Climax*. (New York: B.W. Huebsch, 1909), 18-19.

13. Rosten, *Hollywood, the Movie Colony and the Movie Makers*, 7-12.

14. Raymond Fielding, "The Technological Antecedents of the Coming of Sound: An Introduction," in E.W. Cameron. (ed) *Sound and the Cinema*. (New York: Redgrave Publishing Co., 1980), 5.

15. Ellis, Jack C., *A History of Film*, 2nd ed. (Englewood Cliffs: Prentice-Hall, 1985), 152.

16. Shipman, *The Story of Cinema*, 389.

17. Daniel J. Boorstin, *The Image, or What Happened to the American Dream*. (New York: Atheneum, 1961), 127-8.

18. http://www.filmsite.org/index.html

19. Faith Popcorn, *The Popcorn Report: The Future of Your Company, Your World, Your Life*. (New York: Doubleday, 1991).

20. http://searchsecurity.techtarget.com/sDefinition/0,,sid14_gci956291,00.html.

21. Robert Putnam, *Bowling Alone: The Collapse and Revival of American Community*. (New York: Simon & Schuster, 2000).

22. Time, 14 August 2006, 75.

23. *New York Times*, 10 December 2006: Sec. 2:30.

24. See, for example, David Biedny, "Movie Magic," *MacUser*, August, 1993: 92ff.

25. James Lardner, *Fast Forward*. (New York: W.W. Norton, 1987), 68.

26. *The Wall Street Journal*, 19 September 1989, Bl.

27. See, for example, Robert Putnam's comments, *Bowling Alone: The Collapse and Revival of American Community*.

28. David Denby, "Big Pictures," *The New Yorker*, 8 January 2007: 56, 62.

29. *Minneapolis Star Tribune*, 6 March 1989: 1E.

1. *The New Yorker*, 6 June 2005: 94.

2. George P. Oslin, *The Story of Telecommunications*. (Macon, GA: Mercer University Press, 1992), 227.

3. Daniel Marty, *An Illustrated History of Phonographs*. (New York: Dorset Press, 1981), 18.

4. Marty, *An Illustrated History of Phonographs*, 71.

5. B.L. Aldridge, *The Victor Talking Machine Company*. (Camden, NJ: RCA Sales Corp., 1964), 118.

6. *Harper's Magazine*, September, 1893, 726.

7. Carolyn Marvin, *When Old Technologies Were New*. (New York: Oxford University Press, 1988), 203.

8. Erik Østergaard, http://www.danbbs.dk/~erikoest/nipper.htm.

9. David Lander, "Technology Makes Music," *Invention and Technology*, Spring/Summer, 1990: 63.

10. Andrew F. Inglis, *Behind the Tube: A History of Broadcast Technology and Business*. (New York: Focal Press, 1990), 19-20.

11. Christopher H. Sterling and John M. Kittross, *Stay Tuned: A Concise History of American Broadcasting*. (Belmont, CA: Wadsworth Publishing Co., 2nd ed., 1990), 339-41.

12. Gary Gumpert, *Talking Tombstones and Other Tales of the Media Age*. (New York: Oxford University Press, 1987), 91.

13. Rebecca Ann Lind, "You Can Take It With You: Uses and Gratifications of the Personal Stereo." Unpublished M.A. thesis, University of Minnesota, 1989: 1.

14. Richard Hollander, *Video Democracy*. (Mt. Airy, MD: Lomond Publications, 1985), 132.

15. J.M. Fenster, "How Bing Crosby Brought You Audiotape," *Invention and Technology*, Fall 1994: 58.

16. "John (Jack) T. Mullin. (1913-99) Recalls the American Development of the Tape Recorder," at http://community.mcckc.edu/crosby/mullin.htm.

17. Timothy J. Mellonig, "DCC and MD," in Grant, August E., and Kenton T. Wilkinson, eds., Communication Technology Update, 1993-1994. (Austin: Technology Futures, Inc., 1993), 191-96.

18. Steven Levy, *The Perfect Thing*. (New York: Simon & Schuster, 2006), 34.

19. *New York Times*, 29 June, 2003, op-ed page column by Thomas Friedman.

20. Fred T. Hofstetter, "Is Multimedia the Next Literacy?" *Educators Tech Exchange*, Winter 1994: 7

21. *Newsweek*, 27 February, 1995: 29.

**CHAPTER 8 —
RECORDING:
CAPTURING THE EAR**

22. Forrester Research, posted 16 July, 2003.

23. *New York Times*, 20 April, 2003.

24. Siva Vaidhyanathan, *The Anarchist in the Library*. (New York: Basic Books, 2004), 99.

25. *Time*, 5 May, 2003: 61ff.

26. http://www.gnutella.com/news/4210, posted 3 December 2001.

27. Marshall McLuhan, *Understanding Media: The Extensions of Man*. McGraw-Hill Book Co., 1964, 283.

28. Steven Levy, *The Perfect Thing,*, 207.

CHAPTER 9 —
RADIO:
HEARING VOICES

1. Gavin Weightman, *Signor Marconi's Magic Box*. (London: HarperCollins Publishers, 2003), 56.

2. Stephen N. Raymer, "Fessenden Revisited," *Pavek Museum of Broadcasting Newsletter*, Vol. 4, #4, 1993: 5.

3. Susan J. Douglas, *Inventing American Broadcasting, 1899-1922*. (Baltimore: The Johns Hopkins University Press, 1987), 15.

4. *The Russo-Japanese War*. (Tokyo: Sekai-Bunkei Publishing Co., 1971), 30.

5. Doubt has been cast upon the generally accepted report that the broadcast took place on Christmas Eve. It may have occurred a few days earlier, on December 21, 1906. Similar doubts were not raised about the content of the transmission. See: Donna L. Halper and Christopher H. Sterling, "Fessenden's Christmas Eve Broadcast: Reconsidering an Historic Event," *AWA Review* 19. (2006).

6. *New York Times*, 14 February, 1909: 1.

7. Louise M. Benjamin, "In Search of the Sarnoff 'Radio Music Box' Memo," *Journal of Broadcasting and Electronic Media*, Summer, 1993, and "In Search of the Sarnoff 'Radio Music Box' Memo: Nally's Reply," *Journal of Radio Studies*, volume IX, issue 1. (2002).

8. Robert W. McChesney, "Press-Radio Relations and the Emergence of Network, Commercial Broadcasting in the United States, 1930-1935" *Historical Journal of Film, Radio & Television*, vol 11, issue 1, 1991: 41.

9. Erik Barnouw, *The Sponsor*. (New York: Oxford University Press, 1978), 16.

10. Speech to the Third National Radio Conference, October 1924.

11. *Printers' Ink*, 27 April 1922.

12. James R. Beniger, *The Control Revolution*. (Harvard University Press, 1986), 367.

13. Ithiel de Sola Pool, *Technologies of Freedom*. (Harvard University Press, 1983), 122.

14. David Sarnoff, "Television Progress," *Broadcast News*, December, 1947: 26.

15. George P. Oslin, *The Story of Telecommunications.* (Macon, GA: Mercer University Press, 1992), 283.

16. Douglas, *Inventing American Broadcasting, 1899-1922*, 308.

17. Essay found in de Forest archives, reported in Stephen Greene, "Who Said Lee de Forest Was the 'Father of Radio'?" Unpublished paper, 1991.

18. McChesney, "Press-Radio Relations...": 41.

19. Orange E. McMeans, "The Great Audience Invincible," *Scribner's Magazine*, April, 1923: 411.

20. Robert L. Hilliard and Michael C. Keith, *The Broadcast Century and Beyond: A Biography of American Broadcasting.* (Woburn, MA: Focal Press, 2001), 57.

21. James Rorty, "Radio Comes Through," *The Nation,* 15 October 1938.

22. Disagreement exists over the extent of the "golden age" of radio. For example, Sterling and Kittross, in their excellent *Stay Tuned,* limit it to 1934-1941.

23. Christopher H. Sterling and John M. Kittross, *Stay Tuned: A Concise History of American Broadcasting.* (Belmont, CA: Wadsworth Publishing Co., 2nd ed., 1990), 239.

24. James Gillies and Robert Cailliau, *How the Web Was Born.* (New York: Oxford University Press, 2000), 47.

25. According to *Broadcasting/Cable Yearbook 2002-2003*, there were 4,727 commercial AM stations, 6,051 commercial FM stations, and 2,234 non-commercial FM stations. Other figures: 1,686 TV stations. (1,748 by 2005), 11,800 cable systems, most of them offering 60 or more channels. TV was in more than 105 million (98%) of U.S. homes, of which 91% also had a VCR, 69% also had cable.

26. Michael Wusterhausen, "AM Stereo Radio," in Grant, August E., and Kenton T. Wilkinson, eds., *Communication Technology Update, 1993-1994.* (Austin: Technology Futures, Inc., 1993), 121.

CHAPTER 10 — TELEVISION: LEANING BACK

1. Asa Briggs and Peter Burke, *A Social History of the Media: From Gutenberg to the Internet.* (Cambridge, UK: Polity Press, 2002), 252.

2. Marshall McLuhan, *Understanding Media: The Extensions of Man.* (New York: McGraw-Hill Book Co., 1964), 195.

3. *Newsweek*, 17 October, 1988: 84.

4. Bob Baker, *Los Angeles Times*, 13 April, 2003.

5. *The Economist*, 13 February, 1994: 12.

6. Edmund Carpenter, *Explorations in Communication.* (Boston: Beacon Press, 1960), 165.

7. Neil Postman, *Amusing Ourselves to Death*. (New York: Viking Penguin, 1985), 92.

8. Todd Gitlin, "Flat and Happy," *Wilson Quarterly*, Autumn, 1993: 48.

9. Speech to the 1961 convention of the National Association of Broadcasters.

10. Testimony before the FCC, 1961.

11. *New York Times* article, reprinted in the *Minneapolis Star Tribune*, 5 August, 2004: E5.

12. Christopher Sterling and John Kittross, *Stay Tuned,*. (Belmont, CA: Wadsworth, 1990), 418.

13. Richard Ohmann, *Selling Culture: Magazines, Markets, and Class at the Turn of the Century*. (London: Verso, 1996), 11-12.

14. Steven Johnson, *Everything Bad Is Good for You*. (New York: Riverhead Books, 2005), 159.

15. George A. Wiley, "End of an Era: The Daytime Radio Serial," *Journal of Broadcasting*, Spring, 1961: 110.

16. Leonard Downie Jr. and Robert G. Kaiser, *The News About the News*. (New York: Alfred A. Knopf, 2002), 172.

17. Sterling and Kittross, *Stay Tuned*, 582,

18. Matt Stump and Harry Jessell, "Cable: The First Forty Years," *Broadcasting*, 21 November, 1988: 42.

19. Lloyd Trufelman, Cable Television Advertising Bureau.

20. Larry King, *On the Line*. (New York: Harcourt Brace & Co., 1993), 176.

21. Written on the occasion of CBS's 50th birthday, 1977.

22. Address to Radio Television News Directors Association, 1 January, 1952.

23. E.B. White, *Harper's Magazine*, October, 1938, written when television began to attract public notice for its future potential.

**CHAPTER 11 —
COMPUTERS
AND THE INTERNET:
LEANING FORWARD**

1. Pew Internet & American Life Project, 2005.

2. See, for example, *Wired*, August 2005: 96.

3. *The Digital Futures Report, Year Four*. (Los Angeles:Annenberg School, USC.), 97.

4. Will Wright, "Dream Machines," *Wired*, April, 2006: 112.

5. Martin Greenberger, ed., *Management and Computers of the Future*. (Cambridge: The MIT Press, 1962), 8.

6. Michael Hauben, "The Social Forces Behind the Development of Usenet." http://www.columbia.edu/~rh120/ch106.x03. Also in *Netizens*. (Los Alamitos, CA: IEEE Computer Society Press, 1997), 48.

7. Tim Berners-Lee, *Weaving the Web*. (San Francisco: Harper, 1999), 18.

8. Michael Dertouzos, foreword to Tim Berners-Lee, *Weaving the Web*. (San Francisco: Harper, 1999), ix.

9. *San Francisco Chronicle*, 20 December 2004.

10. *Time*, 8 May 2006: 78.

11. http://www.cnn.com/SPECIALS/2005/online.evolution/

12. *Wired*, February 2005: 65.

13. *Time*, 16 June, 2003: 51.

14. *Murphy Reporter*, Minneapolis: University of Minnesota School of Journalism and Mass Communication, Summer 2006: 10.

15. *The Digital Futures Report*, Year Four. 24.

16. David Glidden, professor of philosophy, University of California, in *Minneapolis Star Tribune*, 30 May, 1989.

17. Michael Hauben, "The Social Forces Behind the Development of Usenet," 123.

18. Abigail Sellen and Richard Harper, *The Myth of the Paperless Office*. (Cambridge, MA: MIT Press, 2002), 13.

19. CBS News, 19 August 2005.

20. Brad Stone, "Right to the Top," *Newsweek*, 9 January 2006: 38.

21. Steven Johnson, *Everything Bad Is Good for You*. (New York: Riverhead Books, 2005), 120.

22. *Time*, 15 August, 1994: 6.

23. *Newsweek*, 17 April 2006: 14.

24. "The Secret World of Lonelygirl15," *Wired*, December 2006: 236-39.

25. Michael Duffy, *Time*, 27 March 2006.

26. Terry Mattingly, Scripps Howard News Service, in *Minneapolis Star Tribune*, 28 June, 2003, B7.

27. *New York Times*, 14 December 2004: A1.

28. Nathan Shapira, et. al., "Problematic internet use: Proposed classification and diagnostic criteria," *Depression and Anxiety*, 17:4, 2003: 217.

29. http://www.caslon.com.au/addictionnote.htm.

30. Steven Levy, *Crypto*. (New York: Penguin Books, 2001), 1.

31. Bruce Mehlman and Larry Irving, Internet Innovation Alliance, *Minneapolis Star Tribune*, 29 May 2007: A9.

32. Quoted in Michael Specter, Kremlin, Inc., *The New Yorker*, 29 January 2007: 61.

33. *Time*, 25 December 2006: 50, 53.

34. Michael Flanagan, Michigan Superintendent of Public Instruction quoted in *Time*, 18 December 2006: 56.

35. *"Small-town school is big on the Web,"* *Minneapolis Star Tribune*, 10 November 2006: A4.

36. *Minneapolis Star Tribune*, 27 November 2006: D1

37. John Matthias and James Twedt, "TeleJustice—Videoconferencing for the 21st Century," 1997, at http://ctl.ncsc.dni.us/bbsfiles/ctc5_rom/208.htm.

38. Marcia Kelly, "Work-at-home," *The Futurist*, November/December 1988: 32.

39. Toffler, *The Third Wave*. (New York: William Morrow, 1980), 210-23.

40. Irving Fang, *A History of Mass Communication: Six Information Revolutions*. (Newton, MA: Butterworth-Heinemann, 1997).

41. See Manuel Castells, *The Information Age: Economy, Society, and Culture.* (New York: Oxford University Press, three volumes, 1996-98.)

42. Peter Leyden, "Teleworking could turn our cities inside out," *Minneapolis Star Tribune*, 5 September, 1993:1A, 16A.

43. *Minneapolis Star Tribune*, 7 January 2004: 1A.

44. *The Digital Futures Report, Year Four*, 21.

45. Lawrence Tesler, vice-president, Advanced Technology Apple Corp.

46. Chris Anderson, *The Long Tail*. (New York: Hyperion, 2006), 2, 5, 17, 27-28.

**CHAPTER 12:
PLAYING
VIDEO GAMES**

1. http://www.videotopia.com/intro.htm

2. Steven Johnson, *Everything Bad Is Good for You*. (New York: Riverhead Books, 2005), 41.

3. Mark J.P. Wolf, ed. *The Medium of the Video Game*. Austin: University of Texas Press, 2000), 177.

4. *Time*, Asia edition, at http://www.time.com/time/asia magazine/2000/0501/japan.essaymurakami.html

5. Brian Southwell and Kenneth Doyle, "The Good, the Bad, or the Ugly?" *American Behavioral Scientist*, 48:4 December 2004, 393.

6. http://news.gamewinners.com/index.php/news/2238/. Posted 9 December 2004.

7. James C. Rosser, Jr., et. al., "The Impact of Video Games on Training Surgeons in the 21st Century," *Archives of Surgery*, Vol 142 no. 2, February 2007: 181-86.

8. Ted Friedman, "Making Sense of Software: Computer Games and Interactive Textuality," in *Cybersociety*, ed. Steven G. Jones. (Thousand Oaks, CA: Sage Publications, 1995). Taken from: http://www.duke.edu/~tlove/simcity.htm.

9. James Paul Gee. *What Video Games Have to Teach Us About Learning and Literacy*. (New York: Palgrave Macmillan, 2004), 13.

10. Will Wright, "Dream Machines," *Wired*, April, 2006: 112.

11. Gee, 207-12.

12. Patricia Marks Greenfield, *Mind and Media: The Effects of Television, Video Games, and Computers.* (Cambridge: Harvard University Press, 1984), 101-2.

13. Geofrey R. Loftus and Elizabeth F. Loftus, *Mind at Play: The Psychology of Video Games.* (New York: Basic Books, 1983), x.

14. J.C. Herz, *Joystick Nation.* (Boston: Little, Brown and Company, 1997), 172.

15. B. De Waal, "Motivations for Video Game Play." MA Thesis, School of Communication, Simon Fraser University, 1995.

16. Van Burnham, *Supercade: A Visual History of the Video Game Age 1971 - 1984.* (Cambridge: MIT Press, 2001), 234.

17. Greenfield, *Mind and Media,* 108-10.

18. K.E. Scheibe and M. Erwin, "The Computer as Altar," *Journal of Social Psychology* 108. (1979), 103-9.

19. Steven Poole, *Trigger Happy: The Inner Life of Video Games.* (London: Fourth Estate, 2000), 166.

20. *The New Yorker*, 6 November 2006: 96.

21. Study headed by Dr. Vincent Mathews, Indiana University School of Medicine, reported by *Newsweek*, 28 November 2006. http://www.msnbc.msn.com/id/15938244/site/newsweek.

22. Craig Anderson, "Violent Video Games and Aggressive Thoughts, Feelings, and Behaviors," in Calvert, *Children in the Digital Ag*e, 102.

23. Testimony in 1993 Congressional hearings, reported in Kent, Steven L. *The Ultimate History of Video Games.* New York: Three Rivers Press, 2001. 471.

24. *Minneapolis Star Tribune*, 24 November 2004: B3.

25. Kaveri Subrahmanyam, Patricia Greenfield, Robert Kraut, and Elisheva Gross, "The Impact of Computer Use on Children's and Adolescent Development," in Sandra Calvert, Amy Jordan, and Rodney Cocking, eds., *Children in the Digital Age: Influences of Electronic Media on Development.* (New York: Praeger, 2002), 24-25

26. David Walsh, president, National Institute on Media and the Family, at the 1993 Congressional committee hearing. *(See note 25.)*

27. Sam Hart, "Gender and Racial Inequality in Video Games," http://www.geekcomix.com/vgh/genracinequal.shtml.

28. Steven Kent, *Minneapolis Star Tribune*, 6 November, 2004: E1,

29. Senate Committee on Commerce, Science and Transportation, 21 March, 2000.

30. Congressional testimony, reported in Kent, *The Ultimate History of Video Games*, 551.

31. Eugene Provenzo, School of Education, University of Kentucky, same 1993 Congressional hearing. *(See note 25.)*

32. *Time*, 28 February 2005: 43.

33. *Wired News*, 17 May 2004.

34. Burnham, *Supercade: A Visual History of the Video Game Age 1971-1984*, 52.

35. Gee, *What Video Games Have to Teach Us About Learning and Literacy*, 204.

36. *New York Times*, 15 October 2006: section 2:14.

37. Brad King and John Borland. *Dungeons and Dreamers: The Rise of Computer Game Culture from Geek to Chic.* (New York: McGraw-Hill/Osborne, 2003), 55.

38. *Newsweek*, 18 September 2006: 47-49.

39. King and Borland, *Dungeons and Dreamers*, 224-25.

40. King and Borland, *Dungeons and Dreamers*, 72.

41. Letter to the editor, *Newsweek*, 2 October 2006: 19.

42. King and Borland, *Dungeons and Dreamers*, 170.

43. *Wired*, April 2006.

44. Sandra Calvert, "Identity Construction on the Internet," in Calvert, op. cit., 68.

45. *Business Week*, 1 May 2006, cover story.

46. Letter to the editor, *New York Times*, 6 May 2007.

**CHAPTER 13 —
BEING PERSUASIVE**

1. Michael Emery, Edwin Emery, and Nancy Roberts, *The Press and America: An Interpretive History of the Mass Media*, 9th ed.. (Boston: Allyn and Bacon, 2000), 35.

2. Letter to Volney, 1802. quoted in Saul Padover, *Thomas Jefferson on Democracy.* (New York: Penguin Books, 1939), 92-93.

3. Letter to his friend Carrington, 1787.

4. Emery, et. al., 124.

5. *Freedom's Journal*, 16 March 1827. In Emery, et. al., 126, 128.

6. G.J. Meyer, *A World Undone: The Story of the Great War, 1914 to 1918.* (New York: Delacorte Press, 2006), 434.

7. See Syd Hoff, *Editorial and Political Cartooning.* (New York: Stravon Educational Press, 1976), 16-26.

8. Observation by Secretary of Labor Frances Perkins, who watched FDR give a radio address, reported in Daniel J. Boorstin, *The Americans: The Democratic Experience.* (Random House, 1973), 475.

9. 2 December 1941.

10. Philippe Schuwer, *History of Advertising.* (London: Leisure Arts, Ltd., 1966), 42.

11. http://www.ciadvertising.org/student_account/spring_01/adv382j/ootvas/paper2/hardsell.htm.

12. James R. Beniger, *The Control Revolution.* (Cambridge: Harvard University Press, 1986), 18.

13. Boorstin, *The Americans: The Democratic Experience*, 145.

14. Richard Ohmann, *Selling Culture: Magazines, Markets, and Class at the Turn of the Century.* (London: Verso, 1996), 106.

15. *Printers' Ink*, October 1895, cited in James Playsted Wood, *The Story of Advertising.* (New York: Ronald Press, 1958), 6-7.

16. C. Edwin Baker, *Advertising and a Democratic Press.* (Princeton: Princeton University Press, 1994), 100.

17. Wood, 13.

18. Wood, 342.

19. *New York Times*, 12 April 2005.

20. Barry Schwartz, *The Paradox of Choice: Why More Is Less.* (New York: HarperCollins, 2004), 53.

21. For a fuller discussion, see C. Edwin Baker, *Advertising and a Democratic Press.* (Princeton: Princeton University Press, 1994), 4 ff.

22. W.F. Ogborn and M.F. Nimkoff, *Sociology.* (Houghton-Mifflin, 1950), 546.

23. Edward L. Bernays, *Propaganda.* (New York: Horace Liveright, 1928), 9-10.

24. *Newsweek*, 5 June 2006: 35.

25. Francis Fukuyama, *The End of History and the Last Man*, 2nd ed. (New York: Free Press, 1993), 7.

26. *Newsweek*, 19 June 1989: 29.

27. Speech to the American Bar Association, London, 1985.

28. Siva Vaidhyanathan, *The Anarchist in the Library.* (New York: Basic Books, 2004), 116.

1. Niels-Jacob Andersen, news editor, Danish Broadcasting Corp., private communication, 23 March 2007.

2. See Olivier Roy, *Globalized Islam: The Search for a New Ummah.* (New York: Columbia University Press, 2004). Cited in Francis Fukuyama, *The End of History and the Last Man*, 2nd ed. (New York: Free Press), 348.

**CHAPTER 14 —
CROSSING
BOUNDARIES**

3. Quoted by David Brooks, *Minneapolis Star Tribune*, 11 February 2006: A17.

4. Fukuyama, *The End of History and the Last Man*, 214.

5. Lawrence Wright, "The Master Plan," *The New Yorker*, 11 September 2006: 53.

6. Aired 21 February 2006.

7. Bernard Lewis, *What Went Wrong: Western Impact and Middle Eastern Response*. (New York: Oxford University Press, 2002), 54.

8. Lewis, 52.

9. James P. Wood, *The Story of Advertising*. (New York: Ronald Press, 1958), 342.

10. Pearse, 34.

11. University of Minnesota Journalism and Mass Communication Professor Emeritus Philip Tichenor, private communication, 7 March 2006.

12. Pearse, 48.

13. Meic Pearse, *Why the Rest Hates the West: Understanding the Roots of Global Rage*. (Downers Grove, IL: InterVarsity Press, 2004), 28.

14. As an example, see Amy Waldman, "Sarendhi Journal," *New York Times*, 28 March 2003, A4.

15. *Bangkok Post*, 23 February 2002, 5.

16. Pearse, 35.

17. Lewis, 73.

18. Lewis, 70.

19. Pearse, 29.

20. Pearse, 49, 109-110.

21. David Kilcullen, quoted in David Packer, "Knowing the Enemy," *The New Yorker*, 18 December 2006: 64.

22. Robert Wright, *Nonzero*, quoted in the *New York Times*, 29 June 2003, op-ed page column by Thomas Friedman.

23. *The New Yorker*, 2 August 2004: 49.

24. Paul Kennedy, *Preparing for the Twenty-First Century*. (Toronto: Harper-Collins Publishers Ltd., 1993), 333.

25. Siva Vaidhyanathan, *The Anarchist in the Library*. (New York: Basic Books, 2004), 78-9.

26. *Minneapolis Star Tribune*, 12 October 1990: 11Ae.

27. *Newsweek*, 20 October 2003: E36.

28. Nayan Chanda, reported by Thomas Friedman, *New York Times*, 6 June 2004, WK 13.

29. Richard Oppel, *New York Times*, 10 August 2003.

30. *The Economist*, 3 February 1996: 54.

31. Thomas L. Friedman, *From Beirut to Jerusalem.* (New York: Farrar, Straus & Giroux, 1989), 33.

32. Associated Press, 8 January 1990.

33. *Minneapolis Star Tribune*, 1 December 2005: A20.

34. 24 February 2003.

35. Bruce Hoffman, Georgetown University terrorism expert, *Newsweek*, 3 September 2007.

1. *Time*, 27 March 2006.

2. Study by the Annenberg Institute of the University of Pennsylvania, 1999.

3. *Time*, 27 March 2006.

4. Edward M. Hallowell and John J. Ratey, *Delivered from Distraction.* (New York: Ballantine Books, 2005), 157.

5. Melissa C. Nelson, et. al. "Longitudinal and Secular Trends in Physical Activity and Sedentary Behavior During Adolescence," *Pediatrics*, Vol. 118 no. 6, December 2006: e-1627-e1634.

6. *Time* Asia edition, found at http://www.time.com/time/asia/magazine/2000/0501/japan.essaymurakami.html

7. For a discussion of this point, see Asa Briggs and Peter Burke, *A Social History of the Media: from Gutenberg to the Internet. (*Cambridge, UK: Polity Press, 2002), 85 ff.

8. *Washington Post*, 23 June 2006: A03.

9. *New York Times* column, reprinted in the *Minneapolis Star Tribune*, 6 November 2006: A9.

10. David Denby, "Big Pictures," *The New Yorker*, 8 January 2007: 60.

11. Lisa Segelman, "The Family Road Trip: Strangers in a Minivan," *Newsweek*, 2 July 2007.

12. Barry Schwartz, *The Paradox of Choice: Why More Is Less.* (New York: HarperCollins, 2004), 2-4.

13. Gregg Easterbrook, *Progress Paradox: How Life Gets Better While People Feel Worse.* (New York: Random House, 2003), xviii.

14. Marshall McLuhan, *The Gutenberg Galaxy.* (University of Toronto Press, 1962), 31.

15. George Will column, 21 June 2001. Located at: http://www.townhall.com/opinion/columns/georgewill/2001/06/21/165862.html.

16. Robert Putnam, *Bowling Alone: The Collapse and Revival of American Community.* (New York: Simon & Schuster, 2000).

**CHAPTER 15 —
ON MEDIATED
COMMUNICATION**

17. Miller McPherson, Lynn Smith-Lovin, and Matthew E. Brashears, "Social Isolation in America: Changes in Core Discussion Networks over Two Decades," *American Sociological Review*, June 2006: 353-75.

BIBLIOGRAPHY

Abrahamson, Albert, *Electronic Motion Pictures: A History of the Television Camera*. Berkeley: University of California Press, 1955.

A

Aldgate, Anthony, *Cinema And History*. London: Scolar Press, 1979.

Aitken, Hugh G., *Syntony & Spark: The Origins of Radio*. New York: Wiley, 1976.

Aldridge, B.L., *The Victor Talking Machine Company*. Camden, NJ: RCA Sales Corp., 1964.

Allen, Marti Lu, *The Beginning of Understanding: Writing in the Ancient World*. Ann Arbor: Kelsey Museum of Archaeology, 1991.

Altschull, Herbert J., *Agents of Power*. New York: Longman, 1984.

American Heritage of Invention & Technology; "Laying a Cable Across the Sea," fall, 1987.

Angelakos, Diogenes, and Thomas E. Everhart, *Microwave Communications*. New York: McGraw-Hill, 1968.

Anderson, Benedict, *Imagined Communities: Reflections on the Origin and Spread of Nationalism*. London: Verso , 1991.

Anderson, Chris, *The Long Tail*. New York: Hyperion, 2006.

Archer, Gleason, *The History of Radio to 1926*. New York: American Historical Society, 1938.

Asimov, Isaac, *Asimov's Biographical Encyclopedia of Science and Technology.*, 2nd revised ed. Garden City, N.Y.: Doubleday, 1982.

_____, *Is Anyone There?* Garden City, N.Y.: Doubleday, 1967.

Atkins, Larry. *More Than a Game*. Manchester: Manchester University Press, 2003.

Augarten, Stan, *Bit by Bit,* Tickenor & Fields, 1984.

Bachlin, Peter, *Newsreels Across The World*. Paris: UNESCO, 1952.

B

Baker, C. Edwin, *Advertising and a Democratic Press*. Princeton: Princeton University Press, 1994.

Baker, W.J., *The History of the Marconi Company*. London: Methuen, 1970.

Bardeche, Maurice, *The History of Motion Pictures*. New York: W.W. Norton & Co., 1938.

Barker, Joel A., *Paradigms: The Business of Discovering the Future*. Harper Business, 1992.

Barnouw, Erik, *A History of Broadcasting In the United States.* 3 vols. New York: Oxford University Press, 1966-70.

_____, *The Sponsor.* New York: Oxford University Press, 1978.

Basalla, George, *The Evolution of Technology.* Cambridge, England: Cambridge University Press, 1988.

Batchen, Geoffrey, *Each Wild Idea.* Cambridge: MIT Press, 2001.

Batra, Rajeev, and Rashi Glazer, eds., *Cable TV Advertising.* Quorum Books, 1989

Beaton, Cecil W.H., *The Magic Image.* Boston: Little, Brown, 1975.

Beaver, Frank E., *On Film: A History of the Motion Picture.* New York: McGraw-Hill, 1983.

Beck, Kirsten, *Cultivating the Wasteland.* New York: American Council for the Arts, 1983.

Begun, S.J., *Magnetic Recording.* New York: Rinehart, 1949.

Beith, John Hay, *The Post Office Went To War.* London: H.M. Stationery Office, 1946.

Beniger, James R., *The Control Revolution.* Cambridge, Mass.: Harvard University Press, 1986.

Berners-Lee, Tim, *Weaving the Web.* San Francisco: Harper, 1999.

Bijker, Wiebe E., Thomas P. Hughes, and Trevor Pinch, *The Social Construction of Technological Systems.* Cambridge, Mass.: MIT Press, 1987.

Blake, G.G., *History of Radio Telegraphy & Telephony.* New York: Arno Press, 1974.

Bliss, Edward Jr., *Now the News.* New York: Columbia University Press, 1991.

Blumenthal, Howard J., *The Media Room.* New York: Penguin Books, 1983.

Boorstin, Daniel J., *The Americans: The Democratic Experience.* Random House, 1973.

_____, *The Image, or What Happened to the American Dream.* New York: Atheneum, 1961.

Brand, Stewart, *The Media Lab.* New York: Viking Press, 1987.

Braun, E., *Revolution In Miniature: The History and Impact of Semiconductor Electronics.* Cambridge, Mass.: Cambridge University Press, 1982.

Brewer, Roy. *The Man Who Loved Letters.* Rowman and Littlefield, 1973.

Briggs, Asa, and Peter Burke, *A Social History of the Media: from Gutenberg to the Internet.* Cambridge, UK: Polity Press, 2002.

Bright, Charles, *Telegraphy, Aeronautics and War.* London: Constable & Co., 1918.

Brittain, James E., *Turning Points In American Electrical History* . New York: IEEE Press, 1977.

Brock, Gerald W., *The Telecommunications Industry.* Cambridge, Mass.: Harvard University Press, 1981.

Broecker, William L., ed., *Encyclopedia of Photography.* New York: Crown Publishers, 1984.

Brooks, John, *Telephone: The First 100 Years.* New York: Harper & Row, 1976.

Buckland, Gail, *Fox Talbot And The Invention of Photography.* Boston: D.R. Godine, 1980.

Bunnell, David, "Tracking the Revolution," *Publish!*, September/October, 1986.

Burch, Robert M., *Colour Printing & Color Printers.* London: Pitman & Sons, 1910.

Burckhardt, Jacob. *History of Greek Culture.* Trans. Palmer Hilty. New York: Frederick Ungar Publishing Co., 1963.

Burke, James, "Communication in the Middle Ages," in David Crowley and Paul Heyer, *Communication in History.* New York: Longman, 1991.

_____, *Connections.* Boston: Little, Brown & Co., 1978.

Burnham, Van. *Supercade: A visual History of the Videogame Age 1971 - 1984.* Cambridge: MIT Press, 2001.

Burrows, A.R., *The Story of Broadcasting.* New York: Cassell & Co., Ltd., 1924.

Bush, Wendell T., "An Impression of Greek Political Philosophy," *Studies in the History of Ideas,* vol. 1. New York: Columbia University Press, 1918.

Butler, Pierce, *The Origin of Printing In Europe.* Chicago: University of Chicago Press, 1940.

Butterworth, William E., *Hi Fi: From Edison's Phonograph To Quad Sound.* New York: Four Winds Press, 1977.

Calvert, Sandra , et. al., eds., *Children in the Digital Age: Influences of Electronic Media on Development* New York: Praeger, 2002.

C

Cameron, E.W., (ed), *Sound and the Cinema.* New York: Redgrave Publishing Co., 1980.

Cantor, Norman, and Michael Werthman, *The History of Popular Culture.* New York: Macmillan, 1968.

Carey, James. "Harold Adams Innis and Marshall McLuhan," *The Antioch Review,* vol. 27, 1967.

Carpenter, Edmund, *Explorations in Communication.* Boston: Beacon Press, 1960.

Carruthers, George. *Paper in the Making.* Toronto: The Garden City Press Cooperative, 1947.

Carter, Harry. *A View of Early Typography.* Oxford: Clarendon Press, 1969.

Carter, John, *Printing And The Mind of Man.* New York: Holt, Rinehart & Winston, 1967.

Carter, T.F., *The Invention of Printing in China and Its Spread Westward.* New York: Ronald Press.

Casmir, Fred L., ed., *Communication in Development.* Norwood, N.J.: Ablex Publishing Corp., 1991.

Castells, Manuel, *The Information Age: Economy, Society, and Culture.* New York: Oxford University Press, three volumes, 1996-9.

Chanan, Michael, *The Dream That Kicks.* Boston: Routledge & Kegan Paul, 1980.

Chappell, Warren, *A Short History of the Printed Word.* New York: Alfred A. Knopf, 1970.

Chase, Scott, "22,300 Miles Closer to Heaven," *Via Satellite,* December 1988.

Christie, Linda Gail, *The Simon & Schuster Guide to Computer Peripherals.* New York: Simon & Schuster, 1985.

Clark, David G., and William B. Blankenburg, *You & Media.* San Francisco: Canfield Press, 1973.

Clark, Kenneth, *Civilization.* New York: Harper & Row, 1969.

Clarke, Arthur C., *Voice Across The Sea.* New York: Harper & Row, l958.

Clarkson, Leslie, *Death, Disease and Famine in Pre-industrial England.* Dublin: Gill and Macmillan, 1975.

Coe, Brian, *The Birth of Photography.* New York: Taplinger Publishing Co., 1977.

_____, *History of Motion Picture Photography.* New York: Zoetrope, Inc., 1981.

Cohn, Angelo. *The Wonderful World of Paper.* London: Abelard-Schuman, 1967.

Collins, Douglas, *The Story of Kodak.* New York: Harry Abrams, Inc., 1990.

Cooke, William F., *The Electric Telegraph: Was It Invented by Prof. Wheatstone?* London, 1857.

Corn, Joseph J., ed., *Imagining Tomorrow* . Cambridge, Mass.: The MIT Press, 1986.

Costigan, Daniel M., *Fax: The Principles And Practice of Facsimile Communication.* Philadelphia: Chilton Book Co., 1971

Cottrell, Leonard. *The Quest for Sumer.* New York: G.P. Putnam's Sons, 1965.

Coursey, Philip R., *Telephony Without Wires.* New York: Wireless Press, Ltd., 1919.

Crawford, William, *The Keepers of Light: A History.* Dobbs Ferry, N.Y.: Morgan & Morgan, 1979.

Crosby, John, *Out of The Blue.* New York: Simon & Schuster, 1952.

Crow, John A., *Greece: The Magic Spring.* New York: Harper & Row, 1970

Crowley, David, and Paul Heyer, *Communication in History.* New York: Longman, 1991.

Cullinan, Gerald, *The United States Postal Service.* New York: Praeger, 1973.

Czitrom, Daniel J., *Media and the American Mind.* Chapel Hill, NC: University of North Carolina Press, 1982.

D Daniels, Peter T., and William Bright, eds., *The World's Writing Systems.* New York: Oxford University Press, 1996.

Davis, Charles, *The Manufacture of Paper.* New York: Arno Press, 1972.

Darnton, Robert, and Daniel Roche, eds., *Revolution in Print: The Press in France 1775-1800.* Berkeley: University of California Press, 1989.

Dayan, Daniel, and Elihu Katz, *Media Events.* Cambridge, MA: Harvard University Press, 1992.

DeForest, Lee, *Television Today and Tomorrow.* New York: Dial Press, 1942.

L. Delaporte, *Mesopotamia: The Babylonian and Assyrian Civilization.* New York: Columbia University Press, 2004.

DeLuca, Stuart M., *Television's Transformation: The Next 25 Years.* San Diego: A.S. Barnes, 1980.

Demaria, Rusel, and Johnny I. Wilson. *High Score!: The Illustrated History of Electronic Games,* 2nd ed., New York: McGraw-Hill/Osborne, 2004.

Denman, Frank, *Television: The Magic Window.* New York: Macmillan, 1952.

Deslandes, Jacques, *Histoire Comparee du Cinema.* Paris: Casterman, 1966.

Didsbury, Howard F. (ed.), *Communications and the Future.* World Future Society, Bethesda, MD, 1982.

"The Difficult Birth of the Typewriter," *American Heritage of Invention & Technology*; spring/summer, 1988.

Dilts, Marion May, *The Telephone in a Changing World.* New York: Longman's Green, 1941.

Disraeli, Isaac, *The Invention of Printing.* New York: The American Institute of Graphic Arts, 1940.

Dizard, Wilson P., *The Coming Information Age.* New York: Longman, 1982.

Dominick, Joseph R., Barry Sherman, and Gary Copeland, *Broadcasting / Cable and Beyond.* New York: McGraw-Hill, 1993.

Douglas, Susan J. *Inventing American Broadcasting, 1899-1922.* Baltimore: The Johns Hopkins University Press, 1987.

Downie, Leonard Jr. and Robert G. Kaiser, *The News About the News.* New York: Alfred A. Knopf, 2002.

Driver, G.R. *Semitic Writing: From Pictograph to Alphabet.* London: Oxford University Press, 1948.

Drucker, P.F., "The First Technological Revolution and Its Lessons," in Burke, J.G., and M.C.

Dryer, Sherman H., *Radio In Wartime.* New York: Greenberg, 1942.

Dunlap, Orrin E., *Communications In Space: From Wireless to Satellite Relay.* New York: Harper, 1962.

_____, *Communications In Space: From Marconi to Man on the Moon.* New York: Harper & Row, 1970.

_____, *Radio's 100 Men of Science.* New York: Harper & Bros., 1944.

Dunn, John, ed., *Democracy: The Unfinished Journey, 508 BC to AD 1993.* New York: Oxford University Press, 1992.

Durant, Will, *The Age of Faith, The Story of Civilization*, Vol. 4. New York: Simon & Schuster, 1949.

_____, *The Life of Greece, The Story of Civilization*, Vol. 2. New York: Simon and Schuster, 1939.

_____, *Our Oriental Heritage, The Story of Civilization*, Vol. 1. New York: Simon and Schuster, 1935.

_____, *The Reformation, The Story of Civilization*, Vol. 5. New York: Simon and Schuster, 1957.

Eaglesfield, Charles, *Laser Light: Fundamentals and Optical Communications.* New York: St. Martin's Press, 1967.

Eakin, eds., *Technology and Change.* San Francisco: Boyd & Fraser, 1979.

Eargle, John. *Handbook of Recording Engineering.* New York: Van Nostrand Reinhold, 1986.

Easterbrook, Gregg. *Progress Paradox: How Life Gets Better While People Feel Worse.* New York: Random House, 2003.

Edgerton, Harold E., *Moments of Vision: The Stroboscopic Revolution in Photography.* Cambridge, Mass.: MIT Press, 1979.

Eisenstein, Elizabeth, *The Printing Press As An Agent Of Change.* Cambridge, Mass.: Cambridge University Press, 1979.

_____, *The Printing Revolution in Early Modern Europe.* Cambridge, Mass.: Cambridge University Press, 1983.

Ellis, Jack C., *A History of Film*, 2nd ed. Englewood Cliffs: Prentice-Hall, 1979.

E

Emery, Michael, Edwin Emery, and Nancy Roberts, *The Press and America*, Ninth Edition. Englewood Cliffs, N.J.: Prentice Hall, 2000.

Ennes, Harold E., *Television Broadcasting: Tape Recording Systems.* Indianapolis: Howard W. Sams & Co., 1979.

Everson, George, *The Story of Television: The Life of Philo T. Farnsworth.* New York: W.W. Norton, 1949.

F   Fabre, Maurice, *A History of Communications.* New York: Hawthorne Books, 1963

Fang, Irving E., *The Computer Story.* St. Paul: Rada Press, 1987.

_____, *Pictures.* St. Paul: Rada Press, 1993.

_____, *Those Radio Commentators!* Ames: Iowa State University Press, 1977.

Fay, Arthur, *Bioscope Shows And Their Engines.* Lingfield: Oakwood Publishing, 1966.

Febvre, Lucien, and Henri-Jean Martin, *The Coming of the Book* . Trans. David Gerard, ed. Geoffrey Nowell-Smith and David Wooten. London: Verso, 1984.

Fedida, Sam, *Viewdata Revolution.* New York: Wiley, 1979.

Fielding, Raymond, *The American Newsreel 1911-1967.* Norman: University of Oklahoma Press, 1972.

_____, *A Technological History of Motion Pictures And Television.* Berkeley: University of California Press, 1967.

Finley, M.I., ed. *The Legacy of Greece.* Oxford University Press, 1984.

The First Decade of Television In Videotown. New York: Cunningham & Walsh, Inc., 1958.

Fischer, Steven Roger *A History of Writing.* (London: Reaktion Books, Ltd., 2001.

Foque, Victor, *The Truth Concerning the Invention of Photography.* New York: Tennant & Ward, 1979.

Forester, Tom, *High-Tech Society.* Cambridge, Mass.: MIT Press.

Forester, Tom, ed., *The Information Technology Revolution.* Cambridge, Mass.: The MIT Press, 1985.

Forkert, Otto, *From Gutenberg To The Cuneo Press: An Historical Sketch...* Chicago: Cuneo Press, 1933.

Fornatele, Peter, *Radio In The Television Age.* Woodstock, NY: Overlook Press, 1980.

Franklin, Harold B., *Sound Motion Pictures.* Garden City: Doubleday, Doran, 1929.

Friedman, Joseph S., *History of Color Photography.* Boston: American Photographic Publishing Co., 1944.

Friedman, Thomas L., *The World Is Flat.* New York: Farrar, Straus, and Giroux, 2005.

Fukuyama, Francis, *The End of History and the Last Man*, 2nd ed. New York: Free Press, 1993.

Fuller, Wayne E. *The American Mail, Enlarger of the Common Life.* Chicago: University of Chicago Press, 1972.

_____, *Morality and the Mail in Nineteenth-Century America*, Champaign, IL: University of Illinois Press, 2003.

Gabler, Edwin *The American Telegrapher: A Social History, 1860 - 1900.* New Brunswick, N.J.: Rutgers University Press, 1988.

Garrett, Albert E., *The Advance of Photography.* London: K. Paul, Trench, Trubner & Co., 1911.

Garson, Barbara, *The Electronic Sweatshop: How Computers Are Transforming the Office of the Future into the Factory of the Past.* New York: Bantam Books.

Gaur, Albertine, *A History of Writing.* London: The British Library, 1987.

Geck, Elisabeth, *Johannes Gutenberg: From Lead Letter to the Computer.* Bad Godesberg: Inter Nationes, 1968.

Gee, James Paul. *What Video Games Have to Teach Us About Learning and Literacy.* New York: Palgrave Macmillan, 2004.

Geldud, Harry M., *The Birth of the Talkies: From Edison to Jolson.* Indiana University Press, 1975.

Gernsheim, Helmut and Alison Gernsheim, *The History of Photography.* London: Oxford University Press, 1955.

Gernsheim, Helmut, *The Origins of Photography.* New York: Thames and Hudson, 1982.

Gibson, James M., and James C. Hall Jr., *Damn Reading!: A Case Against Literacy.* Vantage Press, 1969.

Gillies, James, and Robert Cailliau, *How the Web Was Born.* New York: Oxford University Press, 2000.

Goldberg, Robert, and Gerald Jay Goldberg, *Anchors: Brokaw, Jennings, Rather and the Evening News.* New York: Carol Publishing Group, 1990.

Goldsmith, Alfred N., *This Thing Called Broadcasting.* New York: H. Holt & Co., 1930.

Goldsmith, Arthur, "Reinventing the Image," *Popular Photography*, March 1990.

Goldstine, Herman H., *The Computer from Pascal to von Neumann.* Princeton, N.J.: Princeton University Press, 1972.

Goody, Jack, *Literacy in Traditional Societies.* Cambridge: Cambridge University Press, 1968.

Gorham, Maurice A.C., *Broadcasting and Television.* London: Dakers, 1952.

Gouldner, Alvin W., *The Dialectic of Ideology and Technology*, Oxford: Oxford University Press, 1976.

Grant, August E., and Kenton T. Wilkinson, eds., *Communication Technology Update, 1993-1994.* Austin: Technology Futures, Inc., 1993.

Green, Fitzhugh, *The Film Finds Its Tongue.* New York: G.P. Putnam's Sons, 1929.

Greenberger, Martin, ed, *Management and Computers of Future*, Cambridge: The MIT Press, 1962.

Greenfield, Patricia Marks. *Mind and Media: The Effects of Television, Videogames, and Computers.* Cambridge: Harvard University Press, 1984.

G

Gumpert, Gary, *Talking Tombstones and Other Tales of the Media Age.* Oxford: Oxford University Press, 1987.

Guohao, Li, et. al., *Explorations in the History of Science and Technology in China.* Shanghai Chinese Publishing House, 1982.

H   Hallowell, Edward M. , and John J. Ratey, *Delivered from Distraction.* New York: Ballantine Books, 2005.

Hamilton, Frederick W., *The Invention of Typography.* Chicago: The Committee of Education. United Typothetae, 1918.

Hammargren, Russell James, *The Impact Of Radio On The Newspaper.* M.A. thesis, University of Minnesota, 1934.

Hammer, Mina F., *History of the Kodak and its Continuations.* New York: Pioneer Publications, 1940.

Hammond, John H., *The Camera Obscura: A Chronicle.* Bristol: Adam Hilger, Ltd., 1981.

Hansen, Miriam, *Babel and Babylon: Spectatorship in American Silent Film.* Cambridge: Harvard University Press, 1991.

Hanson, Jarice, *Connections: Technologies of Communication.* New York: Harper Collins, 1994.

Harlow, Alvin F., *Old Post Bags.* New York: D. Appleton, 1938.

_____, *Old Wires and New Waves.* New York: D. Appleton-Century, 1936.

Harpur, Patrick, ed., *The Timetable of Technology.* New York: Hearst Books, 1982.

Harris, William V. *Ancient Literacy.* Cambridge: Harvard University Press, 1989.

Hartmann, Heidi I., Robert E. Kraut, and Louise A. Tilly, eds., *Computer Chips and Paper Clips: Technology and Women's Employment.* Washington, D.C.: National Academy Press, 1986.

Havelock, Eric A. *Preface to Plato.* Cambridge, Mass.: Belknap Press, 1963.

Hawks, Ellison, *Pioneers of Wireless.* London: Methuen & Co., 1927.

Hays, Will H., *See and Hear: A Brief History.* Motion Picture Producers and Distributors of America, 1929.

Haynes, Merritt W., *The Students' History of Printing.* New York: McGraw-Hill, 1930.

Head, Sydney W., Christopher H. Sterling, and Lemuel B. Schofield, *Broadcasting in America,* 7th ed. Boston: Houghton-Mifflin, 1994.

Hellemans, Alexander and Bryan Bunch, *The Timetables of Science: A Chronology of the Most Important People and Events in the History of Science.* New York: Simon & Schuster.

Hendricks, Gordon, *The Edison Motion Picture Myth.* Berkeley: University of California Press, 1961.

Henisch, Heinz K., and Barbara Henisch, *The Photographic Experience, 1839-1914.* University Park: Pennsylvania State University Press, 1994.

Herodotus, *The History.* Trans. David Grene. Chicago: University of Chicago Press, 1987.

Herz, J.C. *Joystick Nation: How Videogames Ate Our Quarters, Won Our Hearts, and Rewired Our Minds.* Boston: Little, Brown and Company, 1997.

Hessel, Alfred. *A History of Libraries*. Trans. Reuben Peiss. New Brunswick, N.J.: The Scarecrow Press, 1955.

Hiebert, Ray, *Impact of Mass Media: Current Issues*, New York: Longman, 1985.

Hilliard, Robert L., and Michael C. Keith, *The Broadcast Century and Beyond: A Biography of American Broadcasting*. Woburn, MA: Focal Press, 2001.

Hindle, Brooke, *Emulation and Invention* . New York: New York University Press, 1981.

A History of Engineering And Science In the Bell System. Vol. 7, Bell Laboratories Series. New York, AT&T, 1975.

Hoe, Robert, *A Short History of the Printing Press*. New York: R. Hoe, 1902.

Hoff, Syd, *Editorial and Political Cartooning*. New York: Stravon Educational Press, 1976.

Hofstadter, Richard, *The Progressive Movement, 1900-1915*. Simon & Schuster, 1963.

Hollander, Richard, *Video Democracy*. Mt. Airy, MD: Lomond Publications, 1985.

Hooker, J.T., ed., *Reading the Past: Ancient Writings from Cuneiform to the Alphabet*. Berkeley: University of California Press, 1990.

House, William C., *Laser Beam Information Systems*. New York: Petrocelli Books, 1978.

Houston, Stephen, ed., *The First Writing: Script Invention as History and Process*. Cambridge: Cambridge University Press, 2004.

Hubbard, Geoffrey, *Cooke & Wheatstone & the Invention of the Electric Telegraph*. London: Routledge & K. Paul, 1956.

Hubbell, Richard W., *4,000 Years of Television*. New York: G.P. Putnam's Sons, 1942.

Hughbanks, Leroy, *Talking Wax or The Story of The Phonograph*. New York: Hobson Book Press, 1945.

Hunter, Dard, *Papermaking: The History and Technique of an Ancient Craft*. New York: Dover Publications, 1978.

Huss, Richard E. *The Development of Printers' Mechanical Typesetting Methods, 1822-1925*. Charlottesville: University Press of Virginia, 1973.

Hutt, Allen, *The Changing Newspaper*. London: Gordon Fraser Gallery., 1973.

Inglis, Andrew F., *Behind the Tube*. Stoneham, MA: Focal Press, 1990. **I**

Innis, Harold A., *The Bias of Communication*. Toronto: University of Toronto Press, rev. ed., 1972.

———, *Empire and Communications*. Toronto: University of Toronto Press, revised ed., 1972.

Isaacs, George A., *The Story of the Newspaper Printing Press*. London: Cooperative Printing Society, 1931.

Jaggard, William, *Printing: Its Birth And Growth*. Liverpool: The Shakespeare Press, 1908. **J**

Jarvie, Ian C., *Hollywood's Overseas Campaign: The North Atlantic Movie Trade, 1920-1950*. Cambridge University Press, 1992.

Jeffrey, Ian, *Photography: A Concise History*. New York: Oxford University Press., 1981.

Jenkins, Reese, *Images & Enterprise: Technology & the American Photography Industry.* Baltimore: Johns Hopkins University Press, 1975.

Jennings, Mary-Lou, and Charles Madge, eds., *Pandæmonium: 1660-1886.* New York: The Free Press, 1985.

Jespersen, James, and Jane Fits-Randolph, *Mercury's Web: The Story of Telecommunications.* Atheneum, 1981.

Johnson, Paul, *A History of the Jews.* New York: Harper & Row, 1987.

Johnson, Steven, *Everything Bad Is Good for You.* New York: Riverhead Books, 2005.

Jussim, Estelle, *Visual Communication and the Graphic Arts: Photographic Techniques in the 19th Century.* New York: R.R. Bowker, 1984.

K Keith, Michael C., *The Radio Station*: Broadcast, Satellite, and Internet 7th ed. Boston: Focal Press, 2007.

Kenyon, Frederic G., *Books and Readers in Ancient Greece and Rome*, 2nd ed. Oxford: Clarendon Press, 1951.

Kennedy, Paul, *Preparing for the Twenty-First Century.* Toronto: Harper Collins Publishers Ltd., 1993.

Kent, Steven L. *The Ultimate History of Video Games.* New York: Three Rivers Press, 2001.

Kielbowicz, Richard, "News Gathering by Mail in the Age of the Telegraph: Adapting to a New Technology," *Technology and Culture*, Jan., 1987.

_____, *News in the Mail: The Press, Post Office, and Public Information, 1700-1860s.* New York: Greenwood Press, 1989.

Kim, W., *A Brief History of Metal Type Printing in the Lee dynasty.* Seoul: Hyangtoseoul, 1958.

King, Brad, and John Borland. *Dungeons and Dreamers: The Rise of Computer Game Culture from Geek to Chic.* New York: McGraw-Hill/Osborne, 2003.

King, Larry, *On the Line.* New York: Harcourt Brace & Co., 1993.

Kingslake, Rudolf, *A History of the Photographic Lens.* Boston: Academic Press, 1989.

Koestler, Arthur, *The Sleepwalkers: A History of Man's Changing Vision of the Universe.* Penguin Books, 1964.

Kosinski, Jerzy, *Being There.* New York: Harcourt Brace Jovanovich, 1970.

Kozol, Jonathan, *Illiterate America.* Garden City, N.Y.: Anchor Press, 1985.

Kramarae, Cheris, ed., *Technology and Women's Voices: Keeping in Touch.* New York: Routledge & Kegan Paul, 1988.

Kramer, Samuel, *From the Tablets of Sumer.* Indian Hills, CO: Falcon's Wing Press, 1956.

L Lander, David, "Technology Makes Music," *Invention and Technology*, Spring/Summer, 1990.

Lardner, James, *Fast Forward.* New York: W.W. Norton, 1987.

Lascia, J.D., "Photographs That Lie," Washington Journalism Review, June 1989.

Laufer, Berthold, *Paper And Printing In Ancient China.* Chicago: Printed for the Caxton Club, 1931.

Layton, Edwin T. Jr., *Technology and Social Change in America*. New York: Harper & Row, 1973.

Lehman, Maxwell, *Communication Technologies and Information Flow*. New York: Pergamon Press, 1981.

Leinwoll, Stanley, *From Spark to Satellite*. New York: Charles Scribner's Sons, 1979

Lenmark, Barbara G., *Some Effects of the Teletypesetter on the Newspaper*. M.A. thesis, University of Minnesota, 1954.

Levy, Steven, *Crypto*. New York: Penguin Books, 2001.

Lewis, Bernard, *What Went Wrong: Western Impact and Middle Eastern Response*. New York: Oxford University Press, 2002.

Lewis, Tom, *Empite of the Air: The Men Who Made Radio*. New York: HarperCollins, 1991.

Lichty, Lawrence, *American Broadcasting: A Source Book on the History of Radio and Television*. New York: Hastings House, 1975.

Litman, Jessica, *Digital Copyright: Protecting Intellectual Property on the Internet*. Amherst, NY: Prometheus, 2001.

Lloyd, G.E.R., "Science and Mathematics," in M.I. Finley, ed., *The Legacy of Greece*. Oxford: Oxford University Press, 1984.

Loftus, Geofrey R., and Elizabeth F. Loftus, *Mind at Play: The Psychology of Videogames*. New York: Basic Books, 1983.

Logan, Robert K. *The Alphabet Effect: The Impact of the Phonetic Alphabet on the Development of Western Civilization*. New York: William Morrow and Co., 1986.

Lowman, Charles E., *Magnetic Recording*. New York: McGraw-Hill, 1972.

Lown, Edward, *An Introduction To Technological Changes In Journalism*. Ann Arbor, Mich.: Published for the Journalism Program, State University of New York at New Paltz by University Microfilms International, 1977.

MacDonald, J. Fred, *Blacks and White TV—Afro-Americans in Television since 1948*. Nelson-Hall Publishers, 1983, p. 89.

_____, *Don't Touch That Dial: Radio Programming in American Life, 1920-1960*. Chicago: Nelson-Hall, 1979.

Macgowan, Kenneth, *Behind The Screen: History and Techniques of the Motion Picture*. New York: Delacorte Press, 1965.

Maclaurin, William R., *Invention & Innovation In The Radio Industry*. New York: Macmillan, 1949.

MacNeil, Robert, *The People Machine*. New York: Harper & Row, 1968.

Manchester, William, *A World Lit Only by Fire: The Medieval Mind and the Renaissance*. Boston: Little, Brown and Company, 1992.

Mander, Jerry, *Four Arguments for the Elimination of Television*. New York: Morrow, 1978.

Marchand, Philip. *Marshall McLuhan*. Ticknor & Fields, 1989.

Marcus, Alan I., and Howard P. Segal, *Technology in America: A Brief History*, New York: Harcourt Brace Jovanovich.

M

Marek, Kurt W., *Archaeology of the Cinema*. New York: Harcourt, Brace & World, 1965.

Marland, E.A., *Early Electrical Communication*. London: Abelard-Schuman, 1964.

Marrou, H.I., "Education and Rhetoric," in M.I. Finley, ed., *The Legacy of Greece*. Oxford: Oxford University Press, 1984.

Martin, Henri-Jean, *The History and Power of Writing*. Trans. Lydia G. Cochrane. Chicago: University of Chicago Press, 1994.

Martin, James, *Future Developments In Telecommunica- tions*. Englewood Cliffs, N.J.: Prentice-Hall, 1977.

_____, *Telecommunications And The Computer,* 3rd ed. Englewood Cliffs, N.J.: Prentice-Hall, 1990.

_____, *Telematic Society: A Challenge For Tomorrow*. Englewood Cliffs, N.J.: Prentice-Hall, 1981

Marty, Daniel, *An Illustrated History of Phonographs*. New York: Dorset Press, 1981.

Marvin, Carolyn, *When Old Technologies Were New*. Oxford: Oxford University Press, 1988.

Mason, William A., *A History of the Art of Writing*. New York: Macmillan Co., 1920.

Maspero, Gaston. *The Dawn of Civilization: Egypt and Chaldæa*, trans. M.T. McClure. London: Society for Promoting Christian Knowledge, 1922.

Matusow, Barbara, *The Evening Stars*. New York: Ballantine Books, 1984.

Maurer, Allan, *Lasers: Light Wave of the Future*. New York: Arco Publishing, Inc., 1982

McClure, M.T., "Appearance and Reality in Greek Philosophy," *Studies in the History of Ideas*, vol. 1. New York: Columbia University Press, 1918,

McLean, Mick, *The Information Explosion: The New Electronic Media in Japan and Europe*. Westport, CT: Greenwood Press, 1985.

McLuhan, Marshall, *Understanding Media: The Extensions of Man*. New York: McGraw-Hill, 1964.

_____, *The Gutenberg Galaxy: The Making of Typographic Man*. Toronto: University of Toronto Press, 1962.

_____, and Bruce Powers, *The Global Village*. Oxford: Oxford University Press, 1989.

McMurtrie, Douglas C. , *The Book*. New York: Dorset Press, 1989.

Mees, C.E.K., *From Dry Plates To Ektachrome Film*. New York: Ziff-Davis Publishing Co., 1961.

Meggs, Philip B., *A History of Graphic Design*. New York: Van Nostrand Reinhold, 1983.

Meyer, G.J., *A World Undone: The Story of the Great War, 1914 to 1918*. New York: Delacorte Press, 2006.

Michaelis, Anthony, *From Semaphore To Satellite*. Geneva: International Telecommunication Union, 1965.

Momigliano, Arnaldo, "History and Biography," in M.I. Finley, ed., *The Legacy of Greece*. Oxford University Press, 1984.

Moran, James, *Printing Presses: History and Development.*. Berkeley, University of California Press, 1973.

Moreau, R., *The Computer Comes of Age.* Cambridge, Mass.: The MIT Press, 1986.

Morison, Stanley. *Politics and Script.* Oxford: The Clarendon Press, 1972.

Morris, Lloyd R., *Not So Long Ago.* New York: Random House, 1949.

Morse, Arthur H., *Radio: Beam & Broadcast.* London: Benn, 1925.

Moseley, Maboth, *Irascible Genius: A Life of Charles Babbage, Inventor.* London: Hutchinson, 1964.

Nasaw, David, *Going Out: The Rise and Fall of Public Amusements.* New York: Basic Books, 1993. **N**

Neale, Steve, *Cinema and Technology: Image, Sound, Color.* Bloomington: Indiana University Press, 1985.

Newhall, Beaumont, *Latent Image: The Discovery of Photography.* Garden City, N.Y.: Doubleday, 1967.

_____, *The History of Photography.* New York: Museum of Modern Art, 1982.

_____, *On Photography: A Sourcebook of Photo History.* Watkins Glen, N.Y.: Century House, 1956.

Nicolson, Adam, *God's Secretaries: The Making of the King James Bible.* New York: HarperCollins, 2003.

North, Joseph H., *The Early Development of the Motion Picture.* New York: Arno Press, 1973.

O'Brien, John E., *Telegraphing In Battle.* Scranton, Pa.: The Reader Press, 1910. **O**

Ogburn, William F. *Social Change.* New York: Viking Press, 1950.

_____, and M.F. Nimkoff, *Sociology.* Houghton-Mifflin, 1950.

Ohmann, Richard. *Selling Culture: Magazines, Markets, and Class at the turn of the Century.* London: Verso, 1996.

Ong, Walter S. *The Presence of the Word: Some Prolegomena for Cultural and Religious History.* New Haven: Yale University Press, 1967.

Oslin, George P., *The Story of Telecommunications.* Macon, GA: Mercer University Press, 1992.

Pan, Jixing, *History of Chinese Science and Technology: Papermaking and Printing.* Beijing: Kexue, **P** 1998.

Pask, Gordon, *Microman: Computers And The Evolution of Consciousness.* New York: Macmillan, l982.

Pattison, Robert. *On Literacy.* Oxford: Oxford University Press, 1982.

Pearse, Meic. *Why the Rest Hates the West: Understanding the Roots of Global Rade.* Downers Grove, IL: InterVarsity Press, 2004.

Pease, Edward C., ed, *Radio: The Forgotten Medium.* New York: Columbia University, The Freedom Forum Media Studies Center, Summer 1993.

Peckham, Morse, *Beyond the Tragic Vision.* New York: George Braziller, 1962.

Peterson, Theodore, *Magazines in the Twentieth Century.* Urbana: University of Illinois Press, 1964.

Petrie, W.M. Flinders. *The Formation of the Alphabet*. London: MacMillan & Co., 1912.

Plato, *Phaedo*, 109B-C, translated and edited by David Gallop. Oxford: Oxford University Press, 1993.

_____, *Phaedrus*, 275, trans. C.J. Rowe, (2nd corrected ed.). Warminster, England: Aris & Rowe, 1988.

Polscher, Andrew A., *The Evolution of Printing Presses From Wood To Metal*. Harper Woods, Mich., Adagio Press, 1968.

Pool, Ithiel de Sola, *Technologies of Freedom*. Cambridge, Mass.: Harvard University Press, 1983.

Poole, Steven, *Trigger Happy: The Inner Life of Videogames*. London: Fourth Estate, 2000.

Popcorn, Faith, *The Popcorn Report: The Future of Your Company, Your World, Your Life*. New York: Doubleday, 1991.

Postman, Neil, *Amusing Ourselves to Death*. New York: Viking Penguin, 1985.

Pound, Arthur, *The Telephone Idea: 50 Years After*. New York: Greenberg, 1926.

Pratt, William K., *Laser Communications Systems*. New York, Wiley, 1969.

Presbrey, Frank, *The History and Development of Advertising*. Garden City, N.Y.: Doubleday, Doran, 1929.

Prescott, George B., *Bell's Speaking Telephone: Its Invention, Construction*. New York: Arno Press, 1972.

Putnam, Robert, *Bowling Alone: The Collapse and Revival of American Community*. New York: Simon & Schuster, 2000.

Q-R   Quigley, Martin, *Magic Shadows: The Story of the Origin of Motion Pictures*. Washington: Georgetown University Press, 1948.

Read, Oliver, and Walter L. Welch, *From Tin Foil To Stereo*, 2nd ed. Indianapolis: Howard W. Sams & Co., 1976.

Redmond, James, *Broadcasting: The Developing Technology*. London: British Broadcasting Corp., 1974.

Rhode, Eric, *A History of the Cinema*. New York: Hill and Wang, 1976.

Rhodes, Frederick L., *Beginnings Of Telephony*. New York: *Harper & Bros., 1929*.

Ritchie, David, *The Computer Pioneers*. New York: Simon & Schuster, 1986.

Robinson, David, *The History of World Cinema*. New York: Stein and Day, 1973.

Rogers, Everett M., *Communication Technology*. New York: The Free Press, 1986.

Rolo, Charles, *Radio Goes To War*. New York: G.P. Putnam's Sons, 1942.

Rosenblum, Naomi, *A World History of Photography*. New York: Abbeville Press, 1989.

Rose, Albert, *Vision: Human & Electronic*. New York: Plenum Press, 1973.

Rosewater, Victor. *History of Cooperative New-Gathering in the United States*. New York: D. Appleton & Co. 1930.

Rosten, Leo, *Hollywood, the Movie Colony and the Movie Makers*. New York: Harcourt Brace & Co., 1941.

Roszak, Theodore, *The Cult of Information*. New York: Pantheon, 1986.

Roy, Olivier, *Globalized Islam: The Search for a New Ummah*. New York: Columbia University Press, 2004.

Rushkoff, Douglas, *Playing the Future: What We Can Learn from Digital Kids*. New York: Riverhead Books, 1999.

Russell, James, *The Impact Of Radio On The Newspaper*. Unpublished M.A. Thesis, University of Minnesota, 1934.

Rybczynski, Witold, *Taming the Tiger: The Struggle to Control Technology*. Viking Press, 1983.

Safley, Thomas, and Leonard Rosenband, eds., *The Workplace before the Factory: Artisans and Proletarians, 1500-1800*. Ithaca: Cornell University Press, 1993.

Salt, Barry, *Film Style and Technology: History and Analysis*. London: Starword, 1983.

Sanderson, Richard A., *A Historical Study*. New York: Arno Press, 1971.

Scarborough, John. *Facets of Hellenic Life*. Boston: Houghton Mifflin Co., 1976.

Scheele, Carl, *A Short History of the Mail Service*. Washington: Smithsonian Institute Press, 1970.

Schiffer, Michael Brian, *The Portable Radio in American Life*. Tucson: University of Arizona Press, 1991.

Schmandt-Besserat, Denise. *Before Writing*. Austin: University of Texas Press, 1992.

Schramm, Wilbur, *The Story of Human Communication: Cave Painting to Microchip*. New York: Harper & Row, 1988.

Schroeder, Peter B., *Contact At Sea*. Ridgewood, N.J.: Gregg Press, 1967.

Schubert, Paul, *The Electric Word: The Rise of Radio*. New York: Macmillan, 1928.

Schuwer, Philippe, *History of Advertising*. London: Leisure Arts, Ltd., 1966.

Schudson, Michael, *Discovering the News*. New York: Basic Books, 1978.

Schwartz, Barry, *The Paradox of Choice: Why More Is Less*. New York: HarperCollins, 2004.

Sellen, Abigail, and Richard Harper, The Myth of the Paperless Office. Cambridge, MA: MIT Press, 2002.

Settel, Irving, and William Lass, *A Pictorial History of Television*. New York: Grosset & Dunlap, 1969.

Shapiro, Neil, *The Small Computer Connection*. New York: McGraw-Hill, 1983.

Shaw, Donald L., "News Bias and the Telegraph," *Journalism Quarterly*, Spring, 1967, pp. 3-12.

Shaw, Thomas, *The Conquest of Distance By Wire Telephony*. New York: AT&T, 1944.

Shiers, George, *The Development of Wireless to 1920*. New York: Arno Press, 1977.

_____, *The Electric Telegraph: An Historical Anthology*. New York: Arno Press, 1977.

_____, *Technical Development of Television*. New York: Arno Press, 1977.

_____, *The Telephone: An Historical Anthology* , New York: Arno Press,1977

S

Shipman, David, *The Story of Cinema*. New York: St. Martin's Press, 1982.

Shlain, Leonard, *The Alphabet Versus the Goddess*. New York: Viking, 1998.

Shurkin, Joel, *Engines of the Mind: A History of the Computer*. New York: Norton, 1984.

Sigel, Efrem, *The Future of Videotext*. White Plains, N.Y.: Knowledge Industry Publications, 1983.

_____, *Videodiscs: The Technology, The Application & The Future*. New York: Van Nostrand, 1981.

Simon, Irving B., *The Story of Printing: From Woodblocks To Electronics*. New York: Harvey House, 1965.

Singer, et. al., eds. *A History of Technology; Vol. 5, The Late 19th Century*. Oxford: The Clarendon Press, 1958.

Singleton, Loy, *Telecommunications in the Information Age*, Cambridge, Mass.: Ballinger Publishing Co., 1983.

Sloan, William, James Stovall and James Startt, *The Media in America: A History*. Worthington, OH: Publishing Horizons, 1989.

Smith, Adele M., *Printing And Writing Materials: Their Evolution*. Philadelphia, published by the author, 1912.

Smith, Anthony, *Books to Bytes: The Computer and the Library*. New York: Gannett Center for Media Studies, 1988.

_____, *Goodbye Gutenberg*. New York: Oxford University Press, 1986.

Smith, F. Leslie, *Perspectives on Radio and Television*. New York: Harper & Row, 1985.

Soley, Lawrence C., *Clandestine Radio Broadcasting*. New York: Praeger, 1987.

Speliotis, Dennis E., and Clark E. Johnson, *Advances In Magnetic Recording*. New York: N.Y. Academy of Sciences, 1972.

Spira, S.F., *The History of Photography: As Seen Through the Spira Collection*. New York: Aperture Foundation, 2001.

Standage, Tom. *The Victorian Internet: The Remarkable Story of the Telegraph and the Nineteenth Century's On-line Pioneers*. New York: Walker Publishing Co., 1998.

Starr, Chester G. *The Origins of Greek Civilization: 1100 - 650 B.C.* Alfred A. Knopf, 1961.

Starr, Paul, *The Creation of the Media: Political Origins of Modern Communications*. New York: Basic Books, 2004.

Stearns, Peter N. *The Industrial Revolution in World History*. Boulder: Westview Press, 1993.

Stein, Dorothy, *Ada: A Life and a Legacy*. Cambridge, Mass.: The MIT Press, 1987.

Steinberg, S.H., *Five Hundred Years of Printing*, 2nd ed.. Baltimore: Penguin Books, 1962.

Stephens, Mitchell, *A History of News*. New York: Viking Press, 1988.

Sterling, Christopher H., and John M. Kittross, *Stay Tuned: A Concise History of American Broadcasting*, 2nd ed.. Belmost, CA: Wadsworth, 1990.

Still, Alfred, *Communication Through The Ages*. New York: Murray Hill Books, 1946.

"The Stormy Birth of the FM Radio," *American Heritage of Invention & Technology*; fall, 1985.

Stump, Matt, and Harry Jessell, "Cable: The First Forty Years," *Broadcasting*, Nov. 21, 1988.

Swift, John, *Adventure In Vision: The First 25 Years of Television*. London: J. Lehman, 1950.

Tansey, Richard G.. and Horst de la Croix, *Art Through the Ages*. Harcourt Brace Jovanovich, 1986.

T

Thomas, David B., *The First Negatives*. London: H.M. Stationery Office.

Thomas, Lowell, *Magic Dials: The Story of Radio and Television*. New York: L. Furman, 1939.

Thomas, Sari, ed., *Studies in Mass Communication and Technology*. Norwood, N.J.: Ablex Publishing, 1984.

Thompson, James W. *Ancient Libraries*. Berkeley: University of California Press, 1940.

Thompson, John S. *History of Composing Machines*. New York: Arno Press, 1972.

Thompson, S.P., *Philipp Reis: Inventor of the Telephone*. Reprint of 1883 edition. New York: Arno Press, 1974.

Toffler, Alvin, *Future Shock*. New York: Bantam Books, 1971.

_____, *The Third Wave*. New York: William Morrow, 1980.

Towers, Walter K., *From Beacon Fire to Radio*. New York: Harper & Bros., 1924.

Trethowan, Ian, *The Development of Radio*. London: British Broadcasting Corp., 1975.

Tsien, Tsuen-Hsien, *Written on Bamboo and Silk.*. Chicago: University of Chicago Press, 1962.

Tubbs, Douglas B., *The Illustrated History of the Camera From 1839 To The Present*. Boston: New York Graphic Society, 1975.

Tuchman, Barbara, *A Distant Mirror: The Calamitous 14th Century*. Alfred A. Knopf, 1978.

Turkle, Sherry, *The Second Self*. New York: Simon & Schuster, 1984.

Turner, Peter, *History of Photography*. New York: Exeter Books, 1987.

Vaidhyanathan, Siva, *The Anarchist in the Library*. New York: Basic Books, 2004.

V

Vincent, David, *Literacy and Popular Culture*. Cambridge: Cambridge University Press, 1989.

Vogt, Ernest, *Radio Technology: Telegraphy, Telephony, Television*. New York: Pitman Publishing, 1949.

Von Felitzen, Cecilia, and Carisson, Ulla, *Children in the New Media Landscape: Games, Pornography, Perceptions*. UNESCO International Clearinghouse on Children and Violence on the Screen, 2000.

Vyvyan, Richard N., *Wireless Over 30 Years*. London: G. Routledge & Sons, Ltd., 1922.

Waterhouse, James, *The Beginnings of Photography. Washington: Smithsonian Institution*, 1903.

W

Watson, Thomas A., *The Birth and Babyhood of the Telephone*. New York: AT&T, 1940.

Weaver, David H., *Videotex Journalism*. Hillsdale, N.J.: L. Erlbaum Associates, 1983.

Weightman, Gavin, *Signor Marconi's Magic Box*. London: HarperCollinsPublishers, 2003.

Westcott, Charles G., and Richard F. Dubbe, *Tape Recorders - How They Work*. Howard W. Sams & Co., The Bobbs Merrill Co., 1974.

Wheeler, Leslie J., *Principles of Cinematography*, 4th ed. London: Fountain Press, 1969.

Wheen, Francis, *Television*. London: Century Publishing, 1985.

White, Roy B., *Telegrams in 1889-and Since!* Princeton, N.J.: Princeton University Press, 1939.

Wiborg, Frank B., *Printing Ink: A History*. New York: Harper & Bros., 1926.

Wicklein, John, *Electronic Nightmare: The New Communications And Freedom*. New York: The Viking Press, 1981.

Wile, Frederic W., *Emile Berliner, Maker Of The Microphone*. Indianapolis: Bobbs-Merrill, 1926.

Wilkinson, Paul, *Terrorism and the Liberal State*. New York: New York University Press, 1986.

Williams, Francis, *Transmitting World News*. UNESCO, 1953

Williams, Frederick, *The Communications Revolution*. Beverly Hills: Sage Press, 1982.

Williams, Raymond, ed., *Contact: Human Communication And Its History*. New York: Thames and Hudson, 1981.

_____, *Televison: Technology and Cultural Form*. New York: Schockben Books, 1975.

Williams, Rosalind, *Notes on the Underground*. Cambridge, Mass.: MIT Press, 1990.

Wilson, Carmen, *Magnetic Recording 1900-1949*. Chicago: John Crerar Library Bibliographic Series, no. 1, 1950.

Winn, Marie, *The Plug-In Drug*. Viking, 1985.

Winsbury, Rex, *New Technology And The Press*. London: H.M. Stationery Office, 1975.

Winston, Brian, *Misunderstanding Media*, Cambridge, Mass.: Harvard University Press, 1986.

Wolf, Mark J.P., ed. *The Medium of the Videogame*. Austin: University of Texas Press, 2001.

Wood, Henry A., *Progress In Newspaper Manufacture*. New York: Wood Newspaper Machinery Corp., 1932.

Wood, James P., *The Story of Advertising*, New York: Ronald Press, 1958.

_____, *Magazines in the United States*, 2nd ed. New York: Ronald Press, 1956.

Wrigley, Maurice J., *The Cinema: Historical, Technical, & Bibliographical*. London: Grafton & Co., 1939.

Wulforst, Harry, *Breakthrough to the Computer Age*. New York: Scribner, 1982.

Wymer, Norman, *From Marconi To Telstar*. London: Longmans, 1966.

Y-Z   Young, L.C., *Materials in Printing Processes*. New York: Hastings House, 1973.

Zilliacus, Laurin, *Mail for the World*. New York: John Day, 1953.

INDEX

A

A TIMELINE
OF COMMUNICATION
AND CULTURE

B.C.E. (BEFORE THE COMMON ERA—*DATES ARE APPROXIMATE*)

45000: In what is now Hungary, a Neanderthal carves on a woolly mammoth tooth.

35000: In what is now Swaziland, a bone with 29 notches, possibly a calendar.

30000: In what is now Germany, someone carves a horse out of a pelvic bone.

In what is now France, Chauvet cave dwellers draw on walls.

25000: Rock painting, female figurines.

23000: In what is now Uganda, the Ishango bone, with complex math markings.

20000: Spain's Altamira caves have red and black drawings of bison and deer.

In the Koonalda Cave, Australia, finger drawings on clay walls.

10000: Notches in bones in Near East presumed to be a lunar calendar.

Writing on skin. Tattooing instruments found in Europe.

9000: Mesopotamia hunter-gatherers settle down; it is the start of agriculture.

8000: In Sumer, clay tokens symbolize goods, like sheep, jars of oil.

6200: Oldest known map, a town plan from Catal Hyk, Turkey.

4800: In Egypt, evidence of astronomical calendar stones.

4004: Bishop Ussher's date, accepted by early Protestants, of the creation of the world.

4000: Egyptian pharaohs listen to flutes and harps.

3800: Nile culture starts.

3760: Start of Hebrew calendar.

3700: In Sumer, tokens representing goods are placed in clay ball envelopes.

3500: In Sumer and Elam, the start of pictographic writing.

Egyptian pharaohs also listen to lyres and a kind of clarinet.

3372: Start of the Mayan calendar.

3000: Sumerians write wedge-shaped cuneiform numerals and ideographic symbols.

Egypt develops hieroglyphic writing.

In the Mediterranean or Near East, an abacus derived from counting boards.

People light the night with candles.

3000: In China, a bamboo flute.

Appalachian dulcimer may have started in the Near East.

2784: Estimated date of the first Egyptian civil year of 12 months, 365 days.

2700: Chinese ink mixes soot, pine smoke, lamp oil, musk, and gelatin from donkey skin.

2640: China produces silk. It will serve as a writing surface.

2600: In Egypt, scribes employ hieratic writing, a condensed, cursive hieroglyphic.

2500: Earliest known glass.

2400: In India, engraved seals identify the writer.

2350: Mesopotamian king uses homing pigeons.

2300: Mesopotamian Semites use cuneiform and base-10 numbering.

Early Britons move from stone age to bronze age.

Akkadian is the diplomatic language of the Near East.

In the Indus Valley (modern Pakistan), Proto-Indian writing.

2200: Oldest existing document written on papyrus.

2000: Ur-Nammu, king of Ur, in Sumeria, creates first known code of law.

In the Fertile Crescent, sundials.

In Sumer, the first known written legend, *Gilgamesh*, a poetic Noah's ark tale.

In Egypt, percussion instruments are played.

Enheduanna, a woman in Mesopotamia, writes first signed text, a hymn.

Vikings toot on trumpets.

Nine Greek muses, responsible for poetry, history, comedy, song, dance.

Place value numeration in Babylonia.

1800: Writing in the Minoan civilization of Crete.

1700: The written law code of Hammurabi, in Babylonia, carved on a stone pillar.

In Crete, the Phaistos disc; symbols printed by pressing into soft clay.

Alphabetic symbols, a few written by Semites in Canaan.

1500: Decimal system spreads through the Near East.

In India, sacred Hindu hymns of the *Rig Veda* are written in Sanskrit.

Indian astronomers write that the Earth is a globe that circles the sun.

Babylonian mathematicians figure out the Pythagorean Theorem.

The Book of the Dead guides wealthy Egyptians into the afterlife.

In the Near East, Hittites play guitar, tamborine, lyre and trumpet.

1450: In Crete, "Linear B" clay tablets show a shift from pictographs to syllables.

1400: Oldest record of writing in China, on bones and tortoise shells.

1350: In Egypt, pharaoh Akhnaton introduces monotheism, but it doesn't survive him.

1300: Thirty Ugaritic alphabetic cuneiform symbols on tablets.

In modern-day Syria, musical notation.

1300: Drum beat codes sound alarms during Shang Dynasty in China.

1259: Egyptians and Hittites sign first written peace treaty.

1250: Moses brings the tablets bearing the Ten Commandments. (Estimate)

1200: The Phoenician alphabet, 22 letters, all consonants.

Egyptians use pigeons for military communication.

1000: Alphabetic writing appears in various parts of the Near East.

In ancient Israel, instrumental music accompanies religious ceremonies.

950: The oldest books of the Bible are written.

900: China's Zhou Dynasty has an organized postal service for government use.

Phonetic alphabet spreads across the Mediterranean.

Oldest extant writing in Western Hemisphere; Olmec stone. (Found in 2006 C.E.)

Beacon fires and smoke signals are used in China.

Start of the writing of the Hindu *Upanishads*.

850: The *Iliad* and the *Odyssey*, 300 years after the Trojan War, ascribed to Homer.

841: Verified Chinese historical chronology begins.

800: In the Near East, leather is a writing surface; rolled as scrolls.

Greeks improve Phoenician alphabet by adding vowels; capital letters only.

Greeks develop choral music.

776: Carrier pigeons bear news of the Olympic games.

775: Chinese astronomers record a solar eclipse, first Chinese proven date.

753: Estimated founding of Rome; start of the Roman calendar.

750: The book of Amos.

Egyptian demotic writing, a cursive derived from hieratic, hieroglyphs.

Greek poet Hesiod writes *Works and Days*, an epic of Greek rural life.

710: In the Egyptian city of Memphis, an account of creation carved in stone.

650: Egyptian papyrus arrives in Greek cities.

Olmecs, a pre-Mayan people, invent first writing system in Americas.

Dionysian festivals among Greeks will lead to drama.

640: A king of Ninevah collects a library, 22,000 clay tablets.

Coins are circulated.

621: Manuscript of Deuteronomy, discovered in Jerusalem.

620: Draco gives Athens a written code of laws, "draconian" in its harshness.

610: Anaximander writes first known book of philosophy.

600: First appearance of Latin.

Thales of Miletus posits that life is dependent upon water.

In India, an early version of a violin.

In Ninevah, a map of the known world, carved on clay tablet.

From Lesbos, Sappho's poetry; it will lead to the term "lesbian."

600: The Near East has coins, clocks, calendars.

Mediterranean cultures agree on left-to-right writing.

585: Thales of Miletus develops physical science, geometry, and a rational worldview.

575: In Babylonian exile, Jewish scholars begin to compile the books of the Bible.

Zarathrustra (Zoroaster) preaches and starts a new religion in the Middle East.

530: In Greece, a belief that mathematics is the study of reality, not just logic.

In Athens, a public library.

528: Buddhism begins as Siddhartha Gautama finds enlightenment.

526: In China, a written code of laws.

500: Chinese government officials use established, speedy courier service.

Heraclitus argues that permanence is an illusion; only change exists.

Chinese philosopher Lao Tze, Taoist founder, is curator of royal archives.

Greek telegraph: trumpets, drums, shouting, beacon fires, smoke, mirrors.

Persia has a form of pony express.

Xenophones examines fossils, speculates on evolution.

Unknown prophet, "second Isaiah," writes, preaches of Yahweh's universality.

In India, the system of numerals that will be known in the West as "Arabic."

In India, the writing of the Vedic hymns is completed.

In present-day Nigeria, the Nok people produce terra cotta art.

The *Analects* of Confucius.

Chinese scholars write on bamboo with reeds dipped in pigment.

Greeks build theaters as drama emerges.

Pythagoras concludes that Earth is a sphere, not flat.

490: Pheidippides dies after bringing to Athens the news of victory at Marathon.

480: Aesop, possibly a freed slave, writes his *Fables*.

475: Parmenides, Greek philosopher, argues that reality is an unchanging substance.

Philosopher Heraclitis posits opposite view that the world is constantly changing.

469: Birth of Socrates, inventor of the art of philosophical dialogue.

458: From Aeschylus, the "father of tragedy," *Oresteia*.

450: Anaxagoras is first Western philosopher to distinguish mind from matter.

Anaxagoras concludes that moonlight is reflected sunlight; explains eclipses.

Herodotus draws a map of the known world.

449: Rome's written Laws of the Twelve Tables cover both civil and criminal matters.

443: Sophocles' *Antigone*.

438: Death of Pindar, arguably the greatest of the Greek lyric poets.

435: In China, a solar calendar.

Phidias sculpts the Zeus, one of the seven ancient wonders of the world.

432: Greek astronomer Meton adjusts the lunar calendar to a solar year.

431: Euripides' *Medea*.

The Athenian ruler, Pericles, delivers his Funeral Oration.

430: Euripides' *The Trojans*.

428: Sophocles, *Oedipus Rex*.

427: Birth of Plato, author of the Socratic *Dialogues* and *The Republic.*

423: Aristophanes' satire, *The Clouds*, caricatures Socrates.

420: Herodotus' *History of the Persian War*; does interviews.

Writings by Hippocrates begin the scientific study of medicine.

Socrates, Democritus locate thought as coming from the brain.

415: Euripides, *The Trojan Women.*

Lysistrata, comedy by Aristophanes.

Protagoras teaches that human beings are "the measure of all things."

409: Sophocles, *Electra.*

405: Euripides' *Bacchae.*

Aristophanes, *The Frogs.*

401: Sophocles, *Oedipus at Colonus.*

400: First illustrated manuscripts.

In India, Panini codifies Sanskrit grammar.

Chinese write on silk as well as wood, bamboo.

Thucydides' *History of the Peloponnesian War.*

In Central America, Zapotec writing.

Greeks use carrier pigeons.

Democritus originates theory that matter consists of colliding atoms.

Xenophon's *Anabasis* tells dramatic tale of Greek army fighting their way home.

399: Socrates drinks poison. Nothing written by famed philosopher survives.

396: Plato's *Apologia* defends Socrates.

387: Plato's *Symposium* uses Socratic logic.

386: Plato founds the Academy

384: Birth of Aristotle.

360: Plato, *The Republc.*

350: From the Greek author Archestratus, a cookbook.

In *Organon*, Aristotle explains logical reasoning.

Diogenes preaches the simple, self-sufficient life.

347: Death of Plato, who leaves an unparalleled mark on Western thought.

340: Aristotle's *Logic*; it will be a source of knowledge for more than 2,000 years.

Aristotle begins musical theory.

335: Aristotle founds his academy, the Lyceum.

323: Theophrastus classifies plant life.

322: Death of Aristotle, the great collector of human knowledge.

320: Greek sculpture spreads across Near East.

312: Start of the ancient Greek calendar, the Seleucid Era.

300: Epicurus starts philosophical school based on simple life that avoids pain.

Indian epic poem, the *Mahabharata*, attains much of its modern form.

300: Euclid's *Elements* explain geometry. *Optics* explains depth perception.

295: Founding of Alexandrian Library. Euclid teaches there.

275: Manetho, Egyptian priest, writes history of Egypt.

260: Aristarchus uses trigonometry to estimate moon's size, distance.

250: Diophantus' *Arithmetica* explains algebra.

Brahmi, the first strictly Indian writing, in King Asoka's edicts.

In Near East city of Pergamum, parchment is made as a writing surface.

The zero appears for the first time, in Babylonian place-value system.

240: Latin literature starts to emerge.

230: Aristarchus of Samos: first scientist to realize that Earth circles the Sun.

220: Archimedes, Sicilian geometrician, leaves records of his many inventions.

213: China's Ch'in emperor, Shihuang, orders destruction of all books.

200: Greek scientist Eratosthenes accurately measures size of the Earth.

Greeks, Romans use wax-on-wood tablets for note taking.

Tipao gazettes are circulated to Chinese officials.

196: Cutting of the Rosetta Stone in hieroglyphics, hieratic, and Greek.

185: In Rome, Plautus and Terence write comedies.

170: Books are written on parchment and vellum, treated animal skins.

165: The book of Daniel.

150: Hipparchus, astronomer, invents trigonometry, calculates length of the year.

The modern Hebrew alphabet, derived from Aramaic cursive letters.

The book of Ecclesiastes.

Paper is placed in Chinese tombs.

Alexandria is the greatest center of Hellenistic and Hebrew culture.

The *Septuagint*, a version of the Old Testament, is translated into Greek.

146: Polybius completes 40 volumes of early Roman history.

Polybius describes complex torch signaling system in use by Greeks.

118: Codification of the Roman constitution is completed.

105: In Alexandria, the first college of technology is founded.

100: Oldest surviving fragment of Bible: Ten Commandments, in Hebrew.

Greek builds recently discovered Antikythera astronomy computer.

80: In China, a collection of biographies of famous women.

67: Sallust writes a history of Rome during the past decade.

63: Marcus Tullius Tiro, ex-slave of Cicero, invents a shorthand system.

59: Julius Caesar orders postings of *Acta Diurna*.

57: Lucretius' 6-volume *De Rerum Natura* extols Epicurean philosophy.

55: Marcus Tullius Cicero writes on rhetoric, *De Oratore*.

54: Cicero on politics, *De Republica*.

51: Caesar's account of the Gallic war; will be read by pupils for centuries.

50:     An early oboe.

47:     Alexandrian Library survives fire set by Julius Caesar's troops; many books lost.

46:     Julius Caesar introduces the solar Julian calendar, with leap years.

44:     Caesar killed. Remarkable life includes writing *Commentaries* and *Civil War*.

39:     In Rome, the first public library, at the Libertas Temple.

37:     Virgil (or Vergil) writes the *Bucolics*, or *Eclogues*.

35:     The *Satires* of Horace.

30:     Virgil writes more poetry of farm life, the *Georgics*.

28:     Rome establishes two large libraries, the Octavian and the Palatine.

19:     Virgil dies; the *Aeneid*, one of the greatest of the epic poems, is unfinished.

13:     Some of the finest lyrical poems of the mature Horace appear.

8:     Horace, greatest of Latin lyric poets, dies after writing *Satires*, *Odes*, *Epistles*.

4:     Likely birth of Jesus, according to modern calculations.

C.E. (COMMON ERA—*MOST EARLY DATES ARE APPROXIMATE*)

0:     Reformed Chinese writing in *li-shu* style prefigures modern Chinese.

10:     Livy's *History of Rome* reflects his admiration for its early civilization.

14:     Rome sets up network of relay runners carrying messages 50 miles in a day.

18:     Ovid dies. Latin poet wrote of myths in the *Metamorphoses* and of love.

20:     Strabo's *Geographia* and histories describe the Mediterranean world.

25:     Mela publishes map of the known world, with climatic latitudes.

37:     Seneca the Elder dies after writing history of Rome.

46:     Paul begins preaching Christianity.

50:     Paul writes his *Epistles*.

        Philo dies after trying to reconcile Greek philosophy, Jewish thought.

60:     Petronius' satirical *Satyricon* describes vulgarity of Roman luxury.

65:     Mark writes the first *Gospel*.

        Lucan's epic poem tells of civil war between Caesar and Pompey.

65:     Suicide of Seneca the Younger, author of *Dialogues* on Stoic thought.

68:     *History of the Jewish War* by a general, Flavius Josephus.

78:     Pliny the Elder dies after compiling the known science of his time.

80:     John completes the last book of the Gospels while in Ephesus.

100:     Tacitus' *Annals of Imperial Rome* describes corrupt emperors.

        Roman couriers carry government mail across the empire.

        Most books of the New Testament are completed.

        In India, Vatsyayana writes of erotic arts, the *Kama Sutra*.

        Mayas adorn pyramids with wall mural painting of mythology.

105:     Chinese imperial eunuch T'sai Lun is officially credited with inventing paper.

113: Pliny the Younger dies; compiled letters describing the life of Rome.

120: Plutarch dies after writing of lives of important Greeks and Romans.

Epictetus' *Discourses* support Stoic concept of calm, disciplined life.

122: Suetonius dies; wrote sensational reports on the lives of *The Twelve Caesars*.

125: Juvenal's *Satires* speak of "bread and circuses" to keep Romans pacified.

150: Ptolemy's *Almagest* puts Earth at center of static universe; errors remain for 1,500 years.

160: Galen's medical treatises will influence but limit medicine for 1,300 years.

Roman Emperor Marcus Aurelius writes Stoic *Meditations* in army camp.

Apuleius' *The Golden Ass*, only Latin fiction to survive in its entirety.

175: Chinese classics are carved in stone that will later be used for rubbings.

180: In China, an elementary zoetrope.

191: Fire destroys Rome's Palatine library.

200: In China, the "suan-pan" abacus; in Japan, the "soroban" abacus.

Scribes start to use uncial script, suitable for writing on parchment.

220: Tertullian supports early Christianity: "It is certain because it is impossible."

230: Japanese begin keeping historical records.

231: In Caesarea, Origen founds school, ties Christianity to Greek philosophy.

235: Dio Cassius dies. His extant histories cover end of republic, rise of imperial Rome.

250: Paper use spreads west from China to central Asia.

270: Plotinus dies after *Enneads* creates foundation of Neo-Platonism.

272: Most of Alexandrian Library destroyed during civil war.

300: First evidence of Christian plays.

In Japan, sumo wrestling.

Chinese couriers during Han Dynasty reach Persia, other far countries.

Goths carve runic alphabet on wood and stone; will continue for 1,000 years.

325: Council of bishops at Nicaea sets course of Catholic Christianity.

338: Jewish calendar is improved by altering length of years.

350: In Egypt, parchment book of *Psalms* bound in wood covers.

Chinese develop xylography, printing of books from wooden blocks.

Chinese bucolic literature flourishes.

370: Rome is said to have 28 public libraries.

386: Singing, including "Hallelujah" hymns, introduced into Christian church.

391: More of Alexandrian Library destroyed; said ordered by Archbishop of Antioch.

393: Church sanctions 27 books of the New Testament; Christian Bible is complete.

400: Writing systems, vocabulary, spread from India to Southeast Asia.

Books cut into pages and bound in codex manner are preferred to scrolls.

Palestinian Talmud, first of two, completed.

A poet, Claudian, writes biased accounts of last days of the Roman empire.

401: Augustine writes his *Confessions*.

405: Jerome translates the Bible into Latin, the Vulgate.

410: Visigoths under Alaric sack Rome.

413: Augustine writes *The City of God*.

415: Murder by monks of woman philosopher Hypatia held to be start of medieval era.

425: Constantinople University is founded.

450: Ink on seals is stamped on paper in China. This is true printing.

Beginnings of Old English; it will last 700 years.

In India, Kalidasa, greatest of classical Sanskrit writers.

476: In India, mathematician Aryabhata writes of roots and powers of numbers.

496: Pope Gelasius I issues a list of banned books.

500: Indian astronomer writes of heliocentric universe, 1,000 years before Galileo.

Indian epic poem, the *Ramayana*, is written.

Peruvians play on drums, flutes, tubas.

Greek and Latin versions of the New Testament in the Codex Bezae.

510: Indian astronomer Aryabhata refers to the zero and place values.

520: The start of Western monasticism will keep learning alive in Christian Europe.

521: Boëthius' *On Music* will be Western standard for 1,000 years.

524: Awaiting execution, Boëthius writes *The Consolation of Philosophy* in prison.

525: Dionysius Exiguus starts "B.C.", "A.D."; incorrectly dates birth of Jesus.

529: Emperor Justinian closes Athenian School of Philosophy, 1,000 years old.

535: Justinian codifies Roman law, the basis of modern civil law.

540: Cassiodorus founds monastery with focus on copying ancient manuscripts.

550: Chess is invented in India.

Buddhism enters Japan, leading to growth of literacy, book publishing.

560: Procopius writes biased first-hand histories of the Byzantine world.

595: In India, calculations done with nine numerals and zero, the decimal system.

598: The first school in England, at Canterbury.

600: Beginnings of Gregorian plainsong chants.

Books printed in China.

Babylonian Talmud, second of two, completed.

600: In China, *The Water Dragon Classic* leads to the study of *fengshui*.

606: Chinese officials establish written examination for civil service positions.

600: Pope Gregory collects church chants; Gregorian Chant named in his honor.

609: Celts play on a stringed instrument, the crwth.

615: The first records of the teachings of Mohammed.

619: In China, large orchestras, with bells, drums, flutes, gongs, guitars.

622: Isidore of Seville's *Origins*, encyclopedic attempt to record world's knowledge.

Start of the Muslim lunar year calendar.

640: Arab invaders find 300,000 scrolls in Alexandrian library.

641:   Invaders shut down Alexandrian book copying, famed school, culture center.

650:   Arab rulers create a news service.

The chapters of the Qur'an (Koran) are collected.

Muslim caliphs set up regular pigeon post, the first news service.

683:   In the Khmer kingdom of Cambodia, the concept of zero appears as a dot.

691:   Dome of the Rock inscriptions are earliest extant quotes from Qur'an.

700:   Sizing agents are used to improve paper quality.

In India, a humorous precursor to the novel, *The Adventures of the Ten Princes*.

Lindisfarne *Gospels* are written, an example of handsome calligraphy.

712:   In Japan, *Kojiki: Records of Ancient Matters*, the sacred book of Shinto.

716:   Codex Amitianus combines Old and New Testaments in 1,030 folios.

731:   In England, the Venerable Bede summarizes most of the learning of his era.

740:   A newspaper is printed in China.

Katakana, one of two syllabic Japanese alphabets.

Moors invade Spain, bringing learning and advanced culture.

750:   The Chinese, with the world's most advanced technology, block-print on paper.

Golden age of Chinese poetry, art.

750:   The Indian zero appears in China, Islamic countries.

751:   Paper made outside of China, in Samarkand, by Chinese captured in war.

760:   Indian numerals, including zero, reach Java.

764:   Japanese Empress Shotoku orders printing of one million Buddhist charms.

765:   Picture books are block printed in Japan.

770:   Oldest surviving printing: a Buddhist prayer for Japanese Empress Shotoku.

771:   Mayan calculation includes place values and the zero.

790:   Schools for religious music in several European cities.

793:   Paper-making moves west to Baghdad at the height of Islamic culture.

800:   Charlemagne crowned first Holy Roman Emperor; signals shift of Christian power.

Irish *Book of Kells*, masterpiece of illumination; now at Dublin's Trinity College.

Charlemagne encourages a revival of learning, the "Carolingian Renaissance."

Western Europe gets a small, neat script style, the "Carolingian Miniscule."

The Gregorian Chant originates in the Frankish Empire.

Government pony express in Charlemagne's Western Europe.

813:   In Baghdad, "House of Knowledge" preserves ancient Greek scientific writing.

816:   In Japan, Kobo Daishi founds Shingon Buddhism center at Mount Koya.

820:   In Baghdad, al-Khwarizmi, develops algebra, algorithms.

830:   Reference is made to a Chinese printed book.

845:   Chinese government prints too much paper money, goes bankrupt.

850:   In Moorish Spain, the *gobar* numerals are used, prefiguring modern numerals.

Arab and Jewish scholars raise European awareness of, interest in, Aristotle.

850: Arab philosopher al-Kindi starts neoplatonic school of Islamic thought.

The Slavs get a writing system; the Cyrillic alphabet will follow.

Church music begins move from monophony to counterpoint, polyphony.

863: Irish philosopher Erigena writes *On the Distribution of Nature*.

Two brothers, both monks, develop the Cyrillic alphabet.

868: The *Diamond Sutra*, block-printed book in China; it's the oldest existing book.

871: Monks begin *Anglo-Saxon Chronicle*, history of England, in Latin.

835: Japanese Buddhist priest, Kûkai, develops hiragana, a second syllabic alphabet.

875: Amazed Western travelers to China see toilet paper.

890: Alfred the Great supervises translation of Latin works into Old English.

900: *The 1001 Arabian Nights* of tales within a tale.

China's Tang Dynasty has courier system with more than 1,600 stations.

940: Jewish philosopher Saadiah translates Hebrew literature into Arabic.

942: Welsh prince orders laws to be written down.

Arabs use kettledrums and trumpets.

950: Paper is made in Damascus and Cairo.

Folded books appear in China in place of rolls.

Women in a Chinese harem invent playing cards.

Lady Li Fu-jen, a Chinese calligrapher, paints on bamboo.

968: In Córdoba, in Muslim-ruled Spain, a university is founded.

972: First woman playwright since ancient Rome, Hroswitha of Gandersheim, dies.

975: In Cairo, studies begin at al-Azhar, now world's oldest university.

First airmail parcel post: pigeons each carry one cherry to Arab caliph.

980: First appearance in Christian Europe (Spain) of Indian-Arabic numerals.

983: An encyclopedia, the *Taiping Yulan*, is produced in China

998: Archbishop Gerbert, scholar and book collector, becomes Pope Sylvester II.

1000: In Japan, Lady Sei Shonagon reveals her amours in *The Pillow Book*.

Epic poem *Beowulf* is written down.

1000: Mayas in Yucatan, Mexico, make writing paper from tree bark.

1002: Murasaki Shikabu's *The Tale of Genji*, is the world's first novel.

1021: Alhazen's study of optics may be first to use empirical, observable science.

1026: Benedictine monk Guido D'Arezzo introduces do-re-mi-fa-so-la scale into singing.

1030: Persian mystic philosopher-physician Avicenna (Ibn Sina) writes *Book of Healing*.

Italian monk Guido d'Arezzo creates solfège system to learn music by ear.

1035: Japanese use waste paper to make new paper.

1038: Arab scholar Alhazen describes a room-size camera obscura.

1048: Pi Sheng, a Chinese commoner, fabricates movable type using clay.

1050: *The Song of Roland* recounts old battle, glorifies French nobility.

In Europe, the harp.

1077:   The *Bayeux Tapestry* completed; depicts the Norman conquest.

1079:   In Persia, Omar Khayyam calculates year's length almost to the minute.

1086:   *The Domesday Book*, census of people and property, reveals life in England.

      Ssu-Ma-Kuang dies after writing history of China, 403 B.C.E. - 959 C.E.

1095:   First Crusade is marker between Dark Ages and Middle Ages.

1100:   Anselm's writings; they will influence Scholastic thought for centuries.

      Gothic Textus script introduced when quill pen is cut at an angle.

      Art and poetry flourish during China's Sung dynasty.

1104:   Gospel of St. John, written in 687 in uncial, found in St. Cuthbert's casket.

1116:   Chinese sew pages to make stitched books.

1126:   In Korea, palace fire destroys library with tens of thousands of books.

      Greek and Arabic scientific books are translated into Latin.

1131:   Persian mathematician Omar Khayyam dies after writing the *Rubáiyát*.

1140:   In Egypt, cloth is stripped from mummies to make paper.

      The University of Bologna, is founded as a center for the study of law.

1142:   French logician Peter Abelard dies; best known for doomed love of Héloïse.

1147:   Crusader taken prisoner escapes with papermaking art, according to a legend.

      Benedictine nun, Hildegard of Bingen, publishes visionary *Scivias*.

1148:   Anna Comnena, daughter of Byzantine emperor, writes history of her time.

1150:   England's Adelard of Bath dies after translating Arabic algebra book into Latin.

      Caliph of Baghdad orders burning of books by philosopher Avicenna.

      Start of 350 years of Middle English.

      Koreans print books from movable type.

1151:   French abbot Suger dies after developing Gothic architecture.

      Papermill built at Jativa, Spain, under the Moors may be first in Europe.

1154:   Monks discontinue *Anglo-Saxon Chronicle* after 183 years.

1155:   Oldest known printed map shows western China.

1158:   Hildegard completes "symphony" of 77 songs.

      Peter Lombard's *Four Books of Sentences* are grounding for Scholasticism.

1161:   Ibn Daud's works establish him as the first Jewish Aristotelian.

1168:   Oxford University is founded.

      Maimonides' *Commentary* on the *Mishnah* shows Aristotelian influence.

1180:   German minnesingers entertain with love songs.

1190:   Aristotelian views of Islamic philospher Ibn Rushd; they will influence Aquinas.

      Maimonides' *Guide to the Perplexed* reconciles Judaism, Aristotelianism.

1194:   Emir of Seville, Spain, burns books of philosophy and logic.

1195:   Pictorial encyclopedia composed and illustrated by Herrad of Landsberg.

1198:   Averroës, Spanish-Arab philosopher, dies; famously wrote on Aristotle.

1200:   The University of Paris is granted its charter, starts mail, messenger service.

1200: Books are copied and sold for profit by stationers, usually at universities.

Tales of love and chivalry, based on an Arab practice, are sung by troubadours.

European monasteries communicate by letter system.

Cymbals join musical performance.

French Dominicans begin the Inquisition to snuff out heresy.

Some religious texts are written in the English vernacular.

1202: Leonardo Fibonacci's *Liber Abaci* establishes Arabic numerals in Europe.

1204: Maimonides dies, revising his 14-volume *Mishneh Torah* to the last.

1215: The *Magna Carta* sets limits on a king's power.

1222: The University of Padua is founded.

1224: The University of Naples is founded.

1225: "The Fibonacci series" introduced in his *Book of Square Numbers*.

1229: The University of Toulouse is founded.

In Toulouse, the Inquisition forbids laymen to read the Bible.

1231: Cambridge University is founded.

1234: Koreans use movable metal type.

1244: The University of Rome is founded.

1253: In Paris, the Sorbonne University is founded.

1262: Birth of Guan Daoshang, most famous of Chinese women artists.

1266: Italian brothers Borgognoni advocate anesthesia, wound cleansing.

1267: Roger Bacon builds a camera obscura to show optical illusions.

Bacon's *Opus Majus* supports empirical study of science, math.

1268: Bacon's *On Experimental Science* supports inductive reasoning.

1270: Syrian scholar compiles an encyclopedia.

Bishop of Paris formally condemns doctrines of radical Aristotelians.

1273: Thomas Aquinas' *Summa Theologica* melds Christian, Aristotelian thought.

1276: At Fabriano, Italy, the first paper mill is built in Christian Europe.

1280: Mechanical clocks using weights and gears gradually replace water clocks.

In China, Kublai Khan establishes a pony express.

1282: In the Fabriano mill, watermarks are added to paper.

1283: Thailand gets its own alphabet.

1285: Eyeglasses are invented in Italy, but correcting only for far-sightedness.

1290: Beatrice, the inspiration of Dante, dies.

French astronomer Guillaume de Saint Cloud describes concept of a camera.

Unknown German author writes epic poem *Lohengrin*.

1298: Marco Polo tells of paper money in China. Few Europeans believe such nonsense.

1300: Wooden type is used in central Asia.

British monk John Duns Scotus writes *Treatise on God as First Principle*.

1305: Taxis family begins private postal service in Europe.

1309: Paper is made in England.

1310: Rainbows are explained as refracted light.

1313: In Florence, Giotto prefigures modern painting.

1321: Dante Alighieri dies after completing his epic poem, *The Divine Comedy*.

1325: Legends of King Arthur are written.

Early organs get pedals.

1328: In England, William of Ockham postulates "Razor" law of parsimony.

1333: Petrarch's discovery of classical manuscripts helps bring on the Renaissance.

1337: Giotto dies. His paintings will influence the great Renaissance artists.

1340: The madrigal, a form of vocal chamber music, originates in northern Italy.

1342: In France, mathematician Levi ben Gershon writes theory of photography.

1350: In Milan, a public striking clock.

Black Death stalks Europe. One in three die.

Lutes are a popular instrument in Europe.

1353: Giovanni Boccaccio's *Decameron* tells tales of earthy love and intrigue.

1360: Before the piano, there was the clavichord and the cembalo.

1373: The Bibliotheque Nationale housed in the Louvre, catalogues 1,000 volumes.

1377: Block printed playing cards in Europe.

1378: In England, the Great Schism; Lollards say lay people can interpret the Bible.

1384: John Wyclif dies after producing copies of English language Bible.

1387: Geoffrey Chaucer writes *The Canterbury Tales*.

1390: The first paper mill in Germany.

1392: Koreans have a type foundry to produce bronze characters.

1395: Improved version of the Wyclif Bible is completed.

1400: In England, allegorical poem *Piers Plowman* criticizes upper class corruption.

1400: From Florence comes the Italic script, a flowing handwriting.

1401: Italian Renaissance in architecture begins in Florence under the Medicis.

1408: Italian sculptor Donatello's *David*.

1415: Czech reformer Jan Hus is burned at the stake in Germany.

1418: The earliest surviving dated woodcut in Europe.

1420: Life is fine for royalty. One recipe calls for 300 doves, 200 chickens, four pigs.

European artists begin painting with oils.

1423: Europeans use xylography (block printing) to produce books.

1430: Block-printed books published in Holland, Germany.

Start of Renaissance music era: sacred music, secular madrigals; lute is favored.

1434: Artist Jan van Eyck paints *Arnolfini Wedding Portrait*.

1436: Leone Alberti writes first book on painting to consider both theory and technique.

1440: Possible date of Johannes Gutenberg's first printing effort.

1441: Painter Fra Filippo Lippi, *The Coronation of the Virgin*.

1441: First artist to use oil-based paints, Jan van Eyck, dies.

1446: The simplifed Korean phonetic alphabet, hangul, with 11 vowels, 28 consonants.

1447: Italian painter Fra Guido Angelico's frescoe, *The Annunciation*.

1448: Gutenberg sets up a printing shop in Mainz.

1450: A few newsletters begin circulating in Europe.

In Germany, Nicholas of Cusa invents concave lenses for near-sightedness.

In England, high point of miracle plays.

Africans carry culture with them as 400 years of slave exports to West begins.

Korea's King Sejong leads a golden age of scientific and humanist learning.

1451: Gutenberg's press prints an old German poem.

1452: Metal plates are used in printing.

Gutenberg begins printing the 42-line Bible in two volumes.

1453: Turks capture Constantinople. Many books disappear from Constantine Library.

1455: First block-printed Bible, the Biblia Pauperum, published in Germany.

1454: Gutenberg prints indulgences, advance pardons for future sins.

1456: Gutenberg's 42-line Bible is illuminated and bound.

Italian painter Piero della Francesca, *The Flagellation of Christ*.

1457: First known color printing, a psalter in Mainz.

1464: The king of France establishes a postal system.

Alberti writes pioneering treatise on sculpture.

1465: *The Doubting of Thomas*, sculpture by Andrea del Verrochio.

French poet, also thief and rogue, Francois Villon dies.

Printed music.

1467: Rome gets a printing press.

1468: Paris gets a printing press.

1472: Dante's epic poem, *The Divine Comedy*, is printed.

1474: German astronomer "Regiomontanus" is the first to use printing for science.

1475: Vatican librarian writes first printed recipes. Hummingbird livers, anyone?

1476: William Caxton brings Gutenberg's invention of printing to England.

1477: Caxton prints *Sayengis of the Philosophres*, the first of a hundred books.

An advertising poster in England.

Hamburg archduke gives diamond to future wife, starting the tradition.

In Florence, the first book with intaglio illustration, *Il Monte Sancto di Dio*.

1480: Caxton prints English fiction by Chaucer, Malory, others.

1482: Marsilio Ficino's *Theologica Platonica* combines Christianity, Platonic thought.

An advertising poster in France.

1484: From Portugal, a manual of sea navigation; tables identify latitudes.

1485: Thomas Malory's, *Morte d'Arthur* creates new legend of King Arthur, knights.

1486: Church-supported *The Hammer of the Witches* attacks witchcraft.

1486: Pico della Mirandola's *Oration on the Dignity of Man* states humanistic view.

1482: Artist Sandro Botticelli, *The Birth of Venus*.

Leonardo da Vinci begins filling notebooks with ideas, sketches.

1485: Alberti's study of architecture is the first printed book on the subject.

1486: Two German monks write a handbook to help identify witches.

1488: A Bible is printed in the Czech language.

1489: German mathematician John Widmann's book introduces "+" , " — " signs.

Aldus Manutius begins career as the greatest publisher of the Renaissance.

1490: Printing of books on paper becomes more common in Europe.

1490: Da Vinci describes principles of the camera obscura.

1492: Great patron of knowledge and art, Lorenzo de Medici, dies at 44.

Columbus sets sail, with Arab geography book, underestimates Earth's diameter.

German map-maker Martin Behaim constructs the first globe.

Profession of book publisher combines type maker, printer, bookseller.

1495: A paper mill is established in England.

1497: In Florence, Savonarola burns books, paintings.

1498: Leonardo da Vinci completes *The Last Supper*.

The toothbrush.

In Venice, the printer Aldus Manutius publishes a book catalogue with prices.

Music is printed in Venice using movable type.

1499: Michelangelo Buonarroti sculpts the *Pietà*.

1500: In England, the growth of middle class literacy.

In England, lead pencils.

1500: Aldus Manutius creates italics.

Book title pages show publisher's imprint, date, page numbers.

In Europe, a portable clock.

Music notation printed with movable type.

During Ming Dynasty China, letter carriers serve private citizens.

By now approximately 35,000 books have been printed, some 10 million copies.

1501: Papal bull orders burning of books that challenge the Church.

Aldo Manuzio designs a small book to replace large codex.

1502: The pocketwatch.

1504: Michelangelo completes his sculpture, *David*.

1506: Leonardo da Vinci finishes painting the *Mona Lisa*.

1507: Map shows the New World, called America, as a separate continent.

1508: Lucas Cranach adds to art of chiaroscuro woodcut engraving prints.

1509: Desiderius Erasmus, *The Praise of Folly*, satirizes behavior of Church clergy.

1510: Venice leads a new art renaissance.

Morality plays are popular in Europe.

1510: The *viola da bracchio*, earliest form of the violin, appears in Italy.

Dutch artist Hieronymous Bosch completes *The Garden of Earthly Delights*.

1511: Raphael completes the Vatican frescoe, *The School of Athens*.

1512: After five years, Michelangelo completes work on the Sistine Chapel ceiling.

1513: Niccolò Machiavelli's *The Prince* offers cold-blooded advice for getting, keeping power.

1514: German artist Albrecht Dürer's engraving, *St. Jerome in His Study*.

1515: Military incursions into Italy help bring the Florentine Renaissance to France.

1516: Sir Thomas More's *Utopia* describes an ideal state, a humanist vision.

Arguably the best poetry of the Renaissance: Ariosto's epic, *Orlando Furioso*.

1517: Martin Luther nails his "Ninety-five Theses" to a church door in Wittenberg.

Luther's Theses are printed in vernacular German, starting the Reformation.

1519: Leonardo da Vinci dies after lifetime of incomparable art and inventive writing.

1520: A written history in Arabic of a city state in East Africa.

1520: One of the world's greatest artists, Raphael, dies at age 37.

1521: Machiavelli's *On the Art of War* intertwines politics and battle.

The Roman Church burns Protestant books.

Cambridge University Press is founded.

1522: Martin Luther publishes German translation of New Testament.

1523: Hans Holbein the Younger, *Portrait of Erasmus*.

1524: The New Testament is published in the Swiss German vernacular.

Erasmus' *Freedom of the Will* attacks Luther's doctrine, upholds moral freedom.

1525: William Tyndale publishes first translation of the New Testament into English.

1526: A Bible is published in Dutch.

1527: A Protestant printer is burned at the stake.

1528: Baldassare Castiglione's book, *The Courtier*, promotes education for women.

1529: In Italy, women appear on stage.

1530: In Rome, the first printed book of madrigals.

A French Bible.

Antonio Correggio paints *Jupiter and Io*.

1533: A postmaster is appointed in England.

1534: Martin Luther finishes translating Old Testament into German vernacular.

With *Gargantua*, physician Rabelais gives his name to debauchery.

1535: Miles Coverdale publishes first English translation of the entire Bible.

John Calvin, *Institution of Christian Religion*, explains idea of elect, damned.

1536: New Testament translator William Tyndale is strangled, burned at the stake.

A newspaper is printed: the *Gazetta* in Venice.

1536: Francesco Guicciardini is first author to consider Italy as one country.

1537: French publishers commanded to send a copy of every book to the royal library.

Henry VIII permits selling of 1,500 Bibles in the English language.

1538: Henry VIII orders a Bible placed in every church in England.

1539: Another Bible appears in the English vernacular, the Great Bible.

In India, mystic poet Guru Nanak dies after founding Sikh religion.

1539: First printer in the Americas, Juan Pablos, brings equipment to Mexico.

1540: Swiss physician Paracelsus argues for pharmaceutical treatment of illness.

1541: A Bible is printed in Swedish.

1543: In Italy, publication of careful anatomical drawings, especially organs.

Andreas Vesalius' *De Fabrica Corporis Humani* corrects Greek medical errors.

Nicolas Copernicus' *De revolutionibus* places sun at the center of our universe.

1544: Spanish and German couriers are allowed to carry private letters.

Illustration of a *camera obscura*, used to trace scenes, is published in Holland.

1545: Garamond designs his typeface.

1547: In England, *The Fyrst Boke of the Introduction of Knowledge.*

1549: In England, the first complete edition of *The Book of Common Prayer.*

1550: Chinese wallpaper brought to Europe.

A Danish Bible is published.

A type maker arrives in Mexico, first in the New World.

Milanese scientist Geralamo Cardano describes a *camera obscura* with a lens.

1552: In Geneva, John Calvin bans dancing, folk medicine, certain clothing.

1553: Michael Servetus burned at stake for *On the Errors of the Trinity.*

1553: Papers are written on blood circulation.

1554: Sculptor Benvenuto Cellini completes *Perseus with the Head of Medusa.*

Anonymous Spanish novel has picaresque theme of wandering rogue.

1555: *Popal Vuh*, holy book of Toltec-Maya, is translated and published in Europe.

In France, Nostradamus publishes his rhymed quatrain prophecies.

1556: Stationers' Company of London gets printing monopoly for all England.

1557: George Wickram writes the first German novel, *Der Goldfaden.*

Estienne du Terte composes a kind of musical suite.

In England, a play is censored: *The Sack-Full of Newes.*

1558: In Elizabethan age, John Knox, a Scot, publishes blast at female monarchs.

Giovanni della Porta recommends camera obscura as an aid to artists.

Child's speller written in England as spelling consistency gradually emerges.

1559: Pope Paul IV creates an *Index of Prohibited Books*; bans books of Erasmus.

1560: The Geneva Bible, supported by dissidents; will influence King James version.

In Italy, the *camera obscura* shrinks from room-sized to portable.

French diplomat Jean Nicot brings tobacco to France. Name gives us "nicotine."

Legalized, regulated private postal systems spread across Europe.

1561: Spanish priest Rúy López writes a book about chess.

1531: A Polish vernacular Bible.

1562: Counter-Reformation attacks secular music; organ will be only church instrument.

1563: In Elizabethan England, Foxe's *Book of Martyrs*, an anti-Catholic propaganda tract.

   The word "Puritan" is coined as an insult to strict Protestant English.

1564: Moscow gets a printing press.

1565: The graphite pencil.

1567: Pieter Bruegel paints *The Peasant Wedding*.

1568: Cartographer Gerardus Mercator draws a projection map of the world.

   Daniele Barbari describes camera obscura with lens and diaphragm.

1568: The Bishops' Bible is printed for Anglican Church.

1569: A Spanish vernacular Bible is printed, but in Switzerland, not in hostile Spain.

   Mercator draws a world map with cylindrical projections.

1570: Women forbidden to sing on stage; castration imitates female voice.

   The Counter-Reformation of the Roman Catholic Church uses printing heavily.

1572: Dutch pigeons carry messages during war with Spain.

1573: Artist Paolo Veronese, *The Feast in the House of Levi*.

1576: Titian paints the *Pietà* in the last year of his life.

1577: Raphael Holinshed's *Chronicle* will give Shakespeare material for plays.

   Giovanni Palestrina composes his most famous mass, *Missa Papae Marcelli*.

1579: El Greco completes painting *The Disrobing of Christ*.

   Thomas North's translation of Plutarch gives Roman material to Shakespeare.

1580: The first of humanist Michel de Montaigne's essays is published.

   Reference made to the English folk song *Greensleeves*. Was Henry VIII composer?

1582: The Gregorian calendar improves on the Julian calendar. Not all adopt it.

   Roman Catholic scholars publish Douay version of the New Testament.

   A dictionary of hard English words is published.

1584: Printing introduced to the New World, in Peru.

1586: Thomas Kyd's *The Spanish Tragedie* may influence Shakespeare's *Hamlet*.

1588: In England, Timothy Bright invents a shorthand.

   Christopher Marlowe's play, *Dr. Faustus*.

   Signal fires report the arrival of the Spanish Armada in the Engish Channel.

   English madrigals, songs of love and sadness, are popular.

1589: Marlowe's play, *The Jew of Malta*.

1590: Hungarians get their own vernacular Bible.

1591: Algebra text by Franciscus Vieta of France introduces *x* and *y*.

1593: William Shakespeare, *Venus and Adonis*.

   A book is printed in the Philippines, *Doctrina Christiana*.

1594: Performances of Shakespeare's *Titus Andronicus*, *The Taming of a Shrew*.

1594: Shakespeare's performance of *The Comedy of Errors*.

In Venice, artist Jacopo Tintoretto finishes *The Last Supper*.

1595: Shakespeare's *Richard II* (possible date).

1596: Edmund Coote writes an English spelling book, arbitrarily chooses spellings.

A Midsummer's Night Dream, *King John* (possible date).

Edmund Spenser's *Faerie Queene* is published.

1597: Shakespeare completes the *Sonnets* (possible date).

The Merchant of Venice (possible date).

Listing of *Romeo and Juliet* in Stationers' Register.

Publication of *Richard III*.

Love's Labor's Lost performed.

Henry IV, parts one and two (possible date)

The Merry Wives of Windsor may have been performed at court.

First real chemistry text published by Libavus of Germany.

1598: First Italian opera, *Dafna*, is performed.

In Denmark, Tycho Brahe's writings advance astronomy.

Reference made to *Two Gentlemen of Verona*.

Possible date of Shakespeare's *Henry V*.

Michelangelo Caravaggio paints *The Calling of St. Matthew*.

1599: The Globe Theatre is built.

In Germany, fixed postal rates.

Julius Caesar is performed.

Much Ado About Nothing, *As You Like It* (estimated date).

1600: Italian philosopher Giordano Bruno burned at the stake for scientific ideas.

Copperplate style of handwriting uses narrow pen nibs to draw fine lines.

William Gilbert's theory tying electricity, magnetism will lead to modern media.

Start of Baroque (Portuguese: "pearl of odd shape") music era, will run to 1750.

English enjoy a new musical instrument, the recorder.

1602: *Hamlet* is entered in Stationers' Register.

Description of a performance of *Twelfth Night*.

Oxford University's Bodleian opens, the first public library in England.

Possible date of a revision of *All's Well That Ends Well*.

1603: In Japan, start of kabuki dance, drama, performed by women.

1604: *Othello*, *Merry Wives of Windsor*, and *Measure for Measure* are performed.

Work begins on the King James version of the Bible.

1605: First regularly published weekly newspaper appears in Antwerp.

1606: *King Lear* and *The Merchant of Venice*.

Ben Jonson's satirical comedy, *Volpone*.

1607: *Macbeth* may have been performed at court.

1607: Modern opera arguably begins with Claudio Monteverdi's *Orfeo*.

1608: *Antony and Cleopatra* and *Pericles* are entered in Stationers' Register.

1609: Johannes Kepler publishes laws explaining elliptical planetary orbits.

Shakespeare's *Sonnets* are entered in Stationers' Register.

Troilus and Cressida is entered in Stationers' Register.

Coriolanus, *Timon of Athens* (possible date).

1610: The Roman Catholic Douay Old Testament follows the 1582 New Testament.

Ben Jonson's play, *The Alchemist*.

1610: Oxford starts to collect a copy of every book printed in England.

1611: The King James version of the Bible is published.

The Winter's Tale and *Cymbeline* are performed.

The Tempest is performed.

1615: Miguel de Cervantes completes *Don Quixote de la Mancha*.

Spanish playwright Lope de Vega, *The Peasant in His Nook*.

1616: In England, George Chapman translates the *Iliad* and the *Odyssey*.

1617: From Scotland, "Napier's bones" are used for calculations.

John Donne's *Songs and Sonnets*.

1620: A book on teaching sign language is published by Juan Pablo de Bonet.

1620: In *Novuum Organum*, Francis Bacon argues for objective scientific induction.

News sheets called "corantos" are sold in Europe.

1622: William Oughtred invents the slide rule.

First ad in an English newspaper, *The Newes*.

1623: Wilhelm Schickard's calculating clock, a forerunner to the computer.

John Donne's memorable line "…for whom the bell tolls" is written this year.

1624: Artist Franz Hals, *The Laughing Cavalier*.

1625: A woman, Francesca Caccini, writes an opera-ballet.

Holland's Hugo Grotius publishes what will be basis of international law.

Spanish playwright Tirso de Molina, *The Trickster of Seville*.

Francesca Caccini, perhaps first woman composer, produces an opera-ballet.

1627: France introduces registered mail as a way to send money.

1628: William Harvey describes the circulation of the blood.

1631: Professional female singers make first appearance in England.

A French newspaper carries classified ads.

1632: Galileo writes his *Dialogo* for the public in support of Copernicus.

In London, a coffeehouse. They will become centers for communication.

1633: Galileo recants during Inquisition trial, is sentenced to lifetime house arrest.

1635: Artist Antony van Dyck, *Lamentation*.

Diego Velázquez paints *The Surrender of Breda*.

Founding of Boston Latin School, first public high school in America.

1636: Harvard University is founded.

1637: French classical dramatist Pierre Corneille's masterpiece, *Le Cid*.

René Descartes' *Discourse on Method* is turning point of modern philosophy.

Painter Nicolas Poussin, *The Rape of the Sabine Women*.

1639: In Boston, someone is appointed to deal with foreign mail.

Puritans ship a printing press to the American colonies.

In Italy, the first comic opera, *Chi Soffre Speri*.

Peter Paul Rubens paints *The Judgment of Paris*.

1640: Some newssheets are printed daily; "corantos" become "diurnos".

Puritan's press in Cambridge, Massachusetts, prints the *Bay Psalm Book*.

1642: Performance of Monteverdi's last and best opera, *L'incoronazione di Poppea*.

Rembrandt van Rijn paints *The Night Watch*.

Puritans close all theaters in England.

1644: John Milton's *Areopagitica* defends freedom to publish.

René Descartes: "Cogito, ergo sum." ("I think, therefore I am.")

1645: Future philosopher Blaise Pascal builds his "Pascaline" calculator.

1646: Kircher, a German Jesuit scientist, builds a magic lantern to project images.

1646: Book describes large camera obscura entered through a trap door.

1648: Swedes attack Prague, seize many books.

1649: Audiences cheer Alessandro Scarlatti's opera, *Gli equivoci nel sembiante*.

1650: From the royal court in Paris, a dance of small steps, the minuet.

Leipzig publishes the first daily newspaper.

Japan, closed to the outside world, creates "No" theater.

In Western music, the overture.

Anglican Bishop James Ussher dates creation from 4004 B.C.; many believe him.

1651: Thomas Hobbes' *Leviathan*: life in nature: "solitary, poor, nasty, brutish, and short."

1653: Parisians can put their postage-paid letters in mail boxes.

Jesuit priest reports Incas use "quipos," colored strings to keep records.

Izaak Walton's *The Compleat Angler* praises the pleasures of fishing.

1655: The word "advertising" is introduced.

1656: Christiaan Huygens constructs an accurate pendulum clock.

English philosopher Margaret Cavendish writes of women's role in society.

1657: In Paris, the earliest fountain pen carries its own ink supply.

A textbook on probability, by Dutch mathematician Christiaan Huygens.

1660: Samuel Pepys begins diary of his life in Restoration England.

1661: Postal service begins within the colony of Virginia.

Bible is published in North America, "Algonquin Indian version."

1662: Church of England's *Book of Common Prayer* includes anthems.

English Parliament declares that censorship is for the public good.

1664: A scientific journal, *Philosophical Transactions*, is published in England.

Molière play *Le Tartuffe* skewers religious hypocrisy, banned by Louis XIV.

1665: Artist Jan Vermeer, *Woman Weighing Pearls*.

Pascal's *Pensees* argues that reason alone is inadequate to satisfy men.

1666: Isaac Newton explains his calculus.

Robert Boyle explains temperature-pressure-volume relations in gases.

Molière's acid pen deals with anti-social people in *Le Misanthrope*.

Leibniz lays foundation for binary calculation.

In Italy, Antonio Stradivari fashions, signs his violins.

After the Great Fire in London, merchants advertise to win back customers.

Isaac Newton publishes his physical laws, notes that light is source of color.

1667: John Milton's *Paradise Lost*. He is paid £10.

1668: John Dryden becomes England's first official poet laureate.

1669: Pepys ends his diary, but it won't be published until 1825.

1670: Pocket watches add minute hands.

Molière's *Le Bourgeois Gentilhomme* ridicules social climbers.

1671: Milton's epic *Paradise Regained* and *Samson Agonistes*.

1673: Mail is delivered on a route between New York and Boston.

In Holland, a paper pulp beating machine.

1674: French tragedian Jean Racine presents his drama *Iphigenia in Aulis*.

1675: Leibniz invents differential and integral calculus.

Concerned about rebellious talk, England's Charles II suppresses coffee houses.

1677: Baruch Spinoza's *Ethics* is published posthumously.

Boston sets up the first organized postal system in the American colonies.

French classicist Jean Racine's best known play, *Phèdre*, is presented, attacked.

1678: Publication of John Bunyan's allegory, *Pilgrim's Progress*.

1679: In London, a business journal is published.

1680: Stradivari makes a cello.

1681: William Dockwra's private penny postal service in London; jealousy will kill it.

1684: In Naples, Scarlatti helps develop operatic structures: aria, overture, recitative.

Robert Hooke lays out plan for visual telegraph; no one tries it.

1685: Johann Sebastian Bach is born.

1686: Leibniz posits a benevolent deity in *Discourse on Metaphysics*.

In Stockholm, Sweden gets a theater.

1687: Newton's *Principia Mathematica*, arguably the greatest scientific book of all time.

1688: The start of the Genroku period, Japan's brilliant flowering of literature.

1689: Henry Purcell composes opera *Dido and Aeneas* for girl's school in Chelsea.

1689: John Locke writes a *Letter Concerning Toleration* of other religions.

1690: Locke's empirical *An Essay Concerning Human Understanding*.

After one issue *Publick Occurrences*, first colonial newspaper, is suppressed.

1691: First papermill in the American colonies, in Germantown, Pennsylvania.

The New England Primer teaches the alphabet plus religious text.

1693: Astronomer Edmund Halley discovers formula for the focus of a lens.

1694: In France, Jean de La Fontaine completes his 12 volumes of animal fables.

In Paris, L'Académie française publishes a dictionary.

1696: By now England has 100 paper mills.

1697: In Holland, Pierre Bayle writes complex *Historical and Critical Dictionary*.

French poet Charles Perrault's *Tales of Mother Goose* tells classic fairy tales.

1698: Public library opens in Charleston, South Carolina.

1700: Protestant German nations adopt the Gregorian calendar promulgated in 1582.

Japan's Chikamatsu Monzaemon writes first tragedies about common people.

1702: Engraving made with three primary colors and black.

1702: In U.S., slaves turn Old Testament stories into spirituals.

1702: The first daily newspaper in the English language, the *Daily Courant*.

1703: Antonio Vivaldi begins composing sonatas, 550 concertos, more than 20 operas.

A newspaper starts publication in Peter the Great's Russia.

1704: Isaac Newton writes on *Opticks*.

Daniel Defoe publishes critical periodical *Review*; foes try to shut him up.

John Harris' *Lexicon technicum*, the first modern encyclopedia.

In the American colonial city of Boston, a newspaper prints advertising.

1705: French horns make their appearance in an opera, *Octavia*.

1709: In London, *The Tatler*, first major magazine.

In Holland, German physicist Gabriel Fahrenheit designs a thermometer.

George Berkeley argues that material objects exist only in our minds.

1710: Berkeley's *Principles of Human Knowledge* explains his "idealism."

German engraver Jakob Le Blon develops three-color printing.

England's copyright act is the basis for protection of intellectual property.

Florence harpsichord maker Bartolommeo Cristofori invents the piano.

1711: Joseph Addison and Richard Steele's *The Spectator* replaces *The Tatler*.

The tuning fork.

Alexander Pope's *Essay on Criticism*.

1712: Invention of steam engine sets the basis for the Industrial Revolution.

1713: François Couperin publishes the first of his harpsichord suites.

1714: Pope's mock-epic poem, *The Rape of the Lock*.

A stamp tax forces the closure of many newspapers in England.

Henry Mill receives patent in England for a typewriter; does not build it.

1716: Italy gets a newspaper, *Diario di Roma.*

1717: George Friederic Handel's *Water Music.*

1719: French scientist Rene de Réaumur proposes using wood to make paper.

Daniel Defoe's *Robinson Crusoe.*

1720: Johann Sebastian Bach composes the *Brandenburg Concertos.*

1721: James Franklin jailed for publishing *New England Courant*; brother Ben takes over.

1722: Defoe's *Moll Flanders.*

British journalists are forbidden to publish Parliamentary debates.

Jean-Philippe Rameau, *Treatise of Harmony*, lays modern music foundation.

1725: Scottish printer develops stereotyping system.

Vivaldi composes *The Four Seasons.*

In London, a circulating library.

1726: Jonathan Swift's *Gulliver's Travels* satirizes aspects of life in England.

1726: Benjamin Franklin starts *The Pennsylvania Gazette.*

Istanbul gets a printing press.

1727: Johann Schulze sees silver nitrate darken, begins science of photochemistry.

1728: An epic poem is written in Swahili.

John Gay's *The Beggar's Opera* is staged.

1729: Swift's sarcastic *A Modest Proposal* suggests eating Irish babies.

J.S. Bach's *St. Matthew Passion* is performed in Leipzig.

1730: John Peter Zenger prints first arithmetic text in American colonies.

1731: In England, *Gentleman's Magazine* calls itself a "magazine."

1732: In Philadelphia, Ben Franklin starts a circulating library.

Franklin begins publication of *Poor Richard's Almanack.* It will run until 1758.

1733: In Madrid, Domenico Scarlatti, son of Allesandro, writes keyboard sonatas.

In Paris, Jean-Philippe Rameau's opera *Hippolyte et Aricie* draws praise, contempt.

1734: Age of Enlightenment begins with Voltaire's *Lettres philosophiques,.*

Alexander Pope's *Essay on Man.*

1735: Viennese musicians begin development of the symphonic form.

Artist William Hogarth completes scenes of *The Rake's Progress.*

John Peter Zenger acquitted of seditious libel.

In Charleston, the start of American musical theater, the ballad opera *Flora.*

1737: *The Biblical Concordance.*

In London, the Licensing Act; the Lord Chamberlain must approve plays.

1739: David Hume expresses empirical philosophy in *Treatise of Human Nature.*

1740: Samuel Richardson's novel, *Pamela,* follows the trials of a virtuous servant girl.

1741: Jonathan Edwards' fiery sermon: "Sinners in the Hands of an Angry God."

Ben Franklin and William Bradford publish first American magazines.

1742: Hume writes *Essays Moral and Political.*

1742: In Sweden, astronomer Anders Celsius also designs a thermometer.

In Dublin, the premiere of Handel's *Messiah*.

Henry Fielding's novel, *Joseph Andrews.*

John Wesley, *Character of a Methodist.*

1748: Hume's *An Enquiry Concerning Human Understanding* challenges faith.

French philosopher Montesquieu will influence American founding fathers.

1749: Henry Fielding's comic masterpiece, *Tom Jones.*

Encyclopedist George Leclerc suggests Earth is older than the Bible indicates.

1750: Russia gets a professional theater.

J.S. Bach dies, signals end of music's Baroque period.

Start of Classic music era, referring to music without folk or popular origins.

1751: Thomas Gray's, *Elegy Written in a Country Churchyard.*

In France, Denis Diderot produces first volume of an encyclopedia.

Hogarth's engraving, *Gin Lane*, lampoons the drunkenness of London's poor.

Benjamin Franklin's *Experiments and Observations on Electricity.*

1752: Canada gets its first newspaper, the Halifax *Gazette.*

Handel composes his final oratorio, *Jephtha.*

Britain, colonies finally adopt Gregorian calendar.

1754: Ben Franklin creates first American cartoon, the "Join, or Die" snake.

1755: Regular mail ship runs between England and the colonies.

Moscow State University is the first institute of higher education in Russia.

Samuel Johnson publishes the great *Dictionary of the English Language.*

1756: In Austria, Wolfgang Amadeus Mozart is born. He will die in poverty in 1791.

1758: Dutch-Japanese dictionary makes Japan more accessible.

1759: Voltaire's *Candide* laughs at the philosophical optimism of Leibniz.

1761: The "father" of symphony, Franz Joseph Haydn, begins career.

1762: Jean-Jacques Rousseau's *Emile* argues for a "natural" education of children.

Rousseau's *The Social Contract* identifies "compact" between men, government.

Christoph Gluck's *Orpheus and Eurydice* transforms opera by emphasizing drama.

1763: English printer John Baskerville publishes a Bible.

1764: Literary salons founded in Paris, London.

Horace Walpole creates the gothic novel with *The Castle of Otranto.*

In Italy, Cesare Beccaria publishes first argument for rehabilitating criminals.

1765: First volume of William Blackstone's *Commentaries on the Laws of England.*

The British Stamp Act taxes newspapers, documents angers American colonists.

English publisher John Newbery brings out a book of Mother Goose rhymes.

1766: Rousseau's quoted "Let them eat cake" is ascribed to Marie-Antoinette, age 11.

Oliver Goldsmith's novel, *The Vicar of Wakefield.*

In England, Nevil Maskelyne publishes *Nautical Almanac*, calculates longitude.

Swedish parliament adopts freedom of the press.

One year after passage, British Parliament repeals unpopular Stamp Act.

1767: Laurence Sterne's, *Tristram Shandy*, gives expanded structure to the novel.

1768: The first of three volumes of the first edition of the *Encyclopædia Britannica*.

1769: Blackstone completes the *Commentaries on the Laws of England*, four volumes.

Watt patents steam engine that will change everything, including communication.

1770: The eraser.

Artist Thomas Gainsborough paints *The Blue Boy*.

In Germany, Ludwig von Beethoven is born.

Goldsmith's poem *The Deserted Village* mourns places ruined by enclosures.

1771: Tobias Smollett's novel, *The Expedition of Humphrey Clinker*.

1772: In France, final volume (28th) of *Encyclopédie*, by Denis Diderot, others.

1773: Goldsmith's witty play, *She Stoops to Conquer*.

1774: Chlorine is discovered; will be used to bleach paper.

Hansard reports of the British House of Commons begin.

1775: Continental Congress authorizes Post Office.

British soldiers' mocking *Yankee Doodle Dandy* adopted by colonial soldiers.

1776: Adam Smith, *An Inquiry into the Nature and Causes of the Wealth of Nations*.

German writers develop "sturm und drang" (storm and stress) movement.

Thomas Jefferson drafts a Declaration of Independence.

Thomas Paine stirs the colonists with his pamphlet *Common Sense*.

1777: Richard Brinsley Sheridan's comedy of manners, *School for Scandal*.

Capt. James Cook, *Voyage towards the South Pole in 1772-5*.

Ammonia is used to block the darkening of silver salts.

1778: Mozart composes the *Paris Symphony*. He is 22.

In Milan, one of the world's great opera houses, La Scala, is built.

1779: In Germany, Gotthold Lessing's drama *Nathan the Wise* is a plea for tolerance.

In Vienna, Gluck's *Iphigénie en Tauride* continues to emphasize drama in opera.

Thomas Jefferson argues unsuccessfully for tax-funded education.

1780: Steel pen points begin to replace quill feathers.

Richard Challoner's translation of Douay Bible, standard for English Catholics.

1781: Immanuel Kant, *Critique of Pure Reason*, will influence future philosophers.

1782: Pierre Choderlos de Laclos, *Liaisons dangereuses*.

Spanish king grants tolerance to gypsies; their music and flamenco come out..

Noah Webster publishes an American speller.

1783: Under Catherine the Great, Russia allows private printing presses.

Pensylvania Evening Post, the first daily newspaper in America.

1783: Heinrich Grellman's *Die Zigeuner* is a rare sympathetic report on Gypsy life.

1784: French book paper is made from vegetation without rags.

Artist Joshua Reynolds, *Mrs. Siddons as the Tragic Muse.*

Capt. James Cook, *Voyage to the Pacific Ocean in 1776-80.*

William Wordsworth starts writing poetry.

Benjamin Franklin invents bifocals.

First mail delivery by coaches, between London and Bristol.

1785: Stagecoaches carry the mail between towns in the United States.

Panorama art reportedly invented in debtor's jail by Robert Barker.

1786: Robert Burns' *Poems* include: "The best laid schemes o' mice an' men..."

Mozart, *The Marriage of Figaro.*

1787: Mozart, *Don Giovanni, Eine Kleine Nachtmusik.*

In the new United States, the Constitution.

Antonio Salieri's best known composition, the opera *Tarare.*

1788: In three months Mozart composes three symphonies, including the *Jupiter.*

In London, *The Times.*

Kant, *Critique of Practical Reason*, explores the "categorical imperative."

Edward Gibbon completes *The Decline and Fall of the Roman Empire.*

1789: Jeremy Bentham's *Principles*: the greatest good for the greatest number.

The French National Assembly votes the *Declaration of the Rights of Man.*

A chemistry textbook is written by Antoine Lavoisier, inventor of periodic table.

New United States proposes *Bill of Rights*, with freedom of faith, speech, press.

In England, the narrative of a former slave is published.

William Blake's *Songs of Innocence.*

Abingdon Press is founded.

French Revolution calls for press freedom, but road will be bumpy.

1790: In England, the hydraulic press is invented.

British adopt secret ship-to-ship code using 10 colored flags, code book.

Mozart, *Così fan tutte.*

The first U.S. copyright law, protection for 14 years.

Edmund Burke writes conservative *Reflections on the Revolution in France.*

1791: James Boswell's *The Life of Samuel Johnson.*

Mozart, *The Magic Flute.*

The Marquis de Sade shocks France with *Justine.*

England gets a new newspaper, the *Observer.*

Thomas Paine defends the French Revolution in *The Rights Of Man.*

The Surprise Symphony, one of more than 100 symphonies by Haydn.

Congress passes the First Amendment.

Philadelphia to N.Y. coded light messages of financial news outrace horses.

1792: In Britain, postal money orders.

J.B. Lippincott begins to publish books.

Mary Wollstonecraft's feminist treatise, *A Vindication of the Rights of Woman.*

The Farmer's Almanac begins more than 200 years of annual publication.

French revolutionary government establishes a ministry of propaganda.

Postal Act promises mail regularity throughout U.S.

Alien and Sedition Acts limit freedom to publish in recently born U.S.

1793: In Germany, business schools for young women.

Johann Schiller's *On Grace and Dignity* criticizes Kant's ethical theories.

The Louvre palace becomes a museum.

1793: Jacques-Louis David paints *The Death of Marat.*

1794: William Blake's *Songs of Experience.*

First letter carriers appear on American city streets.

In Revolutionary France, Claude Chappe sets up semaphore signaling system.

Opening of the first Panorama, forerunner of movie theaters.

Nearly flat rate U.S. postal law mails most newspapers for a penny stamp.

1795: Thomas Paine, *The Age of Reason.*

1796: Madame de Staël's essays inform French nation about the Enlightenment.

American Cookery, the first cookbook by an American, Amelia Simmons.

Burns' *Auld Lang Syne* is published; sung on New Year's Eve.

1797: Paine's *Essays on Religion* see deism as alternative to traditional religion.

In England, a heavy tax is levied on newspapers to limit the radical press.

1798: Aloys Senefelder in Munich invents lithography. He will write about it in 1818.

In England, Thomas Malthus writes his *Essay on the Principles of Population.*

Samuel Johnson's great nephew publishes the first American dictionary.

Nickolas Robert in France invents the "Fourdrinier" paper-making machine.

Coleridge and Wordsworth jointly publish book containing now famous poetry.

1799: From the French Academy of Science, the metric system.

1800: Romantic movement in Europe rebels against rationalism, reason, classicism.

Starting in France, silhouettes are popular; decline when photography arrives.

Mozart's *Requiem* is published.

Friedrich Schleiermacher invents hermeneutics.

Semaphore-like system built between Boston and Martha's Vineyard.

In Germany, a simple sizing process for paper.

Inaugural voyage on the Erie Canal announced by a line of cannons firing.

The popular dances are minuets and quadrilles. Partners barely touch hands.

In Japan, *haiku* verse form gains popularity.

Iron press permits printing on large sheets of paper, thicker fonts.

Wordworth's *Lyrical Ballads* will be the mainfesto of the Romantic movement.

1800: Letter from Portland, Maine, takes only 20 days to reach Savannah, Georgia.

In West Africa, the emir of Gwandu writes religious poetry.

Allesandro Volta's battery provides first long-term source of electricity.

Ludwig von Beethoven's *First Symphony in C Major.*

Parson Weem's *The Life of Washington* creates myths about the first president.

1801: Semaphore system built along the coast of France.

Joseph-Marie Jacquard loom uses punch cards, anticipates computers.

Beethoven's *First* and *Second Piano Concertos.*

Haydn's *The Seasons.*

1801: Thomas Young theorizes that the retina is sensitive to blue, green, and red light.

In Germany, Carl Gauss lays foundation of modern number theory.

Thomas Jefferson begins tradition of annual presidential messages to Congress.

1802: Beethoven's *Second Symphony, Moonlight Sonata.*

Library of Congress established.

Thomas Wedgewood produces silhouettes with silver nitrate, but they darken.

Samuel Hutton's book on changes in earth's crust foreshadows Darwin.

1803: The periodic table of atomic elements is created.

Semaphore code is used on ships.

1804: Beethoven's *Third Symphony (Eroica)* begins music's Romantic period.

Fourdrinier machines put into operation to increase paper output.

1804: Artist Francisco Goya's *Nude Maja* and *Clothed Maja.*

1805: Beethoven's *Fidelio, Fourth Piano Concerto.*

Walter Scott's ballad epic, *The Lay of the Last Minstrel,* is immediate success.

1806: Beethoven's *Fourth Symphony in B Flat, Violin Concerto (Op 61).*

Noah Webster publishes *A Compendious Dictionary of the English Language.*

Carbon paper.

William Wilberforce's 1789 speech in Parliament against slave trade is printed.

1807: Camera lucida is invented, improves image tracing.

Beethoven's *Fifth Symphony, Leonora No. 3, Coriolanus.*

John Wiley & Sons publish books.

Charles and Mary Lamb, *Tales from Shakespeare.*

In Russia, Romani (Gypsies) are allowed to form a music chorus and perform.

1808: In *Speeches to the German Nation*, Johann Fichte encourages nationalism.

Turri of Italy builds a typewriter for a blind contessa.

Beethoven's *Fifth Symphony* and *Sixth Symphony (Pastoral).*

Thomas Moore's *Irish Melodies* advance the cause of Irish nationalism.

Sweden's Berzelius publishes lectures changing awareness of life's processes.

The first war correspondent: Henry Robinson of *The Times* of London.

1809: Beethoven's *Fifth Piano Concerto.*

1809: George Gordon, Lord Byron, *English Bards and Scotch Reviewers*.

John Dickinson invents a cylinder paper-making machine.

Washington Irving's *Rip Van Winkle*, who wakes after 20 years.

1810: An electro-chemical telegraph is constructed in Germany.

Scott's *The Lady of the Lake*.

Postal services consolidated under uniform private contracts.

1811: A printing press is powered by steam.

In France, the forerunner of the Havas news agency is formed.

1811: Jane Austen's *Sense and Sensibility* examines English middle-class morality.

Luddite riots will forever give a name to opponents of advances in technology.

1812: Beethoven's *Seventh Symphony* and *Eighth Symphony*.

Pierre Laplace argues for calculating the probability of natural events.

Byron gains fame with *Childe Harold's Pilgrimage*.

Georg Wilhelm Hegel explains dialectical reasoning in *Science of Logic*.

Brothers Wilhelm and Jacob Grimm write their truly grim *Fairy Tales*.

1813: Austen publishes *Pride and Prejudice*.

Franz Schubert composes the first of nine symphonies.

Byron's *The Bride of Abydos* wins praise.

Troy, NY, *Post* editorial introduces "Uncle Sam" to represent U.S.

Percy Bysshe Shelley's, *Queen Mab*, a poem of social protest.

Jonathan Wyss completes *Swiss Family Robinson*, begun by his father.

Congress authorizes steamboats to carry mail.

1814: In England, a steam-powered press prints *The Times*, 1,100 copies an hour.

Walter Scott publishes *Waverly* (and all future novels) anonymously.

Jane Austen's *Mansfield Park*.

In destroying Washington, D.C., British troops burn down Library of Congress.

Schubert creates the German "lieder" (art songs). He will write more than 500.

Under Napoleon, optical signal system stretches from Belgium to Italy.

Francis Scott Key writes *The Star Spangled Banner*, new words to drinking song.

1815: 3,000 post offices in U.S.

Pigeons carry news of Waterloo; bankers make killing on stock market.

John Vanderlyn's painting of a nude is condemned in New York City.

1816: Post Office carries newspapers for less than 2 cents postage.

Book by John Hoyland, English Quaker, calls for decent treatment of Gypsies.

Joseph Nicéphore Niépce captures a negative image on paper, but it darkens.

Coleridge's *Kublai Khan*, written in 1797, is published.

Gioacchino Rossini's *Barber of Seville*.

Schubert writes his *Fifth Symphony*.

From Vienna to London: the waltz. *Times* calls it indecent touching of arms.

1817: Harper & Row publishing house is founded.

David Ricardo's *Principles of Political Economy* considers economics a science.

1816: American Bible Society founded; wants to put *Bible* in every American home.

1818: In France, the first dictionary on *The Language of Flowers*.

Stamped letter paper is sold in Sardinia.

In England, Thomas Bowdler's *Family Shakespeare* has rude words expurgated.

Mary Wollstonecraft Shelley writes *Frankenstein*.

1818: Jane Austen's novels *Persuasion, Northanger Abbey* published posthumously.

Lord Byron's *Don Juan* is published.

Schubert's *Sixth Symphony*.

Scott's novels *Rob Roy, Heart of Midlothian*.

Arthur Schopenhauer writes pessimistic *The World as Will and Representation*.

In Sweden, Berzelius isolates selenium; its electric conductivity reacts to light.

1819: John Herschel publishes work on photographic chemical processes.

Napier builds a rotary printing press.

Hans Oersted's electromagnetism discovery; will be essential to communication.

Charles LaTour's noisemaker adds to world history of warning signals.

In France, freedom of the press.

1820: Arithmometer, forerunner of the calculator.

Walter Scott's *Ivanhoe*.

In *Principles of Political Economy*, Malthus urges delay of marriage.

Washington Irving, *The Sketch Book*.

John Keats' *Ode on a Grecian Urn* is the height of literary romanticism.

1821: In England, Charles Wheatstone reproduces sound.

The Saturday Evening Post. It will publish weekly until 1969.

Thomas De Quincey's *Confessions of an English Opium Eater*.

Carl Maria von Weber's opera, *Der Freischutz*.

The *Manchester Guardian* begins publication.

Artist John Constable, *The Hay Wain*.

Thomas Jefferson's *Autobiography* expresses debt to ideas of John Locke.

Free public high school opens in Boston. Free education will aid literacy.

1822: Jean Champollion deciphers hieroglyphics by translating the Rosetta Stone.

Diorama paintings, lit in dark room, are a forerunner of projection cinema.

Biologist Jean-Baptiste Lamarck argues that species transmit acquired traits.

Franz Schubert's unfinished *Eighth Symphony*. He dies in 1828, age 31.

Joseph Niépce is able to photograph an engraving superimposed on glass.

Bowdler "bowdlerizes" the Old Testament of sexy or "irreligious" passages.

1823: Beethoven's *Ninth Symphony (Choral)*.

In Britain, a medical journal, *The Lancet*, is published.

1823: Clement Moore's poem, "A Visit from St. Nicholas," introduces Santa Claus.

Charles Babbage builds a section of a calculating machine, a "difference engine."

Percy Bysshe Shelley's *Posthumous Poems* published.

In England, Ronalds builds a telegraph in his garden; no one is interested.

1824: The Cherokee people get their own alphabet, 85 letters. Literacy booms.

British physicist Peter Mark Roget describes persistence of vision.

1825: Persistence of vision shown with the Thaumatrope, disk with image on each side.

Pepys Diary is published 156 years after he stopped writing it.

Russian poet Aleksandr Pushkin's *Boris Godunov*. Permission to publish in 1830.

Height of Japan's *ukiyo-e* period, wood-block prints of the "floating world."

In France, a law makes sacrilege a capital offense.

1826: James Fenimore Cooper's novel, *The Last of the Mohicans*.

Age 17, Felix Mendelssohn composes overture to *The Midsummer Night's Dream*.

Promoting adult education, the Lyceum Movement grows in the U.S.

1827: Using a camera obscura, Niépce makes a true photograph on a pewter plate.

Eugenè Delacroix paints *The Death of Sardanapalus*.

Heinrich Heine's early poetry published in *Book of Songs*.

Wheatstone constructs a kind of microphone and a kind of image scanner.

First African-American newspaper, *Freedom's Journal*.

1828: First Native American newspaper, *Cherokee Phoenix*.

Ladies' Magazine, first successful American magazine for women.

1828: Gioachino Rossini's *William Tell Overture*.

In Belgium, the Anorthoscope is a forerunning of a motion picture projector.

The first volume of John James Audubon's 10-volume *The Birds of America*.

Webster's *American Dictionary of the English Language*, for educated adults.

London's University College: professorship of English Language and Literature.

1829: Louis Daguerre joins Niépce to pursue photographic inventions.

Charles Wheatstone also invents the concertina.

The first of 13 volumes of the first edition of *The Encyclopedia Americana*.

William Burt gets the first U.S. patent for a typewriter.

In Paris, *The Poetical Works* of Coleridge, Shelley, and Keats are published.

1830: Calendered paper is produced in England.

Godey's Lady's Book, a second U.S. magazine targeting women readers.

Book of Mormon published, the basis of a religion founded by Joseph Smith.

Railway, Manchester to Liverpool, uses 5-needle telegraph.

Hector Berlioz' *Symphony Fantastique* breaks with traditional form.

1831: Essayist Thomas Carlyle writes his spiritual autobiograhy, *Sartor Resartus*.

William Lloyd Garrison publishes abolitionist newspaper, *The Liberator*.

Victor Hugo's novel, *The Hunchback of Notre Dame*, is best seller.

1831: Pushkin's novel in verse, *Eugene Onegin*; it will become a Tchaikovsky opera.

Stendhal's novel, *The Red and the Black* sensitively examines French society.

Hegel's *Lectures on the Philosophy of History*.

Artist Jean-Baptiste Corot, *View of the Forest of Fontainebleau*.

G. & C. Merriam start book publishing firm.

Vincenzo Belli stages his opera *Norma*.

Faraday's research in electromagnetism will lead to world of communication.

The Quarterly Journal of Education begins publication.

1832: Houghton, Mifflin publishing house established.

In England, Philip Watt invents sewing machine, can bind books.

Byron's poetry, letters, journals are published posthumously.

Publication of the poems of Wordsworth, Tennyson.

Phenakistoscope in Belgium and stroboscope in Austria herald the movies.

Wheatstone builds a stereoscopic, but non-photo, viewer.

Paper jackets are wrapped around book covers.

Frédéric Chopin's *Mazurkas (op 6)*.

Johann Wolfgang Goethe completes *Faust*, dies. It speaks to eternal yearnings.

1833: A penny buys a newspaper, the *New York Sun*, opening a mass market.

Mendelssohn composes *Fourth Symphony in A*.

In Japan, Hiroshige's drawings: *Fifty-three Stages of the Tokaido Highway*.

In Germany, the Weber and Gauss telegraph line runs for nearly two miles.

Prussian general Karl von Clausewitz' *On War* published posthumously.

Mendelssohn's, *Italian Symphony*.

1834: Edward Bulwer-Lytton's popular novel, *The Last Days of Pompeii*.

The zoetrope, a toy using a rotating drum, gives the illusion of movement.

Lithographer Honoré Daumier, *Rue Transnonain*.

A Bohemian peasant girl invents the polka.

Babbage conceives the analytical engine, forerunner of the computer.

Louis Braille creates a raised-point code to help the blind to read.

1835: Penny press expands with James Gordon Bennett's newspapers.

Hans Christian Andersen publishes his *Fairy Tales*.

New York Herald founded, starts to build a reference library of books.

Lucia di Lammermoor, most famous of Gaetano Donizetti's 60-plus operas.

In England, W. H. Fox Talbot produces his first photographs, the first negative.

P.T. Barnum begins his career.

Alexis de Tocqueville's *Democracy in America* looks at the new country.

1836: First of phenomenally successful *McGuffey Readers*, moral tales for youth.

In Russia, Gogol writes *The Inspector General*.

German playwright Georg Buchner, *Woyzeck*.

1836:   Ralph Waldo Emerson's essay on *Nature* starts transcendentalist movement.

1837:   Wheatstone and Cooke patent an electric telegraph in England.

Rowland Hill's pamphlet on postal reform; will have global influence.

Charles Dickens becomes famous with publication of *The Pickwick Papers.*

1837:   Leigh Hunt publishes book of poems, including "Jenny Kissed Me."

Isaac Pitman's *Stenographic Soundhand* introduces shorthand.

Nathaniel Hawthorne, *Twice Told Tales.*

Start of Little, Brown, publishing house.

Samuel Morse exhibits pendulum telegraph, but Alfred Vail invents Morse Code.

In Massachusetts, Horace Mann starts campaign for public school system.

Thomas Carlyle publishes *The French Revolution.*

Daguerre creates daguerreotype.

1838:   *New York Herald* opens bureaus in Europe.

In England, Wheatstone explains depth perception, but mirror stereoscope fails.

G.P. Putnam's Sons, book publishers.

Dickens' *Oliver Twist.*

Germany's K.A. Steinheil finds that grounding can aid telegraph transmission.

1839:   John Herschel's hypo fixative stops darkening of photographs.

Cameras manufactured for sale, the Giroux Daguerreotype.

Daguerre's paper to Royal Society begins photography craze.

Stereoscopic photos—stereographs—are shot.

Dickens' *Nicholas Nickelby.*

The New York Philharmonic.

India gets an experimental electrical telegraph 21 miles long.

Chopin completes composition of 24 *Preludes.*

In Russia, Jacobi invents electrotyping, the duplicating of printing plates.

Electricity runs a printing press.

In London, a commercial telegraph line sends messages.

Fox Talbot's calotype method prints photographs from paper negatives.

Marie Henri Stendahl's novel, *The Charterhouse of Parma.*

1840:   Charles Darwin publishes *Voyage of the H.M.S. Beagle.*

German paper makers experiment with wood pulp.

Richard Henry Dana exposes seamen's life in *Two Years Before the Mast.*

Richard Wagner's first successful opera, *Rienzi.*

Dickens, *The Old Curiosity Shop.*

Donizetti's opera, *The Daughter of the Regiment.*

Anarchist Pierre Proudhon opposes both property and equality for women.

In China, thousands of post offices handle letters, packages, remittances.

England starts penny post. Stamps are cheap, so people write more letters.

1841: Petzval of Austria builds an f/3.6 lens, the first designed for photography.

In the U.S., Volney Palmer is the first ad sales agent.

New York Tribune begins publication.

Dickens' *Barnaby Rudge.*

The satirical magazine *Punch* starts to publish.

Thomas Cook, a Baptist minister, opens a travel agency.

Robert Browning's cynical poem, *Pippa Passes.*

James Fenimore Cooper's adventure novel, *The Deerslayer.*

Edgar Allan Poe's *The Murders in the Rue Morgue* starts modern detective story.

Wagner's fourth opera, *Der fliegende Holländer (The Flying Dutchman).*

Ralph Waldo Emerson's humanistic essay, *Self-Reliance.*

The first type-composing machine goes into use in London.

Phineas Barnum opens his museum in New York City.

First American women university graduates.

1842: *Illustrated London News* begins publication with engravings.

Charles E. Merrill, book publisher, opens for business.

In England, Alexander Bain demonstrates a crude fax machine.

Another use for paper: the first commercial Christmas card.

Alfred Lord Tennyson's *Morte de Arthur.*

In Russia, Mikhail Glinka's opera, *Russlan and Ludmilla*, is hissed by audience.

Cyanotype film printing: white image on blue background. Still used.

1843: Donizetti's comic opera, *Don Pasquale.*

In the U.S., the photographic enlarger.

A photo portrait studio is opened in Edinburgh, Scotland.

John Stuart Mill publishes *System of Logic.*

Wheatstone telegraph installed alongside railroad in England.

Denmark's Søren Kierkegaard's *Either-Or* will become a basis of existentialism.

Dickens' *A Christmas Carol*, a huge success, and *Martin Chuzzlewit.*

Byron's daughter, Ada Lovelace, explains concept of computer programming.

The Economist is founded.

On an American stage, the first blackface minstrel show.

British Algae, an album illustrated with photographs, is produced by Anna Atkins.

Congress gives Morse funds to build an experimental telegraph line.

Rubbery "gutta percha" is found in Malaya, a future submarine cable wrap.

Exchanging Christmas cards becomes popular.

Thomas Hood's *Song of the Shirt* stirs anger at working conditions of women.

Edgar Allan Poe writes the first modern mystery story, *The Gold Bug.*

1844: William Makepeace Thackeray, *Barry Lyndon.*

Samuel Morse's telegraph connects Washington and Baltimore.

1844: In Germany, paper is made from wood pulp.

A camera is designed to take panoramic photographs.

A newspaper is published in Thailand.

Electrotyping in book printing makes plates of type and woodcuts.

Fox Talbot publishes *The Pencil of Nature,* first book with photographs.

Alexander Dumas' *The Three Musketeers.*

1845: U.S. postal reform bill lowers rates, regulates domestic and international service.

The typewriter ribbon.

Rules are written for a popular pastime: baseball.

Submarine cable is laid across the English Channel.

Mathew Brady opens a portrait studio in New York.

Telegraph message leads to capture of murderer in London.

Friedrich Engels, *The Conditions of the Working Class in England.*

Horace Mann leads movement to improve U.S. public education.

Wagner's opera, *Tannhäuser.*

Benjamin Disraeli begins career as a novelist, with *Sibyl.*

Edgar Allan Poe writes his most famous poem, *The Raven.*

Dickens' *The Chimes* and *The Cricket on the Hearth.*

1846: In Germany, Zeiss begins manufacturing lenses.

In France, Prosper Merimee's play, *Carmen*; it will lead to Bizet's opera.

Richard Hoe's cylinder press produces 8,000 sheets an hour.

Herman Melville's first novel, *Typee,* life among South Seas cannibals.

Printing telegraph is forerunner of ticker tape.

Dickens' *Dombey And Son.*

Edward Lear publishes his *Book of Nonsense.*

Dumas' *Man in the Iron Mask* and *Count of Monte Cristo.*

Hector Berlioz' *Damnation of Faust.*

Henry Rawlinson deciphers cuneiform writing, key to Babylonian history.

1847: Ralph Waldo Emerson, *Poems.*

Honoré de Balzac: *Cousin Bette*

The first Merriam-Webster dictionary.

Congress sells demonstration line; first use of telegraph as business tool.

Charlotte Brontë's *Jane Eyre* criticizes limited options for women.

Emily Brontë's *Wuthering Heights*; doomed love and revenge.

William Makepeace Thackeray's *Vanity Fair* is serialized.

George Boole's *Mathematical Analysis of Logic*; basis for computer programs.

Henry Wadsworth Longfellow's epic poem, *Evangeline.*

1848: Forerunner of the Associated Press is founded in New York.

Wagner's opera *Lohengrin.*

1848: *The Communist Manifesto*, a pamphlet by Karl Marx and Friedrich Engels.

Elizabeth Gaskell's *Mary Barton*, reveals misery of industrial age England.

Egg whites are discovered to hold photo negatives on glass plates.

Spiritualism becomes popular; alleged communication with the dead.

Walt Whitman starts the newspaper *Brooklyn Freeman*.

John Stuart Mill, *Principles of Political Economy*.

The first two volumes of Thomas Babington Macaulay's *History of England*.

Dante Gabriel Rossetti begins England's Pre-Raphaelite poetry movement.

Jacob Grimm publishes *History of the German Language*.

1849: The photographic slide.

Antonio Meucchi demonstrates what may (or may not) be a telephone.

Photographs of Egyptian pyramids begin travel photography.

Dickens' *David Copperfield*.

Gustave Courbet paints *The Stone Breakers*.

First edition of *Who's Who*.

Twin-lens camera can take pictures for stereoscopic viewing.

The term "advertising agency" is used by Volney B. Palmer.

Henry David Thoreau's essay, "The Duty of Civil Disobedience."

1850: Number of U.S. public libraries triples in 25 years.

Elizabeth Barrett Browning publishes *Sonnets from the Portuguese*.

Mathew Brady publishes collection of photographs of famous Americans.

Auguste Comte, French philosopher, founds discipline of sociology.

In China, foreign nations operate the postal systems.

Alfred Lord Tennyson's lyrical poem, *In Memoriam*, is published anonymously.

Olive Gilbert's *Narrative of Sojourner Truth*, former slave, is published.

A new use for paper, the paper bag.

Jean-François Millet paints *The Sower*.

Robert Schumann's *Third Symphony*, the *Rhenish*.

The New York Times founded as the *Daily Times*.

Ballroom dances divided into "round dancing" and "square dancing."

Antonio de Torres Jurado invents the modern guitar.

Submarine cable briefly connects England and France.

Songs of Labor, of New England, arguably John Greenleaf Whittier's best work.

Nathaniel Hawthorne, *The Scarlet Letter*.

P.T. Barnum sets a razzle-dazzle tone with newspaper ads and handbills.

1851: Soap is mass marketed.

Herman Melville's novel of the obsessive search for the great whale, *Moby Dick*.

In London, Frederick Bakewell demonstrates fax machine to send pictures.

Hawthorne, *The House of the Seven Gables*.

1851: In the U.S., paper is made from wood fiber.

Stereoscope stirs public excitement at a London exhibition.

Sojourner Truth gives "Ain't I a Woman" speech in face of jeers by hostile men.

In Japan, type molds are designed to replace traditional wood printing blocks.

The Erie railroad depends on the telegraph.

Scott Archer invents wet-plate photography process.

In England, Talbot takes a flash photograph at 1/100,000 second exposure.

U.S. newspaper postage cut in half; free distribution within county.

The Reuters news agency is founded.

Giuseppe Verdi's *Rigoletto* is staged.

Fire damages the Library of Congress.

Stephen Foster composes *Old Folks at Home* for a minstrel show.

1852: Peter Mark Roget assembles his *Thesaurus of English Words and Phrases.*

Harriet Beecher Stowe's *Uncle Tom's Cabin* increases abolitionist support.

Postage stamps are widely used.

Telegraphic fire alarm system adopted in Boston, will spread worldwide.

E.P. Dutton, book publisher.

Dickens' *Bleak House.*

Massachusetts is first state to enact compulsory education law.

Verdi's *Il Trovatore.*

1853: Envelopes are made by a paper folding machine.

London Stock Exchange sets up first pneumatic tube message delivery.

Duplex system doubles telegraph wire capacity.

European optical signalling system has 556 stations.

Richard Wagner publishes the librettos to *The Ring Cycle.*

Franz Liszt's *Sonata in B Minor* changes the structure of the sonata.

Verdi continues his operatic magic with *La Traviata.*

1854: Telegraph brings news of the Crimean War.

In Paris, *Le Figaro.*

Thoreau publishes *Walden.*

Patent issued for a flexible film roll holder.

Bourseul in France builds an experimental telephone.

Carte-de-visite process simplifies photography.

Dickens' *Hard Times.*

Wagner's opera, *Das Rheingold.*

Curved stereotype plate obviates column rules; wide ads follow.

George Boole develops logic system that future computers will depend on.

1855: Prepayment of letters made compulsory in the United States.

Walt Whitman publishes, at his own expense, *Leaves of Grass.*

1855: In London, the *Daily Telegraph*.

The Bondwoman's Narrative, a novel apparently written by a former slave.

First edition of John Bartlett's *Familiar Quotations*.

French diplomat Joseph Gobineau publishes racist book on Nordic supremacy.

The stopwatch.

Photographers Roger Fenton and James Robertson go to Crimean War.

Longfellow's *Song of Hiawatha*.

Registered letters enter service.

Photo studios offer cheap, finished-while-you-wait ambrotypes.

Charlotte Brontë dies in childbirth before completing *Emma*.

Dickens' *Little Dorrit*.

Publication of the collection of legends known as *Bulfinch's Mythology*.

A privately owned newspaper is published in Sierra Leone.

1856: Poitevan starts photolithography.

Origin of Rand, McNally.

Electric clocks.

Photojournalism begins with pictures of the Crimean War.

Portugal gets a railroad and a telegraph line.

500,000 stereoscopes sold in Europe in two years, one million stereographs.

Photographer Mathew Brady starts trend with large-type newspaper ads.

First full-page ad runs in a newspaper, the *New York Ledger*.

Blotting paper replaces sand boxes.

Another Wagnerian opera, *Die Walküre*.

Machine folds paper for books, newspapers.

1857: A machine to set type is demonstrated.

Currier & Ives prints go on sale.

Harper's Weekly magazine features engraved illustrations.

Reports from Germany's Neanderthal Valley: bones of a pre-modern man.

Gustave Flaubert's *Madame Bovary* leads to immorality trial; he is acquitted.

Thomas Hughes, *Tom Brown's School Days*.

Elizabeth Barrett Browning's "novel in verse," *Aurora Leigh*, praised, attacked.

In France, Scott's phonautograph is a forerunner of Edison's phonograph.

Atlantic Monthly is published.

Anthony Trollope's *Barchester Towers*.

Les Fleurs du mal, the only poetry published during Charles Baudelaire's life.

Matthew Arnold, new professor at Oxford, writes poetry and literary criticism.

1858: Mailboxes appear on American streets.

First effort at transatlantic telegraph service fails.

Work begins on the *Oxford English Dictionary*.

1858: Eraser is fitted to the end of a pencil.

In London's Covent Garden, an opera house goes up.

George Eliot (Mary Ann Evans) writes *Adam Bede*, first of eight novels.

1859: Camera gets a wide-angled lens.

The telautograph is another precursor to recorded sound.

Edward FitzGerald publishes *The Rubáiyát of Omar Khayyám*.

A novel by an African-American woman, Harriet Wilson, is published.

Gounod writes an opera about the legend, *Faust*.

Dickens' *A Tale of Two Cities*.

Telegraph crosses U.S. from Atlantic to Pacific.

Jacques Offenbach's comic opera, *Orpheus in the Underworld*.

Tennyson's *Idylls of the King*.

Wagner's opera, *Tristan und Isolde*.

George Meredith's novel, *The Ordeal of Richard Feverel*.

Charles Darwin's *On the Origin of Species* sells out in a day, but creates fury.

John Stuart Mill's *On Liberty* is a far-seeing liberal exposition.

1860: Pony Express carries mail between St. Joseph, Missouri, and Sacramento.

Dickens' *Great Expectations*.

Panoramic photography is improved by using curved glass plates.

260 magazines are published in the United States.

"Dime novels," printed on cheap, rough paper, sell well.

New York *Herald* creates the first "morgue" of newspaper clippings.

Frenchman Rene Dagron invents "microfilm" technique using glass plates.

Eliot's *The Mill on the Floss*.

The first aerial photographs are taken from a balloon over Paris.

1861: The first American Ph.D. is awarded by Yale University.

German inventor J.P. Reis demonstrates a kind of electric telephone.

Charles Reade's picaresque novel, *The Cloister and the Hearth*.

Telegraph brings Pony Express to an abrupt end.

Julia Ward Howe composes "Battle Hymn of the Republic."

Kinematoscope by U.S. inventor Coleman Sellers, is a crude movie projector.

George Eliot publishes her best loved novel, *Silas Marner*.

First chemical means to color photography.

Mathew Brady and others begin to photograph the American Civil War.

Aerial balloonist sends telegraph message.

Heliostat message, using sun and a mirror, sent 90 miles at Lake Superior.

Patent issued for a single-lens reflex camera.

James Clerk Maxwell shows that red, green, and blue are the primary colors.

1862: Verdi stages his opera *La Forza del Destino*.

1862: In Italy, Caselli sends a drawing over a wire.

Ivan Turgenev's nihilist novel, *Fathers and Sons*.

In the U.S., paper money.

Jean-Auguste Ingres paints *The Turkish Bath*.

The first of philosopher Herbert Spencer's 10 volumes of *Principles*.

Victor Hugo's *Les Misérables*.

1863: Abraham Lincoln's Gettysburg Address, arguably history's greatest speech.

William Bullock invents the rotary web-fed letterpress.

Edward Everett Hale, *The Man Without a Country*.

Early phonograph: a machine that records what a piano plays.

The Football Association Laws lets everyone play the same game.

Painter Edouard Manet shocks with nude *Luncheon on the Grass*.

Typotelegraph sends fax messages between London and Liverpool.

Large U.S. cities get free home delivery of mail.

First international postal conference held in Paris.

1864: "Railway post office" sorts mail on trains.

Innocenzo Manzetti invents what may be a telephone; seeks no patent.

Dickens' *Our Mutual Friend*.

Maxwell publishes electromagnetic theory that leads to radio wave discovery.

Postal money orders sold in U.S; $1.3 million in 6 months.

Jules Verne's *Journey to the Centre of the Earth.*

1865: Experimental photograph is developed inside a camera.

"Lewis Carroll" publishes *Alice's Adventures in Wonderland*.

Mark Twain gets fame with "The Celebrated Jumping Frog of Calaveras County."

In Paris, the beginnings of the International Telegraph Union.

Two San Francisco newspapers, *Examiner* and *Chronicle,* publish.

Botanist Gregor Mendel, writing on heredity, begins science of genetics.

Louis Pasteur publishes his theory that germs spread disease.

West Virginian Mahlon Loomis manages a kind of wireless communication.

After adult novels mailed to Civil War troops, Congress votes obscenity law.

Paris and Berlin build networks of pneumatic tube telegram delivery.

Most U.S. states have laws guaranteeing tax-based public education.

Pantelegraph transmits faxes commercially between Paris and Lyon.

Web offset press prints both side of a continuous roll of paper at once.

1866: Western Union dominates U.S. wires.

In Sweden, before the Nobel Prizes, Alfred Nobel invents dynamite.

Photos of Yosemite Valley will help pass laws to protect U.S. scenic places.

In Prague, *The Bartered Bride*, an opera by Bedrich Smetana, is staged.

Atlantic cable ties Europe and U.S. for instant communication.

1866: Prussia uses telegraph to coordinate its armies in war against Austria.

Fyodor Dostoevsky's *Crime and Punishment.*

The Black Crook, a musical play, foreshadows musical comedies.

1867: Christopher Sholes of Wisconsin builds a Type-Writer.

Double-column advertising in newspapers.

Karl Marx publishes *Das Kapital.*

Johann Strauss' waltz, *The Blue Danube.*

The West sees Japanese art at the Paris Exposition.

Prussia nationalizes Taxis mail service.

Charles Gound's opera, *Romeo and Juliet.*

Louisa May Alcott's novel, *Little Women.*

Henrik Ibsen's drama, *Peer Gynt.*

Wagner's opera, *Die Meistersinger von Nürnberg.*

The first Japanese magazine, *Seiyo Zasshi* (*The Western Magazine*).

1868: A communication necessity: the stapler.

Dostoevsky's *The Idiot.*

Start of Allyn & Bacon, book publishers.

Edward Grieg's *Piano Concerto in A Minor.*

U.S. government for the first time tries to define obscenity.

Thomas Edison patents a vote recorder.

In Philadelphia, the N.W. Ayer & Son full-service advertising agency.

Tchaikovsky's *First Symphony* is well received. He is 28.

1869: From France, color photography, using the subtractive method.

Cardiff Giant hoax inspires comment, "There's a sucker born every minute."

Leo Tolstoy's *War and Peace* is published.

Horatio Alger begins publishing rags-to-riches novels.

Biologist Thomas Huxley coins the term "agnostic."

The American Women's Home is best-selling book of household advice.

John Stuart Mill and Harriet Taylor, *On the Subjection of Women.*

Matthew Arnold's *Culture and Anarchy* labels him "the apostle of culture."

From Austria, postcards.

Edison patents stock ticker and printing telegraph.

Mark Twain, *The Innocents Abroad.*

James Russell Lowell, *The Cathedral.*

1869: John Hyatt's invention of celluloid will lead to phonograph records, telephones.

The *People's Literary Companion,* the first mail-order periodical.

American Newspaper Directory estimates newspaper circulation.

1870s: States pass laws to protect scenery from ad sign painters.

1870: More than 5,000 newspapers are published in the U.S.

1870: Stock ticker comes to Wall Street.

Two from Jules Verne: *20,000 Leagues Under the Sea* and *Mysterious Island*.

Léo Delibes' ballet, *Coppélia*.

William Jackson's Yellowstone photographs aid efforts to preserve U.S. heritage.

Once and future prime minister Benjamin Disraeli publishes last novel, *Lothair*.

Dickens does not live to complete *The Mystery of Edwin Drood*.

Bret Harte writes Western stories, like "The Luck of Roaring Camp."

Wood pulp is widely used to make paper.

Pigeons carry microphotographed secret messages in Franco-Prussian War.

Telegraph across Europe and Asia connects London with Calcutta, 11,000 km.

French postal authorities use hot air balloons during siege of Paris.

1871: Artist James Whistler, *The Artist's Mother*.

Japan gets a newspaper, Yokohama *Mainichi Shimbun* (*Daily Newspaper*).

Verdi's opera *Aida* premieres in Cairo.

Arguably the toughest newspaper interview ever, Stanley meets Livingston.

Wagner's opera, *Siegfried*.

British Dr. Richard Maddox proposes gelatin from bones as photo emulsion.

Darwin's scholarly *Descent of Man* raises indignation about monkey ancestors.

Eliot begins serialization of her *Middlemarch*.

In Boston, the *Globe* publishes.

Lewis Carroll (mathematician Charles Dodgson) writes *Through the Looking Glass*.

Jules Verne's novel, *Around the World in 80 Days*.

Louisa May Alcott's novel, *Little Men*.

P.T. Barnum opens a circus, calls it "The Greatest Show on Earth."

1872: Dentist Mahlon Loomis gets patent for wireless invention, but was it radio?

James McNeill Whistler paints a portrait of his mother.

Simultaneous transmission from both ends of a telegraph wire.

Under Meiji Restoration, Japan embarks on drive to expand book publishing.

Mark Twain, *Roughing It*.

George Smith deciphers cuneiform tablets containing the epic of *Gilgamesh*.

Susan B. Anthony casts a ballot and is arrested for it.

The Montgomery Ward mail order catalog.

Erewhon (anagram of "Nowhere"), Samuel Butler's satire of English life.

Bruckner's *Second Symphony*.

1873: U.S. postcard debuts; costs one penny.

Illustrated daily newspaper appears in New York.

Report about selenium, resistance, and light is a step toward television.

British children are required to go to school.

Typewriters get the QWERTY pseudo-scientific keyboard.

1873: Lord Kelvin calculates the tides with a machine.

In Ireland, May uses selenium to send a signal through the Atlantic cable.

Remington starts manufacturing Christopher Sholes' typewriter.

Anthony Comstock gets government O.K. to inspect mails for vice.

French astronomer Pierre Janssen designs a photographic "revolver."

1874: Quadriplex telegraph system allows four messages to travel over single wire.

Baudot telegraph code prints using five channels of paper tape.

Pictures from an Exhibition by Modest Moussorgsky.

A Civil War Union Army bugle tune is officially named "Taps."

Verdi's *Requiem* is performed.

After much rejection, Mussorgsky's opera, *Boris Godunov*, performed.

The peak of Viennese operetta: Johann Strauss II's *Die Fledermaus*.

Wagner's *Götterdämmerung* completes the *Ring of the Nibelungen*.

Second Symphony wins Peter Tchaikovsky public acclaim.

In France, the first show of the impressionist painters.

Thomas Hardy's novel, *Far from the Madding Crowd*, appears serially.

1875: Universal Postal Union formed in Berne, Switzerland.

In England, William Crookes builds a forerunner to the cathode ray tube.

In France, the praxinoscope, an optical toy, a step toward movies.

Mary Baker Eddy's *Science and Health*, cornerstone of Christian Science.

Edison invents the mimeograph while trying to improve telegraph tape.

French composer Georges Bizet's opera, *Carmen*, has unsuccessful opening.

Gilbert & Sullivan's *Trial by Jury*.

U.S. has 257 public libraries.

Cheap book reprints published in series called "libraries."

Peter Ilyich Tchaikovsky's *Third Symphony* (*Polish*), *First Piano Concerto*.

In the U.S., George Carey designs a selenium mosaic to transmit a picture.

1876: "Mr. Watson, come here. I want you." Bell invents the telephone.

Elisha Gray files phone patent application the same day Bell does.

National Baseball League is founded.

Mark Twain's *The Adventures of Tom Sawyer* considers fence painting.

French poet Stéphane Mallarmé's "The Afternoon of a Faun" will inspire Debussy.

Feminist Annie Besant's *The Legalisation of Female Slavery in England*.

Amilcare Ponchielli's opera, *La Gioconda*.

Tolstoy's *Anna Karenina*.

Melvil Dewey develops a library book classification decimal system.

Edgar Degas paints *The Glass of Absinthe*.

The player piano.

Herbert Spencer applies evolution to society, coins "the survival of the fittest."

1876: In Norway, Edvard Grieg composes the *Peer Gynt Suite*.

Tchaikovsky's *Marche Slav*.

Johannes Brahms' *First Symphony*. He labored over it for 15 years.

1877: Brahms' *Second Symphony*.

Edwin Holmes builds a telephone switchboard.

Eadweard Muybridge photographs horse in motion, forerunner of movies.

Bell "photophone" uses light to transmit audio, anticipates fiber optics.

A weather map is printed in an Australian newspaper.

In France, Charles Cros invents the phonograph.

In America, Edison also invents the phonograph.

French composer Camille Saint-Saëns' opera, *Samson and Delilah*.

Impressionist Camille Pissarro, *Red Roofs*.

The Fixation of Belief sets Charles Peirce as a founder of American pragmatism.

Robert Louis Stevenson writes his first stories; many written from a sick bed.

In Japan, ten years after the first magazine is published, there are 200.

Tchaikovsky's ballet, *Swan Lake*.

The *Washington Post* starts printing.

Emile Berliner invents the microphone. So does David Hughes.

Anna Sewell's much loved novel, *Black Beauty: The Autobiography of a Horse*.

1878: Karl Klic produces a commercially successful means of photogravure printing.

Portuguese professor Adriano de Paiva writes proposal for a video system.

Edison invents a better microphone.

Thomas Hardy's novel, *The Return of the Native*.

Gilbert & Sullivan's operetta, *HMS Pinafore*.

Telephone directories are issued.

In New Haven, Connecticut, a telephone central exchange.

A photograph is reproduced using halftone method.

Full page newspaper ads.

A Cincinnati stenographer's school teaches typing with ten fingers, not two.

Joseph Pulitzer begins empire with the *St. Louis Post-Dispatch*.

Emma Nutt becomes the first woman hired as a telephone operator.

Punch cartoon imagines "telephonoscope": global, interactive, flat-panel HDTV.

Founding of Johns Hopkins University Press.

Dry-plate photography replaces messy, inconvenient wet plates.

Thomas Edison gets a patent for a phonograph talking doll.

First of 300 patents issued for acoustic "string" telephones.

Quaker Oats, the first mass-marketed breakfast food.

1879: Starting in Lowell, Massachusetts, telephone numbers replace names.

Benday process aids newspaper production of maps, drawings.

1879: Dostoevsky's novel, *The Brothers Karamazov*.

George Eastman builds a machine to mass produce photographic dry-plate film.

Gilbert & Sullivan's *The Pirates of Penzance*.

Henry James, *Daisy Miller*.

National Bell Telephone Company is formed.

Henry George, *Progress and Poverty*, calls for a single tax on land.

Tchaikovsky's opera, *Eugene Onegin*, based on Pushkin.

An electric telescope is designed to capture moving images.

Henrik Ibsen's *A Doll's House* shocks audiences when Nora leaves her husband.

Addition to communication and culture: the electric light bulb.

Postal law separates periodical rates from advertising matter.

1880: Civil War General Lew Wallace's novel, *Ben Hur*.

Muybridge's Zoopraxiscope projects photographic images in motion.

Tchaikovsk's *1812 Overture*.

Emile Zola's realistic novel, *Nana*.

Sculptor Auguste Rodin begins *Gates of Hell*, never completes it.

Offenbach dies before completing *Tales of Hoffmann*.

France's Leblanc theorizes transmitting a picture in segments.

An American, John Paine, writes a symphony, *In Spring*.

A halftone photograph, "Shantytown," appears in a newspaper.

Antonin Dvořák's *First Symphony*.

Parcel post.

National Bell, others merge into American Bell Telephone Company.

Advertising copywriter becomes an occupation.

The U.S. has about 50,000 telephones.

From Italy, Carlo Collodi's tale for children, *Pinocchio: The Story of a Puppet*.

Birth of Helen Keller, who will learn to communicate by sign language.

Telephone pay stations are opened in New York.

John Powers, the first skilled ad copy writer.

Richard Strauss, age 16, wins acclaim with *Symphony in D Minor*.

A dispatch is telegraphed from a field of battle (the Second Afghan War).

1881: Tchaikovsky's *Violin Concerto in D*.

The *Los Angeles Times*.

France gets press freedom; this time it lasts.

The first photographic roll film.

The Electric Telescope, a book about television, intrigues readers.

In London, the Savoy Theater is built to house Gilbert & Sullivan operas.

Women enter the business world via the typewriter.

A revised edition of the New Testament is published.

1881: Business offices acquire typewriters, begin to look modern.

Paris Exposition lets visitors listen to opera over telephone headsets.

Bell and Tainter's Graphophone; has better sound than Edison phonograph.

Selford Bidwell sends electronic image by telegraph using photoelectric cell.

1882: Mark Twain's novel, *The Prince and the Pauper.*

Gilbert & Sullivan's operetta, *Iolanthe.*

Wagner's final opera, *Parsifal.*

In England, a twin-lens camera goes into production.

Emma Lazarus' sonnet is inscribed on the pedestal of the Statue of Liberty.

In England, the first wirephotos.

Etienne Jules Marey designs a rifle-like camera that shoots 12 photos per second.

Walt Whitman's *Leaves of Grass* is banned in Boston.

1883: After many rejections, Anton Bruckner succeeds with *Seventh Symphony.*

Edison stumbles onto "Edison effect"; later, basis of broadcast vacuum tubes.

Annie Besant, *The Bitter Cry of Outcast London*, exposes industrial poverty.

Stevenson's *Treasure Island.*

Newspapers are folded by machine.

Pulitzer buys the *New York World* from financier Jay Gould.

Buffalo Bill Cody opens his Wild West Show.

Nietzsche, *Thus Spake Zarathustra.*

Mark Twain's recollections, *Life on the Mississippi*, first typed book manuscript.

Henrik Ibsen's play, *An Enemy of the People.*

1884: In Germany, Paul Nipkow's scanning disc, early version of television.

People can now make long distance phone calls.

The electric tabulator.

The Stebbing Automatic Camera, first production model to use roll film.

Jules Massenet's opera, *Manon.*

Lewis Waterman designs a practical fountain pen that doesn't blot.

The letter "A" of the *Oxford English Dictionary* is finished; volume published.

Mark Twain's *Adventures of Huckleberry Finn.*

1885: Fingerprints are used for identification.

Dictating machines are bought for offices.

American Bell Telephone Co. creates AT&T for its long distance business.

H. Rider Haggard's *King Solomon's Mines.*

Transparent film negatives are sold.

U.S. Post Office offers special delivery.

Scottish game of golf crosses the Atlantic.

Mail rates for publications drop to a penny a pound.

Franz Liszt completes nineteen *Hungarian Rhapsodies.*

1885: Tchaikovsky's *Manfred Symphony*.

Vincent van Gogh paints *The Potato Eaters*.

Richard Burton's *The Arabian Nights* sets imaginations aflame.

Gilbert & Sullivan's operetta *The Mikado*. It will infuriate Japanese.

Trains are delivering newspapers daily.

"Nellie Bly" begins career as exposé reporter.

Emile Zola's *Germinal*, about a bitter coalminers' strike in France.

Robert Louis Stevenson's *A Child's Garden of Verses* and *Prince Otto*.

William Dean Howells, *The Rise of Silas Lapham*.

1886: Sapphire stylus improve sound.

Little Lord Fauntelroy, a novel by Francis Burnett.

Pointillist painter George Seurat, *Bathing at Asnières*.

Tokyo's Imperial University is founded.

Berne Convention sets up international copyright agreements.

Thomas Hardy's novel, *The Mayor of Casterbridge*.

Friedrich Wilhelm Nietzsche, *Beyond Good and Evil*.

Stevenson's *The Strange Case of Dr. Jekyll and Mr. Hyde* and *Kidnapped*.

Rudyard Kipling begins a long writing career with *Departmental Ditties*.

One-third of all books published in U.S. are cheap paperbacks.

Ottmar Mergenthaler's Linotype at *New York Tribune* replaces setting type by hand.

Amos Dolbear gets patent for wireless communication using induction.

1887: Cellulose photographic film on a roll is developed by New York clergyman.

William Randolph Hearst gets his first newspaper, the *San Francisco Examiner*.

Montgomery Ward mails out a 540-page catalog.

Annie Sullivan meets Helen Keller; will develop touch teaching for the blind.

St. Nicholas Magazine, best of early children's magazines; will publish until 1943.

Berliner gets music from a flat "gramophone" disk stamped out by machine.

Thomas Edison assigns engineer W.K.L. Dickson to create a motion picture camera.

In Chicago, with a broomstick and an overstuffed ball: softball.

Comptometer multi-function adding machine is manufactured.

Impressionist Pierre Renoir, *The Bathers*.

Alexander Borodin dies before finishing his opera, *Prince Igor*.

Arthur Conan Doyle writes his first short story about Sherlock Holmes.

Ads appear in magazines.

Nietzsche, *On the Genealogy of Morals*, calls for heroic morality, supermen.

1888: A new magazine: *National Geographic*.

Wisconsin telegraphy teacher George Parker designs a new pen.

Printer's Ink, a newspaper for the advertising industry.

Cesar Franck composes the *Symphony in d Minor*.

1888: "Kodak" box camera makes picture taking simple. The "snapshot" is born.

In London, the *Financial Times*.

Considered an office machine, the phonograph is franchised in territories.

Edison tries to record movies on a wax cylinder like his phonograph.

Richard Strauss' tone poem, *Don Juan*.

McGraw-Hill begins book publishing.

Heinrich Hertz proves that radio waves exist.

Experimental motion pictures are recorded on sensitized paper rolls.

The first beauty contest is held in Spa, Belgium.

The Kodak box camera, $25, takes 100 pictures on a roll.

The coin-operated public telephone, patented by William Gray.

Tchaikovsky's *Fifth Symphony*.

Nikola Tesla invents alternating current.

John Loud patents ballpoint pen; never manufactured.

Nikolai Rimsky-Korsakov's tuneful symphonic suite, *Scheherazade*.

Edison's phonograph is manufactured for sale to the public.

Oberlin Smith sets forth theory of magnetic recording.

Lehigh Valley Railroad adopts wireless telegraph; uses induction coil.

1889: Eleven years after patent, Edison mass produces a phonograph doll.

William Dickson reportedly synchronizes motion pictures with phonograph.

John Philip Sousa's "Washington Post March" honors the newspaper.

Andrew Carnegie, "The Gospel of Wealth"; endows 2,800 libraries, much else.

Mark Twain's *A Connecticut Yankee in King Arthur's Court*.

Eastman sells cellulose roll film.

The Wall Street Journal.

Coin-operated phonographs are placed in bars, arcades, the first jukeboxes.

Richard Strauss' tone poem, *Death and Transfiguration*.

Robert Louis Stevenson's *The Master of Ballantrae*.

Columbia Phonograph Company issues one-page music record catalog.

1890: Herman Hollerith counts the U.S. population with punch cards.

A.B. Dick markets the mimeograph.

William James' *Principles of Psychology* moves the field toward science.

Rimsky-Korsakov and Glazunov complete Borodin's opera, *Prince Igor*.

Oscar Wilde's *The Picture of Dorian Gray* is serialized in *Lippincott's Magazine*.

Typewriters are in common use in offices.

The $1 Brownie camera; film is 15 cents a roll.

In Germany, Karl Ferdinand Braun invents the cathode ray tube.

James Frazer's *The Golden Bough* draws parallels between myth and Christianity.

First juke box: coin-operated cylinder phonograph with 4 listening tubes.

1890: In England, Friese-Greene builds the kinematograph camera and projector.

In France, Branly's coherer conducts radio waves.

How the Other Half Lives by Jacob Riis alerts public to life in city slums.

Tchaikovsky's ballet, *Sleeping Beauty*.

Emily Dickinson's first book of *Poems*.

Pietro Mascagni's opera *Cavalleria rusticana*.

In Paris, Theatrophone subscribers can hear live performances by phone.

1891: Diazotype put photographs onto fabric.

Large press prints and folds 90,000 4-page papers an hour.

Telephoto lens is attached to the camera.

Guy de Maupassant goes insane after writing novels, plays, 300 short stories.

An international agreement on copyright.

J. Walter Thompson, first advertising account executive.

Thomas Hardy's *Tess of the D'Urbervilles*.

A mortician, Almon Strowger, develops automatic phone switching exchange.

Edvard Grieg writes two suites for Ibsen's play, *Peer Gynt*.

Photographers can load camera film in daylight, not just in a darkroom.

Impressionist Claude Monet, *Haystacks*.

Herman Melville writes the tragic novel *Billy Budd*, unpublished until 1924.

Ibsen's play, *Hedda Gabler*.

American Express issues travelers cheques.

The first international phone call via submarine cable, London - Paris.

Founding of precursor to the Outdoor Advertising Association of America.

Sears mails 8,000 postcards with imitation handwriting; gets 2,000 orders.

Edison and Dickson construct the peep-show Kinetoscope, 46 frames per second.

1892: Parker Pen Company begins business, based on patent for a new fountain pen.

4-color rotary press.

Frederick Ives invents natural color photographic system.

Artist Mary Cassatt, *The Bath*.

Wilde's play, *Lady Windermere's Fan*, is a success.

Portable typewriters.

Paul Cézanne paints *The Card Players*.

Invented in Iowa, the Addressograph enters the office.

Tchaikovsky's ballet, *The Nutcracker*.

Ruggiero Leoncavallo's opera *Pagliacci*.

Kipling's *Barrack-Room Ballads* are published.

Arthur Conan Doyle's stories published as *The Adventures of Sherlock Holmes*.

Automatic telephone switchboard comes into service.

Chicago editor's "Who or what? How? When? Where?" advice is 5W start.

1892: *The Ladies' Home Journal* decides to refuse ads for patent medicine.

1893: Dickson builds a motion picture studio in New Jersey.

In Budapest, Telefon Hirmondo, pre-broadcast news and entertainment.

Finnish composer Jean Sibelius writes *The Swan of Tuonela.*

From France, first color photo of a living person.

Jacob Riis' *Children of the Poor* shakes complacent New Yorkers.

Coca Cola is registered as a trademark by a pharmacist in Atlanta.

Norwegian artist Edvard Munch, *The Scream.*

Magazine circulation war creates mass national readership in the U.S.

Dickson's Kinetograph camera uses perforated film to sync with shutter.

Robert Louis Stevenson's novel, *David Balfour.*

Dvorák's final *Symphony No. 9, From the New World.*

On a Paris stage, the striptease.

Brazilian priest Landell de Moura allegedly invents voiced radio.

Englebert Humperdinck's opera, *Hansel and Gretel.*

Tchaikovsky conducts premiere of *Sixth Symphony (Pathetique).*

Antonin Dvorák's *Fifth Symphony in E Minor (The New World).*

1894: Emile Berliner sells 1,000 gramophones, 25,000 records.

Kipling's *The Jungle Book.*

In New York City, Edison opens a Kinetoscope movie parlor.

Wilde succeeds again with another play, *The Importance of Being Earnest.*

The word "spaceship" appears in print.

English satirist Max Beerbohm writes letters in the style of Oscar Wilde.

George Bernard Shaw's *Arms and the Man.*

Claude Debussy's *Prelude to Afternoon of a Fawn.*

1895: E.A. Wallace Budge translates *Egyptian Book of the Dead, Papyrus of Ani.*

Stephen Crane, *The Red Badge of Courage.*

Single-lens reflex cameras are popular, but expensive.

Frederic Remington's sculpture, *Bronco Buster.*

France's Lumière brothers' portable movie camera can also print, project films.

In Italy, teenager Guglielmo Marconi sends a radio signal more than a mile.

Richard Strauss, *Til Eulenspiegel's Merry Pranks, Thus Spake Zarathustra.*

In Berlin, Max and Emil Skladanowsky show a 15-minute motion picture.

In a Paris cellar, a paying audience sees Lumière's motion pictures projected.

In Louisville, Ben Harney introduces ragtime music.

Vitascope adds intermittent motion loop to movie projector.

Artist Francis Barraud paints *His Master's Voice*, with Nipper listening.

Hearst takes over the *New York Morning Journal.*

In England, Friese-Greene invents phototypesetting.

1895: William Butler Yeats, lyrical Irish poet, publishes *The Lake Isle of Innisfree*.

Gustav Mahler's *Second Symphony*.

Thomas Hardy's novel, *Jude the Obscure*.

Dial telephones go into Milwaukee's city hall.

1896: Adolph Ochs buys dying *New York Times*, begins path to greatness.

To date, 450,000 typewriters have been manufactured.

Underwood model permits typists to see what they are typing.

John Philip Sousa pens *Stars and Stripes Forever*.

The Monotype sets type by machine in single characters.

In London, the *Daily Mail* begins publishing.

Hilaire Belloc's *The Bad Child's Book of Beasts*.

Giacomo Puccini's opera, *La Bohème*.

Edison short film, *The Kiss*, called immoral by critics.

Maryland enacts first shield law for journalists.

Alfred Nobel creates the Nobel Prize.

The film company Gaumont is founded.

Electric power is used to run a paper mill.

Edison Vitascope, designed by Thomas Armat, brings film projection to U.S.

Edison's Kinetoscope comes to Japan.

The first comic strip, *The Yellow Kid*, in the *New York American*.

In Britain, the motion picture projector is manufactured.

Trading stamps.

Hollerith founds the Tabulating Machine Co. It will become IBM in 1924.

X-ray photography.

Fannie Farmer's Boston Cooking School Cookbook.

An estimated 150,000 typewriters are in use in the U.S.

Anton Chekhov's *The Seagull* barely survives disastrous opening night.

Rural free delivery (RFD) is inaugurated in the United States.

Hard resinous shellac phonograph disks replace hard rubber.

Nikola Tesla invents a spark radio transmitter.

Theodor Herzl, *Der Judenstaat*, begins Zionist movement.

English poet A.E. Housman, *A Shropshire Lad*.

Turned down by Italy, Guglielmo Marconi takes radio gear to England.

1897: Newspaper comic strips are collected and sold, precursor to comic books.

The term "public relations" is used in book, *Year Book of Railway Literature*.

In England the Marconi Company is set up for wireless telegraphy business.

In Germany, Braun improves the Crookes' tube with fluorescence.

Eldridge Johnson patents an improved, inexpensive disk gramophone.

Music record sales grow; mostly classical and Tin Pan Alley songs.

1897: In England, postmen deliver mail to every home.

Edison patents a movie projector.

The Katzenjammer Kids begin cartoon antics.

Bram Stoker's horror novel, *Dracula*.

Fire kills 125 people watching a motion picture in a Paris theater.

Cyrano de Bergerac, a play by Edmond Rostand.

A new book publishing firm starts, Doubleday.

General Electric creates a publicity department.

Kipling's *Captains Courageous*.

Paul Gaugin in Tahiti paints *Nevermore*.

World's first cinema, just for films, is built in Paris.

1898: Lumière boasts a catalogue of more than one thousand short films.

Newspapers, led by Hearst and Pulitzer, help push U.S. into war with Spain.

Émile Zola's article "J'Accuse" shakes France.

H.G. Wells' novel *The War of the Worlds* brings the Martians.

Rodin sculpts *The Kiss*.

Peking University is founded.

Henry James' short novel, *The Turn of the Screw*.

Photographs taken by artificial light.

A loudspeaker is invented.

Elizabeth Cady Stanton's *The Woman's Bible* urges suffragist cause.

New York State passes a law against misleading advertising.

Oscar Wilde, out of prison, writes *The Ballad of Reading Gaol*.

Sound is recorded magnetically on wire by Valdemar Poulsen of Denmark.

Notre Dame professor sends a wireless telegraph message for one mile.

World total of working telegraph wire: almost three million miles.

1899: California passes law to regulate political cartoons.

Magnetic sound recording.

Western Union boasts nearly one million miles of wire, 22,285 offices.

Marconi radio gear installed in British warships, signals across English Channel.

Economist Thorsten Veblen coins the term "conspicuous consumption."

American Marconi Company incorporated; forerunner of RCA.

Nathan Stubblefield claims to transmit voice by radio, but he will die in poverty.

Edward Elgar composes *The Enigma Variations*.

Telephone company reorganizes; AT&T takes over parent American Bell.

Debussy composes *Nocturnes*.

Scott Joplin popularizes ragtime music; starts the first dance craze.

Cakewalk dance is popular, grows out of black slave ridicule of white dancing.

The first Japanese-made film.

1900:   The *Oxford English Dictionary* letters "A" to "H" are published.

Visitors to Paris Exposition fascinated by huge Muliplex Grand Graphophone.

U.S. has 2,150 daily newspapers, 478 tri- or semi-weeklies, 14,717 weeklies.

French coin a new word: *télévision*.

The Dentsu ad agency is founded in Japan.

American country music grows from English, Scottish, Irish ballad roots.

Artist Homer Winslow, *On a Lee Shore*.

English handwriting experts establish the art of calligraphy.

Theodore Dreiser's novel *Sister Carrie* shocks public morality.

Rodin completes *The Thinker*.

Swedish playwright Johan Strindberg, *The Dance of Death*.

Lyman Frank Baum's *The Wonderful Wizard of Oz*, first of Oz book series.

Kodak's $1 Brownie puts photography within almost everyone's reach.

Michael Pupin's loading coil reduces telephone voice distortion.

Estimated 1,800 magazines are being published in the United States.

Total newspaper circulation in U.S. passes 15 million daily.

562 cities in U.S. have more than one daily newspaper; New York City has 29.

In Paris, the *Guide Michelin*.

Much of Europe and Japan begin to make movies.

Phonograph cylinders continue to outsell discs by wide margin.

Phonograph records add paper labels.

Eldridge Johnson produces double-sided phonograph records.

In London, the *Daily Express*.

Giacomo Puccini composes *Tosca*.

Joseph Conrad's novel, *Lord Jim*.

University of Wisconsin experiments with radio transmissions.

On Broadway, *Floradora* introduces what will become the chorus line.

Sigmund Freud's *The Interpretation of Dreams*.

Start of modern music era.

Max Planck introduces quantum theory hypothesis.

Chekhov's play, *Uncle Vanya*.

Russian scientist Constantin Perskyi coins the term "television."

Henri Matisse begins the Fauvist movement in painting.

In Finland, the tone poem *Finlandia*, composed by Jean Sibelius.

First overseas phone call, from Key West to Havana.

1901:   High school graduates face something new: College Board entrance exams.

Andrew Carnegie begins to build public libraries across the U.S.

Rudyard Kipling's *Kim*, an Irish orphan traveling through India.

Up From Slavery by Booker T. Washington.

1901: Oliver Heaviside's theory of ionosphere leads Marconi to Atlantic signaling.

"Red Label" records of classical music go on sale, first in Russia.

At the Moscow Art Theater, Stanislavsky introduces his acting method.

Communication improves when the hearing aid is patented.

In Germany, Braun discovers that a crystal can detect radio waves.

Pablo Picasso begins his "blue period."

Serge Rachmaninoff composes the *Second Piano Concerto.*

First electric typewriter, the Blickensderfer.

Thomas Mann achieves fame with first novel, *Buddenbrooks.*

First Nobel Prize in Literature: poet Sully Prudhomme, France.

In Newfoundland, Marconi receives a radio signal—the letter "s"—from England.

1902: Germany's Zeiss invents the four-element Tessar camera lens.

Etched zinc photoengravings.

Reginald Fessenden builds a radio wave detector.

William James, *The Varieties of Religious Experience*, study of human nature.

In France, magician George Méliès' *A Trip to the Moon* tells fantasy in film.

Los Angeles theater succeeds by showing movies only, no vaudeville.

Nobel Prize in Literature: historian Christian Mommsen, Germany.

Muckraking begins with a Lincoln Steffens article in *McClure's Magazine.*

Arthur Conan Doyle's *Hound of the Baskervilles.*

Images can be transferred by photoelectric scanning.

Claude Debussy's opera *Pelléas et Mélisande* brings impressionism to music.

Anton Chekhov's *Three Sisters*, a play of hope and human flaws.

Maxim Gorky's novel, *The Lower Depths.*

London *Daily Mirror* now illustrates only with photographs, not drawings.

Henry James' *The Wings of the Dove* contrasts European, American societies.

Oldest extant Biblical writing acquired: Ten Commandments on papyrus.

U.S. Navy installs radio telephones aboard ships.

Film can be developed in a machine without a darkroom.

Germany's Arthur Korn displays photoelectric (non-contact) fax system.

Alfred Stieglitz publishes *Camera Work* to promote photography as art.

Rudyard Kipling's *Just So Stories* for children.

Vivaphone, Chronophone, and Kinetophone synchronize sound and film.

Edward Elgar composes *Pomp and Circumstance.*

Unable to find publisher, Beatrix Potter self-publishes *The Tale of Peter Rabbit.*

French novelist André Gide establishes reputation with *The Immoralist.*

Transpacific telephone cable connects Canada and Australia.

In Europe, 10-inch "Red Seal" records feature tenor Enrico Caruso.

Owen Wister, *The Virginian.* "When you call me that, smile!"

1903:   Pacific Cable completed. Message circles the globe in 12 minutes.

An entire Verdi opera is recorded on 40 single-side disks.

Henry James, *The Ambassadors*, serialized in magazine, then published as book.

Jack London, *The Call of the Wild*, one of his most popular adventure books.

The Story of My Life by the remarkable Helen Keller, blind and deaf.

The Life of an American Fireman begins narrative documentary film.

Victor Herbert's operetta, *Babes in Toyland*.

Russian scientist K. Tsiolkovsky publishes theory of rocket propulsion.

Technical improvements in radio, telegraph, phonograph, movies, and printing.

Nobel Prize in Literature: poet Martinus Bjørnson, Norway.

W.E.B. Du Bois writes *The Souls of Black Folks*, his best known work.

Arnold Schönberg's symphonic tone poem, *Pelleas und Melisande*.

Cheap crayons are mass produced in the United States.

Patent issued in Germany for a miniature camera to be carried by a pigeon.

The Great Train Robbery introduces editing, creates demand for fiction movies.

1904:   E.F. Alexanderson's huge alternator adds distance to radio signals.

Ambrose Fleming invents the diode tube, improves radio communication.

Offset lithography becomes a commercial reality.

The comic book.

Panchromatic film, sensitive to all visible colors.

Jack London, *The Sea-Wolf*, another of more than 50 books.

Lincoln Steffens's *The Shame of the Cities* exposes municipal corruption.

"Muckraker" Ida Tarbell's exposé, *History of the Standard Oil Company*.

Giacomo Puccini's opera, *Madame Butterfly*.

Cabbages and Kings, the first collection of O. Henry's short stories.

Lewis Hine shocks with photographs of America's immigrants, child labor.

Advertising discovers hard-sell.

Photograph is sent by telegraph wire.

Joseph Conrad, *Nostromo*, arguably his best novel.

Nobel Prize in Literature: Frédéric Mistral, France; José Echegaray, Spain.

Chekhov's *The Cherry Orchard* brings modern realism to the stage.

The telephone answering machine.

G.K. Chesterton, *The Napoleon of Notting Hill*, one of his early novels.

In Austria, music is transmitted by radio.

1905:   Alfred Stieglitz and Edward Steichen open photo art gallery in New York City.

In Berlin, Isadora Duncan opens the first school of modern dance.

German lyric poet Erich Maria Rilke achieves fames with *Das Stundenbuch*.

In Pittsburgh the Nickelodeon movie theater opens; concept grows fast.

In Vienna, Franz Lehar's operetta, *The Merry Widow*.

1905: 2.2 million telephones in Bell system.

George Bernard Shaw's play, *Man and Superman*.

Max Weber, *The Protestant Ethic and the Spirit of Capitalism*, challenges Marx.

Photography, printing, and post combine in the year's fad, picture postcards.

Painesville, Ohio, phone company transmits music recital to 1,000 listeners.

In France, Pathé colors black and white films by machine.

In New Zealand, the postage meter is introduced.

New York police close Shaw's *Mrs. Warren's Profession* after one showing.

Popular actors used to advertise a product, Murad Cigarettes.

George Santayana begins philosophical writing with *The Life of Reason*.

Nobel Prize in Literature: novelist Henryk Sienkiewicz, Poland.

A small advance that holds: the fountain pen adds a pocket clip.

Publication of Albert Einstein's *Special Theory of Relativity*: $E=MC^2$.

Richard Strauss' shocking opera, *Salome*, presents the dance of the seven veils.

Bus timetables are printed.

Phonograph records may be 6 ⅔", 7", 8", 10", 11" 12", 13 ¾", or 14" wide.

In Chicago, the jukebox, playing flat records, is invented.

The Victrola turns the phonograph into furniture.

German inventor Alfred Korn telegraphs pictures.

1906: International Radiotelegraph Union is founded.

Uncle Remus and Br'er Rabbit, book of short stories by Joel Chandler Harris.

Motion picture screen aspect ratio of 1.33 : 1 accepted as international standard.

Maxim Gorky's novel *The Mother* awakens revolutionary feelings in Russians.

In Britain, new process colors books cheaply.

50-cent hardcover potboilers published in series for young adults.

Kinemacolor movie process enjoys some success.

Lee De Forest's three-element vacuum tube, the audion, puts voices on the air.

Nobel Prize in Literature: poet Giosuè Carducci, Italy.

In Michigan, yellow pages advertise business listings.

75.000 subscribers cancel *The Ladies Home Journal* over VD articles.

Dunwoody and Pickard build a crystal-and-cat-whisker radio.

Phonograph records become thinner, less scratchy.

International agreement on radio is hammered out in Berlin.

An animated cartoon film is produced, *Humorous Phases of Funny Faces*.

Jack London continues adventure novel successes with *White Fang*.

Fessenden plays violin over radio and talks to startled ship wireless operators.

An experimental sound-on-film motion picture.

Upton Sinclair's *The Jungle* exposes filthy, dangerous meat packing industry.

1907: Bell and Howell develop a film projection system.

1907: Multiple-reel movies are produced.

A photograph is transmitted by wire across France.

Dialogue titles are added to silent films.

Chicago enacts first movie censorship law. Other cities, states will follow.

Pure Food and Drug Act passed after exposé in *Collier's* magazine article.

Franz Kafka's first writing; most will be published after his death in 1924.

Lumière brothers invent still color photography process.

De Forest broadcasts music from phonograph records.

Marconi starts transatlantic radio service with Ireland to Newfoundland leg.

A photocopier is marketed.

Ziegfeld Follies musical stage shows; will run to 1931.

Canadian Robert Service publishes verse like "The Cremation of Sam McGee."

Irish playwright John Synge, *The Playboy of the Western World*.

Irving Berlin publishes the first of more than 800 tunes.

Movies figure out how to do slow motion.

U.S. cavalry tests wired mobile phone; horse's flank provides the ground.

A daily newspaper comic strip: "Mr. Mutt" in *San Francisco Chronicle*.

Commercial fax system for photos operates between Paris, London, and Berlin.

George Bernard Shaw's *Major Barbara* satirizes unbridled capitalism.

Christmas stamps are sold to raise money for tuberculosis research.

In Russia, Boris Rosing develops theory of electronic television.

Florenz Ziegfield sets Broadway ablaze with first annual *Follies*.

Rudyard Kipling receives the Nobel Prize in Literature.

1908: A trust, the Motion Picture Patents Co., is set up to control U.S. movie making.

Nobel Prize in Literature: philosopher Rudolf Eucken, Germany.

In France, Gabriel Lippmann improves color photography, wins Nobel Prize.

The Christian Science Monitor begins publication.

With Schönberg and Ives, atonality influences classical musical composition.

Safety film replaces highly flammable cellulose nitrate base for stills.

Kenneth Grahame's *Wind in the Willows* introduces Toad and companions.

Artist Gustav Klimt, *The Kiss*.

Gideon Society votes to place Bibles in all hotel rooms.

D.W. Griffith starts to introduce variety in movie film composition.

Lucy Montgomery, *Anne of Green Gables*, life on Prince Edward Island.

1909: In Paris, Serge Diaghelev begins modern ballet with the *Ballets Russes*.

Sergei Rachmaninov composes *Piano Concerto No. 3* for American tour.

Tschaikovsky's *Nutcracker Suite* is recorded and packaged, the first album.

Radio distress signal saves 1,700 lives after ships collide.

In France, Charles Pathé creates the newsreel.

1909: The *New York Times* publishes the first movie review.

In San Jose, California, Charles "Doc" Herrold starts a radio station.

Isaac Albéniz composes *Iberia* for piano.

First woman to win Nobel Prize in Literature: Selma Lagerlöf, Sweden.

Marconi and Braun share Nobel Prize in Physics for wireless development.

First broadcast talk; the subject:women's suffrage.

Major revision of the U.S. Copyright Act protects authors, composers.

Founding of McGraw-Hill, book publishers.

Mann Act passed after "Daughters of the Poor" published in *McClure's*.

Protestant churches create National Board of Censorship for movies.

1910: Daily newspapers in U.S. peak at 2,200.

Edison's kinetophone attempts to create motion picture talkies.

Sweden's Elkstrom invents "flying spot" camera light beam.

Gustav Mahler composes *Das Lied von der Erde*, his best known work.

Nobel Prize in Literature: Johann Heyse, Germany.

Henri Matisse, *The Red Studio*, helps break down academic painting standards.

The first live remote broadcasts: operas *Cavalleria Rusticana* and *Pagliacci*.

Dance music is recorded.

Movie "stars" created when Florence Lawrence becomes "the Vitagraph Girl."

Bertrand Russell and Alfred North Whitehead, *Principia Mathematica*.

U.S. requires radio transmitters on some ships; first U.S. radio law.

Krazy Kat appears in a comic strip. The bricks start flying.

Victor Herbert's operetta, *Naughty Marietta*.

Igor Stravinsky's *Firebird Suite*.

The start of Hallmark Cards.

Market research begins, targeting audiences.

24% of adult Americans have fewer than 5 years of schooling.

13.5% of Americans have completed high school; 2.7% have college degrees.

Radio hobby craze; Quaker Oats boxes used to build crystal-cat whisker sets.

DeForest's radio carries Enrico Caruso's voice from the Met; heard at sea.

Neon tube development will aid mechanical television.

5.8 million phones in Bell system, more than doubled in 5 years.

D.W. Griffith sets up shop in California at a place called Hollywood.

1911: In China, theatres get raised platforms.

Rotogravure aids magazine production of photos.

Emma Goldman expresses outspoken credo in *Anarchism and Other Essays*.

Nobel Prize in Literature: playwright Maurice Maeterlinck, Belgium.

Photoplay, first movie fan magazine.

A Cincinnati broadcaster gets the first U.S. radio license.

1911:   Stravinsky's ballet *Petrushka* hailed in Paris premiere.

J.M. Barrie's *Peter Pan* flies through the air.

Charles Ives' piano sonata *Concord* introduces wider public to atonal music.

Keystone Kops' folly delights audiences, especially cop-fearing immigrants.

Richard Strauss' *Der Rosenkavalier* is staged.

Ambrose Bierce's cynical take on humanity, *The Devil's Dictionary.*

Postal savings system inaugurated.

The *Concise Oxford Dictionary* is published.

Pablo Picasso's cubist collages challenge traditional art.

The first of G.K. Chesterton's *Father Brown* mysteries.

Edith Wharton, *Ethan Frome,* tale of hardship, romance on New England farm.

Early movie star, Danish actress Asta Nielsen, crossed gender boundaries.

Marc Chagall paints *I and the Village.*

1912:   Germans develop single-exposure panoramic camera borne by a spy homing pigeon.

U.S. passes Radio Act to control radio broadcasts; licenses are easy to get.

Carl Jung's *Psychology of the Unconscious* helps found analytical psychology.

Shaw's updated fable, *Androcles and the Lion,* considers religious belief.

Riders of the Purple Sage starts Zane Grey's series of Western potboiler novels.

Motorized movie cameras replace hand cranks.

Thomas Mann, *Death in Venice,* marked by symbolism, allegory.

The Speed Graphic camera is introduced. It will become newspaper standard.

Maurice Ravel's ballet, *Daphnis and Chloe.*

Early Cubist artist Juan Gris, *Homage to Picasso.*

George Moore's *Ethics* will influence many modern philosophers.

Nobel Prize in Literature: playwright Gerhart Hauptmann, Germany.

Howard Armstrong's regeneration circuit boosts radio reception.

Universal Pictures Corporation is formed.

First mail carried by airplane.

Titanic sinking leads to U.S. government controls on radio transmission.

A chemist coins the term "vitamine."

Queen Elizabeth, starring Sarah Bernhardt, is first feature-length movie.

University of Minnesota tries to broadcast football games by wireless telegraph.

Edison records music on cylinders with a diamond stylus for better acoustics.

1913:   Armstrong discovers that audion tubes can transmit; De Forest didn't know.

Hollywood becomes America's movie production center.

Painter Georges Rouault, *Three Judges.*

Matisse coins the term "cubism."

The rumba, based on African-Latin roots, bumps to the United States.

Indiana passes law to regulate cartoons.

1913: Prentice-Hall book publishing firm is founded.

Movies get longer; *Quo Vadis* runs for nine reels, about two hours.

Non-European wins Nobel Prize in Literature: poet Rabindranath Tagore, India.

Tagore writes his best known work, *Sadhana*, echoing sacred Hindu ideas.

The portable phonograph is manufactured.

Radio sound is recorded on cylinders.

Gertie the Dinosaur, the first animated cartoon, requires 10,000 drawings.

D.H. Lawrence's autobiographical *Sons and Lovers* dwells on physical love.

Billboard magazine publishes its first list of most popular songs.

For professional photographers, sheet film instead of glass plates.

Igor Stravinsky's *Le Sacre du printemps* explores dissonant modern music.

George Bernard Shaw's play *Pygmalion*; it will one day lead to *My Fair Lady*.

In the *New York World*, the first crossword puzzle.

African oral tradition is preserved in a written poem, *Epic of Liyongo Fumo*.

Edison starts making disks; cylinder recordings are on the way out.

Records are even thinner (¼-inch) with Bakelite.

AT&T pledges universal phone service, expands to rural areas.

1914: 1,300 journals, 140 daily newspapers in U.S. targeted to ethnic populations.

World War I opponents make use of mass media for propaganda.

Radio message is sent to an airplane.

WCTU demands federal film censorship.

Wireless telegraph baseball game by innings: N.Y. Giants vs. Memphis Turtles.

In the U.S., Robert Goddard begins rocket experiments.

Amateur radio licenses in most countries are suspended when WW I breaks out.

From Hollywood, a full-length comedy, *Tillie's Punctured Romance*.

Underground cables link Boston, New York, and Washington.

First transcontinental telephone call.

James Joyce's short story collection, *Dubliners*.

ASCAP founded to protect music copyrights.

Charlie Chaplin creates cinema's most enduring character, the little tramp.

Cliffhanging serials like "The Perils of Pauline" enthrall movie audiences.

Mack Sennett fills the screen with slapstick and skimpy costumes.

Grand cinema houses replace nickelodeons.

For the first time, no Nobel Prize in Literature is awarded.

Silk screening in San Francisco, based on earlier English invention.

New York vaudeville leads the steps to ragtime music with the foxtrot.

Tarzan of the Apes by Edgar Rice Burroughs, potboiler novelist's first success.

Federal Trade Commission regulates advertising.

1915: Wireless radio service connects U.S. and Japan.

1915: Edith Sitwell publishes book of poetry.

Comstock retires after burning "60 train cars" of books, photos, drawings.

Einstein adds the *General Theory of Relativity*.

The 78 rpm record.

Supreme Court denies First Amendment protection for movies.

Aerial photography improves for use in World War I.

Americans average 40 phone calls a year.

Long distance phone lines connect New York and California.

Radio-telephone carries voice from Virginia to the Eiffel Tower, Paris.

Nobel Prize in Literature: Romain Rolland, France.

Somerset Maugham's partly autobiographical novel, *Of Human Bondage*.

The Birth of a Nation sets new standards for film art, but is racist; leads to riots.

ASCAP created to organize Tin Pan Alley.

Hollywood begins star system. Charlie Chaplin goes from $125 to $10,000 weekly.

Actress Audrey Munson starts a trend: she takes her clothes off on screen.

Edgar Lee Masters' tombstone verse, *The Spoon River Anthology*.

Vacuum tube amplifiers aid coast-to-coast phone transmission.

Sonar.

1916: From Spain, Vicente Ibanez' antiwar novel, *The Four Horsemen of the Apocalypse*.

Cameras get optical rangefinders.

The electric loudspeaker.

Ferdinand de Saussure's *Course in General Linguistics* helps found linguistics.

Charles Ives' best known symphony, the *Fourth*.

The electric clock.

Purported date of David Sarnoff's radio music box memo.

Norman Rockwell draws his first *Saturday Evening Post* cover.

Nobel Prize in Literature: poet Carl von Heidenstam, Sweden.

James Joyce's fictional autobiography, *A Portrait of the Artist as a Young Man*.

Radios get tuners.

God and the State by Russian anarchist Mikhail Bakunin.

Béla Bártok's ballet, *The Wooden Prince*.

De Forest broadcasts presidential election returns.

Research proceeds for a sound-on-film recording system.

1917: Jazz is recorded by Dixieland Jazz Band, an all-white group.

Ottorino Respighi composes *The Fountains of Rome*.

U.S. Espionage Act dooms socialist magazine *Masses*.

Austrian painter Egon Schiele's *The Embrace*.

Photocomposition begins.

Lenin's *State and Revolution* tells how to put Marx's theories into practice.

1917: Pulitzer Prizes are created.

Jazz spreads across American cities.

Nobel Prize in Literature to two Danes: Karl Gjellerup, Henrik Pontoppidan.

Condenser microphone aids broadcasting, recording.

The American Association of Advertisers.

Albert Einstein identifies stimulated emission, theoretical basis for lasers.

A Chicago movie theater adds a new feature: air conditioning.

U.S. enters WW I; amateur radio transmitters shut down; Navy controls radio.

The Uncle Sam *I Want You* poster brings thousands of recruits to World War I.

Erik Satie's ballet, *Parade.*

Trench Pen puts ink pellets inside fountain pen to aid writing by soldiers.

Police in Japan order cinemas to separate seating for men and women.

The American Association of Advertising Agencies

1918: Dr. Marie Stopes' *Married Love* discusses the hidden world of sex.

All U.S. states require education through elementary school.

Wireless radio widely used by armies, navies in war.

First regular airmail service: Washington, D.C. to New York.

Howard Armstrong's superheterodyne circuit improves radio reception.

Nobel Prize in Literature: no award.

Oswald Spengler, *The Decline of the West.*

Willa Cather, *My Antonia*, a view of the immigrant experience.

U.S. Army publishes a newspaper: *Stars and Stripes.*

A recording of war: a gas shell bombardment.

Multiplexing increases telephone transmission capacity.

Two million phonographs, 100 million records are sold annually.

Germans get first version of Enigma code machine.

Valdemar Poulsen's wire recording patent expires; Germans improve on it.

Pulitzer Prizes for journalism, history, and biography are awarded.

In Russia, Communists send agit-prop trains to hinterlands with propaganda.

1919: Shortwave radio is invented.

Sherwood Anderson's novel, *Winesburg, Ohio.*

Nobel Prize in Literature: poet Carl Spitteler, Switzerland.

Flip-flop circuit invented; will help computers to count.

The Algonquin Round Table of writers, wits, holds its first luncheon.

The *New York Daily News* is published

Italian artist Amedeo Modigliani, *Reclining Nude.*

Pulitzer Prizes are added for poetry, drama, and fiction.

Maugham's *The Moon and Sixpence*, novel based on Paul Gaugin's life.

AT&T places dial telephones in offices and homes; new switching systems.

1919: Jazz establishes itself in a new home, Chicago.

Upton Sinclair's *The Brass Check* pillories American journalism.

Americans spend more on records than on books, musical instruments.

Ten Days That Shook the World: John Reed witnesses Russian Revolution.

With war's end, amateur radio transmitters return, now with vacuum tubes.

In Pittsburg, Frank Conrad builds a radio station, later KDKA.

H.L. Mencken, *The American Language*.

Manuel de Falla's ballet, *The Three-Cornered Hat*.

Radio Corporation of America, RCA, comes out of American Marconi Co.

Phonofilm, an optical sound-on-film process, is patented.

1920: The press release.

AT&T, GE, RCA patent agreement permits radio equipment manufacturing.

First cross-country airmail flight in the U.S.

H.G. Wells' *The Outline of History*.

German film expressionsim is established with *The Cabinet of Dr. Caligari*.

Agatha Christie writes first of Hercule Poirot detective novels.

Pittsburgh department store sells ready-made radio sets.

Detroit station 8MK begins regular broadcasting on August 20.

Pittsburgh's KDKA begins broadcasting with election returns on November 2.

German psychiatrist Karl Binding calls for killing those who are "dead weight."

After 21 years, Japanese movie makers start using actresses.

Japan has become the world's second largest book-publishing nation.

Hugh Lofting's charming *Story of Dr. Doolittle* talks to the animals.

Edith Wharton's *The Age of Innocence* depicts callous New York society.

Sound recording is done electrically. "Talkies" will follow.

Charles Jenkins invents "prismatic rings," precursor to his mechanical TV.

In England, Marconi creates the first short wave radio connection.

Sinclair Lewis ridicules middle-class America in *Main Street*.

Start of Négritude, French language anti-colonial literary movement.

XWA, Montreal, begins first regularly scheduled North American broadcasts.

Nobel Prize in Literature: novelist Knut Hamsun, Norway.

Eugene O'Neill's play, *The Emperor Jones*, the tale of a black anti-hero.

Stanley and Helen Resor introduce psychological ad research.

1921: Broadcast of Dempsey-Carpenter fight widens awareness of radio.

Baseball's World Series is reported by radio.

Deep sea telephone cable laid, Havana to Key West. Longest undersea cable.

With Bessie Smith's first record, this decade will see the flowering of the blues.

Quartz crystals keep radio signals from wandering.

The word "robot" enters the language via Karel Capek's play *R.U.R.*

1921: Italian playwright Luigi Pirandello, *Six Characters in Search of an Author.*

Cleveland Playhouse becomes first U.S. resident professional theater.

D.H. Lawrence's *Women in Love* examines sexual, psychological relationships.

Western Union begins wirephoto service.

Nobel Prize in Literature to French novelist Anatole France.

Eugene O'Neill's play *Anna Christie* opens; will win Pulitzer for drama.

Britain gets its first radio station.

Skywriting.

Jaroslav Hašek, *The Good Soldier Švejk,* satire of World War I.

Photographs can be transmitted by wire across the Atlantic.

Arnold Schoenberg develops 12-tone music notation.

Radio becomes family fun as hobbyists turn in headphones for speakers.

Public address amplifiers and loudspeakers are used in military ceremony.

Sergei Prokofiev's opera, *The Love for Three Oranges*, is performed.

At the movies: Chaplin's *The Kid* and Valentino's *The Sheik.*

Many radio licenses are issued. Many radio "firsts," especially in sports.

Hendrik Willem Van Loon's *The Story of Mankind* is widely read.

1922: In one year, from 80 radio licenses to 569.

Only three radio broadcasting frequencies are available in the U.S.

Katherine Mansfield's short story collection, *The Garden Party.*

American introduces radio to the Philippines.

Nervous Hollywood censors itself with own film review board, the Hays Office.

100,000 radio sets manufactured in U.S.

Commerce Secretary Herbert Hoover holds first of four radio conferences.

Paul Klee paints *Twittering Machine.*

T.E. Lawrence ("of Arabia") privately publishes *Seven Pillars of Wisdom.*

A commercial is broadcast. U.S. radio will be built on "toll broadcasting."

Muzak, developed by George Squier.

Herbert Kalmus introduces two-color Technicolor process for movies.

Joyce's *Ulysses* develops stream-of-consciousness writing.

T.S. Eliot's *The Waste Land* considers the sterility of modern life.

Nobel Prize in Literature: dramatist Jacinto Benavente, Spain.

Eugene O'Neill's play *The Hairy Ape*, a comedy of ancient and modern life.

Ludwig Wittgenstein's *Tractatus* argues that much of philosophy is nonsense.

15-year-old Philo Farnsworth designs a television "image dissector."

Hermann Hesse's *Siddhartha* searches for the meaning of life.

German historian Oswald Spengler completes *The Decline of the West.*

The BBC goes on the air.

Walter Lippmann, *Public Opinion.*

1922: Movie tickets sold weekly in the U.S.: 40 million.

Emily Post publishes *Etiquette*, 627 pages of advice.

The Reader's Digest begins its monthly run.

First licensed educational radio station: WOI, Ames, Iowa.

Germany's UFA produces a film with an optical sound track.

Singers desert phonograph horn mouths for acoustic studios.

Little Orphan Annie enters the comic pages.

The first portable radio and an experimental car radio.

On a Schenectady, NY, station, the first radio drama is presented.

Sinclair Lewis' *Babbitt* adds a name to the lexicon of insults.

Comic Monthly magazine reprint of comic strips foreshadows comic books.

New York Philharmonic concert is broadcast.

RCA radio-faxes a photo across the Atlantic Ocean in six minutes.

Robert Flaherty's *Nanook of the North* is the first feature film documentary.

Emmanuel College in Michigan is first school to get a radio license.

Ku Klux Klan at height of ability to terrify African-Americans, supporters.

1923: Argentine poet, critic, short-story writer Jorge Luis Borges' first book.

Vladimir Zworykin patents electronic camera tube, the iconoscop*e*.

Ribbon microphones become the studio standard.

Neon signs.

Kodak manufactures a 16 mm movie camera for amateurs.

A picture, broken into dots, is sent by wire.

A book, *Crystallizing Public Opinion*, helps give stature to public relations.

Nobel Prize in Literature to Irish poet W.B. Yeats.

A.C. Nielsen Company measures radio audiences for advertisers.

In the U.S., creation of the National Association of Broadcasters.

Shaw's *St. Joan* argues that she had to die; the world was not ready for her.

16 mm nonflammable film makes its debut.

Half a million radios are sold in U.S., a five-fold increase in one year.

"Jelly Roll" Morton composes jazz.

A speech by President Warren Harding is broadcast.

Several radio stations hook up by phone to form a temporary network.

Harlem's Cotton Club presents all-black entertainment to all-white audiences.

Time, the weekly newsmagazine.

Newspaper editor H.V. Kaltenborn introduces radio commentary, but opinion angers AT&T.

Reversal film eliminates negatives, eases home movie photography.

Novelist Willa Cather and poet Edna St. Vincent Millay win Pulitzer Prizes.

Kodak introduces home movie equipment.

Darius Milhaud's ballet, *Creation of the World*.

1924: Edna Ferber's Pulitzer Prize novel, *So Big*.

King George V speech broadcast over BBC radio.

Bell system has more than 15 million telephones.

Sean O'Casey's play, *Juno and the Paycock*.

On Broadway, operettas *Rose Marie* and *The Student Prince*.

Low tech achievement: notebooks get spiral bindings.

E.M. Forster's novel about British colonial mentality, *A Passage to India*.

Herman Melville's 1891 *Billy Budd* finally published; will lead to opera, film.

Nobel Prize in Literature to Polish epic poet Wladyslaw Reymont.

Eugene O'Neill continues to dominate theater drama with *Desire Under the Elms*.

Ottorino Respighi composes *The Pines of Rome*.

Thomas Mann, *The Magic Mountain*.

P.G. Wodehouse, *Jeeves*, punctures pompous British upper class.

In Germany, the first precision 35 mm still camera, a Leica.

Radio program sent coast-to-coast over telephone lines.

Founding of Simon & Schuster, book publishers.

Radio hook-ups broadcast Democratic, Republican conventions.

The Eveready Hour is the first sponsored radio program.

At KDKA, Conrad sets up a short-wave radio transmitter.

E. Howard Armstrong builds first portable radio, a gift to his bride.

The first Walt Disney cartoon, *Alice's Wonderland*.

Daily coast-to-coast air mail service.

In New York, the Juilliard School of Music opens.

In the U.S., 1,400 stations are broadcasting to 3 million radio sets.

Almost daily sports broadcasts.

K. Jansky's radio astronomy reports of "star noise" published, ignored.

George Gershwin writes his symphonic jazz *Rhapsody in Blue*.

Pictures are transmitted between London and New York.

Two and a half million radio sets in the U.S.

All-electric recorder and phonograph are built.

1925: Commercial picture facsimile radio service across the U.S.

Der Prozess (tr. as *The Trial*) by Franz Kafka.

Alban Berg's *Wozzek* removes tonality from opera.

The Scopes "monkey trial" is broadcast.

Theodore Dreiser, *An American Tragedy*.

The Goodyear blimp floats ads through the sky.

Expatriate American poet Ezra Pound begins his *Cantos*.

John Dos Passos, *Manhattan Transfer*, a novel of life without meaning.

Random House begins book publication.

1925: Western Electric creates Vitaphone, a sound-on-disk film system.

A British radio broadcast is heard in the United States.

From the new Soviet Union, Dmitri Shostakovich, *First Symphony*

Harold Ross starts *The New Yorker*.

Electrical recordings go on sale.

Virginia Woolf's novel, *Mrs. Dalloway*.

F. Scott Fitzgerald's *The Great Gatsby*, a novel of the tragedy of success.

Grand Ole Opry begins in Nashville as "WSM Barn Dance."

Thomas Mofolo's *Chaka the Zulu* is written in the Sotho language.

Arrowsmith, a novel by Sinclair Lewis of a life devoted to medicine.

Charlie Chaplin's film, *The Gold Rush*.

Romani (Gypsy) writers union is founded in Soviet Union, then is suppressed.

The first volume of Adolf Hitler's *Mein Kampf*, written in prison.

Sergei Eisenstein's *Battleship Potemkin* establishes film montage technique.

George Bernard Shaw wins Nobel Prize in Literature.

Earl Biggers introduces the fictional detective Charlie Chan.

In London, the demonstration of a televised image. The first image: **$**

A moving image, the blades of a model windmill, is telecast.

From France, a wide-screen film.

Transcontinental radio hook-up carries Coolidge inaugural to 24 stations.

Ben-Hur costs nearly $4 million, an unheard-of price to make a movie.

The first broadcast soap opera: *The Smith Family*.

John Logie Baird demonstrates first TV system, using mechanical scanning.

Warner Bros. starts experiments to make "talkies."

From Nashville, the "Grand Old Opry."

1926: The first featherweight phonograph stylus.

Kodak manufactures 16 mm film stock.

Commercial picture facsimile radio service across the Atlantic.

Will Durant's *The Story of Philosophy* will sell millions of copies.

Some radios get automatic volume control, a mixed blessing.

The Book-of-the-Month Club starts: cut-rate books by subscription.

A.A. Milne writes of Christopher Robin, Winnie the Pooh, and Piglet.

The Scholastic Aptitude Exam (SAT) is administered.

In U.S., first 16 mm movie is shot.

Burma Shave signs dot U.S. highways.

Playwright Sean O'Casey, *The Plough and the Stars*.

Kafka, *The Castle*.

Swing music originates in New York.

The first radio jingle is for Wheaties.

1926: Sigmund Romberg composes *The Desert Song*.
Ernest Hemingway's first novel, *The Sun Also Rises*.
Ring Lardner, *The Love Nest and Other Stories*.
Robert Goddard launches the liquid-fuel rocket.
Paul Henry de Kruif's *Microbe Hunters* is surprising best seller.
Sinclair Lewis wins Pulitzer for *Arrowsmith*, refuses it.
Enough Rope, Dorothy Parker's first book of verse.
Rudolf Valentino funeral hysteria, suicides, show emotional power of film.
Giacomo Puccini's *Turandot* is produced posthumously.
Richard Rodgers and Lorenz Hart bring *The Girl Friend* to Broadway.
Nobel Prize in Literature: novelist Grazia Deledda, Italy.
Martha Graham, barefoot, leads American modern dance movement.
NBC is formed and takes over AT&T Red Network.
Charles Jenkins transmits TV signal between cities.
Edna Ferber's novel *Show Boat* will become Broadway musical, hit film.
Don Juan, the first publicly shown "talkie," premieres in New York.
Bell Telephone Labs transmit film by television.
Coin-operated radios in public places, 5 minutes for 5 cents.
Unregulated radio stations drown each other out, beg for government controls.
Poet Langston Hughes, *The Weary Blues*.
Weather map is televised experimentally.

1927: Advertising locks in as the economic base of U.S. radio broadcasts.
BBC commissions a music composer, Gustavu Holst.
NBC begins a second radio networks, NBC Blue.
The Literary Guild book club.
CBS is formed. Radio broadcasting is becoming a mass medium.
New U.S. Federal Radio Commission regulates radio transmission, not content.
Electric plugs and single knob tuning make radio listening more than a hobby.
Live test TV by mechanical scanning, 2" x 2.5", of Herbert Hoover's face.
Sinclair Lewis attacks religious hypocrisy in *Elmer Gantry*.
Grand Ole Opry debuts.
Kafka's novel *Amerika* is published three years after his death.
The film *Napoleon* tries wide-screen and multi-screen effects.
Nobel Prize in Literature: philosopher and essayist Henri Bergson, France.
Martin Heidegger's *Being and Time* will help found modern existentialism.
Philo Farnsworth assembles a complete electronic TV system.
Jolson's *The Jazz Singer* is the first popular "talkie."
The Hardy Boys series of novels for boys.
Movietone offers newsreels in sound.

1927:   Rose Bowl game is broadcast.

Hermann Hesse's novel *Steppenwolf*, a fable about the split in human nature.

U.S. Radio Act declares public ownership of the airwaves.

Negative feedback makes hi-fi possible.

Thornton Wilder's Pulitzer Prize novel, *The Bridge of San Luis Rey*.

The Academy of Motion Picture Arts and Sciences is founded.

John Logie Baird sells first recorded TV images, 30-line Phonovisor.

In Paris, Marcel Proust completes his 16-volume *Remembrance of Things Past*.

Two-way AT&T radio phone service, U.S. to London, $75 for 5 minutes.

1928:   The teletype machine makes its debut.

Rudolf Carnap, *Logical Structure of the World*, logical positivism philosophy.

In Germany, Fritz Pfleumer creates audio tape: magnetic powder on paper, film.

Television sets are put in three U.S. homes, programming begins.

General Electric builds a television set with a 3" x 4" screen.

Baird invents video disk to record television; sends TV signal across Atlantic.

Gershwin's tone poem, *An American in Paris*.

Advertising agencies are producing most sponsored network programs.

Maurice Ravel composes his best known work, *Bolero*.

Anthropologist Margaret Mead startles readers with *Coming of Age in Samoa*.

First Oscars (for 1927 and 1928): *Wings*, Emil Jannings, Janet Gaynor.

Also at the movies: Chaplin's *The Circus*, *7th Heaven*.

Nobel Prize in Literature: novelist Sigrid Undset, Norway.

O'Neill's play, *Strange Interlude*.

Voice of Firestone on NBC.

NBC creates permanent transcontinental radio network.

Decline and Fall, Evelyn Waugh's satiric novel about British upper crust.

Stephen Vincent Benet writes the Pulitzer winning poem, John Brown's Body.

Home radios use ordinary electric current instead of batteries.

Disney adds sound to cartoons; *Steamboat Willie* introduces Mickey Mouse.

In an experiment, television crosses the Atlantic.

The newest dance craze: the Charleston.

The *Oxford English Dictionary*, begun in 1858, is finished: 15,487 pages.

Lawrence's *Lady Chatterly's Lover* will be banned for years over sex content.

In Schenectady, N.Y., the first scheduled television broadcasts.

Amos 'n' Andy broadcasts to huge audiences. Even movies are interrupted.

Syndication of recorded shows begins with *Amos 'n' Andy*.

Times Square gets moving headlines in electric lights.

IBM adopts the 80-column punched card.

Kurt Weill, Bertolt Brecht break theater's 4th wall: *The Threepenny Opera*.

1928: Daven mechanical TV disk can scan 3 standards: 24, 36, and 48 lines/sec.

Experimenter Charles Jenkins heralds future of television as "radio movies."

1929: Erich Maria Remarque's pacifist novel, *All Quiet on the Western Front*.

In London, the first TV station is built, experimental transmission only.

Sinclair Lewis' novel, *Dodsworth,* explores the pain adultery can bring.

Founding of the Vienna Circle; it will influence philosophy.

Experiments begin on electronic color television.

The Museum of Modern Art opens in New York.

Oscars for 1928, *The Broadway Melody*, Warner Baxter, Mary Pickford.

Also at the movies: *The Divine Lady, The Patriot, In Old Arizona, Alibi*.

Telegraph ticker sends 500 characters per minute.

The Rise of the Goldbergs on NBC.

The first 4-color comic publication, *The Funnies*, but not quite a comic book.

Ship passengers can phone relatives ashore.

Brokers watch stock prices soar, crash on an automated electric board.

Something else new: the car radio. But you have to stop to mount an antenna.

Zworykin demonstrates the *kinescope* cathode ray tube for TV receivers.

Phonograph manufacturers phase out hand-cranked models.

German novelist Thomas Mann awarded the Nobel Prize in Literature.

Popeye the Sailor and *Tarzan* swing into the comic strips.

Television studio is built in London.

President Hoover's has a phone on his desk; he had used a booth in the hallway.

Bell Labs produces color TV mechanically.

24 frames/second established as sound motion picture camera standard.

The film *Hallelujah* introduces post-synchronization.

The Charles Boni Paper Books have paper covers.

Thomas Wolfe's novel, *Look Homeward, Angel*, desperation to leave small town.

Les Paul, age 14, creates forerunner of the electric guitar.

William Faulkner's novel *The Sound and the Fury*: a family falls apart.

Archibald Crossley starts a radio network rating service.

Hemingway's *A Farewell to Arms* extends his reputation.

Winston Churchill completes 4-volume *The World Crisis*, about WW I.

Air mail is flown from Miami to South America.

Bertrand Russell shocks tradition with *Marriage and Morals*.

Hollywood makes its first original musical, *The Broadway Melody*.

"Prime time" enters the radio lexicon.

1930: Hollywood tightens self-censorship with the Motion Picture Code.

Photo flashbulbs replace dangerous flash powder.

On Broadway, George and Ira Gershwin's *Girl Crazy*.

1930:   *The Better Homes and Gardens Cookbook* sells the first of 15,000,000 copies.

Lowell Thomas begins first regular U.S. network newscast.

TVs based on British mechanical system roll off factory line.

Most nations use radio to educate. The American School of the Air is U.S. effort.

Movie cartoon character Mickey Mouse gets a comic strip.

U.S. customs officials seize James Joyce's *Ulysses* as obscene.

Nancy Drew, the teenage detective, starts 30 novels of sleuthing.

Vannevar Bush's partly electronic computer can solve differential equations.

Blondie and Dagwood join the daily comics.

Communist Leon Trotsky's writings are banned in Boston.

José Ortega y Gasset's *The Revolt of the Masses* will lead to his exile from Spain.

A practical, affordable car radio goes on sale.

From AT&T, high quality insulated phone wire.

Police get a 3-state interconnected teletype hookup.

Grant Wood paints the *American Gothic*.

Radio station programs for children.

Radio adventure show, *The Shadow*.

American School of the Air on CBS.

Dashiell Hammett invents the hard-boiled detective with *The Maltese Falcon*.

Sinclair Lewis becomes the first American to win the Nobel Prize in Literature.

Published photos show Americans the hard times of the Depression.

Broadway gets professional stage lighting.

The March of Time on CBS.

NBC sets up experimental TV transmitter in New York.

Dick and Jane "See Spot Run."

12 million U.S. homes have radios.

Hays Office creates Production Code; most Hollywood producers ignore it.

Oscars for 1929, *All Quiet on the Western Front*, George Arliss, Norma Shearer.

Also at the movies: *The Big House, Bulldog Drummond, Disraeli*.

BBC transmits a play by television, 240 lines/sec of resolution.

1931:   Dick Tracy arrives in newspaper comics as "Plainclothes Tracy."

RCA broadcasts experimental TV image of familiar Felix the Cat.

Jenkins Radiovisor uses slotted, spinning wheel to send experimental TV image.

Commercial teletype service.

Annual U.S. radio advertising: $31 million as depression worsens.

Scotch Tape.

Metropolitan Opera broadcasts an entire opera.

Scrabble.

Most popular radio orchestras: Guy Lombardo, Paul Whiteman.

1931: Most popular radio singers: Kate Smith, Rudy Vallee.

New radio singers: Bing Crosby, the Mills Brothers.

Radio soap opera: *Lum 'n' Abner*.

Salvador Dali's painting, *Persistence of Memory*, shows limp, hanging watches.

At the New York Group Theater, Lee Strasberg introduces method acting.

Popular news commentators: Walter Winchell, Lowell Thomas, H.V. Kaltenborn.

U.S. Radio Commission flexes muscle, orders two Chicago stations off the air.

Bigoted radio priest Charles Coughlin splits with CBS, goes independent.

Effort by black journalist fails to cancel radio program *Amos 'n' Andy*.

In Berlin, lone genius Konrad Zuse invents a computer, but is ignored.

"Hill-and-dale" vertical phonograph record introduced.

Two-way radio phone service from U.S. to Hawaii.

Radios sit in two of every five U.S. homes.

Metropolitan Opera with Milton Cross begins its long weekly radio engagement.

Electronic TV broadcasts in Los Angeles and Moscow.

Laura Ingalls Wilder's *Little House on the Prairie* will become a classic.

Pearl Buck's novel *The Good Earth* looks at peasant poverty in China.

Allen DuMont improves the cathode ray tube.

George Gershwin and George S. Kaufman's Pulitizer winner, *Of Thee I Sing*.

Little Orphan Annie will be one of many children's daily radio programs.

Exposure meters go on sale to photographers.

William Faulkner's *Sanctuary* examines Southern aristocracy.

Stephen Vincent Benét, *Ballads and Poems, 1915-30*.

The Star Spangled Banner becomes U.S. national anthem.

Bell Labs experiment with stereo recording.

Artist Georgia O'Keefe, *Red, White, and Blue*.

Nobel Prize in Literature: poet Erik Karlfeldt, Sweden.

Oscars, 1930, *Cimarron*, Lionel Barrymore, Marie Dressler.

Also at the movies: *Min and Bill, Front Page, Trader Horn. City Lights*.

NBC experimentally transmits 120-line screen.

Germany manufactures audio tape recorders.

1932: Court ruling allows James Joyce novel *Ulysses* into U.S.

Allen DuMont secretly develops radar for U.S. Army.

James Hilton's novel about Shangri-La, *Lost Horizon*.

Jack Benny goes on the air, the first of many variety comedy shows.

Novelist John Galsworthy wins the Nobel Prize in Literature.

Lindbergh baby kidnapping shows power of radio news to capture listeners.

Walter Winchell goes on the air for NBC Blue.

The *Times* of London uses its new Times Roman typeface.

1932: Aldous Huxley's sci-fi classic, the dystopian *Brave New World.*

Radio patent medicine pitchman "Dr." Brinkley nearly elected Kansas governor.

Stereophonic sound in a motion picture, *Napoleon.*

Oscars: *Grand Hotel*, Wallace Beery and Frederic March (tie), Helen Hayes.

Also at the movies: Laurel and Hardy's *Music Box*, documentary *Man of Aran.*

Zoom lens is invented, but a practical model is 21 years off.

Visagraph translates print into embossed pages so blind can read, see pictures.

Electric-eye enables typesetting machine to scan print without operator.

BBC broadcasts television four days a week.

Dashiell Hammett's novel, *The Thin Man,* will become movie series.

Ed Sullivan Show on CBS.

NBC allows recorded programs on its owned stations, but not the network.

Herbert Kalmus develops optical and dye 3-color Technicolor process.

Jack Benny and Fred Allen begin their long running radio shows.

Flowers and Trees, first to use 3-color Technicolor, also first Oscar for cartoon.

Noel Coward's play, *Design for Living.*

Erskine Caldwell's novel of rural poverty, *Tobacco Road.*

For home movies: 8 mm cameras and film.

NBC and CBS allow prices to be mentioned in commercials.

Song "It Don't Mean a Thing If It Ain't Got That Swing" foretells swing era.

Radio City Music Hall opens in Manhattan.

1933: The first magazine for men, *Esquire.*

Multiple-flash sports photography.

U.S. newspapers pressure AP to cut service to radio, start "Press-Radio War."

Radio stations fight back with own reporters; UP, INS continue radio service.

Erskine Caldwell writes another best seller, *God's Little Acre.*

Nazis use "big lie" technique in mass media propaganda.

Adolf Hitler, Joseph Goebbels employ power of radio to influence the masses.

The first *King Kong* sends the giant ape up the new Empire State Building.

Franz Werfel's best known novel, *The Forty Days of Musa Dagh.*

The Lone Ranger arrives. He and Tonto will ride the radio waves until 1954.

Starting long radio runs: *Ma Perkins; Jack Armstrong, the All-American Boy.*

Russian émigré Ivan Bunin wins the Nobel Prize in Literature.

O'Neill's *Ah, Wilderness*, a comedy from the playwright of tragedies.

Singing telegrams.

In just 90 minutes over special line, CBS reports attempted assassination of FDR.

FDR begins radio Fireside Chats, bypasses hostile newspapers.

Oscars for 1932, *Cavalcade*, Charles Laughton, Katharine Hepburn.

Also at the movies: *42nd Street, I Am a Fugitive from a Chain Gang.*

1933: Philo Farnsworth displays electronic television.

Nazis begin burning of books.

Dorothy Day founds *The Catholic Worker*, supports pacifism, social causes.

The first real comic book, *Funnies on Parade*, on the newsstands.

Despite title, Gertrude Stein is author of *Autobiography of Alice B. Toklas*.

Drive-in movie theater opens in Camden, New Jersey.

The Breakfast Club begins its radio run on NBC Blue.

1934: *Mary Poppins*, a children's book by P.L. Travers.

A bookseller's catalogue is devoted to detective fiction.

On NBC: *The Aldrich Family*.

Laurens Hammond builds an electric organ to replace the pipe organ.

Henry Miller's *Tropic of Cancer*, banned in U.S., is published in Paris.

Associated Press starts wirephoto service.

Tender is the Night, a novel by F. Scott Fitzgerald.

Radio phone service from U.S. to Japan, but plagued by fading, interference.

The jitterbug dance craze.

Wurlitzer and Seeburg make eye-catching jukeboxes.

On Broadway, Cole Porter's musical, *Anything Goes*.

James Hilton's novel about a beloved teacher, *Goodbye, Mr. Chips*.

Robert Graves' novel, *I, Claudius*, describes excesses of ancient Rome.

International Telecommunication Union merges telegraph, radio groups.

International agreement assigns broadcast spectrum.

Catholic Legion of Decency pressures Hollywood to adopt Production Code.

In Germany, a mobile television truck roams the streets, catches Nazi rally.

In Scotland, teletypesetting sets type by phone line.

"High fidelity" records are advertised.

Bumper stickers appear on automobiles.

Oscars: *It Happened One Night*, and its stars, Clark Gable, Claudette Colbert.

Also at the movies: *The Thin Man*, *Of Human Bondage*.

William Saroyan catches eyes with "The Daring Young Man on the Flying Trapeze."

Arnold Toynbee publishes the first of 12 volumes of *A Study of History*.

Federal Radio Commission becomes Federal Communications Commission

Benny Goodman on NBC's *Let's Dance* starts big band swing era on radio.

Flash Gordon docks on the comic pages. The movie serial follows in two years.

Terry and the Pirates, including the Dragon Lady, battle in a comic strip.

Nobel Prize in Literature: playwright and novelist Luigi Pirandello, Italy.

Mutual Broadcasting System becomes fourth U.S. radio network.

Playwright Lillian Hellman, *The Children's Hour*.

1934: Agatha Christie, *Murder on the Orient Express*, one of more than 80 novels.

Mikhail Sholokhov's novel, *And Quiet Flows the Don*, translated into English.

FCC is created to regulate U.S. broadcasting and telecommunication.

Half of the homes in the U.S. have radios.

Surrealist painter René Magritte, *The Human Condition*.

From Cincinnati, WLW broadcasts nationally with 500,000 watts of power.

Li'l Abner, Daisy Mae, and the rest of Dogpatch in the newspapers.

Soviet Union makes a television broadcast.

1935: Alcoholics Anonymous and its well-publicized 12-step program.

Albert Einstein co-invents first automatic light adjustment camera.

Germany begins TV programming with 180-line resolution.

BBC chooses electronic television over mechanical after six-month trial.

New Fun Comics begins the creation of original comic book cartoons.

Film *Becky Sharp* exhibits improved three-color Technicolor system.

George Gershwin's jazz opera, *Porgy and Bess*, debuts on Broadway.

Playwright Robert Sherwood, *The Petrified Forest*.

In England, Penguin Press sells paperbacks.

First telephone call made around the world.

Thomas Wolfe's *Of Time and the River* continues semi-autobiographical tale.

Howard Armstrong introduces FM radio, but its real future is 15 years off.

German single lens reflex roll film camera synchronized for flash bulbs.

IBM's electric typewriter comes off the assembly line.

Martin Block's *Make Believe Ballroom* introduces disk jockeys.

T.S. Eliot's play, *Murder in the Cathedral*.

On radio: *Fibber McGee and Molly*.

U.S. radio stations win "Press-Radio War" started by newspapers.

Two plays from Clifford Odets: *Waiting for Lefty* and *Awake and Sing*.

Demagogues on U.S. radio: Huey Long, Charles Coughlin, Gerald L.K. Smith.

All-electronic VHF television comes out of the RCA lab.

Kodachrome is the first successful amateur color film.

Your Hit Parade starts long NBC run, sponsored by Lucky Strike.

In Nazi Germany, magnetic tape and Magnetophone recorder are developed.

Oscars: *Mutiny on the Bounty*, Victor McLaglen, Bette Davis.

Also at the movies: *The Informer, Naughty Marietta, Ruggles of Red Gap*.

Sponsors develop, control U.S. radio programs.

Philosopher Goerge Santayana's only novel, *The Last Puritan*, popular success.

Nobel Prize in Literature: no award.

Two-way speaker system becomes a standard for cinemas.

Tweeter and woofer reduce loudspeaker distortion.

1935: John Steinbeck attains reputation with *Tortilla Flat*, stories about California.

Our Oriental Heritage, the first of Will Durant's 15 volumes of history.

1936: William Faulkner's *Absalom, Absalom!* examines Southern attitudes toward race.

A.C. Nielsen acquires M.I.T. audimeter.

Gang Busters starts radio run on CBS.

Electronic speech synthesizer mimics human speech.

American playwright Eugene O'Neill wins Nobel Prize in Literature.

John Maynard Keynes' *General Theory of Employment, Interest and Money*.

H.V.Kaltenborn broadcasts a Spanish Civil War battle live.

Sergei Prokofiev composes *Peter and the Wolf*, beloved by children.

Electric guitars.

On radio: *The Green Hornet*.

Dale Carnegie's best seller, *How to Win Friends and Influence People*.

An actor, Eddie Albert, is hired to write, produce and star in television dramas.

Irish law bans advertising any birth control devices.

Margaret Mitchell's *Gone With the Wind*; may be most popular novel ever.

Robert Benchley's humorous essays, *My Ten Years in a Quandary*.

Pulitzer awarded for Broadway play, *You Can't Take It with You*.

BBC starts world's first regular television service, three hours a day.

Berlin Olympics are televised closed circuit.

In U.S., daily test broadcasts of 300-line cathode ray TV.

Philco demonstrates 345-line TV with transmission of 7 miles.

Republican National Committee invents negative radio campaign soundbites.

Bell Labs invents a voice recognition machine.

In Mexico City, Diego Rivera completes the mural, *The History of Mexico*.

Oscars: *The Great Ziegfeld*, Paul Muni, Luise Rainer.

Also at the movies: *Modern Times*, Our Gang's *Bored of Education*.

The March of Time is honored for its newsreels.

Henry Havelock Ellis completes monumental *Studies in the Psychology of Sex*.

Life magazine is published; introduces photo essays.

CBC, the Canadian Broadcasting Corporation, goes in the air.

BASF/AEG audio tape recording of a live concert.

Inside Europe is first of a series of political *Inside* books by John Gunther.

33 million radio sets in the U.S.

Rodgers and Hart's musical, *On Your Toes*, with "Slaughter on Tenth Avenue."

In England, a symphony concert is tape recorded.

Co-axial cable connects New York to Philadelphia.

Fanny Brice introduces radio audiences to *Baby Snooks*.

Ventriloquist Edgar Bergen introduces Charlie McCarthy to radio listeners.

1936: Porky Pig joins the animated cartoon barnyard.

Alan Turing's "On Computable Numbers" describes a general purpose computer.

1937: George Stibitz of Bell Labs invents the electrical digital calculator.

John Steinbeck's novel, *Of Mice and Men*, tragedy of two drifters in California.

Decades of exposé reporting finally pay off with passage of child labor law.

Sarnoff hires Italian conductor Arturo Toscanini to lead new NBC Symphony.

Oscars: *The Life of Emile Zola*, Spencer Tracy, Luise Rainer.

Also at the movies: *Dead End*, *Good Earth*, *Lost Horizon*, *Captains Courageous*.

The first full-length animated film, Disney's *Snow White and the Seven Dwarfs*.

Pulse Code Modulation points the way to digital transmission.

Film *One Hundred Men and a Girl* puts nine music channels on one track.

The forerunner of the Minox spy camera, with fingernail-size negative.

NBC sends mobile TV truck onto New York streets.

One of Agatha Christie's best, *Death on the Nile*.

NBC has 111 affiliate stations; CBS has 105.

The Shadow, weekly network radio drama; will appear until 1954.

Pablo Picasso paints the *Guernica*, showing the horrors of war.

Artist Georges Braque, *Woman with a Mandolin*.

FCC sets channel aside for TV broadcasts.

Crash of the zepplin Hindenburg is captured on a recording, then broadcast.

More than half of all American homes now boast a radio.

Chester Carlson invents the photocopier, Xerography process.

NBC refuses government talk on venereal disease.

Look magazine starts; will run until 1971.

Radio soap opera, *The Guiding Light.*

British testers judge electronic television superior to mechanical.

BBC transmits final mechanical television program.

Nobel Prize in Literature: novelist Roger du Gard, France.

J.R.R. Tolkien opens up a fantasy world with *The Hobbit*.

On Broadway, Rodgers and Hart, *Babes in Arms* and *I'd Rather Be Right*.

Karen Blixen, under pseudonym Isak Dinesen, writes *Out of Africa*.

Theodore Geisel, "Dr. Seuss," begins writing, illustrating books for children.

1938: Thornton Wilder's Pulitzer Prize play, *Our Town*.

Churchill completes 4-volume biography of ancestor, Duke of Marlborough.

Lewis Mumford's *The Culture of Cities* argues for old values in modern society.

Jean-Paul Sartre writes his absurdist first novel, *Nausea*.

Strobe lighting.

Information Please! on NBC Blue.

John Dewey's *Logic: The Theory of Inquiry* argues his view of epistemology.

1938: Baird demonstrates live TV in color.

Imported from Argentina: the tango.

Radio broadcasts can be taped and edited.

Aaron Copland composes *Billy the Kid.*

50 million radio sets in the U.S.

President Roosevelt creates a cheap mail rate category for books.

Robert Sherwood stages *Abe Lincoln in Illinois*, a Pulitzer Prize winner.

Nobel Prize in Literature: American Pearl Buck for novels of Chinese peasants.

Surprise U.S. radio hit: *Information Please.*

Oscars: *You Can't Take it with You*, Spencer, Tracy, Bette Davis.

Also at the movies: *Boys Town, Jezebel, Angels with Dirty Faces, Pygmalion.*

The first of C.S. Lewis' *Chronicles of Narnia* religious allegories.

Two Hungarian brothers named Biro invent practical ballpoint pen in Argentina.

CBS World News Roundup ushers in modern newscasting.

DuMont markets electronic television receiver for the home.

Orson Welles' radio drama, *The War of the Worlds*, panics thousands.

From Krypton, *Superman* lands in *Action Comics* #1.

The Grand Ole Opry radio show is now nationally famous.

Blondie and Dagwood move from comic strip to first movie.

More than 80 million movie tickets (65% of population) sold in U.S. each week.

1939: Mechanical television scanning system abandoned.

Karen Horney's *New Ways in Psychoanalysis* dismisses Freudian "penis envy."

Era of jazz composers, including "Satchmo" Armstrong and "Duke" Ellington.

The Man Who Came to Dinner, Broadway hit by Kaufman and Hart.

AC bias control improves tape recorded sound.

Christopher Isherwood's novel, *Goodbye to Berlin*; it will lead to *Cabaret.*

New York World's Fair shows TV to the public; President Roosevelt speaks on TV.

Both houses of U.S. Congress get radio broadcasting galleries.

If *Superman* can do it, why not *Batman*?

NBC starts first regular daily electronic TV broadcasts in the U.S.

Katherine Anne Porter's short story collection, *Pale Horse, Pale Rider.*

Lillian Hellman's play, *The Little Foxes.*

I Love a Mystery on NBC.

Raymond Chandler's first detective novel, *The Big Sleep.*

Air mail service across the Atlantic.

U.S. radio networks pledge minimum of horror, excitement in war coverage.

Rudolph, the Red-Nosed Reindeer, joins the Christmas festivities.

Nobel Prize in Literature: novelist Frans Sillenpää, Finland.

Baseball game is televised: Princeton vs. Columbia.

1939: *Young Doctor Malone* joins radio soap opera lineup on NBC Blue.

Lost Horizon is first novel published in paperback.

Many TV firsts: sports coverage, variety show, feature film.

Oscars: *Gone with the Wind*, Robert Donat, Vivien Leigh.

Also at the movies: *The Wizard of Oz, Stagecoach, Goodbye, Mr. Chips.*

James Joyce's *Finnegan's Wake* may be the most incomprehensible novel ever written.

The wire recorder is invented in the U.S.

John Steinbeck, *The Grapes of Wrath*, describes Dust Bowl migration.

Multiphone expands jukebox choices from 20 tunes to 170 using phone lines.

Radio brings the public first reports of World War II events.

Western Union introduces coast-to-coast fax service.

Pocket Books enters paperback market.

1940: 5.5% of U.S. adult males, 3.8% of females have college diplomas.

Nobel Prizes will not be awarded during most of World War II.

Zenith experiments with mechanical color wheel television.

Burma-Shave roadside ads.

Radio hit shows include Jack Benny, Eddie Cantor, Burns and Allen, Major Bowes.

24% of American adults have completed high school.

William Saroyan's prize-winnng drama, *The Time of Your Life.*

On Broadway, Cole Porter's *Panama Hattie.*

W.B. Yeats' *Last Poems* published a year after his death.

Richard Wright's *Native Son* describes growing up with racism.

Teletypewriter, calculator tied by phone line to demonstrate remote computing.

First broadband carrier for multiple phone calls.

For phonograph recording, a single-groove stereo system is developed.

Hemingway's *For Whom the Bell Tolls*, a novel of the Spanish civil war.

Faulkner's first novel of the Snopes trilogy, *The Hamlet.*

Churchill's radio speeches encourage battered Britons, others.

Carson McCullers' first novel, *The Heart Is a Lonely Hunter.*

Graham Greene's *The Power and the Glory*, a "whiskey priest" in Mexico.

Peter Goldmark at CBS demonstrates electronic color TV.

Fantasia introduces a kind of stereo sound to American movie goers

On Broadway, Rodgers and Hart, *Pal Joey.*

Two radio quiz shows debut: *Truth Or Consequences* and *Take It Or Leave It.*

"Downhill skier" starts Charles Addams' career at *The New Yorker.*

Start of Peabody Awards for broadcasting excellence.

Chaplin's *The Great Dictator* parodies Hitler and Mussolini.

Fibber McGee opens his closet door, and begins a national tradition.

Oscars: *Rebecca*, James Stewart, Ginger Rogers.

1940: More than 28 million U.S. homes have radios.

At the movies: *Gaslight, The Philadelphia Story, The Grapes of Wrath.*

Also at the movies: the first of the six Bob Hope - Bing Crosby "Road" films.

U.S. gets first regular TV station, WNBT, New York; estimated 10,000 viewers.

Bugs Bunny cartoons.

Radio adventure program for kids: *Captain Midnight.*

Big bands dominate popular music.

Democratic, Republican national conventions are on radio.

Regular FM radio broadcasting begins in a small way.

Shostakovich's *Leningrad Symphony*, the *Seventh*, honors WW II resistance.

First of Upton Sinclair's 11 Lanny Budd novels looking at 20th century's events.

In France, discovery of Lascaux caves reveals fine paleolithic animal drawings.

1941: Eugene O'Neill's play, *A Long Day's Journey into Night.*

FCC sets U.S. TV standards.

William Shirer, *Berlin Diary*, chronicles rise of Nazis.

Noel Coward's play, *Blithe Spirit.*

Lillian Hellman's play, *Watch on the Rhine.*

Touch Tone dialing tried in Baltimore.

FCC decision to shift FM bandwidth makes existing sets obsolete.

Citizen Kane experiments with flashback, camera movement, sound techniques.

A Moscow cinema gets stereo speaker system.

Bertolt Brecht's anti-fascist play, *Mother Courage and Her Children.*

Microwave transmission.

NTSC 525-line standard approved by FCC for television.

In "Mayflower" decision, FCC rules that broadcasters cannot editorialize.

The push button telephone.

Mohandas Gandhi explains passive resistance in "Constructive Programme."

IBM offers a typewriter with proportional spacing.

Pocket Books begins first mass distribution system for books.

Radar placed on U.S. Navy warship.

In U.S., 13 million radios manufactured. War will shut down production.

Motorola manufactures a two-way AM police radio.

An illustrated copy of the *Iliad* starts trend to classics with art.

In New York, the first television commercials.

McCullers, *Reflections in a Golden Eye;* Southern heat, will be major film.

FCC's chain broadcasting report weakens network domination of the air.

Walter Winchell is the most popular radio newscaster.

Oscars: *How Green Was My Valley*, Gary Cooper, Joan Fontaine.

Also at the movies: *Sergeant York, The Maltese Falcon, Dumbo.*

1941: *Wonder Woman* follows *Superman* and *Batman* into the comic books.

Konrad Zuse's Z3 in Germany is the first computer controlled by software.

CBS and NBC start commercial TV transmission; WW II intervenes.

Comic strip characters *Pogo* and *Sad Sack* cheer American readers.

Americans hear never-to-be-forgotten radio broadcast of Pearl Harbor attack.

Arthur Koestler's *Darkness at Noon*, a dispirited novel of the Soviet world.

Record 90 million hear F.D.R. broadcast to nation after Pearl Harbor.

War needs freeze commercial TV development.

Radio networks on 24/7; heavy on news.

1942: Warring nations use radio as propaganda tool.

U.S. war censorship code outlaws man-in-the-street, other ad-lib interviews.

U.S. Office of Censorship bans any mention of weather in baseball broadcasts.

Magnetic recording tape.

Dorothy Parker's witty *Collected Stories*.

Supreme Court reverses, offers movies some First Amendment protection.

Thornton Wilder wins third Pulitzer with play, *The Skin of Our Teeth*.

Atanasoff and Berry in Iowa build the first electronic digital computer.

Poet Robert Frost wins fourth Pulitzer Prize.

Kodacolor Film for prints is the first true color negative film.

Voice of America, Office of War Information, Armed Forces Radio.

Congress votes F.D.R.'s cheap book rate order into postal law.

Oscars: *Mrs. Miniver*, James Cagney, Greer Garson.

Also at the movies: *Yankee Doodle Dandy*, *Pride of the Yankees*, *Prelude to War*.

Albert Camus's novel, *The Stranger*, touches on absurdities in man's habits.

"Chattanooga Choo Choo" becomes the first "gold" record.

C.S. Lewis' satire on salvation, *The Screwtape Letters*.

Artist Edward Hopper, *Nighthawks*.

1943: After more than 4,000 episodes, radio's *Amos 'n' Andy* is canceled.

Oklahoma! advances theatrical musicals by dealing with serious subjects.

Being and Nothingness, expounds Sartre's philosophy of existentialism.

Repeaters on phone lines quiet long distance call noise.

Armed Services Editions of books published for American troops.

Belá Bartók explores musical harmonies with *Concerto for Orchestra*.

NBC separates from Blue Network.

In *The Myth of Sisyphus*, Camus expands on the meaninglessness of life.

Norman Rockwell draws *The Four Freedoms* cover of *The Saturday Evening Post*.

French writer and aviator Antoine de Saint Exupéry's *The Little Prince*.

Betty Smith's novel, *A Tree Grows in Brooklyn*.

1943: Artist "Grandma" Moses, *Sugaring Off.*

British code breaking machine Colossus cracks Germany's Enigma code.

Ayn Rand's novel of libertarian thought, *The Fountainhead.*

In Havana night club, swing meets Cuban music: the mambo.

Wire recorders help Allied radio journalists cover WW II.

Comic book publishers are selling 25,000,000 copies a month.

The "walkie-talkie" backpack FM radio.

The newest dance craze: the jitterbug.

William Saroyan's novel and film, *The Human Comedy*, a family in wartime.

Broadway musical *One Touch of Venus*; music by Kurt Weill; book by Ogden Nash.

Oscars: *Casablanca*, Paul Lukas, Jennifer Jones.

Also at the movies: *For Whom the Bell Tolls, The Ox-Bow Incident, Desert Victory.*

1944: Harvard's Mark I, first digital computer to be put in service.

Two new radio shows: *Ozzie & Harriet* and *Roy Rogers.*

Hooper replaces Crossley as dominant radio ratings company.

Economist Friedrich Hayek, *The Road to Serfdom*, rips communist planning.

Smokey the Bear starts fighting forest fires.

On Broadway, Leonard Bernstein's musical, *On the Town.*

Anne Frank dies in Bergen-Belsen. Her diary will survive.

After 16 years, Thomas Mann completes *Joseph and His Brothers.*

Somerset Maugham's novel, *The Razor's Edge.*

Sartre's play, *No Exit*: "Hell is other people."

One-fifth of network radio time is given to news.

Radio network censors cut sound on Eddie Cantor song.

Networks cancel commercial programs during presidential conventions.

Colette continues sensitive novels about women with *Gigi.*

John Hersey's novel, *A Bell for Adano,* finds humanity in midst of war.

Oscars: *Going My Way*, Bing Crosby, Ingrid Bergman.

Also at the movies: *Gaslight, Lifeboat, Meet Me in St. Louis, The Fighting Lady.*

First U.S. radio network censorship: sound cut on Eddie Cantor show song.

NBC presents first U.S. televised network newscast, a curiosity.

Aaron Copland composes *Appalachian Spring;* will win Pulitizer Prize.

With Norway free, the Nobel Prize in Literature to Johannes Jensen, Denmark.

1945: Richard Wright's searing coming-of-age novel, *Black Boy.*

Benjamin Britten composes *A Young Person's Guide to the Orchestra.*

Capt. John Mullin "liberates" two German tape recorders; starts U.S. industry.

Perhaps radio's most eloquent moment: Murrow's report on Buchenwald.

Gallup Poll asks, "Do you know what television is?" Many don't.

Arthur Clarke envisions geosynchronous communication satellites.

1945: In Sweden, *Pippi Longstocking*, the tale of a free-spirited girl, is published.

U.S. has 2,000 miles of co-axial cable.

It is estimated that 14,000 products are made from paper.

Nobel Prize in Literature: poet Gabriela Mistral, Chile, first Latin American.

The entire nation sits by the radio to attend FDR's funeral.

Millions tune in daily to hear news as World War II comes to an end.

Evelyn Waugh, *Brideshead Revisited*, arguably his best non-satiric novel.

Tennessee Williams' play of shattered hope, *The Glass Menagerie*.

In Russia, Dmitri Shostakovich's *Ninth Symphony* is performed.

Another Rogers and Hammerstein Broadway smash, *Carousel*.

Oscars: *The Lost Weekend*, Ray Milland, Joan Crawford.

Also at the movies: *Mildred Pierce, Spellbound, The True Glory, Henry V.*

Arthur Godfrey joins CBS radio network, stays 27 years.

Much improved television camera, the image-orthicon.

Art Linkletter on CBS radio.

FCC assigns VHF spectrum of channels 2 – 13.

The Klipschorn folded horn speaker.

Starting its long life on NBC radio: *Meet the Press.*

American Broadcasting Co. emerges from sale of NBC Blue in 1943.

Vannevar Bush conceives idea of hyperlinks, hypermedia.

George Orwell's *Animal Farm* lampoons totalitarianism, communism.

1946: Jukeboxes go into mass production.

Founding of Bantam Books.

Seven thousand television sets are sold in the U.S.

John Hersey, *Hiroshima*, effects of atom bomb on six lives.

The *Photon*, the first practical phototypesetting machine.

University of Pennsylvania's ENIAC heralds the modern electronic computer.

Dr.Benjamin Spock's *The Common Sense Book of Baby and Child Care.*

In St. Louis, automobile radio telephones connect to telephone network.

Arthur Godfrey's Talent Scouts starts 12-year run on CBS radio.

Soap operas enter television with *Faraway Hill.*

On Broadway, *Brigadoon, Annie Get Your Gun.*

Louis-Conn heavyweight title fight is telecast to 100,000 viewers.

U.S. Army Signal Corps reports bouncing radar signal off moon, getting echo.

Carson McCullers' novel, *The Member of the Wedding*, a girl's coming of age.

Oscars: *The Best Years of Our Lives*, Frederic March, Olivia De Haviland.

Also at the movies: *It's a Wonderful Life, The Yearling, The Razor's Edge.*

In France, the debut of the Cannes Film Festival.

U.S. nationwide telephone numbering plan.

1946:   The New York City Ballet starts to dance.

RCA, NBC demonstrate rival color television systems.

Italian cinema counters Hollywood glitz with neo-realism in *Open City*.

Nobel Prize in Literature: Swiss German novelist Herman Hesse.

Bertrand Russell's *History of Western Philosophy*.

U.S. has 1,000 licensed AM radio stations.

U.S. population: 141 million; movie tickets sold weekly: 100 million.

After WW II freeze, U.S. radio manufacturers turn out 15 million sets this year.

Westinghouse "Stratovision" on airplane bounces TV signal 250 miles.

CBS experiment sends color TV program 450 miles over coaxial cable.

Robert Penn Warren's novel about Huey Long, *All the King's Men*.

A television network soap opera: *Faraway Hill*.

Television Arts and Science Academy is formed.

1947:   James Michener's writing career starts with *Tales of the South Pacific*.

Charles Ives wins Pulitizer for *Symphony No. 3*.

Dialectic of Enlightenment introduces public to Frankfurt School of thought.

Seven U.S. East Coast TV stations begin regular programming.

Two million radios can receive FM.

Television network service expands with line from New York to Boston.

A State of the Union address, by President Harry Truman, is televised.

World Series is telecast. Yankees beat Dodgers.

Poet W.H. Auden wins Pulitzer Prize for "Nones."

The Diary of Anne Frank is published.

Two more radio shows for kids: *Lassie* and *Sgt. Preston of the Yukon*.

American television viewers watch commercials.

Edwin Land's Polaroid camera prints pictures in a minute.

The Dead Sea Scrolls are discovered in a cave.

Allen Funt begins his foolery with *Candid Microphone* on ABC radio.

Primo Levi's *If This Is a Man* (in U.S.: *Survival in Auschwitz*)

Meet the Press shifts from radio to TV; will be television's longest running program.

André Gide wins the Nobel Prize in Literature.

From Chicago, *Kukla, Fran & Ollie* entertain children.

Dennis Gabor, Hungarian engineer in England, invents holography.

The transistor, invented at Bell Labs, will replace vacuum tubes.

On Broadway, Tennessee Williams' play, *A Streetcar Named Desire*.

The zoom lens covers baseball's world series for TV.

NBC cuts to dead air when Fred Allen tells joke about NBC vice presidents.

U.S. House Un-American Activities Committee attacks entertainment industry.

Oscars: *Gentleman's Agreement*, Ronald Colman, Loretta Young.

1947:   Also at the movies: *Miracle on 34th Street, The Farmer's Daughter, The Egg and I.*

FCC decrees national standard for television receivers.

Mickey Spillane's *I, the Jury*, points to new direction for potboilers.

Howdy Doody starts a 13-year television run.

History on radio: *You Are There.*

Groucho Marx quiz show, *You Bet Your Life.*

Telephone area codes.

A record 97% of all AM stations in U.S. are affiliated with a network.

1948:   Founding of the Public Relations Society of America.

Wilbur Schramm's Source-Message-Channel-Receiver commmunication model.

On radio: Ted Mack's *Original Amateur Hour.*

On TV, *CBS Evening News, Ed Sullivan Show, Candid Camera, Arthur Godfrey.*

From RCA, a 16-inch television display tube.

Radio's *Candid Microphone* becmes TV's *Candid Camera.*

CBS and NBC begin nightly 15-minute television newscasts.

Truman Capote's first novel, *Other Voices, Other Rooms.*

TV coverage of GOP convention via airplane Stratovision.

Newsreels come to TV with *Camel Newsreel Theatre.*

WFIL-FM, owned by Philadelphia newspaper, transmits fax editions twice a day.

Evelyn Waugh's novel, *The Loved One*, savages the funeral industry.

Norman Mailer's novel of World War II, *The Naked and the Dead.*

Bell system has 30 million telephones.

Alfred Kinsey's *Sexual Behavior of the Human Male* delivers some shocks.

LP ("long playing") record runs 25 minutes per side; old record: 4 minutes.

Poet W.H. Auden's Pulitzer Prize winning dramatic poem, *The Age of Anxiety.*

The Tony Awards begin, with awards for the best in 1947 theater.

Leo Fender invents the electric guitar.

Milton Berle's *Texaco Star Theater* sends sales of television sets soaring.

From RCA, the Ultrafax system can transmit one million words per minute.

Shannon and Weaver of Bell Labs propound information theory.

B.F. Skinner, *Walden Two*, a utopia based on operant behavior.

French ink maker Marcel Bich introduces the Bic ballpoint pen.

Hollywood switches to nonflammable film.

Two radio sitcoms: *Our Miss Brooks* and Lucille Ball's *My Favorite Husband.*

From the United Nations, a *Universal Declaration of Human Rights.*

Public clamor for television begins; FCC freezes new licenses.

CBS raids NBC for radio, TV top talent.

Western Union manufactures 50,000 Deskfax machines for fax transmission.

Community Antenna Television, CATV, forerunner to cable TV.

1948: Airplane re-broadcasts TV signal across nine states.

Alan Paton's novel of South Africa, *Cry, the Beloved Country*.

Oscars: *Hamlet*, Laurence Olivier, Jane Wyman.

Also at the movies: *Johnny Belinda*, *The Snake Pit*, *Red River*.

Charlie Brown, Lucy, and the other *Peanuts* begin as *Li'l Folks*.

Cole Porter's Shakespearean musical, *Kiss Me Kate*, on Broadway.

European nations import quotas on foreign films hit Hollywood.

Artist Andrew Wyeth, *Christina's World*.

Nobel Prize in Literature: poet T.S. Eliot.

Theory developed for check-bits to detect errors in phone switching.

Intruder in the Dust continues Faulkner's examination of Southern prejudices.

1949: Network TV established in U.S.

Arthur Miller's Pulitzer Prize play, *Death of a Salesman*.

Presidential inauguration is televised.

Simone de Beauvoir, in *The Second Sex*, discusses male oppression.

Rodgers and Hammerstein's *South Pacific* on Broadway; wins Pulitzer.

Edward Murphy's law is a guide to communication and everything else.

The Emmy Awards for television begin, with 1948 programs.

RCA offers the 45 rpm record; Columbia has 33 ⅓ rpm LP.

Look magazine says radio is doomed; instead, *Look* will die.

James Michener writes semi-autobiographical *The Fires of Spring*.

Milton Berle hosts the first telethon.

NBC prime-time, half-hour TV soap opera: *One Man's Family*.

Supreme Court decision splits movie studios from theater chains.

Hollywood studios begin to produce television programs.

Nobel Prize in Literature: American novelist William Faulkner.

FCC Fairness Doctrine reverses 1941 Mayflower; stations must carry opinions.

The McIntosh amplifier improves home listening.

Dragnet starts on NBC radio.

AT&T phone combines ringer and handset, volume control.

George Orwell's novel of a bleak, fascist future, *1984*.

Nelson Algren's novel of drug addiction, *The Man with the Golden Arm*.

The Lone Ranger gallops onto television screens.

Oscars: *All the King's Men*, Broderick Crawford, Olivia De Haviland.

Also at the movies: *Twelve O'Clock High*, *Battleground*, *Champion*.

Hollywood tackles race issue in *Pinky*, but plays safe with a white actress.

Italian neo-realism continues with *The Bicycle Thief*.

Talent, money, energy move from radio to television.

Whirlwind at MIT is the first real-time computer.

1949: Library of Congress awards annual Bollingen Prize for living poets.

The acoustic suspension loudspeaker.

New on TV: *Captain Video, Easy Aces, Ripley's Believe It or Not, Voice of Firestone.*

Shirley Jackson's story of sheeplike behavior, "The Lottery."

The United States has 98 television stations.

Poet Stephen Spender's essays on communism, *The God That Failed.*

These Are My Children, NBC televised soap opera.

New York - Chicago co-ax lines: three channels westbound, two east.

British EDSAC computer stores programs in memory, switches programs.

1950: More than 3 billion tickets sold at U.S. movie theaters.

New on TV: *Truth or Consequences, What's My Line, Burns and Allen, Jack Benny.*

Party lines make up 75 percent of all U.S. telephone lines.

Networks knuckle under to *Red Channels*; blacklist "subversives."

Sid Caesar and Imogene Coca, *Your Show of Shows*, on TV.

Flow-Matic, the first English language data-processing compiler.

CBS broadcasts in color to 25 television sets.

The FCC adopts the CBS color TV standard, changes its mind three years later.

Vidicon camera tube improves television picture.

Many popular soap operas, prime-time radio shows shift to television.

Nobel Prize in Literature: mathematician and philosopher Bertrand Russell.

Dennis the Menace torments Mr. Wilson in the comics.

CBS sets up TV news bureau in Washington, D.C.

From Earl Hilton, the credit card.

What's My Line? starts 17-year television run.

John Hersey's *The Wall* documents persecution, courage in the Warsaw ghetto.

Playright William Inge, *Come Back, Little Sheba*; film followed in 1953.

Ray Bradbury's, *The Martian Chronicles* expands science fiction themes.

John von Neumann influences design of computer logic.

Eugène Ionesco's play, *The Bald Soprano*, a classic of the theater of the absurd.

Changeable typewriter typefaces in use.

Gian Carlo Menotti wins Pulitzer for opera, *The Consul.*

Kodak Colorama exhibited at Grand Central station, 18 feet wide x 60 feet high.

Oscars: *All About Eve*, José Ferrer, Judy Holliday.

Also at the movies: *Born Yesterday, Sunset Boulevard, Harvey.*

Nielsen's Audimeter tracks television audiences.

Children's programming on Saturday morning television.

English translation from Swedish of Astrid Lindgren's *Pippi Longstocking.*

Xerox photocopiers roll off the assembly line.

Average U.S. home has two radios.

1950: Party lines make up 75 percent of all U.S. telephone lines.

Carson McCullers' *The Member of the Wedding* goes to Broadway.

Irving Berlin's Broadway musical, *Call Me Madam*.

Soviet Union starts jamming foreign radio broadcasts.

1951: *Paint Your Wagon* opens on Broadway.

Color television sets go on sale.

Radio program *My Favorite Husband* moves to TV as *I Love Lucy*.

Disk jockey Alan Freed introduces the term *rock 'n' roll*.

The Nagra tape recorder adds precision, quality sound to silent cameras.

Edward R. Murrow's *See It Now* debuts on television, shows coast-to-coast images.

J.D. Salinger's *The Catcher in the Rye* will become a symbol of adolescent angst.

Todd Storz and Bill Stewart create Top 40 radio music format.

Herman Wouk's novel, *The Caine Mutiny*, brings us Captain Queeg.

Marine biologist Rachel Carson, *The Sea Around Us*.

Truman Capote's novel, *The Grass Harp*.

Direct Distance Dialing (no operator for long distance) begins in New Jersey.

Marianne Moore's *Collected Poems*.

Isaac Asimov's novel, *Foundation*.

New on TV: *I Love Lucy, Dragnet, Search for Tomorrow*, NFL games.

Roger and Hammerstein's *The King and I* on Broadway.

Grace Hopper discovers the first computer bug, a real moth.

British film censors add an X rating.

William Buckley's *God and Man at Yale* argues conservative philosophy.

Hannah Arendt's influential book, *The Origins of Totalitarianism*

The Ballad of the Sad Café, a collection of Carson McCullers' short stories.

Nobel Prize in Literature: poet Pär Fabian Lagerkvist, Sweden.

Estes Kefauver's Senate hearings on harmful media influences.

Cinerama will briefly dazzle with a wide, curved screen and three projectors.

FCC approves test in Chicago of Phonevision subscription TV, $1 for a movie.

Still cameras get built-in flash units.

TV version of *Amos 'n' Andy* has all-black cast, but is criticized for stereotyping.

First transcontinental telecast. President Truman addresses the nation.

Oscars: *An American in Paris*, Humphrey Bogart, Vivien Leigh.

Also at the movies: *A Streetcar Named Desire, Quo Vadis, The African Queen*.

From Japan, a classic film: *Rashomon*.

Bing Crosby's company tests videotape recording.

A new beauty competition: Miss World.

CBS presents 4 hours of color TV, but only CBS execs, engineers have sets.

UNIVAC I is the first mass-produced computer.

1951: Comics Bob & Ray buck TV trend, start two-year radio show.

Nicholas Monsarrat's novel of the North Atlantic in WW II, *The Cruel Sea*.

Clifford Odets' play, *The Country Girl*.

Americans can dial long distance calls directly instead of needing operator.

One and a half million TV sets in U.S., a tenfold jump in one year.

Eric Hoffer, *The True Believer*, connects psychology of political extremes.

1952: FCC ends freeze, opens UHF band, reserves education channels.

Eisenhower-Stevenson race sharply increases political commercials.

3-D movies makes the audiences duck.

Sony sells a miniature transistor radio.

Agatha Christie's play, *The Mousetrap*, will run for years.

EDVAC takes computer technology a giant leap forward.

Ralph Edward's *This Is Your Life* moves from radio to television.

UNIVAC projects the winner of the presidential election on CBS.

Atomic bomb test in Nevada shown live on television.

In *The Courage to Be*, Paul Tillich applies existentialism to theology.

The Revised Standard Version of the *Bible*.

French playwright Jean Anouilh, *The Waltz of the Toreadors*.

American Bandstand broadcasts begin.

Richard Nixon's "Checkers speech" on TV saves VP candidacy.

Television sets in about 19 million U.S. homes.

NBC-TV offers a magazine-format program, the *Today* show.

The Supreme Court gives movies First Amendment free speech protection.

Claude Shannon uses electric mouse and maze to prove computers can learn.

Oscars: *The Greatest Show on Earth*, Gary Cooper, Shirley Booth.

Also at the movies: *High Noon, Ivanhoe, Viva Zapata!*

British postwar comedy: *The Lavender Hill Mob, The Man in the White Suit*.

Studio control of stars erodes as James Stewart signs independent contract.

MAD magazine starts a nonsense trend.

John Cage makes *Water Music* with non-traditional instruments.

RCA's Bizmac has first computer database.

New on TV: *Ozzie and Harriet, American Bandstand, Guiding Light, Superman*.

Lucille Ball, pregnant, plays pregnant on TV, but can't say "pregnancy."

The word "anchorman" is used at CBS Television News.

Huge EDSAC computer programmed to play tic-tac-toe.

Edna Ferber's novel of Texas, *Giant*; will be popular film.

Nobel Prize in Literature: French novelist François Mauriac.

Hemingway's *The Old Man and the Sea*, the lonely struggle of an old fisherman.

John Steinbeck's novel *East of Eden*, a Biblical tale set in California.

1952: *Charlotte's Web*, a tale for children, by E. B. White.

National Association of Broadcasters writes a code of ethics.

Samuel Beckett presents his absurdist play, *Waiting for Godot*.

Mary McCarthy, *The Groves of Academe*, sardonic view of faculty politics.

Wise Blood, Flannery O'Connor's novel of bizarre Southern life.

First Off-Broadway hit, a revival of Tennessee Williams' *Summer and Smoke*.

The first magazine-format TV program, *The Today Show*, with Dave Garroway.

Jackie Gleason's *The Honeymooners* starts a two-decade TV run.

Ralph Ellison's novel of African-American despair, *Invisible Man*.

Grace Hopper develops the first computer compiler.

1953: *TV Guide*; initial press run is 1.5 million copies.

Watson and Crick uncover the structure of DNA.

44 million viewers tune in *I Love Lucy* for a baby's birth.

Playboy arrives, with Marilyn Monroe stretched out on the cover.

James Baldwin's first novel, *Go Tell It on the Mountain*.

Winky Dink and You on TV offers a kind of interactivity to kids.

Also on TV for kids: *Romper Room.*

Ludwig Wittgenstein, *Philosophical Investigations*.

Color TV set costs $1,157; too expensve for most people.

The pre-recorded reel-to-reel tape at 7 ½ ips goes on sale.

A book, *The Wonderful World of Insects*, is phototypeset.

Magnetic core memory is installed in a computer, the Whirlwind.

Hollywood hopes wide-screen CinemaScope will counteract TV.

Nobel Prize in Literature: Winston Churchill.

Arthur Miller's play, *The Crucible*, a parable of the McCarthy witch hunts.

Broadway musical, Cole Porter's *Can-Can*.

New on TV: *Major League Baseball Game of the Week*.

FCC adopts NTSC color standard developed by RCA; drops CBS standard.

Conelrad emergency radio system tested across U.S.

Blue Poles, abstract expressionism by Jackson Pollock.

Educational TV station KHUT, Houston.

Paddy Chayesfky's play, *Marty*. Even the homely need love.

William Inge's play, *Picnic*, drama in a small Kansas town.

Ray Bradbury's novel of censorship and fascism, *Fahrenheit 451*.

Voice of America increases broadcasts to Soviet Union, Eastern Europe.

Oscars: *From Here to Eternity*, William Holden, Audrey Hepburn.

First telecast Oscars.

Also at the movies:1921: *Shane, Stalag 17, Roman Holiday*.

1953: Walt Disney's True Life Adventures: *Bear Country, The Living Desert.*

  Jacques Cousteau, *The Silent World.*

  Saul Bellow's early novel, *The Adventures of Augie March,* a search for identity.

  The Moon Is Blue uses the word "virgin," leads to picket lines.

  Bill Haley records first rock hit, *Crazy Man Crazy.*

  One American, two Russians figure out how to harness what will be the laser.

  Novelist Kingsley Amis' satire on English academia, *Lucky Jim.*

  CATV system uses microwave to bring in distant signals.

  Kinsey's *Sexual Behavior of the Human Female* delivers more shocks.

1954: Regular color TV broadcasts begin in U.S. using NTSC standard.

  Sporting events are broadcast live in color.

  Stereo music tapes go on sale.

  New on TV: *Face the Nation, Lassie, Disney, Father Knows Best,* NBA games.

  Cha-cha-cha, an offshoot of the mambo, is popular.

  William Golding's novel *Lord of the Flies* looks at childhood "innocence."

  Radio sets in the world now outnumber copies of daily newspapers.

  Saul Bellow's novel *The Adventures of Augie March* wins National Book Award.

  Texas Instruments produces transistors commercially.

  Supreme Court rules against separate education for blacks and whites.

  U.S. shaken by Edward R. Murrow TV documentary on Sen. Joseph McCarthy.

  Kodak introduces Tri-X, high speed black-and-white film.

  Oscars: *On the Waterfront,* Marlon Brando, Grace Kelly.

  Also at the movies: *The Caine Mutiny, Sabrina, The Country Girl, Rear Window.*

  James Michener's novel *Sayonara,* World War II Japanese-American love story.

  Christie's play, *Witness for the Prosecution.*

  Pre-recorded open-reel stereo tapes go on sale, $12.95, from RCA Victor.

  54% of American homes have television sets.

  Frederic Wertham's *Seduction of the Innocent* sees meance in comic books.

  Nobel Prize in Literature: Ernest Hemingway.

  From CBS President Frank Stanton, a network editorial.

  Churchill completes 6-volume history of World War II.

  Army vs. McCarthy hearings televised to captivated American viewers.

  In U.S., television revenue surpasses radio revenue.

  Tolkien continues his fantasy with *The Fellowship of the Ring.*

  U.S. Senate committee holds hearings on societal effects of televised violence.

  IBM writes a computer operating system for the 704.

  New on TV: *The Tonight Show,* hosted by Steve Allen.

  Made in Japan, a portable transistor radio, the Regency TR-1.

  U.S. television revenue exceeds radio revenue for the first time.

1954: Disney ends Hollywood freeze, leads studios in producing television programs.

1955: Movie studios open their vaults for television rentals, sales.

Network affiliation of AM radio stations in U.S. drops to 50%.

Dumont television network gives up.

Radio's *$64 Question* becomes TV's *$64,000 Question*.

Teletypesetting, using paper tape, diffuses among American newspapers.

William Buckley starts *The National Review*.

From Esterbrook in England, the felt-tip pen.

New on TV: *Lawrence Welk, Mickey Mouse Club, Wyatt Earp*.

President Eisenhower's news conference is televised.

William Inge's play, *Bus Stop*, followed a year later by Marilyn Monroe film.

TV programs for children: *Howdy Doody* and *Kukla, Fran and Ollie*.

Frankfurt School founder Herbert Marcuse writes *Eros and Civilization*.

Hobbit characters return in Tolkien's *The Lord of the Ring*.

Gunsmoke starts along the trail to be longest running TV western.

Vladimir Nabokov's scandalous novel of middle-age lust for "nymphet" *Lolita*.

Flannery O'Connor's short story collection, *A Good Man Is Hard To Find*.

Todd-AO process for musicals continues Hollywood's wide-screen efforts.

Comic book code censors horror, hurts sales, hits industry hard.

Archaeologists set carbon dating base year; other years: BP (before present).

Nobel Prize in Literature: novelist Halldór Laxness, Iceland.

Tests begin to provide massive digital communication via fiber optics.

Guinness Book of Records publishes.

First rock 'n' roll song to top the chart: Bill Haley's "Rock Around the Clock."

A View from the Bridge, another Pulitzer Prize play by Arthur Miller.

African film-making starts in Paris with *Afrique sur le Seine*.

Patricia Highsmith, *The Talented Mr. Ripley*, first of the series about the con man.

Oscars: *Marty*, Ernest Borgnine, Anna Magnani.

Also at the movies: *East of Eden, Mister Roberts, The Rose Tattoo*.

On Broadway: Tennessee Williams' *Cat on a Hot Tin Roof*.

Research shows TV viewing correlates inversely with education, income.

1956: Chet Huntley, David Brinkley bring star system to U.S. TV newscasting.

Ampex builds a practical videotape recorder for TV networks, stations.

CBS evening news videotaped on West Coast for 3-hour delay rebroadcast.

Milton Friedman's study of quantity theory begins modern monetarism.

Bell's test Picturephone sends one image every two seconds.

Swedish director Ingmar Bergman's world fame starts with *The Seventh Seal*.

My Fair Lady begins six-year run on Broadway.

1956: In Japan, Yukio Mishima's novel, *Temple of the Golden Pavilion*.

First transatlantic telephone calls by submarine cable.

Zenith sells a cordless remote for TV.

Two new CBS soap operas: *As the World Turns, The Edge of Night*.

Westerns are popular televised drama.

M.I.T. builds a transistorized computer, the TX-O.

Oscars: *Around the World in 80 Days*, Yul Brynner, Ingrid Bergman.

Also at the movies: *Anastasia, The King and I, Bus Stop*.

John Osborne's play, *Look Back in Anger*.

IBM ships a hard drive, the 5 MB. 305 RAMAC, as big as two refrigerators.

Foreign language films get an Oscar category. This year: Italy's *La Strada*.

Nobel Prize in Literature: Spanish exile poet Juan Jiménez.

Elvis Presley spreads rock to a world audience with first film, *Love Me Tender*.

Allen Ginsburg's poem of beatnik angst, "Howl."

Liquid Paper is created on the kitchen table of a Dallas secretary, Bette Graham.

Peyton Place steams up the bestseller list.

Transistors go into car radios.

The first hard disk random access drive is created at IBM.

The pager. Hospitals are quick to buy.

On Broadway, from Voltaire, Leonard Bernstein's musical, *Candide*.

John F. Kennedy's short biographies, *Profiles in Courage*.

Hush-a-Phone court ruling forces AT&T to allow outside equipment in network.

1957: Supreme Court's *Roth* decision sets community standards for obscenity.

Leonard Bernstein's *West Side Story* opens on Broadway.

Iran bans rock 'n' roll music.

American Bandstand on network TV.

Lawrence Durrell begins *Alexandria Quartet*, point-of-view novels, with *Justine*.

Noam Chomsky's *Syntactic Structures* pioneers transformational grammar.

John Cheever's novel, *The Wapshot Chronicle*, skewers wealthy suburbia.

Nabokov's witty, erudite novel, *Pnin*.

CBS-TV offers *Perry Mason*.

Jack Kerouac's novel, *On the Road*, expresses the beat generation.

Isaac Bashevis Singer's novel, *Gimpel the Fool*, translated from Yiddish.

Nobel Prize in Literature: Albert Camus.

James Agee's posthumous novel, *A Death in the Family*, wins Pulitzer.

Samuel Beckett's existential play, *Endgame*, mingles anguish with humor.

Soviet Union's Sputnik 1 beep-beeps from space.

Sputnik 2 carries a dog, Laika, on a one-way space journey.

FORTRAN becomes the first high-level computer programming language.

1957: A surgical operation is televised.

Idealized American family on TV: *Leave it to Beaver*.

Oscars: *The Bridge on the River Kwai*, Alec Guinness, Joanne Woodward.

Also at the movies: *Peyton Place, Sayonara, 12 Angry Men*.

Italians again win foreign language film Oscar: *The Nights of Cabiria*.

First book to be entirely phototypeset is offset printed.

A computer is part of a movie plot: *Desk Set*, with Tracy and Hepburn.

In Ghana, effort begins to recover and record African oral tradition.

Sputnik launch sets off alarm about U.S. math and science education.

Many television programs switch to color.

1958: Federal funds voted to improve science, math teaching.

International News Service is taken over by United Press. It's now UPI.

Videotape delivers color.

Leon Uris, *Exodus*, novel of the founding of Israel; will become film.

Seymour Cray at Control Data builds a transistorized computer.

Stereo LP records go on sale.

Quiz show fraud rocks U.S. television.

Data moves speedily over regular phone circuits.

Live television drama is replaced by videotaped programs.

Broadcast is bounced off a rocket; it is pre-satellite communication.

First successful U.S. satellite, Explorer I, sends signals about Van Allen Belt.

Noam Chomsky and George Miller co-author *Finite State Languages*.

95% of prime-time audiences choose network programs.

Number of drive-in theaters in U.S. peaks near 5,000.

Oscars: *Gigi*, David Niven, Susan Hayward.

Also at the movies: *Cat on a Hot Tin Roof, The Old Man and the Sea, South Pacific*.

Foreign language film Oscar: French comedy *Mon Oncle*.

Cliffsnotes.

In Tokyo, a dramatic structure to relay broadcast signals, the Tokyo Tower.

Early version of *Pong* uses analog computer, oscilloscope.

The Smurfs, created by Belgian cartoonist Peyo.

Cable carries FM radio stations.

Cinéma verité (also called "direct cinema") documentary technique.

Playwright Harold Pinter, *The Birthday Party*.

Experiments begin to create the modem.

Posthumous publication of Giuseppe Tomasi di Lampedusa, *The Leopard*.

Billboard's "Hot 100" chart lists the hits.

Economist, presidential adviser John Kenneth Galbraith, *The Affluent Society*.

Joan Míro completes ceramic murals for the UNESCO building, Paris.

1958: Defense Department creates ARPA, precursor of the Internet.

      Churchill finishes 4-volume *History of the English-Speaking Peoples*.

      The microchip; it will enable the computer revolution.

      Soviet Union forces novelist Boris Pasternak to refuse Nobel Literature Prize.

      Truman Capote's novel, *Breakfast at Tiffany's*; it will become a hit film.

      Physicist Werner Heisenberg explains his uncertainty principle.

      From Europe, ALGOL, a programming language for math, science.

      New on TV: *Peter Gunn, Donna Reed, The Invisible Man, Concentration*.

      Durrell continues with *Balthazar* and *Mountolive*. *Clea* will arrive in 1960.

1959: Magnetic ink character recognition developed to process checks.

      Jack Kilby of Texas Instruments builds an integrated circuit.

      The Grammy Awards, starting with 1958 music.

      New on TV: *Rocky and Bullwinkle, Dennis the Menace, Twilight Zone, Untouchables*.

      NBC offers a western in color; *Bonanza* will run for 14 years.

      Grace Hopper writes the COBOL programming language for business.

      James Michener, *Hawaii*, mixes truth and fiction across the centuries.

      U.S. rules D.H. Larence novel, *Lady Chatterley's Lover*, not obscene.

      Playwright Jean Genet, *The Blacks*.

      Barbie dolls.

      Public is shocked to learn that most big-money TV quiz shows are fixed.

      Disk jockey payola scandals smear radio broadcasting.

      Post Office tries, abandons effort to move mail by submarine-fired missiles.

      From Ampex, a mobile videotape recorder.

      Boris Pasternak's *Dr.Zhivago*; published in Italy despite Soviet pressure.

      William Burroughs' novel about drug addiction, *Naked Lunch*.

      Mordecai Richler's novel, *The Apprenticeship of Duddy Kravitz*.

      Nobel Prize in Literature: poet Salvatore Quasimodo, Italy.

      Local announcements, weather data, and local ads go on cable.

      Saul Bellow's *Henderson, the Rain King*, a study in alienation.

      E.B. White's *The Elements of Style*; will be best-selling writing guide for decades.

      Princess telephones in 5 colors go on sale.

      An all-transistor radio can fit into a shirt pocket.

      Xerox manufactures a plain paper copier.

      Bell Labs experiments with artificial intelligence.

      High speed Ektachrome film.

      Ionesco's absurdist play, *The Rhinoceros*.

      Television sets in more than 46 million U.S. homes.

      On Broadway, Stephen Sondheim's musical, *Gypsy*.

1959: Lorraine Hansberry's *A Raisin in the Sun*, first Broadway play by black woman.

Oscars: *Ben-Hur*, Charlton Heston, Simone Signoret.

Also at the movies: *The Diary of Anne Frank, Some Like It Hot, Pillow Talk*.

Foreign language film Oscar: *Black Orpheus*, France.

French SECAM and German PAL compete with American NTSC television standard.

Günter Grass' novel *The Tin Drum* is regarded as an immediate classic.

Satirists Bob and Ray are top radio attractions.

Philip Roth's first novel, *Goodbye, Columbus*, wins National Book Award.

1960: Echo I, a U.S. balloon in orbit, reflects radio signals to Earth.

The ATM, invented by Luther Simjian.

New on TV: *Andy Griffith, Bugs Bunny, Route 66, My Three Sons*.

Animated cartoon, *The Flinstones*, comes to prime time; will stay there until 1987.

Off-Broadway, *The Fantasticks* begins a 42-year-run.

90% of American homes have television sets.

John Barth's *The Sot-Weed Factor* parodies historical novels.

Kennedy-Nixon debates draw huge numbers of viewers, voters.

Theodore Maiman uses a synthetic ruby to build first true laser.

Taking a food order by telephone, Domino's delivers a pizza.

Voice communication for people who cannot talk: an electronic larynx.

Little Shop of Horrors film; will grow to a play, another film, animation.

In Rhode Island, an electronic, automated post office.

Gulf Oil sponsors unscheduled news bulletins on NBC-TV.

Harvest of Shame, arguably U.S. television news' finest documentary.

AT&T installs first electronic switching system.

A movie gets Smell-O-Vision, but the public just sniffs.

Lerner and Loewe's Broadway musical, *Camelot*.

William Shirer's *The Rise and Fall of the Third Reich*.

In England, the world's longest running TV soap, *Coronation Street*.

Oscars: *The Apartment*, Burt Lancaster, Elizabeth Taylor.

Also at the movies: *Exodus, Spartacus, Psycho, Elmer Gantry*.

Foreign language film Oscar: *Virgin Spring*, Sweden.

The first of the John Updike *Rabbit* novels: *Rabbit, Run*.

Electronic music is established through Karlheinz Stockhausen, others.

The Post Office experiments with facsimile mail.

PLATO, a computer-based method of education.

A hologram is constructed.

Nobel Prize in Literature: French poet Saint-John Perse.

Henry Miller completes trilogy, *Sexus, Plexus*, and *Nexus*.

Tiros I is the first weather satellite.

1960: Chubby Checkers' twist becomes dance craze.

Parker 45 fountain pen takes refill cartridges.

Americans, Britons simultaneously develop packet switching transmission.

Telephone-averse Parisians use pneumatic tubes for love letters.

Mattel's Chatty Cathy doll speaks 11 phrases in random order.

John Coltrane leads jazz new wave.

1961: *Franny and Zooey*, a collection of Salinger's short stories.

Poet Robert Frost recites "The Gift Outright" at JFK's inauguration.

IBM Selectric "golf ball" typewriter.

Robert Heinlein's science fiction novel, *Stranger in a Strange Land*.

The French Catholic *Bible de Jerusalem* is published.

FCC Chairman Newton Minow calls television a "vast wasteland."

Nobel Prize in Literature: poet, novelist Ivo Andric, Yugoslavia.

Time-Life Books begin publication.

Tennessee Williams' play, *Night of the Iguana*.

John Steinbeck, *The Winter of Our Discontent*, his twelfth novel.

Boxing match test shows potential of pay-TV.

FCC approves FM stereo broadcasting; spurs FM development.

Franz Fanon writes his influential, anti-colonial *The Wretched of the Earth*.

A wireless microphone is used in a movie, *Mutiny on the Bounty*.

Bell Labs tests communication by light waves.

Sony markets a helical scan videotape recorder.

Henry Miller's *Tropic of Cancer* in U.S. 27 years after banning.

Harper Lee wins Pulitzer Prize for *To Kill a Mockingbird*.

The Carousel Projector aids lecturers.

Fairchild Semiconductor makes integrated circuits commercially.

Silicon chips.

New on TV: *The Avengers, Ben Casey, Dr. Kildare, Bozo the Clown, Wide World of Sports*.

Instant videotape playback in slow motion.

Low tech: Letraset makes headlines at home simple.

British novelist Muriel Spark's *The Prime of Miss Jean Brodie*.

Oscars: *West Side Story*, Maximilian Schell, Sophia Loren.

Also at the movies: *Breakfast at Tiffany's, Splendor in the Grass, El Cid*.

Foreign language film Oscar: *Through a Glass Darkly*, Sweden.

The time-sharing computer is developed.

President Kennedy allows TV news to cover his press conferences live.

Julia Child et. al, *Mastering the Art of French Cooking*. Best seller for years.

Novelist Joseph Heller tells us about *Catch-22.*

Trinidad novelist V.S. Naipaul, *A House for Mr. Biswas*.

1961: Novelist Walker Percy, *The Movie Goer.*

TV viewers see Alan Shepard's sub-orbital flight at start of manned space race.

1962: Marshall McLuhan's *The Gutenberg Galaxy* sees limits for the print media.

Poet Sylvia Plath's fictional memoir, *The Bell Jar,* published under pseudonym.

Edward Albee's lacerating play, *Who's Afraid of Virginia Woolf.*

The Telstar satellite sends television across the Atlantic.

Katherine Anne Porter's novel, *Ship of Fools.*

On CBS-TV, *The Beverly Hillbillies.*

Estimated 44% of world's population are illiterate.

Benjamin Britten's *War Requiem* is sung at reconstructed Coventry Cathedral.

Rachel Carson's *Silent Spring*; it will lead to ban on DDT, other pesticides.

Spacewar can be played by competitors on a variety of computers.

Cable companies import distant signals.

Helen Gurley Brown's best-seller, *Sex and the Single Girl.*

FCC requires UHF tuners on new television sets.

Comsat created to launch, operate global satellite system.

Oscars: *Lawrence of Arabia*, Gregory Peck, Anne Bancroft.

Also at the movies: *To Kill a Mockingbird, The Miracle Worker, The Longest Day.*

Dr. No begins the James Bond series.

Foreign language film Oscar: *Sundays and Cybèle*, France.

Anthony Burgess' novel, *A Clockwork Orange*; it will become a film classic.

Broadway hit, Sondheim's *A Funny Thing Happened on the Way to the Forum.*

Eull Gibbons writes a best seller advising people to find food in forests, parks.

Touch Tone phones are a hit at the Seattle World's Fair.

Soundtrack of *West Side Story* tops the music charts for 54 weeks.

AT&T introduces T-1 multiplex service in Skokie, Illinois.

Packet-switching networks.

Telstar, first international communication satellite, transmits an image.

Michael Harrington's *The Other America* revives interest in school lunches.

Plastic insulation for phone lines.

New on TV: *The Jetsons*, Merv Griffin, Johnny Carson.

Nobel Prize in Literature: American novelist John Steinbeck.

The Reivers is published in the year Faulkner dies.

Mariner II sends radio signals from Venus.

Ken Kesey's *One Flew Over the Cuckoo's Nest* introduces Nurse Ratched.

John Glenn's earth orbit is televised; 135 million viewers.

FCC sees a demonstration of cellular technology.

Andy Warhol paints many images of Campbell's Soup cans, Marilyn Monroe.

John Steinbeck's *Travels with Charley*, vignettes of life in the United States.

1962: Alexander Solzhenitsyn, *One Day in the Life of Ivan Denisovitch*, tells of Gulag.

1963: James Baldwin's essays, *The Fire Next Time*, stirs concerns about racial tensions.

Raise High the Roof Beam, Carpenters, more of J.D. Salinger's short stories.

Nobel Prize in Literature: Georgos Seferis, Greece.

Maurice Sendak's prize-winning children's book, *Where the Wild Things Are*.

From Phillips of Holland comes the audio cassette.

Presidents of U.S., Nigeria have phone conversation via satellite.

Yukio Mishima's allegorical tale, *The Sailor Who Fell From Grace with the Sea*.

Postal ZIP codes.

Instant replay.

New on TV: *Doctor Who, The Fugitive, Richard Boone, General Hospital, Let's Make a Deal*.

TV is now principal source of news in U.S., according to Roper Poll.

Instamatic cameras with drop-in cartridges; more than 50 million will be sold.

Douglas Engelbart gets a patent for the computer mouse.

In the U.S., the Emergency Broadcast System, with periodic air tests.

CBS and NBC TV newscasts expand from 15 to 30 minutes in color.

Barbara Tuchman wins a Pulitzer for *The Guns of August*.

Jacques Cousteau, *The Living Sea*.

The Beatles shake up music.

81 million telephones in the United States, 159 million worldwide.

Hannah Arendt's *Eichmann in Jerusalem* speaks of "the eerie banality of evil."

Sony offers an open-reel videotape recorder for the home, $995.

Betty Friedan's *The Feminine Mystique* energizes the feminist movement.

Polaroid instant photography adds color.

Communications satellite, Syncom II, goes into geo-synchronous orbit.

Oscars: *Tom Jones*, Sidney Poitier, Patricia Neal.

Also at the movies: *Cleopatra, Hud, Lilies of the Field, How the West Was Won*.

Foreign language film Oscar: Federico Fellini's *8 ½*, Italy

TV news "comes of age" in reporting JFK assassination.

Julia Child cooks on television as *The French Chef*.

Martin Luther King gives "I have a dream" speech.

First live televised murder: Jack Ruby shoots Lee Harvey Oswald.

On educational TV: *The French Chef*, with Julia Child.

1964: *Peyton Place*, televised soap opera, moves to prime-time.

TTY developed out of personal need by deaf physicist Robert Weitbrecht.

Anti-war protest folk music is popular.

On TV, *Gilligan's Island, Jeopardy, Bewitched, Munsters, Man from U.N.C.L.E.*

V.S. Naipaul's critical view of modern India, *An Area of Darkness*.

Michener's *The Source* traces a location in Israel through history.

1964: Artist Roy Lichtenstein, *Good Morning, Darling.*

Olympic Games in Tokyo telecast live globally by satellite.

Picturephone tested: Disneyland to N.Y. World's Fair. Public unimpressed.

IBM's OS/360 is first mass-produced computer operating system.

The PDP-8, first minicomputer, first to use integrated circuit technology.

Mariner IV sends television images from Mars.

Oscars: *My Fair Lady*, Rex Harrison, Julie Andrews.

Also at the movies: *Mary Poppins, Dr. Strangelove, Zorba the Greek.*

Foreign language film Oscar: *Yesterday, Today and Tomorrow*, Italy.

From Dartmouth: BASIC programming.

Russian scientists bounce a signal off Jupiter.

IBM Selectric typewriter has reusable magnetic tape.

Ken Kesey's *Sometimes a Great Notion;* will be award-winning film.

Saul Bellow's novel *Herzog;* will win the International Literary Prize.

First version of Moore's Law: microprocessor speed will double each year.

Intelsat, international satellite organization, is formed.

Nobel Prize in Literature: Jean-Paul Sarte, who declines it.

Japan's NHK begins HDTV development.

The first televised negative political ad skewers Barry Goldwater.

"Pirate" ships broadcast off English coast, challenge BBC monopoly.

Marshall McLuhan's *Understanding Media* describes the global village.

Transpacific submarine telephone cable service begins.

Arthur Miller, *After the Fall*, fictional play about ex-wife Marilyn Monroe.

Ayn Rand's *The Virtue of Selfishness* argues for "ethical egoism."

A local area network (LAN) is created for atomic weapons research.

1965: "Bobo doll" study indicates effects on small children of televised violence.

Computer-based telephone digital switching replaces electromagnetic system.

Nobel Prize in Literature: Russian novelist Mikhail Sholokhov.

African-American, Bill Cosby, stars in a TV show, *I Spy.*

Jerzy Kosinski's *The Painted Bird* looks at the plight of Gypsies in the Holocaust.

Author Ian Fleming dies, but James Bond carries on in books, films.

Ford offers 8-track tape players on next year's model cars.

Mobile radio telephone service widely available in the U.S.

Vietnam War becomes first war to be televised.

9 of 10 U.S. telephones can use direct distance dialing.

Western Electric uses lasers in industry.

British ban televised cigarette advertising.

Videotape recorders sold in huge numbers for home use.

Electronic phone exchange gives customers extra services.

1965: Radio astronomy research supports Big Bang Theory.

Satellites begin domestic TV distribution in Soviet Union.

Color news film.

New on TV: *Green Acres, Hogans Heroes, I Dream of Jeannie, Get Smart.*

Commercial communications satellite Early Bird (Intelsat I) orbits.

Kodak offers Super 8 film for home movies.

Cartridge audio tapes go on sale for a few years.

ABC World News Tonight.

Oscars: *The Sound of Music*, Lee Marvin, Julie Christie.

Also at the movies: *Dr. Zhivago, Cat Ballou, A Thousand Clowns.*

Foreign language film Oscar: *The Shop on Main Street*, Czechoslovakia.

Most broadcasts are in color.

Non-sequential hypertext is created. It will one day build the Internet's links.

FCC rules bring structure to cable television.

Westinghouse Phonovid stores TV sound, pictures on phonograph records.

Solid-state equipment spreads through the cable industry.

The Autobiography of Malcolm X.

Ralph Nader's *Unsafe at Any Speed* attacks Detroit's auto industry.

1966: Doctoral dissertation is printed by a computer.

Star Trek goes into orbit.

In China, the Cultural Revolution.

Recent movies are played on prime time.

Public records collection, LexisNexis, founded as the Data Corporation.

Quotations from Mao Tes-Tung. Millions read *Little Red Book.*

Star Trek launches on television.

Old Metropolitan Opera House closes; opera moves to Lincoln Center.

Bernard Malamud's novel, *The Fixer*, of a poor man influenced by Spinoza.

Truman Capote's *In Cold Blood* uses narrative style for non-fiction.

William Buckley hosts *The Firing Line*, erudite, conservative discussion on TV.

Linotron can produce 1,000 alphanumeric characters per second for printing.

Charles Kao's waveguide light theory will lead to communication channels.

TV viewers are treated to close-ups of the moon, courtesy of Surveyor 1.

The Amateur Computer Society organizes personal computing.

Neorealistic style gives *The Battle of Algiers* a documentary look.

Nobel Prize in Literature shared by Jewish writers Nelly Sachs, Shmuel Agnon.

Marc Chagall's murals are installed at the new New York Met.

Oscars: *A Man for All Seasons*, Paul Scofield, Elizabeth Taylor.

Also at the movies: *Who's Afraid of Virginia Woolf?, Alfie, Hawaii, Blow-Up.*

Foreign language film Oscar: *A Man and a Woman*, France.

1966:   Flora Nwapa's *Efuru* is the first novel by a black African woman.

Periscope is the first arcade game to cost a quarter, not a dime.

TV version of *Amos 'n' Andy* called racist, removed from airwaves.

Xerox sells the Telecopier, a fax machine.

John Barth's comic novel, *Giles Goat-Boy*, the tale of a would-be messiah.

Nations of the world choose among competing TV standards: NTSC, PAL, and SECAM.

SABRE airline reservation system is an early data communication network.

FCC blocks cable television wiring in large cities.

Star Trek is beamed to home screens.

1967:   Newspapers, magazines start to digitize production.

Nobel Prize in Literature: Miguel Asturias, Guatemalan writer of Indian life.

Dolby eliminates audio hiss.

In New York the *World-Telegram* goes out of business.

Marshall McLuhan, *The Medium Is the Message*.

New on TV: *Washington Week in Review, Carol Burnett Show*.

Computers get the light pen.

From IBM, the floppy disk.

Tom Stoppard's first play, *Rosencrantz and Guildenstern Are Dead*.

Jacques Derrida's philosophy "deconstructs" Western rationalist thinking.

Pre-recorded movies on videotape sold for home TV sets.

On Broadway, *Thoroughly Modern Millie*.

Fairness Doctrine allows anti-cigarette ads; tobacco industry pulls own ads.

ADVENT, a text-based adventure game.

Adult, underground comics arrive with R. Crumb's *Zap Comix*.

Oscars: *In the Heat of the Night*, Rod Steiger, Katherine Hepburn.

Also at the movies: *The Graduate, Cool Hand Luke, Bonnie and Clyde*.

Foreign language film Oscar: *Closely Watched Trains*, Czechoslovakia.

Gabriel García Márquez' novel, *One Hundred Years of Solitude*.

Cordless telephones enter the phone system.

U.S. mandates Daylight Savings Time.

ABC Radio divides into four networks.

Newspapers introduce computers into their operations.

Congress creates Corporation for Public Broadcasting; adds federal support.

ABC joins CBS and NBC in presenting 30-minute television newscasts.

William Styron's, *The Confessions of Nat Turner*, criticized, praised.

Novelist Joyce Carol Oates, *A Garden of Earthly Delights*.

New magazines include *Rolling Stone* and *New York*.

1968:   Gore Vidal's novel of gender switching, *Myra Breckenridge*.

60 Minutes starts ticking.

1968: On Broadway: the rock musical *Hair.*

FCC is given jurisdiction over cable TV.

It seems we live in *Mister Rogers' Neighborhood.*

Norman Mailer, *Armies of the Night,* wins Pulitzer and National Book Award.

TV photographers lug two-inch-tape portable videotape recorders.

FCC approves attaching non-Bell equipment to phone system.

Magnetic-stripe credit cards.

Hollywood adopts an age-based rating system; at first: G, M, R, X.

Hand-held cameras used at national political conventions.

Hawaii Five-O starts 12-year TV run.

Noam Chomsky influences linguistics with *Language and Mind.*

Tom Stoppard's play, *The Real Inspector Hound.*

Joan Didion, *Slouching Towards Bethlehem.*

On TV, *Laugh-In* is modeled on British *That Was the Week That Was.*

Andrew Webber's first hit, *Joseph and the Amazing Technicolor Dreamcoat.*

Jürgen Habermas' *Knowledge and Human Interests* argues critical theory.

Intelsat completes global communications satellite loop.

Kawabata Yasunari becomes first Japanese to win Nobel Prize in Literature.

Tom Wolfe, *The Electric Kool-Aid Acid Test.*

Approximately 200 million TV sets in the world, 78 million in U.S.

Oscars: *Oliver!*, Cliff Robertson, Katherine Hepburn.

Also at the movies: *2001: A Space Odyssey, Funny Girl, Rosemary's Baby.*

Foreign language film Oscar: *War and Peace*, U.S.S.R.

U.S. movie attendance drops to 20 million tickets weekly (10% of population).

Eldridge Cleaver's *Soul on Ice*, on racism, written in prison.

Sony develops the Trinitron color television tube.

Action for Children's Television (ACT) organization is created.

U.S. adopts "911" as national emergency telephone number.

An Intel 1 KB RAM microchip reaches the market.

Douglas Englelbart links keyboard, keypad, mouse, windows, and more.

First digital wireless network, Linkabit, created in San Diego.

1969: PASCAL.

New on TV: *Monty Python's Flying Circus, Brady Bunch.*

Supreme Court's *Red Lion* decision supports Fairness Doctrine.

Public Broadcasting Service (PBS) is created.

Nobel Prize in Literature: Irish playwright Samuel Beckett.

RCA SelectaVision plays pre-recorded cassettes, but cannot record.

Sony brings out ¾" U-Matic, first videotape cassette editing system.

Astronauts send live color photos from the moon to worldwide audience.

1969: First words broadcast from the moon: "That's one small step..."

Department of Defense commissions ARPANET for research into networking.

Audio music tapes sold with Dolby Noise Reduction.

Vice President Agnew accuses network television newscasts of bias.

Kenneth Thompson creates the Unix Operating System for computers.

UCLA computer sends data to Stanford computer, foreshadowing Internet.

Oscars: *Midnight Cowboy* (X-rated), John Wayne, Maggie Smith.

Also at the movies: *True Grit, Butch Cassidy and the Sundance Kid, Easy Rider.*

Foreign language film Oscar: *The Brothers Karamazov*, U.S.S.R., and *Z*, Algeria

The Saturday Evening Post stops publishing after 148 years. TV blamed.

Children can visit *Sesame Street.*

Novelist Kurt Vonnegut, *Slaughterhouse Five.*

Novelist Michael Crichton's first best-seller, *The Andromeda Strain.*

James Dickey's novel, *Deliverance.*

Mario Puzo's novel, *The Godfather.*

CompuServe goes into business.

John Fowles' novel, *The French Lieutenant's Woman.*

Philip Roth's *Portnoy's Complaint* shocks with sexual caricatures.

Joyce Carol Oates' award winner, *them.*

Pop-art movement's Claes Oldenburg makes large sculptures, like *Lipstick.*

The Woodstock music festival.

1970: Congress outlaws tobacco ads in broadcasting.

Heller, *Good As Gold*, a novel examining a man's self-loathing, obsession.

On Broadway, *Jesus Christ Superstar.*

On television, *Monday Night Football.*

Germaine Greer's *The Female Eunuch*, adds to feminist literature.

The Protestant *New English Bible* and the Catholic *New American Bible.*

Postal Reform Bill makes U.S. Postal Service self-supporting.

Corning Glass Works spins out optical fiber clear enough for light pulses.

Kate Millet's *Sexual Politics* stirs feminist thinking.

Teams of players compete in shooting games on Internet.

FCC refuses to extend Fairness Doctrine to anti-war, environmental groups.

In Germany, a videodisc is demonstrated.

IBM System 370 allows time-sharing, online computing.

Eudora Welty's novel *Losing Battles* imagines two days in a Mississippi town.

Alohanet, first wireless computer networking system, University of Hawaii.

Picturephone commercial service begins in downtown Pittsburgh.

U.S. Post Office and Western Union offer Mailgrams.

The Mary Tyler Moore Show starts 7-year run on CBS-TV.

1970: Also New on TV: *All My Children, Flip Wilson Show, Partridge Family.*

Huntley-Brinkley Report becomes *NBC Nightly News.* Chet Huntley retires.

55% of American adults complete high school; slightly more females.

Controversial Japanese author Mishima Yukio commits ritual suicide.

Louis Rukeyser's *Wall Street Week* starts 32-year run on TV.

Phil Donahue Show starts 26-year run.

Oscars: *Patton*, George C. Scott (refuses Oscar), Glenda Jackson.

Also at the movies: *Five Easy Pieces, Love Story, Airport, M*A*S*H.*

Foreign language film Oscar: *Investigation of a Citizen Above Suspicion*, Italy

Mr. Sammler's Planet wins Saul Bellow another National Book Award.

Big Bird of *Sesame Street* gets a *Time* cover.

Probably starting in New York: the disco hustle.

National Public Radio (NPR).

Picturephone services offered in downtown Pittsburgh.

AP sends news by computer.

Nobel Prize in Literature: Russian novelist Alexander Solzhenitsyn.

Film *Jane Eyre* made with new Dolby noise reduction.

Canadian filmmakers invent giant projector IMAX system.

FM stations target population segments, introducing "narrowcasting."

Mini-Moog synthesizers sold to touring rock bands.

Some FM stations offer stereophonic music.

FCC forces television networks out of syndication business with "Fin-Syn" rules.

U.S. movie ticket sales drop from 3 billion plus in 1950 to under 1 billion.

Arcades go into shopping malls.

1971: *Computer Space* competes in taverns against pinball machines, fails.

Software patent issued for computerized telephone switching system.

Nobel Prize in Literature: Pablo Neruda, Chilean poet.

Newspapers switch from hot metal letterpress to offset.

National Public Radio.

Email.

FCC orders broadcasters to "ascertain community needs."

National Science Foundation begins two-year videotex test.

Laser printer created by Xerox.

PBS imports *Masterpiece Theater* shows from Britain.

ARPANET, Internet forerunner, has 22 university, government connections.

Project Gutenberg starts to enter great documents, literature online.

Herman Wouk's *The Winds of War* is a best-seller, will become a mini-series.

Intel builds the 4004 microprocessor, "a computer on a chip."

Oscars: *The French Connection*, Gene Hackman, Jane Fonda.

1971:   Also at the movies: *Klute, The Last Picture Show, Fiddler on the Roof.*

Foreign language film Oscar: *The Garden of the Finzi-Continis*, Italy.

World swallows hoax of primitive Philippine Tasaday tribe of cave dwellers.

Wang 1200 is the first word processor.

Gerry Trudeau introduces *Doonesbury.*

Texas Instruments sells a popular portable electronic calculator.

New York *Times* publishes "The Pentagon Papers."

American television grows more socially conscious with *All in the Family.*

Masterpiece Theatre arrives from Britain.

In Washington, D.C., the Kennedy Center for the Performing Arts opens.

John Rawls, *A Theory of Justice*, seminal work in modern philosophy.

Elizabeth Janeway, *Man's World, Woman's Place.*

AM-FM radios are installed in new cars.

Jerzy Kosinski's satire on television viewing, *Being There.*

World watches as terrorists seize Israeli athletes at Munich Olympics.

On National Public Radio, *All Things Considered.*

Fiddler on the Roof closes; longest running Broadway musical.

1972:   *Ms.* magazine.

Videocassette movies for sale or rent in stores.

In Philippines, Marcos' martial law throttles one of Asia's freest presses.

C, a programming language for the Unix operating system.

Sony sells a videotape system for the home, the Betamax.

Deep Throat starts porn movie industry explosion.

Historian Daniel Boorstin publishes the first of his 3-volume *The Americans.*

European manufacturers (Decca, Phillips, AEG) bring out the video disc.

A satellite is used for live television transmission.

Washington Post begins Watergate reporting that will bring down president.

Public demonstration of ARPANET.

HBO starts pay-TV service for cable.

New FCC rules lead to community access channels.

Polaroid camera can focus by itself.

Digital television comes out of the lab.

The BBC offers "Ceefax," two-way cable information system.

"Open Skies": any U.S. firm can have communication satellites.

Landsat I, "eye-in-the-sky" satellite, is launched.

Nobel Prize in Literature: German novelist Heinrich Böll.

On television: *M*A*S*H*, Waltons, Maude, Bob Newhart, Sanford and Son.*

Philadelphia *Inquirer* builds a computer database for a news story.

Atari's *Pong*, a hit in arcades, taverns, starts video game industry.

1972:   Satellites used for television news reports.

Oscars: *The Godfather*, Marlon Brando, Liza Minelli.

Also at the movies: *Cabaret, Deliverance, The Poseidon Adventure.*

Foreign language film Oscar: *The Discreet Charm of the Bourgeoisie*, France.

Sony's Port-a-Pak, a much more portable video recorder.

From Canada, a programmable word processor with a video screen, the AES 90.

The Xerox Alto, first computer with a mouse and a graphical interface.

The Godfather sets box office record of $1 million a day for first month.

FCC ends six-year ban on installing cable TV in large cities.

1973:   George Carlin's "Seven dirty words" results in court slap for Pacifica Radio.

Starting in Columbus, Ohio, TV cable homes get identifiable addresses.

Nobel Prize in Literature: Australian novelist Patrick White.

Cell phone is invented.

Another popular network soap opera, *The Young and the Restless.*

Burr, best-selling historical novel by Gore Vidal.

$575 buys you a computer kit with a microprocessor, the Scelbi-8H.

Oscars: *The Sting*, Jack Lemmon, Glenda Jackson.

Also at the movies: *The Exorcist, Last Tango in Paris, American Graffiti.*

Foreign language film Oscar: *Day for Night*, France.

Non-compatible video player formats lead several manufacturers to fail.

IBM's Selectric typewriter is now "self-correcting."

For television stations, electronic news gathering (ENG) starts an era.

Vonnegut writes more dark humor, *Breakfast of Champions.*

Erica Jong's *Fear of Flying* shocks with her language.

Complex Thomas Pynchon novel, *Gravity's Rainbow,* wins National Book Award.

Fairchild builds an image-forming CCD chip, 100 rows x 100 columns.

Xerox sets up a LAN (local area network) called Ethernet.

Super 8 home movie cameras with magnetic striping for sound.

Newspaper editors get computer terminals.

Watergate exposure by press will lead to Nixon resignation next year.

Reggae music spreads out from Jamaica.

AP plans to store news photos in its computers.

Computer in England, another in Norway connect to ARPANET.

An American family, the Louds, come apart on national television.

People magazine steps out.

New on TV: *Barnarby Jones, Kojak, Schoolhouse Rock.*

CGI (computer-generated imagery) used in movie *Westworld.*

AP, UPI start to install computer terminals in all U.S. bureaus.

Playgirl gives women the eye candy men get from *Playboy.*

1974: Telephone "hot line" is set up between the White House and the Kremlin.

Arcade video game Tank uses ROM chips to store graphics.

International digital voice transmission.

Carrie is the first of Stephen King's blockbuster gothic novels.

Robert Pirsig's oddly titled novel, *Zen and the Art of Motorcycle Maintenance.*

In England, the BBC transmits Teletext data to TV sets.

Alexander Solzhenitsyn, *The Gulag Archipelago: 1918-1956.*

Coaxial cable can carry 108,000 phone conversations at the same time.

Satellite transmission of mailgrams.

New on TV: *Happy Days, Little House on the Prairie.*

President Nixon. resigns; 110 million viewers watch.

Wall Street Journal successfully transmits an edition by satellite.

Nobel Prize in Literature: Swedish novelists Eyvind Johnson, Harry Martinson.

Telnet offers commercial packet data service.

James Michener, *Centennial*, a fictional account of a Colorado town.

Heinrich Böll, *The Lost Honor of Katharina Blum.*

Magazine article on $439 Altair kit inspires many computer hobbyists.

Oscars: *The Godfather, Part II*, Art Carney, Ellen Burstyn.

Also at the movies: *The Towering Inferno, Chinatown, Blazing Saddles.*

Foreign language film Oscar: *Amarcord*, Italy.

U.S. newspapers start to replace reporters' typewriters with terminals.

Punk rock music emerges in Britain, with themes of nihilism, anarchy.

"Teacher-in-the-Sky" satellite begins educational mission.

The word "Internet" enters the lexicon.

Dolby Labs demonstrates Surround Sound and Pro Logic for movies.

Board game *Dungeons & Dragons* introduces multi-player role play.

Atari's *Tank* shows beginnings of graphic design in video games.

1975: 100,000 coin-operated video games in U.S.

Home version of *Pong* from Atari.

Magnavox adds sound and scoring for Odyssey 200.

Microprocessor used in Taito's *Gunfight.*

Saturday Night Live starts TV run. So does *Good Morning America.*

Also on TV: *Wheel of Fortune, The Jeffersons, Welcome Back, Kotter.*

Two new soap operas: *Ryan's Hope, One Day at a Time.*

Philips demonstrates an optical videodisc system.

The microcomputer, in kit form, develops a market of young hobbyists.

Oscars: *One Flew Over the Cuckoo's Nest*, Jack Nicholson, Louise Fletcher.

Also at the movies: *Jaws, Nashville, Funny Lady, Dog Day Afternoon.*

Steven Spielberg's *Jaws* will be the first film to earn more than $100 million.

1975: Foreign language film Oscar: *Dersu Uzala*, U.S.S.R.

Peter Singer's *Animal Liberation* informs public of humane treatment.

Feature film, *Lisztomania* has Dolby Stereo optical soundtrack.

HBO's "Thrilla' from Manila," nationwide by satellite, begins pay cable boom.

Substantial entertainment production for cable channels.

Playwright David Mamet, *American Buffalo*.

In Maine, the last manual telephone company switchboard is put away.

HBO bounces signal off satellite to reach cable systems and customers.

Bill Gates and Paul Allen start a company they call Micro-Soft.

Frances Lappé's *Diet for a Small Planet* opposes meat, sells 1.5 million copies.

Venera 9 sends pictures of the surface of Venus.

In Los Angeles, the first computer store; it sells assembled computers.

Nobel Prize in Literature: poet Eugenio Montale, Italy

Saul Bellow's comic novel *Humboldt's Gift* wins Pulitzer Prize.

On television, *Saturday Night Live*.

Paul Theroux's travel by train through Asia, *The Great Railway Bazaar*.

New Yorkers read Reuters news via teletext and videotex on cable.

In France, a test of the Antiope text-only teletext service via TV signals.

E.L. Doctorow's historical novel, *Ragtime*; will become 1998 Broadway musical.

U.S. television networks agree to set a "family hour" free of sex and violence.

Tom Wolfe writes about the astronauts, *The Right Stuff*.

Citizens band (CB) radio service available for public use.

Gunfight, an arcade video game for two players, uses a microprocessor.

1976: Digital still-store can access 1,500 stills in random order.

Apple computer founders design popular video game *Breakout*.

Court rules that "family hour" on television is unconstitutional.

U.S. Copyright Act extends protection.

Barbara Walters becomes first woman to anchor a U.S. TV nightly network newscast.

CB radio use leaps as FCC lifts license requirement.

Alex Haley's search for his ancestors is published as *Roots*.

Nobel Prize in Literature: American novelist Saul Bellow.

The Apple I. Steve Jobs sells his VW van to raise manufacturing funds.

Queen Elizabeth II is the first head of state to send an email message.

The Cray-1 supercomputer can do 240 million calculations per second.

Small satellite dishes go into residential backyards.

On Broadway: *Evita*.

New on TV: *Scooby Doo, Laverne and Shirley*.

"Electric Pencil," the first popular microcomputer word-processing program.

Dolby Stereo goes into movie theaters.

1976: Viking II sends color photos from Mars.

FCC reserves line 21 on television sets for closed captions.

Trials begin on TCP/IP protocol for Internet.

Ted Turner delivers programming nationwide by satellite.

Sony's Betamax and JVC's VHS battle for home market. Sony will lose.

Steadicam, a camera stabilizing system.

In England the BBC starts Ceefax, a teletext and videotex system.

Oscars: *Rocky*, Peter Finch, Faye Dunaway.

Also at the movies: *Network, All the President's Men, Taxi Driver*.

Foreign language film Oscar: *Black and White in Color*, Ivory Coast.

A still camera, Canon AE-1, uses a microprocessor.

U.S. Copyright Act revison considers photocopying, fair use, interlibrary loans.

Channel F for the TV set, using a game cartridge.

Death Race 98 raises public complaints about video games.

1977: Toy company Mattel manufactures hand-held LED video games.

Atari 2600 with joystick offers many games.

Columbus, Ohio, residents try 2-way cable experiment, QUBE.

Oscars: *Annie Hall*, Richard Dreyfuss, Diane Keaton.

Also at the movies: *Star Wars, Saturday Night Fever, Looking for Mr. Goodbar*.

Foreign language film Oscar: *Madame Rosa*, France.

Marilyn French's *The Women's Room*, a novel of feminist frustration.

Andre Blay begins business of renting videotapes.

New on TV: *Three's Company, The Love Boat, CHIPs, Eight is Enough, Lou Grant*.

Star Wars released in 46 theaters equipped with Dolby Stereo.

Atari introduces a programmable home video game system in a cartridge.

The Apple II microcomputer is a best seller. Also:Commodore Pet, TRS-80.

Annie Hall adds to writer-director Woody Allen's list of works.

Nobel Prize in Literature: Spanish poet Vicente Aleixandre.

John Cheever's novel, *Falconer*.

Toronto *Globe and Mail* offers public access to newspaper text database.

As a TV miniseries, *Roots* draws 130 million viewers over 8 nights.

Disco music becomes the rage.

King's novel, *The Shining*; like *Carrie*, it will become a hit movie.

Nintendo begins to sell computer games.

In Chicago, AT&T transmits telephone calls by fiber optics.

MCI ends AT&T exclusivity for long distance phone service.

Apple II's floppy disk drive leads to writing of many software programs.

1978: Cellular radio gets spectrum allocated to cable channels 70 to 83.

1978: RCA introduces the Selectavision video disc.

John Irving's novel, *The World According to Garp*.

Another Michener novel, *Chesapeake*, Maryland history, semi-fiction across time.

From Japan's Konica, the point-and-shoot, autofocus camera.

BBS (Bulletin Board Software) lets computers communicate via phone modems.

Wide tests of cellular telephones.

AM stereo system gets FCC green light.

In England, the start of a videotex and teletext system called Oracle.

Nobel Prize in Literature: Jewish short story writer Isaac Bashevis Singer.

Broadcasting finds many uses for computers.

In Japan, the Captain videotex service begins public tests.

Intel offers a 16-bit microprocessor.

120 million watch *Holocaust* drama on TV.

Toni Morrison's novel, *Song of Solomon*.

PBS goes to satellite for delivery, abandoning telephone lines.

Oscars: *The Deer Hunter*, Jon Voight, Jane Fonda.

Also at the movies: *Coming Home, Superman, Midnight Express, The Wiz*.

Foreign language film Oscar: *Get Out Your Handkerchiefs*, France.

Herman Wouk's *War and Remembrance*, a best-seller, will lead to mini-series.

Electronic typewriters go on sale.

ABC offers its news magazine show *20/20*.

Also on TV: *Dallas, Taxi, Mork and Mindy, Diff'rent Strokes, WKRP in Cincinnati, Paper Chase*.

Hewlett-Packard begins development of inkjet printer.

AT&T tests a cell phone system in Chicago.

Games like *Space Invaders* draw teenagers to arcades.

Louise Brown, the first test tube baby.

Will Eisner's *A Contract with God* is the first graphic novel.

Atari's arcade game *Football* introduces video game sports genre.

Atari's *Lunar Lander* arcade game originally designed for space program.

Speech recognition machine has a vocabulary of 1,000 words.

Wordstar, an early, successful word processing program.

News groups arrive on the Internet.

Prestel videotex provides data by television on command in England.

Rap music goes beyond the streets of New York.

Game players discover the Internet, especially multi-user potential.

From Holland comes the digital videodisc read by laser.

On Broadway, a Sondheim musical, *Sweeney Todd*.

Canada tests Telidon videotex.

Star Raiders video game anticipates space-combat simulators.

1978: In Japan, first cell phone network.

1979: Atari 400 and 800 model game computers.

V.S. Naipaul, *A Bend in the River*, questions accuracy of history.

Sony's Betascan shows picture in fast forward mode.

A spreadsheet program, VisiCalc, turns small businesses on to computers.

Nobel Prize in Literature: Greek poet Elytis Odysseus.

Motorola's 68.000 microprocessor contains 68,000 transistors.

Oscars: *Kramer vs. Kramer*, Dustin Hoffman, Sally Field.

Also at the movies: *Apocalypse Now, Norma Rae, All That Jazz, The Black Stallion*.

Foreign language film Oscar: *The Tin Drum*, West Germany.

Computerized laser printing is a boon to Chinese printers.

From England, a text-only Multi-User Dungeon (MUD) game.

William Styron's, *Sophie's Choice*, a horrific novel of Nazi atrocity.

Sony Walkman tape player starts a fad.

CompuServe comes online.

USENET begins.

For TV news watchers: *Nightline, Nightly Business Report, CBS Sunday Morning*.

Four-player video game, *Atari Football*.

New cable channels: C-SPAN, Nickelodeon, ESPN, The Movie Channel.

Galxian arcade game, introduces three-channel RGB color.

Asteroids, arcade game that publicly records initials of high scorers.

Adventure has an "Easter Egg," a hidden room with designer's name.

WordStar, an early, successful word processing program.

1980: Reporters use 25 lb. Osborne portable computer on assignments.

The PC hard drive, holds 10 MB.

Ted Koppel's *Nightline* emerges from ABC's nightly Iran hostage coverage.

The Right Stuff, about astronauts, by Tom Wolfe;; will be hit film.

Norman Mailer's *Executioner's Song* examines life of killer Gary Gilmore.

Sears sells closed-caption decoders for television.

20% of U.S. homes have cable TV; 1% have VCRs.

New on TV: *That's Incredible!, Magnum, P.I.*

Normally secretive China televises trial of the "Gang of Four."

Gary Larson's *The Far Side* comic panels.

Zork attracts players to adventure games.

The Minitel telephone system begins in France; it will be used for decades.

James Michener, *The Covenant*, traces South Africa from bushmen to apartheid.

In France, a holographic film shows a gull flying.

Of every ten books sold in the U.S., seven are paperbacks.

A former movie star, Ronald Reagan, is elected president of the United States.

1980: Intelsat V relays 12,000 phone calls, 2 color TV channels.

Sears sells decoders for closed captioning for television.

Public international electronic fax service, Intelpost, begins.

Consultants determine news policy at many U.S. television stations.

Atlanta gets first fiber optics system.

New York Times, *Wall Street Journal*, Dow Jones put news database online.

In Germany, the Telekom videotex system begins tests.

CNN, 24-hour news channel, begins reports from Atlanta to 172 cable systems.

Black Entertainment Television (BET) is added to cable network programming.

The Learning Channel, Bravo, USA Network.

Sony introduces the consumer camcorder.

Umberto Eco's novel, *The Name of the Rose*, infuses fiction with semiotics.

Voyager 1 sends back images of Saturn and its moons, one billion miles away.

From 3M: Post-it notes.

International committee (CCITT) sets compatibility standards for fax machines.

Oscars: *Ordinary People*, Robert De Niro, Sissy Spacek.

Also at the movies: *Raging Bull*, *Coal Miner's Daughter*, *Private Benjamin*.

Foreign language film Oscar: *Moscow Does Not Believe in Tears*, U.S.S.R.

Addressable cable TV converters pinpoint individual homes.

Nobel Prize in Literature: Polish-American poet Czeslaw Milosz.

The public sees a computer digital imaging system.

Michael Crichton's *Congo*: lost city, diamonds, vicious ape men.

Lasers are used to set type.

Atari's *Battlezone* introduces 3-D arcade game. Army will adapt for training.

Berzerk introduces arcade video games that speak.

1981: *Centipede*, first arcade video game designed by a woman, Dona Bailey.

Pac-Man and *Donkey Kong* dominate the arcade video game world.

Americans spend $5 billion to play arcade video games.

Galaga is one of the first video games with a bonus stage.

Japan's NHK demonstrates analog HDTV system.

In Sri Lanka, Sinhalese police burn irreplaceable library of Tamil history.

On Broadway, *Cats*.

From Sony, the Mavica, a filmless "still-video" camera, but only a prototype.

Paul Theroux's novel, *The Mosquito Coast*; it will become a film.

New cable channel: Eternal Word Network.

CNN Headline News.

Deregulation and longer license periods make life easier for broadcasters.

Wave system eliminates feedback distortion from telephone calls.

Hill Street Blues begins era of gritty television cop shows.

1981:   If evening soap *Dallas* is such a hit, why not *Dynasty* and *Falcon Crest*?

       MTV, a music video channel, goes on cable 24/7.

       The IBM PC, the 5150 with 16K memory; cost: $1,500.

       Apartheid-controlled South Africa starts TV channel for black audience.

       Nobel Prize in Literature: British immigrant Elias Canetti.

       450,000 transistors fit on a silicon chip 1/4-inch square.

       Hologram technology improves, now in video games.

       From Microsoft, the MSDOS 1.0 operating system.

       The laptop computer is introduced by Tandy.

       Most modems run at 300 bits/sec.

       Oscars: *Chariots of Fire*, Henry Fonda, Katherine Hepburn.

       At the movies: *On Golden Pond, Reds, Raiders of the Lost Ark*.

       Foreign language film Oscar: *Mephisto*, Hungary

       The mouse pointer is attached to computers.

       In England, Prestel videotex adds email service.

       BITNET connects university mainframe computers worldwide.

       The *Donkey Kong* computer game swings off the shelves.

       Some malls in Canada provide touchscreens for shoppers.

       ADA, a programming language named in honor of Ada, Lady Lovelace.

1982:   *Ms. Pac-Man* attracts girls as well as boys to home video games.

       From Japan, a camera with electronic picture storage, no film.

       Sony of Japan and Philips of the Netherlands bring out the compact disc.

       USA Today typeset in regional plants by satellite command.

       Oscars: *Gandhi*, Ben Kingsley, Meryl Streep.

       Also at the movies: *E.T., Tootsie, The Verdict, Missing, Das Boot*.

       Foreign language film Oscar: *Volver a Empezar* (*To Begin Again*), Spain.

       Return of the Jedi plays in theaters equipped for its THX sound system.

       Caller ID.

       From Carnegie Mellon U. professor Scott Fahlman: emoticons. :-)

       New cable channels: Weather Channel, Playboy Channel.

       Kodak camera uses film on a disk cassette.

       The film *Tron* goes inside a video game.

       Commodore 64 introduced; popular with game players.

       Noisy arguing thrives on prime time: *Crossfire, The McLaughlin Group.*

       Ian Hancock's *Land of Pain* tells little known, tortured history of the Gypsies.

       Nobel Prize in Literature: novelist Gabriel García Márquez, Colombia.

       James Michener, *Space*, a story of the American space program.

       5.5 million PCs have been sold.

       Cheers gets off to a shaky start on network TV, but recovers.

1982:   *Late Night with David Letterman.*

From 9th grade practical joker Richard Skrenta, something new: a computer virus.

Also on TV: *Cagney & Lacey, Knight Rider, St. Elsewhere, Family Ties, Bob Newhart.*

Vectrex video game computer is introduced.

Alice Walker's novel, *The Color Purple.*

Thomas Keneally's novel, *Schindler's List,* starts as *Schindler's Ark.*

England's Prestel videotex system adds *Newsweek* content for subscribers.

1983:   Laser disk technology used in *Dragon's Lair,* an arcade video game.

Nobel Prize in Literature: British novelist William Golding.

Time names the computer as "Man" of the Year for 1982.

TV news anchor Christine Craft stirs industry with discrimination suit.

Joseph Heller, *God Knows,* comic novel about King David.

CDs (compact discs, not certificates of deposit) go on sale.

Pole Position, an arcade driving game, puts teens behind the wheel.

More than 500 cartridge games are released.

Michener examines *Poland* across the centuries, mixing fact and fiction.

Apple's Lisa, the first microcomputer with a graphical user interface.

Compaq builds the first fully compatible IBM clone.

New on TV: 1983: Final episode of M*A*S*H* draws record share of TV viewers.

NES game console comes to U.S. with *Super Mario Bros.,* a huge hit.

Intercity fiber optic phone transmission begins: New York to Washington.

Lasers and plastics improve newspaper production.

Audio music cassettes outsell LP records.

Alleged discovery of Hitler's diaries; proves to be a forgery.

Lotus 1-2-3 spreadsheet program.

American Public Radio network.

Vanessa Williams wins, breaks Miss America contest race barrier.

Computer chip holds 288,000 bits of memory.

ZIP + 4, expanded 9-digit ZIP codes, and postal bar codes are introduced.

Internet domains get names instead of hard-to-remember numbers.

AT&T forced to break up; 7 Baby Bells are born.

Cisco Systems starts network router manufacturing business.

Oscars: *Terms of Endearment,* Robert Duvall, Shirley MacLaine.

Also at the movies: *The Right Stuff, Silkwood, The Big Chill, Flashdance.*

Foreign language film Oscar: *Fanny & Alexander,* Sweden.

Compaq builds the first fully compatible IBM clone.

TCP/IP becomes standard for Internet communication between computers.

MILNET, for military sites, splits off ARPANET.

American videotext service starts; fails in three years.

1984: Trucks used for SNG (satellite news gathering).

New cable channels: Lifetime, A&E, AMC.

Machine translates basic Japanese into basic English, but makes many mistakes.

Portable compact disk player arrives.

On television: *The Cosby Show., Miami Vice, Kate & Allie, Hunter, Murder, She Wrote.*

Jay McInerney's novel, *Bright Lights, Big City.*

Michael Jackson album *Thriller* has sales of 37 million copies.

Arguments over teaching evolution break out across U.S.

National Geographic puts a hologram on its cover.

William Gibson coins the term "cyberspace" in his novel *Neuromancer.*

Experimental television set can be worn on the wrist.

Japanese introduce high quality facsimile over phone lines.

Several large U.S. newspapers offer online text versions.

Apple Macintosh and IBM PC AT are introduced.

On Broadway: *Glengarry Glen Ross.*

Canon sells an electronic still camera.

3 1/2-inch disk drive.

From Russia, *Tetris.*

AT&T fiber optic cable service extends from Boston to Washington.

FCC eases rules on multiple ownership of media in same market.

The 32-bit microprocessor.

Video cameras are sold widely.

Irish singer Bob Geldof begins raising funds for Africa's famine victims.

CD-ROM disk can hold 270,000 typewritten pages of data.

Broadway Pulitzer musical, Sondheim's *Sunday in the Park with George.*

Oscars: *Amadeus*, F. Murray Abraham, Sally Field.

Also at the movies: *Places in the Heart, The Killing Fields, The Natural.*

Foreign language film Oscar: *Dangerous Moves*, Switzerland.

Hollywood amends ratings; now G, PG, PG-13, R, X.

The one-megabyte memory chip.

FCC lottery for cell phone spectrum, starts bidding frenzy; 25,000 users in U.S..

CONUS relays news feeds for stations on Ku-band satellites.

Nobel Prize in Literature: Czech poet Jaroslav Seifert.

Novelist John Updike, *The Witches of Eastwick.*

Playwright Sam Shepard, *Fool for Love.*

Novelist Tom Clancy, *The Hunt For Red October* and *Red Storm Rising.*

From Florida, Radio Marti beams anti-Castro propaganda to Cuba.

The Tonight Show introduces multi-channel stereo to regular TV.

1985: Ownership of VCRs rises rapidly to 20% of U.S. households.

1985: Rock band recordings raise money for African relief.

Michener, *Texas*, major historical events once again in fictional settings.

New cable channels: Home Shopping Network, Discovery Channel, VH-1.

Desktop publishing becomes familiar.

World has 340,000 cell phone users.

Bret Easton Ellis' novel of his generation, *Less Than Zero*.

Cray-2 supercomputer does 1.2 billion calculations per second.

Historian Daniel Boorstin, *The Discoverers*.

Western novelist Larry McMurtry, *Lonesome Dove*.

In Soviet Union, mass communication opens up under "glasnost" policy.

Nobel Prize in Literature: French novelist Claude Simon.

Cell phones go into cars.

Studs Terkel, *The Good War*, wins Pulitzer, an example of oral history.

"Live Aid" for Africa shows power of rock music and communication.

The first of the *SimCity* series of video games.

Images can be broken into digital bits.

Minolta 7000, an auto-focus 35 mm single lens reflex camera.

Microsoft ships the Windows 1.0 operating system.

Synthetic text-to-speech computer pronounces 20,000 words.

Television broadcasts can be heard in stereo.

U.S. TV networks begin satellite distribution to affiliates.

British transputer allows computer parallel information processing.

Typical modem speed now 2,400 bits/second.

At Expo, a Sony TV screen measures 40 x 25 meters.

Sony builds a radio the size of a credit card.

America Online founded as Quantum Computer Services.

Publication of last of Anaïs Nin's diaries.

In Japan, 3-D television experiment; no spectacles needed.

New on TV: *Golden Girls, Dennis the Menace, MacGyver, Moonlighting, Larry King Live.*

Oscars: *Out of Africa*, William Hurt, Geraldine Page.

Also at the movies: *Witness, The Color Purple, Prizzi's Honor, Ran, Rambo.*

Foreign language film Oscar: *The Official Story*, Argentina.

The 12-hour Holocaust documentary, *Shoah*.

Pay-per-view channels open for business.

Kids can't get enough of *Super Mario Brothers* computer game.

New videotape formats: 8 mm and VHS-C.

50 newspapers now offer online access to news texts.

1986: Digital Audio Tape (DAT).

Canon filmless camera, the RC-701, goes into production.

1986:	HBO, Cinemax scramble their signals to foil off-air thieves.

Maus comic books, about the Holocaust, published.

U.S., Europe veto Japanese analog HDTV; will develop digital system.

Over objections, black-and-white movies are "colorized."

Nigerian poet-dramatist Wole Soyinka wins Nobel Prize in literature.

Oscars: *Platoon*, Paul Newman, Marlee Matlin.

Also at the movies: *The Color of Money*, *Children of a Lesser God*, *Aliens*.

Foreign language film Oscar: *The Assault*, Netherlands.

A fourth U.S. television network, Fox, is added to ABC, CBS, NBC lineup.

Laser printers start to replace dot matrix and daisy wheel printers.

Reference book, *Academic American Encyclopedia*, produced as CD-ROM.

The LISTSERV mailing list program for Internet-based interest groups.

Live coverage of Challenger explosion stuns viewers.

International standards set for audio, video, digital recording.

On Broadway, *Les Miserables*; in London, *Phantom of the Opera*.

Comic books turn grim and violent with *The Dark Knight Returns*.

Patriot Games, another of Tom Clancy's best-selling novels.

Final supplement of *Oxford English Dictionary*. Work began in 1858.

Television is on for more than seven hours a day in average U.S. home.

Margaret Atwood's dystopian novel, *The Handmaid's Tale*.

Japanese introduce Game Boy, with 8-bit operating system.

Oprah Winfrew Show on television.

Cable shopping networks meet two public desires: TV and shopping.

Voyager 2 sends back images of Uranus.

Cable and discs bite into TV network dominance.

New on TV: *Oprah*, *L.A. Law*, *Matlock*, *Pee-wee's Playhouse*, *Designing Women*.

Congress passes Electronic Communications Privacy Act.

Computer-created *Luxo Jr.* is first of Pixar's virtual studio films.

1987:	FCC repeals most of the Fairness Doctrine. Personal Attack Rule remains.

Tom Wolfe's first novel, *The Bonfire of the Vanities*.

Nobel Prize in Literature: Russian exile poet Joseph Brodsky.

Half of all U.S. homes with TV are on cable.

Fortunes paid for Van Gogh art. He had traded paintings for meals.

The Simpsons animated cartoon is introduced on Fox TV.

Toni Morrison's Pulitzer novel, *Beloved*.

Fourth major U.S. television network: Fox.

After his death, Soviet Writers Union rehabilitates Boris Pasternak.

One million cell phone subscribers in U.S.; many more in other nations.

1987:   From Japan, the *anime* sci-fi cartoon film.

Oscars: *The Last Emperor*, Michael Douglas, Cher.

Also at the movies: *Wall Street, Moonstruck, Fatal Attraction, Lethal Weapon.*

Foreign language film Oscar: *Babette's Feast*, Denmark.

Global teleconference on hunger links 50,000 people in 79 cities.

More than 10,000 Internet Service Providers (ISPs).

Government deregulates cable industry.

New on TV: *Married... with Children, 21 Jump Street, Full House.*

ADSL (Asymmetric Digital Subscriber Line).

IBM offers a computer with VGA, giving a choice of 262,144 colors.

Computer application programs Excel and PageMaker.

From Fuji in Japan, the "QuickSnap" disposable camera.

People Meter improves Nielsen rating accuracy.

Bill Atkinson's hypercard carries on Vannevar Bush's hyperlink vision.

Dolby Pro Logic speakers are made for the home market.

National Science Foundation starts NSFNET; it will replace ARPANET.

1988:   The Digital Disk Playback (DDP) system uses uncompressed digital sound.

Sony introduces the Pocket Discman.

Who Framed Roger Rabbit? feature film combines live action, animation.

Tennessee Senator Albert Gore proposes U.S. research and education network.

Stephen Hawking's explanation of the universe, *A Brief History of Time.*

First transatlantic telephone call over fiber optics line.

Government brochure mailed to 107 million addresses.

Prodigy dial-up service.

Leading radio music format: adult contemporary.

The first Nobel Prize in literature written in Arabic won by Naguib Mahfouz.

Oscars: *Rain Man*, Dustin Hoffman, Jodie Foster.

Also at the movies: *Die Hard, Big, Do the Right Thing, A Fish Called Wanda.*

Foreign language film Oscar: *Pelle the Conqueror*, Denmark.

Self-service fax machine can be accessed by credit card.

"Hacker" and "Worm" enter the Internet lexicon. First data crime reported.

Two long-running TV documentary series start: *48 Hours, America's Most Wanted.*

Roseanne breaks ground on TV with a plain-talking blue collar family.

Also on TV: *Murphy Brown, Garfield and Friends.*

Steve Jobs offers the futuristic NeXT computer. It will not survive.

Jarkko Oikarinen of Finland writes the Internet Relay Chat software program.

Internet T1 backbone completed; soon proves inadequate for traffic surge.

James Michener, *Alaska*, another blockbuster from ancient times to the present.

In *Foucault's Pendulum*, Umberto Eco offers a novel with levels of meaning.

1988: CDs now outsell vinyl records.

The Last Temptation of Christ film is condemned by Christian groups.

Salman Rushdie's novel, The Satanic Verses, enrages Muslims.

98% of U.S. homes have at least one television set.

In Japan, an ISDN, International Service Digital Network.

New cable channel: TNT.

After 38 years, Soviet Union abandons jamming of foreign radio signals.

MP3 (Motion Picture Experts Group 1, Layer 3) for music, video files.

1989: Ayatollah Khomenei orders death for Salman Rushdie, who is not in Iran.

Microsoft's Corbis Corp. starts gathering, digitizing millions of photographs.

AT&T claims speech recognition machine understands 300 billion sentences.

Amy Tan's best-selling novel of Chinese women, The Joy Luck Club.

SimCity attracts new players, especially women, to "god games."

Researchers try to index the exploding Internet; can't keep up.

Another Tom Clancy military best-selling novel, Clear and Present Danger.

Caribbean is examined across time in typical James Michener style.

TV Guide cover sneaks Oprah Winfrey's head on Ann-Margaret's body. They're caught.

More than 100,000 Internet hosts.

New Sony videotape format: Hi8.

Photos can be digitally manipulated on a home computer.

Nintendo racks up an annual profit of $1 billion.

Nobel Prize in Literature: novelist Camilo José Cela, Spain.

E.L. Doctorow, Billy Bathgate, fact and fiction among Thirties gangsters.

New Revised Standard Version of the Bible replaces Revised Standard Version.

NHK begins regular broadcasting of analog HDTV programs.

With 5 million Minitels, France is the world's most wired nation.

Nintendo's Game Boy is a hand-held gaming device.

Channel One enters schools with free TV sets, programs, and commercials.

The Sega Genesis console.

Additions to TV news magazines: Primetime, Inside Edition.

Baywatch tests limits on showing skin.

Also on TV: COPS, Family Matters, Doogie Howser, M.D.

The Abyss wins Oscar for visual effects that include advanced CGI.

For newspapers: Dilbert, Dogbert, Catbert, The Boss, and their co-workers.

The Sound Blaster card adds to the video game excitement.

Study blames video games for decline in health of schoolchildren.

Tiananmen Square massacre demonstrates power of media to inform the world.

Oscars: Driving Miss Daisy, Daniel Day-Lewis, Jessica Tandy.

Also at the movies: When Harry Met Sally, Glory, Field of Dreams.

1989:   Foreign language film Oscar: *Cinema Paradiso*, Italy.

Voyager 2 sends back images of Neptune.

Pacific Link fiber optic cable opens, can carry 40,000 phone calls.

B.F Skinner, *The Origins of Cognitive Thought*, delves into behaviorist theory.

Vacationers can buy single use, throwaway cameras.

1990:   Many telephone, broadcasting monopolies move to competition, privatization.

With *Iron John*, writer Robert Bly starts a back-to-masculinity movement.

Michael Crichton's blockbuster novel, *Jurassic Park*.

Entertainment Weekly magazine.

The second edition of the *Oxford English Dictionary*, book form or CD-ROM.

Flyaway SNG aids foreign reportage.

Kodak introduces the Photo CD player.

New on TV: *Seinfeld, Northern Exposure, Twin Peaks, Law & Order, Beverly Hills 90210.*

New cable channel: CNBC.

IBM sells its Selectric division, a sign of the typewriter's passing.

The Video Toaster, a low cost video effects tool.

Video games go non-linear with *Super Mario Bros. 3.*

By now, most 2-inch videotape machines are gone.

Oscars: *Dances With Wolves*, Jeremy Irons, Kathy Bates.

Also at the movies: *Pretty Woman, GoodFellas, Total Recall, Ghost.*

Foreign language film Oscar: *Journey of Hope*, Switzerland.

Dick Tracy is first 35 mm feature film with a digital soundtrack.

Videodisc returns in a new laser form.

Average U.S. home has five radio sets.

From IBM, a line of workstations using RISC chips.

World Wide Web originates at CERN in Europe. Tim Berners-Lee writes program.

Norman Mailer, *Harlot's Ghost*, looks at two generations in the C.I.A.

Adobe Photoshop 1.0 for the Macintosh, an image manipulation program.

85% of American adults have completed high school.

Average American cable customer has a choice of 33 channels.

Nobel Prize in Literature: poet, essayist Octavio Paz, Mexico.

Television Marti joins Radio Marti to send U.S. propaganda to Cuba.

Hollywood replaces X rating with NC-17.

Congress passes Children's Television Act.

Seinfeld starts television run.

1991:   Sony's PlayStation game console.

TV tabloid talk shows: *Jerry Springer, Jenny Jones, Maury Povich.*

Also on TV: *Home Improvement, Rugrats, Silk Stalkings.*

1991: Internet made available for commercial use.

Douglas Coupland writes novel about *Generation X*.

Recordable compact disk drivers, CD-Rs, reach the market.

Hypertext Markup Language (HTML) written; helps create the World Wide Web.

Motion Picture Assoc. says only 16% of American movies fit for kids under 13.

Nobel Prize in Literature: South African novelist Nadine Gordimer.

FCC widens AM frequency band.

Sega's arcade game *Time Traveler* comes close to true holograms.

In Europe, Internet sites more than triple in one year, pass 100,000.

CNN dominates news coverage worldwide during Gulf War.

The Web gets "servers."

New cable channels: Comedy Central, Court TV, Encore.

Live TV news switching between world capitals during Gulf War looks simple.

Denver viewers can order movies at home from list of more than 1,000 titles.

Moviegoers astonished by computer morphing in *Terminator 2*.

User-friendly Gopher offers point-and-click navigation of Internet files.

Baby Bells get government permission to offer information services.

Multichannel Multipoint Distribution Systems (MMDS) get more spectrum space.

Collapse of Soviet anti-Gorbachev plot aided by the Internet.

The start of grunge music.

V.P. Dan Quayle outraged by fictional Murphy Brown out-of-wedlock baby.

English scientists build optical amplifiers into fiber cable network.

More than 4 billion cassette tape rentals in U.S. alone.

Oscars: *The Silence of the Lambs*, Anthony Hopkins, Jodie Foster.

For the first time, a cartoon, *Beauty and the Beast*, is up for best picture Oscar.

Also at the movies: *Thelma & Louise*, *Bugsy*, *City Slickers*.

Foreign language film Oscar: *Mediterraneo*, Italy.

Civilization, a turn-based, strategy-driven video game.

Motorola works on a communication system to reach every point on the globe.

Data is transmitted through optical fiber at 32 billion bits per second.

3 out of 4 U.S. homes own VCRs; fastest selling domestic appliance in history.

Tom Clancy, *The Sum of All Fears*, shows chilling foresight of Mideast terrorism.

Howard Stern fined $705,000 for on-air indecency.

An x-ray photograph is taken of the brain recalling a word.

Condoms advertised on U.S. television screens.

Philips introduces the Compact Disk Interactive (CD-I) player for music, video.

1992: The Sony Mini-Disc, a recordable magneto-optical disc.

Dateline NBC and *World News Now* join U.S. TV news program lineup.

65 million personal computers have been sold.

1992: Rodney King beating videotape shot by amateur adds "visualanties" to lexicon.

Compact disk music sales pass cassette tapes.

New cable channels: Sci-Fi Channel, Cartoon Network.

Broadcast station ownership rules eased still more.

The Michelangelo virus, originating in Europe, disables computers worldwide.

The Internet Society is formed to coordinate Internet activities.

U.S. cable mogul John Malone predicts 500-channel future.

Cable TV revenues reach $22 billion.

Sega's *Mortal Kombat* video game is offered in two versions, one bloody.

Michelangelo is first virus to reach national attention.

Daniel Boorstin's *The Creators*, a history of what and how people created.

Text-based browser opens World Wide Web for general usage.

British end Oracle teletext and videotex service.

At least 50 U.S. cities have competing cable services.

Maus comics about the Holocaust wins Pulitzer Prize.

Oscars: *Unforgiven*, Al Pacino, Emma Thompson.

Also at the movies: *Chaplin, The Player, The Crying Game*.

Foreign language film Oscar: *Indochine*, France.

Two more from James Michener, *Mexico* and *The World Is My Home*.

Alors! Disneyland comes to Paris.

Ten million cell phone customers in U.S., a tenfold jump in 5 years.

New Web terms: HTTP and URL.

AOL reports it has 200,000 subscribers.

Number of newspapers offering online news rises to 150.

At Bell Labs, an English-Spanish translator recognizes 450 spoken words.

After first President Bush speaks, 25 million viewers try to phone in opinions.

Nobel Prize in Literature: West Indian poet, playwright Derek Walcott.

Toni Morrison's novel, *Jazz*.

Stamps sold by automatic machines.

Delphi offers dial-up service to the Internet.

Digital AM radio broadcasting is tested.

1993: "Spiders" search the Internet looking for key words.

Nobel Prize in Literature: African-American novelist Toni Morrison.

Compaq brings out Concerto, a pen-based notebook PC.

Rumors fly that cell phones cause brain cancer; sales continue to soar.

World conference adopts MPEG-2 standard for digital television pictures.

IMAX 3D digital sound system goes into a New York theater.

Nokia sends text messages between mobile phones.

Computer-generated (CGI) dinosaurs roam the earth in *Jurassic Park*.

1993: Oscars: *Schindler's List*, Tom Hanks, Holly Hunter.

Also at the movies: *The Fugitive, The Piano, Sleepless in Seattle*.

Foreign language film Oscar: *Belle Époque*, Spain.

Senate committee hearings on video game violence.

Foreign box office movie revenue pulls ahead of domestic revenue.

NBC News causes ethical blast by staging a GM truck explosion.

Hollywood film edited on non-linear editing computer system.

David Letterman and Conan O'Brien start late night TV shows.

Also on TV: *X-Files, Dr. Quinn, Power Rangers, Frasier, NYPD Blue*.

Demand for "V-Chip" to block out violent and sexual television programs.

From Intel, the Pentium chip.

Served on cable TV: the Food Network.

Apple Newton, a PDA, recognizes handwriting on its screen.

Picturephone updated to put faces on computer screen for transmission.

Graphical user interface, Mosaic, is developed for the World Wide Web.

1 in 3 Americans do some work at home instead of driving to job.

Photojournalists, studio photographers switch to specialized digital cameras.

Nokia sends text messages between mobile phones.

The first versions of the video games *Doom* and *Myst*.

1994: *Warcraft* introduces real-time strategy into a narrative video game.

M.I.T. student charged with wire fraud for file swapping system.

S.A.T. takers permitted to use calculators for the math exam.

Hewlett Packard combines printer, fax, and copier in one machine.

After 25 years, U.S. government privatizes Internet management.

Two million computers connected to the Internet.

Sega's *Daytona USA* complex video arcade game can have 8 players.

Radio stations open World Wide Web locations.

Digital satellite TV service, DirecTV, offered in the U.S.

FCC approves Advanced TV standards, including HDTV and SDTV.

WWW growth mushrooms. Pizza Hut starts taking orders on the Web.

200 workstations worldwide get Rolling Stones concert on Internet "MBone."

The Netscape Navigator replaces Mosaic as a World Wide Web browser.

The Zip drive, with removable storage of up to 100 MB.

Radio HK, a 24-hour Internet-only radio station.

Superbowl telecast pulls in nearly 135 million viewers.

The most popular radio format in the U.S. is country music.

New on TV: *Friends, ER, Chicago Hope. Touched by an Angel*.

Sensible World of Soccer advances play, views of sports video games.

Yahoo search engine is started by two Stanford graduate engineering students.

1994:   Chain bookstores outsell independents in the U.S. for the first time.

   Internet mass marketing brings "spamming" into the lexicon.

   Real Audio allows online audio listening in near real time.

   To reduce Western influence, a dozen nations ban or restrict satellite dishes.

   FCC raises one-company ownership to 20 AM, 20 FM radio stations.

   DBS (Direct Broadcast Satellite) signals to 18-inch home dishes.

   Oscars: *Forrest Gump*, Tom Hanks, Jessica Lange.

   Also at the movies: *Pulp Fiction, Nell, The Client, Speed, The Lion King*.

   Foreign language film Oscar: *Burnt by the Sun*, Russia.

   Forrest Gump uses digital photo tricks to insert person into historical footage.

   New cable channels: FX, IFC, TCM, Home & Garden, Starz!, Game Show Network.

   Prodigy bulletin board fields 12,000 messages after L.A. quake.

   Magazines known as "'e-zines" are published on CD-ROM disks.

   Competitors agree on a standard for high definition TV.

   Almost 1/3 of all American homes have a computer.

   Nobel Prize in Literature: Japanese novelist, essayist Kenzaburo Oe.

   Banner ads appear on Internet websites.

   Time Warner creates WB television network.

   Video game industry forms Interactive Digital Software Association.

   Internet use rises sharply as major online providers open portals to public.

1995:   Total annual sales of video games: $3 billion.

   Phone calls over the Internet: VoIP.

   Amazon.com starts selling books online, will become Web's hottest retailer.

   Videotape project lets prisoners read books to their children.

   Personal Communication Service (PCS) digital wireless phones.

   UPN television network created by Paramount and Universal studios.

   Direct Broadcast Satellites (DBS) beam digital programs to home dishes.

   Tokyo Wars advances arcade video games with two 32-bit microprocessors.

   U.S. population continues to increase, but newspaper readership declines.

   New on TV: *JAG, Drew Carey, Jeff Foxworthy, MADtv, Xena the Warrior Princess*.

   Nobel Prize in Literature: Irish poet Seamus Heaney.

   Toy Story is the first totally digital feature-length film.

   Experimental CD-ROM disk can carry a full-length feature film.

   Sony Playstation and Sega Saturn use 32-bit systems for home video games.

   "Internet addiction" is identified.

   Oklahoma City bombing sends many to the Internet for details.

   Sony demonstrates a flat TV set.

   WebTV formed to combine television and the Internet.

   The Java programming language for websites.

1995: DBS feeds are offered nationwide in U.S.

ABC, CBS sold. New networks: WB and UPN.

Howard Stern, Infinity Broadcasting pay added indecency fine of $1.7 million.

The FCC allows radio stations to operate with no one there.

Want a .com? It will now cost $50 a year. .edu and .gov still free.

62% of U.S. homes have cable TV.

Denmark announces plan to put much of the nation online within 5 years.

Major U.S. dailies create national online newspaper network.

Oscars: *Braveheart*, Nicolas Cage, Susan Sarandon.

Also at the movies: *The Bridges of Madison County, Leaving Las Vegas, Babe*.

Foreign language film Oscar: *Antonia's Line*, The Netherlands.

Lamar Alexander chooses the Internet to announce presidential candidacy.

In Cleveland, the Rock and Roll Hall of Fame and Museum opens.

The average U.S. home has nearly six radios.

Caller ID now nationwide in U.S.

30 million Internet users worldwide.

Audio of live events can be heard on the Internet.

Worlds Chat, a 3-D online chatroom introduces communication avatars.

TV images of black/white reactions to O.J. Simpson verdict polarize U.S.

Mortal Kombat becomes a movie.

Disney swallows ABC; Westinghouse swallows CBS.

1996: *Lara Croft, Tomb Raider*, the video game.

From Microsoft: Hotmail.com, a Web-based email site.

The shooter game *Quake* allows users to create their own levels.

U.S. has 40 million cell phone subscribers, up from 1 million in 9 years.

AT&T splits off Lucent Technologies and NCR.

World Exposition is a world's fair held on the Internet.

The stripped-down Net computer arrives.

Opinions on TV from *The Daily Show, The O'Reilly Factor, Hannity & Colmes*.

Larry Page, Sergey Brin create Backrun, predecessor to Google.

In Athens, archæologists uncover the ruins of Aristotle's Lyceum.

Digital Associated Press cameras send Super Bowl pix to newspapers in minutes.

More than 100,000 World Wide Web sites, and growing fast.

45 million Internet users, including 30 million in U.S.

New cable channels: MSNBC, Animal Planet, Fox News Channel, Sundance.

Optical fiber cable line stretches across the Pacific.

Web-TV tunes television sets to the Internet via the TV-set-top box.

Yahoo goes public. In three years its market value will be $70 billion.

Advanced Photo System provides drop-in film loading, choice of print formats.

1996: Computer makers sell flat-panel displays.

South African factory makes Bayliss radio receivers operated by windup spring.

Telecommunication Reform Act: phone, cable, broadcast companies compete.

Telecom Act also removes caps on radio station ownership; expansions follow.

Oscars: *The English Patient*, Geoffrey Rush, Frances McDormand.

Also at the movies: *Evita, Shine, Fargo, Jerry McGuire*.

Foreign language film Oscar: *Kolya*, Czech Republic.

Advantix film for still cameras combines analog and digital technology.

Japanese newspaper Mainichi Shinbum delivers its editions online.

Typical modem is 14.4K bits/sec., but new sales are for 28.8K modems.

Michael Crichton's blockbuster about aircraft construction, *Airframe*.

American Psychological Assoc. correlates TV violence, aggressive behavior.

U.S. Postal Service handles nearly 600 million pieces of mail daily.

A pocket telephone/computer comes on the market.

Sesame Street gets a Russian version.

28% of U.S. public libraries offer Internet access.

TV host Oprah Winfrey boosts book sales with monthly book club.

Several large newspapers offer Web access to their archives.

The FCC approves a digital HDTV standard.

Microsoft releases Explorer 3.0 Web browser.

Nobel Prize in Literature: poet Wislawa Szymborska, Poland.

DVDs are introduced.

Nintendo produces 64-bit *Super Mario 64* home video game.

America Online has 5,000,000 subscribers.

Dell's "e-tailing" sells assemble-to-order computers on the Internet.

From Netscape: the cookie.

Loosening of rules allows multiple station ownership of radio, TV in same city.

1997: Film *Titanic* uses computer images to show people falling off sinking ship.

DVD players and DVD movies are on the fast track to success.

The Supreme Court finds the Communication Decency Act unconstitutional.

Exploding growth: more than 4,000 ISPs in the U.S. and Canada alone.

"Spam" means more than canned meat.

The View brings a panel of women to discuss current issues.

Internet, DVD movies, video games bite deeper into TV audience.

Streaming audio and video are available on the Web.

ARIN, the American Registry for Internet Numbers.

Raunchy cartoons for adults on TV: *South Park, King of the Hill*.

Also on TV: *Ally McBeal, Buffy the Vampire Slayer, Oz*.

"Heaven's Gate" cult sets up website before committing mass suicide.

1997: More than 50 million Americans, Canadians use the Internet.

Palm produces the first handheld device with the Palm OS.

Nearly 8 of 10 U.S. public schools have Internet access.

Elton John's "Candle in the Wind" sells 32 million copies in 37 days.

IBM computer defeats world chess champion Garry Kasparov.

Email spreads hoax of Kurt Vonnegut "sunscreen" commencement speech.

From Kodak, the first point-and-shoot digital camera.

Optical fiber cable lines now stretch around the world.

Pathfinder's Mars pictures released; NASA website gets 46 million hits.

U.S. television adopts age-based ratings; news, sports excluded.

Nobel Prize in Literature: playwright Dario Fo, Italy.

AOL boasts 10 million subscribers.

Another cable channel for women: WE.

PAX-TV makes it seven TV broadcast networks.

2,600 U.S. newspapers have Internet sites or dial-up connections.

Oscars: *Titanic*, Jack Nicholson, Helen Hunt.

Also at the movies: *As Good As It Gets*, *Wag the Dog*, *The Full Monty*.

Foreign language film Oscar: *Character*, The Netherlands.

Novelist Charles Frazier's *Cold Mountain*.

43% of U.S. homes have computers.

FCC hands out huge amount of spectrum for digital television promise.

Film *Titanic* costs $300 million to make, market; will earn more than twice that.

Ultima Online, a massively multiplayer online role-playing game (MMORPG).

1998: Sony's *Everquest* multiplayer online game attracts thousands worldwide.

HP introduces the Jornada PDA (personal digital assistant).

Boorstin's history, *The Seekers*, examines man's quest for understanding.

Multi-billion-dollar mergers involve broadcasting, cable, publishing.

About 800 drive-in theaters still remain open in the United States.

Music industry up in arms as fans download MP3 sound files for free.

Harry Potter and the Sorcerer's Stone, the first of the J.K. Rowling series.

Oscars: *Shakespeare in Love*, Roberto Begnini, Gwyneth Paltrow.

Also at the movies: *Saving Private Ryan*, *The Truman Show*, *Pleasantville*.

Foreign language film Oscar: *Life Is Beautiful*, Italy.

Megapixel cameras available at consumer level.

New on TV: *Sex and the City*, *Will & Grace*, *Dawson's Creek*, *Becker*.

"Sonny Bono Act" extends copyright to lifetime plus 70 years.

SPJ awards given for public service to online journalism.

Drudge Report, an online website, breaks news of Clinton-Lewinsky affair.

The Last Broadcast is the first feature film made with desktop editing.

1998: Associated Press sells online archive service to newspapers.

Google emerges from Backrub.

3,250 newspapers, 1,280 TV stations now have online websites.

Justice Department sues Microsoft for monopolistic practices.

Estimated number of World Wide Web pages: 300 million.

Estimated number of Web pages added each day: 1.5 million.

Plans laid by universities, industry, government for Internet2.

150 million Internet users estimated at year's end, half in the U.S.

The Pentium II processor incorporates 7.5 million transistors.

Apple unveils the colorful iMac computer.

Net users are judges of a TV sports event: world champion ice skating.

Traffic on the Internet, network of networks, is doubling every 100 days.

AOL reports it has 14 million subscribers.

Postage stamps downloaded from the Web, then printed, go on sale in the U.S.

First digital TV programs are broadcast in the U.S.

1 of 3 Americans now use the Internet.

New cable channels: Cinemax, Biography, BBC America.

Britain abandons telegrams in favor of email.

Associated Press once had 1,500 telegraph operators, now has four.

Nobel Prize in Literature: José Saramago, Portugal.

Tom Clancy: *Rainbow Six*; good guys use latest military gadgets to foil terrorists.

V-Chips go into television sets.

Survey: average American with a computer uses it more than 5 hours weekly.

Americans average 2,300 phone calls a year.

HDTV broadcasts begin in the United States.

Cable channels start using digital compression technology.

Internet economy gets its own weekly magazine, *The Industry Standard*.

In U.S. alone, 70,000 book titles this year, 50.000 publishers.

Some cable systems upgraded to permit hundreds of channels.

FCC's E-Rate program makes Internet access cheap for libraries, schools.

Iridium worldwide satellite cell phone service born, but will soon die.

An HDTV station goes on the air in the United States.

Netscape makes public its code for Mozilla, an open-source browser.

The Digital Millennium Copyright Act.

Video game *Metal Gear Solid* offers mixed message about smoking.

The Legend of Zelda earns more in six weeks than any movie.

1999: Video games bring in more money than movie box offices do.

Columbine High School killings focus spotlight on video games.

Music industry releases record 38,900 titles this year.

1999: Jon Johansen, 15, of Norway manages to break movie DVD copy protection.

Number of U.S. daily newspapers drops to 1,483; total 56 million circulation.

Baby Bells offer long distance phone service.

Free downloading of music, videos increases sharply. Millions do it.

Americans are buying average of 8 books a year, 3 times pre-WWII.

Nielsen, Arbitron start World Wide Web rating service.

$35,000 *Blair Witch Project* shows potential of low cost video production.

Virus after virus attack computers. "Melissa" is the worst yet.

FCC allows one company to own 2 TV, 6 radio stations in same big city.

150 million Internet users can access more than 800 million web pages.

Home video games expand with Sega Dreamcast 128-bit operating system.

World worries about Y2K bug; great sums spent to solve the problem.

Michael Crichton visits medieval France for sci-fi novel, *Timeline*.

Mule train still delivers mail down the south face of the Grand Canyon.

New on TV: *The Sopranos, West Wing, SpongeBob SquarePants.*

Ten million Web servers throughout the world.

Nobel Prize in Literature: German novelist Günter Grass.

Oscars: *American Beauty*, Kevin Spacey, Hilary Swank.

Also at the movies: *Matrix, The Insider, The Hurricane, The Sixth Sense.*

Non-English language film Oscar: *All About My Mother*, Spain.

The Ikonos satellite can detect an object on Earth as small as a card table.

On television: *Who Wants to Be a Millionaire?*

TiVo offers personal television control.

2000: Sony Playstation 2 uses DVD for home video games.

40 million mobile wireless users worldwide, most in Europe, Asia.

Use of common office paper in U.S. rises almost 15% since 1995.

Report: the most performed song of the 20ᵗʰ century: "Happy Birthday."

"Y2K" bug tamed, but it was expensive.

Oxygen joins Lifetime and WE as a cable channel appealing to women.

Microprocessors outdo Moore's Law with Intel's 1.5GHz.

Website created to ease public search of U.S. government locations.

"Beenz" issued as an online currency resembling trading stamps.

British "newscaster" Ananova joins other virtual performers on TV, the Net.

Stephen King's novel *Riding the Bullet* is best seller via Net downloads only.

Online Journalism Awards to be given in international competition annually.

The dot.com industry boom busts.

Crusoe chip triples laptop battery life.

More than 3,000,000 blank CDs are sold every month.

2000: School libraries in several states challenged over "satanic" *Harry Potter* books.

One in four American adults hold college degrees.

FCC approves Viacom/CBS merger.

Seven new Web domain names approved, including .info, .pro, .biz.

"Love Bug" virus infects 45 million computers worldwide.

Experimental IBM microprocessor bit is a molecule with five fluorine atoms.

5.1 billion emails are sent in the U.S; 8.2 billion worldwide.

FCC authorizes low power, non-commercial FM radio stations.

Feature film *Quantum Project* is produced for Internet distribution, not theaters.

3G (3rd generation) licenses sold for wireless internet.

Microchip inventor Jack Kilby wins Nobel Prize in Physics.

In Japan, Internet cell phones are sold; 40,000 new subscribers daily.

Bluetooth lets computers converse via low power radio signals.

Microsoft gives the mouse an optical sensor.

From Japan, the camera-phone.

Children's Online Privacy Protection Act becomes U.S. law.

U.S. government sets up website for official documents.

Reality TV shows like *Survivor* are big hits in U.S.

Queer as Folk breaks new TV ground.

Also on TV: *Gilmore Girls, CSI, Curb Your Enthusiasm., Malcolm in the Middle.*

Digital cameras cut deeply into analog camera sales.

Oscars: *Gladiator*, Russell Crowe, Julia Roberts

Also at the movies: *Traffic, Erin Brockovich, Chocolat, Almost Famous*

Non-English language film Oscar: *Crouching Tiger, Hidden Dragon*

65% of all people in Finland own mobile phones, lead the world.

9-minute video, *George Lucas in Love*, premieres on the Internet.

Japanese work on Internet-access glove, choker; downloaded talking ebook.

Supreme Court ends Personal Attack Rule, last vestige of Fairness Doctrine.

Court limits Napster's Internet file-sharing of music.

Congress passes the Children's Internet Protection Act.

Extremely rapid diffusion: 85% of U.S. households own VCRs.

U.S. Postal Service opens Internet postal store.

Nobel Prize in Literature: Gao Xingjian of China.

More than 3 million blank, recordable CDs are sold monthly.

More dollars spent on cable advertising than on TV broadcast ads.

DVD players become world's fastest selling home electronics device.

Sony's PlayStation 2.

Average American cable customer has a choice of 61 channels.

In U.S. alone: 100 million cell phone subscribers.

2000: Seventy million computers connected to the Internet.

Singles spend $7 million for online dating services.

2001: In U.S., FBI arrests Russian who cracked eBook encryption.

E-books on book-size electronic units have only modest success.

New cable channels: Hallmark, National Geographic, ABC Family.

Napster reaches a peak of 77 million users before shutdown.

Patriot Act allows examination of library, Internet use.

Waking Life, a film shot live, then converted into Roboscope animation.

Average American adult watches 4 hours of TV daily.

Movie box office receipts in U.S. climb to $8.4 billion.

From *Harry Potter* to *Crouching Tiger*, special effects rock audiences.

Intelsat becomes private company, not an inter-governmental organization.

Ixus digital camera produces color prints without computer.

Time names Albert Einstein the Person of the Century.

Satellite radio; XM begins broadcasting.

AT&T develops Natural Language Understanding: voice recognition.

Lara Croft, Tomb Raider, the movie.

Anna Kournikova virus jams email boxes around the world.

Code Red and Nimda worms bring major damage to computer networks.

Azerbaijan switches from Cyrillic to Latin alphabet, angering Russians.

Much maligned TV newscasts receive praise for reports of New York terrorism.

Final Fantasy, a life-like, computer-generated feature film.

AT&T improves speech synthesizer, uses several languages.

Personal headsets display movies, video games, spreadsheets.

USB 2.0 connectors, will become computer standard.

Instant messaging, short messaging service (SMS), grows in popularity.

LexisNexis offers 2.8 billion searchable documents from 30,000 sources.

More than half of all Americans now use the Internet.

Mac OS X operating system.

New on TV: *Fear Factor, Alias, Scrubs, Reba, Smallville, 24, The Amazing Race*.

A state, Nevada, legalizes online gambling.

Internet has thousands of online radio stations.

V.S. Naipaul, Trinidadian of Indian descent, wins Nobel Prize in Literature.

U.S. TV networks, magazines among targets of anthrax terrorists.

Oscars: *A Beautiful Mind*, Denzel Washington, Halle Berry.

Also at the movies: *Lord of the Rings, Gosford Park, Moulin Rouge, Shrek*.

Non-English language film Oscar: *No Man's Land*, Bosnia-Herzogovina.

Oscar category created: Best Animated Film. Feature Film Award.

The iPod music player.

2001: From Microsoft: the Xbox game player.

World watches horror of 9/11.

2002: A Wi-Fi-equipped laptop, the Tablet PC also recognizes writing.

"Googlewhacking" fad looks for odd word combinations in Internet sites.

On the Web, creators of online journals, or "web logs," now "blog on."

UK workers spend more time with email than with their children.

Politically Incorrect remark by Bill Maher leads to ABC cancellation.

Sirius follows XM as second satellite radio channel.

Comic book publishers join to express views on 9/11 destruction.

Apple computer can create movies in DVD format.

Making DVD movies becomes affordable for the average household.

New on TV: *American Idol, Monk, The Shield, Dr. Phil, Without a Trace.*

MTV reportedly reaches 250 million homes worldwide.

Feature film, *Attack of the Clones*, produced entirely in digital format.

Hungarian Jewish Holocaust survivor Imre Kertész: Nobel Prize in Literature.

U.S. Supreme Court says 1996 Child Pornography Act is unconstitutional.

Pop-ups and pop-unders clutter computer screens.

Worldwide PC sales pass one-billion mark.

DVD burners are popular for storing downloaded movies.

From England, roll-up screens for computers, television sets.

Cheap, hand-held computers are a big sales item.

Amazon.com stocks more than 350,000 titles.

Star Wars: Attack of the Clones, first big budget film shot with digital cameras.

Sony's PlayStation2, Microsoft's Xbox, Nintendo's GameCube attract devotees.

"Klez" is the most destructive computer network worm yet.

DVD sales pass VCR sales; 40+ million U.S. homes have DVD.

Oscars: *Chicago*, Adrien Brody, Nicole Kidman.

Also at the movies: *Gangs of New York, The Pianist, The Hours, Adaptation.*

Non-English language film Oscar: *Nowhere in Africa*, Germany.

Animated film Oscar: *Spirited Away*, Japan.

Documentary feature Oscar: *Bowling for Columbine.*

70% of U.S. households could have broadband service; 15% use it.

Nearly 21,000 DVD titles in circulation, 7,000 introduced this year.

South Africa's *Sesame Street* introduces an HIV-positive muppet.

Music industry earns $33 billion worldwide.

Estimated 100 million computer users have file sharing software.

Friendster sets up Internet social contact network.

Google News, an automated service without human editors.

2003: Sales of recorded CDs drop 10% for a second year.

2003: 239 million computer games are sold.

Auckland, New Zealand, has city-wide, high-speed wireless network.

Nobel Prize in Literature: John Coetzee, South African novelist, essayist.

Oscars: *The Lord of the Rings*, Sean Penn, Charlize Theron.

Also at the movies: *Pirates of the Caribbean, Mystic, Cold Mountain.*

Non-English language film Oscar: *The Barbarian Invasions*, France.

Oscar for animated film: *Finding Nemo.*

From Apple Computer: the browser Safari.

New on TV: *Bill Maher, Ellen DeGeneris, Last Comic Standing, Nip/Tuck, Las Vegas.*

A fifth of all Russians reportedly use cell phones.

DVD movie sales bring in more money than box offices.

Cell phones add computer and Internet capabilities.

Supreme Court approves porn filters in federally funded public libraries.

Intelsat has more than 20 communication satellites in orbit.

Internet becomes integral part of political campaigning.

Hollywood releases are heavy on special effects, violence, sequels.

U.S. law limits telemarketers by "Do not call" phone list.

New cable channel: Spike TV.

Apple's G5 64-bit processor contains 58 million transistors.

Flash mobs, organized on the Net, start in New York, spread worldwide.

Destructive computer worms and viruses sharply increase.

The online iTunes Music Store offers songs for 99 cents.

Some U.S. states tax Internet bandwidth.

zip-codes.com offers ZIP code information online.

Popularity of blogs increases sharply.

Second Life offers a parallel universe.

The IP phone is a mini-computer that can transmit movies.

One-third of books bought in U.S. are romance novels.

Amazon.com scans texts of 120,000 books for Internet users.

An estimated one million camcorders worldwide.

Harry Potter books attacked as satanic, but also defended.

International piracy of films is rampant.

Dan Brown's best seller, *The Da Vinci Code.*

Estimated 5 trillion unwanted messages set on the Internet.

A world summit on the Information Society meets in Switzerland.

European Union requires Internet companies to tax downloads.

World has 159 million cell phone users.

French Ministry of Culture bans the word "email." Wants "courriel."

Cost to business of computer viruses estimated at $55 billion.

2003: Two AARP magazines far outstrip all others in circulation.

Cable TV offers TiVo-like features: storing, skipping commercials.

Intelsat has more than 20 communication satellites orbiting worldwide.

2004: HD car radios go on sale.

Digital AM and FM signals with CD-quality.

98% of all U.S. homes have color television.

Worldwide cell phone revenues surpass fixed-phone revenues.

Market grows for VOIP broadband Internet phone service.

Nobel Prize in Literature: Elfriede Jelinek, Austria novelist.

RCA sells 61-inch-wide TV sets 6.5 inches thick.

Survey identifies the cell phone as the chief American love/hate object.

2-D and 3-D photos taken by Rover vehicles beamed back from Mars.

Mel Gibson's *The Passion of the Christ*, is a hit, but is called anti-semitic.

FCC fines radio stations for obscene language on the air.

Google gets 138,000 requests a minute in 90 languages.

Three out of four Americans use the Internet.

Congress raises fines for TV indecency; considers action on TV violence.

1 in 5 people under 30 say Internet is their main information source.

Oldsters, minority groups reduce the "digital divide," go online.

$21 billion spent on online ads in U.S. alone.

The Polar Express uses sensors to convert live action to animation.

More U.S. information services are outsourced to India, elsewhere.

Survey: U.S. women spend more online game time than men, teens.

The iPod holds 10,000 tunes, but fits into a shirt pocket.

95% of U.S. public libraries offer Internet access.

U.S. public library attendance up 17% in six years.

The Sims 2 advances story games for computers.

Motion capture in *The Polar Express* shows animated version of actor.

Con artists use "phishing" to trick people to reveal personal data.

Wi-fi cell phone/cameras are replacing some computers.

1.5 billion cell phones worldwide.

New on TV: *Deadwood, Trading Spouses, Lost, Desperate Housewives, Boston Legal.*

Multi-million dollar mapping programs now cost less than $100.

University in San Diego offers degree in wireless communication.

London police use tiny, hidden wireless cameras to catch drug dealers.

Employers can use GPS tracking to see if service workers are on the job.

Apple wireless station plays iTunes over home stereo systems.

PDA sales fall sharply in favor of cool "smart" cell phones.

"Cabir," the first virus to infect cell phones, arrives via Bluetooth.

2004: Violent video games *Halo 2* and *Grand Theft Auto: San Andreas* sell millions.

Supreme Court rejects Internet porn ban as free speech violation.

Video games are 30 years old. Average age of player: 29.

More than half of all Americans play video games.

Oscars: *Million Dollar Baby*, Jamie Foxx, Hilary Swank.

Also at the movies: *The Aviator, Ray, Sideways, Finding Neverland*.

Non-English language film Oscar: *The Sea Inside*, Spain.

Animation Oscar: *The Incredibles*.

"Podcasting" coined as term for Internet delivery of radio-style content.

Google Gmail advances email service in many languages.

2005: Cyber identity theft increases.

Chicken Little released as 3-D digital movie; shot at 144 fps.

Verizon buys MCI; SBC and AT&T connect.

2 billion mobile phone customers worldwide.

Camera phones create instant citizen photojournalists.

Movie box office drops to 25 million tickets weekly; 36.000 screens.

Average U.S. homes can get 96.4 cable channels, but watch 15.4.

Two iPod Photo players combined as 3-D "stereopod."

Wikipedia has 750,000 online encyclopedia articles in 50 languages.

Oscars: *Crash*, Philip Seymour Hoffman, Reese Witherspoon.

Also at the movies: *Brokeback Mountain, Syriana, Capote, Munich*.

Non-English language film Oscar: *Tsotsi*, South Africa.

Animation Oscar: *Wallace & Gromit in The Curse of the Were Rabbit*.

BPL (Broadband over Power Lines), emerges for Internet access.

YouTube post its first video.

512 TV stations broadcast in digital high definition.

Cyberathletes win $1 million prize money in video game competition.

Nobel Prize in Literature: Harold Pinter, British playwright.

Newsweek criticized for photograph of Martha Stewart's head on model's body.

New on TV: *The Office (U.S. version), Colbert Report, Dancing with the Stars, Prison Break*.

Episode of NBC's *Medium* shot in 3-D.

2006: "Kama Sutra" worm attacks computers seeking porn sites.

Muslims riot over cartoons of Mohammed in Danish press.

Western Union gets out of telegram business.

Uproar over cell phone financial records available for sale.

An estimated 30 million readers of millions of blogs daily.

Google adds instant messaging; competes with AOL and Yahoo.

Da Vinci Code film stirs Christian religious anger.

Internet "telemedicine" allows doctors to see patients at a distance.

2006: Blu-ray optical discs hold five times regular DVD storage.

Push email sends an alert when a letter arrives.

Deadline set for broadcasters to be digital-only and surrender extra spectrum.

Estimated total hits to blogs each day: 30 million.

At CBS, Katie Couric is first principal female anchor of TV evening newscast.

TV networks place their most popular programs on the Web.

Viruses can infect Macs, considered almost immune until now.

Movie *Bubble* opens simultaneously in cinemas, on DVD, cable.

Skype Internet phone system reports 100 million customers.

From Shure, earphones that can be switched to pick up street noise.

Mac computers can run Windows XP operating system.

Nobel Prize in Literature: Orhan Pamuk, Turkey.

Phone companies deliver video by IPTV (Internet Protocol Television).

Fold-up fabric contains wireless full-size keyboard for PDAs, phones.

High definition tapeless, digital memory camcorders on sale.

Hand-cranked $100 computer designed for students in developing countries.

World of Warcraft video game has 6 million online players worldwide.

More wi-fi hotspots; citywide hotspots planned.

New on TV: *Top Chef, The Unit, Ugly Betty, Friday Night Lights.*

Nintendo game controller responds to hand, body movements.

U.S. broadcasters face increased fines for programs deemed indecent.

Battle in Congress over "net neutrality" regarding website access.

John Updike's novel, *Terrorist.*

Average American watches 4 hours 35 minutes of TV daily, a record.

Bill Gates decides to give up day-to-day control of Microsoft.

Video editing is done online; scenes can be "borrowed."

In Tokyo test, pointing a cell phone yields sightseeing information.

In U.S., women buy most of the video games sold for mobile phones.

On TV, *To Catch a Predator* stings online sex prowlers.

Congress holds hearings on online safety concerns for children.

Study reports growing loneliness of Americans.

Sony Reader's improved display revives interest in e-books.

UCLA brain research shows problems with studying while TV is on.

Espresso Book Machine offers cheap on-demand publishing.

Cell phones, iPods, and laptops considered terrorist detonation devices.

Number of drive-in theaters in U.S. rises to 658.

In Mexico, archeologists find 3,000-year-old Olmec writing on stone slab.

100 million websites with domain names and content.

Average American encounters an estimated 3,000 marketing messages daily.

2006: Nintendo game Wii remote waved like a magic wand.

In a year and a half, YouTube posts 100 million videos; adds 70,000 daily.

DirecTV experiment lets viewers choose baseball game camera angles.

Hundreds of millions of dollars paid for MySpace.com and YouTube.com.

Oscars: *The Departed,* Forest Whitaker, Helen Mirren.

Also at the movies: *Babel, Letters from Iwo Jima, The Queen, Little Miss Sunshine.*

Animation Oscar: *Happy Feet.*

Ex-Vice President Al Gore's *An Inconvenient Truth* on global warming wins Oscar.

Foreign language film: *The Lives of Others*, Germany.

Gold Rush, a television-style reality quiz show on the Internet.

Image Metrics' animated figures mimic emotions on actors' faces.

Time Person of the Year: You, for taking control of your media. Web 2.0

2007: iPhone surfs Web, emails, plays videos and tunes, makes phone calls, takes pictures.

Mobile TV service for cell phones builds a customer base.

Wikileak.org, an open-source site for government documents.

Nielsen research reports that rich, poor watch different TV shows.

Of video game players, more are adult women (30%) than boys under 18 (23%).

Netflix has 6.7 million subscribers for online movie rentals.

Another computer worm: W32.Rinbot.H.

Cell phone can now tune into television programs.

Cost of a first-class U.S. postage stamp rises to 41 cents.

More than 700 U.S. radio stations have converted to HD.

Internet oversight agency rejects proposal for .xxx porn site designation.

New on TV: *Who Wants to be a Fifth Grader?*

Pakistani cleric threatens suicide bombing to support anti-smut campaign.

Students email, blog on MySpace.com during massacre at Virginia Tech.

Radio, TV talk show host Don Imus fired over insensitive comment.

FCC asks Congress for power to regulate TV violence.

More than six million "residents" of *Second Life*, but not all are active.

A.M.A. decides it's not ready to call excessive video game play an "addiction."

Last 20 minutes of *Harry Potter* film available in 3-D at IMAX theaters.

China combats online game addiction; cuts points in half after three hours play.

The last of the seven-volume *Harry Potter* series is published.

Nation of Estonia is nearly shut down by botnet attack. Web War One?

CNN and YouTube sponsor Web 2.0-style political debate.

IBM researches a way to store data on a single atom.

Fred Thompson's presidential candidacy halts *Law & Order* TV reruns.

Teenage hacker breaks iPhone code within months of its release.

17-year-old Ashley Qualls earns millions via MySpace.com business.